Cold Case Homicides

The Third Edition of *Cold Case Homicides* remains a vital resource for students and professionals alike, offering a comprehensive guide to the investigation and resolution of unsolved cases. Updated with the latest advancements, this edition emphasizes the evolving landscape of cold case work, including cutting-edge forensic tools, the expanding role of digital and mobile evidence, and the transformative impact of DNA technologies, especially forensic genealogy and familial matching. Readers will gain insight into the most recent techniques for leveraging public records, social media, and data analysis in cold case reviews. Richly illustrated and grounded in practical application, the text underscores how emerging technologies and a reassessment of earlier missteps can breathe new life into dormant investigations. Whether used in academic settings or by active investigators, this edition demonstrates how today's tools and methodologies can bridge gaps left by past limitations, bringing justice and closure to long-unsolved crimes.

Rachel H. Walton: Dr. Rachel Walton brought over 35 years of California law enforcement experience and 15 years of college-level instruction, with expertise in homicide, cold cases, arson, and fraud. She led a landmark 13-year reinvestigation of a 1920s homicide that resulted in a posthumous pardon for a wrongfully convicted man. A sought-after speaker, she presented to the FBI Academy, RCMP, NCIS, AAFS, and others. Dr. Walton earned her Ed.D. from the University of San Francisco with the first academic research on solvability factors in cold case homicides, and was the author of *Cold Case Homicide: Practical Investigative Techniques.*

Frank P. Tona: Frank P. Tona is a Lieutenant with the Charles County Sheriff's Office in Maryland, one of the oldest law enforcement agencies in the United States, where he has served since 2002. He holds a B.S. in Criminal Justice from SUNY Brockport and an M.P.A. from Norwich University. Lt. Tona is a Board Member of the Mid-Atlantic Cold Case Homicide Investigator's Association, a Fellow at the Future Policing Institute, and a member of the Vidocq Society and International Homicide Investigators Association. He also serves as an adjunct instructor at Norwich University, John Jay College, Franciscan University, and the University of Maryland Global Campus.

CRC SERIES IN
PRACTICAL ASPECTS OF CRIMINAL AND FORENSIC INVESTIGATIONS

VERNON J. GEBERTH, BBA, MPS, FBINA *Series Editor*

Practical Military Ordnance Identification
Tom Gersbeck

Practical Cold Case Homicide Investigations Procedural Manual
Richard H. Walton

Autoerotic Deaths: Practical Forensic and Investigative Perspectives
Anny Sauvageau and Vernon J. Geberth

Practical Crime Scene Processing and Investigation, Second Edition
Ross M. Gardner

The Counterterrorism Handbook, Fourth Edition: Tactics, Procedures, and Techniques
Frank Bolz, Jr., Kenneth J. Dudonis, and David P. Schulz

Practical Forensic Digital Imaging: Applications and Techniques
Patrick Jones

DiMaio's Forensic Pathology, Third Edition
Vincent J.M. DiMaio and Kimberley Molina

Bloodstain Pattern Analysis with an Introduction to Crime Scene Reconstruction, Fourth Edition
Tom Bevel, Ross Gardner, and Tom J. Griffin

Practical Aspects of Rape Investigation, Sixth Edition: A Multidisciplinary Approach
Edited by Ann Wolbert Burgess and Robert R. Hazelwood

Practical Bomb Scene Investigation, Fourth Edition
James T. Thurman

Cold Case Homicides, 3rd Edition: Practical Investigative Techniques
Rachel H. Walton (†) and Frank P. Tona

For more information about this series, please visit: www.routledge.com/Practical-Aspects-of-Criminal-and-Forensic-Investigations/book-series/CRCPACFINVE

Cold Case Homicides

Practical Investigative Techniques

Third Edition

Edited by
Rachel H. Walton and Frank P. Tona

CRC Press
Taylor & Francis Group
Boca Raton London New York

CRC Press is an imprint of the
Taylor & Francis Group, an **informa** business

Photo credit: Personal collection of Rebecca Green Hulun, daughter of Washington, DC Metropolitan Police Det. Richard Green.

Third edition published 2026
by CRC Press
2385 NW Executive Center Drive, Suite 320, Boca Raton FL 33431

and by CRC Press
4 Park Square, Milton Park, Abingdon, Oxon, OX14 4RN

CRC Press is an imprint of Taylor & Francis Group, LLC

First edition published by CRC Press, 2006.
Second edition published by CRC Press, 2017.

ISBN: 978-1-032-54195-2 (hbk)
ISBN: 978-1-032-54194-5 (pbk)
ISBN: 978-1-003-41563-3 (ebk)

DOI: 10.4324/9781003415633

Typeset in Minion Pro
by codeMantra

In memory of Rachel H. Walton, Ph.D. (1947–2025) A dedicated criminal investigator, a gifted mind, and a cherished friend. Your contributions to the cold case community were invaluable, and your absence is deeply felt. This book stands as a testament to your insight, your passion, and your enduring legacy.

In memory of Frank A. Colaprete, Ed.D. (1962–2023) My mentor, colleague, and friend. Your guidance shaped not only this work, but the path that led me here.

To Melissa, Matthew, and Emily. Your love, strength, and patience carry me through every chapter of my life.

Contents

Preface to the Third Edition

Cold Case Homicides: Practical Investigative Techniques, 3rd ed.

By R.H. Walton and F.P. Tona

The persistent investigation of cold case homicides remains one of the most challenging and compelling areas of law enforcement. These cases—long unresolved yet never forgotten—represent the enduring responsibility of the criminal justice system to seek the truth, hold offenders accountable, and bring long-overdue justice to victims and their families. In this Third Edition of *Cold Case Homicides: Practical Investigative Techniques*, we continue our commitment to equipping investigators, analysts, forensic professionals, and criminal justice students with the evolving tools and strategies necessary to address these complex cases.

Since our previous edition, the field has advanced significantly. This edition reflects those developments with new chapters and revised content grounded in modern investigative practice, forensic innovation, and inter-agency collaboration. Among the most notable additions is an examination of digital forensics in cold case investigations. These records are now essential tools in recreating timelines, confirming alibis, and identifying suspect movements, often years after the crime occurred. We explore the utility, limitations, and evidentiary considerations of mobile data in reinvigorating dormant cases.

We also introduce a chapter on victim advocacy, recognizing the indispensable role that survivors and family members play in cold case resolution. No longer passive observers, victims today are engaged partners in justice, supported by advocacy programs and legal rights that empower their participation in every phase of the process. The power of the public cannot be underestimated. In this edition, we explore the growing use of social media platforms in cold case investigations. Whether through awareness campaigns, crowdsourcing of tips, or public engagement, social media has become a crucial channel for generating leads and maintaining visibility for unsolved homicides.

Closely linked is our expanded treatment of open-source intelligence (OSINT), the use of publicly available digital information to support cold case inquiries. OSINT now plays a pivotal role in identifying persons of interest, locating witnesses, and uncovering patterns or affiliations that were previously obscured by time.

We introduce a new chapter on the use of K9 units, particularly in searches for human remains in aged crime scenes. The value of properly trained detection dogs, used in conjunction with environmental and archaeological methods, has proven instrumental in uncovering remains and evidence that have been long hidden or buried.

In this edition, we introduce our readers to the ever-evolving use of investigative genetic genealogy (IGG). This revolutionary tool has solved some of the most infamous cold cases in history, and we explore not only the science and methodology but also the ethical, legal, and constitutional issues that now frame its use.

This edition also includes a comprehensive chapter on professional networking and resource allocation. Cold casework cannot be done in isolation. We emphasize the importance of building professional relationships across agencies, disciplines, and geographic boundaries while offering practical guidance on maximizing limited resources and securing external support.

In addition, we offer a fully updated discussion of forensic anthropology, with emphasis on new techniques in skeletal analysis, isotope studies, trauma reconstruction, and facial approximation, methods that continue to aid in identifying unknown victims and interpreting crime scenes decades after the fact.

Another key update focuses on the role of forensic crime laboratories. These facilities are no longer confined to reactive testing but serve as collaborative partners in reexamining evidence, reprocessing biological samples, and implementing cutting-edge techniques such as probabilistic genotyping, DNA mixture deconvolution, and advanced fingerprint analysis.

The challenges of managing cold case investigations also fall to agency leaders. For this reason, we present a newly revised chapter for law enforcement executives, offering a roadmap for creating, staffing, funding, and sustaining cold case units. This chapter provides practical strategies for institutionalizing cold case work within an agency's operational priorities, ensuring continuity, accountability, and measurable results.

Finally, this edition includes a detailed case study on the successful investigation and prosecution of Joseph James DeAngelo, the Golden State Killer. This landmark case illustrates the impact of persistence, collaboration, and the marriage of traditional detective work with modern forensic science.

We also recognize the expanding role of academia in cold case investigations. University-based cold case centers, academic partnerships, and student-led reviews are becoming valuable allies to law enforcement, injecting fresh analytical perspectives and research-based methodologies into complex investigations.

The Third Edition of *Cold Case Homicides* brings together the best elements of previous volumes while embracing new tools, techniques, and philosophies. We hope that this work will serve not only as a practical guide for those engaged in the pursuit of justice but also as a source of inspiration, reminding readers that time does not diminish the importance of truth and that every case matters.

Acknowledgment

In Memoriam: Dr. Rachel Walton
Pioneering Cold Case Investigator, Educator, and Author
July 15, 1947–February 1, 2025

Dr. Rachel Walton, a pioneer in cold case homicide investigations and a respected educator, passed away on February 1, 2025. With more than 35 years of distinguished service in California law enforcement and over 15 years of teaching at the college and university level, Dr. Walton left a lasting impact on both the investigative and academic communities.

Dr. Walton began her law enforcement career in 1971 with the Humboldt County Sheriff's Office before moving to the Humboldt County District Attorney's Office in 1986. Her extensive investigative expertise covered a wide range of complex cases, including homicide, cold case homicide, arson, white-collar crime, elder abuse, and fraud. She was perhaps best known for her pioneering work in cold case homicides, including her groundbreaking reinvestigation of crimes dating back to the 1920s. Her 13-year pursuit of justice ultimately led to identifying a surviving perpetrator and securing a posthumous pardon, on the grounds of innocence, for a man wrongfully convicted and imprisoned for decades.

Dr. Walton earned her B.S. in Natural Resources from Humboldt State College in 1969, her M.A. in Education from the University of San Francisco in 1978, and her Doctor of Education from the same university in 2005. Her doctoral dissertation was the first academic study to identify solvability factors in cold case homicide investigations, research now widely cited and used by law enforcement agencies and scholars worldwide.

Throughout her illustrious career, Dr. Walton was a dedicated mentor and educator, sharing her expertise at numerous national and international forums. Her lectures and presentations reached audiences at the FBI Academy, Naval Criminal Investigative Service, Royal Canadian Mounted Police, National Institute of Justice, American Academy of Forensic Sciences, and the Vidocq Society, among many others.

A Fellow of the American Academy of Forensic Sciences and a proud member of the Vidocq Society, Dr. Walton was also the author of the influential book *Cold Case Homicide: Practical Investigative Techniques* (CRC Press, 1st ed., 2006), along with subsequent second and third editions, as well as numerous scholarly articles and professional publications.

Dr. Rachel Walton's legacy is built on perseverance, innovation, and a steadfast dedication to justice. Her work has inspired generations of investigators and scholars, and it continues to guide those committed to solving the most difficult cases. She will be greatly missed by colleagues, students, and the broader law enforcement and forensic science communities. I am honored to have known her and, more importantly, to call her my friend.

Frank P. Tona
La Plata, Maryland
August 2025

Foreword

Cold Case Homicides: Practical Investigative Techniques (Third Edition)

Thomas Hargrove

Most Americans are astonished to learn that there are more than 300,000 unsolved homicides committed in the United States since 1970. This number is similar to the total combat deaths the nation experienced in World War II. Yet domestic murder has become a conflict that we seem to be losing.

Folks are even more surprised to hear that murders have become less likely to be solved over time. Back in the 1960s, police reported to the Federal Bureau of Investigation that they were arresting homicide offenders more than 90% of the time. But we hit an all-time-low clearance rate in 2022 when only 52% of murders resulted in an arrest.

This tremendous decline in murder clearance rates seems to run counter to everything the public has been told about modern crime investigative techniques. Aren't there new forensic miracles that are clearing murders using rapidly advancing science like DNA analysis to identify the killer's familial genealogy? It certainly runs counter to fictional TV crime shows where most murders are solved within 60 minutes by beautiful actors portraying detectives who stand in front of giant, glittering computer monitors.

The truth is that law enforcement in the United States suffers from a profound decline of resources of every kind. We don't have enough detectives, experienced investigators, and forensic technicians who can spend many hours culling a crime scene. We don't have enough beat cops available to knock on doors asking folks what they saw and heard a few hours ago when one of their neighbors was gunned down. These "neighborhood sweeps" are becoming less common. Crime labs are often underfunded, understaffed, and use outdated equipment, hindering their capacity to process evidence efficiently. It is not uncommon for detectives to experience lab backlogs of months – and even years – for processing ballistics, blood, and other critical evidence.

But law enforcement faces even more basic challenges. We have an imperfect design of governance. Unlike most other Western democracies, America suffers from a complex system of overlapping jurisdictions with conflicting responsibilities. We have local, county, state, and federal authorities that rarely act in concert to resolve day-to-day criminal activity.

A few years ago, I had lunch with the senior homicide investigator for the nation of Denmark. While we were digging into our salads, just to make conversation I asked how many murders occur in Denmark annually. "About 50 a year," he said, almost causing me to drop my fork. Now more interested, I asked how many are cleared through the offender's arrest. "We clear about 49 of them," he responded. "I know this because every one of them crosses my desk." If a case has gone unresolved after a few weeks, he routinely would telephone the local investigators to ask if they needed more resources of any sort. He'd even offer to leave his office in Copenhagen to lend a hand.

Denmark is similar in population size to the state of Maryland. Both have about 6 million people. But Maryland suffers more than 500 killings every year, a rate more than 10 times that of Denmark. While detectives in Denmark make an arrest about 98% of the time, police in the "Old Line State" cleared an average of just 43% of murders over the last five years.

The truth is that there is a strong correlation between homicide clearance and occurrence. As murders become less likely to be cleared, homicides become more common. If killers are allowed to walk the streets, nothing good happens. Uncaught killers are available to kill again. Why not? It might be "dope" or "rad" or even "fab" to tell your friends that you are officially a serial killer. Uncleared murders also prompt more murder since family and friends may feel obliged to take the law into their own hands to avenge a killing gone cold with police.

Murder begets murder. Especially unsolved murder.

The only practical means law enforcement has to interrupt this most vicious of cycles is to arrest killers. High clearance rates can dissuade would-be killers. We've seen massive numbers of murder decline dramatically in places like New York City, Santa Ana, California, and Los Angeles. At the same time, we've seen places with low clearance rates rack up ever-increasing body counts in places like Baltimore, Chicago, New Orleans, and Saint Louis.

The key to producing results lies with leadership that promotes a coordinated response by multiple levels of government. Consider the statewide clearance rates of California and Texas. Police in the Lone Star State historically clear 72% of the murders, compared to California's more anemic 62%. Why? Many Texas observers point, with pride, to the close working relationship between the fabled Texas Rangers and local police. Detectives have even been known to brag "I'm working with the Rangers on this one!"

The state with America's highest clearance rate is Wyoming. Of course, it helps to be rural. Communities where everyone knows everyone are more likely to know who the likely suspects are. But judiciary leaders in the Wyoming Legislature are also quick to praise the very close working relationship between local police and the Wyoming Division of Criminal

Investigation. State investigators are willing, when asked by local police, to take the lead on a local murder. This close partnership certainly contributed to Wyoming's stellar statewide clearance average of 84%. Killers would be well advised to practice their trade elsewhere.

The best approach to dealing with cold cases is to avoid them. Data clearly shows that the probability of clearing a homicide declines dramatically with time. Cases that have gone unresolved after a year will probably remain so. Evidence generally becomes harder to collect with each passing day. Witnesses' memories quickly fade. Those few cold cases that do get solved should be celebrated as Blue Moon events.

What should America do with that ever-growing backlog of unsolved murders? The many hundreds of thousands of families and friends of cold case victims are becoming a political force who are difficult to ignore in a democratic society. Congress, aware of the problem, in 2022 passed the Homicide Victims' Families Rights Act which empowers close relatives of a cold case murder victim under federal jurisdiction to request a case review by someone who was not part of the original investigation. Such reviews have been known to produce positive results when fresh eyes go over the so-called "Murder Book" looking for new approaches. I've personally witnessed that such reviews have resulted in the arrest of killers.

Authorities around the nation are considering, and a few are actively assembling, statewide databases of unsolved murders. They look to criminologists and organizations like mine, the Murder Accountability Project, for help. Despite often overworked volunteers and other limited resources, they hope that this assistance will help prioritize their cold case mountains to give them one more chance to solve uncleared murders.

Books like this one can offer practical suggestions for how to build a "solvability matrix" to score each case so that those limited human resources can be wisely assigned. Machines are now capable of conducting reviews of complex issues. Were all forensic tests completed and reported to local and national databases for DNA, ballistics, and fingerprints? Have previously unavailable witnesses turned up? Did the spouse of a murder suspect get a divorce? Have business partners since separated? Have any of the principals in the investigation experienced subsequent criminal difficulties in other cases?

We've seen that police departments can reverse the trajectory of their communities. Vicious circles can become virtuous cycles. As arrests become more common, would-be killers rethink their career choices. Leaders of street gangs will change their MO if they come to believe murder is bad for business. As murders become less common, detectives can focus more effectively on their declining case load. The Department of Justice recommends that homicide detectives not work more than five cases at a time. Yet in many communities, detectives juggle 10 and even 20 cases a year. If that caseload comes down, detectives will have the time to solve more and more of their backlog, which prompts fewer and fewer murders in the future.

Despite the daunting size of that cold case mountain, there is hope.

Thomas K. Hargrove
Founder and Chairman
Murder Accountability Project
www.murderdata.org

Contributing Authors

Ryan Backmann
Project Cold Case
Atlantic Beach, Florida

Trevor Buchanan
Geolocation Investigative Team,
Lexis-Nexis Risk Solutions
Alpharetta, Georgia

Anthony R. Cardoza
San Diego County, CA Medical Examiner's Office
San Diego, California

Thomas A. (Tad) DiBiase
United States Capitol Police
Washington, DC

Louis N. Eliopulos
Naval Criminal Investigative Service
Quantico, Virginia

John Elliott
Charles County, MD Sheriff's Office
La Plata, Maryland

Christopher Flanagan
Mid-Atlantic Cold Case Homicide Investigators Association
Leesburg, Virginia

Fiona Gabbert
University of London
London, United Kingdom

Thomas K. Hargrove
Murder Accountability Project
Washington, DC

Jay W. Henry
Utah Department of Public Safety (ret.)
Salt Lake City, Utah

Lorraine Hope
University of Portsmouth
Portsmouth, United Kingdom

Steve Johnson
Truth2Lies Analysis Group, LLC.
Mesa, Arizona

David Keatley
Murdoch University
Murdoch, Australia

Erin Kimmerle
University of South Florida
Tampa, Florida

Ashley Link
Innovative Forensic Investigations
Emporia, Virginia

Kirk Luther
Carleton University
Ottawa, Canada

Kathy Mackay
Utah Department of Public Safety-Statewide Information & Analysis Center
Salt Lake City, Utah

David MacNeil
Watertown Police Department
MacNeil Investigations & Forensic Consulting
Watertown, Massachusetts

Jennifer Moore
Innovative Forensic Investigations
Emporia, Virginia

Sharon Pagaling-Hagan
California Department of Justice-Violent Crime Profiling Unit
Sacramento, California

Heather Price
Thompson Rivers University
Kamloops, Canada

Kacy Robinson
K9 Handler, Fide Canem Cold Case, Inc.
Brigham City, Utah

Bret Sayer
K9 Handler, Fide Canem Cold Case, Inc.
Brigham City, Utah

Anne Marie Schubert
Sacramento County, California (2014–2022)
Schubert Strategies
Auburn, California

Norman D. "Skip" Sperber
San Diego County, CA Medical Examiner's Office
San Diego, California

Wayne Thomas
Ravenwood Cognition Limited
Edinburgh, United Kingdom

Todd VanCantfort
Public Safety & Resiliency Associates
Washington, DC

Paul Wagner
NBC4
Washington, DC

Introduction

RACHEL H. WALTON

It is hard to imagine that it has been more than 20 years now since Vernon Geberth, retired lieutenant commander in homicide of the NYPD and editor of the forensic series for CRC Press, viewed a cold case presentation I made at a conference of the American Academy of Forensic Sciences. While passing each other on the escalators at the host hotel, he told me he wanted me to write a textbook on practical cold case homicide investigation. Having recently retired from my 34-year association with the badge, an adventure which began as a young college student in 1968 who became a reserve police officer and followed this up with more than three decades as a California deputy sheriff and district attorney investigator, I was in the middle of my studies in pursuit of my doctoral degree.

Fate, chance, and luck have a funny way of altering life, sometimes for the good and sometimes otherwise but altering the course of one's life, nevertheless. A chance conversation on a street corner in 1983 while a young deputy on patrol, that a woman had died and in the years before death told others that she always regretted giving false testimony accusing a young Native American of sexual assault, became the genesis for my first exposure to what would become perhaps the oldest active homicide investigation in the nation. Technically perhaps, it was not a "cold case." I just believed that if someone lied and someone went to prison, they should have their name cleared. I did not know that it entailed multiple murders, alleged rapes, and official corruption at the highest levels, and would ultimately consume me through obsessive, compulsive, perhaps neurotic, behavior. It became a personal research endeavor: "Did Jack Ryan commit the crimes for which he spent more than 40 years in prison and on parole?" Unbeknownst to me, I was stepping into a sordid part of history, crimes set in the middle of Prohibition more than 20 years before I was born. Done on my own time until it became official, I conducted more than 400 interviews, 265-plus of these were with persons between the ages of 65 and 94. I learned a lot about life, and criminal investigation. I had never conducted a homicide investigation before; I was a patrol deputy, but one with an insatiable sense of justice and who loved history and doing research.

My decades-long efforts identified two surviving killers from this high-profile double homicide case in 1925, and in 1996, the governor of California granted what is perhaps the nation's first posthumous pardon on the grounds of innocence of its kind for that Native American, who spent

DOI: 10.4324/9781003415633-1

more than 40 years in prison and on parole for crimes which he did not commit. These efforts, detailed in the final pages of this book, catapulted into speaking invitations for, among others, the FBI Academy at Quantico, NCIS, California Association of Criminalists, the Royal Canadian Mounted Police, and so many more.

It was this exposure to investigators far more experienced than I that, when confronted with cold case re-investigations but encountering missing files, absent evidence, and other issues, stymied some, as they concluded that they were the only ones encountering such obstacles, and that to move forward, they had to—proverbially speaking—"re-invent the wheel." These many conversations stimulated my return to academia and to ultimately write the first dissertation of its kind on identification of solvability factors in 21st-century cold case homicide investigation.

But I had no idea on how to write a book. I was a "cow county" deputy sheriff at heart, and I had never even thought about it until Vernon approached me. I thought I had to learn all the topics which involved the various forensic and other disciplines in order to write all the chapters until he set me straight—ask the experts to contribute chapters.

To all of these I—perhaps I should say "we" as this includes you, the reader—owe such a sense of gratitude. Such a sense is not just for me but for all our cold case investigative team members around the nation—indeed, as time would show, around the world. This is not, and has never been nor ever will be, my book. It is OUR book.

Time marches on, and so it has with cold case homicide investigations. The book went into a second edition in 2017, and now this third edition. Never in my wildest imagination did I ever conceive of writing a book such as this, nor of the success that it would bring. Sadly, our nation is not the same in many regards as it was in 2006, or even 2017. We face unprecedented challenges in national security and integrity of government, but cold case investigators move forward regardless. The legal and forensic horizons are ever changing. If we thought the advent of the use of DNA in the criminal investigative paradigm was a game changer, I doubt that any of us imagined the role and impact that the integration of computer databases and investigative genetic genealogy (IGG) would bring to the field of unsolved homicides, unidentified human remains, and long-term missing persons. We owe so much to so many, but it is the soldiers in the fields—the investigators and their forensic and legal partners—who bring us new tools to combat the oldest of crimes: murder. Our author Anne-Marie Schubert, as district attorney in Sacramento, spearheaded the Golden State Killer case and the first real thrust of this valuable tool into the public spectrum.

Every cold case resolution, whether it be by arrest and conviction, identification of a deceased perpetrator, or identification of unknown remains, is a win. It is a win for the investigators, the agency, the families … and above all, for society. When I began my journey toward full professorship at Utah State University 17-plus years ago, I reflect on how I have learned in all things. I learn best from actually "doing." I did so with my 1925 case and have sought to use what I learned (sometimes the hard way) to help others learn. In teaching, our best teachers are not the highly paid conference speakers, but other teachers, and above all, the students themselves. It is our colleagues in all things, including life itself. Such is the *practical* aspect of life.

One does not write books such as this for large sums of money—leave that to true crime and romance writers. To me the biggest payoff has been emails and comments such as "… after reading your book we re-designed our cold case unit …" It is the innumerable similar expressions that our work has achieved what Vernon envisioned and demanded—a text on "practical" cold case homicide investigation. I hope he is as pleased with these contributions to attempting to achieve whatever passes for "justice" in our world for victims and their families and friends.

This edition will be my "last hurrah" so to speak. But the message must be carried on. To this end, in 2018, I asked Lieutenant Frank Tona of the Charles County Sheriff's Office in Maryland to join me in this edition. I first met Frank in 2012 when I was co-instructing at a cold case investigation seminar in San Antonio, Texas, sponsored by the outstanding Virginia Center for Policing Innovation. He impressed me with his enthusiasm and from-the-heart passion and dedication to resolving the unresolved. We stayed in touch over the years, and I have watched his achievements and progress through untold number of conversations, emails, visits, his involvement with the Vidocq Society and with the Mid-Atlantic Cold Case Homicide Investigator's Association (MACCHIA). As I considered this passing of the gavel, it was my opinion that he possessed and had demonstrated the critical components to ultimately contribute to and lead in the future of our groundbreaking achievement—tenacity, passion, strength of character, and dedication.

Dr. Rachel H. Walton
Price, UT
2024

I

The Investigation

The Cold Case Problem

1

RACHEL H. WALTON
AND FRANK P. TONA

Introduction

The purpose of this chapter is to present a brief overview of the background of homicide in the United States, how it has been identified and recorded, and the emergent basis for practical unsolved homicide investigation. In addition, this chapter will also review trends and patterns of twentieth- and twenty-first-century homicides in the United States, and how these affect the later day investigations and operations of homicide investigators assigned to investigate unsolved, *cold case* homicides in the twenty-first century. In this author's experience, these eras from the 1960s to the present day harbor the bulk of such cases as may confront current investigators. This chapter will review homicide and homicide data to identify the scope of unsolved murders in the United States at this time and will provide an overview of the trends and advances in the forensic sciences and their application to cold case homicide investigation. The chapter will conclude by reviewing circumstances that contribute to cases growing cold and to recent trends to reinvestigate such cases.

What's in a Name: Hot versus Cold Case Homicide

The very use of the term "cold case" is controversial among homicide investigators and others associated with the investigation of unsolved murders. Such terminology may suggest to some that unsolved cases are unworkable and impossible and offer no hope for future solution. This term may convey a false impression to family and friends of unsolved murder victims that their cases do not count anymore, that their case will never be resolved, and that as a result, their case is old and "cold" and has been forgotten. Counter to this philosophy is the use of the terms unsolved or unresolved when it comes to referencing such murder cases. As will be discussed in future chapters, the wounds of murder are sub-surface in the hearts and minds of those who have suffered the violent loss of a loved one or a close friend, and "closure" is a misnomer. Like the proverbial pebble cast upon still waters, the ripple effect continues. Despite what media and others may suggest at times, for families and friends there is no closure.

DOI: 10.4324/9781003415633-3

A common perception of cold case homicides is that they are unsolved murders previously reported to law enforcement and investigated but that failed to result in the identification and arrest of a suspect and filing of criminal charges. Due to the passage of time and lack of investigative leads, they are no longer actively pursued by investigators. To the best of my knowledge, the popular application of the phrase and the concept of "cold case" homicide has been attributed to the news media in the Metro Dade region of Florida.

A high-profile rape–murder of an 11-year-old girl during a surge in homicides in the 1980s prompted the homicide section to assign a four-man team of highly experienced detectives to solve the case. They did so, and the concept of a special team of investigators to work unsolved cases that others do not have time to work grew. The effort was the first of several successes for the "Pending Case Squad." The media, however, coined a new term and called them the "Cold Case Squad." The name stuck. Similarly, "cold" has been used in countless western and police movies when describing a trail or a search for someone.

The Los Angeles County Sheriff's Department (California), however, has maintained its Unsolved Unit in the Homicide Bureau since the 1970s. In the past two decades, numerous law enforcement agencies have formed their own cold case squads, with detectives and investigators tasked to reinvestigate previously investigated yet unsolved murders.

Some of these will be presented in the following chapters.

Media focus and attention on this topic in the past decades have brought about public awareness of this aspect of homicide investigation. In a positive manner, this attention has heightened media coverage, and the use of social media platforms has significantly raised public awareness of this facet of homicide investigations. This increased attention has had several positive effects, including:

- Fostering public interest in revisiting older unsolved cases, leading to potential breakthroughs.
- Garnering public understanding and support for law enforcement efforts to allocate resources to cold case investigations.
- Encouraging individuals with knowledge of unsolved homicides to come forward with information.
- Prompting law enforcement agencies to take a proactive approach in reexamining cold cases.
- Serving as a stark reminder to individuals who have thus far evaded justice that law enforcement remains committed and vigilant, ensuring that their cases are not forgotten or overlooked.

Conversely, hot homicides are those murders that are known to law enforcement and are in the initial, active investigation phase. Most commonly in this scenario,

- A murder or finding of a body is reported to law enforcement.
- Officers and investigators respond to the scene.
- Witnesses are located and interviewed.
- Forensic services are enlisted.
- The victim is identified.
- The cause and manner of death are established.
- Investigators seek to identify what happened and who did it.
- In doing so, they write reports and document their actions, building the case—and their knowledge—day by day.

These actions result in the identification and arrest of a suspect and filing of criminal charges. If not, the case may become an unsolved homicide.

Once the media coins a term, we are often stuck with it whether we like it and agree with it or not. The term "cold case homicide" has come to be collectively understood by the public and the media as an older, unsolved murder. What is considered "cold" to one investigator or to one law enforcement agency, however, may not be shared by other investigators or agencies.

For the purposes of this book, murder is the intentional killing of one human being by another without legal justification or excuse. While it is the least frequent of violent crimes, it is also the ultimate crime against the person. In our culture, we value life and do not want anyone to get away with murdering another person. For the protection of society and the rule of law, it is incumbent upon the police to identify those who kill and for the criminal justice system to adjudicate their actions in accordance with the law.

In both hot and cold homicide scenarios, investigators routinely seek to answer the questions:

- What happened?
- Who is my victim?
- Who had the opportunity to do it?
- How did it happen?
- Why did it happen?
- Where did it happen?

As in a hot homicide investigation, cold case investigators seek to learn why the victim was killed and who had the means, opportunity, and motive to do so (MOM). Over the centuries, these motives have not changed. People still commit murder for love, for money or power, in anger or rage, or for retribution of a real or imagined wrong. Cold case investigators may also consider:

- Murder-suicide
- Thrill killing
- Self-defense
- Random killing
- Sex and sadism
- Love triangles
- Jealousy
- Drug connection
- Political terrorism

What + How + Why + When = Who?

Whichever the case, there is no one-best-way or one-size-fits-all method of investigation. Each cold case is investigated on its own merits based upon the remaining written record and the circumstances surrounding the crime. Modern cold case investigation teams apply professional law enforcement practices with forensic knowledge and technology. This combination has been successfully applied to revisiting unsolved murders dating back 20, 30, …, even 50 years, or more.

"I treat a cold case the same as a fresh homicide…I still have to answer the same questions" …. Detective Wally Hendricks, Carbon County Sheriff's Office, Utah.

"Iceman"

The circumstances and cause of death surrounding Iceman illustrate several lessons for those who would examine cold cases. Iceman, or Iceman Ötzi, was a well-preserved human being whose mummified remains were discovered frozen face down in a glacier approximately 11,000 feet above sea level in the Ötztal Alps bordering Italy and Austria in September 1991. The reporting parties were two German hikers. It was initially believed that he was a hiker who had died from a fall, or perhaps perished from hypothermia or drowning.

Figure 1.1 illustrates an artist's rendition of what Iceman Ötzi may have looked like based upon examination of the remains. He has a beard, a coat made of natural material, and a bow and arrows.

Examination of the remains, clothing, and possessions—he was armed with an unfinished bow, arrows, and dagger—indicated that he was approximately 46 years old and had died approximately 5,300 years before. The find ultimately became a media sensation and attracted the interest of the public and researchers worldwide, perhaps not unlike media attention in high-profile cases today. Initial theories and findings regarding the cause and manner of death—including suggestions that he was a human sacrifice—have been revised based upon still ongoing investigation and research, and now suggest

Figure 1.1 Iceman Ötzi. (© South Tyrol Museum of Archaeology, http://www.iceman.it.)

the circumstances surrounding his final meal, movements, and events preceding his death, information desirable in cold case investigations.

Forensic examination revealed an arrow point in his left shoulder. Years later, however, one of the two people who discovered the body subsequently stated that when first observed, Iceman was clutching a knife in his right hand. Such information, as in more recent cold case homicide investigations, brought a fresh examination and interpretation of the deceased and of the events surrounding his death.

A knife had been found at the scene but was apparently dislodged when the mummified remains were removed. A cold case investigator seeking to examine this case would inquire if there were any photographs taken in situ, before the body was moved. When later placed in Iceman's clenched hand, the knife did fit. Examinations revealed what appeared to be a defensive wound on his right hand, a gash on his left hand, a slash on his right forearm, and bruising on his torso. Deoxyribonucleic acid (DNA) examination of his effects revealed different sequences of ancient human DNA. DNA from his cloak, a broken arrow point, the arrow shaft, and his knife blade did not match Iceman's DNA.

Modern forensic and legal-medico disciplines involved included DNA, plant morphology, metallurgy, archaeology, odontology, anthropology, and more. These disciplines are not infrequently used today by homicide investigators, in both hot and cold cases. Ultimately, examiners concluded that he had been involved in a fight. He had been shot with an arrow from behind while fighting with at least one other assailant and most likely bled to death from the arrow wound, although scientists now believe the fatal wound was a blow to the head (Owen 2013). In many ways, this was the coldest of cold cases.

Murder in the Twentieth and Twenty-First Centuries

The number of unsolved murders which have occurred in the United States during this time frame is unknown. No comprehensive databases for reporting or recording murder existed in the United States throughout much of the twentieth century. While some states, such as Utah and Washington, have now implemented statewide databases to identify and track unsolved homicides, no such government resources exist today that accurately track unsolved cases on a national basis. Historically, the Vital Statistics Division of the National Center for Health Statistics (NCHS) recorded mortality information resulting from death certificate information as received from coroners and/or medical examiners.

In the early years of the twentieth century, some states reported death certificate information, while others did not. It was not until the 1930s that vital statistics reporting became fully national. Prior to this time, the reliability and presence of this information depended on which cities and states participated. While some eastern cities such as Boston and Washington, DC, furnished such information in the late nineteenth century, Georgia reportedly did not begin to provide this information until 1922, and Texas followed suit in 1933. Beginning in the mid-1930s, data based on law enforcement and mortality have been increasingly more reliable than the sporadic data of the first third of the century (NCHS 2004).

In the early part of the century, coroners in some locales in the United States practiced a fee-for-service program for enumeration. By this method, they were paid in part depending upon the manner of death they decreed for each death. A fee schedule was linked to the cause of death reported, irrelevant of the difficulty or length of time of the case. In the case of murder, the fee was often to be collected from the convicted perpetrator. One can only imagine that when a body was found with multiple gunshot wounds in the back, and with no known suspect in sight, the cause and manner of death may have been recorded as other than murder. I have reviewed some murder cases going back to the 1930s in which I wondered about the true circumstances of death.

In 2015, the National Institute of Justice (NIJ) assembled a team of subject matter experts to assess and review the status of these investigations nationwide and suggest protocols and mechanisms which could assist local law enforcement in resolving these cases. This comprehensive examination and review of successful national practices centered upon the formation of a specialized cold case investigation unit and included suggestions regarding utilization of vetted civilians, victim-witness trained personnel, means to obtain public support, and many more. Published in 2017, this 158-page report is a comprehensive model based upon the years of practical experience by the team members. It may be found on the web as NIJ Office of Justice Programs report NCJ252016.

Figure 1.2 shows the multi-colored cover of the report with various mini-images of items related to criminal justice and forensics such as evidence bags, rows of boxes containing case files, forensic personnel in white lab coats and a gavel.

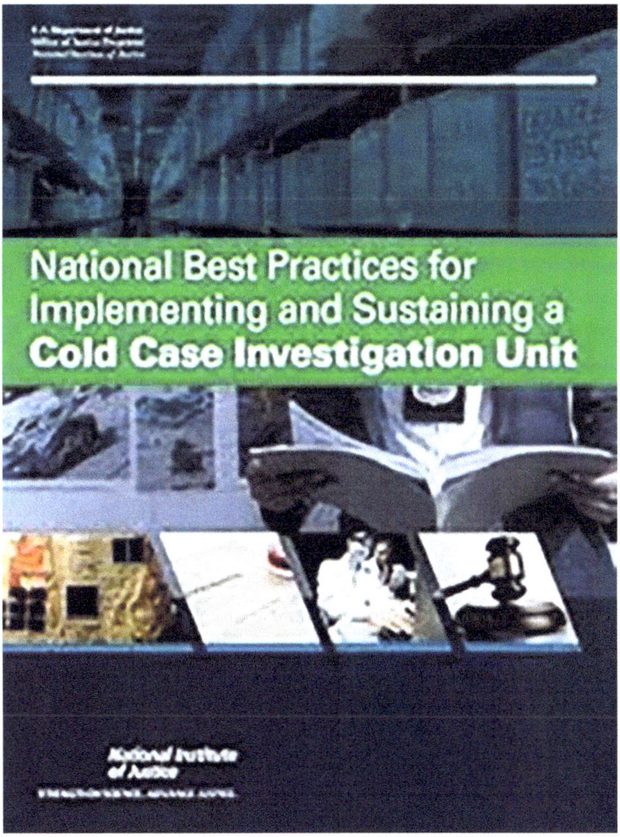

Figure 1.2 Cover of NIJ. (National Best Practices for Implementing and Sustaining a Cold Case Investigation Unit.)

Modern Crime Reporting

According to the U.S. Department of Justice, Bureau of Justice Statistics (BJS), homicide is of interest not only due to its severity but also because it is a reliable barometer of all violent crime and is a crime most likely to be reported and investigated (BJS 1.5.04). No other crime is measured as precisely and accurately as homicide. In addition, homicide is one means by which the public gauges police operation and efficiency. In 1929, the International Association of Chiefs of Police established a system to begin to uniformly collect law enforcement statistics and record national crime information. This was done in such a way as to standardize variations in which crimes were defined in various regions of the country.

The following year, the Bureau of Investigation (later renamed the Federal Bureau of Investigation or FBI) initiated the Crime in the United States: Uniform Crime Reporting (UCR) program. Subsequently, law enforcement data at the national level began to be compiled in 1933 (FBI UCR 8.22.04). This program has continued to today with advancements in collection and reporting formats.

Sources of early murder data are sometimes questionable or incomplete. Not every jurisdiction and police agency participated in this program in the early 1930s, nor do they today. The program's initial objective was to provide an accounting of the nature and extent of criminal activity and was intended to serve as an administrative tool for better criminal justice management within law enforcement agencies. In the succeeding decades, the UCR has become a source to gauge the country's social order and is referenced by urban planners and scholars.

Under the UCR system, the FBI Criminal Justice Information Services (CJIS) division publishes an annual report, Crime in the Nation. The data for this report are gathered from reports submitted by law enforcement as known to law enforcement. In the period 2021–2023 the program began migrating to a new data collection system, the National Incident-Based Reporting System (NIBRS). Other publications include Law Enforcement Officers Killed and Assaulted (LEOKA), and Hate Crime Statistics, among others. Contribution of data is still voluntary, however, and not all law enforcement agencies may participate. This change resulted from recognition that the original reporting system did not include sufficient victim–offender information and much more concerning specific instances of a crime. This information is reported directly to the FBI or through respective centralized state agencies and summarizes the amount of crime reported the previous year. It includes expanded homicide, property crime, arrest data, and much more. Today, NIBRS and the UCR are continually evolving systems.

Rates and Trends, 1900–2000 Homicide Rates

Population and demographic changes and post-turn-of-the-century immigration changed the nation. During this period, much of the nation underwent transformation from agrarian and rural to more urban in nature, and the big cities saw concentrated pockets of those with similar ethnic and cultural origins. The crime patterns and trends that originated during this period have in part become the basis for police, legal, and forensic practices today. During this period, the murder rate has varied significantly.

This is reflected in Figure 1.3.

Figure 1.3 is a timeline graph of homicide rates per year from 1900 to 2000. The compilation of homicide data from death certificates for the whole of the twentieth century makes it possible to view rises and falls in the homicide rate, the number of homicide victims per 100,000 population. This can be viewed against a backdrop of national events, and certain major occurrences appear to have contributed to changes in the crime rate during the century. According to the National Vital Statistics System, the murder rate rose from almost 1 homicide per 100,000 population to a peak of 9.8 in 1933; it fell to a low of 4.5 per 100,000 population between 1934 and 1958 and rose to peak at 10.2 per 100,000 population in 1980.

Post–World War I (WWI) events saw increased reporting on crime by the national press and reaction from state and federal governments. National Prohibition, that period between 1920 and 1933 when America went dry,

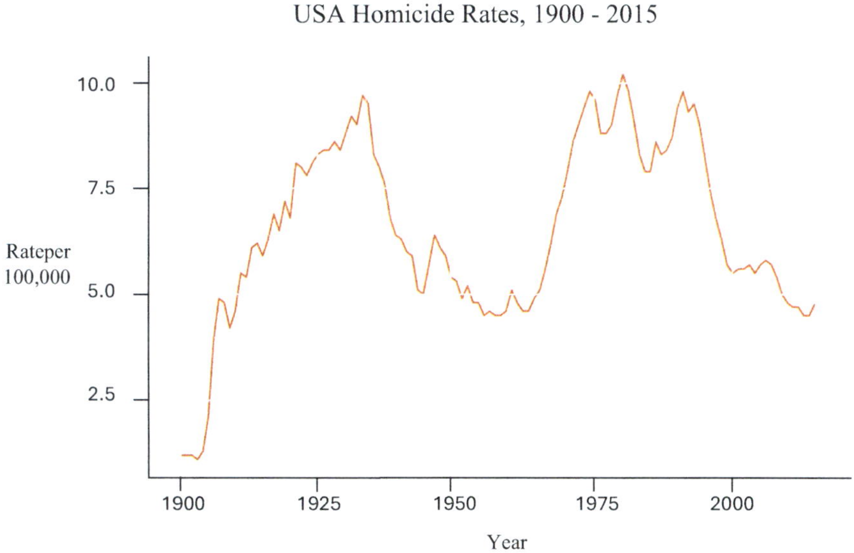

Figure 1.3 Homicide rate, 1900–2000. (Courtesy of National Center for Health Statistics Vital Statistics, n.d.)

brought organized crime to the forefront of national attention and the efforts of federal law enforcement to assume a stronger role in criminal investigation. In part due to the use of machine guns by gangsters and others during this period, America witnessed the origins of national gun control through the beginning of the National Firearms Act in 1934, which regulated private possession of fully automatic firearms. High-profile crimes such as the 1932 Lindberg abduction brought forth federal legislation addressing kidnapping as well as the federal Bank Robbery Act of 1934. These and others paved the way for future federal legislation encompassing a wide variety of topics in the later part of the century.

The subsequent period witnessed the recovery from the Great Depression and America's entry into WWII in 1941. These events affected the homicide rate, as evidenced by a sharp decline during the war years and a short-time rise thereafter. The rates fell during the 1950s, but the maturity of the postwar baby boom began to emerge in the early 1960s. At this time, the homicide rate began to rise sharply. Subsequently, this increase occurred against a backdrop of the Vietnam War and the sharp increase in drugs and gangs. This period gave rise to increasing numbers of unresolved murders.

Clearance Rates

Clearance rates are the number of homicides that are cleared or solved. Acting as a national clearinghouse for such homicide data, the FBI uniform crime report also describes the conditions by which a homicide case is considered solved or cleared (closed) for crime report purposes. Each of these is a potential option in closing a cold case investigation. While a law enforcement agency may close a case through administrative action, it may not be necessarily cleared as an offense for purposes of the UCR or NIBRS.

These are as follows:

- When at least one person is arrested, charged with the commission of an offense, and turned over to a court for prosecution.
- By exceptional means. This occurs when circumstances beyond the law enforcement agency's control preclude the agency from placing formal charges against an identified offender.

To clear a crime in this manner, an agency must have (1) identified the offender, (2) enough evidence to support an arrest, (3) identified the offender's location, and (4) a reason outside the agency's control that does not allow the agency to arrest, charge, and prosecute an offender. These circumstances may occur when the offender dies by suicide or is justifiably killed by police or citizenry. Official closure of the case may also result when the victim refuses to cooperate with the prosecution after the identification of the offender or denial of extradition because the offender committed a crime in another jurisdiction and is being prosecuted.

Law enforcement agencies like to reflect high clearance rates for homicide and other violent crimes. In some instances, however, reviews have found that cases were "closed by arrest," but charges were subsequently not filed or were dismissed at a preliminary hearing. The true numbers of how many murders have occurred in the United States in any given period is unknown. Crime in the Nation reports those offenses known to police, but somewhere in between these crimes known to police and those that occurred and are unknown is the Dark Circle of murder numbers.

During these last decades, however, another trend became evident. This trend is a foundation for cold case investigators today: the number of homicides cleared by arrest has been declining. In 1965, the homicide clearance rates were approximately 93% and has shown a precipitous decline to 2022 to an estimated 52.3%.

However, it's important to note that clearance rates can vary significantly from one city to another and can be influenced by factors such as whether an agency reported crime statistics to the FBI, the quality of police investigations, community cooperation, resources allocated to solving homicides, and the complexity of the cases.

Figure 1.4 is a graph provided by Mr. Tom Hargrove, Founder and Chairman of the Murder Accountability Project (MAP), a private organization which tracks America's unsolved homicides. This graph reflects the FBI's CJIS clearance estimate from 1965 to 2022.

Thomas K. Hargrove is a retired Washington, DC-based investigative journalist and former White House correspondent. While working as a national correspondent for the Scripps Howard News Service, Hargrove developed an algorithm that uses FBI homicide data to identify clusters of murders with an elevated probability of containing serial killings. Authorities in Youngstown, Ohio, and Gary, Indiana, opened new homicide investigations in 2010 because of Hargrove's findings. The algorithm's identification of 15 unsolved strangulations in Gary was corroborated in 2014 with the arrest of Darren Deon Vann, who confessed to killing women for decades and then took police to abandoned properties in Gary where the bodies of six previously unknown strangulation victims were recovered.

He founded the nonprofit MAP in 2015. This private organization maintains a database to track unsolved homicides and suspicious deaths nationwide and focuses on analyzing patterns and trends in unsolved homicides to

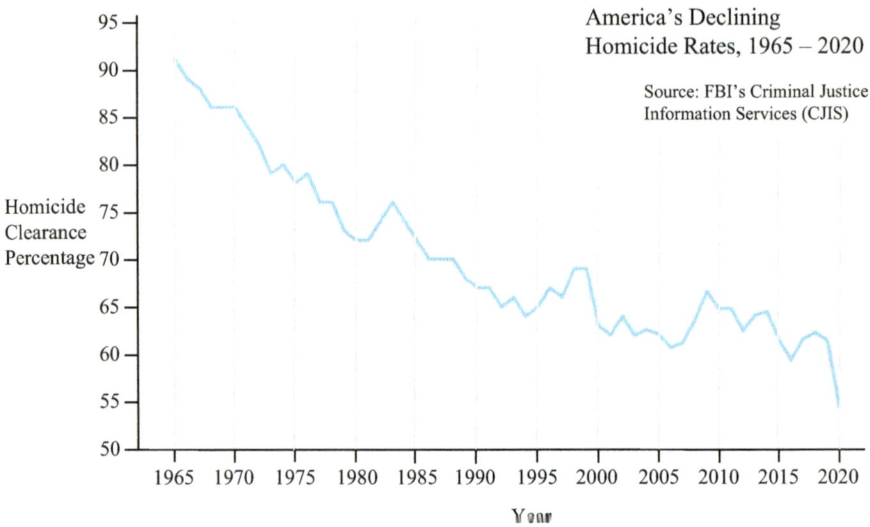

Figure 1.4 Graph, "America's Declining Homicide Clearance Rates 1965–2022." The exact number of homicides cleared cannot be finitely determined. (Mr. Tom Hargrove, Murder Accountability Project.)

assist law enforcement agencies in their investigations. Hargrove is available to answer questions from police officers or the press and can be emailed at hargrove@murderdata.org or by phone at 571-606-5999.

Figure 1.4 is a line graph showing a line reflecting estimated homicide clearance rates from 1965 to 2022, the line beginning in the upper left corner in the year 1965 and reflecting a downward trajectory to 2022.

Years	Total Homicides	Total Uncleared
Uncleared homicides 1965–2023	1,413,427	334,652
Uncleared homicides 1970–2023	1,343,610	327,075
Uncleared homicides 1980–2023	1,110,342	286,830
Uncleared homicides 1990–2023	844,872	228,508

Need new illustration to visually demonstrate homicide clearance rates, especially pre-post COVID Got it as Figure 1.4.... See MAP – "Floyd effect" homicides up 30%.

Background of Current Cold Case Problem

Analysis of long-term trends reported by the suggested that the homicide rate doubled from the early 1960s to the late 1970s, peaking at 10.2 per 100,000 population in 1980, and falling off only to rise again in the late 1980s and early 1990s to peak at 9.8 per 100,000 in 1991. By 1997, the nation's murder rate fell to the lowest level in 3 decades. Most of this occurred in cities with more than 1 million inhabitants, where the rate fell from 35.5 per 100,000 population in 1991 to 20.3 per 100,000. Nationally, murder rates declined to 5.5 per 100,000 by 2000, levels last seen in the mid-1960s (BJS 2005).

This decline allowed many law enforcement agencies the opportunity to dedicate resources to the re-examination of previously unsolved, cold case homicides and unidentified persons. Time and experience are now showing us that many of the cold cases with potential for reinvestigation have fallen within these periods, or later, due to significant changes in investigative and forensic practices. However, the increasing numbers of homicides and other violent crimes in the years since the turn of this century have counterbalanced this as agencies strive to keep pace with current crime levels.

In 2017, in their national best practices guide for implementing and sustaining a cold case unit, the guide suggested that there were more than 180,000 unsolved homicides nationwide since 1980, and researcher James Adcock used UCR and supplemental homicide reporting data to suggest a figure of 230,355 unresolved homicide cases for 1980–2014 (Adcock, J. as reported in Best Practices Guide). This is significant for understanding the cold case problem in the United States as estimates suggest that approximately 40%–50% of the murders nationwide have remained unsolved (NIJ Best Practices). It is important to note that arrests made after the initial reporting would impact the total number of unsolved cases, but as this information is not tracked outside of the investigating agency, this information is not known. However, these numbers indicate the potential scope of the problem.

Figuratively speaking, as each decade advances, it may be fair to say that 1 decade's worth of unsolved cases falls off at the back end, due to this passage of time.

"One of the most troubling aspects of cold cases is that we do not know precisely how many exist."—NIJ Best Practices Guide

As can be seen by this review, the bottom line IS we just do not know how many unsolved homicides exist in America. On top of this data, the question is asked "what impact does the expansion of drug cartels in the past 20 years have on these numbers?" This begs the question as to how many deaths have occurred due to the rise in the fatal use of fentanyl in the past decades. Are these murders? Were they investigated as a criminal homicide?

Advances in Forensic Science

Trace evidence, the idea that there occurred a transfer of telltale evidence from an offender to a victim or a crime scene, was formally advanced in the early twentieth century by Edmond Locard (1877–1966). A Frenchman, Locard was the founder of the anthropometric service within the Lyon Police Service shortly before WWI. Locard later served as an educator in forensics and strongly advocated analysis and examination of microscopic "trace" evidence. He noted that inculpatory evidence of a perpetrator was to be found in the examination of soil and dust, and that examination of clothing, shoes, underclothing, body parts (including skin, hair, and nails), as well as weapons and vehicles would reveal a telltale linkage between the offender and the scene or the victim. If the offender did not bring something to the scene, he certainly took something away, and proper forensic, microscopic examination would reveal it. Thus, the foundations of trace, or microscopic, evidence are to be found in the contact between people, places, and objects. With the advent of DNA technology late in the century, Locard's theories are consistent with our use of this advanced technology.

Blood and Serology

Scientific investigation in the nineteenth century, as it was, recognized the forensic potential for detecting blood at crime scenes and upon the clothing of suspected perpetrators. At the beginning of the twentieth century, science lacked a reliable method of distinguishing between bloodstains of an animal and of a human. Bloodstains did not mean much in most investigations, as a claim could be made that they came from a nosebleed or an animal, depending upon the need of the suspect. Science could not reliably differentiate.

This changed in 1901, however, when Paul Uhlenhuth discovered a method to distinguish human blood from that of animals. This was the beginning of the branch of science of serology. The precipitin test, as it came to be known, soon became a benchmark in scientific criminology. About this same time, Karl Landsteiner reasoned the existence of different blood types and the compatibility or incompatibility among certain groups of people. He identified three blood groups, A, B, and C. Shortly thereafter, C became AB, and O was recognized. Thus, the four groups we know today were identified in the first years of the twentieth century. The use of this knowledge was primarily applied to paternity issues, however. For criminal cases in America, the science did not go far beyond separating animal from human during the first half of the century. Blood spatter, or blood pattern analysis, likewise was generally not recognized for its forensic value at this time.

Firearms Identification and Other Evidence

The concept of matching a fired projectile to a specific firearm dates at least to the eighteenth century. More formal, albeit less scientific, application of this concept began to surface in the later part of the 1900s and early twentieth century. A series of high-profile crimes during the first quarter of the century focused America's attention on the application of science to the criminal justice process and the courtroom. On April 15, 1920, an armored car robbery in Braintree, Massachusetts, resulted in the shooting deaths of a guard and a paymaster. Police arrested shoe factory worker Nicola Sacco and itinerant fish peddler Bartolomeo Vanzetti, and they were charged with the murders. This was the era of the Red Scare, and both men were active anarchists. Racial and political overtones transcended the legal aspects of the case, and it attracted international attention.

Forensic examination presented by the prosecution affirmed that their weapon fired the fatal shots, and both were sentenced to death. Others disagreed. In the courtroom process, those who testified for the prosecution that fired projectiles and shell casings came from a specific weapon were countered by experts for the defense that the suspect weapon did not fire the items. After lengthy legal appeals and controversy surrounding witness identification and forensic presentations in the courtroom, both men were executed in 1927. In this and other cases, juries were left to believe or disregard the testimony of "experts." During this period, anyone with a microscope and a camera could hold themselves out to be a "criminologist," and the field was marked by charlatans and frauds. The expert witness had come to stay.

In June 1925, the *Saturday Evening Post* reported upon the advances in forensics as pertaining to firearms examinations and "fingerprinting" of bullets. The public was informed of the advances in matching fired projectiles to specific firearms and of a new device, the comparison microscope. This piece of equipment was developed by Charles Waite, a former New York attorney general's investigator; John Fisher, a student of physics; chemist Howard Gravelle; and reserve army officer Calvin Goddard, MD. It utilized two lens systems, which, when combined with prisms, allowed an examiner to bring two images side by side for comparison. Thus, an examiner could compare a suspect projectile and a known exemplar together under conditions more conducive to accurate comparison and analysis than previous methods. Goddard and others advanced the use of forensic sciences and the establishment of formal schools for training others in the application of science to the courtroom and in the criminal investigation process. Goddard and others were the harbingers of professional standards in the area of identifying characteristics of spent bullets and shell casings, and upon examination of firearms for forensic purposes. Should we just condense this way down?

On the West Coast in this same time period, Edward O. Heinrich (Figure 1.5) offered law enforcement and the courtroom process the results of years of formal academic training and experience in the physical sciences. He was, perhaps, America's first academically trained forensic scientist. Upon graduation from the University of California at Berkeley with a degree in chemistry in 1908, Heinrich began to apply the field to areas in criminal investigation. As a generalist, his practice included a variety of forensic skills, including questioned document and firearms examination. During the ensuing decades, he was employed to examine evidence in a multitude of high-profile murders and other cases. Upon his death in 1953, his life works including case files, notebooks, photo archives, and other records were bequeathed to his alma mater. Evidence is where you find it.

This old photograph shows the scientist with camera photographing a pistol. Behind him is a bookshelf with books.

Cold case investigators can benefit from Heinrich's example. When reviewing cold cases in which any or all the law enforcement or forensic participants have passed away, it is suggested that investigators identify those who may possess their files and records and establish what records may still exist and review them. In the 1954 "Boulder Jane Doe" case described elsewhere in this book, investigators located the original pathologist, who still retained a copy of the autopsy report.

In 2007, the detective in the 1970 Sharon Jones rural Utah murder case study presented in Chapter 3 located the surviving magistrate who held a preliminary hearing for the suspect 40 years before as well as a former court clerk who retained a copy of the court records from that proceeding. My investigation into the 1925 murders and subsequent alleged rapes discovered the existence and location of Heinrich's case files, which included extensive notes, reports, and photographs. Among these records was the forensic case file for the homicide case. Figure 1.5 illustrates Heinrich's file photograph of Ryan's jacket. An examination of the bloodstains by a blood expert and physician identified human and nonhuman stains, a fact supporting Ryan's account and discounting the prosecution.

Accompanying notes and newspaper accounts reported that the pins were used to denote the direction of blood spatter. This file and its contents provided detailed information about case events and case forensics.

Figure 1.6 shows a leather jacket with pins through spots in the shoulder area, the points of the pins showing the direction of the pattern.

As do many such investigations, methods and techniques used involve thinking outside the box. Successful cold case investigations are often concluded because of investigators who are resourceful and use imagination not normally associated with hot homicide investigations. In the 1920s, local and state government agencies slowly began to build crime labs that

Figure 1.5 Criminalist E. O. Heinrich. For the first half of the twentieth century, Edward Oscar Heinrich advanced the forensic sciences by his application of science and technology in many high-profile criminal and civil cases. (Courtesy of Duayne J. Dillon, DCrim.)

Figure 1.6 Jack Ryan's jacket. In 1925, technology only allowed differentiation between human and animal blood. In this report concerning analysis of blood found on a suspect's jacket, Dr. Ernest Victors determined that both human and animal blood were present on the jacket. This ran counter to the prosecution's theory that only human blood was present and helped exonerate the defendant, who had a logical explanation for the presence of both types. (Courtesy of University Archives, Bancroft Library, University of California, Berkeley.)

could analyze physical evidence. In 1932, using a borrowed microscope, the origins of the FBI laboratory were born. By the middle of the century, the facility was conducting examinations for federal agencies and local and state law enforcement agencies. At this laboratory and others, forensic examinations included those related to firearms, serology, toolmark, paint, questioned documents, tire treads, shoe prints, and forensic geology. The field had come a long way in a short time. Just as investigators in pre-WWII era saw such dramatic changes in forensic technology back then, so too have current cold case investigators today, as crime laboratories have expanded upon these and many other forensic disciplines, most noteworthy being DNA.

By the late 1940s, the FBI laboratory was conducting forensic examinations in a variety of fields, ranging from firearms examination to fingerprints to paint analysis. Since the 1930s, the FBI laboratory has set high standards for forensic examination of evidence. (Author's collection.) Figure 1.7 shows the cover of magazine *FBI Law Enforcement Bulletin* with FBI seal in the center of the page.

Figure 1.7 1949 FBI Law Enforcement Bulletin.

Forensic Sciences and Advanced Technology

In the 1950s, scientific breakthroughs laid the groundwork for significant advances in forensic and criminal investigation processes at the end of the century. In 1953, American scientist James Watson and Britain Francis Crick demonstrated the double helix of the DNA molecule. This was the beginning of the ability to identify individuals not by grouping, as in ABO serology, but now down to the individual. In 1986, British scientist Alec Jeffries first applied DNA identification to the criminal investigative process. His efforts resulted in the identification and capture of a perpetrator for the rape–murders of two young girls in England by linking biological evidence left at the crime scene to a local baker. The forensic value of DNA quickly became apparent, but not just for conviction of criminal defendants. In 1989, the first U.S. DNA database was created, and in that year, David Vazquez reportedly became the first person in the United States exonerated through postconviction DNA testing. The forensic value of DNA became a highlight of forensic advances in the latter half of the century.

In 1992, the FBI introduced the Combined DNA Index System (CODIS). This system was designed to be a national database for linking crimes to criminals through DNA. In 1995, O. J. Simpson was acquitted of murder in a high-profile case despite strong DNA evidence against him. Evidence collection and custody issues were scrupulously analyzed in court and in the media, and as a result, methods of handling and testing of evidence underwent significant analysis and change. By 1994, 42% of the U.S. prosecutor's offices reported using DNA evidence in a felony case at least once, and by 2001, 68% reported such use (Prottas and Noble 2007, p. 310).

Perhaps more than any other aspect of forensic science, the use of DNA in criminal investigations has expanded beyond what even its earliest advocates might not have imagined. As will be covered in subsequent chapters, touch DNA, investigative genetic genealogy (IGG), DNA phenotyping of one's features to produce a potential image of the contributor of that DNA, and so much more have exploded upon the forensic landscape.

Other disciplines came into their own during the latter half of this century. In 1954, Marilyn Sheppard was murdered in Cleveland, Ohio. The investigation and subsequent trial became a media circus. Her husband, Dr. Sam Sheppard, was tried for her murder and convicted. Sheppard insisted throughout his life that a "bushy-haired" intruder committed the crime, knocking him unconscious and murdering his wife. He was convicted at trial, but the verdict was overturned on appeal due to undue publicity and violation of due process. At a second trial 10 years later, University of California forensic scientist Paul Kirk analyzed bloodstains and patterns at the crime scene. In a detailed report, he concluded that Sheppard's version was credible, and that the killer was left-handed. Kirk's role in this notorious crime enhanced forensic and public awareness of blood spatter analysis. After serving 10 years in prison, Dr. Sheppard was acquitted at a second trial and died in 1970. This case further illustrates the value of determining the disposition of the case files, notes, and records of case personnel. In the late 1990s, legal action was brought to clear Dr. Sheppard's name. Two vials of blood from the crime scene were discovered in the property acquired by one of Kirk's students who had acquired some of the famed scientist's property after his demise. It became a focal point in the resultant civil action. See Figure 1.8.

Sheppard Evidence Turns Up in Bay Area

Blood from 1954 slaying in 2 vials

Associated Press

Cleveland

Missing blood evidence from the Dr. Sam Sheppard murder case has resurfaced in the Bay Area, potentially offering new clues as to whether he committed the slaying that inspired TV's "The Fugitive."

A court order says the material in Walnut Creek — forgotten for decades — includes two vials containing bloodstains taken from a wardrobe door in Marilyn Sheppard's bedroom after her 1954 slaying.

Sam Sheppard

Sheppard spent 10 years in prison for the beating death of his pregnant wife. He was acquitted at a second trial in 1966 and died four years later.

The doctor insisted throughout his life that a "bushy-haired intruder" knocked him unconscious and killed his wife.

Sheppard's estate, on behalf of the couple's only son, Sam Reese Sheppard, who lives in Oakland, is now suing the state of Ohio in civil court, claiming wrongful imprisonment.

The wardrobe bloodstains are "of huge significance," Terry Gilbert, an attorney for the younger Sheppard, said yesterday. "It is a potential source of blood from a third-party suspect in the murder room itself, something that we have not had yet in this case."

County prosecutors maintain that too much time has passed and too much evidence has been lost to make a definitive conclusion about the killer.

Cuyahoga County Common Pleas Judge Ronald Suster ordered last week that the bloodstains be sent back to Cleveland from Walnut Creek, where they are in the hands of forensic scientist John Murdoch.

Murdoch was a student at the University of California at Berkeley of Paul Kirk, a forensic scientist hired by the Sheppard family.

In 1955, Kirk collected samples and analyzed bloodstains at the crime scene. He concluded that Sheppard's blood was not present in the room.

From the shape of the bloodstain on the wardrobe, he also deduced that it came from the killer touching it, rather than from blood spattered from Marilyn Sheppard.

Kirk died in 1970, and when his office was later cleaned out, Murdoch received a box of material related to the case, including the vials with the bloodstains, Gilbert said. Murdoch, who now works for the federal Bureau of Alcohol Tobacco and Firearms, learned through another scientist about the current case and contacted the Sheppard team last month.

Murdoch was at a meeting in Maryland yesterday and could not be reached.

Figure 1.8 San Francisco Chronicle news story about Sam Sheppard. It is suggested that cold case investigators seek to identify the disposition of the forensic collections of deceased forensic scientists involved in now-cold-case investigations. (San Francisco Chronicle.) Newspaper article. (Sheppard Evidence Turns Up In Bay Area.)

Role and Influence of the Media

Traditional media such as newsprint and radio/television have been supplemented by a new phenomenon, social media. Whatever the form, media has affected investigative efforts in the field as well as events in the nation's courtrooms. The results have directly impacted the public perception of law enforcement and forensic science.

Cops and the Media

In the early 1950s, television began to supplement and replace newsprint as a prime source of America's news. Television shows about the police, including M Squad and Dragnet, popularized and glamorized the police role, especially homicide detectives. This popularization, however, sometimes misinformed the public and tainted their view of the homicide investigation process, and of police work in general. Early television shows such as The Andy Griffith Show and Car 54, Where Are You? portrayed law enforcement in a comical and unrealistic setting. While vast differences did, and do, exist between large metropolitan agencies and their rural counterparts, these images have carried to this day in the minds of the baby boomer and subsequent generations through reruns of these episodes. More recently, social media and traditional media microanalysis of law enforcement actions has further contributed to public (mis)understanding of the police investigative role. Perception is reality, and these events may impact cold case investigators. In older cases, perception of the police from movies or television may affect the willingness of some to speak to the police about events long ago and to cooperate with cold case investigators. These perceptions may also carry over into the jury pool in a courtroom.

Television shows about police work saturated the airwaves during the last quarter of the century. Programs from the 1960s and 1970s such as Adam-12 and Police Story gave insight into police practices and professionalized the law enforcement image. In the last decade of the century, television programs such as NYPD Blue and Law and Order impacted the way America viewed law enforcement and the court process. True-life television coverage of events such as the Los Angeles–based Symbionese Liberation Army (SLA) shootout and the Rodney King and O. J. Simpson episodes also contributed to America's perception of police and police practices.

The 1990s and the beginnings of the twenty-first century marked a turning point in television and Hollywood's script-based portrayal of law enforcement. Programs such as Cops and America's Most Wanted portrayed the reality of law enforcement and reminded viewers that the world of police work is sometimes brutal and violent, and the police investigation process cannot be accomplished between commercials. In this evolution, however, a new trend emerged that has impacted homicide investigations and the courtroom process, and cold case investigations. This was the marriage of television with the courtroom and forensics.

Television shows based on advances in forensic sciences such as CSI, Cold Case, and Cold Case Files emerged as among the most popular and watched in television. (However, I have never seen a crime scene investigator or technician come to a scene or the laboratory in leather pants and high heels.) Together with television coverage of ongoing investigations and live courtroom proceedings, these elements have combined to impact the public's perception about forensics and police work in general (and particularly homicide investigation). As a result, advances in forensics as well as law enforcement investigative methods are perhaps more closely scrutinized now than in decades past.

This is significant for cold case investigators as they must build upon the work of others performed during a different period and perhaps with a different level of expectation, and subsequently develop it to meet today's standards. Previous evidence identification and collection practices may directly affect their ability in these cold case investigations. Such has contributed to the "CSI Effect," the media-based perception of what police and forensics can and cannot do and which is carried into the courtroom by potential jurors who are negatively influenced by these.

Further, media coverage of "wrongful convictions" and research and publicity about those factors that contributed to the conviction of innocent persons for crimes that they did not commit has further placed the criminal justice process under the microscope of public scrutiny. While past investigation and forensic practices have been identified as contributing factors in these miscarriages of justice, some media have contributed to the dissemination of misinformation and enhanced misconception by the public in this regard.

Influence of Law Enforcement Culture, Organization, and Practices

The changing landscape of American law enforcement has challenged and affected the ability of cold case investigators to resolve unresolved "cold case" homicides. In the late 1960s, most of the nation's 40,000 police forces had 10 or fewer personnel. In many instances, organizational structure and practices had not changed perceptively for decades. In the past, coordination among agencies was sometimes sporadic and informal, and rivalries and jealousies between some police departments and sheriff's departments negatively impacted the resolution of crimes, including murders. Unfortunately, in this writer's experience, such have carried over even to this day in some locales. The result is a lack of communication and coordination. This fragmentation plays into the ability of perpetrators to commit their crimes, cross jurisdictional boundaries, and get away.

In 2022, the NIJ Report noted that "almost half (46%) of all local police departments employed fewer than 10 full-time-equivalent sworn officers" (NIJ Report NCJ305187, November 2022). As with other occupations, time and experience make for a better and more efficient individual. Coupled with the fact that homicide investigation may be the quintessential example of the necessity and role of on-the-job training, smaller departments had fewer homicides and thus officers could not or did not obtain the requisite "hands-on" training necessary.

Following WWII, many states increased selection and training standards for police-empowered personnel. In the mid-1970s, some agencies were implementing variations of community policing and redesigning their organizational structure. Some agencies, such as in Lakewood, Colorado, experimented with the abandonment of the police uniform in favor of less militaristic-style attire. Many, however, remained entrenched in the traditional hierarchy of patrol, traffic, detectives, and administration (Figure 1.9). Standards for selection of detectives varied, and it was not uncommon that such personnel, especially in smaller agencies, were promoted for reasons other than demonstrated investigative ability. Knowledge of past organizational structure, culture, and records and evidence practices is of importance to cold case investigators, and this will be discussed in further chapters.

America has long resisted any attempts to create a national, uniform police agency as is found in Europe and other countries. This is a condition crime writer Joseph Wambaugh has termed the "Balkanization" of the United States and is a contributing factor in the amount and nature of the cold case homicide problem in the United States. The landscape of American law enforcement is comprised of city police departments operating within an incorporated jurisdiction while county sheriffs are responsible for investigating crimes that occur within the unincorporated regions of the state in which the county is located. In addition, states operate their own agencies with statewide jurisdiction to investigate crimes, including murder, and these may be known as state police, state troopers, or other names. Further, murders committed on federal reservations may not be reflected in local statistics, and instead, these case files are in the custody and control of agencies such as the FBI or Naval Criminal Investigative Service or other military policing/investigation units.

As a result, multiple jurisdictions each with their own hierarchy, policies, ranks, rules, and procedures practiced their own brand of communication—or

Figure 1.9 A 1950s uniformed police officer/dispatcher. (Courtesy of El Segundo Police Department.) A police officer at a desk with a radio microphone to contact officers by radio.

in some cases, lack thereof. Similarly, each agency maintains its own system of information retention and retrieval, as well as property and evidence rules, procedures, and methods of evidence storage. Failure in intra-agency and interagency communications has been a contributory factor to the cold case problem.

Evolving forms of business technology also impacted law enforcement. The advent of microfiche and microfilm impacted department record keeping and retrieval, as well as transition from film photography to digital imaging. In the early 1980s, the personal computer began to revolutionize the way the world worked. Law enforcement recognized the advantages to computerizing records and communications, and a new means of recording and retrieving information evolved. These changes occurred in police agencies of all sizes, creating new sources of potential data retrieval for those investigating homicides and other serious crimes. Unfortunately, in some cases, as these records were converted to other formats, it was not uncommon for agencies to destroy the original records. In the 1970s, this writer's captain destroyed hundreds of older black-and-white booking photos, photos which should have been retained for future use by investigators when building a "6-pack" photo lineup. He saw no sense in it. These events merged to lay the foundation for a new type of homicide investigation and murder investigator, the cold case detective.

Roots of the Unsolved Problem Today

The highest homicide rates of the twentieth century occurred during its last 2 decades. FBI Agent Charles L. Regini summarized the background and nature of the cold case problem in his August 1997 report in the FBI Law Enforcement Bulletin. During this period, traditional patterns and trends were impacted by the rise in gangs and drugs, stranger killings, or drive-by shootings. The growth in drug-related homicides, crimes much more time consuming and difficult to solve, provided new challenges to law enforcement. During this era, murder became more vicious, senseless, and random. The link between victim and killer became more blurred, and motives were uncommonly thin. In addition, killers were not infrequently killed before they could be identified or located. Further, insufficient investigation allowed uncharged killers to be released back on the street to continue to kill.

During this period, traditional investigative approaches, such as focusing on motive, were less effective in solving these cases. Practical difficulties of identifying and locating witnesses, overcoming their hostility, and obtaining their confidence posed additional problems beyond the normal realm. Fear of retribution impacted efforts to secure witness cooperation and obtain needed testimony in court. Additionally, the lifestyles of many of these witnesses impacted credibility and compounded the difficulties in investigation and prosecution.

The ability of law enforcement to adequately investigate the sharp rise in homicides decreased under the onslaught as a steady stream of fresh murders taxed overworked investigative, forensic, and medical examiner resources. This was especially true in some of the nation's largest cities, but also in smaller jurisdictions and more rural areas. Available resources were not sufficient to keep up with the surge and spike in homicides. As a result, many agencies found themselves unable to supply the necessary fiscal, technological, educational, or manpower resources necessary to efficiently and adequately address each new homicide. In some cases, less experienced personnel lacking the skill and practice were assigned to investigate homicides (Eliopulos). The growth in stranger-to-stranger homicides further exacerbated the problem, as traditional homicide investigation focused on identifying a known victim–offender relationship.

What Are Cold Cases?

Cold case is a concept, and as such, there is no one standard definition of a cold case homicide. Definition of what is a cold case can vary from agency to agency, thus impacting any statistical attempt to identify such cases even within one state. Such was the problem in Arizona that a state-commissioned task force required law enforcement agencies to "use the same definition of a 'cold case homicide' to attempt to conduct a statewide survey" (Arizona Cold Case Task Force 2007 as cited in NIJ Best Practices p. 1).

An Arizona statute in 2014 defined that a cold case "…means a homicide or a felony sexual offense that remains unsolved for one year or more after being reported to a law enforcement agency and that has no viable and unexplored investigatory leads" (Justia U.S. Law 2014 as reported in NIJ Best Practices 2017, p. 1).

These may well be described as those homicides that others, perhaps more experienced, tried to solve and could not. These are homicides previously reported to law enforcement and investigated, yet lacking resolution. These are cases in which a suspect may have been known to the investigators, yet there was insufficient evidence for arrest and charging. These also include those cases in which no perpetrator has been identified, and the case is a whodunit.

Cold case homicides are among the most difficult and frustrating cases facing investigators. In addition to being previously reported and investigated, such cases may include homicides:

- In which the primary investigator has transferred or otherwise been detached from the case and the case is not currently assigned to an investigator
- In which no current investigative activity is taking place, due to lack of investigative leads or information
- At least a year old that have had no activity on them for at least 1 year, or a case in which the primary investigator has been transferred from the unit and it needs to be reassigned to a new investigator

In this writer's experience, this definition varies, and the specific designation of what constitutes a cold case rests with guidelines used by the individual law enforcement agency responsible for the investigation of the crime. Theirs is the definition they design to designate the parameters for those cases to be classified and investigated as cold case homicides within the agency. Some specify that a lengthy period of time must have elapsed since the commission of the crime. Others require that 1 year must have passed and/or a change of personnel involved in the investigation process must have occurred. Among the various definitions of a cold case homicide or cases to be investigated as cold case murders are those with parameters that include:

- Unsolved cases prior to a specific time (i.e., 1990).
- Unsolved cases during specific intervals (i.e., 1960–1995).
- Long-term missing-persons cases that have a high probability of being a homicide.
- Cases wherein enough time has passed that the perpetrator begins to feel confident enough to speak freely about his/her involvement, suggestively 4–5 years or more.
- Homicide cases older than 3 years from the date of the offense in which no arrests have been made.
- Homicide cases older than 3 years from the date of the offense that are "closed–active" or cases that were closed by arrest of a suspect, but the charges were dismissed without the suspect going to trial.
- Homicide cases less than 3 years old from the date of offense (including closed but active) in which all leads have been reasonably exhausted and investigation or assignment as a cold case homicide has been authorized by a responsible authority.
- Homicide cases in which the date that the death was ruled a homicide by the medical examiner's office is greater than 1 year after the original event that led to the decedent's death. This would include those cases wherein the victim dies more than 1 year after the fatal injuries were sustained.
- Undetermined deaths of a suspicious nature older than 1 year following the death.
- Any case linked to a case under active investigation by a cold case investigation unit.
- A case at least a year old that has had no activity on it for at least 1 year.

Why Cases Go Cold

Conventional wisdom in a homicide investigation holds that time is of the essence. For decades, this perception has guided investigators in their approach to homicide investigation. It holds that if a murder is not solved within the first 24–72 hours, the chances of solving the case rapidly diminish. Why? At the outset,

- Witnesses were still centrally located and easier to locate.
- Their recollection of events was fresh and most accurate.
- Those who may have been involved or had knowledge had not had a chance to get their stories and alibis straight among themselves.
- The chances of identifying and retrieving evidence are strongest at the outset. With the passage of time, the potential to identify evidence may diminish, or it may be damaged, lost, or destroyed (Figure 1.10).

A bell curve graph can be used to reflect the course of an investigation of a cold case over a period of many years through a service of continuous curves representing investigation and reinvestigation events (Figure 1.10).

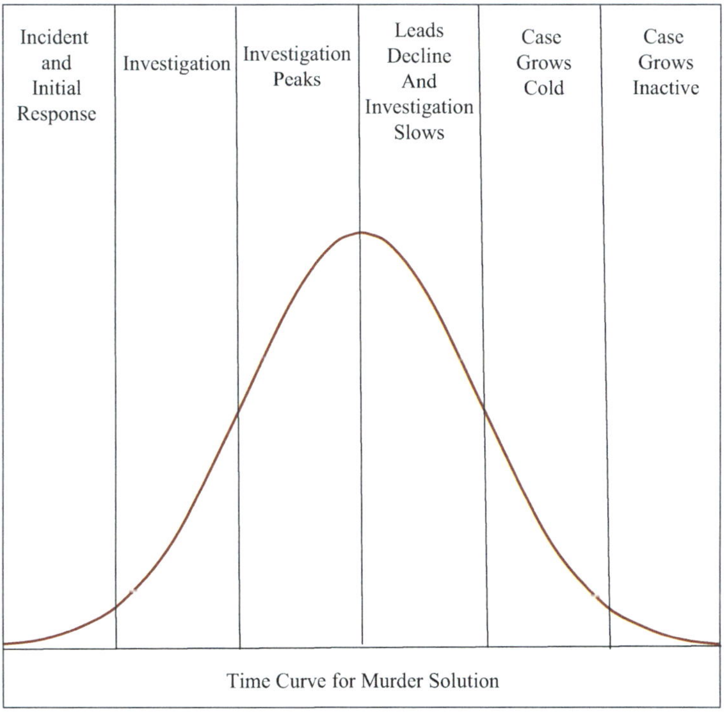

Figure 1.10 Cold case bell curve. Cold case homicide investigation may best resemble the traditional bell curve. When the case is reported and investigation begins, it follows through until leads taper off, and the investigation slows. As other cases consume agency resources, the case grows cold and inactive. At any time, the bell curve may again incline when new information comes in. It is not unusual that some cold case homicides, solved and unsolved, have shown a series of bell curves. (Credit: author.)

Two primary factors may affect a homicide case becoming a cold case. Awareness of these by cold case investigators may contribute to their understanding of the strengths and weaknesses of the initial investigation in their cold case investigation. These are (1) case factors over which police have no control and (2) organizational factors within the law enforcement agency over which the police have control (Wellford, C. and Cronin, J).

Case factors over which the police have no control include:

- Lack of physical evidence
- Lack of witnesses or cooperating witnesses
- Inability to identify victim
- Weapon used
- Gang or drug related
- Crime scene location (public versus private)
- Previous technology inadequate to fully analyze evidence

Organizational factors within the law enforcement agency may include:

- Initial response and documentation
- Initial investigation and gathering of evidence
- Number of detectives originally assigned to case
- Detective's case load
- Leads not followed up
- Retirement
- Promotion and transfer
- Leadership and organization commitment
- Budgetary and financial considerations
- Personnel management
- Politics and personal agendas

Cases Most Likely to Go Cold

Those cases most likely to go cold include cases involving:

- Missing persons
- Gang/drug related
- Immigrants, transients, and the homeless
- Unidentified
- Suicides
- Accidental
- Unclassified
- Unsolved murders of police officers (Figure 1.11)

Figure 1.11 Billboard—Who Killed Mike? Unsolved murders of police are among some of the hardest to solve. Officer Mike Edwards was murdered in 1974, and the case remains unsolved.

Use of media is one means to elicit information from the public in some of the more difficult cases. (Courtesy of Detective Rick Jackson, Los Angeles Police Department, Los Angeles, California.)

Figure 1.11 shows a highway billboard sign with the picture of a murdered police officer and the words "Who Killed Mike?"

How Old Is Cold?

Some departments have arbitrarily decreed that absent compelling information and circumstances, they will not proactively review cases prior to a specific date or year. This is in part due to the rationalization that the chances of the perpetrator remaining alive, witness availability, and similar case factors are minimal or nonexistent. It is also in part due to optimizing use of available resources. Also factored into this set of guidelines is the easily recognizable availability of biological evidence suitable for DNA analysis or latent fingerprint evidence. Those that have expressed this parameter to me most often cite varying time periods in the 1970s to 1990s as the arbitrary cutoff date, yet these cases—even some dating to the 1950s—continue to be reported in media today due to advances in forensics and other factors. This issue will be addressed in future chapters.

1946 Case Study: Murder of Police Officer John Milledge

On the night of November 1, 1946, Miami police officer John Milledge, 48 years old, was on duty and patrolling near a city park in which a football game was being played. Milledge was among the first black officers appointed to the department, during a time when racial segregation was a predominant factor in life in the South. The presence of black police officers was a new concept in the city, and these officers were primarily assigned to predominantly the same racial areas. While on patrol, Milledge caught some local juveniles trying to sneak into the game. He reportedly struck some with his nightstick, and they ran away. A short time later, an unknown assailant fired one shot from a .22-caliber weapon and struck Milledge in the neck. He died shortly thereafter at a local hospital. Witnesses reported seeing "some young negroes" nearby who might have been responsible, and another witness reported that one was carrying a rifle (Figure 1.12).

During the initial investigation, officers contacted two witnesses, who advised them that on the night of the shooting, an individual known locally as "FATS" came to their residence and asked for a ride out of town. He was given a ride and never seen again. FATS became a prime suspect in the shooting, and officers learned that his true name was Leroy Strachan. Officers learned he may have gone to New York City, but he was never located or contacted

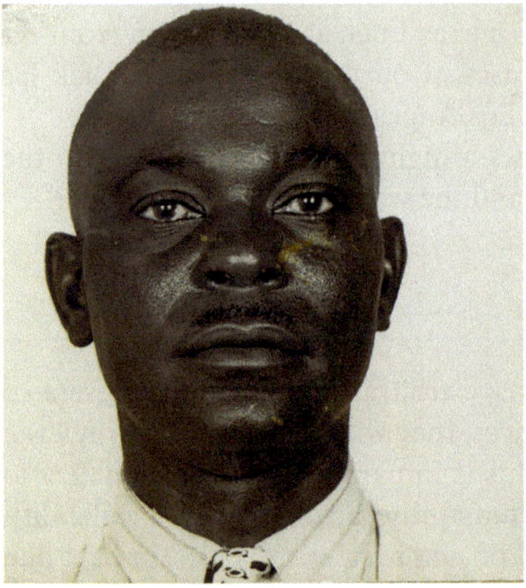

Figure 1.12 Miami police officer John Milledge, one of the first African American police officers in Miami, Florida, was shot in an ambush in 1946. His murder was not solved until 1990, following revelations by a witness who had lived in fear of revealing what she knew. With the death of another, the witness now came forward. Change in relationships and no longer being in fear of another are significant solvability factors in solving cold case homicides. (Courtesy of Miami Police Department.)

during the initial investigation. Other potential suspects were investigated, and the case went cold until 1989.

On July 27, 1989, 43 years after the murder, an anonymous caller to the local Crime Stoppers program indicated knowledge about the murder of a black police officer. The call was forwarded to the homicide unit of the City of Miami Police Department. The caller identified herself and gave a sworn statement. The caller was an elderly witness, a female, who lived near the park. She reportedly was plagued by her conscience and wanted to tell what she knew but had withheld all these years.

On the night of the shooting, the witness was sitting on her porch with a male friend. A black teenager ran to her porch, almost out of breath. He was carrying a rifle. The witness described the teenager as having a bad eye. Upon seeing the rifle, her male friend went inside the house, and shortly afterward, they learned a policeman had been shot. The witness initially misidentified the name of the teenager with the gun but noted that the teenager had a brother who was a close friend of her companion. She stated that her companion subsequently told her the teen had left town. The witness further stated that she learned the teen had gone to New York, but she was afraid of her male companion and remained silent all these years. He had recently died.

The case was reopened and assigned to Detective George Cadavid of the Cold Case Squad of the City of Miami Homicide Unit. Cadavid had been assigned to homicide for the past 10 years and assigned to this unit for approximately 2 years. Cadavid located the original case file within the police department and reviewed the names of those contacted during the initial investigation.

During his investigation, he reinterviewed some of these witnesses from 1946. Among those reinterviewed was the same male witness who gave FATS a ride out of town shortly after the shooting. With the passage of time, the witness now provided further detail of the events of that night, information not furnished to the police four decades before. He stated that on the night of the shooting, which he remembered well, his brother and sister came home upset over the shooting of the officer. Later that night, FATS came to their house, nervous and scared, and wanted a ride out of town. During this conversation, FATS told the witness he had shot the officer. The witness stated that he now knew FATS as Leroy Strachan and that Leroy had a problem with one of his eyes. Except for the name, this information was consistent with information from the new witness.

Cadavid located Strachan, now age 62, in New York City. He learned that Strachan did have a problem with his left eye. A meeting was arranged, and Strachan gave a taped statement. Strachan stated that on the night of the shooting, he and others tried to sneak into the game. Milledge caught them and hit a few of them with his nightstick. Strachan ran to a friend's house and retrieved a .22-caliber rifle. He and the friend returned to an alley across from the park, and his friend handed him the weapon. He yelled for other boys in the alley to move, and he fired one shot at the officer. He then ran home and left Miami the next day for New York. Strachan was indicted by a grand jury for the murder of Officer Milledge and arrested in New York City on February 15, 1990.

The police and assistant state attorney recommended waiver of the death penalty. Mitigating factors considered that Strachan had no significant criminal history prior to the murder, he was 18 years old at the time of the murder, and he had not had any criminal activity for the subsequent 43 years, in which he had been a law-abiding citizen with a wife and family. It is reported that some family members of the victim further believed that Strachan deserved a break. Strachan subsequently pled guilty to manslaughter and was given credit for 19 months in custody time served and 400 hours' community service each year for 5 years and placed on 7 years' probation.

This case illustrates the following cold case issues:

- Unsolved murder of police officer
- Media crime reporting program
- Tip from citizen due to conscience
- Department maintained case file
- Procedural assignment to experienced cold case detective
- Change in relationships due to passage of time
- Original investigation identified perpetrator yet never followed up
- Youthful age of offender
- Reinterview of original case witnesses
- New information by other witnesses
- Perpetrator now a religious person and admitted guilt
- Time, place, and social setting
- Legal, charging, and "justice" considerations

Suggested Readings and Bibliography

Abrahamson, S. (2002). *Using DNA to solve cold cases*. Washington, DC, N. I. o. Justice. U.S. Department of Justice: 22.

Anonymous. (2002). *Cold case homicide*. Sacramento, C.P.T. Network, California Commission on Peace Officer Standards and Training.

AP. (1997). Sheppard evidence turns up in Bay Area. *San Francisco Chronicle*: A2.

Barcus, H., Heurich, C., Ritter, N., Schwarting, D. E., and Walton, R. (July 2019). *National Best Practices for Implementing and Sustaining a Cold Case Investigation Unit* (NCJ 252016). Washington, DC: U.S. Department of Justice, Office of Justice Programs, National Institute of Justice.

Block, E. B. (1958). *The wizard of Berkeley*. New York, Coward-McCann, Inc.

Block, E. B. (1979). *Science vs crime: The evolution of the police lab*. San Francisco, Cragmont Publications.

Bureau of Justice Statistics. (2005). *Criminal victimization, 2004* (NCJ 207251). U.S. Department of Justice.

Cadavid, G. (1991). *Homicide investigation F90-6184*. Miami, Miami Police Department.

Carroll, R. (2002). Wounds suggest iceman was stabbed in the back, fought attacker. *The Guardian Unlimited*.

Cooper, A., and Smith, E. (n.d.). *Homicide trends in the United States, 1980–2010*. Bureau of Justice Statistics. https://www.bjs.gov/content/pub/pdf/htus8008.pdf. Retrieved June 22, 2016.

Cooper, A., and Smith, E. L. (n.d.). *Homicide trends in the United States, 1980–2008*. Annual Rates for 2009 and 2010. Report NCJ236018, November, 2011.

Eliopulos, L. (2003). *Death investigators handbook: Expanded and updated edition*. Boulder, CO, Paladin Press.

Ellis, K. (2004). *Kansas City cold case squad solves string of murders*. Police Executive Research Forum 18: 1, 7.

FBI. (1970). *Crime in the United States 1970: Uniform crime reports*. Washington, DC, U. S. D. o. Justice.

FBI. (2001). *Crime in the United States 2000: Uniform crime reports*. Washington, D.C., U.S. Government: 424.

FBI. (2002). *Crime in the United States 2001: Uniform crime reports*. Washington, D.C.

FBI. (2014). *2014 Crime in the United States: Expanded Homicide Data Table 10*. Murder Circumstances. https://www.fbi.gov. Retrieved June 21, 2016.

Fowler, B. (2000). *The Iceman's last meal*. NOVA Online.

Fox, J. A., and Zawitz, M. (2003, January). *Homicide trends in the United States: 2000 update*. Washington, DC: U.S. Department of Justice. NCJ 197471. Retrieved from https://bjs.ojp.gov/content/pub/pdf/htus00.pdf

Geberth, V. (1996). *Practical homicide investigation: Tactics, procedures, and forensic techniques*. New York, CRC Press.

Goddard, C. (1936). A history of firearms identification. *Chicago Police Journal* XI: 1–14.

Houck, M. M., Ed. (2001). *Mute witness: Trace evidence analysis*. New York, Academic Press.

Hargrove, T. (n.d.). *Project cold case: Cold case homicide statistics*. Retrieved from https://www.projectcoldcase.org/cold-case-homicide-stats/. December 18, 2016 and personal interview.

Hargrove, T. (2011). Scripps news. *Personal Interview*. June 11, 2010.

Hargrove, T. (2010). Murder mysteries: Investigating America's unsolved homicides. *Scripps news.com*. https://www.murderdata.org/p/data-docs.html. Retrieved June 11, 2010.

Hargrove, T. (2025). Murder accountability project. *Personal Interview*. March 4, 2025.

Lane, R. (1997). *Murder in America: A history*. Columbus, Ohio State University.

Lorenzi, R. (2003). Details emerge of Iceman Otzi's death. *Discovery News*.

McCall, P. L., and Zahn, M. A., Eds. (1999). *Trends and patterns of homicide in the 20th-century United States. Homicide: A sourcebook of social research*. Thousand Oaks, SAGE Publications.

National Center for Health Statistics Vital Statistics. (n.d.). *Homicide rate 1900–2000: Rate per 100,000 population.* https://www.ojp.usdoj.gov/bjs/glance/hmrt.htm. Retrieved January 5, 2004.

Norrgard, D. L. (1969). *Regional law enforcement: A study of intergovernmental cooperation and coordination.* Danville, IL, Interstate Printers and Publishers, Inc.

Nyberg, R. (1999). Investigations: Cold case squads re-activate old investigations. *Law and Order* 47(10): 127–130.

Owen, J. (2013). 5 surprising facts about Otzi the Iceman. *National Geographic.*

Prottas, J., and Noble, A. (2007). Use of forensic DNA evidence in prosecution offices. *Journal of Law, Medicine, and Ethics* 35(2): 310–315.

Regini, C. L. (1997). The cold case concept. *Law Enforcement Bulletin* 66(8): 1–6.

Statistics, B. of. J. (1983). *Report to the nation on crime and justice.* Washington, DC, U.S. Department of Justice.

Stout, W. W. (1925). Fingerprinting bullets: The expert witness. *Saturday Evening Post:* 6–7, 193, 194, 197.

Stout, W. W. (1925). Fingerprinting bullets: The expert witness. *Saturday Evening Post*: 18–19, 163, 165, 166, 169–170.

Thompson, G., and Williams E. (2003). The thin blue line's: New front line. *San Diego Union*: G1, 5, 6.

Thorwald, J. (Unk). *Crime and science: The new frontier of criminology.* New York, Harcourt, Brace & World, Inc.

Turner, R., and Kosa, R. (2003). *Cold case squads: Leaving no stone unturned.* Washington, DC, Bureau of Justice Assistance Bulletin, U. S. D. o. Justice: 2–7.

Van Natta, D. (1991). NY Man to plead guilty in 1946 Miami cop killing. *Miami Herald* 1: 14A.

Wambaugh, J. (2002). *Fire lover.* New York, Avon Books.

Wellford, C., and Cronin, J. (2000). Clearing up homicide clearance rates. *National Institute of Justice Journal* 243: 3–7.

Case File Review

2

RACHEL H. WALTON
AND FRANK P. TONA

Introduction

Cold case investigation begins with review of the case file. The investigation of a cold case homicide is different from the investigation of a "hot" homicide in many ways. Cold case investigation is *proactive*, versus the *reactive* nature of a hot case. The cold case investigation initially builds upon the documented work of others, utilizing case files that may vary in the degree of completeness and record retention over the ensuing years. In addition, cold case investigation exploits the elements of time and technology in conjunction with advanced investigative techniques. While every case and each victim's family deserve the ultimate opportunity to see that justice in some form or another is rendered on their behalf, available resources require that investigation of cold cases must be selective, focused, and targeted in its method.

This chapter will begin with a review of the qualities of investigator most suitable for cold case homicide investigation, and discussion of the influence and impact of time and technology as it pertains to cold case homicide investigation. This chapter will address the influence of past law enforcement methods in cold case investigation and how to approach a file and assess file contents. In addition, this chapter highlights administrative considerations for cold case investigation and will further discuss how to organize and prioritize multiple cases for subsequent investigation.

Causes for Review and Reactivation of Cold Cases

Identification of a single cold case to be selected for re-examination may be due to any of the following factors:

- Inquiry, single or repeated, by a family member or friend of the victim. As time passes, the parents, siblings, or others may periodically contact the police to inquire if anything new has arisen on their case. Family inquiries may cause a fresh review of the case.
- New information brought forth by family or friends of victim. With the passage of time, friends and family of the victim may hear or otherwise obtain information that furnishes a new lead to investigators.

DOI: 10.4324/9781003415633-4

- New information furnished by a member of the public.
- Institutional knowledge of detectives. With the passage of time, detectives go on to other cases, but for the most part, do not forget those cases they could not solve. As the years become decades, other investigators may transfer in and out of homicide and the case may have been rendered inactive due to leads. But those who initiated the investigation, or later followed it up, remember the unsolved. Through intentional or casual communication with homicide supervisors, homicide detectives, or others within the department, something is said that causes the case to be pulled and subject to a fresh review.
- Individual investigator curiosity.
- Secondary information from other investigations, often drug or organized crime related.
- Those in trouble with the law providing information to mitigate their legal burden.
- Media report.
- Political pressure.
- Sometimes purely by accident.

Preliminary Considerations in Cold Case Investigation

Cold Case Investigator Attributes

It is estimated that almost every law enforcement agency in the United States has unsolved homicide cases in their files. These are cases other investigators worked, but that went unsolved for various reasons. If they had been easy, they would have been solved. With the passage of time, however, and a fresh review by a new set of eyes coupled with advances in technology, these cases may offer fresh leads. Case review is more than just opening a file folder or carton. The review begins with *mental attitude* or *mindset* by the investigator. In addition, it includes awareness of the changes wrought by *time* in technology and personal relationships. This review involves:

- The ability to think and act objectively.
- The ability to ask the right questions.
- A positive "can-do" spirit.
- Knowledge of modern investigative methods.
- Knowledge of advances in science and technology.
- Ability to work collaboratively with other investigators, forensic experts, and legal professionals.

Case file review also entails *teamwork*. The days of the one-man homicide ace-detective following gut instinct are over. Cold case homicide investigation is a team effort between law enforcement, the prosecutor's office, the medical examiner/coroner's office, and the laboratory. Each of these is an important component in the re-opening and investigation of a cold case file. In addition, cooperation and communication within the law enforcement community are required, not the territorialism or proprietary of "*It's my case.*"

To proceed expediently, investigators assigned a cold, unsolved homicide may be faced with a variety of start-up decisions and options to make to proceed expediently. Depending upon the age of the case, many factors may immediately present themselves. Some of these may appear daunting, or even insurmountable. The older the case, the greater potential for missing reports and missing or degraded evidence, deceased investigators, witnesses, and other obstacles. The law enforcement agency may have changed physical locations one or more times. Each time files, evidence, or property is moved increases the possibility that these items will be lost, misplaced, or even destroyed. Administrative and budgetary issues may also impact the presence or absence of these items. Cases that have been inactive for a few years for lack of leads present a different arena than those revived after 20 or 30 years, or more. Those more recent are likely to be written on forms and in formats currently in use, thus facilitating investigator efforts.

Remember, a cold case investigation builds upon the previous work of others.

Who will investigate cold case homicides is an immediate concern to law enforcement supervisors and administrators, as well as the investigators themselves. Whenever possible, but not necessarily, those assigned to cold case homicide investigation should be experienced homicide detectives. These investigations are often prolonged, and it is important to note that all the problems and frustrations experienced in a hot homicide may be multiplied many times over in cold case investigation and resultant court proceedings.

Desirable cold case investigator attributes would include:

- Knowledgeable of the mechanics of homicide investigation.
- Knowledgeable in the variations in homicide law.
    - Knowledge of the use of forensic sciences and up-to-date advances.
    - Skilled in interview techniques.
    - Excellent oral and written communication skills.
    - Knowledge and experience in use of informants.
    - Open minded.
    - Strong deductive and reasoning skills.
    - A good listener.
    - Creative and innovative.

Figure 2.1 Los Angeles Sheriff's Homicide Bulldog patch. Cold case investigation requires "Bulldog" tenacity. (Courtesy of Sgt. Richard Longshore, Los Angeles County Sheriff's Department.)

- Knowledgeable in crime scene reconstruction.
- Experienced in use of computers and report writing.
- Knowledgeable of courtroom procedures and testimony.
- Able and willing to work in a team atmosphere.
- Knowledgeable of department resources, procedures, and protocols.
- Good health and stamina.
- Motivated and enthusiastic.
- Patient, analytical, and bulldog *tenacious* (Figure 2.1).

In our experience, it appears to be a consensus among those involved in the investigation of cold case homicides that not all homicide investigators are suited to cold case investigation. Why? Cold case investigations are tedious and require an investigator who can sit for hours, review old papers, and analyze people, events, relationships, and time sequences. This is cerebral analysis. In some older cases it may be helpful to task a more senior investigator who may have knowledge and experience in the time frame of the crime, as well as trends in department systems over the years. Younger, less experienced investigators may seek faster paced activity.

While a background in homicide investigation is highly beneficial for cold case detectives, it is not an absolute requirement. Cold case investigations often require a broad range of skills, including forensic analysis, interviewing techniques, and a deep understanding of criminal behavior, which can come from various investigative backgrounds, such as burglary, missing persons, or sexual crimes. Detectives with experience in different investigations bring varied perspectives and techniques that can uncover new angles and leads in cold cases. Examples include detectives with specialized knowledge in forensic science, digital forensics, or cybercrime, which can be crucial, especially when re-examining old evidence with new technology. Detectives from fraud or financial crime backgrounds may excel in following complex paper trails and uncovering hidden connections, which can be pivotal in solving cold cases.

The use of senior, experienced homicide investigators for cold case homicide investigation draws upon aspects of investigative ability that can only come from practice. These more experienced investigators:

- Know what the case needs to move forward.
- Know what the prosecutor needs to prosecute the case.
- Has established contacts and rapport with the prosecutor's office.
- Has established contacts and rapport with coroner/medical examiner office.
- Through experience have statewide and nationwide contacts.
- Through membership and participation in homicide investigator associations and training programs have expanded fields of contact.
- May recognize information overlooked or blatantly obvious in case file.

Each of these is important in all stages of file review and case investigation. *WHAT* you know is sometimes not as important as *WHO* you know.

Homicide investigation is part scientific, but also part subjective. With experience comes the ability to "*feel*" or "*read*" a case beyond the words on paper. It is an ability to feel the "*pulse*" of the case. Selection of the wrong individual can further compound the difficulty in case solution. In the end, it will be the investigator who combines time, technology, and old-fashioned shoe leather to solve a cold case homicide.

Age + Experience = Wisdom

Investigators assigned to investigate cold cases must be cognizant that they may have no control over the cases they work, depending upon the political climate of their agency or community. Similarly, they may have little say in how their agency prioritizes what cases are more important and which are not as important. Conversely, however, investigators may have a say in which cases they re-investigate due to their experience and ability to separate those cases with a higher potential for solution from those with a lesser possibility of being solved with given resources.

Time

Modern cold case investigation turns the previous liability of time into an asset. While law enforcement traditionally labored under a conventional wisdom that murders unsolved after 48–72 hours were increasingly more difficult to close, the pendulum of time in cold cases has now reversed this adage. Time, once so unforgiving in homicide investigation, may now be an ally to law enforcement efforts to solve cold cases. This change is due primarily to two factors:

- Change in relationships and
- Advances in technology.

In a hot homicide scenario, witnesses or those with knowledge about the crime often remain silent due to a relationship with or fear of the perpetrator; their own lifestyles and standards; or fear of, hostility toward, or noninvolvement with the police.

With the passage of time, relationships change. Not uncommonly in these cases, people *want* to tell what they know yet cannot bring themselves to pick up the telephone and call the police. In some cases, all it takes is for an investigator to take the *initiative* and knock on their door. We have been a part of several cases where performing a proper neighborhood canvas yielded new witnesses or information not previously known. In a cold case scenario,

- The friendship that once existed between perpetrator and those with knowledge of the crime may have ended. It may now be adversarial.
- Marriages and former lover–partnership relations may have ended, perhaps on a sour note.
- Business relationships dissolve.
- Formerly hostile witnesses are no longer hostile.
- Religion may have entered the life of one with information or knowledge of the crime.
- Conscience may have become a factor in the lives of those with information or knowledge of the crime.
- People mature. Witnesses may have moved away from the influence of the perpetrator and lifestyle at the time of the murder. They may have married, raised a family, and become a better person.
- Witness no longer fears the perpetrator. This may be due to time having made the witness a stronger person, or the perpetrator a weaker person. Or the perpetrator may be dead.
- Perpetrator may become comfortable and talk to others about crimes committed in the past.

Technology

Advances in technology have enabled:

- More precise examinations of evidence than was available in the past.
- DNA profiles to now be extracted from amounts of biological material previously insufficient in quantity for DNA analysis.
- DNA profiling to offer a strong potential as an investigative aid.
- DNA databanks such as the Combined DNA Index System (CODIS) to allow for comparison of known and unknown genetic profiles between crime scenes and identified or unidentified perpetrators.
- Expanded fingerprint and biometric identification capabilities. Advanced fingerprint methods can now lift prints from surfaces once considered unprintable. Among these are cyanoacrylate fuming ("superglue") and laser systems for lifting and reading fingerprints. Fingerprint databanks such as Next-Generation Identification (NGI) and Integrated Automated Fingerprint Identification System (IAFIS) allow for inputting and comparing fingerprints on a national level.
- Other databanks such as the National Integrated Ballistic Information Network (NIBIN) for comparing spent shell casings and projectiles or projectile fragments.
- The use of Open-Source Intelligence (OSINT) sites to gather data and locate individuals.
- Expanded, computer-based communications and information exchange.
- Enhanced cellular phone technology.
- Geographical profiling.
- The rise of digital technology has led to the capability of retrieving and analyzing data from electronic devices.
- Use of Investigative Genetic Genealogy (IGG), which combines traditional genealogical research methods with DNA analysis to solve crimes, identify remains, and resolve unknown cases.
- Body-worn cameras and widespread surveillance provide real-time recording of crime scenes and interactions with suspects and witnesses.

Time + Technology

Time and technology have combined in a manner no one anticipated a few decades ago. This includes the perpetrator *and* the police, however. Perpetrators who considered themselves knowledgeable, or lucky, in seemingly leaving no trace of them did not anticipate DNA or computer databanks. Similarly, *neither* did the police. In too many instances, evidence in homicide cases was discarded after a period of time, and records were destroyed. The mindset of many who have committed murder is such that they become confident after the passage of the years, and many have moved to other regions of the country away from where they committed their crimes. Some have gone on to raise families and become accepted or respectable members of their community. In many instances, the original investigators moved on in their careers, retired, or have passed away. There is no free pass for those who kill; however, those who murdered may try to forget and put their past behind them, others have not. The family and friends of the murder victim never forget, and in most cases, neither does law enforcement. Awareness of these factors is important before an investigator opens the file.

Time may not be an ally in some cases, however. If a case is 40–50 years old, is it plausible to expect that witnesses or a suspect may still be alive? Yes, it is. We must never assume such without looking deeper as cases 40 and 50 years old are now being resolved which once might not have been given a cursory review. Regrettably, however, experience has demonstrated that some senior administrative and command officers have taken the position to not review cases of this vintage that do not have available DNA evidence.

Even with a thoroughly documented case and evidence in file, does the case warrant an initial effort? In a situation such as this, a review may be justified. It is imperative investigators seek a resolution in these cases and offer a sense of justice for the families and friends of the victims. Many have waited decades without answers or accountability, and solving these cases can provide much-needed relief and sense of knowing. The investigation will involve locating friends, relatives, and other associates of the decedent. In addition, any subsequent investigation would seek to locate medical, or law enforcement personnel involved in the initial investigation. These are concerns to be considered in the initial review. Closing unsolved homicides where the perpetrator is deceased can still be highly beneficial for several reasons. That sense of knowing for families may provide a sense of justice to the victims' families and loved ones. Even posthumously, knowing the perpetrator's identity can help families move forward and find peace. That investigators can establish the facts and identify the perpetrator(s) contributes to the accuracy and completeness of the historical record. This can also clear the name(s) of individuals who may have been wrongfully suspected or accused during the initial investigation. It restores their reputation and provides relief to their families. Finally, identifying deceased perpetrators can help law enforcement recognize patterns or links to other unsolved cases, potentially solving unknown crimes.

What *if* the perpetrator in a 40-year-old homicide was 15–19 years old at the time of the crime? That person would be in their late 50s now. Given longevity and other factors in modern life, this person may still be a suitable prospect for investigation and prosecution. Several notable investigations and convictions in these circumstances have occurred and continue to do so. These include the case of Miami Police Officer John Milledge illustrated in Chapter 1, and that of Clyde Wilkerson discussed elsewhere in this text.

A cold case should be evaluated upon the reasonable merits of the case and not necessarily rejected solely due to age.

Administrative and Supervisory Concerns

Hot case homicides generate law enforcement response as well as media publicity. The media is often in contact with family and friends of the victim, and this is relayed in sound bites or newspaper stories. This in return generates a response from the law enforcement agency. In higher profile cases, such as the 2022 Idaho College Murders, the sheriff or chief of police often faces the media to assure the public and answer questions.

In cold case investigations, however, the family and friends usually do not know when a case is re-activated until contacted by law enforcement. In turn, the media usually does not become aware of cold case investigations until an arrest is made. The public likes to hear that somebody did **not** get away with murder. The resultant publicity reflects positively on the agency and not uncommonly, law enforcement uses this time to reassure the public they are doing all they can to track down killers in unsolved cases and protect the public. Such news may also stimulate others to come forward with information on the case, or on another case. These come with a cost, however.

Cold case investigations may, and often do, incur expenses and resources exceeding those normally found in hot homicide investigation. Further, results may be longer in coming. In addition to the normal frustrations encountered when working homicide cases, additional frustration for investigators results when an agency tasks investigators to work these cases but does not supply the necessary logistics. Agencies are often dependent on yearly budget cycles and administrators prioritize specific needs for their departments; unfortunately, cold case murders are not included or given the attention they deserve. The leadership and organizational commitment by an agency to investigate cold cases requires awareness and acceptance that such investigations often include:

- Added travel expenses. By this time, suspects, witnesses, and others with important information may have scattered about the country. This may apply to former and retired officers and investigators as well. All witnesses and investigators will have to be located and re-interviewed, often face to face. These interviews and other investigation costs will require added travel, lodging, transportation, and related expenses.

- Overtime and associated expenses for investigators due to travel, telephone, and investigation.
- Use of other personnel and resources.
- Potential for increased laboratory costs and/or other evidentiary related expenses. All physical evidence will need to be reprocessed.
- Conflicts within the agency. There may be those who would contest revisiting cold cases when resources are drained from investigation of current cases or other individual agendas or priorities occur within the department.
- Impact on the workload or case load of others.

In addition, one cold case investigation may be the precursor to other cold case investigations. These investigations are often cross-jurisdictional. Investigation in these cases may lead investigators to spend time and travel to nearby or more distant law enforcement agencies. In other instances, the information spawned in one cold case may lead to re-opening other cases within the department or in other agencies. It has not been unusual that information developed in the investigation of one cold case has also identified a serial killer. Such was the case of prolific killer Samuel Little, a drifter with a long criminal history, including charges of assault, attempted rape, and robbery. He operated across multiple states, making his pattern of crime difficult to trace. In 2012, Little was arrested on narcotics charges in Kentucky. His DNA was collected and entered into the FBI's CODIS. DNA matches linked him to three unsolved homicides in Los Angeles, California, dating back to the late 1980s. The victims, all women, had been beaten and strangled, matching Little's known modus operandi. After the DNA matches, the Los Angeles Police Department (LAPD) and the FBI began to re-examine other cold cases. Little's movements and criminal history were scrutinized, revealing a pattern consistent with unsolved murders across the United States. In 2018, Texas Ranger James Holland obtained a confession from Little, who began to divulge details about other murders. Over the next few months, Little confessed to 93 murders committed between 1970 and 2005. Little provided detailed descriptions and drawings of his victims, many of whom were marginalized individuals whose deaths were not thoroughly investigated at the time.

Cold case homicide investigation is especially time consuming and labor intensive. The very nature and intensity of these investigations necessitates focus upon the written case and subsequent investigation. A cold case investigation begins with a review of the written record, often complex in size. Where once we submitted homicide cases in one or two 3-ring binders, if that, cases comprising thousands of pages of documentation may now take up multiple banker-boxes in volume.

In this regard, a cold case investigation builds upon the degree of thoroughness and completeness of previous investigators. It is also built upon the missed opportunities. This focus is necessary for an investigator to begin to digest and understand a multitude of names, dates, relationship, and who-said-what, as well as evidence and property considerations. This is the beginning of the investigative plan. It is a disservice to the investigator, the victims, and to the agency to distract the investigator's focus from the cold case investigation.

Because these investigations originate with review of a written record and not through on-the-spot, ground-floor-up activity, investigation as occurs with a hot homicide, investigators must have conducive working conditions and agency support to accomplish their task. While some agencies may assign multiple cold cases to an investigator or teams of investigators, other agencies may assign one cold case to one investigator or one team. In either circumstance, one case at a time has been described as an excellent ratio. This allows *focus*. In either situation, cases are worked to solution or until they can be worked no further. It is highly desirable that investigators assigned to cold case investigation are not distracted or assigned other duties during these investigations.

When investigators are tasked by the administration to investigate cold cases, they must be free to do so with a minimum of resistance from other administrative personnel (who sometimes have no investigative experience and understanding of what homicide investigation entails). On some occasions, investigators have been directed to investigate a cold case by the head of the agency or other supervisory personnel, only to be stonewalled and rebuffed by those in charge of the budget and other agency resources. This creates added and unnecessary tension and is detrimental to the goal of the investigation. Not to mention the negative impact it has on morale and interpersonal relations.

Opening the File

Where Is the Case File?

Locating the original case file and original evidence is sometimes not as easy as it could be in cold case investigation. Personnel changes, individual filing habits (quirks), case-numbering system changes or procedures, facility changes, and passage of time may complicate the simple effort of retrieving a case file or evidence. Investigator experience and knowledge of past practices and patterns of the agency may be beneficial to a cold case investigator in this sequence. Beginning in-house, investigators may look in numerous places, including:

- Agency records storage area where records are normally filed.
- Homicide Bureau or specially designated storage facility for homicide files, solved and unsolved.
- Agency property room (as well as for evidence logs and physical evidence).
- Off-site warehouses or storage facilities.
- Some police departments use digital records management systems (RMS) to store and manage case files. These systems can include scanned copies of old paper files and digital records.
- Reports from law enforcement forensic laboratories may often be stored separately within the confines of their secure facilities.
- Some files might be stored in state archives if the police department or municipality can no longer store them.
- Law enforcement agencies increasingly use cloud-based storage solutions for their RMS.

Don't hesitate to ask those who have been around for a long time if they know of any records or other places where records may have been stored over the years. Long-time secretaries and clerks are many times the *best* sources of information on many different subjects. If you don't ask the question, you will not get the answer.

File Condition

Subjectively, initial appearance of the case organization may offer an insight into the ease and potential time and resources necessary for case review and subsequent investigation. Is it together in three-ring binders (Figure 2.2) or labeled envelopes and folders? Or is it a collection thrown haphazardly into a box? Or … *is* there a file?

Cases may be encountered in any one of three categories, or a combination of completeness:

1. *Organized:* An organized file suggests that the case will be complete and laid out in an orderly manner. Review of an organized file may begin with little or no re-organization by the assigned investigator. This facilitates investigator review and absorption of the case. This case may have summaries of events, evidence, and of those involved in the case. These will assist in the investigator coming up to speed in a shorter period than otherwise. No matter which category the file appears to fall into, a cold case investigator will strive to ensure that all relevant records are identified and recovered.

   Caution is warranted, however, that if or when reports or similar material seemingly not connected to the case under review is

Figure 2.2 Organized case file. An organized case file makes cold case investigation more efficient and effective. (Courtesy of Detective Richard Rouleau, El Cajon Police Department.)

found, do not necessarily discard its connection to the case at hand. Someone along the line may have felt this was related to the case. Whether these reasons are documented or not, do not disregard this earlier thought.

As an example, detectives Jon Wooddell and Robert Anderson of the El Cajon, California, Police Department were re-investigating a cold case homicide that occurred in their city in 1965. Co-mingled with the homicide investigation case were reports and records from other seemingly unconnected sexual assaults during this same time period. Upon review, however, these reports suggested that their predecessor decades before had believed there might be a connection between these crimes. These detectives ultimately succeeded in identifying and convicting serial killer-rapist Clyde Wilkerson in 2003 for their homicide. This case is discussed further in Chapter 4.

2. *Disorganized:* These are not infrequently encountered in older unsolved cases and may be encountered in departments of all sizes. These are characterized as reports and other material dumped loosely into a box or file folders (Figure 2.3). These cases may have gone through a sequence of investigators over the decades and documents may be such as to suggest an uncertainty as to completeness. There may be notations or other writings on reports and documents that do not appear to be those of the original author of the document, and authorship is unknown. This compounds the efforts of

(a)

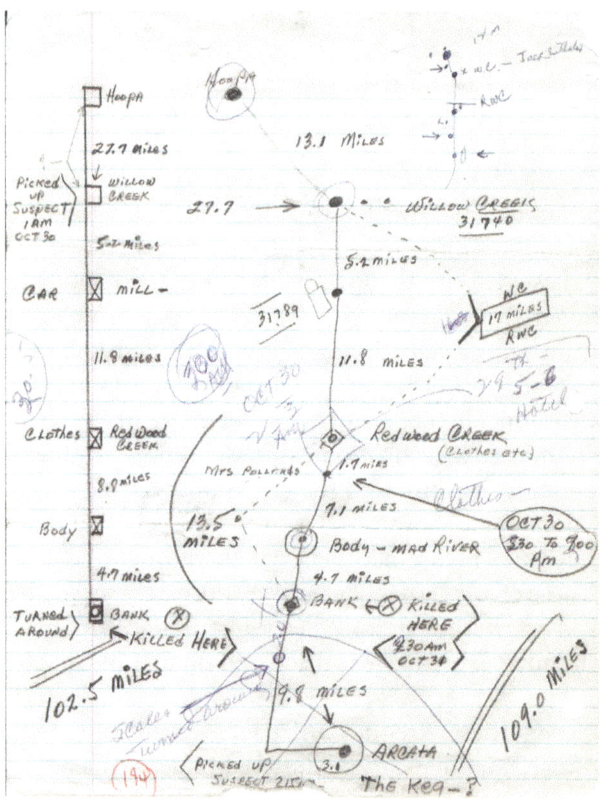

(b)

Figure 2.3 Disorganized File. (a) Disorganized files are not uncommon. Over the years, contents are scattered and dumped loosely into a box or folder. Inside these files may be found original biological or physical evidence, photos, or even bullets. (b) Old crime scene map with numerous notation and lacking authorship. (Author's collection.)

later investigators to determine who wrote these remarks and the significance of that document. Even in an unorganized case file, crucial pieces of evidence might be present but overlooked. This evidence could include unreturned "while you were out" messages, witness statements, forensic reports, or physical evidence that was not fully analyzed with modern techniques. An unorganized case file might contain information that, when cross-referenced with other cases or data, reveals patterns or connections to other crimes. Don't judge a book by its cover is an important quote here. These files should not be disregarded because they may contain critical information that, if properly examined, can lead to the resolution of the case.

3. *Missing:* These are circumstances in which no case file may be retained in the department records. It has happened. In one study by the late Robert Keppel, Ph.D., data was collected on all unsolved and solved murders in the State of Washington between January 1981 and December 1986. Of the 1,309 murder victims, 38 homicide case files were "missing" and could not be located by records personnel of the responsible agencies. This obviously poses a potential problem for investigators, and this situation has been related to the authors by investigators for other agencies.

   Cold case investigators will often invoke methods not normally associated with homicide investigations and may successfully reconstruct events and a case file. Reconstruction of these case files may begin with review of the death certificate, media reports, and interviews with family and friends of the victim. Other methods to reconstruct these cases will unfold throughout this text.

Additional reasons for files to be missing include:

- Lost due to changes in physical storage location. This may occur when an old police station or courthouse is torn down, and files are lost when records are moved. In these cases, it might be prudent to attempt to identify who may have had access to the homicide files and inquire if the files were taken for someone's personal reading.
- Destroyed due to fire, flood, or other natural disaster at the storage location.
- Inadvertently misfiled or co-mingled elsewhere.
- Theft or intentional removal or destruction.
- There *never was* a case file. Yes, it has happened. Those assigned to investigate a death never wrote reports. As a result, there is no file to be found.

Organizing the Disorganized File

The first step in this instance is to organize the remaining record. It is not uncommon to find that these cases, as well as some organized cases, have items of evidentiary value co-mingled with the reports and documentation. This would include film negatives, x-rays, physical items, and other case material. In at least one case known to these authors, a detective found a spent bullet and a shell casing. There was no documentation however, and it was unknown if this was related to the case or not. Other cold case files have contained women's panties, hairs and fibers, and other items of potential physical or biological evidentiary value. If items of evidentiary value are present, contact the appropriate evidence specialist and follow evidence handling procedures.

Because of the potential for original evidence being in the files or case boxes, investigators may consider that the opening of the file or box in cold cases be done in a laboratory or similarly secure setting, using appropriate coverings in case items with potential trace evidence are present. Teamwork begins with the file review, so work with your laboratory associates to ensure that you do not handle any items and potentially destroy or contaminate any evidence. These items should be secured and handled in conjunction with evidence handling practices and department procedures.

When working with your lab and legal partners in a cold case investigation, make them feel as if they are part of the team. Giving them a sense of ownership and keeping them informed will be appreciated.

Next, organize the paperwork into chronological order. Consider the sequence of how you would begin a current homicide investigation. Begin with those records reflecting the initial report of the crime and work forward. This gives you the basis of when and how the crime came to be reported and insight into how it progressed. This is the beginning of the "*who/what/when/where/why and how*" of the case. This may present a problem in some instances as investigative actions may have occurred on one date while the report was not written until days later and other interviews and actions occurred in-between. Note the date of the interview or action in relation to when the report was written. In addition, it is not uncommon to find multiple witness interviews on one document or sequence of a single report. The object of this process is to reconstruct the sequence of reported events and steps in the investigation. This will facilitate investigator review and provide a logical basis for understanding what happened and moving forward with the review or investigation. At the same time, it would be useful to note that which you believe is missing and to begin to construct an investigative plan as the file is reconstructed.

Keep in mind that this sequence reflects events as earlier investigators came to know them, and do not be judgmental or critical with the advantages of hindsight. Current investigators will have to spend additional time sorting documents, often having to review, assemble, and re-connect disconnected reports. Special attention, requiring additional time, must be paid to making sure that papers are reassembled correctly, and often there may be multiple copies of each report or there may appear what seem to be multiple copies, but are in fact slightly different.

Case Study

The following rural county sheriff's office homicide case was reviewed in 2002 and consisted of a cardboard box upon which was written the victim's name and the 1958 case number. The victim was a white female in her 40s, a part-time prostitute and waitress in a blue-collar town in the Pacific Northwest. Most of the reports were separate from the file folders also found in the box, and many of these were unstapled and loose. There was no order to the documents and contents were scattered loosely in the box. In addition, someone later had re-numbered in red letters all the report pages. The significance of this is unknown due to lack of documentation. The file folders themselves contained many notes and notations written by numerous, unidentified persons. *Who were they? When were they written? What did this mean?*

Figure 2.3a illustrates an older disorganized file. Figure 2.3b is an older hand-drawn map of the crime scene areas, showing the point where the body was found, various distances, and locations. Drawn in multiple colors and handwritings, it was apparently drawn by multiple and unidentified persons over an unknown period of time.

Photographs of the victim and other unidentified persons were scattered in the box, as well as original x-rays and personal property of the victim. Numerous envelopes of film negatives of the crime scene, victim's vehicle, and other subjects were also scattered, although it appeared none had been printed. There was an absence of documentation of the significance of what the photos may have intended to show. In addition, letters from unidentified individuals concerning a variety of topics were found in the file, including letters suggesting firsthand knowledge of events in the crime. There was no documentation to denote the status of any investigation regarding these claims.

The documents, when reassembled, revealed a pattern of investigation that began with a missing person's report to the local police department in an incorporated city, and the finding of her body 6 months later in a remote location within the sheriff's office jurisdiction. Involvement of multiple jurisdictions in investigations is not an uncommon sequence of events, even today. After the initial investigation span of approximately 1 year, the case went cold. Review by local investigators was sporadic after the first year with no sign of proactive review in the succeeding decades.

Of noteworthy importance, no evidence, property, or photo logs were contained in the box. A handwritten note dated in 1979 from the property clerk to the district attorney, however, explained why: "*...because the case is now 20 years old and will never be solved, request permission to destroy all the evidence in this case.*" Permission was granted by the prosecutor.

In 2002, all the original case investigators and several witnesses were still alive. Despite lack of physical evidence, cases such as this might be solved due to changes in relationships with passage of time. Such scenarios and their variations have been encountered by cold case investigators seeking to locate old case files and evidence. The ease in which investigators may quickly come up to speed in understanding the sequence of known events and subsequent investigation is initially dependent upon how the file was organized and maintained. This degree of organization may indicate a carry over into the care and preservation of evidence also.

Other Considerations

Past Patterns and Practices

During initial review of older cases, an investigator should not be alarmed if the case file appears, physically, rather thin compared to more recent case volumes. That does not necessarily mean that it is incomplete; such may have been the accepted standard at the time. Since the 1960s, professional advancement in police and investigative practices and procedures has expanded many folds. Older cases offer a glimpse into the past but once subjected to follow-up investigation incorporating modern techniques and protocols, such files quickly become much more massive in physical size and content. Other cases from the same time may occupy many carton boxes or file cabinet drawers. It is not the size, but the *quality* that counts.

This is one area, however, that in many instances exemplifies the difference between past and present law enforcement investigative practices. Understanding these may be of importance to cold case investigators. Each law enforcement agency has traditionally set its own policies, practices, and standards for, among other things, investigating homicides and documenting these investigations. Beginning in the middle of the twentieth century, many states began mandating changes and implementing standardization in the selection and training of law enforcement officers. This ultimately carried over into adoption of uniform means and methods of documentation and recording in police reports. This has been, and still is in some areas, an evolving process.

In 1930, the FBI began collecting crime data reported by the nation's law enforcement. This became the *Crime in the United States: Uniform*

Crime Report (UCR). It was revised in the 1980s and became the National Incident-Based Reporting System (NIBRS). It provides more detailed and comprehensive data on each reported crime incident, including homicides. Unlike the summary-based UCR, NIBRS includes information on the circumstances of the offense, the relationship between victims and offenders, and the use of weapons. In addition, agencies have begun the use of digital case management systems allowing for more efficient data entry, storage, and retrieval.

In many past instances some law enforcement agencies did NOT have policies regarding required documentation in homicide investigations. As a result, what was, or was not, recorded depended upon the individual investigator and the degree of supervision or department policies and procedures. Some investigators wrote detailed investigative reports, while others wrote a minimum if anything at all.

Who the victim was may, in some instances, have factored into the scope and quality of the initial investigation. Prostitutes, minorities, and known offenders or "troublemakers" may not have had the diligence applied to their investigations as found in other homicide investigations. Circumstances such as cases where the victim was murdered in one jurisdiction and remains were placed in another jurisdiction can bring their own set of challenges. In one case, the victim was a not a member of the community. As a result, law enforcement officials and an elected sheriff did not prioritize the case, ultimately telling investigators to concentrate on cases involving members of that jurisdiction.

For example, Samuel Little's murders involved killing victims in one location and often dumping their bodies in another, which significantly complicated the investigations and delayed his capture for many years. Samuel Little led a transient lifestyle, frequently moving across state lines and living in various locations. This mobility allowed him to commit crimes in multiple jurisdictions, making it difficult for law enforcement agencies to connect the dots.

Little targeted vulnerable women, often prostitutes or those with high-risk lifestyles. He would typically pick them up in one location, commit the murders in a secluded place, and then dispose of their bodies in different areas: sometimes across state lines. This dispersal of crime scenes and bodies hindered the investigations as different police departments often did not communicate or share information effectively.

The separation of crime scenes (where the victims were killed) and dump sites (where the bodies were found) created jurisdictional challenges. Different law enforcement agencies were responsible for the investigation of the murder and the discovery of the body, often without realizing the connection between the two events.

In addition, it may not be uncommon to find that investigation reports were more synopsis-oriented than detail-specific in their construction. Some agencies required no documentation in a homicide investigation unless a suspect was developed, and as a result, written reports may be non-existent. The entire case record might have been kept in the notes and notebooks of the individual detectives, and when that person retired, the notebooks went with them if the department did not require such to be turned in (see Figure 2.4). I have spoken to "old time" detectives who would tap their shirt pocket or their head and stress that they carried their investigation "right here."

Figure 2.4 Newspaper story of lynched teen. In some instances, homicide victims were buried without an autopsy. Forensic exhumation is one technique to be considered when re-activating a case in which no autopsy was made (credit- to be determined.) Old investigator's notebook

Another area in which these practices have occurred was documentation of a neighborhood canvas. In decades past, if a witness reported nothing of importance, there was no requirement for any documentation. Thus, the witness who reported nothing was not identified. If no one was home, no attempt for follow-up contact may have occurred. It was not unusual for investigators to detail uniformed officers to conduct the canvas, and in short, any documentation of a neighborhood canvas may be a hit or miss affair. Even so, new residents or individuals who were overlooked or reluctant to come forward during the initial investigation might now provide valuable information. People who were present at the time of the crime may recall details that seemed insignificant initially but can be critical with new investigative context. It is not uncommon to find witnesses in these cases who were never interviewed by law enforcement. Additionally, the authors have been involved in canvases where individuals had valuable information but did not choose to come forward until investigators came to them. Further discussion of this is found in Chapter 4.

When opening a cold case file, never discard any papers, worn out file folders, or other items in the file or box that may appear unrelated or of no use in the case investigation. In many states, any item(s) found in a case file can and will be deemed discoverable in a criminal case. This should be noted in the report of the initial review. A defense attorney may ask if this occurred at some point and perhaps try to stress that the real killer's name was discarded.

Older Technology

When reviewing older files, investigators may encounter types of formats not normally seen today, including audio, image, or recording formats. Reports may be handwritten or typed on typewriters. Older homicide files may include both types. Forms may be primitive by today's standards or lacking altogether. Word processors began to attain widespread use within law enforcement in the early to mid-1980s.

- *Onion skin paper*: This is a very thin, almost transparent type of paper that was used for making multiple copies of the same document and became popular in the typewriter era (see Figure 2.5). It is characterized by being very fragile and tears easily. Most often encountered in a typewritten format, reports on this paper were made using carbon paper. Carbon paper is a black paper that when struck on the top side of the paper leaves the impression in dark ink on a piece of paper adjacent to the bottom side. Manual (non-electric) typewriters could often make three to five legible copies using these

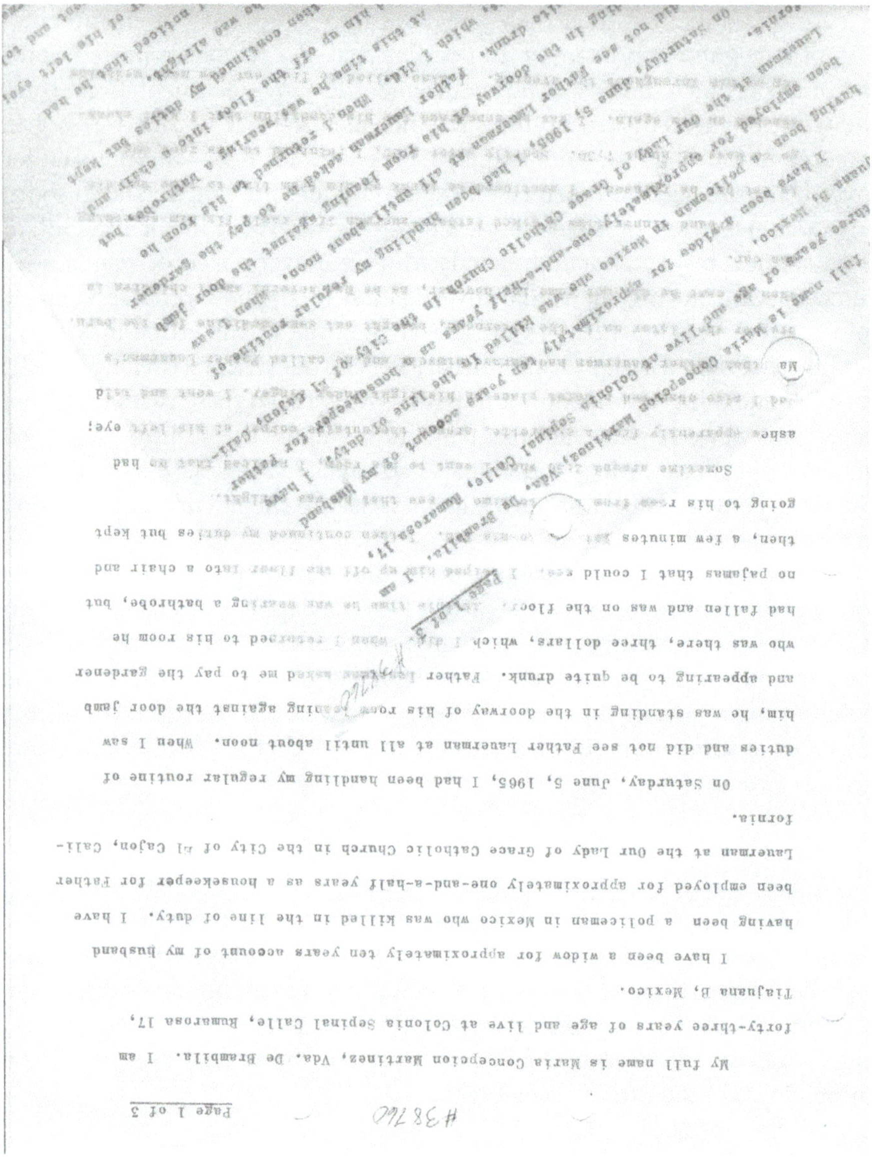

#38760 Page 1 of 3

My full name is Maria Concepcion Martinez, Vda. De Brambila. I am forty-three years of age and live at Colonia Sepinal Calle, Rumarosa 17, Tiajuana B, Mexico.

I have been a widow for approximately ten years account of my husband having been a policeman in Mexico who was killed in the line of duty. I have been employed for approximately one-and-a-half years as a housekeeper for Father Lauerman at the Our Lady of Grace Catholic Church in the City of El Cajon, California.

On Saturday, June 5, 1965, I had been handling my regular routine of duties and did not see Father Lauerman at all until about noon. When I saw him, he was standing in the doorway of his room leaning against the door jamb and appearing to be quite drunk. Father [illegible] asked me to pay the gardener who was there, three dollars, which I did. When I returned to his room he had fallen and was on the floor. [illegible] time he was wearing a bathrobe, but no pajamas that I could see. I helped him up off the floor into a chair and then, a few minutes [illegible] continued my duties but kept going to his room [illegible] he was alright.

Sometime around [illegible] I noticed that he had ashes [illegible] of his left eye;

Figure 2.5 Carbon copies on onion skin paper. Older case files will contain copies made with carbon paper, and these are often encountered on onion skin paper, a semi-transparent, fragile paper. (Courtesy of El Cajon Police Department.)

formats. The copy most immediate to the original face sheet is usually most legible and the quality of print declines with the additional copies. This format is not uncommon in reports written prior to the mid-1980s.

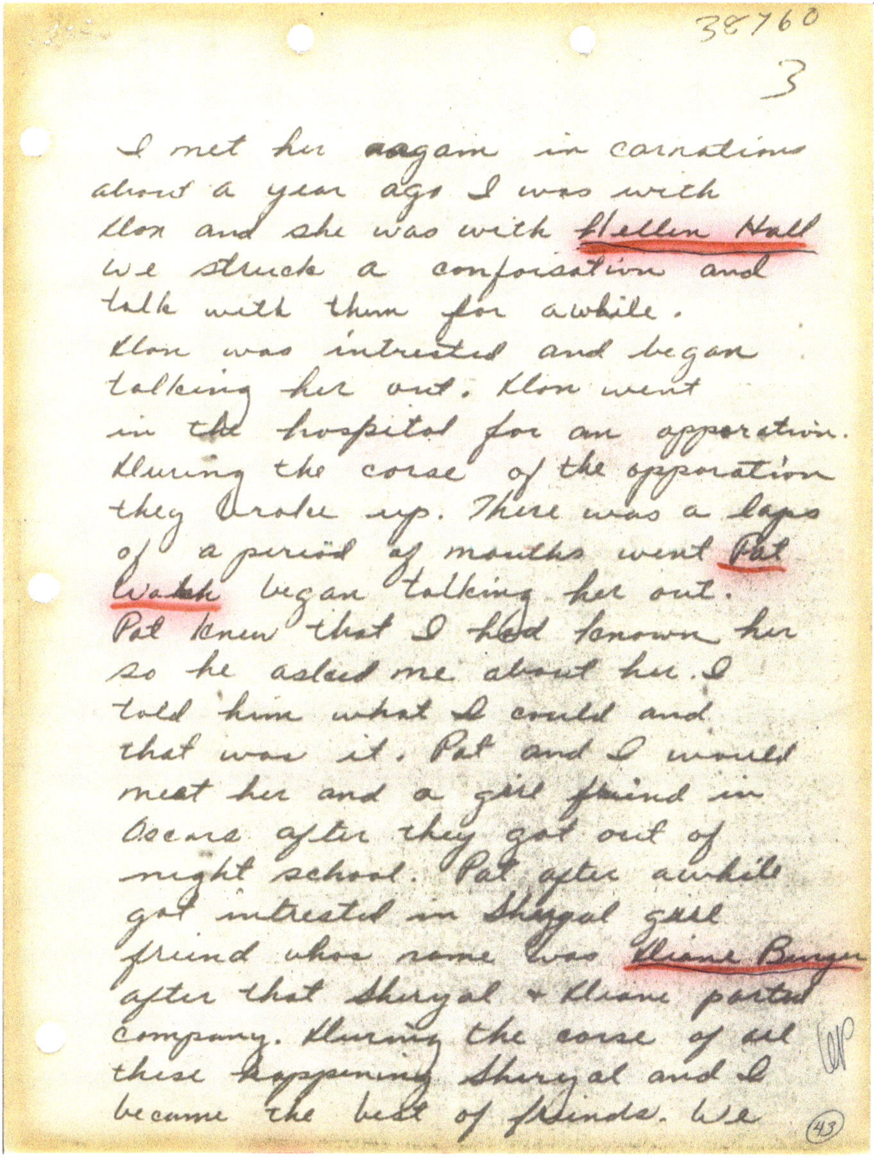
38760
3
I met her again in carnation
about a year ago I was with
Don and she was with Hellen Hall
We struck a converation and
talk with them for awhile.
Don was intrested and began
talking her out. Don went
in the hospital for an opperation.
During the corse of the opporation
they broke up. There was a laps
of a period of months went Pat
Walsh began talking her out.
Pat knew that I had known her
so he asked me about her. I
told him what I could and
that was it. Pat and I would
meat her and a girl friend in
Oceans after they got out of
night school. Pat after awhile
got intrested in Sheryal girl
friend whos name was Diane Berger
after that Sheryal + Diane parted
company. During the corse of all
these happening Sheryal and I
became the best of friends. We
43

Figure 2.6 Thermal paper. Note the reddish-brown tinge to this paper. With time the writing will fade almost completely. (Courtesy of El Cajon Police Department.)

- *Thermal paper*: This style of copy paper uses a heat source to impregnate the words and images onto the paper. It was invented in the mid-1960s, and variations of it are still used today in facsimile machines (Figure 2.6). A characteristic of this paper is that it begins to fade after a few years or so, depending upon its composition and conditions to which it has been exposed, such as light and heat. Documents reproduced on thermal paper may be identified by an overall brownish tinge to the paper, and a reddish-brown tinge to the letters. In addition, the paper may have a semi-glossy sheen. These have been encountered in reviewing reports from the 1950s and 1970s, and this was one of the earlier forms used in office-style duplicating machines to reproduce reports or other documents now found in some older cold case files.

When thermal paper copies are found in a file, it is suggested that these be photographed, or their images otherwise preserved due to the continuing degradation which may occur. In addition, a cold case investigator may ask *"Where is the original?"* This may suggest possible sources for follow-up and/or to retrieve further case documents, material, or identify other contacts. Why were copies made and who were the recipients?

- *Photostat:* The term is a trademark name for a style of photocopier and copies of documents made by this process that may still be found in older cold case files. The device is a large camera which takes a photograph of the object. A paper negative is processed in developer, washed, and dried in a drier. The result is white letters on a black background, whereas the original of the document was black letters, such as from a typewriter, on a white background (see Figure 2.7).
- *Shorthand*: Shorthand is a method of taking notes and reporting dialogue using a handwritten series of figures and spaces. It is a process that is formally learned through specialized training and

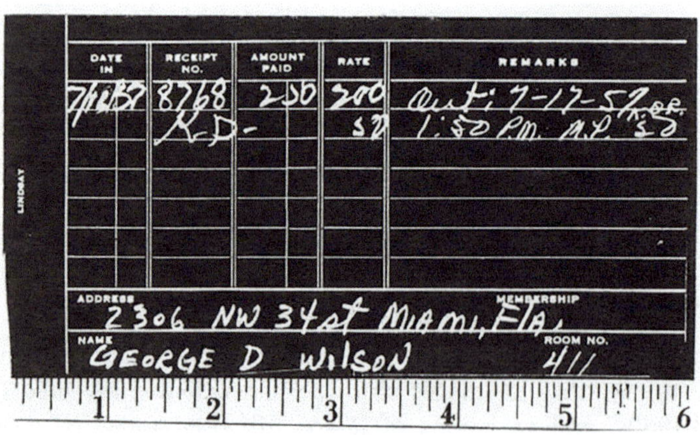

Figure 2.7 Photostat copy. This was essentially a paper negative produced by a particular camera. (Courtesy of Mr. Paul Edholm.)

> experience and was a commonplace form for taking dictation or recording statements or testimony in business and in the legal profession for many decades. The use of shorthand in the legal system dates to at least the late 1800s. In the days before courtroom reporting became mechanized, trained clerks recorded question and answer sessions and court proceedings using paper and pencil or pen. In some older cold cases, investigators have encountered the stenographers' notes being retained in the file. These are often the result of interrogation and interviews between investigators and witnesses or suspects.

These notes may be encountered in loose sheet form, or in spiral or similar bound tablets. In addition, there have been different styles of shorthand. Should these be encountered in reviewing cold case files, the local court reporter's office may be able to assist in deciphering and/or transcribing these notes. In addition, they may know the whereabouts or disposition of the original stenographer as well. A cold case investigator may seek to identify the stenographer who took the notes to inquire as to what they are and ask:

- Is this a complete statement or a partial statement?
- Was a transcribed report made? (Is it in the file or does the stenographer have a copy?)
- Does the stenographer retain any other records pertaining to this case?

As noted in the Jones case study in Chapter 3, publicity surrounding a 1970 murder of a young mother brought about a call to the investigating detective. It was a case investigation that began in 2009 with only five newspaper clippings, the original medical examiner's report, and some faded Polaroid photos. The suspect had previously been charged with the murder but was released at the preliminary hearing. Upon reading about this re-investigation, the original stenographer contacted the detective and furnished her original notes taken during the course of the hearing. It was a treasure trove of information unknown at the time to the detective. The suspect pled guilty in 2016 and died in prison in 2024.

Additionally, while opening and reviewing a cold case file, investigators may discover different colored copies of report forms. When these are found, investigators may seek to determine the number of copies in the original form, and their dissemination routes. This may lead investigators to other sources of case information. An example is shown in Figure 2.8. Investigators should ask: *Who was the recipient? Why did they need, or get, a copy? Do they have additional documentation relevant to this case?*

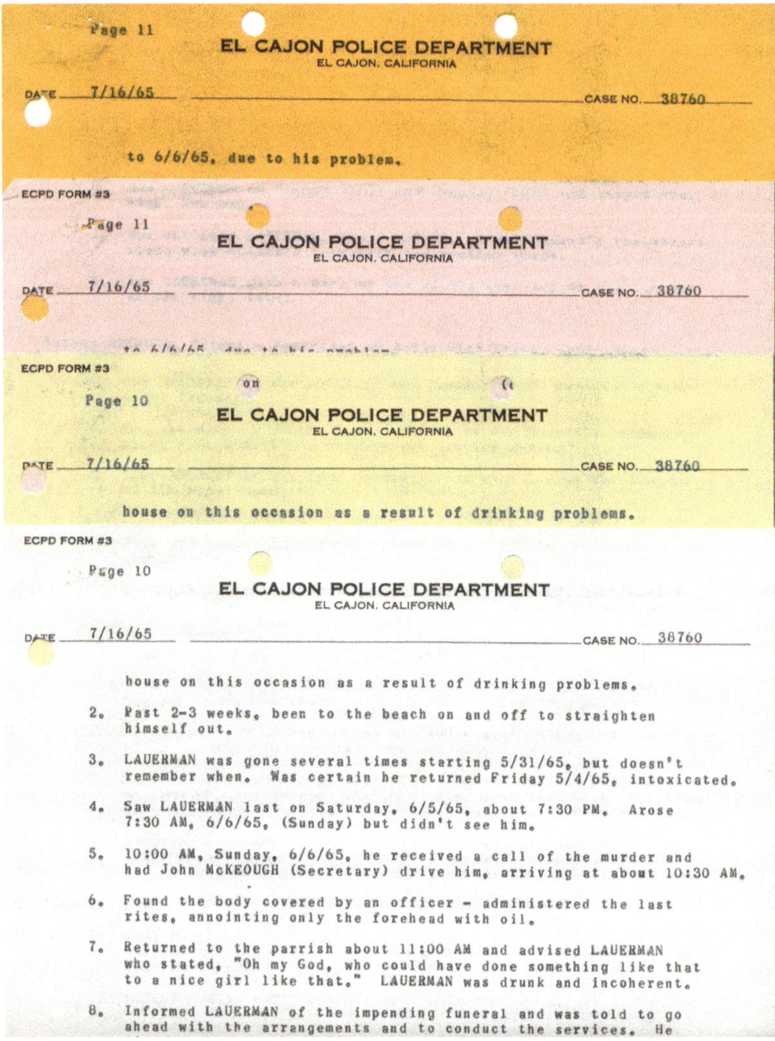
Page 11

EL CAJON POLICE DEPARTMENT
EL CAJON, CALIFORNIA

DATE 7/16/65 CASE NO. 38760

to 6/6/65, due to his problem.

ECPD FORM #3

Page 11

EL CAJON POLICE DEPARTMENT
EL CAJON, CALIFORNIA

DATE 7/16/65 CASE NO. 38760

ECPD FORM #3

Page 10

EL CAJON POLICE DEPARTMENT
EL CAJON, CALIFORNIA

DATE 7/16/65 CASE NO. 38760

house on this occasion as a result of drinking problems.

ECPD FORM #3

Page 10

EL CAJON POLICE DEPARTMENT
EL CAJON, CALIFORNIA

DATE 7/16/65 CASE NO. 38760

house on this occasion as a result of drinking problems.

2. Past 2-3 weeks, been to the beach on and off to straighten himself out.

3. LAUERMAN was gone several times starting 5/31/65, but doesn't remember when. Was certain he returned Friday 5/4/65, intoxicated.

4. Saw LAUERMAN last on Saturday, 6/5/65, about 7:30 PM. Arose 7:30 AM, 6/6/65, (Sunday) but didn't see him.

5. 10:00 AM, Sunday, 6/6/65, he received a call of the murder and had John McKEOUGH (Secretary) drive him, arriving at about 10:30 AM.

6. Found the body covered by an officer - administered the last rites, annointing only the forehead with oil.

7. Returned to the parrish about 11:00 AM and advised LAUERMAN who stated, "Oh my God, who could have done something like that to a nice girl like that." LAUERMAN was drunk and incoherent.

8. Informed LAUERMAN of the impending funeral and was told to go ahead with the arrangements and to conduct the services. He

Figure 2.8 Colored police report forms. When colored forms are found in a file, cold case investigators should determine who may have received the copies. These recipients may retain case documents or other material. (Courtesy of El Cajon Police Department.)

Preliminary File Review

The goal of a preliminary file review is to:

- Put each file into such a condition that an investigator can (1) move forward with that file anytime following the review, (2) see a concise summary of the facts and physical evidence, and (3) begin working that case without having to track down missing information or reports.

- Create a concise summary of the facts and physical evidence as well as results of forensic examinations previously performed upon the evidence. This summary may be downloaded into appropriate computer systems, thus allowing for an immediate review of the case without having to physically locate the file.
    - Update all identifying information pertaining to witnesses, suspects, and other persons of interest, allowing for the possibility of linking these persons to other cases or alerting other investigators who have contact with these persons of their involvement in this case.
    - Download case information into Violent Criminal Apprehension Program (VICAP) or other local, state fusion centers, or regional information sharing sites such as the RISS (Regional Information Sharing Sites) network, like MAGLOCLEN (Middle Atlantic-Great Lakes Organized Crime Law Enforcement Network).
    - Allow for rapid identification of cases for future forensic potential when new technology becomes available.
    - Identify investigative leads.
    - Prioritize cases based upon leads and evidence.

Review of cold case homicide files and selection of those cases for investigation may further occur through organizational circumstances. Agency leadership, size and number of unsolved homicide cases may factor into this analysis. Not infrequently, the decision to undertake a preliminary file review may address legal considerations as well as personal relationship and evolving technological changes.

It is important investigators do not disregard cases without biological evidence during a review process. Many techniques used to solve cases without biological evidence have much to do with tactically efficient police work, rather than DNA evidence. While there isn't a definitive, up-to-date statistic on the percentage of cold cases without biological evidence, cold case investigators should not overlook these cases. As discussed earlier in this chapter, the presence or absence of biological evidence varies widely depending on various factors. Agencies are increasingly revisiting old cases and re-examining evidence using modern investigative methods, which may yield new leads or even solve cases that were previously unsolvable due to a lack of biological evidence. Ultimately, while the percentage of cold cases without biological evidence may be significant, the evolving landscape of criminal investigation coupled with old-fashioned gumshoe police work can resolve some of these cases.

This review may also be the result of selecting (1) of a few cases or (2) a systematic review of all unsolved homicides.

Preliminary guidelines in a case file review may include these evidentiary considerations:

- There is a known suspect, and physical evidence appears to have been preserved.
- There is no known suspect, but physical evidence has been preserved.
- There is no known suspect, and physical evidence is lacking or not preserved in a manner that facilitates re-examination through advanced technology.

Initial Legal Considerations

When conducting an initial case file review, whether it is a single case or during a systematic review of all unsolved cases, cold case investigators should consider potential legal issues. While there is no statute of limitations on first-degree murder, there may be limitations to prosecution on lesser degrees of murder. Review and potential reactivation of cold case homicides may involve other legal issues as well. In conjunction with representatives of the prosecutor's office, considerations during the review process may include:

- Degree of homicide.
- Jurisdiction or venue.
- Changes in the law since time of offense.
- Previous invocation of Miranda Rights.
- Statute of limitations of premeditated versus manslaughter.
- Speedy trial.
- Evidence code then and now.
- Chain of custody of evidence.
- Suspect status (deceased or incarcerated).
- Sexual assault statute of limitations (if this component is present).
- Allegation of prior offenses.
- Ex post facto considerations.
- Enhancements.
- Possible change of punishments.

Arrest and successful prosecution of those responsible for the murder is the goal of police and prosecutors. These cases are circumstantial cases at present and cold case investigators should bear in mind that investigation and prosecution will fully illustrate the difference between "*probable cause*" and "*beyond a reasonable doubt.*" Good communication between law enforcement and local prosecutors is critical when examining legal questions and serves to build rapport for the future. Keep in mind that prosecutors and judges may need to be *educated* in cold case investigation.

Cold case investigators may, in some instances, need to overcome prosecutorial belief that every possible hypothesis of innocence must be overcome. This is not normally done during current homicide cases and is not necessarily so in cold case investigation and prosecution. Identifying prosecutors to assist in these cases early in the process facilitates the exchange of information and may speed up obtaining search and arrest warrants in the future. Good communication at this time will not put the investigator in a position of calling a prosecutor at 3 a.m. in the morning and hearing "*...you're calling me now on a 20-year-old case?*"

Remember, the case is not done until you get a conviction.

Systematic Review of All Cases

In this method of file review, all unsolved homicide cases (and sometimes suspicious deaths or other cases of concern) are identified, reviewed for potential solvability, and prioritized for further investigation. The methods and procedures utilized in this process are applicable to a single case file review as well. During this process, reviewers may include:

- Current homicide detectives.
- Retired homicide detectives hired back—"*hire backs*"—by the organization to review these cases. This is an option that an agency may utilize in lieu of assigning detectives with current, full case loads. When this method is used, however, it should be noted that one of the advantages in a file review is to have someone *unfamiliar* with the case do the review. A fresh pair of eyes means a fresh perspective, something that may not be possible should the original detective be hired back and assigned his or her own unsolved case.
- Civilian volunteers with homicide investigation experience. In 2002, the Charlotte, North Carolina, Police Department inaugurated a program to review unsolved homicide cases dating to 1979. After concerns addressing confidentiality and potential judicial obstacles were resolved, these volunteers were assigned a case based on solvability factors such as DNA and fingerprints as well as examination for potential relationship changes. The volunteers reviewed their assigned cases and developed an organized case file. They prepared lead sheets addressing forensic evidence and suggested persons to interview. As a result of their work, a case summary was prepared for homicide detectives, and the case was given back to a detective

for continued follow-up. The agency has reported favorably upon this method. A further example is illustrated in Chapter 11 [cold case unit chapter].

- College students vetted by their local or state law enforcement agency. This practice is becoming increasingly more popular and has yielded success. For example, Western Michigan University's Cold Case Investigation Program involves students from the Department of Anthropology and the School of Criminal Justice. Under the guidance of faculty members and forensic experts, and the Michigan State Police, students work on real cold cases, analyzing evidence, conducting interviews, and developing investigative strategies. Dr. Michael Arntfield's Cold Case Society at the University of Western Ontario is another wonderful example of using college students and faculty from multiple disciplines, to analyze unsolved murders.

Qualifications to Review Unsolved Cases

Those persons selected to review unsolved homicide cases should be knowledgeable in homicide investigation, law, and technology. In addition, they should be:

- Knowledgeable in current computer software relating to case review including VICAP and agency case management systems.
- Knowledgeable of current sources for research of witnesses, suspects, and principals involved in unsolved cases.
- Knowledgeable in locating current sources for all evidence and coroner/medical examiner documentation.
- Knowledgeable in operating applicable agency computer software to document their activity.

Solvability Factors

Cold case reviews focus on people (as victims, witnesses, or suspects) and evidence (physical or biological). These are the elements that may solve it. Solvability factors are those facts and circumstances of a case that influence its potential to be solved. These reviews commonly seek to maximize the potential to be gained from (1) changes in relationships that may now result in persons providing necessary information to law enforcement or (2) utilization of advanced technology in the examination and analysis of physical or biological material. Ultimately, these solvability factors may be incorporated into the parameters that are defined when a systematic case review program is instituted.

Technology as a solvability factor includes systems such as the following:

- DNA/CODIS.
  - Potential suspect DNA recovered.
  - Potential probative victim DNA recovered.
  - Detection of previously unidentified unknown DNA profile.
  - No DNA evidence recovered.
- AFIS (Automated Fingerprint Identification System)/IAFIS
  - Identified fingerprints recovered.
  - Unidentified fingerprints recovered.
  - No fingerprints recovered.
- NIBIN, DRUGFIRE (an automated, computerized forensic firearms identification system).
  - Shell casings recovered.
  - Bullets recovered.
  - Linked to another crime.
  - No firearm evidence recovered.
- VICAP potential link to another crime.

People as potential solvability factors may be:

- Suspect and/or person of interest.
  - Arrested but released.
  - Named, no arrest.
  - Incarcerated/other charge.
  - Under investigation/other charge.
  - Seen but unidentified.
  - Deceased.
  - No suspects.
- Witness.
  - Witness under investigation/trial.
  - Witness incarcerated.
  - Multiple eyewitnesses.
  - Previously uncooperative.
  - Previously did not tell all.
  - Other.

These solvability factors have been summarized as a Homicide Case Review Solvability Chart by the Washington, D.C. Metro Police Department and are shown in Figure 2.9.

Those homicides that have a sexual assault/biological evidence or fingerprint component often present the highest potential for solvability.

Defining Parameters for a Systematic Review

Parameters may be based on elements of time, technology, and encompassing time periods. Some agencies conduct a systematic review by:

Homicide case review solvability chart

Suspect		**Comments**
Arrested but released	☐	______
Named, no arrest	☐	______
Incarcerated/other charge	☐	______
Under investigation/other charge	☐	______
Deceased	☐	______
Seen but unidentified	☐	______
No suspects	☐	______
Witness		
Witness under investigation/trial	☐	______
Witness incarcerated	☐	______
Multiple eye-witnesses	☐	______
Other	☐	______
Firearm evidence		
Shell casings recovered	☐	______
Slugs recovered	☐	______
Linked to another crime	☐	______
No firearm evidence recovered	☐	______
Fingerprint evidence		
Unidentified prints recovered	☐	______
No fingerprint evidence recovered	☐	______
DNA evidence		
Potential suspect DNA recovered	☐	______
Potential probative victim DNA	☐	______
No DNA evidence recovered	☐	______
Other crimes		
Potential link to another crime	☐	______
Misc. solvability factors		
______	☐	______
______	☐	______

Figure 2.9 Washington, D.C. Metropolitan Police Department Solvability chart. (Courtesy of Detective Jim Trainum.)

- Re-examining all unsolved cases beginning with those most recently unsolved (cases prior to a date 1–3 years in the immediate past or similar criteria). The Kansas City, Missouri, Police Department (KCPD) has utilized this method.
- Selecting a specific encompassing period. For example, those cases unsolved between, for example, January 1, 1960, and December 31, 1995.

In addition, these selection criteria may be combined with:

- Selection of those cases in which there exists a potential to exploit changes in personal relationships due to passage of time.
- Selection of those cases in which evidence exists that may be exploited by advanced technology.

A systematic review is often conducted by an agency that has a large backlog of unsolved homicides. In conducting this style of review, an agency may seek to learn:

- How many qualifying cases are there in the agency?
- Where are these cases located?
- Do case summaries currently exist?

This method of review has also resulted in:

- Identification of cases reflected in the records as "unsolved" that are solved, but records were not current. Thus, the agency had fewer cold cases than initially thought and records are updated.
- Identification of cases considered "unsolved" that had progressed through the identification of a suspect and issuance of an arrest warrant but that the warrant had not been entered into state/national computer systems.
- Identification of cases wherein an arrest warrant had been issued but erroneously recalled and needed to be reissued.
- Recognition of previously unrecognized patterns in homicides and/or sexual assaults.
- An updated database that identifies the offense and other designated criteria. This may include:
  - Victim.
  - Date of offense and/or report.
  - Suspect name, description, and vehicle.
  - Presence of physical or biological evidence.
  - Physical location and availability of case and/or evidence.

This method is appropriate for any jurisdictional size, and agencies of many different sizes have utilized such a method to review their unsolved homicide cases. No agency, however, has unlimited resources and these efforts will be affected by time, number of personnel, and other available resources. While a larger department may assign more personnel to review cold cases, it most likely will have a proportionally larger number of cold cases to investigate. Similarly, smaller departments may assign one, two, or more detectives to review a smaller number of cases. They may be assigned on a full- or part-time basis to review unsolved cases. In either method, a systematic review represents a commitment by the agency to address all unsolved homicides.

Case Prioritization by Homicide Category

During a systemic review, homicides may be prioritized by type or category of homicide. These could include:

- *Sex-related*: Due to DNA/CODIS potential, sexual assault-related murders may present the highest rate of solvability, depending upon existence and preservation of biological evidence.
- *Stabbings*: Possibility of biological evidence/DNA left by suspect.
- *Beating and strangulation*: Possibility of DNA transfer from suspect.
- *Shootings*: Largest category but small potential for DNA or physical evidence; potential of firearms-related evidence.
- *Closed cases*: Cases closed by arrest but should be considered whether charges were later dropped. Also, whether more than one suspect may have been involved.

Objectives Clearly Stated

In conducting a systematic review, the goal of the review should be clearly stated and understood by those who are tasked to conduct the review: (1) Is the goal of the review to obtain convictions, or (2) is the goal of the review to solve and close unsolved cases regardless of whether a conviction can be obtained?

If the purpose of the review program is to obtain convictions and the *statute of limitations has expired*, an agency may desire to save the resources for those cases more likely to result in a conviction. If the goal of the review is to solve and close unsolved cases regardless of whether a conviction can be obtained, an agency may opt to review all cases that qualify under its guidelines. This may be an important consideration during investigations of serial killers, whose criminal depredations may span years or decades.

Identifying Unsolved Cases

Using a systematic approach, each unsolved homicide is given a preliminary review and subsequently prioritized or ranked for the possibility of successful investigation potential. When conducting a systematic review of all unsolved homicide cases, it is important to thoroughly and methodically identify all unsolved homicides within the agency. Sources of information to identify potential unsolved cases, or to assist in corroboration of unsolved cases, would include:

- Local agency logbooks.
- Computer databases.
- Rejected cases.
- Dismissed cases.
- Autopsy logbooks and coroner or medical examiner records.
- Crime laboratory logbooks.
- Retired homicide investigators.
- Prosecutor records.
- State Bureau of Vital Statistics.
- Local Recorder's Office.
- Undetermined, or other manner of death or suspicious circumstance.

Suggested Preliminary Case Review Procedure

The following is a synopsis of several cold case review protocols utilized by various law enforcement agencies. The cold case reviewer would consider (1) reports and documents, (2) evidence, and (3) review and updated condition of case file. In-depth discussion of these topics will occur in further chapters.

Reports and Documents

- Locate all case files and reports.
- Read all reports and documents to determine if workable information exists.
- Listen to all audio tapes and determine if transcripts should be made or existing ones are accurate. Consider making back-up copies for case work and minimizing usage of original tapes.
- Review all video recordings. Similarly, consider preserving originals and make duplicate.
- Where possible, contact original detectives to obtain their perspective and an overview to determine whether information exists that is not reflected in the case file. During this contact, the reviewer should seek to determine whether the former detective has any notebooks, case files, photos, or other memorabilia from this case and to recover these.

During this contact, the previous detectives' work must not be criticized or belittled. Other events or activities that may have been concurrent with their investigation at the time are not known. In some uncommon circumstances, detectives have declined to cooperate based upon personal and professional circumstances at the time of their departure. Remember, the advantage of the new investigation is the perspective of a fresh look and caution is suggested so as to not necessarily limit one's objectivity in the investigation.

- The reviewer should determine whether contact needs to be made, or should be made, with the victim's family. This is perhaps the most frequently asked question detectives may ask themselves or others. Contact may be necessary to establish whether new information exists that was not known to original investigators, and this may be especially true in gang or drug-related homicides. This subject will be discussed elsewhere in this text.
- The reviewer would prepare recommendations for a follow-up assigned investigator to obtain possible information from any specialized law enforcement units, such as gang units, narcotic investigative units, or other groups.

During the case file review, reviewers and investigators may begin to formulate their investigative plan by considering factors that may include:

- Totality of information known about the crime, including but not limited to:
    - Date, time, location.
    - Name of victim.
    - Brief profile of victim.
    - Finding of body.
- Identified or developed suspects:
    - Known relationship to victim.
    - Known prior contacts with victim.
    - Current location.
- Agency jurisdiction for investigation of the offense.
- Previous investigation(s).
- Autopsy and medical examiner records.
- Motive, opportunity, and means (MOM).
- Witness information.
- Known physical evidence that may link a potential suspect to the crime.

- New forensic technologies that may assist in developing known physical evidence.
- What impact does the passage of time have on the case?
- Does this case have a *pulse?*

Evidence Review

- The reviewer would determine if evidence existed. Locations to find physical or biological evidence may include:
  - Agency evidence/property room.
  - Coroner or medical examiner office for original slides, swabs, victim clothing, or other evidence. Even when agency biological evidence has been discarded, lost, or otherwise cannot be located, check with the coroner/medical examiner for duplicate slides/swabs that may have been retained in their case file.
  - Public or private crime laboratories (previously submitted or tested evidence and lab reports).
  - Hospital or medical facilities (rape kits, medical reports, slides).
  - Courthouse property rooms.
  - Prosecutor's offices (previous trial or investigations).
  - Possession by retired investigators, including case notes and details not found in files.
  - Other investigating agencies.

It is incumbent during a preliminary cold case file review, or during a subsequent in-depth case examination, to identify the location of the evidence and to *personally* inspect and examine it. During this inspection and review, the cold case investigator seeks to:

- Identify the physical existence of the evidence.
- Identify the physical location of the evidence.
  - Confirm the identity and description of the evidence.
  - Confirm that all evidence is properly packaged and stored.
  - Physically examine it to check for degradation, damage, or other conditions.
  - Confirm quantity [drug evidence] or amount [if money].
  - Determine that physical evidence and property are concurrent with written case records.
  - Examine chain of custody issues to ensure integrity of the evidence.
  - Ensure that all evidence is present and accounted for.
  - Document this activity.
  - Determine and recommend what analysis may be available for existing evidence, such as DNA, AFIS, etc.

"John Doe" Warrants

During the initial file review, DNA-related legal issues may be identified. Due to advances in this technology, "John Doe Warrants" may be a viable option. This is the method of issuing an arrest warrant for a DNA profile obtained from analysis of unsolved crime scene evidence. The warrant is issued for the DNA identifier, absent the name of the profile holder. This innovative approach was pioneered by Deputy District Attorney Norm Gahn in Milwaukee, Wisconsin. The method has allowed charges to be filed and permit old cases, primarily sexual assaults, to be prosecuted when the person matching the "John Doe" DNA profile is subsequently identified by name. "John Doe" DNA warrants are one way to permit cases to remain active and allowing them the chance to be solved through future DNA technology and databases.

Review and Update of Case File

- Ensure that the "Murder Book" is complete and updated with all necessary reports (Figure 2.10).
- Locate and inspect all photos and negatives and ensure that they are in satisfactory condition for court purposes.
- Identify and ensure that all coroner's or medical examiner's reports and photographs and other documents are in the file and in satisfactory condition for court purposes.

Figure 2.10 LAPD Murder Investigation summaries. The larger the agency, the greater the possibility of higher numbers of unsolved homicides. (Courtesy of Detective Rick Jackson, LAPD.)

Figure 2.11 Detective's notebook. (Courtesy of Sgt. Richard Longshore, Los Angeles County Sheriff's Department.)

- Ensure that all available investigator's notebooks and case notes are in the file and not with the original investigator (see Figure 2.11).
- Ensure that all evidence is documented and accounted for, and that requests for needed examination or re-examination are completed and filed. In addition, the reviewer would ensure that a complete copy of the evidence list, including location, is present in the case file.
- Locate and inspect all maps and diagrams to ensure that they are present and suitable for court purposes.

Case Synopsis and Assessment Report

Upon completion of the file review, the reviewer would prepare a complete and accurate summary of the case for entry in specified agency computer systems. This synopsis provides a review of events, of the persons involved, and summary of the evidence and the case.

- *Solved cases*: If the case has been solved or resolved, the reviewer would prepare a closing supplemental report and dispose of evidence (with the approval and supervision of the homicide unit supervisor or commander, or agency policy and procedures).
- *Unsolved cases*: If the case is unsolved, the reviewer would ensure that the case is ready to be handed off to an assigned investigator for active follow-up investigation. This might include:
  - Written recommendations and offer of a comprehensive investigative plan that would suggest a high probability for the arrest and prosecution of responsible suspect(s) for criminal homicide.
  - Indication of a reviewer's preparation to give an oral overview of the case and presentation of proposed investigative plan.
- Solved cases with arrest warrants outstanding: The reviewer would evaluate the case and locate and confirm evidence.
  - Ascertain and determine what information exists in file to positively identify and locate the defendant named in the outstanding arrest warrant.
  - Ensure that certified copies of identification which positively identifies the named defendant in the outstanding warrant exists in the case file. This documentation may include:
    - Certified copy of driver's license photo with fingerprint verification.
    - Latent fingerprint card.
    - Other (passport, etc.).
  - Recommend or ensure VICAP update when new information is received.
- Prepare a written, comprehensive recommendation so the case can be assigned to a specialized unit for active investigation. In these cases, it is important to realize the necessity for *due diligence* and to document these efforts for future legal activity.
- Be prepared to present an oral briefing or overview of case as necessary.
- Update case management system.
- Ensure that warrant is valid and entered into state or national computer systems.

Figures 2.12 and 2.13 are examples of forms used in the review process by the Unsolved Unit of the Los Angeles County Sheriff's Department, California. Additional report forms are used for case assessment, evidence evaluation, and examination of evidence. This process is described further in this chapter.

Prioritization Schedules

Once the preliminary case and evidence reviews have been completed, a priority of likelihood for solution building upon the following criteria may be considered. This prioritization schedule will assist in filtering those cases

CASE STATUS AND REVIEW

File #:		Date Received:	
		Date Received:	

Victim Name(s):

Location of case file:

(Library # or who has it)

Investigator responsible for	1.	
the case or investigation:	2.	
(Not the Reviewer)	3.	

INFORMATION FOR CASE NARRATIVE UPDATE:

Don't rewrite case summary or narrative unless necessary. Just write additions or update narrative already in case management system.

☐	FURTHER INVESTIGATION		**(Check these only if done by Reviewer)**
☐	ACTIVE WITH NO WORKABLE INFORMATION	☐	CASE ASSESSMENT REPORT (6 Pages)
☐	SOLVED	☐	POOR-BOY INVENTORY SHEET
☐	**(Mark Only If Requesting Lab Work)**	☐	MURDER BOOK
☐	EVIDENCE-FIREARMS	☐	SUPPLEMENTARY REPORT SUBMIT
☐	EVIDENCE-DNA	☐	CLOSE/OUT SUPP. REPORT
☐	EVIDENCE-PHYSICAL		

REVIEWED BY: DATE:

Figure 2.12 Case Status and Review Summary. (Courtesy of Lt. Joseph Hartshorne, Los Angeles County Sheriff's Department.)

WITNESS LIST	FILE #	

NAME/DESCRIPTION	ADDRESS/PHONE	RELATION TO CASE	REF PAGE

REVIEWER	FILE #	

DATE	TIME	FOLLOW-UP

Figure 2.13 Case Assessment Report. (Courtesy of Lt. Joseph Hartshornem Los Angeles County Sheriff's Department.)

(Continued)

CASE ASSESSMENT REPORT

FILE #		CRIME:			
Murder Book:	☐ Yes ☐ No	Library #		Crime Status:	
Date of Occurrence:		Time of Occurrence:		Day of Occurrence:	

LOCATION:		TYPE OF LOC:	

VICTIM:		CC#	
DESCRIPTION:			

ADD'L VICTIMS:	

SUSPECT( ):		IN CUSTODY: ☐ YES ☐ NO
DESCRIPTION:		

ADD'L SUSPECTS:	

****

CASE SUMMARY:

FILE #		REVIEWER:	

Figure 2.13 (*Continued*) Case Assessment Report. (Courtesy of Lt. Joseph Hartshornem Los Angeles County Sheriff's Department.)

(*Continued*)

FILE #		SUSPECT ( ) OF ( )

NAME:		PHOTO: ☐ YES ☐ NO

AKA'S:		DOB:	

Marks / Scars / Tattoos:	

PHYSICAL:

Sex		Race		Height		Weight		Eyes		Hair	

IDENTIFIERS

ID/DL#		CII#		FBI#	

SS #		OTHER	

RESIDENCE:	

Date Arrested		Booking #		Charges:	
Case #		Charges Filed			
Arrest Warrant Issued ☐ YES ☐ NO			Warrant Status ☐ Cleared ☐ Outstanding		
Court Action:					
Sentence:					
ADDITIONAL INFORMATION:					

Figure 2.13 (*Continued*) Case Assessment Report. (Courtesy of Lt. Joseph Hartshornem Los Angeles County Sheriff's Department.)

(*Continued*)

WITNESS LIST	FILE #	

NAME/DESCRIPTION	ADDRESS/PHONE	RELATION TO CASE	REF PAGE

REVIEWER	FILE #	

DATE	TIME	FOLLOW-UP

Figure 2.13 (*Continued*) Case Assessment Report. (Courtesy of Lt. Joseph Hartshornem Los Angeles County Sheriff's Department.)

that offer the highest potential for solvability with given resources from those with a lesser chance of solution. The following examples reflect three different types of prioritization schedules, and various agencies use variations and modifications of these.

Five-Part Schedule

Priority 1: These are those cases in which an offender has been identified, and an arrest warrant has been issued. These are those cases that have "*fallen through the cracks.*" Further, this review will ensure that the arrest warrant is still valid and properly entered into the National Crime Information Center (NCIC), or an Unlawful Flight to Avoid Prosecution (UFAP) warrant has been obtained. Follow-up investigation to locate the suspect will be necessary and this investigation may ultimately draw upon forensic artistry or media alerts or national television broadcast in attempts to locate the suspect. Investigation may necessitate review of all evidence to ascertain its existence, location, and condition as well as witness location and potential re-interviews.

Priority 2: There is a known suspect, and physical evidence has been preserved. Modern technology, including DNA, AFIS, and other technologies, may be enlisted to develop significant information that perhaps was previously not technically feasible. In some cases, evidence was not processed. Review and follow-through might result in successful prosecution.

Priority 3: There is no known suspect, but physical evidence has been preserved. Modern technology may potentially identify the suspect(s). An example would be identifying a DNA profile in conjunction with the CODIS system.

Priority 4: There is no known suspect and insufficient physical evidence, but there are witnesses who were not previously available who may now provide material information that can assist in suspect identification and case advancement. These cases may involve situations in which witnesses could not be initially located and interviewed or who now need to be re-interviewed. Investigation may be extensive.

Priority 5: There are no known witnesses and no known physical evidence that can assist in identifying the suspect(s). These are those cold case investigators and former NCIS laboratory director Louis N. Eliopulos term a "*snowball's chance in hell.*"

By the very nature of these cases, the reality of cold case review and prioritization may be affected by who the victim is, degree of heinousness, media influence, and election politics.

Four-Part Schedule

Priority 1: Suspect(s) have been previously identified. A warrant of arrest has previously been issued. A suspect has been identified by forensic methods. These cases are given the highest priority for re-investigation.

Priority 2: There are witnesses who can assist in identifying the suspect(s). Information has developed which identifies possible suspect(s). Evidence has been developed which can assist in identifying suspect(s). Initial investigation identifies witnesses who could not be located and/or need to be re-interviewed. These cases will be re-investigated.

Priority 3: Evidence has been preserved and modern technology, AFIS, DNA, and other methods can be utilized to process and analyze evidence. These cases will be reclassified depending on the results of the additional laboratory analysis.

Priority 4: There are no known witnesses who can assist in identifying suspect(s). There is no physical evidence that can assist in identifying suspect(s). These cases will not be re-investigated.

Three-Part Schedule

This is a three-tiered level of investigative prioritization that is evidence and case specific based. It may also be known as a *high-medium-low* system. The following is an example used by the Texas Rangers:

High: There exist(s) viable investigative option(s) that can be expected to generate leads and/or suspects.

Moderate: There exist(s) reasonable investigative option(s) that might generate leads and/or suspects.

Low: Remote investigative option(s) exist(s), and these are not expected to generate viable leads and/or suspects.

In this method, a case may also be d*eclined* due to (1) the absence of any viable investigative option(s) or (2) case facts strongly suggest that something other than a violent crime (i.e., suicide) has occurred.

Those agencies adopting a system utilizing a high-medium-low method of prioritization may also adopt a policy of investigating all high-range cases before investigating cases offering a moderate potential for solution. This option can be rationalized based upon number of cases and available resources. In turn, all moderate range cases may be investigated before dedicating resources to those cases exhibiting a low potential for solvability.

Investigative efforts, due to case numbers and resources, may never arrive at the moderate level of priority or the low level of priority. Similarly, those agencies utilizing a number tiered system may also choose to investigate those that offer the most potential before moving to those offering a lesser potential, based upon investigative resources.

The result, however, may be that some cases are not re-investigated.

Agency Samples

Morris County, New Jersey, Prosecutor's Office Method

Figure 2.14 identifies ten solvability factors previously used by the Morris County, New Jersey, Prosecutor's Office to determine the priority of investigation of cold case homicides. This method utilizes a point system to rank and subsequently prioritize a cold case homicide in comparison with other unsolved homicides. Final determination of investigative priority, however, rests with the County Prosecutor, Chief of Investigations, or their designee. This method is in keeping with identifying all unsolved homicides, management of agency resources, and optimization of investigative resources.

Kansas City, Missouri, Police Department Method

In 2002, the KCPD was scrutinized as a result of evidence disappearing in a pending homicide trial. The chief of police formed a cold case squad

Factor #	Factor	If Yes, Add	If No, Add
1	Has the death been ruled a homicide?	+1	−9
2	Can the crime scene be located today and is it in Morris County?	+1	−9
3	Has the victim been identified?	+5	−3
4	Is there significant physical evidence that can identify a suspect?	+5	0
5	Is the evidence still preserved and available?	+1	−5
6	Can any evidence be reprocessed to yield further clues?	+5	0
7	Are the critical witnesses still available?	+7	0
8	Are their leads documented in the last 6 months?	+2	0
9	Are there named suspects in the file?	+5	0
10	Is there behavior in this crime that is unusual or significant enough to warrant a behavioral assessment that may identify the offender(s)?	+1–5	0

Figure 2.14 Morris County New Jersey Solvability Factors Table. This agency has identified 10 factors to be considered in the re-opening of an unsolved case and the resulting prioritization. (Courtesy of Deputy Chief of Investigations James Gannon.)

and tasked the detectives with two purposes: (1) detectives were to examine unsolved homicides to look for new leads, and (2) detectives were to audit each item of evidence and property from their assigned cold cases. In this regard, they were to determine its physical location and proper maintenance. Cases were reviewed from 2001 and working backward. The philosophy driving this directional sequence considered maximization of resources. Older cases present more difficulty due to lack of witness availability, evidence considerations, and other factors.

The Department wanted the unit to be operational within a short period of time, and established a method to determine which cases would be re-investigated. Their procedure included:

1. Each unsolved homicide would be reviewed by a detective not originally assigned to the investigation. They felt that fresh eyes offered a fresh perspective to the case.
2. A case overview document would be prepared upon completion of the review. This overview document would cover:
   - Crime scene information overview.
   - Physical evidence description, condition, and location.
   - Victim/victimology information.
   - Overview of witness statements.
   - Citizen/informant Information.
   - Suspect information.
   - Availability of new forensic technology.
   - Impact of passage of time (is it a plus or negative).

Upon this review, a conclusion highlighting new information or details about the evidence would be prepared. It was the responsibility of the assigned detectives to physically locate property and evidence and to document their findings, including date and time. In addition, the conclusion specified the disposition of the case, including whether it was (1) submitted for prosecution, (2) maintained by the cold case squad for investigation, (3) exceptionally cleared, or (4) archived due to lack of follow-up leads or evidence.

If the preliminary interview suggested the likelihood of a successful investigation and solution to the crime, a more formal review and investigation would be conducted by an assigned investigator. The KCPD adopted a point system to identify cases to be worked. This system assigns a weighted value to 23 individual categories (see Figure 2.15). While 50 points are the possible, cases examined with as little as 2 points and as many as 24 points have been successfully cleared. This format has proved to be a valuable tool for their detectives, although the overall value as a solvability indicator is unknown. The unit reported solving 22 cold case homicides within the first year of the method's implementation.

OFFENSE NUMBER

VICTIM

DATE OF CRIME

EVIDENCE		YES	PT.	NO	UNK	N/A
1	FINGERPRINTS RECOVERED?		2			
2	PRINTS CHECKED THROUGH AFIS?		-			
3	ANY PRINTS AFIS QUALITY?		3			
4	PRINTS AVAILABLE ON POSSIBLE SUSPECT?		2			
5	TRACE EVIDENCE RECOVERED FOR DNA ANALYSIS?		4			
6	DNA ANALYSIS REQUESTED?		-			
7	DNA PROFILE OBTAINED FROM ANALYSIS?		3			
8	DNA SAMPLE OBTAINED FROM SUSPECTS?		2			
9	MURDER WEAPON RECOVERED?		4			
10	PROJECTILES/CASINGS RECOVERED?		2			
11	CHECKED THROUGH NIBIN SYSTEM?		-			
12	NIBIN IDENTIFCATION MADE?		2			
13	VICTIM'S PROPERTY TAKEN IN CRIME?		2			
14	STOLEN PROPERTY ENTERED IN NCIC?		4			

WITNESS (S)		YES	PT.	NO	UNK	N/A
15	EYEWITNESS (S) TO THE CRIME?		3			
16	COOPERATIVE WITNESS (S) ?		2			
17	HOSTILE WITNESS (S)?		1			
18	GOOD WITNESS (S) DEVELOPED IN CANVASS?		2			

SUSPECT (S)		YES	PT.	NO	UNK	N/A
19	SUSPECT(S) NAMED BY WITNESS(S)?		4			
20	DOES EYEWITNESS(S) KNOW SUSPECT(S)?		2			
21	SUSPECT(S) DEVELOPED IN INVESTIGATION?		2			
22	CAN WITNESS(S) IDENTIFY SUSPECT(S)?		2			
23	IS SUSPECT(S) STILL IN KANSAS CITY?		2			

TOTAL SOLVABILITY POINTS (50 possible)	
Det.	Date

Figure 2.15 Kansas City, Missouri, Solvability Points Table. The KCPD utilizes a 23 factor table that utilizes a point system for categories of evidence, witness, and suspect in the determination of a priority ranking system for re-investigation. (Courtesy of Sgt. Rick Jackson, Kansas City, Missouri, Police Department.)

Los Angeles County Sheriff Method

Beginning in July 2000, the Los Angeles County, California, Sheriff's Department undertook a systematic review of all identified unsolved homicides that occurred from January 1, 1980, through December 31, 1999. Approximately 3,000 unsolved homicide cases were initially believed to exist within these parameters. The concept of this program was to determine whether the passage of time since the murder had occurred may lead to the identification of a suspect in selected cases. The parameters for this concept involved (1) utilization of advances in forensic technology, including DNA, fingerprint visualization techniques, NIBIN, or DRUGFIRE firearm databases; (2) previously unknown witnesses that may now come forward; (3) previously reluctant witnesses that may now be more likely to cooperate; and (4) a multi-year review that may reveal previously unknown homicide patterns.

The sheriff's department employed six retired sheriff's homicide detectives, "hirebacks," and devised a protocol by which they were to identify and score those cases that held potential for solution. In addition to their previous experience within the Homicide Bureau, requirements for selection included knowledge of current scientific capabilities and proficiency with law enforcement databases and other computer technology. These re-hired detectives underwent a 24-hour training program and began to review these unsolved homicides.

This training instruction entailed (1) locating and cataloging homicide file contents from within sheriff's department sources; (2) instruction in computer software for the FBI's National Center for Analysis of Violent Crime (VICAP) and department case management systems; (3) instruction in research sources for locating witnesses, suspects, and principals in unsolved cases; (4) locating all evidence and coroner's office documentation, and (5) writing and filing a "Case Assessment Report" as shown previously in Figures 2.12 and 2.13, summarizing their case review activity.

A case review was then completed for each unsolved homicide case. The procedures utilized in this review included (1) location and receipt of case file; (2) listening to all audio tapes and determining whether transcripts should be made, or existing ones are accurate; (3) contacting original investigators, if possible, for case overview and to determine whether additional information exists that is not in the case file, in addition, to recover any notes or notebooks still retained by the original investigator; (4) determining whether contact needs to be made with family of victim to establish whether new information exists that was not known to original investigators; and (5) preparing recommendation to sheriff's homicide investigator as whether to obtain information from other specialized law enforcement units.

These examiners would systematically review and update the condition of the case file (Figure 2.15). This would include ensuring the following:

- Case file folder had the appropriate information required by the Homicide Bureau and that it was up to date and complete.
- All photos and negatives were located and in satisfactory condition for investigative and court purposes.
- All coroner's reports, photos, and other documents were present in the file, complete, and in satisfactory condition for court presentation.
- All original investigator notes and notebooks were in the file and not still retained by the investigator.
- All evidence is accounted for, and its location is determined, as well as need for re-evaluation and re-examination.
- All progress reports were up to date and in the file.
- All maps and diagrams were inspected and in satisfactory condition for court presentation.

The reviewing detective would then prepare a case assessment report. This would provide updated information and recommend any necessary field work and investigation. As a result, the file would be as complete as possible and, in a condition, to turn over to a homicide investigator with an oral briefing.

The agency identified in excess of 2,000 homicide cases that were unsolved, and as a result of the filtering process based upon parameters of time, changes in relationships, and technology, identified approximately 600 cases for further investigation. A number of the cases have been subsequently solved.

Figure 2.16 is an example of another cold case protocol.

Conclusion

Today's cold case homicides are solved by old-fashioned "shoe leather" detective work in combination with the passage of time, advanced technology, and changes in relationships. Cold case investigators begin by finding and reviewing the original case file, a feat sometimes more difficult than it may first appear to be. These files are found in a variety of conditions. For those agencies with large numbers of unsolved cases, a systematic review may be a viable method of filtering those cases with a potential for solvability with available resources from those with a lesser possibility. After the cases are reviewed, they may be prioritized, thus providing a means for the agency to proactively move forward with cold case investigations. The following chapters discuss in-depth file reviews and investigative methods that may assist in the solution of cold case homicides.

COLD CASE PROTOCOL

Victim's Name ____

Race _____ Sex _____ DOB __________

Date of Incident _______________ Incident Case # _______________

Day of Week __________ Time of Day __________

Case Materials Available?

	No	Yes
Initial Offense Report	_____	_____
Detectives Notes	_____	_____
Original Detective Available for interview	_____	_____
Crime Scene Photos	_____	_____
Crime Scene Diagrams	_____	_____
Autopsy Report	_____	_____
Body Diagram	_____	_____

Lab

	No	Yes
Was any evidence recovered	_____	_____
Was evidence analyzed	_____	_____
If Yes, results identify anyone besides Victim	_____	_____
Was evidence analyzed within last 5 years	_____	_____
Any remaining evidence NOT analyzed	_____	_____
Is there any DNA evidence, not the Victims	_____	_____
If Yes, is DNA profile in CODIS	_____	_____
Is there fingerprint evidence, not the Victim's	_____	_____
If Yes, is it in AFIS & IAFIS	_____	_____
Any other trace evidence recovered	_____	_____
Weapon recovered	_____	_____
If firearm, projectile	_____	_____
Casing(s)	_____	_____
If Yes to either, entered into IBIN/NIBIN	_____	_____
Was weapon analyzed for evidence	_____	_____
If Yes, any forensic/investigative value	_____	_____

Witnesses

	No	Yes
Any known witnesses	_____	_____
If Yes, were they formally interviewed	_____	_____
Written notes _____ Audio _____ Video _____		
Were criminal record checks conducted	_____	_____
Any criminal activity since this offense	_____	_____
Any witnesses NOT interviewed	_____	_____
Are witnesses still in area?	_____	_____

Figure 2.16 Cold case file review protocol. This protocol identifies some of those points to be considered when conducting both a case file review as well as during the investigation itself. (Courtesy of Detective Timothy Keel, Baltimore Police Department [ret'd].)

(Continued)

Potential Person(s) of Interest	**No**	**Yes**
Any potential persons of interest identified	____	____
Persons Name ____________________	DOB ________	
Prior criminal record ____________________		
Type of offenses(s) ____________________		
Any arrest since this offense	____	____
Financial Records checked	____	____
Relationship to Victim	____	____
Former paramours at time of incident	____	____
If Yes, bio info ____________________		
Arrest info ____________________		
Current contact info ____________________		
Anyone offered a polygraph/CVSA that refused	____	____
Cell Phones		
Did victim have a cell phone	____	____
Were records obtained	____	____
Were cell site tower dumps obtained	____	____
Were records analyzed	____	____
Was a time line created	____	____
Any type of crime analysis from neighborhood created	____	____
Media		
Any newspaper or television coverage	____	____
Website created	____	____
Crime Stopper flyer out	____	____
Reward offered	____	____

Potential Motive for Offense

Drugs ____ Robbery ____ Retaliation ____

Sexual ____ Personal ____ Unknown ____

Synopsis of case :

____

____

____

____

____

Good Potential for Leads Fair Lead Potential Poor Lead Potential

Figure 2.16 (*Continued*) Cold case file review protocol. This protocol identifies some of those points to be considered when conducting both a case file review as well as during the investigation itself. (Courtesy of Detective Timothy Keel, Baltimore Police Department [ret'd].)

This differs significantly from the book.

Many persons and agencies contributed to the preparation of this edition, but the principles remain today although names and forms may change…all are now retired.

In the preparation of this chapter, I would like to especially thank Former Ranger Tony Leal and Ranger John Martin of the Texas Rangers; Sgt. John Jackson of the Kansas City, Missouri, Police Department; Sgt. John Neff of the Austin, Texas, Police Department; Deputy Chief of Investigations

James Gannon of the Morris County, New Jersey, Prosecutor's Office; and Lt. Joe Hartshorne and the late Sgt. Richard Longshore of the Los Angeles County Sheriff's Department for their invaluable assistance. In addition, the KCPD method was drawn from a discussion of the Kansas City cold case squad by Sergeant Kate Ellis of that agency in the July 2004 issue of "Subject to Debate," published by the Police Executive Research Forum, and interview with department personnel. Discussions of the methods used by the Charlotte, NC, Police Department were drawn from an article by Mike Adams in the July 2003 issue of "Subject to Debate," and from CMPD Sgt. Darrell Price (ret.).

Suggested Readings

Adams, M. (2003). *Cold case squad: Partnering with volunteers to solve old homicide cases.* Washington, DC: PERF.

Adams, M. (July 2002). *Subject to debate.* Washington, DC: Police Executive Research Forum: P. 1, 7.

Anonymous. (2002). *Cold case homicide.* Sacramento, CA, C. P. T. Network, Commission on Peace Officer Standards and Training.

Barmazel, S. (1996). Murder on coyote flat. *California Lawyer 16*(5): 42–45, 86–87.

Bowker, M. (1994). The case of the fateful fingerprints. *Readers Digest:* 91–96.

Eliopulos, L. N. (2003). *Death investigators handbook: Expanded and updated edition.* Boulder, CO, Paladin Press.

Ellis, K. (2004). *Kansas City cold case squad solves string of murders.* Washington, DC, Police Executive Research Forum. **18**: 1, 7.

Geberth, V. (1996). *Practical homicide investigation: Tactics, procedures, and forensic techniques.* New York, CRC Press.

Keppell, R. D. and J. G. Weis (1994). Time and distance as solvability factors in murder cases. **Journal of Forensic Sciences 39**(2):386–401.

NIJ. (2002). *Using DNA to solve cold cases* (Commission report No. NIJ 194197). Washington, DC, National Institute of Justice.

Nyberg, R. (1999). Investigations: Cold case squads re-activate old investigations. **Law and Order 47**(10): 127.

O'Brien, C. (1993). *30 Years Later, prints meet match.* Los Angeles Times, Los Angeles, CA.

Roletti, A. (1992). *Team's task is to lo ok at long-unsolved murders.* San Diego, San Diego Union-Tribune: B-1, B-4.

Spraggs, D. (2003). *How to…open a cold case.* Policemag.com: 29–3.

Tona, F. (2012). Cold cases with no DNA…no problem. *Law and Order Magazine, Hendon Publishing* 60(09): 82–84.

Reading the Book
Learning the Case

3

RACHEL H. WALTON
AND FRANK P. TONA

Introduction

"Read the book. Before you do anything, read the *whole* Book!" With these words, the late Sergeant Rudy Ortega of the Unsolved Unit, Los Angeles County Sheriff's Department, summed it up. Before you begin to investigate a cold case, read the case file to see what you have, and what's already been done. As you do so, you will begin to *reconstruct the case* and formulate an *investigative plan* in your mind. You will read what is known about the victim, and about the circumstances of the crime. You will read how it was initially handled, who responded, and what was learned in the initial investigation. You may readily identify a weakness in the investigation – perhaps witnesses who appear to be less than truthful or may have been holding back, or identification of evidence that may now offer more potential due to advanced technology. As you do so, your experience will begin to identify any potential gaps, areas that you may seek to fill.

Through understanding the case file, you are *informally* reconstructing the crime, the crime scene, and post-crime behavior. This contrasts with a formal reconstruction as might be undertaken at a later stage of investigation. This is the beginning of the new investigation as you seek answers to questions you would normally ask in a homicide investigation but are now asking years or even decades since. These questions include:

- What happened?
- How did it happen?
- When and where?
- Who found the body?
- Who had a motive?
- Did anyone gain financially from the victim's death?
- Do the witness statements, or those of others, make sense?
- Where are the witnesses now?
- Has the passage of time affected the willingness of others to cooperate?
- What evidence did they have?
- Does the evidence "fit" the crime?

 DOI: 10.4324/9781003415633-5

- What would a timeline of events reveal?
    - Have there been any relationship changes that may now be exploited?
    - If a suspect was developed, where is that suspect now?
    - Is the suspect in custody?
    - What other crimes did the suspect commit before, or after, this crime?
    - Who might he or she have talked to about this crime?
    - What relationship changes may have occurred in the suspect's life?

In doing this, you will see what was done by the investigators. You may also see what they did not do. You may initially sense no weakness in the case, that the original investigators did everything humanly possible at the time but were not able to make the case. It is now your turn, and you will try to exploit the advantages of time and technology to solve the case. Maybe now a re-examination of the physical or biological evidence will reveal critical information not known before, or an informant can be generated or a witness enticed to tell *all* they know.

As you do, keep an *open mind* and do not necessarily be drawn into the theories and avenues of focus of the original investigators. Do not pass judgment on those investigators who came before you. We have experienced those cases, personally and through discussion with other cold case investigators, in which the focus of our predecessors was incorrect. They may have had wrong information, or circumstances at the time may have suggested they were on the right track. There have been those cases, unfortunately, in which the initial investigators focused on individuals with less regard for truth or fact and perhaps guided by personal feelings or other motives. Remember what you do not know, such as the political environment or the organizational culture of the law enforcement agency tasked with the initial investigation. The factors outside the control of the investigators may have negatively impacted the investigation. Above all, keep an open mind!

This chapter considers these and other issues that may be addressed by the cold case investigator as they proceed with the investigation. If the case has been assigned to the investigator because of a systematic review, it may be in order and a synopsis or summary has been compiled from which the investigator may readily obtain an overview of the case elements. A suggested investigative plan may already be outlined, but this is a suggestion only. Cold case investigation is cerebral and what may have sounded good at the time to a reviewer may now not seem as necessary or beneficial as it once did. All investigators have their own approaches. If a cold case investigator assumes the investigation without the benefit of a prior review, this chapter offers further assistance in understanding the file and moving forward with the investigation. If the re-investigation is the result of specific information that has come to the attention of law enforcement, this chapter and the next address potential avenues to approach the case and its investigation.

Initial Considerations

No one person is an expert in every field, and those in law enforcement are no different. When studying the case file, keep in mind the various disciplines and experts that are used in homicide investigation today, and their possible role in a cold case investigation. Among these are:

- Criminal investigative analysis
- Legal and prosecutorial considerations
- Crime scene reconstruction personnel
- Forensic laboratory
- DNA (human/plant/animal)
- Technology databases such as Combined DNA Index System (CODIS)/Next-Generation Identification (NGI)/automated fingerprint identification systems (AFIS/IAFIS), National Integrated Ballistic Information Network (NIBIN)/National Missing and Unidentified Persons System (NAMUS), and state and local databases and resources
- Blood pattern experts
- Evasion detection/polygraph
- Specialty crime investigators or experts such as forensic document analysis and handwriting
- Medical examiners and forensic pathologists
- Firearm examiners
- Advanced fingerprint technology
- Forensic odontology
- Forensic anthropology
- Forensic botanists
- Forensic artistry
- Child abuse experts and resource organizations
- Non-government resources, including private forensic laboratories
- Media
- Other technical and specialty support resources
- Digital forensics examiners
- Investigative genetic genealogy (IGG)

The Case File

The case file contains the written record of the investigation, including all interview reports, photographs, evidence collection and analysis reports, and other documentation. The previous chapter discussed methods and sources to determine that all known records have been assembled. It is imperative that all records be identified and collected for the re-investigation. Some of the sources of these are:

- In-house agency file systems where records are normally kept
- Archives on site or off-site storage areas
- District attorney/prosecutor's office
- Property/evidence storage
- Coroner/medical examiner office
  - Reports
  - Biological or physical evidence
  - Coroner's inquest
- Local laboratory
- State or Federal Bureau of Investigation (FBI) laboratory or other federal crime laboratories
- Retired investigators
- Other agencies involved in a joint investigation of the homicide
  - Local
  - State
  - Federal

When reading the file does it appear complete and is it in order? As you study the file you are beginning your investigation.

- What do you know about your victim?
- Victim's lifestyle?
  - Friends and associates?
  - Relationships?
  - Use of social media and the internet?
- By what circumstances did the victim come to be a victim?
- What do you need to learn about your victim?
- What do you know about any developed suspect?

Where to Start

Our experiences and those of most cold case investigators with whom we have spoken suggest that a cold case file review should begin at the start of the case. In other words, at the beginning. Whether it begins with the initial missing person's report or locating a body or report of shots fired, start at the earliest time and date of related events. The reasoning behind this is that the cold case investigator can see the investigation as it unfolded, as the events occurred, and how the pieces began to fall into place. In doing so, you may see open windows that need to be closed.

Very few investigators, however, prefer to start investigating a cold case by working *backward*. That is, once the file is in chronological order, they prefer to work backward from the most recent investigative activity to the initial report of the crime and related events. This chapter addresses the investigation in a *forward* manner from the beginning of the crime to the latest activity and to the rejuvenated investigation.

As you begin, do you have questions? Write notes down *now.* When you read it a second time, the same thought may not be repeated exactly as it was and may become a different thought pattern altogether. Quite often, our first thoughts are the best. Although many of your questions will be answered as you read further, these initial questions and thoughts are the beginning of your investigation. If they are not answered when you finish reading the book, they become the basis of your investigative plan. This plan is one that identifies and organizes your investigative action. It is based upon what has been done and what you determine *needs* to be done. Based on the complexity of the case, you may have to read and re-read the file(s) multiple times. As mentioned earlier in this book, you are learning from the work of others.

Start to think about your own organization, also.

At the outset, place a fresh page with a photograph of your victim at the start of the file. This is the person you now represent, the victim for whom you may be last chance for what passes for justice in our society.

Biography Sheet

With many cold cases, there are a lot of people – and their roles and relationships – to come to know. Many, if not all, will need to be located, contacted, and re-interviewed. Consider a biography sheet for everyone (see Figure 3.1). This document contains summary information about an individual and provides a quick resource for the cold case investigator in lieu of reading through numerous documents. In addition, it may be used to document those who are now deceased, and other pertinent information.

As the cold case investigation progresses, investigators may learn of relationships between persons that were previously unknown *or have developed*, and this may be significant. This is a good place to note it for future investigative knowledge. As an example, an investigator was investigating a case and contacted a man believed to have knowledge about the past events at his rural residence. After some time had passed, he identified a woman

INDIVIDUAL BIOGRAPHY SHEET

Case No. ____________ Case Name ______________

[ ] New Witness
[ ] Original Participant
[ ] Relative of Participant
[ ] Other
[ ] Role

NAME:

DOB: __________________ POB: ______________

DOD: __________________ POD: __________________

Current Address:

Current Telephone:

Previous Addresses/Time of Offense:

PHOTO/DRIVERS LICENSE

Father: Address/Phone:

Mother: Address/Phone:

Notes:

Figure No. _________

Figure 3.1 Individual biography sheet.

whom he believed had critical information about the same event and drove to contact her. As he approached her rural residence, the investigator realized that he was not very far from the man's location he had been to in the past. Upon interviewing the new witness, the investigator casually mentioned that he had been to the nearby location in the past and inquired if she knew the man. Whereupon the current witness said, "Oh yes, that was my uncle." This one comment tied together a number of people and opened a whole new understanding of previously unknown familial relationships that were critical to the case. Knowledge of relationships is just as important in cold case investigations as in hot cases – especially some gang-related homicides – and this procedure is one means of quickly documenting who is related to whom.

This document may be used for:

- Victim
- Victim's family members, friends, and associates
- Witnesses and other parties
- Suspect
- Suspect family members, friends, and associates
- Law enforcement officers
- Forensic/laboratory personnel
- Others for a quick reference as necessary

Information to be included:

- Case number (old and new as necessary)
- Case name
- Individual role
    - New witness
    - Original participant
    - Relative of participant
    - Other
    - Role
- Name
- Also known as (AKA)
- Date of birth (DOB)
- Place of birth (POB)
- Date of death (DOD)
- Place of death (POD)
- Current address
- Current telephone
- Previous addresses/time of offense
- Subject's picture or copy of driver's license
- Father
- Address/telephone
- Mother
- Address/telephone
- Ex-wives or husbands or other partners
- Relationship to others in case if known

July

Sun	Mon	Tue	Wed	Thu	Fri	Sat
	1	2	3	4	5	6
7	8	9	10	11	12	13
14	15	16	17	18	19	20
21	22	23	24	25	26	27
28	29	30	31			

1957

Figure 3.2 Computer-generated monthly calendar.

If you establish and use a computer database for your investigation, this information may be included within your case file on the computer system.

Calendars

Consider preparing a calendar of the month and year of the crime, as well as one of the months preceding and the month(s) following. Such calendars are readily available on many desktop computer programs or other sources (see Figure 3.2). Confirming accuracy may be accomplished by comparison to a period newspaper from the time of the crime or original investigation. These serve several purposes, including:

- Allow investigator to picture sequences of events as they unfolded by day of the week.
- Allow investigators to correlate witness statements to dates, days, and times.
- Illustrate potential incongruencies.
- Graphically enhance investigator comprehension of the crime events and subsequent investigation.
- Aid witness recall. During witness re-interviews in the cold case investigation, it may serve as an aid to assist the witness in recall of events and time sequences. This may be especially true when interviewing senior citizens. For instance, they may not recall the *date* of an activity, but that the activity occurred on "*Wednesday* before her body was found." The calendar assists the witness in establishing a correct orientation of events.

- At the conclusion of the investigation, such a calendar may contribute to preparing timelines or computerized presentations to present the case to superior officers or the prosecutor.

In-House Changes

A complete case file is essential to moving forward. Knowledge of past filing systems and practices within the agency is important in locating and gathering all relevant written and evidentiary material. This includes records filing, maintenance and storage, as well as evidence filing and storage practices. This knowledge may be learned from more senior members of the agency as well as past employees. When reviewing property lists and property records, know how the evidence section filed and cataloged evidence and paperwork during the case and subsequent time period. When possible, investigators should seek to learn:

- Information intake systems and dispatch procedures in place at time of reporting of crime
- 911 or similar recordings that might still be available
- Information recording systems (handwritten logs or computer generated)
- Agency daily activity logs. Availability, and accessibility, of these day-to-day records of reported crimes and other activities may be of importance in reconstructing the crime or similar relevant time-frame events
- Any "purges" or destruction of agency records since the offense

The Case Number

Depending upon the age of the case, note whether this number style corresponds to the form still in use by the agency. If not, identify when the department or agency changed numbering systems since the homicide, and consider its relevance to the case under investigation. Identify all case file numbers associated with this case, past and present, and ensure that files and evidence are searched for and located under all identified numbers. During the review and inspection of each report and document, ensure that the file or case number is accounted for. If there were additional victims, check whether separate case numbers were issued and ensure that all relevant case files pertaining to the cold case have been identified and collected.

Similarly, if the laboratory or evidence facilities have changed numbering systems, check under all numbers also. When gathering and reviewing coroner or medical examiner files, similarly, ascertain whether there have been any changes in numbering systems. In these locations, changes in numbering systems may preclude a complete search and recovery of all pertinent records and evidence.

In the case of physical evidence such as rape kits or bullets and expended cartridge casings, inquire if at any time, personnel filed large groups of property under a *single* case number. This has happened, usually when suspects are unknown.

During the course of testimony in a high-profile involuntary manslaughter case at trial in July 2024, it was reported that the defense learned that an individual had brought investigators at the sheriff's office a box of cartridges several months earlier, which he suspected might be of evidentiary value in the case. The evidence technician reportedly booked them under a separate case number within the sheriff's office and not that of the case in trial. A sheriff's office technician reportedly testified that the items were "catalogued separately from the case and thus not included in the case inventory or tested to see if …they matched the lethal round." A former prosecutor in the case reportedly had reviewed the ammunition and determined that it had "no evidentiary value." It is well to remember that what is *not* of evidentiary value to one party or side in a legal matter may definitely *be* of evidentiary value to the opposing side. When the defense learned of this, while in trial, they filed a motion for dismissal based upon *Brady v. Maryland (373 U.S. 83 (1963))*. The case was dismissed with prejudice, meaning charges could not be refiled (CNN News July 12, 2024, via internet).

File Contents

While the layout of a "Murder Book" and file conditions varies between agencies, the contents detail what was done during the initial and follow-up investigations. These records serve to reconstruct the crime scene as well as the investigation. Consider that the older case files may contain all or portions of the following and these are areas to be studied and addressed in your investigation:

- *Case chronological record*: Often over the period of years or decades, case chronological records and summaries will be compiled by a sequence of investigators. These are informative, but view these with caution: As in any instance when someone interprets and reports the work of others, misinterpretation and misreporting may result, albeit unintentionally. Always try to know and use *original* source documentation wherever possible. We also suggest making a working copy and keeping the original source documentation separate from your working case file. Upon completion of the cold case investigation, the compilation of a detailed timeline and chronological record will assist those who review the completed case, as well as the prosecutor, in understanding what may often be a decades-long series of events, relationships, and technology advancements.

- *Crime scene*: Nature and extent of crime scene documentation. This would include sketches, photos and reports.
  - Initial responding officer actions and observations
    - Was blood dry or wet upon arrival?
    - Did the responding officer see or smell anything unusual upon arrival?
  - Weather conditions at the time
  - Who were the technicians that responded?
  - How was evidence identified – or not?
  - What evidence collection and preservation methods were used?
  - Who turned any lights on or off?
  - Were windows and doors checked?
  - Was there evidence of what we today call "staging?"
- *Crime scene log*: Nice in theory, not always done, especially in older cases. When, and if, this document is in the case file, identify and interview:
  - Those who preserved the scene and their subsequent documentation
  - Subsequent officers and other agency personnel present
  - Others recorded in the log
  - Other recorded events or unusual circumstances

  As with all other law enforcement or other persons involved in the response or investigation, identify and re-interview, inquiring whether they retain any notes, photographs, or other records, and any *undocumented* observations or thoughts on the crime. When re-interviewing original-scene officers and investigators:
  - Ask what they first saw
  - Discuss what they did and what evidence they recovered or did not recover
  - Review original reports with each
    - Were there discrepancies?
    - Was the original report complete?
    - Can they add any further thoughts?
    - Were there observations or perceptions that they did not report?
- *Crime report(s)*: Include initial responding officer and investigator reports. Although previously described, keep in mind that older case file reports may be much different by today's standards. Changes may include the following:
  - Personal identification information lacking specific detail. This compounds cold case investigator's efforts to identify "John Smith" and to re-locate for follow-up interview

- Synopsis versus detailed style of reporting
- Lack of reports
- Look for information on how the crime came to be reported, including
  - Who discovered the body?
  - Who made the call or notified police?
- *Property and evidence report*: Review all property reports and compare these to what was seized and has since been maintained. How complete, and how detailed, are these reports? Consider the source of seizure and its relationship in the crime. During your physical inspection of each item, note whether its weight (i.e., narcotics) or other description is sufficiently detailed. If money was seized, does the amount in evidence correspond to the original documentation?
- *Forensic logs and reports*: Review the evidence gathered at the time and cross-check to other evidence and property logs. Does the case file reflect all copies of logs and reports? Compare any original requests for forensic examination to what was done, or not done, and to copies maintained by the forensic facility. Inquire whether they retain:
  - Examination notebooks
  - Work journals
  - Photographs and diagrams
  - Reports
  - Biological material slides

  Consider what may be accomplished by re-examination utilizing advanced technology. When reviewing this with laboratory personnel, explore advances such as DNA testing now as opposed to serology grouping in previous decades or earlier DNA methods. Tread lightly as many investigators tend to inquire about the newest type of examination for the case. Carefully discuss what forensic examinations were previously completed prior to deciding on the latest methods as well as the quantity of suspected DNA evidence remaining and the requirement of the laboratory to preserve one-half of the sample. Consider the present ability to identify palm prints or fingerprints or trace evidence that was technically not possible at the time. If a knife recovered from a suspect was tested for the victim's DNA yet none was found, advanced technology now is able to recover victim DNA from *within* the hilt of the knife or handle due to advances in short tandem repeat (STR) DNA technology (see Figure 3.3).
- *Vehicle reports*: Identify all vehicles involved in the case and their disposition. Were they released to family members or sold at auction? Consider running the Vehicle Identification Number or license plate through motor vehicle registrations to re-locate vehicle if title

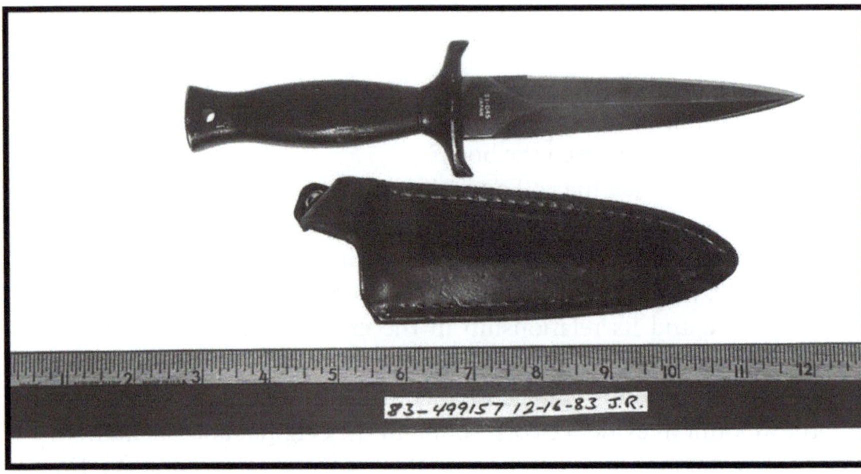

Figure 3.3 Knife with scabbard and wooden scale.

has changed hands. This may be useful in reconstructing the crime scene, or other events. If the vehicle is unable to be located, consider online web searches for similar vehicles through car collector clubs, local car clubs, auto enthusiasts, etc. Also, consider model years post 2017, as newer vehicles have online diagnostic systems capable of forensic examinations. Vehicles hold a vast amount of data that can be used to uncover critical information during an investigation and help determine what happened, where it occurred, and who was involved

- *Related crime reports*: When reviewing names and reports, note whether other crime reports may be associated with this offense. Were there co-victims whose case may have been assigned a separate case number? Were there other victims at the same period as the homicide, or other cases suspected by original investigators to be related?
- *Follow-up and progress reports*: During the review of these reports, the original investigator's focuses and theories may become evident. Are there numerous reports of interviews with one or a few subjects? Does the same name re-appear? Are there investigator synopses detailing case progress, including their thoughts and theories?
- *Crime scene canvass*: Was a canvass completed? Are the records present? How complete and thorough was it?
- *Victim information*: Victim information found in the file may or may not provide insight into motive or their possible contributing role to the homicide. Keep in mind that there is often a strong possibility that the victim and their attacker knew one another or were acquainted.

An original profile of the victim may be portrayed in the reports through interviews with family, friends, co-workers, classmates, teacher, and others. Consider the width and depth of what is known about the victim as found in the case file and consider follow-up investigation to learn more about the victim. Considerations may include the following:

- Was a psychological autopsy addressed?
- Identify significant personal relationship at time of offense.
- Previous or other relationships, past and present.
- Perhaps more so than men, females have a "*best*" or close friend in which they may confide and share private thoughts, including secrets, fears, or other intimate information. This person is not necessarily a family member and may include their hairdresser or similar person. When re-interviewing previously known witnesses or persons with knowledge about the victim, seek to identify and interview (or re-interview) victim's best or closest friends. What *more* might they say now?
- When viewing photos which include the victim and other persons are in the photo, identify these people and ascertain if they are known to the investigation.
- Developing greater insight into victim's background and biographical information.
- Criminal history including probation and parole reports.
- Other civil or criminal reports previously reported by victim or family.
- Any reported stalking of victim, or other suspicious activity reports.
- What *don't* you know about your victim and the circumstances.

- Suspect/person of interest information
    - Statements to investigators at time of initial investigation and any subsequent interviews. Statements to other persons, including any media interviews or statements.
    - Alibis and witness statements.
    - Photos or forensic artist/composite drawings.
    - Criminal history including probation and parole reports pre- and post-event.
    - Current custody status.
    - Custody history to identify past incarcerations and identify possible cellmates, institution intelligence reports etc.
    - Other identified relationships that may now be changed due to passage of time, including friends, intimate partners, spouses, business associates.

- *Photo lineups*: Were photo lineups conducted in previous investigation? Are they in the file? Who were they shown to? What identifications were made? What reports were generated as a result of these lineups? What processes were utilized during the procedure? Were any admonitions given to witnesses similar to current practice?
- *Witness statements and lists*: Are the reports of these statements sufficiently detailed? During the review of witness statements, including listening to recorded interviews, cold case investigators should note closely what questions were asked and what answers were given (and how these were subsequently documented). Did the response answer the question asked?
  - What was not asked may be more important than what was asked.
  - Note the number of interviews with repeat witnesses or suspect. Consider statement analysis of repeat interviews as noted below.
  - Is there sufficient information to identify and re-locate the witness?
- *Crime scene notes and canvass surveys*: Are these preserved in the file? Review and cross-check to the crime scene log, if possible. Identify officers or crime scene personnel who may have made or maintained any notes, surveys, or other documents not in the file.
- *Crime scene sketches*: Are these present in the file? Rough sketch or finished sketch? If so, are they detailed and to scale? In older cases, these may be general overviews and not measurement specific. Consider that in some agencies, other city or county resources may have been called upon for assistance in this regard (see Figures 3.4 and 3.5). These might include:
  - City/county engineers
  - Public works
  - Private architects/draftsmen
  - State architects, engineers, or draftsmen
- *Crime scene photos*: Does the case file reflect a number of photographs that sufficiently detail the crime scene in macro and micro detail? Are they adequately documented to reflect the following?
  - What do they represent (see Figure 3.6)?
  - What is the significance of the photo (see Figure 3.7)?
  - When was it taken?
  - By whom was it taken?
  - Is what you now see as evidence shown in photos yet was never collected?
- *Ambulance run records*: Were ambulance and similar emergency personnel identified and interviewed? Were their run records obtained?
- Medical records

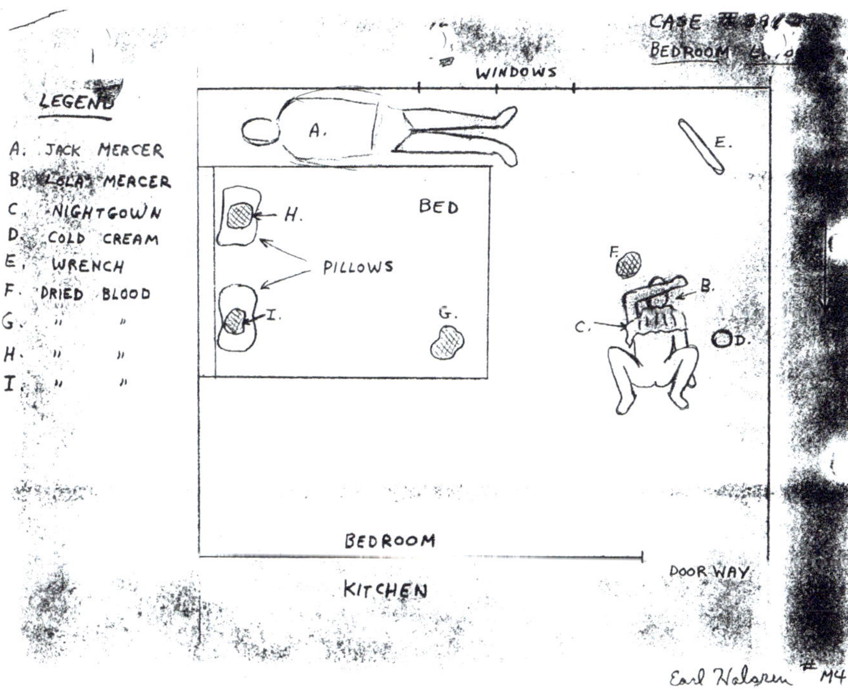

Figure 3.4 1960s crime scene sketch.

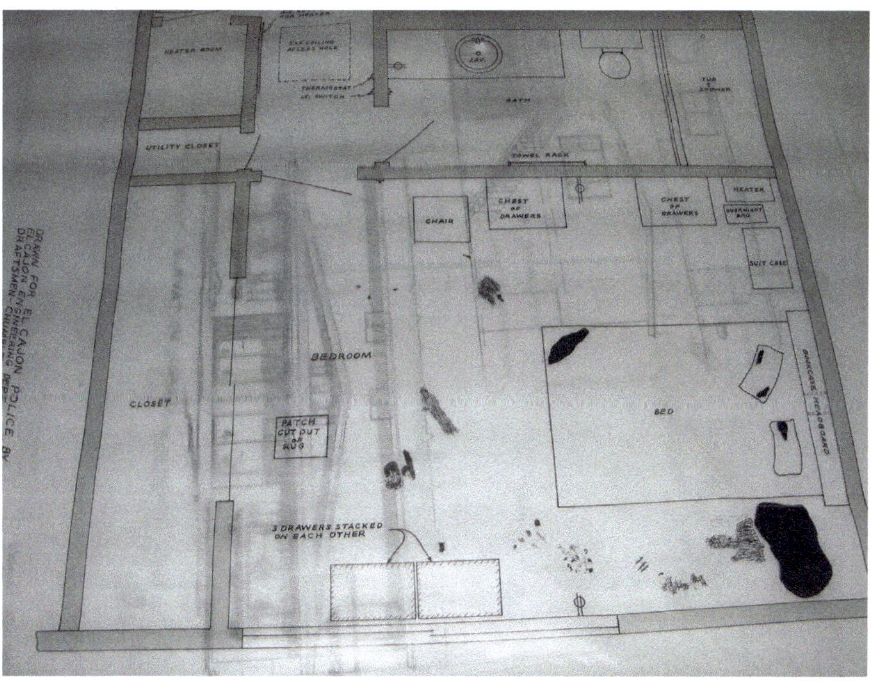

Figure 3.5 Finished crime scene diagram.

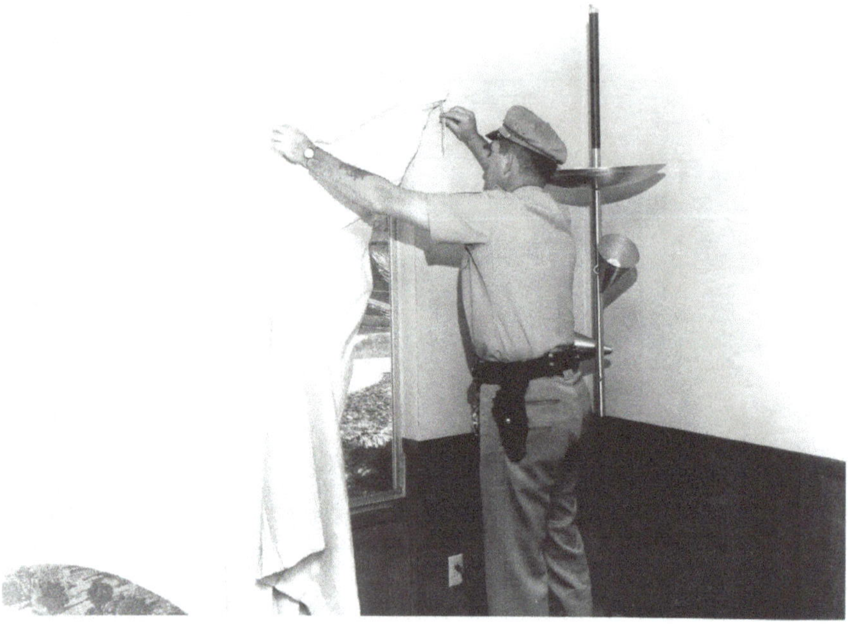

Figure 3.6 Officers in crime scene.

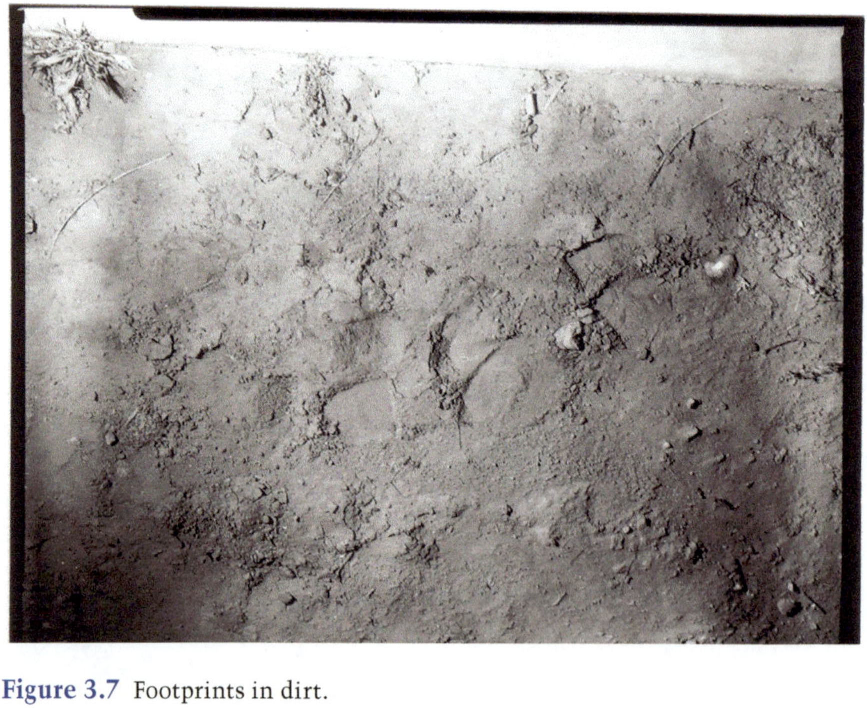

Figure 3.7 Footprints in dirt.

    - Emergency room records
    - Doctor reports
- Coroner's records
    - Autopsy report
    - Toxicology reports
    - Photos
    - Retained clothing or other physical evidence
    - Retained biological samples such as swabs
- *Death certificate and obituary*: These documents may not always be found in the cold case file. They may provide valuable information for the course of investigation. They are further described in this edition's Chapter 6 on Obituaries.
- Communications
    - Initial crime report intake information
    - Original 911 or other telephonic records and/or recordings
    - *Old teletypes*: Prior to computers, these were terminals similar to a typewriter, which generated printed documents and were used to broadcast information from one law enforcement agency to another nationwide
    - Press releases
    - Newspaper clippings
    - Police bulletins
- *Affidavit for search warrants*: Affidavits contain detailed case information about known case events and investigator knowledge at a specific time during the investigation when the affidavit is drafted and submitted to a magistrate when requesting a search warrant. Is there evidence in the case file that affidavits for search warrants were ever prepared?
    - Are these documents still retained in the file?
    - Were they served?
    - Do court clerk or court copies remain?
    - Are there search warrant returns listing any property recovered?
- *Investigation notes*: Are any, part, or all in the file? During the follow-up interviews, cold case investigators should seek to gather all remaining notes from initial responding officers, investigators, and other persons connected with the case or its investigation. It is critical that cold case investigators approach their case review and subsequent investigation with an open mind. While one may be aware of and consider original investigators' focus and theories, investigators must let facts guide their re-investigative efforts

Additional Considerations

Case Organization

While "Reading the Book," it is suggested that investigators make a duplicate copy of all documents and use these for organizing their working case documents.

While investigators have their own method of doing so, many find that it is helpful to segregate persons, or topics, into groups and to proceed in this manner. In this context, a cold case investigator can identify all persons whose names are reflected in the reports, and subsequently identify a plan of action that needs to take place with each. This will illuminate the process of the original investigation as well as identify those who need to be re-interviewed.

These persons may be categorized as follows:

- Law enforcement
- Medical and ambulance
- Crime scene and evidence
- Coroner/medical examiner
- Laboratory and forensic
- Witnesses
- Victim family, friends, and associates
- Suspects/persons of interest
- Legal
- Other persons or topics developed during the course of previous and current investigation

Some investigators find that it is helpful to organize the file utilizing a simple system of file folders that address each individual or topics (e.g., evidence) by category. All reports, news clippings, and any document mentioning the individual name can be included in this file. As the records are reviewed and filed, this simple system may bring together relationships or identify inconsistent or contradictory statements, as well as illuminate the full role of the individual in the investigation. This is a simple system, albeit may ultimately consume boxes of files. Each investigator has a system that "works," however. What works is what is best.

Homicide investigators, and cold case homicide investigators, are guided by experience, training, and decades of insight into human nature. From this experience comes intuition and "gut feeling." When reviewing the case reports, keep in mind the following:

- Were the right questions asked of the right people?
- Which interviews are less than incomplete now in context with the investigation to date?
- Who might have more to say now than what the original report said?

Listen to original taped interviews, and make working copies for the investigation. Evidence review protocols of some agencies prescribe those original tapes be copied first to preserve the original tapes. Do you perhaps hear something on the tape the original investigators did not? If there is a transcript, is it complete? Is it accurate? A simple phrase may be something that slipped out but was not caught by the investigator. Look for anonymous letters and phone calls or messages that were not returned.

Re-examination of Evidence

The importance of re-examining all physical and biological evidence is discussed throughout this book. This is necessary to update and confirm examination results due to technological or other changes. The results of these examinations may influence the investigative plan and direction of the investigation. Because of the age of many unsolved homicides, successful prosecution may depend greatly upon the use of scientific evidence. Despite old lab reports attesting that no trace evidence (such as semen) was found, or that the results are inconclusive or negative, you should *re-test*. Re-examination using the latest technology and forensic know-how not only provides updated results, but it also provides the prosecution with an expert to subpoena when it comes time for trial.

The investigator should keep in mind that the presence of the potential evidence in the case under review and findings of original examination are subject to (1) mistaken filing, tagging, or other association of the evidence with the case under review; (2) original error on the part of the examiner, including mis-identification or inaccurate conclusions based upon, among other factors, the state of the art of techniques and procedures in effect at the time of the examination; and (3) other factors that have arisen due to passage of time. Unfortunately, there have been a few instances in the last decades of the twentieth century whereby forensic laboratory personnel have committed gross ethical and criminal violations in their testimonies in court or taking narcotic evidence for their own use or addictions. These have resulted in wrongful convictions of innocent persons and subsequent dismissal of numerous, most often narcotic-related cases.

As a result of a fresh analysis, potentially new exculpatory or inculpatory evidence may be discovered. A previous negative finding for presence of semen that, upon re-examination, provides a DNA profile resulting in a CODIS hit can significantly alter the direction of the investigation. Re-examination of evidence can save investigators valuable time and other resources when review of the evidence discounts that which was previously thought possible. This includes circumstances in which suspect items were believed associated with a homicide when in fact they were not. Conversely, re-analysis may yield new information through discovery of new evidence that may assist police in identifying the suspect(s) and solution of the case.

Case History

While searching the evidence room for evidence in another case, officers in a small California police department discovered an old Colt's revolver in a box with evidence from another case (see Figure 3.8). The case number on the evidence tag indicated that the weapon was associated with a case number that was not known to the agency. Documentation was sparse, but also found in the box was the original investigator's notebooks for an unsolved homicide that had occurred in the early 1980s.

A transcript of an interview marked with the case number of the other agency was also located in the box. These items suggested that this case encompassed investigation by at least one or more jurisdictions. Contact with the other agency discovered that their case file remained, although the original recording from which the transcript was made was no longer in their custody. Their reports, plus the original investigator's notebook, were the beginnings of a cold case homicide investigation. When contacted, the original investigator, now retired, recalled little of the case. Officers began by reviewing all the names in the investigator's notebook, reports from the other agency, and reviewing the remaining physical evidence remaining in the evidence room.

Figure 3.8 Colt .32-20.

Also recovered from the box was the victim's clothing. The victim had been recovered from a large body of salt water when released to the medical examiner. The clothing was subsequently bagged in plastic and returned to the agency. It was stored in this condition for almost 20 years. It had not been properly dried for storage and was now in a moldy condition.

Cold case homicide investigation builds on the life and career experience of cold case investigators. An X-ray showing a number of bullets in the torso was also found in the box (see Figure 3.9). When an experienced cold case investigator reviewed the X-ray and was given a description of the revolver, it immediately appeared doubtful whether the bullets were fired from this weapon. Observation of the bullets in the X-ray indicated that they were round-nose projectiles. The Colt was now an antique and was chambered for the 32WCF round. This frontier-era cartridge saw double duty as a rifle cartridge in tubular feed, lever action style rifles which necessitated the use of flat nose bullets. When it was suggested that the weapon be re-examined to determine whether it could have fired the bullets, modern forensic examination corroborated my review, and the weapon was discovered to have no relationship to the crime. The case remains open.

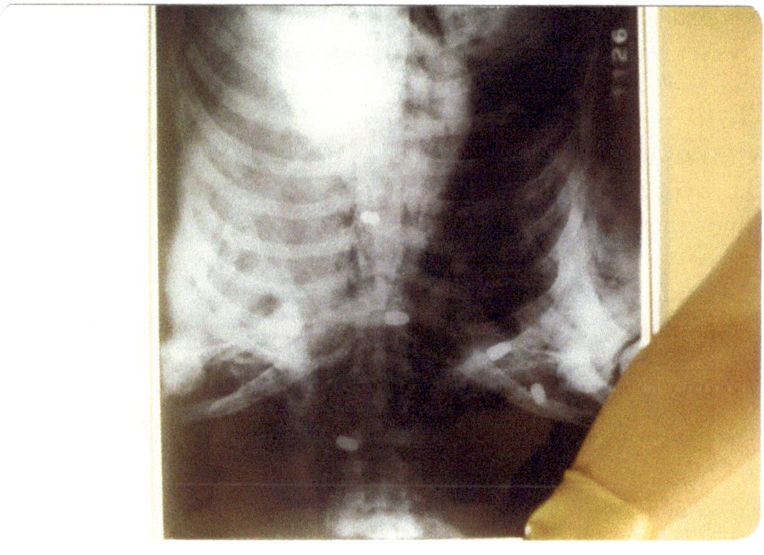

Figure 3.9 X-ray.

Photos and Photo Analysis

While the value of crime scene photos in homicide investigation has long been recognized, nowhere is this perhaps more important than in the process of *Reading the Book*. During this process, the investigator is mentally reconstructing the crime and the case. The presence of sharp, quality photos that thoroughly document the crime scene in micro and macro detail provides investigators with the best representation of what the scene looked like years or decades before. While investigator or witness memory can serve to augment words on paper, nothing takes the place of original crime scene photos.

Excluding early large format box cameras of the early 1900s, crime scene photographs most likely to be encountered in older cold case files today were taken using 35mm silver nitrate-based film which had to be chemically developed to create a "negative" which reflected the image and was used to make a print of the image. The film and developing process was costly to agencies, and sometimes less than a desirable number of photographs were taken. Older case files have been observed in which there are a minimum number of crime scene photographs, especially detailed crime scene photographs.

In addition, the written record to support and authenticate these photographs may be lacking in detail, if present at all. When this occurs, investigators have photographs that may not necessarily be fully relied upon for future courtroom value due to lack of authenticating documentation. They are, however, valuable for investigative purposes as quite often the subject or topic that the photograph seeks to represent may be apparent. In other cases, however, it may not be as shown in Figure 3.7.

When reviewing the photo file, it is prudent to identify agency photographic protocol at the time of the original homicide investigation. Who took the crime scene photos? Was it...

- Full-time photographic and crime scene/evidence personnel?
- Responding officers responsible for own crime scene processing?
- Contract or on-call photographers from local camera shop?
- Local news media photographers?
- Others?

Depending upon agency size, organization, and other factors, there may or may not have been a formal agency crime scene photographer or a photograph protocol. What was done may have varied from scene to scene, depending on the circumstances and availability of a photographer. In reviewing the photographic record, consider whether it reflects:

- Identity of the photographer
- Date and time of photograph
- Exact location
- Written record of detail being photographed
- Compass orientation
- Camera and film description
- Specialized equipment used
- Weather and light conditions
- Processing sequences including chain of custody
- Development record including number of prints
- Print distribution
- What were the processing standards? Was the film automatically developed or was it developed and printed only at the discretion of the investigators, or the photographer?
- Where were the negatives stored?
- Where are the copies now?

If the photographer is known and available:

- Meet with the person to review each photo.
- Attempt to learn what additional information the photographer may have to offer that is not already known.
- Inquire if the photographer has any additional photos not found in the case file and does the photographer maintain any notes or other records of the crime or photography session?

Review of available case file photographs will reveal whether they are ground-based photos or aerial photos (see Figure 3.10) and whether they are black and white or color.

Aerial Photos

While the concept and earliest experiments at aerial date to the mid-nineteenth century, aerial photos have been practically utilized in some regions of the United States since the 1920s for government and private purposes. They became more commonplace in the 1940s and 1950s with re-flights often updating the photo files taking place every so many years. Aerial photos may be very useful in reconstructing a crime scene decades later, especially in those areas where urban growth has re-defined the landscape. Local tax assessor's offices are sometimes the best sources of aerial photos. While they were most likely obtained from private contractors, these offices may have

Figure 3.10 Aerial photograph.

photos going back many decades. If they do not have what you are looking for, they may be able to advise sources of older local region aerial photos. Other sources of these photos include:

- Local governments, including city and county planning departments
- Local universities and colleges
- State highway departments
- Utility companies
- Local large industries and developers
- Railroads
- Bureau of Mines
- Bureau of Reclamation
- U.S. Army Corps of Engineers
- National Park Service
- U.S. Geological Survey
- U.S. Forest Service
- Bureau of Land Management
- U.S. Department of Agriculture including National Agriculture Imagery Program
- National Environmental Satellite, Data, and Information Service
- NASA
- Space imaging corporations

Photo Degradation

When reviewing the crime scene photographs in older cases, consider doing so with one knowledgeable in applicable forensic or image enhancement techniques. Due to age, crime scene photographs may be faded. This is especially true in older instant development photographs, such as those commonly referred to as Polaroids®. This problem is also encountered in 35 mm color photos. When faded or less legible photos are found in file, consider consulting with in-agency photographic or forensic resources, state or FBI crime laboratory, universities, or other resources.

Other Considerations in Photo Analysis

- Carefully study the photo to see what it *really* shows you in relation to what you know from reading the case reports.
- Study the photo from the center out – normally the subject of the photo is centered in the image.
- Enlarge/blowup photos. This often reveals significant detail not otherwise noticed. This can often be accomplished by just scanning the image and increasing the view percentage on a desktop computer.
- Consider re-printing from negatives without cropping the picture. Cropping may have removed vital detail from the photo.
- Is there evidence of "posing" the scene?
- Evidence that victim killed, dragged, or carried to location?
- Number of perpetrators.
- Weapon used.
- Opportunity or planned.
- Ingress and egress for victim and suspect.
- Drag marks, including direction.
- What evidence do you see in the photo that you do not have today?
- Suggestion of motive.
- Possibility of witnesses.
- Remember – the primary scene is the body
  - State of decomposition
  - Insect activity
  - Wounds or mutilation
  - Secondary scene around the body
  - Tertiary or third level including blood spatter in surrounding area.

Take all photos and put them in sequence of the events during the crime. What does it tell you? Do you see anything not reflected in reports?

If persons are present in the photo, identify and re-interview to ascertain scene value and meaning of the photograph. In past decades, it was not unusual or uncommon for officers and investigators to stand in the crime scene or related locations as pictures were being taken. Other persons that might be found in crime scene photographs might be family members, coroner/medical examiner personnel, fire and ambulance personnel, or news photographers. Or they might be suspects.

Review the photos with a crime scene reconstruction expert. What do they see that perhaps you do not?

For example, a cold case investigator had the occasion to review a series of photographs from a late 1970s homicide. These were 35 mm color photographs, and many were now fading. The female victim had been left in a remote area that had previously been used for body dumps. A suspect had been identified in the case, but evidence to place him at the scene was lacking. Photographs of the suspect, a biker, taken prior to the homicide had been recovered during the initial investigation. When the victim's body was recovered, a man's belt was wrapped around her legs and had been left behind, as if the suspect may have been interrupted or scared of while disposing of the body. The buckle was multi-sided and irregular in shape and had the name and logo of a popular motorcycle brand embossed on it in a wavy manner. In addition, the leather belt also was stamped with an ornate pattern. Although other circumstantial evidence was present, the prosecutor wanted more evidence to link the suspect to the victim, and to the scene.

Review of the photographs recovered from the suspect identified some photos of him wearing a belt and belt buckle seemingly identical to the belt and buckle recovered with the victim's body. This was forwarded to the laboratory for further analysis, which suggested that the buckle and belt recovered with the victim were consistent with that worn by the biker suspect in the photograph.

Photos Can Turn Up in the Strangest of Places

During review and investigation of cold case homicides, originals or copies of photographs not in the case file have turned up in places normally beyond the practical range of sources explored by cold case investigators. Sometimes this is the result of publicity or word-of-mouth information resulting from investigator actions. They have been found in:

- Old newspapers no longer in publication
- Off-campus university publications
- Pawn shops and second-hand stores
- *True Detective* and similar crime magazines or news magazines (see Figure 3.11)
- Private collections of local current or retired photographers

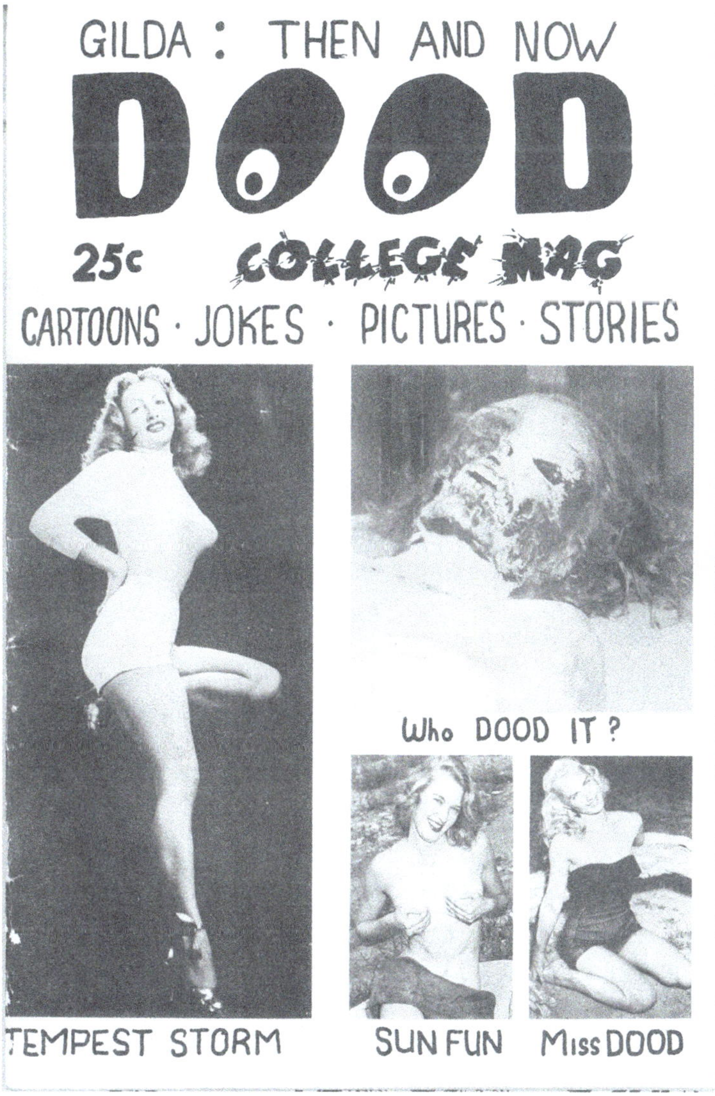

Figure 3.11 *DOOD* magazine.

- Historical societies
- YouTube®, Facebook®, and other social media sites or internet platforms
- Family photograph albums of those who participated in the crime or its investigation. When interviewing family members, witnesses, and others, inquire if they have any photographs regarding the case and its investigation (see Figure 3.12).

Figure 3.12 Family album picture.

Practical Statement Analysis

See Chapter 16 for full presentation on statement analysis. The following is a practical synopsis based upon the author's experiences.

When a case file contains multiple (more than one) statements by the same individual, or follow-up investigation results in additional statements, it may be useful to combine these in an individual file and to subject them to line-by-line scrutiny that may reveal discrepancies and inconsistencies. As an example, use of the phrase "I did…" during the initial interview that subsequently changes to "I did not…" when re-interviewed in proximity to the original statement, or during a cold case investigation, years or decades later. While this avenue of approach is not uncommon in normal day-to-day interviews, in cold case investigation identification of such inconsistencies may be even more valuable. While this sounds simple, consider that some cold cases consume cartons of files concerning the crime, evidence, and witness statements. Also consider that while cold case investigators are the best in the field, they are not machines. When the statements are spread out over a sequence of files, the full impact and value of what they say may not necessarily be realized. If individuals have been interviewed, then re-interviewed, over a period, their statements may reveal these variations, variations that may be a segue to breaking down the discrepancies and learning the truth.

Sources of statements are not necessarily confined to just interview statements given to police during the specific investigation. There are other sources of potential statement information that may offer opportunities to identify these discrepancies and variations. Among these are

- Initial police interview
- Follow-up police interview
- News media interviews or statements
- Statements made to other parties, including their own family or the family of the victim
- Written memorabilia including diaries, notes, or book and short story drafts
- Interviews to investigators from other agencies
- Probation and parole statements
- Wiretap conversations
- Civil actions including deposition statements
- Criminal trial actions including testimony
- Coroner's inquest testimony
- Post-arrest interviews

Case Study

LORETTA JONES HOMICIDE

Price, Utah
July 31, 2017

Helper Arts Festival, Helper, Utah

On August 15, 2009, Carbon County Sheriff's Office Detective David Brewer's life changed forever. Attending a street art festival one Saturday afternoon, the former U.S. Marine, small business owner, and 16-year veteran sheriff's detective encountered Heidi Jones-Asay, then 43 years old. Heidi and Brewer knew each other as they had gone to high school together, and they began discussing what she had been doing in the subsequent years. When Heidi learned he was now a sheriff's detective, she began talking about the unsolved murder of her mother, Loretta Jones, which occurred in the nearby town of Price when she was 4 years old. Brewer later admitted that inwardly he rolled his eyes; this was not the first time people cornered him and asked him to investigate a particular case. But after listening to what she had to say, he was intrigued and invited her to call his office on Monday. She did.

Time and Place

Carbon County, Utah, is in the southeastern region of Utah, a still somewhat remote region noted for its red and white rock formations and ancient Indian art. This area was noted for its coal mining and tourism, such being the core of the local economy. In 1970, the county was home to almost 16,000 residents, and the county seat, Price City, consisted of little over 6,000 residents. Nine miles northwest, Helper sat at the foot of a mountain range and was so named as during the early days of railroading the Union Pacific railroad sent extra engines there to "help" coal trains traverse the rugged mountain passes. Rows of false fronted buildings gave the town an Old West appearance along its one main business street. Other small communities were scattered around the region, and the main street doubled as a segment of the narrow, two-lane highway which snaked over the mountains from Helper toward the fertile valleys south of Salt Lake City. This main travel route helped keep the area somewhat isolated and travel was always an arduous and dangerous journey. By 1970, the town was in the final throes of open prostitution and other similar abeyances of the law, which had escaped the close attention of officials elsewhere in Utah due to its remoteness.

Background of Case

Heidi called Brewer in his office on Monday. As she lived further north, they conversed and emailed until they could meet. Brewer had done some checking but could find no record or documentation from this case, which was not surprising after all these years. Brewer would later learn that there was an unusual agreement between the police department and the sheriff's office at the time of the murder; the city police investigated misdemeanors only and all felonies were investigated by the sheriff's office. When she later came to his office and as he listened to her story unfold, the man who wanted to be a police officer from the early days of his youth unknowingly began a 7-year quest which would consume him in his tenacious pursuit of someone who had gotten away with murder 39 years before.

Brewer learned, however, that this had been a decade's long quest by Heidi herself, a series of unsuccessful efforts to garner official interest and investigation into her mother's death. In April 2009, she had driven by her mother's old house and learned from a neighbor that the police had reopened the case. Contacting the department, Heidi learned that while they had done some follow-up investigation, she was told that they had done everything they could except contact the original suspect.

Heidi told Brewer how, when she was 4 years old, she looked through the keyhole of her bedroom door on the morning of July 31, 1970, and saw the body of her mother on the living room floor. Their small house was located just north of the railroad tracks on the south side of town in Price. She ran outside and told a neighbor boy "*I think my mommy is dead.*" The neighbor called the police department.

Brewer had never investigated a case under such circumstances before and was a bit hesitant, but what Heidi brought him changed that. Black-and-white crime scene photos the family had taken and retained now painted a picture of what she was describing. She showed him pictures of the living room with the victim's blood on the floor and the layout of the furniture, which the family still retained in storage. These were real crime scene photos. Real evidence. It was the beginning. He subsequently searched all the county buildings for any records related to the crime, but despite numerous searches, found nothing.

Heidi related how she knew Tom Egley, the man police had suspected of killing her mother, and that he had been introduced to her mother a short time before. She told Brewer she had seen Egley in the living room with her mother earlier that evening of the homicide, and how she would later tell the police "*It was Tom that killed my mom!*" Egley, Brewer was to learn, was a 30-year-old drifter who lived at the New House Hotel, a rooming house on Main Street in Helper and who had reportedly begun a relationship with Loretta … a relationship that began while his pregnant girlfriend stayed in their boarding house room. Heidi further told him how Egley had been arrested but was later released after a preliminary hearing in the Price City Circuit Court. Brewer would later say that since no case file or evidence was apparently retained, he assumed that they had the wrong man, and he excluded Egley from the case at the start and treated it like a new case.

Where to Go and How to Start

Detective David Brewer learned that the Price City Police Department had begun an initial re-review of the Jones case a year before, in March 2008. Their original case file, however, had disappeared and the current file consisted of four newspaper clippings from the time of the crime as printed in the local Sun Advocate newspaper. At the request of the chief of police, an officer and this writer had interviewed the last known surviving investigator connected with the original case, retired Price City Police Chief Art Paloni that previous March. Suspicious of their motives, Paloni was initially reluctant to discuss the matter, insisting that – as one of the rumors which persisted in this town since the crime – she was sexually familiar with many of the men in the town and had kept a "black book." Although he spoke derogatorily of the victim, he could offer no proof. Paloni said he had no remaining files, but did, however, provide original copies of the same newspaper articles the police agency maintained. These faded copies were a significant source of names, places, photographs, events, and other related reporting and enabled Walton to draft a five-page suggested investigative plan.

Paloni told the visitors that he did not think Egley did it, and named another man named "Tom." Asked why, he could not recall, just that he believed the man did it and not Egley. Paloni died shortly thereafter, and like hot homicide investigations, Brewer would chase down local tales and urban legends and eliminate them one by one. The medical examiner's report and autopsy photographs had been obtained but the police department administration, upon learning there were no remaining vaginal swabs and thus no DNA, closed the investigation. The city police department advised that Egley was in Colorado to the last of their knowledge and provided him with what they had.

Newspaper Review – Beginning of the Case File

Reading the copies of the newspapers, Brewer learned that Sheriff Albert Passic and Price City Police Chief Art Paloni personally handled the investigation. Indeed, later newspaper stories would show the two officers in the crime scene as well as reporting case investigation information not preserved anywhere else. The August 6, 1970, edition of the Sun Advocate reported how Loretta was found by her daughter at approximately 11:40 a.m. She had been stabbed 17 times in the back and twice in the chest, the report said, and her neck was slashed. No weapon had been found nor was there evidence of forced entry, although evidence of sexual assault was noted.

Brewer wondered how Egley first came to the officer's attention, and reading further, the detective learned that an anonymous phone call led authorities to question Tom Egley. "*Who was this informant?*" According to the reports, Egley was questioned on August 3rd, and admitted to knowing the victim and of being in Price that night. He requested an attorney, however, and refused to take a polygraph. Brewer also noted that an attempted abduction of a 10-year-old girl occurred that same night, just three blocks from the Jones's residence. Police brought in a man from Provo, Utah, whom they suspected of this, but the victim failed to identify him and Egley denied any involvement in this attempted abduction. In this story, Sheriff Passic stated the attending physician put the time of the murder between 10:00 p.m. and 1:00 a.m.

The article reported that physical evidence was sent to the FBI laboratory for analysis. But it did not say what the evidence was, however, and this became a question never fully answered during the remaining investigation. A check with the FBI laboratory elicited the response that their files on this case had been purged in the mid-1990s. Thus, the newspaper reports became the basis for this case file and ultimately the resolution of this case.

On September 3, 1970, the newspaper provided follow-up information on the case. Egley had been arrested and charged with the murder of Loretta Jones. According to the report, police stated they had the FBI lab results, which gave them their required probable cause to arrest Egley. As he was indigent, Egley was provided court-appointed counsel, and on August 31st had been ordered held without bail. Preliminary hearing was set for October 8, 1970, but this date was postponed to November 6th due to the discovery of a new witness and that all the FBI reports were not yet received, as well as Chief Paloni being unavailable until that time.

On November 12, the same newspaper would report that Egley was not held to answer on the murder charge, and that Judge Platis ruled the state had not provided sufficient evidence to hold Egley over for trial. He was released. Brewer would later track down the long-retired jurist. Judge Platis stated that he remembered the case well as it was his first murder case and went on to relate how the evidence was not sufficient. Although he did not recall what witnesses testified about, he said the prosecution only had fibers for evidence and that these could be easily explained away. He believed Egley was guilty but that if he held Egley to answer on the murder, the prosecution would have lost in trial and Egley would be beyond prosecution. Following up, Detective Brewer located the original stenographer who recorded the preliminary hearing, but she said she did not keep any of the records. Years later, she would make a startling discovery.

The newspaper reports were so informative and so detailed that Brewer now had basic information – names and a timeline of dates and events – with which to formulate his investigative plan.

Brewer discovered that Heidi had written to the courthouse in 1989 seeking records in her mother's case, only to be told that the files had been retained for the legal time period required, then disposed of. Purging of such being so often the nemesis of cold case investigations. The court clerk, however, did have file cards – "minute entries" – of the preliminary hearing which he photocopied and sent her. These cards added to the mountain of information the detective was assembling now, a mountain which came more and more into focus as new information continued to be found.

These cards identified the original witnesses who testified, but not what they testified about. In addition to those of the officers, these names included Becky Jo Hillard, Parley Jones, Ed Wilson, M.D. (later found to be the state medical examiner), Charles Kirkwood, and a Margret Hamilton, the latter two residents in Helper. In addition, the minute entry for the preliminary hearing revealed physical evidence, including pink shorts and a pair of panties, a plastic bag with a small rug, a plastic bag with Levi's and a t shirt, and a signed statement by Kirkwood. From the medical examiner's records, he learned that after the autopsy, the examiner had returned to the sheriff's office the victim's bra, shirt, a container of blood, pubic hairs, eyelashes, eyebrows, scalp hair, fingernails, and a vaginal swab with semen present. Brewer also learned that the deputy who handled the evidence at the time of the crime was still alive, but when contacted, the retired lawman advised that he had placed it in the evidence room and had no further information on its disposition. Detective Brewer now had even more questions without answers.

The Victim's Family

Having no idea as to who his surviving witnesses were, or what new witnesses might yet be identified, Detective David Brewer now continued to reconstruct the case from scratch. In the months and years to follow he would have numerous conversations with Heidi, and he now began with interviews of her other family members, starting with Loretta's mother, Ludeen. "*An awesome lady*," he would later say. Ludeen had been very protective of her daughter's memory and Brewer had many visits with her, ones in which he was always welcome and always ended with hugs and tears. Brewer came to realize how the hurt in these cases, even when almost 40 years old, was still as fresh as the day it happened, and he was determined to pursue this case to the end. He was their last chance.

Heidi's aunt Linda recalled the police coming to the house a day or two after the murder, and distinctly remembered Heidi telling the police, "*Tom did it, he hurt my mom*." Likewise, Heidi's aunt Carolyn also recalled the police visit and Heidi telling them "*Tom killed my mom*." Loretta's other sister, Lila, similarly recalled Heidi telling the police "*I saw Tom stab my mom and she fell to the floor*." These statements were critical, as Heidi now had no recollection of telling this to the police. This was, after all, 39 years before. It could become an evidentiary issue, however, hearsay within hearsay.

Visiting the Crime Scene

Detective Brewer visited the Jones house the following month. Upon arrival, he noticed that it appeared almost unchanged since the day of the crime. The homeowner, upon told of his purpose, invited him in. Brewer discovered that the original linoleum on the floor still was in place, although it was now covered with carpet, and he wondered if the suspect may have injured himself, as so often happens in stabbing cases. The owner offered to let him pull up the carpet, but having no authorization from his agency to replace it, he passed on the offer. By visiting the scene, and reviewing the photos Heidi had provided, he visualized the scene as it appeared that July night decades before. It gave him a "feel" for the time and the place.

The detective repeated his searches of county locations for evidence and documents, including an old safe in the old courthouse basement. He wanted that missing swab and the other evidence. Egley was still excluded from the investigation as he attempted to investigate the other "Tom" Chief Paloni had told his visitors that he suspected. Loretta had gone to high school with this man, and his name had been in Loretta's diary with entries between 1961 and 1965. Rumors of another diary, a "black book" of her relations with various city officials and prominent businessmen, grew up around this case, and there was confusion about "Tom" and the other missing diary. This diary was never located.

His investigation now had the small community talking, and Detective David Brewer provided information to the Sun Advocate newspaper in hopes to further this conversation. Urban legends had grown up around this case, including that there was a mafia connection (the east coast mafia DID reportedly have interests locally at that time), and that there was more than one suspect. These rumors included talk that high-ranking officials had disposed of her reported "black book" and even that serial killer Ted Bundy was responsible. Bundy did pass through Utah, murdering a young woman south of Salt Lake City, but that was 4 years after Loretta's murder. Brewer investigated all these as far as he could – "*Red Herrings*" as they are known in criminal investigations.

From people talking, he learned of "Red." Red operated the Sportsman's Bar in Helper, and when contacted told how he employed Egley to work odd jobs and allowed him to stay in his hotel. Egley would work there as well. Importantly, Red remembered Egley having a girlfriend, Marilyn. He also recalled that the night of the murder, Egley was seen with blood on his person. He told the detective that "Betty," who used to run his bar, might know Marilyn. He tracked Betty down, and when contacted, she remembered Egley and told the detective that she had hired him for odd jobs. She also recalled Egley's girlfriend was "Marilyn" but no last name, although Marilyn was pregnant and had a baby in Price.

Betty also recalled that Egley liked *True Detective* magazines. This information would become critical intelligence for Brewer's investigation. Knowing that relationships can change with time, Brewer searched for Marilyn and eventually located her in Kansas. "*She told me she had nothing to say,*" Brewer recalled, "*but that if I wanted to waste my time, to come down.*" Thus began one of many road trips for the detective and his partner, Roger Taylor.

It was not a waste of his time. Marilyn related how Egley came home around 3:00–4:00 a.m. that morning, later than his usual 1:00–1:30 a.m. hours. Egley had to yell at her from the street to let him in, and she remembered being mad at him for coming home late. She said he went in and took a bath in his clothes, then put them in a bag and went to bed. Asked where he had been, he told her that he took "*…that girl and her daughter hamburgers.*" The next morning, he asked if she had laundry, and said he would take them across the street to the laundromat. She recalled that he would NEVER do laundry, that this was so out of character for him. He returned without the clothes, which he had put in the bag, telling him he threw them away because they had holes in them. She reiterated his interest in detective magazines.

Marilyn remembered visiting Egley in jail, in fact had his baby while he was in custody. She also related how Egley's attorney wanted her to marry Egley so that she would be legally excused from testifying against him in court. She also recalled that the police had contacted Egley in Helper during their initial investigation, and when they requested the clothes he was wearing, Egley told her he gave them different clothes. Marilyn always thought he had committed the murder.

The minute records had identified Becky Jo Hillard. To his surprise, this last surviving original witness lived in the same house as she had the night of the murder. Brewer was now experiencing a significant issue when investigating cold cases – missing evidence, deceased witnesses, and unknown witnesses. From her, he learned she was the neighbor who called the police that morning when told of Loretta's death.

Margret Hamilton, now deceased, was also listed in the minute records. She owned and operated the Highway Rendezvous bar on the highway between Price and Helper. She was a friend to Betty, and when interviewed, Betty informed the detective that Margret had told her how, in the early hours of the following morning, Egley had come to the bar. When he entered, Hamilton had reportedly exclaimed, "*Tom, where did you get all that blood on you?*" or similar. Egley responded that he had been painting for Betty. Betty said she never had him paint anything red. Apparently not realizing this, Egley went to the bathroom, and when he came out, got a ride to Helper by a patron.

Betty further told how she had a clear view from the bar to the laundromat across the street, where a burn barrel was located. Betty told Brewer how, on the day following the murder, she saw Egley burning something in the burn barrel. Later she asked him about the clothes the police came to get, and he admitted that he did not give them the clothes he had been wearing. There was talk of fibers, but Egley said he could explain that away as he had been to Loretta's house before. Betty further stated that Sheriff Passic had asked her to visit Egley in jail, in hopes that he would say something, but that he told her "*shhh…bugged.*" Betty again spoke of Egley's fascination with true crime stories, and how people got away with them.

Despite his efforts, Brewer was finding no physical evidence that could be analyzed by modern technology. He remembered that the crime scene photos Heidi had provided showed a passageway between the living room and kitchen, with rows of hanging beads covering the opening. Theorizing that the perpetrator had cut himself, he learned Ludeen still had them. Forwarded to the Utah Bureau of Forensic Services, however, the beads failed to provide any inculpatory evidence.

Sometimes in homicide investigations, it is the little things that get overlooked or ignored which can turn out to have been significant leads lost. Brewer was intrigued by the burn barrel issue, and he obtained aerial photographs of the Helper area at the time of the crime. If corroborated, this would be one more piece of strong circumstantial evidence. Some of his colleagues, however, thought he was chasing ghosts, and teased him about this. The tenacious detective, however, located a former employee who had worked at the described laundromat between 1960 and 1972. Shown the aerial photo, she pointed out the location and told how the burn barrel was close to the south side door of the building, and that peopled burned things there regularly.

The detective was also not willing to overlook the attempted abduction of the little girl. The now grown victim told how she was riding her bicycle in the area in front of her home, located between the hamburger stand and the Jones residence, about dusk. She had bubble gum in her mouth and recalled two things that became significant to Brewer. Her abductor, wearing a white t-shirt and jeans, smelled of burgers and when he grabbed her, she spit the gum into his hand. He let her go and she screamed. She suggested the detective speak to her brother, Robert.

When contacted, Robert told of seeing a man in a weird hat, wearing white t-shirt and jeans, sitting on the sidewalk curb one-half a block from where he and a friend were. The time was about 9:00 p.m. and the man was eating a hamburger. When the man approached them, they went into the house, but then heard the girl scream and instantly came running out. They chased this same man in the direction of Loretta's home, three blocks away, but lost him. Robert told the detective that he later identified Egley in a police lineup as the same man they saw, and he chased.

By now, Detective Brewer was learning a lot about Egley. He was from Rocky Ford, Colorado. He had served in the navy but was discharged for sleeping at his post. He was a drifter with a criminal record, doing odd jobs, and had had multiple relationships. It was now time to visit Tom Egley.

In March 2010, Brewer and Taylor drove to Rocky Ford. Brewer would later tell how, when they arrived at Egley's mobile home he invited them in, and that "*he knew why we were there.*" The interview began with small talk. The detectives asked if he knew why they were there and if it bothered him to talk about this case. Egley told the officers that he had moved to Helper for work, and when the job ended, stayed there doing odd jobs. Marilyn moved in with him, and he admitted he dated Loretta less than a month. He stated he was arrested for the murder because he refused the polygraph. He did not, however, recall going to Loretta's house "*that*" night, saying he had never been to her home. He also remembered going to Price and eating a hamburger on the curb. To Brewer, this was a meaningful statement. An "ah-ha" moment. The victim's stomach contents at autopsy were consistent with hamburger ingredients.

Knowing that Egley read true crime magazine stories, Brewer mentioned fibers being found, and asked again if he had been to Loretta's home? "*Not many times, more than once, less than 5*" Egley recalled. When DNA and swabs were mentioned, Egley did not "*think*" he had sex with her that night, "*no.*" "*I just don't remember having sex with her that night,*" he said. Asked if he would take a polygraph, Egley declined, saying they had their chance originally. During the interview, Egley stated he "*did not think this would be brought up again,*" and when DNA was mentioned again, replied "*I don't remember having sex with her…that night…I sure don't…I ain't saying I didn't but I don't remember it.*"

Egley was now back up on Detective Brewer's radar. He theorized that Egley fled the Jones house out the back door and through the brush to the railroad tracks just behind the house. From there he walked along the railroad tracks back toward Helper. The route was through rural farmland and scattered residences, and it was now dark. He stopped at the Highway Rendezvous bar, now identified in the assessor's photos and by his investigation as 7.1 miles from Loretta's home. It was here witnesses saw him in red-stained clothes. He left the bar and returned to his room at the New House Hotel about 2:00–3:00 a.m., yelling at Marilyn from the street to let him in. Later in the morning of July 31st, he went to the laundromat, across the street and 368 feet to the south. It was here Betty saw him burning the clothes from a distance of 124 feet away. Egley then left the laundromat and walked south, re-crossed the street, and went to the Sportsman's Bar, a block south of the New House Hotel, where he told Betty he was burning the clothes he had on "*that night*" as they had holes in them.

Detective Brewer had exploited the passage of time and changes in relationship to establish his case. Helper was little changed since that night, the original buildings and Main Street much as they were in 1970. He constructed an elaborate timeline of events from approximately 8:45 p.m. on July 30 through about 3:00 a.m. on July 31. Throughout this, he had the benefit of another solvability factor in such cases – supportive leadership. Despite working this in time away from other duties, his sheriff gave him his full support.

Brewer had previously presented a PowerPoint presentation of his work to the district attorney, and in 2010, took his case to his county prosecutor for review and filing. He believed they had a strong circumstantial case. He never anticipated that he would not hear back from the prosecutor for 4 years.

During this period, his career took a detour. Promoted to sergeant in 2012, Brewer was transferred back to patrol. He would not let go of this case, however, and juggled further investigation between his other duties. On July 21, 2014, Brewer received a message from the prosecutor. "*Please be advised that this office is declining prosecution on this matter.*" It was a hard blow. In 2015, however, he became the day sergeant supervising the detective division…he now had time to do further work on the case.

Experience has shown time and again that fresh eyes and perspective often open doors for further avenues of investigation. In April 2016, Detective Brewer attended a cold case seminar in Salt Lake City and presented his case to an audience of experienced law enforcement. He was asked by one of the other investigators if he had considered a forensic exhumation. He had, but had declined to do so as he did not wish to upset Ludeen. By now, however, the "awesome" woman had passed away, and he decided to go forth. Brewer knew that Egley was aware of DNA and would be following any and all developments on the case. *Reverse "CSI Effect?"*

EXHUMATION

A forensic or investigative exhumation is a lawfully sanctioned disinterment of human remains, and is legally accomplished by search warrant processes, court orders, varying statutes authorizing such, or permission of the family of the deceased. Due to advances in DNA and other forensic disciplines in the past few decades, this investigative procedure has become more common than it once was. Such procedure is often used to obtain DNA from the deceased or conduct a second autopsy. The results of such an effort cannot be accurately predicted, however, and only when the site is opened can investigators assess the potential of their efforts. When told of his plan, Heidi's response was "*where's the shovel*?" Permission was granted.

The Lost Scrolls

Before doing so, however, Brewer called his county prosecutor to advise of this pending action. It was then that he was informed by the prosecutor that his office had had the original transcripts of the 1970 preliminary hearing for 4 months. They had not said a word to Brewer about it. An office staff member, a friend of the Jones family, told him to "*drop it.*"

When previously interviewed, the court stenographer had said she had no records as she did not keep such things. The former reporter later found she had kept the transcript of the preliminary hearing of this case, however, and had taken them to the country prosecutor instead of the detective. Review of the document brought forth new questions, and discussed evidence that had been presented in court, including the victim's panties and other items. Items now apparently long gone. These records assisted identifying original persons, many of whom were now deceased. The later included several witnesses, all original attorneys involved in the case, the state medical examiner, and others. The document further tightened his timeline of events that fatal night.

Neighbor Hillard had seen Loretta sitting on her front porch at 9:00 p.m. Parley Jones (now deceased) was Loretta's father and had a warehouse behind Loretta's house. Jones had testified the lights were on about 9:45 but off at 10:05 p.m. Chief Paloni had described the crime scene in detail, and that Egley had admitted calling Jones that night. The medical examiner told of a defensive wound on Loretta's wrist. A Charles Kirkwood (now deceased) testified that he gave Egley a ride to Price that night, and that Egley wore a polka dot hat, white shirt, and Levi's. Margret testified he wore a white t-shirt that had red spots on it.

On June 7, 2016, Detective Brewer, a local mortician, and representatives from the state crime laboratory gathered at Loretta's grave in the tiny settlement of Elmo, in Emery County just south of Carbon County. The medical examiner had declined to attend, but also present was a member of the local media. The grave was shaded by a tree and lay on a gentle slope downhill from an irrigated hay field. Glancing uphill at the slope, Walton was not hopeful that their effort would be successful as was Detective Brewer. As the backhoe operator was attempting to remove the concrete vault, however, the bucket smashed it, and hundreds of gallons of water poured out. The remains were transported to a secure sheriff's office facility where, upon opening, the vault was found to be full of water and the casket had collapsed. It was obvious there would be no remaining DNA or opportunity for a secondary autopsy. Characteristic of the man he is, Brewer did not want to think of Loretta laying in the cold facility all night by herself…so he spent the night by her remains. Throughout this investigation, Brewer had had unfailing support from his sheriff, but now a new sheriff had been elected and continued the unwavering support of his efforts.

The next day, Loretta was reinterred in a new casket donated by local Mitchell's Funeral Home, a ceremony attended by family and a dedicated investigator. The exhumation had a desired effect, however, as Detective Brewer shortly learned that news of the event had reached Egley through media reports. That same night after the graveside ceremony, a friend of Heidi's from Rocky Ford called Heidi, and told her that she had a friend, Sheryl, who lived near Egley. Heidi learned that Egley had called Sheryl and asked if she could watch his dogs because he felt the cops would be there for him any day. Brewer felt that Egley might now become dangerous and notified the Otero County Sheriff's Office for officer safety reasons in case they had any contacts with Egley.

In the aftermath of the ceremony, Brewer received a call from a Jones family friend, telling the detective that Loretta had written her killer's name in her own blood on the floor before she died. It was too Hollywood to believe, and he asked her to draw it as she remembered the linoleum. Re-inspection of the photo with 4-year-old Heidi showed a void from the victim's arms, and a closer look revealed "T.O." on the floor. In the transcript Brewer now had, Chief Paloni had testified that her hand appeared to be moving in blood. She had died before she could complete it.

The phone calls kept coming. Brewer received a call from Laura, also in Otero County, Colorado. She was a neighbor to Egley and told how he had asked if she could adopt his dogs out, telling her that officers were coming for him. She further told how Egley had asked her if she knew how long DNA could stay in the body. When she told him to take a polygraph, he told her "*…they will just have to prove I did it.*" She told the detective "*You have your man.*"

At this point, Detective Brewer and his new partner, Wally Hendricks, took their case to the Utah Attorney General's Office. Providing them with a copy of the investigation, he told the officials he was not waiting any longer and was going back to Colorado. A parting comment from the officials was "*...then bring us back a confession.*"

The sheriff's faith in his detective was unwavering, so his administrative support for another road trip to Colorado was strong. Sheriff Jeff Wood gave the detective a county credit card and told him "*don't come back until you get what you want.*"

David Brewer had a good circumstantial case now, and Egley was obviously worried. He had Betty's sworn statement about burning his clothes, and had told her he did go to Loretta's that night, while telling Brewer he did not. Nearing Rocky Ford, Brewer did not want to be seen in town just yet, so he and Hendricks stayed in La Junta, 11 miles from Rocky Ford. There they met with Laura at the hotel. Laura and Egley were friends, she said, and saw each other almost every day. She had previously recorded several conversations with Egley. Knowing this, the detectives provided her with some case information to see what his reactions would be and provided her with a "script" of some information to elicit his responses.

Later in the evening, Laura called. "*You gotta hear this, he just confessed,*" she said. Listening to the recording, the two lawmen heard Egley say, "*I don't remember stabbing her, but I did cut her throat.*" The detectives had to listen to this several times to believe what they heard.

The next day, Brewer and Hendricks re-visited Egley at his residence, and again, he was welcoming. They did tell him they were leaving today without him. Egley then volunteered that while he did not remember stabbing her, he did remember cutting her throat. After being read his rights and knowingly waiving them, Egley told how he did go to Price that night to see Loretta; that he had had consensual sex with her previously, but that night she turned him down. He said he stabbed her in the chest when she exited the kitchen, but did not remember stabbing her in the back 17 times. He kissed her good-bye and left. He knew Loretta had a little girl but did not see Heidi that night.

After filling in some gaps during their interview, the detectives prepared to leave. As they did so, they asked him if there was anything he wanted them to convey to Heidi. Egley replied, "*Tell her I'm sorry I killed her mom.*" For Egley, it seemed to be a release. In the aftermath, he provided two written letters to Laura, acknowledging what he did. These letters showed his satisfaction with Brewer's investigation, including that he did bathe that night with his clothes on...something some of Brewer's colleagues had found hard to believe. And he did admit to chasing the little girl, but did not catch her.

On August 18, 2016, an arrest warrant was issued for Tom Egley for the 1970 murder of Loretta Jones. Detective Brewer had coordinated the arrest in Rocky Ford with the U.S. Marshal's Service, and Egley was arrested peacefully shortly after the judge signed the warrant. They flew Egley to the Salt Lake City airport, where Brewer was waiting…waiting with pink handcuffs to put on the man who so brutally murdered a young woman a lifetime ago. Once back in Price, and represented by defense counsel, Egley pled guilty to the murder and was sentenced to 10 years to life, based upon the Utah statute of 1970. His first parole hearing was not until 2036.

In her impact statement to the court, Heidi brought tears to this writer's eyes and those in the courtroom, telling Egley how her mother was never there for her first kiss, her prom, and other events. She told of the void in her life due to his selfish actions, but Egley was non-responsive as the courtroom listened in hushed silence. Perhaps telling more about himself than he realized, he retained a bit of defiance as he told the judge that he "*…cannot believe you are worried about it after 46 years.*"

On November 29, 2016, Tom Egley entered the Utah State Prison, wearing another set of pink handcuffs. These were later inscribed "S*it pax Have evos*" *(let there be peace)* and presented to Heidi Jones-Asay by Detective David Brewer. The handcuffs worn by Egley when he was returned to Carbon County to be held for his actions now hang on the wall over the detective's desk.

"NEVER GIVE UP"

Detective Brewer will tell others how "*I lived this case; it became embedded in me.*" This is not an uncommon experience for cold case investigators, who have often spent years working and living their cases. He will tell of his overwhelming belief in the case and his attachment to it as soon as he heard the story from Heidi. Detective Brewer's determination and tenacity steadfastly demonstrate that the lack of forensic evidence should not be a deterrent to re-investigating unsolved, cold case murders. Nor should size of a police jurisdiction be a hindrance when victims have tenacious investigators and effective leadership. Shoe-leather detective work, experience, and resolve solved countless crimes before the advent of the advanced technology we enjoy today, and this case should serve as an inspiration to others, a model of what can be accomplished when one starts with almost nothing but tenacity and determination. Tom Egley died in prison in 2024.

> "*Some people's heroes wear capes…mine wear Kevlar.*" – *Heidi Asay Jones*

Works Cited

Eliopulos, L. N. (2003). *Death Investigator's Handbook.* Boulder, CO: Paladin Press.

FBI. (n.d.a). *VICAP.* Retrieved November 29, 2018, from https://www.fbi.gov/news/stories/vicap-links-murders-to-prolific-serial-killer-112718

FBI. (n.d.b). *How We Investigate*. Retrieved November 28, 2018, from https://www.fbi.gov/services/cirg

Schubert, A. (2017). The prosecution of cold case murders. In R. Walton, Ed. *Cold Case Homicides: Practical Investigative Techniques* (pp. 151–164). Boca Raton: CRC Press.

Stein, S. K. (2017). Cold cases: An exploratory study into the status of unresolved homicides in the USA. *Investigative Sciences Journal*, 9(2), 1–19.

U.S. Government Census of Population and Housing. (n.d.). Decennial Census of Population and Housing. Retrieved https://www.census.gov/programs-surveys/decennial-census.html

Walton, R. (2005). *Identification of Solvability Factors in Twenty-First Century Cold Case Homicide Investigation*. Unpublished dissertation. San Francisco, CA.

Walton, R. (2016). Investigation of long-term missing persons as cold case homicides: An American perspective. In S. J. Morewitz, & C. Colls, Eds. *Handbook of Missing Persons* (pp. 233–249). Switzerland: Springer.

Walton, R., & Henrie, M. (2011). *Summary Report and Findings Utah Unsolved Homicide Assessment 1965–2005*. Price: Research, Utah State University Eastern, Sociology Social Work and Anthropology.

Walton, R. H. (2017). *Cold case Homicides: Practical Investigative Techniques* (2nd ed.). Boca Raton, FL: CRC Press.

Winsor, M. (2018, November 20). Retrieved from https://abcnews.go.com/US/investigators-announce-significant-break-decades-cold-case-murder/story?id=59314962

Significant Cold Case Issues

This case history offers a significant number of issues for cold case investigators.

- Organizational leadership and commitment to proactive cold case homicide investigation
- Case re-activation because of effort initiated by victim's family through casual conversation with a law enforcement official
- Absence of original investigation documentation, physical evidence, or photographs, despite intensive search
- Witness re-contacts and changes in relationships
- Although the original case investigators were deceased, small town cold case investigator was able to re-investigate this case and through the efforts of Utah State Attorney General and local prosecutor, to obtain plea of guilty by perpetrator of almost 46-year-old rape-murder
- Re-interviews with suspect and recording of immediate reaction and responses to questions, including statements and body language
- Informant development
- Interstate law enforcement cooperation so necessary in these cases

- Interview preparation by investigators including photographs and records to show suspect
- Denials and apparent selective memory loss feigned by suspect
- Investigator knowledge of suspect background and interview methodology
- Dedication and perseverance of cold case investigators
- Fate and luck

We wish to extend our deepest gratitude to Carbon County Sheriffs Jeff Wood and Detective Sergeant David Brewer for providing the material used in compiling this case history as well as their work in this case. I further wish to acknowledge the leadership role these sheriffs demonstrated in this cold case homicide investigation, and to express my gratitude for his assistance in providing this case material. This investigation is a credit to cold case homicide investigation and to law enforcement, no matter the size or location of the agency.

Investigation

4

RACHEL H. WALTON
AND FRANK P. TONA

Introduction

The investigation sequence and methods in a cold case homicide investigation will vary, depending upon several factors. These factors include those forces that caused this specific case to be re-examined (i.e., specific information has come forward regarding this specific case) and individual methods of investigation based on each investigator's training and experience, as well as perceived investigative plan based upon file review. As no two hot homicides are investigated exactly in the same manner, neither are cold case homicides. Each takes place within an overall similar framework, however. This framework includes people, places, and evidence.

This chapter explores various considerations that may be involved in the re-investigation of a cold case homicide. Not all cases will use the methods or sources of potential information presented here. Perhaps they will use others. In addition, investigators may "color outside the box" as they utilize combinations of other means and methods.

Reconstructing the Crime and Investigation

After reading and studying the case file, the cold case investigator is familiar with the *documented* record that has been preserved. This includes what officers and investigators did, what witnesses and others said, what evidence was collected, analyzed, and preserved, and what was photographed. In this way, the investigator has *informally* and *informationally* reconstructed the crime scene. During the investigation, it may be appropriate to further consult with qualified reconstruction experts to *formally* reconstruct the crime. Investigators today also have at their disposal a myriad of different resources to assist them in the reconstruction of the crime. This can include the utilization of open-source intelligence sites, data-mining sites, social media platforms, using drones, and digital forensic capabilities for unsolved cases post-2015. Reconstruction will depend upon the nature of the crime, the

DOI: 10.4324/9781003415633-6

types of events that occurred, and the questions that need to be answered. This may involve physical reconstruction and/or psychological reconstruction (victim and suspect). Such reconstruction may involve:

- Gunshot trajectory
- Muzzle to target distance
- Ejection pattern and other firearm-related analyses
- Blood spatter patterns
- Sharp object, including depths, angles, clothing damage, defense wounds, and ante- or postmortem injuries
- Arson and fire burn
- Furniture and objects
- Vehicle impact
- Vehicle tire and skid mark patterns
- Clothing and/or article patterns

Visit the Crime Scene

Reports and photographs provide the cold case investigator with a two-dimensional, informational view of the crime scene and the crime. In my experience, nothing serves to orient the investigator and the investigation, more forcefully than a visit to the crime scene. Decades later, the scene may be little changed from when only a rural cabin stood (see Figures 4.1 and 4.2), or condos may now stand in place of an old office building. Regardless, returning to "the scene of the crime" provides an insight that words and photographs cannot quite equal. For example, Google Earth provides a feature called Historical Imagery, which allows users to view past satellite and aerial images of a location. By accessing this feature, you can see how a particular area has changed over time. Google Earth doesn't exactly provide "maps" in the traditional sense (like road maps) from history, but rather satellite and aerial images. This can offer an insightful glimpse into the past, allowing the investigator to gain a sense of what the area was like when the incident occurred. While reading the case may allow the cold case investigator to feel the "pulse" of the crime, visiting the scene allows one to *feel* the scene of the crime (see Figure 4.3).

Reconstructing the Scene

If the location has changed, consider reconstructing the scene through interviews with those who knew the scene and use of other sources of photographs.

- Family or family members of victims (if crime occurred in or near residence)

Figure 4.1 Scene of the crime, 1925. In some cold cases, the area that contained the crime scene is preserved only in photographs found outside the case file. These can provide investigators an insight into what the scene looked like at the time, and aid in informational reconstruction of the crime. Pictured here is the scene of a 1925 homicide case re-activated in the 1980s. (Courtesy: Irvine collection.)

Figure 4.2 Scene of the crime, 1988. Although the ravages of time may alter the original scene of the crime, photographs and returning to the scene with original participants or witnesses may further investigator understanding and provide information not found in the case file. In this photo, a member of the 1925 posse returns to the scene of a murder with the author to walk through the events from over 60 years before. (Author's collection.)

Figure 4.3 Crime scene 1965 and 2001. Vegetation changes and remodeling are not uncommon in decades following a homicide. In many cases, current homeowners have allowed law enforcement to re-enter the residence to familiarize themselves with the "ins and outs" of the scene. Contact of scene owners or those who control access may be a delicate situation as they may have had no knowledge of the prior homicide. (Courtesy of Anderson/ECPD.)

- With neighbors of scene
- In city planning or building departments, including aerial photos
- In newspaper or local magazines
- In other media
- In historical societies
- In libraries
- In private collections
- Online communities, such as Reddit, or social media groups focused on a particular town or region might have users who can share old photos or point you to resources

When Visiting the Scene of the Crime

Revisit all scenes that are known to be associated with the crime. These may include:

- Homicide location
- Body recovery location(s)
- Victim's residence or last-known location
    - The social and cultural dynamics of the neighborhood may have shifted. Investigators should consider how these changes may affect witness recollections, the availability of new witnesses, or patterns in criminal activity
- Suspect residence or last-known location
- All locations where evidence was located
- Consider geographic profiling
- Consider behavioral assessment of both victim and suspect

Time and Distance

- Note the ingress and egress for victim and suspect
- Visit at the time of day or night the crime occurred
    - Lighting?
    - Who may have been present?
    - Where?
    - Businesses hours or routine activities by others that might have allowed for unknown witnesses to be present
- For a different perspective, visit in the daytime if crime was at night and vice versa
- Take the crime scene pictures with you and orient yourself and the pictures to the scene
- Observe surrounding terrain or buildings

- Look up, down, and around
- Slope and lay of the land
- Compare witness statements to the scene. Do they appear realistic as to what they said, did, and saw?
- Is evidence still present? For instance, a rural location, tall grass, and brief scene investigation, or perhaps evidence was missed and never recovered
- Have witnesses or reporting party walk through the scene with you (see Figure 4.2)

The Neighborhood Canvass

According to homicide expert Vernon Geberth, a neighborhood canvass is the door-to-door questioning of those in the general area after a crime has been committed to gain information about the specific incident. During this brief contact and interview with residents and others, officers or investigators attempt to locate witnesses or individuals who might provide information about the specific incident. Although this knowledge may not appear important to them, when coupled with other information known to investigators, it may play a significant role in an investigation. The canvass or a re-canvass, according to Geberth, may provide:

- An actual eyewitness to the crime
- Information about the circumstances of the crime
- An approximate time of occurrence and/or estimate of time of death
- Information about the deceased, including identity, habits, friends
- Information about unusual observations or individual behavior at the time
- Information about a suspect, or even identity of a suspect
- A motive for the crime

Normally, but not always, a canvass is conducted shortly after the crime or incident. A canvass may have been done by the investigators, but also may have been done by other officers who would then forward the names and addresses of potential witnesses to the investigators along with a summary of what the witness may have to offer. The investigators would then conduct a more thorough, detailed, interview. It is well to remember that due to passage of time, a re-canvass may identify those who were never interviewed and/or those who may now be more cooperative and divulge what they know. The original canvass may not have reached everyone in the area, particularly if residents were absent or unaware of the crime. Years later, new people may have moved in, and former residents who were once hesitant to speak may now be more willing to come forward. Over time, people often reflect on past events and may remember something they initially overlooked or didn't think was important.

Individual and community perspectives on law enforcement, the crime, and individuals involved may have evolved. Public sentiment can affect how open or forthcoming people are with investigators. A renewed investigation may stir up community interest and lead to the sharing of forgotten or new information. In some cases, a person of influence or authority in the area may have discouraged others from talking. Changes in leadership or power dynamics can free witnesses to speak openly. Re-canvassing allows for these details to surface, especially if witnesses have had time to process the event.

The physical environment of the crime scene may have changed since the initial investigation. Re-canvassing helps investigators understand how the area has developed, which may influence the crime scene analysis. A new building, change in landscaping, or road construction might provide new hiding spots or sightlines that were not considered previously. New public infrastructure such as security cameras, streetlights, and other public infrastructure might have been added since the crime occurred. By revisiting the area, investigators may discover that new technology could have recorded relevant information, even retroactively.

With the rise of social media and digital communication, people may have shared information online that wasn't accessible during the original investigation. Investigators can now ask about old messages, posts, or digital interactions that might provide new clues. Cell phone towers and data were not as commonly analyzed in older cases. When re-canvassing, investigators might request mobile data from individuals or check for any overlooked digital evidence.

A neighborhood canvass could be a hit-or-miss affair, depending upon the diligence of those assigned this duty, or other priorities. If a neighborhood resident had nothing to offer, the canvassing officer may have not written anything down. If a resident was not home, no one may not have gone back. It is critical to review if a canvass was initially completed, did any of the investigators go back to those residences missed. Re-engaging with individuals who were missed during the initial canvass is a proactive step that can yield significant benefits in a cold case murder investigation, potentially transforming previously overlooked details into critical evidence that leads to solving the case. Some agencies may have used a form, a canvass questionnaire, during this activity, and case file review should attempt to identify this practice. Not uncommonly, however, the canvassing officer used their notebook or perhaps an index card to make note of any information. Transmission to the investigators of the identity of persons to be contacted could be verbal and subsequently forgotten and never followed up.

In one instance, a man hit his wife, and she died. A neighbor, who knew the couple well, approached uniformed officers at the scene and stated that she had information the investigators should be aware of. She was told that investigators would contact her. Some weeks later, she telephoned the police agency to state that she had never been contacted and possessed information regarding the couple that police should be aware of. She was never contacted.

Approximately a year later, the case was going to trial. The suspect stated he had never hit his wife before. District attorney investigators were conducting pre-trial investigation about the crime when they were approached by the same neighbor. The neighbor then told of past domestic violence toward the victim and how, just days before the homicide, observed the suspect hit her so hard he knocked the victim across the room. At this time, he voiced words to the effect that next time he would kill her. The suspect pled guilty.

Reconstructing the Canvass

Going back to a neighborhood years or decades after the crime may yield valuable information. If the results of a neighborhood canvas have been found in the file, use this as a starting point to begin. Which addresses were checked? Which were not? Go to the neighborhood and look around. Look for neatly maintained, older homes. Attempt to identify the older residents of the neighborhood and elicit their help. Choose a time of day that most optimizes the chance to find people at home. When reconstructing a canvass, ascertain if the address or numbering sequences may have changed since the time of the crime.

Start going door-to-door as you would a primary canvass today. Attempt to identify those who may have been living in the neighborhood at the time of the crime. In some instances, the original resident may have moved but the current resident may be their tenant or know how to contact them. In some circumstances, a relative may now live there, if not the same resident from the time. Experience has shown witnesses still residing in the same location as at the time of the offense 45 years or more after the incident. In the Wilkerson case study which follows, witnesses from the 1960s still resided in the same residence in 2002 as when they first reported information to police.

Call the telephone number in the report. Check the address.

Remember, while some may possess knowledge of the crime or persons involved, they can't bring themselves to pick up the telephone to call but may just be waiting for the investigator to knock on their door to tell all they know. It has happened.

When conducting the canvass, start at the point where the crime occurred. Look around, from what locations might someone see something? Don't forget to look up, also. Consider the time of day, or night, of the crime.

To reconstruct the neighborhood for a canvass, consider:

- City/county directories for the time period
- Public works for street maps
- New public infrastructure changes (lights, cameras, etc.)
- Planning department
- Public utilities
- Local historical societies
- Fire department
- Post Office
- Local resident input

Suggested Questions

- Did you reside here at the time of the crime?
- Knowledge of crime?
- Know anyone involved?
- Firsthand knowledge of events or the crime?
- Heard of anything about the crime or individuals over the years?
- Did anybody move away suddenly after the crime?
- Any suspicious persons at that time, or other suspicious events?
- Any similar crimes before or after?
- Do you suspect anyone of this crime?
- Is there anything else you think might be important for us to know?
- Have you spoken to anyone else about what you witnessed?
- Are there any other neighbors or individuals who might have seen or heard something?

After the canvass, check criminal histories on any names that may have developed.

City/County Directories

City or county directories are publications produced by commercial companies that provide information about people living within the boundaries as designed by the directory (see Figure 4.4). These directories and their variations have been around since the late 1800s and offered in many locales nationwide, both urban and rural. These publications are especially useful in reconstructing information about physical locations, including neighboring

Figure 4.4 City directories. These published directories offer cold case investigators a variety of information about people and the local community during previous decades. Such directories date to the nineteenth century in many areas and are useful in researching people and places and for may be useful in construction of timelines. (Author's collection.)

addresses and intersections as well as personal data about individuals. The cold case investigator should keep in mind that, like other print sources, the information to be found in these sources is only as good as the original source of information.

These directories were compiled and published on an annual basis, often by larger commercial publishers. They were sold commercially, often by subscription, and may have been produced in association with local chambers of commerce. These directories offered commercial and demographic information about a community, as well as personal information about its occupants. Among these directories, one may find:

- Alphabetical directory of business names
- Alphabetical directory of private citizens
- Directory of householders
- Occupants of office buildings and other business places
- Street name and number guide
- Numerical telephone directory
- Classified advertising
- Other miscellaneous information

For example, if an investigator knows that subject of interest operated a barber shop in San Diego, California, in a particular year, a review of the city directory for that year would include a list of barber shops in alphabetical order, as compiled by this data source. Although city or state licensing and business operation records may normally be destroyed or discarded after a prescribed length of time, city directories offer a means to locate reported information about people and places in a specific time period (see Figure 4.4).

As a source of personal information, city directories offer a cold case investigator a thumbnail picture of people. Persons are listed in alphabetical order by last name, first name, middle initial, name of spouse (common law, "significant other" or other non-married co-habitants may not be included in these older listings), address, place of employment, and/or occupation. The listing of a spouse or employment information may offer cold case investigators additional names or sources of information heretofore unknown, especially in older cases.

These directories detailed the numerical sequencing of streets and intersections. In addition, they listed individual house numbers, name of occupant, and telephone number (see Figure 4.5). City or county directory listings may also include not only the address of apartment structures, but also the names of individual occupants and their telephone numbers. The passage of time between

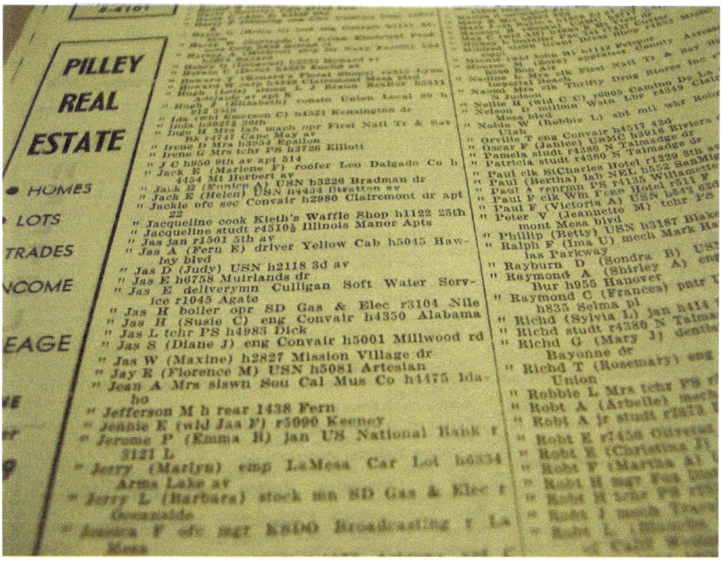

Figure 4.5 City directories may be useful in several facets of cold case investigation. In addition to listing people by name and phone number, they also provide sequential street address information. This may aid in identifying neighbors to a particular address or in reconstructing an area cold case canvass. (Author's collection.)

the period when the information was obtained and when it was published, however, may impact the accuracy of this information. This may be especially true in more transient populations. These listings may be useful when attempting to reconstruct addresses and occupants surrounding a subject location or crime scene. Development of this information may provide cold case investigators with names and addresses of persons not reflected in original police reports or statements. This information might be useful in preparing diagrams showing scene locations or when used in conjunction with aerial photographs. The directories might also offer confirmation or non-confirmation of information and aid in constructing timelines and occupational profiles.

Sources of old city directories may include:

- In-agency archives and library
- Local libraries
- Local chamber of commerce
- Local historical societies
- Local law enforcement agency archives
- Local offices of the FBI and other federal agencies

Telephone Directories

The style and format of published, soft cover telephone directories have changed in the decades since the 1940s. Older telephone directories may list persons by last name, full first name, middle initial, physical location address for the specified telephone number, and the telephone number. In more recent decades there has been a transition from such inclusive personal information to a listing that includes last name, first initial, and telephone number only. Therefore, telephone directories may offer more assistance to cold case investigators in some older cases than more recent editions.

Telephone directories may provide cold case investigators with information useful when:

- Establishing residency confirmation or disconfirmation, or locations of suspects, witnesses, or other persons
- Cross checking or indexing telephone numbers
- Yellow pages business information

Victim and Family Considerations

Contacting the Victim's Family

Cold case investigators hold differences of opinion as to investigator-initiated contact with a victim's family. To contact or *not* to contact depends upon the circumstances of the case, and the investigative plan of action as it is conceived and carried out. While perhaps no such contact is planned at the start of the cold case investigation, circumstances may change and contact then becomes necessary.

When contacting the family of a victim in these investigations, keep in mind that the pain and anxiety, the feelings from that first day of the crime, are just below their emotional surface. The family never forgets. To the family of homicide victims, the hurt is still present, even after 60 years or more. In the initial period after the crime, they sought answers from the police, from friends, and from each other. How they *perceived* their treatment by law enforcement can affect how they react to a renewed investigation. Their feelings may run the scale from desiring no contact with authority to full cooperation. On some occasions, they may not wish the case to be re-opened, and to just "let it be." There may be reasons for this, and these might include family secrets or matters they do not want exposed, or culpability by a family member.

If contact is made with family, consider utilizing the services of Victim/Witness Unit. When a cold case is solved, involve this unit with the family in the post-arrest and media interest phase.

Reasons to Contact Victim's Family

- Over the years, the victim's family may have learned direct information or have secondhand information that may be of interest to the investigation. They may also have previously contacted law enforcement investigators who may not have given them the perception that their information was not considered valuable at the time. This information may or may not have documented in the file. In later years, with other information subsequently known, that information may now be more valuable.
- To obtain diaries, notes, photographs, or other material that now may be of importance to the investigation. These may identify previous relationships, relationship status, other friends and acquaintances, or identify specific concerns or fears held by the victim (see Figure 4.6).
- To learn more about the victim and circumstances at the time of the homicide.
- To identify or learn further of other persons of interest who may have surfaced during the initial or subsequent investigation.
- To verify or eliminate other information from consideration.
- To inform the family that their case has not been forgotten.
- To stimulate communications in the family or immediate circle of friends.

Arguments against Contacting Victim's Family

- Raises false hopes and expectations.
- Family or members begin to call every day to learn if anything is new.

Figure 4.6 Knowledge of the victim may come from many sources. During a cold case investigation, investigators seek to learn as much as they can about victim's movements prior to the crime, as well as previous relationships. Contact with the family may provide notes, letters, and diaries with information previously unknown to investigators. In this 1925 case, a letter from the victim to her brother provided personal information and detailed a relationship that was important in the case reconstruction eight decades later. (Author's collection.)

- Family begins to discuss it and word may get to the suspect(s) and they further cover their tracks.
- If there are concerns about potential retaliation from suspects or associates, contacting the family could put them at risk.
- If the cold case goes nowhere and remains unsolved, they do not ride another emotional roller coaster.
- A family member may be involved in the case, or may be the suspect.
- Families may have differing opinions or dynamics that could lead to conflict or confusion about the case if not handled carefully.

Learning More about the Victim (and the Suspect)

When studying the unsolved case, investigators try to learn as much about their victim as they can. This in turn *may* begin to identify the suspect. Consider the *Victimology* in the course of investigation and try to come to know who the victim was before the murder and identify and assess what role they may have played in this chain of events. Apply your experience as you would a fresh case.

- *Physical*: This includes evidence transfer from the crime and recovered at the scene, at autopsy, or other circumstances. Interview the autopsy pathologist for case review and discussion. This may include:
  - Seminal or other body fluids
  - Bruises
  - Bitemarks
  - Bullet wounds and tracks
  - Contact distance
  - Defense wounds
  - Blood spatter or patterns
  - Foreign objects
  - Hair and fibers
- *Lifestyle*: This is learned through observations, interviews, and document analysis and may assist in learning more about the victim as well as contributing to the identification of a suspect. As a suspect is identified, these considerations may also apply to building the case.
  - Physical residential or work environment
  - Environment where the crime occurred
  - Notes, diaries, letters
  - Social media footprint
  - Church associates
  - Employment
  - Circle of friends, acquaintances, and co-workers
    - Any outliers
    - Anybody moves away suddenly
    - Anybody undergoes noticeable lifestyle change
  - Anyone who had access to victim
  - Then-current relationships and prior relationships (including former spouses)
  - Fears and phobias
  - Mental and physical history
  - Behavior changes
  - Hobbies and sports
  - Habits and routines
  - Neighbors
  - Social clubs and organizations
  - Physical abilities and capabilities
  - Hairdressers
  - Financial profile and credit check
  - Review of credit card records including spending and last uses or usage profile
  - School or work problems

- Telephone records or cell phone records reviewed
- Sexual fetishes or interests
- Sexual orientation
- Drug and alcohol abuse
- Cellmates and co-defendants
- Probation and parole reports
- Institution intelligence reports
- Violence or illegal activity in background
- Enemies and adversaries
- Former business partners and associates
- Social services
- Civil files
- Known trial testimony

Other Family Dynamics

- Did any family ever hire private investigators?
  - Were witnesses contacted by private investigators?
  - Were private investigators used in any aspect of the case (civil or criminal)?
- Who benefited financially from the victim's death?
  - Life insurance
  - Mortgage insurance
  - Review Last Will and Testament and Probate File or Trusts
  - Business insurance policies (family or partners as beneficiaries)
  - Property transfers or money movements
- Identify family tree
  - Use of obituary
  - Publicly available genealogy sites
  - Siblings
  - Stepparents and relations
  - Other relations including "*Black Sheep*" that may tell what others will not

Interviews and Re-interviews

Re-interviewing witnesses is an important component of the re-investigation of cold case homicides. By this process, investigators seek to

- Affirm previous witness statement and update contact and identifier information
- Obtain information *held back* by previously identified witnesses who may now tell more due to changes in their own lifestyle, maturity,

distancing from the previous crowd they ran around with, or no longer fearing the suspect
- Identify previously unidentified witnesses or associates of suspect
- Obtain cooperation of previously uncooperative witnesses

Interview Sequence

Cold case investigators may consider the order of the witness interview process.

- Begin with law enforcement and other officials as necessary.
- Consider those witnesses on the outside periphery of those initially contacted and work toward the center, those most immediate to the victim. Those on the outside may know more than they told or have heard information over the years. Of course, remember that the more people you contact, the increased likelihood the word may get back to the suspect.
- Material witnesses. Prior to contacting material witnesses, compile as much background information on them as possible. Ascertain any pending legal difficulties, including custody, probation, or parole status.
- Run background checks on *all* subjects, including witnesses, family members, or others involved in the case as you would if the case was a fresh homicide. Use the advantage of time to obtain further insight into various individuals.

During the background and interview process, look for

- Lifestyle changes. These include downhill slides as well as improved lifestyle and relationships, or religious embracement.
- Movements out of city, county, or state. It has been my interesting observation that many of those who commit their crimes in the vicinity of where they were raised may often move out of state, and those who commit their crimes far from where they were raised may return to their comfort zone of family and friends.
- Arrests.
- Violence.
- Changes in personal relationship or inability to maintain relationships. Keep in mind that former friends, lovers, and secretaries can be the most valuable sources of information. Identify these when possible and as necessary.
- Other evidence of self-destructive behavior.
- Be careful not to give out more than you receive!
    - Your job is to get information, not give it!

Additional Background Resources for Victim and Suspect Information and Development

- Marriage and divorce records
- Real estate records including grantee/grantor
- Birth certificate
- Social media platforms
- Open-source intelligence sites
- Civil liens and judgments
- Local fire/police/ambulance reporting as victim/witness/suspect
- Assessor
- Treasurer/tax collector
- City/county clerk
- Professional licensing and certification
- Trade unions
- Post Office
- Schools
- Local voter registration

Modus Operandi (M.O.) in the Twenty-First Century—"Thoughtprints"

In his international bestseller, *Black Dahlia Avenger: A Genius for Murder*, retired Los Angeles Police Department Homicide Detective Steve Hodel introduces us to the term "thoughtprints." Beginning in 1999, Hodel began to research the possibility that his father, the late Dr. George Hodel, was responsible for one of the most infamous unsolved homicides in Los Angeles history, the 1947 "Black Dahlia" murder. In doing so, he uncovered compelling evidence that suggested his father was responsible for this and other unsolved murders. During his investigation, he conceived the idea of "thoughtprints" and provides this definition: Our thought patterns determine what we do each day, each hour, each minute. While our actions may appear simple, routine, and automatic, they really are not. Behind and within each of our thoughts is an aim, an intent, a motive.

The motive within each thought is unique. In all our actions, each of us leaves behind traces of our self. Like our fingerprints, these traces are identifiable. I call them thoughtprints. They are the ridges, loops, and whorls of our mind. Like the individual "points" that a criminalist examines in a fingerprint, they mean little by themselves and remain meaningless, unconnected shapes in a jigsaw puzzle until they are pieced together to reveal a clear picture.

If we are careful and clever in committing our crime, we may remember to wear gloves and not leave any fingerprints behind. But rarely are we clever enough to mask our motives, and we will almost certainly leave behind our thoughtprints. A collective of our motives, a paradigm constructed from our individual thoughts, these illusive prints construct the signature that will connect or link us to a specific time, place, crime, or victim.

In his book, Hodel cites numerous examples of Dr. George Hill Hodel's thoughtprints. I asked Hodel if he might provide us with a few examples of thoughtprints, and if he would explain how they might be useful to cold case investigators. Here is his response: First let me clarify a misconception. Thoughtprints have absolutely nothing to do with anything psychic or metaphysical. They can apply to any crime. However, in the specialized field of homicide investigation, they should be thought of as a tool to complement M.O. and signatures.

As with the "Zodiac" unsolved murders in the San Francisco area in the 1960s and early 1970s, the slayer in the Black Dahlia case taunted police with notes and documents mailed to the news media. Figure 4.7 shows notes mailed to a local newspaper after the homicide. I believe the sender reveals training as a journalist and crime reporter through the pasted headline "copy" he sent to the press and the police as the "Black Dahlia Avenger." During the investigation, I learned that my father had training as a journalist and crime reporter for newspapers.

Figure 4.7 Murder weapon and lubricant. The murder weapon was brought to the scene of the crime, and afterward, released back to its owner. This was a not uncommon practice, perhaps depriving cold case investigators in some instances the chance to apply advanced technology in some cases. (Courtesy of Anderson/ECPD.)

In another instance, as illustrated in Figure 4.8, the careful posing of the victim's arms and body mimicked the surrealist photograph, The Minotaur, created by Dr. Hodel's friend Man Ray. This artist's photograph illustrated a nude woman bisected at the waist (see Figure 4.9). The nude victim was found bisected at the waist and similarly posed.

Within months of the murder, George Hodel's 11-year-old daughter asked him to help her name her play doll. Interviewed decades later, the woman recalled that Hodel told her to name the doll, "Elizabeth Ann." As revealed during my investigation, The Black Dahlia's dossier from the FBI revealed the victim's name as Elizabeth Ann Short.

In another instance, I discovered a witness statement that described attendance at a "Hollywood" party at George Hodel's Hollywood house. The witness told officers that the doctor used lipstick to write words on the bare breasts of a partygoer. After concluding that the evidence strongly suggested Dr. Hodel stomped a woman to death months later, my research indicated that Dr. Hodel wrote a taunting message to the police on her nude body—using lipstick.

The concept of thoughtprints can best be utilized by cold case investigators, by providing them a fresh start, and emphasizing the need to "think outside the box." I suggest that investigators should look for connections in a suspect's background, profession, or personal life. These could link him or her, to the crime, the victim, or the location. One of the best sources for finding potential thoughtprints comes through the re-interview of close friends.

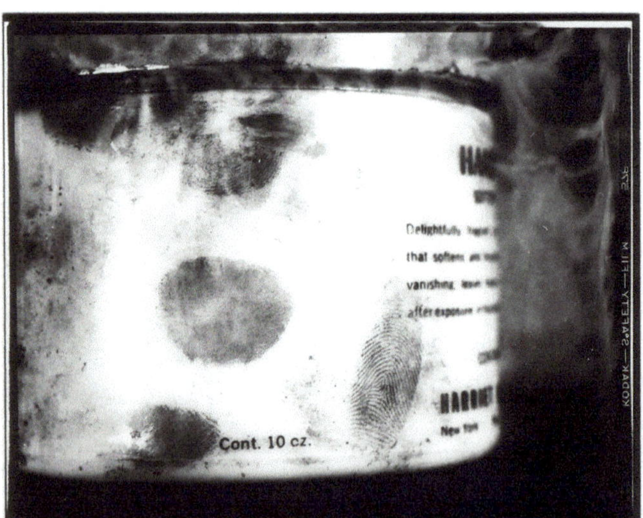

Figure 4.8 Cold cream container. Although latent prints were observed on the jar, it was broken when crushed in a vice being used to hold it. (Courtesy of Anderson/ECPD.)

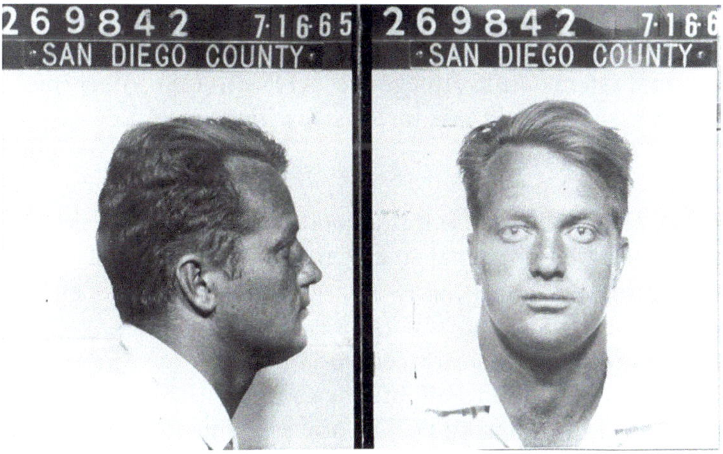

Figure 4.9 Serial killer Clyde Wilkerson after his 1965 arrest for rape. Authorities could not link him to the homicides and rapes at this time. Only the advent of DNA and the tenacity of determined investigators allowed this case to be solved. (Courtesy of Anderson/ECPD.)

In very cold cases, careful research and review of all newspaper articles from the period can be invaluable. In the Dahlia-related serial killings from the 1940s, I extracted the documented statements of over 75 witnesses, and after placing them in chronological order, discovered they yielded critical information on both the victim and the suspect. Another huge potential source for latent thoughtprints is the original crime scene photographs. Investigators can re-scan them at high resolution, then magnify and zoom in, and conduct a present-day "walk-through," right from a laptop. Re-examine the scene, inch by inch, quadrant by quadrant.

Good luck and good hunting.
Steve Hodel, LAPD (ret.)
Los Angeles, California
January 2005

Additional Investigative Means and Methods for Suspect Development

Time and changes in relationships as well as technology are the primary solvability factors identified in the successful resolution of cold case homicides. Many of these topics discussed in victim and witness development in this chapter are applicable to further suspect development. As the suspect is recognized, many of these investigative avenues may prove useful to the investigation.

In addition to re-examination of evidence and use of databases such as Combined DNA Index System (CODIS) and Automated Fingerprint Identification System (AFIS)/Integrated AFIS (IAFIS), other means and methods may assist the cold case investigator. These include:

- Wiretaps
- Off-line National Crime Information Center (NCIC) checks
- Law enforcement criminal intelligence services at local, state, and federal level
- Law enforcement computer databases
- Corrections institution/incarceration records
- Corrections institution staff interviews
- Psychological profiling and behavioral assessment
- Cellmate informants and street informants
- Accomplices and co-defendants in prior criminal activity
- Internet searches
- Physical surveillance
- Use of Grand Jury
- Federal Organized Crime Statutes
- Undercover operations
- Search warrants
    - Home and work computer
    - Telephone records
    - Cell phone records
    - Social media footprints

When investigating crime, remember crime is like water. Crooks, for the most part, are inherently lazy. Like water, they will take the path of least resistance. Don't make more out of a particular crime than it is. The easiest answer, that makes sense, is usually the answer.

– Tony Leal, former Texas Ranger

Interview Considerations

Once the suspect has been identified, and located, several considerations occur as investigators attempt to conduct an interview, or to effect arrest.

Chief among these is a consideration of arrest *then* interview, or interview and *then* followed with arrest. At this stage of the investigation the interview process should involve both law enforcement and prosecutorial perspectives. Department policy may subscribe parameters, and each has its own perspective and concerns although ultimately the same result.

Law Enforcement Perspective

- Is the interview *within* the investigating agency jurisdiction or outside, including out of state?
    - If out of state or jurisdiction, arrangements must be made with appropriate authorities
    - Contact strategy
        - Direct approach
        - Indirect approach (i.e., the Freiburger case study)
    - Availability of surreptitious video or recording devices
- Type of setting for interview (formal or informal)
- Recording or video options (including agency/legal requirements) or availability
- Custodial Interview. Arrest and then interview with possibility of suspect invoking Miranda Rights
- Non-custodial interview
    - Further inculpatory statements that may conflict with previous statements
    - Observations and appraisal of demeanor and the person
    - Negative statements
    - Admissions or confession
- Use of *forensic* psychologist or behavioral analysis to frame interview questions, techniques, and tactics
- Strategize how to approach suspect
- Strategize WHO will interview suspect
    - Selection of investigator most likely to elicit suspect's cooperation and not alienate suspect from the start. As an example, perhaps it would not be wise to utilize an African American investigator to interview a White Supremacist. Or would it?
    - Interviewer must be thoroughly familiar with *all* aspects of the case

Strategize Interview and Interrogation

- Determine suspect's interview style. Identify and interview previous authorities who have interviewed suspect to see how he reacts. What "pushes his buttons" and what does not
    - Police officers and investigators
    - Probation and parole officers
    - Former prosecutor insight
    - Pull all prior reports and read interviews
    - Former psych reports
    - Listen to previous interview tapes

    - Determine what works and what does not
        - Confrontation
        - Accusation
        - Bluff—be careful!
        - Use of props such as photo of
            - Victim
            - Crime scene
            - Grave
- Suspect's interview and interrogation history
    - How many arrests?
    - Circumstances?
    - Locations?
    - Custodial or non-custodial?
    - When/how long ago was suspect's last interview or law enforcement contact?
- Time span since crime
    - Suspect's lifestyle then/now
    - Stability as expressed through family, relationships, religion, children, and career
    - Known or identified medical/mental conditions
    - Known criminal history since the cold case homicide
- Methods that have appeared to be successful

The element of Surprise is a prime consideration for a successful interview.

Prosecution Perspective

- Ideally would like (recorded) admissions or confession with corroborating evidence
- Must consider additional evidence admissibility problems due to passage of time
- Must consider how suspect's post-crime behavior may affect jury. If suspect went on to become a respectable member of the community, church, and family figure, prosecutor must keep jury focused on the *deed* and *accountability*
- May strongly conflict with police perspective

Arrest Considerations

Most law enforcement agencies have guidelines, policies, and procedures for arrest and apprehension of suspects in violent crimes. If the arrest is to occur within your jurisdiction, you would most likely invoke normal arrest procedures. This is an area where history of the case and investigation, and post-crime behavior coupled with investigator experience and perceptions influences how, when, and where the arrest is to be made. These options may range from negotiated surrender to high-risk entry tactics. In this arrest situation, you would consider potential:

- Hazard assessment
    - Time of day or night
    - Type of location
    - Firearms
    - Possibility of pursuit
    - Neighbors
    - Pedestrian or other vehicular traffic
    - Hostage potential
- Tactical plan
    - Totality of knowledge of the suspect, previous arrest history, propensity for fight or flight
    - Assistance from specialized units, allied investigation agency, or neighboring agency
    - Surveillance and reconnaissance of suspect and location
    - Approach. Best method to minimize hazards and execute surprise
    - Communications systems
    - Availability of ambulance and medical personnel
    - Briefing and personnel assignment
    - Coordination
    - Execution of plan
- Cold case considerations
    - Advanced age and potential medical condition of suspect and wife
    - Search warrant (sealed until service to minimize leaks)
        - Documents and memorabilia pertaining to the crime
        - Documents to establish identity as same person in original investigation
        - Documents that show dominion and control of residence or location
        - Diaries, records, letters, notes correspondence that may indicate suspect knowledge of victim or relationship, or commission of the crime
        - Travel and movement documents
        - Documents that exhibit suspect's original handwriting
        - Documents or photos that show interest in any aspects of the crime, i.e., bondage, torture, etc.
        - Photos of subject then and now
        - Firearms and ammunition or other weapons
        - DNA
        - Other items particularly related to the offense

Case Study—Wilkerson

El Cajon is a bedroom community along the interstate highway that runs east out of San Diego, California. The city has long maintained its own police department, as have many similar communities in the region, including neighboring La Mesa. The larger San Diego Police Department and county sheriff's office border these small Southern California departments in a patchwork of jurisdictional boundaries. On June 6, 1965, a 19-year-old mother was murdered in her bottom floor apartment in El Cajon. She had been out with friends until approximately midnight, and one of these friends stayed with her until approximately 3:00 a.m. Before dawn, an intruder entered through a sliding glass door and beat her with a cocktail-mix bottle. He then used a drapery cord cut (see Figure 3.6) from a living room window to strangle the victim, and then raped her. The victim was left in a "staged" position, with candles left to burn in a "last rite" orientation and a candle was inserted into her vagina. The apartment was ransacked, although there was no sign of a struggle. The contents of the victim's purse were dumped on the living room floor, although cash and jewelry were not taken. The only items taken were a camera and a crucifix.

The homicide was discovered when neighbors saw the victim's young son wandering outside her apartment the next morning. She was found partially sprawled across the corner of her bed, and her legs kept her propped up off the floor. Evidence recovered at the scene indicated that she had been sexually assaulted, and that evidence decades later provided a DNA profile. While processing the crime scene, investigators recovered the ligature, and it was booked into evidence. There it remained for over three decades.

Two weeks later, on June 23, a husband, age 63, and his 57-year-old wife were preparing for bed in their apartment when an intruder entered the residence. Armed with a long-handled socket wrench (see Figure 4.7) he had stolen in a vehicle burglary a short time before, he beat the husband to death, raped the wife, and beat her viciously with the wrench before leaving her for dead. An open jar of hand cream was next to her, and cream smeared about her vagina. Her legs were doubled underneath her with the heels of her feet resting on her buttocks and her legs spread apart. She was found about 20 hours later when neighbors heard her moans and cries. Numerous individuals were investigated and cleared, but despite the best efforts of numerous detectives and other personnel, no suspects were identified. Serology and fingerprints (see Figure 4.8) were the two primary means of identification utilized at this time, and no leads were developed. The socket wrench was released to its owner, and the other evidence was boxed up and put into storage.

The next month, a man in a nearby community of La Mesa reported to police that his son had seen a suspicious man emerging from some bushes. When asked what he was doing, the man replied that he was looking for his lighter. The boy did not believe him and told his father. They copied the license number from the man's red Triumph and called police. Not long after, a similar looking man was seen near a red Triumph in La Mesa outside the apartment of a 23-year-old nurse. Before dawn, the nurse heard noises within her apartment and dialed the Operator. The suspect broke into her apartment and attempted to rape and murder her. As she fought him off, the Operator heard the fight and called police, but the suspect was gone on arrival. Based on the boy's observation and witness information regarding the red Triumph, Clyde Wilkerson, a recently released parolee, was brought in for questioning.

Wilkerson was arrested and charged for this crime after the victim positively identified him as her assailant. Although questioned in the two homicides and rapes, there was no evidence to link him to these crimes. He was convicted on the La Mesa offense in November 1965 and sentenced to 5 years to life in prison (see Figure 4.9). He subsequently paroled to Oklahoma in 1973.

In the meantime, the homicide cases remained unsolved.

In 1997, El Cajon Police Department (ECPD) Lieutenant Pat Sprecco began to assign some of the older, unsolved crimes to investigators. He believed that advanced forensic technology might assist in resolving some of these crimes. In January 1999, Detective John Wooddell received the homicide case of the young mother. Sometime after, Detective Robert Anderson observed a box of news clippings about the case of the older couple and began reading them. Neither case file contained a *death certificate* for the victims (see Chapter 9). Their reviews of the cases, however, had to be accomplished while carrying their normal case load and other assigned duties. While each began working their respective cases separately, they soon had reason to believe they might be connected. During their review of the evidence, they found that items were co-mingled between the two cases, suggesting that earlier detectives had considered them linked. Wilkerson was the apparent linchpin.

During this review, they encountered a situation not uncommon in cold case investigation. Although items were individually tagged and bagged, some from one case were mixed with the other case. Loose reports, photographs, correspondence, and other material were dumped into boxes and there was no apparent chain of custody. Some pages of some reports were lost and never found. During this process, Anderson contacted other agencies mentioned in the reports to ascertain if they possessed related documents (see Figure 2.9). The district attorney's office still retained reports, as did the Probation Department. In addition, the California Department of Justice retained important documents and reports.

The detectives began by putting everything on a table and sorting the two cases. In this process, they began to re-assemble the record *chronologically.* As they reviewed the reports, they observed a lack of uniformity in reporting. Reports were handwritten or typed (misspellings not infrequent), and there was a noticeable lack of identifying information to be used in their efforts to re-locate persons. Thermofax paper documents were fading badly, and onion skin carbon paper documents were fragile to handle. In addition, certain report entries were not "politically correct" by today's standards, with detectives' opinions freely inserted into the reports. In those days, suspects were not "alleged." Like the photos, the case was black and white to some earlier investigators, but the focus ultimately shifted with the later investigation.

The *photo review* similarly showed investigative actions far different from today. Officers handled crime scene evidence without gloves (see Figure 3.6) or stood in the middle of the crime scene smoking a cigarette while the picture was taken. The photos were more generally more overall than specific in nature. Similarly, crime scene sketches and diagrams were lacking by today's standards (see Figure 4.10). The sketches showed no measurements or other detail, but for the present, did provide an overview of the scene as encountered by responding investigators.

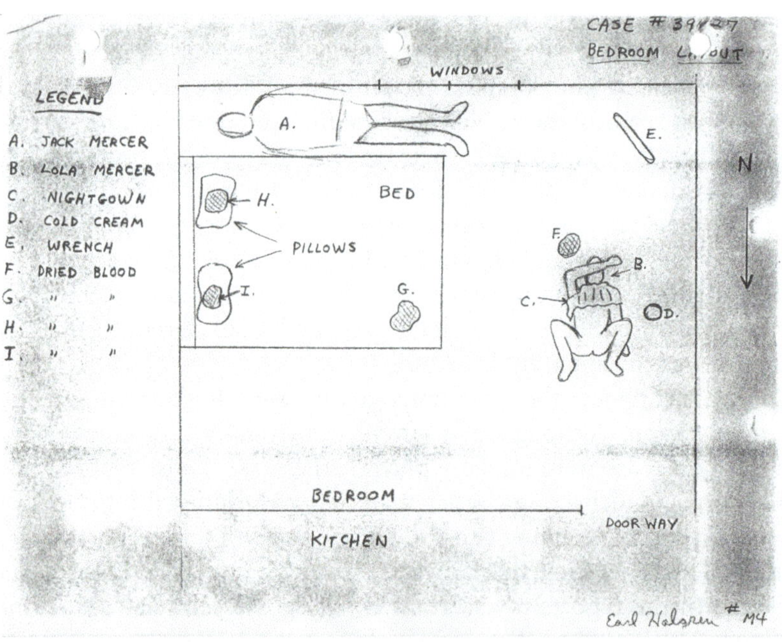

Figure 4.10 Crime scene sketch. Like other sketches of the period, no measurements were included on the sketch. This sketch, when combined with the minimal number of photographs, does depict the crime scene. (Courtesy of Anderson/ECPD.)

During their review and investigation to locate persons and documents, Anderson discovered that *city engineers* had subsequently diagramed the scene. These drawings had been entered into evidence (see Figure 3.5). Thus, the investigators recovered more detailed drawings to supplement the photo record, and which could be utilized to more accurately reconstruct the scene. Although they were unable to locate the engineer who drew the diagrams, they did locate his supervisor, who was able to *authenticate* the period work as a course-of-business document.

An additional record of the crime and investigation was discovered when Wooddell contacted the media and discovered that a local television station still retained film footage from broadcasts of the period. As this was previously aired material, the station converted the footage to a video tape and furnished it to the investigators. A similar review of the newspapers was conducted by Anderson. Microfilm copies were located, and many hours were spent in the library reviewing old newspaper reports, to identify overlooked witnesses and information, as well as to learn what was in the public domain. Some of the newspaper reports provided better witness identification than did the police reports, as reporters interviewed neighbors and reported in the detail of the period. Not unlike today. These were copied and placed in the file.

The investigators continued to search for original persons who figured in the initial investigations. They located and brought on board *original detectives* who were elated at the re-investigation of their original, unsolved cases. Among those contacted was one detective who had interviewed Clyde Wilkerson in 1965. In addition, they located the boy who had observed Wilkerson emerge from the bushes, a grown man now living in his father's same house as in 1965.

Like other smaller agencies, the El Cajon department utilized the San Diego County Sheriff's department crime laboratory to conduct forensic examinations. Very early in the investigation, the detectives consulted with a DNA specialist in the Sheriff's Crime Lab, Criminalist Connie Milton. Anderson was interested in DNA recovered from his crime scene. He had read the reports that earlier detectives suspected Clyde Wilkerson and wanted to locate him to obtain a sample of his DNA. At this stage of the investigation, the two detectives were in constant contact, yet handled aspects of their own investigations independently as time allowed.

Review of the remaining case file indicated that period investigators had suspected family members of the couple, and reports indicated that polygraph examinations had been utilized to clear them (the actual polygraph reports were not found in the file). The polygraph examinations had been administered by police officers and not by State Department of Justice personnel as was often the case during this time for smaller agencies. Similarly, the polygraph was mentioned as being used in the young mother's case, but further documentation was again lacking.

In Wooddell's investigation, events were a bit more complicated. During the file review and investigation, cold case investigators seek to develop as much information on the victim as they can, and to learn more through the *victimology.* They attempt to identify anything the victim may have done that contributed to their victimization, and subsequently, to the identification of the perpetrator. While the more elderly couple's case was an apparent "whodunit," the victim's family was fully cooperative in the investigation. In Wooddell's case, the cooperation was less. The little boy found wandering outside the crime scene was now an ex-con, and when located, did not want anything to do with police or the investigation. "Let it be," he told investigators.

In addition, Wooddell's investigation revealed that some earlier detectives had a different prime suspect, a Catholic priest. Apparently, the young mother was being tutored in catechism. The priest, an alcoholic, had made comments to various persons in the bars he frequented that he was responsible for her death. When word of this reached period detectives, they began to focus on him as a suspect. "*Responsible*" equated in some minds to "*I killed her.*" The earlier detectives tried relentlessly to pursue the church representative, without success. He repeatedly denied that he killed her, and ultimately, the church transferred the priest to another locale outside the easy reach of local law enforcement. The man died in 1972, and the question remained for cold case investigators decades later—was he the guilty person? There was one way to find out: DNA.

A *forensic exhumation* is a legal process to dis-inter a body, and this process is presented in future chapters (see Chapter 22). Early in the investigation, the investigators had involved deputy district attorney Dan Lamborn in their investigation effort. Detective Wooddell sought a court order to exhume the body, and this was accomplished. DNA *excluded*, once and for all, the priest as a source of the DNA in the victim. In addition, it was also necessary to dis-inter the other victims as well, and permission was granted by family members in lieu of court action. As in similar cases, there were other suspects, and these were tracked down and tested, with negative results. Slowly, everyone was eliminated except for Clyde Wilkerson.

Wilkerson was a career criminal: one we now recognize as a serial killer. He had a lengthy rap sheet and the only time he was not committing crimes was when he was in custody for previous offenses. A long-distance truck driver, Wilkerson's livelihood took him all around the nation, and to this day, there is no way of knowing how many other murders he is responsible for. He was arrested in Oklahoma in 1973 on suspicion of robbery, although charges were later dropped, and in April 1976, convicted and sentenced for rape in Arkansas. After serving 7 years in prison, he was paroled in 1983.

In June 1985, he was arrested in Texas on suspicion of aggravated assault, and in March 1987, convicted of selling a controlled substance in Florida and sentenced to 3 years in prison, including time for violating parole.

As he began to focus on Wilkerson, Anderson formulated a *timeline* to assist in the investigation (see Figure 4.11a and b).

TIMELINES, LINKAGES, AND VISUAL INVESTIGATIVE ANALYSIS CHARTS

A useful and valuable tool in many situations, a timeline is an asset in homicide cases, perhaps even more so in cold case homicide investigations. These cases often involve developing, and understanding, an abundance of dates, times, events, places, and more. In a hot homicide scenario, investigators develop the information firsthand and absorb it as it happens. In a cold case investigation, the information is contained not only in the often volumes of reports and other files, but also in the development of the investigation. Timelines and Visual Investigative Analysis (VIA) charts can show the linkages, time flows, and relationship between people, places, and events, and aid in the visual informational reconstruction. They can take an apparent unconnected series of events and graphically illustrate a clear visual picture of the entire case, relating apparently unrelated events and activities. Such aids can illuminate an individual's presence, or motive. This method can highlight missing details and information and show investigators where to focus their efforts to fill these gaps. They can help reduce duplication of effort and increase investigative efficiency. In addition, they are highly effective for prosecutor and court presentations.

The concept of VIA reportedly originated in the mid-1960s by the Los Angeles Police Department, the source of many advanced law enforcement concepts and techniques. This notion evolved from previous approaches, the Critical Path Method (CPM) and the Program Evaluation and Review Techniques (PERT). The VIA idea was picked up by the California Department of Justice and the Federal Law Enforcement Training Center at Glynco, Georgia, and has now become a standard investigative tool. VIA methods involving the concept of networking were first incorporated in a major criminal investigation because of the Robert Kennedy assassination in 1968, and in the early 1970s in the still-unsolved Zodiac killings of the late 1960s and early 1970s.

Timelines may be especially useful in understanding victim and suspect movements and how they converge.

The ability to construct useful timelines has been enhanced greatly by computers. What was once done on legal pads or rolls of butcher paper—and found in older cold case files—is now accomplished on desktop computer software (see Figure 4.12). The sources of information for detailed time and date entries can include:

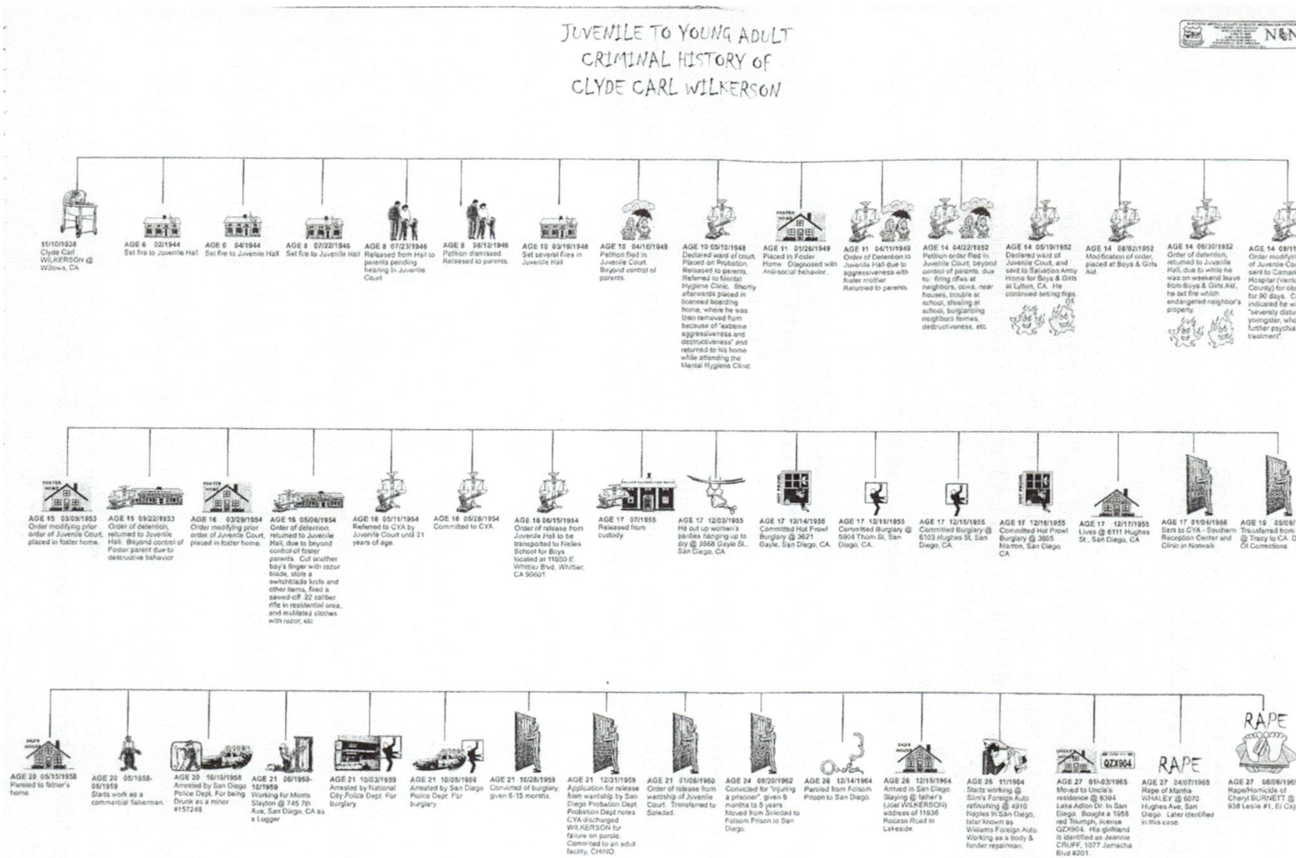

Figure 4.11 (a) and (b) Clyde Wilkerson timeline. Timelines are an invaluable tool for investigators, prosecutors, AND juries. They illustrate, and illuminate, more than words can say. (Courtesy of FBI.)

Figure 4.12 Clue Management Program. The Los Angeles County Sheriff's Department provides free software to law enforcement agencies to assist in clue management. This program is well suited to cold case homicide investigation. (Courtesy of Detective Gerry Biehn, Los Angeles County Sheriff Unsolved Unit.)

- Law enforcement reports
- Booking sheets
- Witness statements
- Probation and parole documents
- Rap sheets
- Telephone and cell phone records
- Residence locations
- Employment records
- Trip logs
- In-custody records
- Public utility records
- Traffic/parking tickets
- Driver's license
- Department of motor vehicle registrations and related documents
- Receipts (motel, gas, grocery, etc.)
- Suspect statements
- Diaries, notes, and journals
- Accomplice and informant information

As the detectives discovered, Wilkerson began his life of crime at an early age, displaying behavior that later criminal profilers would come to identify as not uncommon among violent predators. This included setting fires and mutilating animals. Much of his teen years was spent in juvenile reformatories and foster homes. Every event and every known movement were now being compiled into a timeline that chronicled the life and movements of Clyde Wilkerson. Overviews provided investigators with a profile of his life, and specific timelines such as monthly trucking route, broken down by date, time, and location, were compiled (see Figure 4.13).

TEXAS

Date	Time	Location-City	State	Date	Time	Location-City	State
09/03/99	21:36:00	Waxzahachie	TX	12/05/99	5:38:00	Horizon Cy	TX
09/03/99	22:32:00	Waxahachie	TX	12/05/99	10:11:00	Saragosa	TX
09/03/99	22:40:00	Red Oak	TX	12/05/99	15:02:00	Ingram	TX
09/14/99	5:10:00	Horizon Cy	TX	12/06/99	5:21:00	Kirby	TX
09/14/99	10:36:00	Van Horn	TX	12/06/99	7:33:00	San Antonio	TX
09/14/99	15:44:00	Sweetwater	TX	12/06/99	10:48:00	Kirby	TX
09/15/99	0:11:00	Weatherford	TX	12/06/99	15:35:00	San Antonio	TX
09/15/99	1:19:00	Blue Mound	TX	12/06/99	15:56:00	Kirby	TX
09/15/99	7:53:00	Ft Worth	TX	12/06/99	19:18:00	San Antonio	TX
09/15/99	9:03:00	Ft Worth	TX	12/06/99	19:46:00	Kirby	TX
09/15/99	11:35:00	Rockwall	TX	12/07/99	5:58:00	Sealy	TX
09/20/99	15:30:00	Cumby	TX	12/07/99	9:44:00	Hilshire V	TX
09/20/99	19:33:00	Rockwall	TX	12/07/99	10:46:00	Houston	TX
09/21/99	7:14:00	Irving	TX	12/08/99	5:21:00	Marshall	TX
09/21/99	13:18:00	Irving	TX	12/10/99	5:16:00	Amarillo	TX
09/21/99	13:33:00	Mesquite	TX	12/17/99	5:50:00	Carthage	TX
09/21/99	15:06:00	Rockwall	TX	12/17/99	7:34:00	Burke	TX
09/21/99	15:27:00	CadoMills	TX	12/17/99	9:47:00	Hillshire V	TX
10/08/99	10:28:00	Alanreed	TX	12/17/99	16:45:00	Houston	TX
10/16/99	7:23:00	Post	TX	12/17/99	16:47:00	Hilshire V	TX
10/16/99	9:11:00	Hermleigh	TX	12/17/99	17:49:00	Jacinto Cy	TX
10/16/99	15:13:00	Elgin	TX	01/16/00	5:41:00	Amarillo	TX
10/17/99	10:16:00	Houston	TX	03/09/00	10:01:00	Tyler	TX
10/18/99	10:00:00	Heights	TX	03/09/00	11:27:00	Tyler	TX
10/18/99	11:24:00	Houston	TX	03/09/00	15:56:00	Strawn	TX
10/18/99	13:49:00	Cheek	TX	03/10/00	5:52:00	Pecos	TX
11/07/99	0:00:00	Amarillo	TX	03/10/00	8:47:00	Van Horn	TX
				03/10/00	10:56:00	Horizon Cy	TX

Figure 4.13 Timeline. Timelines are constructed from multiple sources of information and may portray a period of 1 day to weeks to months or years and decades.

As his profile developed, Anderson sought interstate assistance from the San Diego office of the FBI. The FBI and U.S. Marshal's Service are excellent cold case homicide investigative resources, and team members often sit on agency or regional cold case task forces.

Locating suspects can sometimes be difficult, at other times relatively easy. Based upon case file information for suspected places he might reside, Anderson conducted a driver's license search of various states where Wilkerson might be licensed—if he was still alive. When they located him, he was 62 years old and living in Arkansas.

Investigation revealed that Wilkerson had long been employed as an Arkansas-based truck driver. Anderson obtained a court order for employment records, and with FBI assistance obtained Wilkerson's employment application and route invoices. Then Arkansas agent inquired whether the company still retained any envelopes in which Wilkerson had mailed their invoices. They did.

Anderson conducted a further background check on Wilkerson, one that sought to determine any *relationships* that may now yield information about the crimes. Anderson located and interviewed the officers who had interviewed Wilkerson's Oklahoma rape victim, but when he attempted to interview a relative of Wilkerson, the door was slammed in his face.

Chain-of-custody documentation and collection protocols have evolved significantly over the past decades, and while reviewing the evidence, Detective Anderson had discovered a thermos bottle that they suspected contained original cotton swabs. Unopened, for fear of contaminating any potential evidence, the thermos was sent to the FBI lab. Like many investigations nationwide, events of 911 impacted many facets of police work, and changed the priorities for FBI operations. This investigation was no different, and ultimately, the thermos was returned unopened. Wooddell re-contacted Criminalist Milton.

When reviewing the original forensic reports, Milton had not suspected any usable evidence to remain. The method used in rape examinations during the time of the crimes was no longer even a part of a modern sexual assault examination. She considered that, for lack of another container, an examining physician had emptied his thermos and stored evidence in it. It was not the usual evidence container, even then.

Inside the thermos were glass vials containing cotton swabs and a dried residue (see Figure 4.14). Examination revealed the presence of sperm, but the source of the sperm was unknown. After more than 30 years, Connie Milton extracted and typed the DNA. Although Wilkerson had been questioned after both rapes and murders, there had not been enough evidence to link him to the crime scenes at the time.

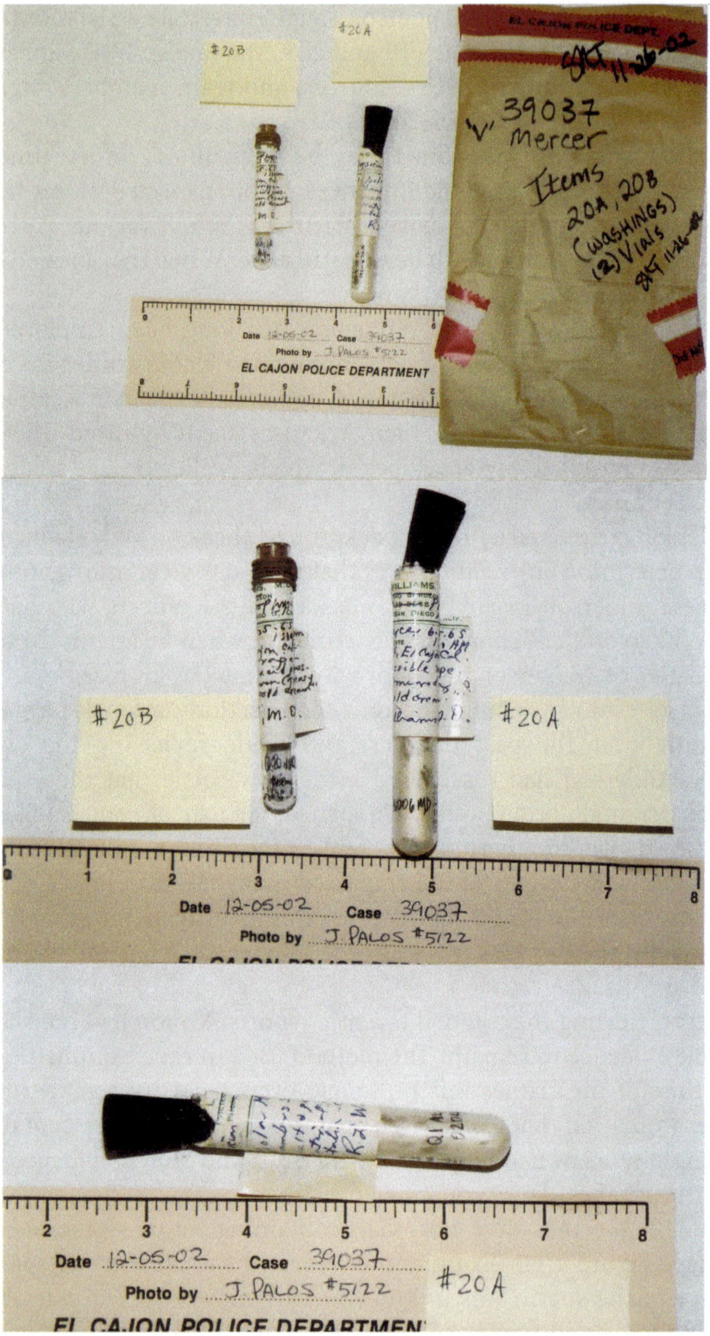

Figure 4.14 These 1965 vials containing cotton swabs were recovered in a coffee thermos that had been used to contain them for over 30 years. Criminalist Connie Milton was able to extract and type DNA, closing the forensic net on serial killer Clyde Wilkerson. (Courtesy of Anderson/ECPD.)

Criminalist Milton had previously processed the semen evidence found on the bed sheet collected at the scene from where the young mother was raped and murdered. On a Saturday afternoon, she made the match. She now had the DNA from the trucking company envelopes as well as from the murder of the couple and the young mother. Clyde Wilkerson was the common denominator among the samples from the victims as well as the trucking company envelopes.

The case had taken over 37 years to reach this point. Technology had now enabled law enforcement to make an identification from sources almost a nation, and decades, apart. It had taken 3 years to complete the re-investigation, one complicated by a process of eliminating numerous other potential suspects as the focus narrowed on Wilkerson.

Not unheard of in cold cases, Anderson and Wooddell were only a couple of years old at the time of the crime, and those who collected the evidence decades before were now quite elderly or deceased. This case was no different in that regard. Milton had not even been born when the murders occurred. Her skills, however, now identified Wilkerson's DNA print as having been at both crime scenes. The frequency of occurrence of this DNA profile for Caucasian males was now estimated at one in 57 quadrillion.

An arrest warrant was obtained, and the detectives, Deputy District Attorney Lamborn, District Attorney Investigator Steve Baker, and the San Diego-based FBI agent, traveled to Benton, Arkansas. With the cooperation of local authorities, Wilkerson was arrested without incident on his rural property on October 29, 2002 (Figure 4.15). Time had not improved his social behavior, however, and arresting officers discovered a small methamphetamine lab when he was taken into custody (Figure 4.16).

Post-Arrest Interview

In cold cases, investigators have the advantage of being able to compile background history on an identified suspect and to study all aspects of the crime. As have other cold case killers, Wilkerson claimed no memory of the events, admitting that *if* he had committed these vicious crimes, he would surely have remembered. "If you get arrested, you remember it. If you don't get arrested, you don't," he said. As far as any other crimes, he told them, they would have to prove that on their own and stopped talking.

During the arrest period, identification and interview of those who know the suspect is a suggested tactic. At the time of Wilkerson's arrest, District Attorney Investigator Steve Baker interviewed a tenant who resided on Wilkerson's property. On his own, the tenant then contacted Wilkerson in jail. He asked Wilkerson if he had committed the crimes. "Yeah, but it took 'em 37 years to catch me," the tenant later reported his landlord had said.

Wilkerson was returned to San Diego. On March 17, 2003, almost 40 years after his crime spree, Clyde Carl Wilkerson pled guilty in a plea agreement

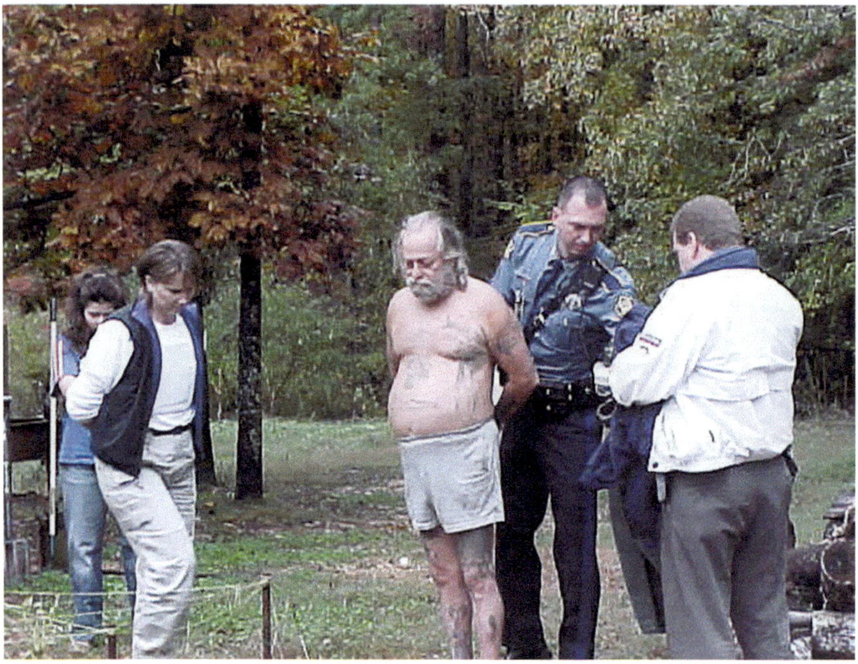

Figure 4.15 Clyde Wilkerson at his arrest. Thanks to the efforts of detectives, prosecutors, and criminalists, a serial killer's decades-long rampage came to an end. Wilkerson was arrested and subsequently pled guilty to one 1965 California murder as well as a 1975 Oklahoma murder. The investigation into his activities has continued. (Courtesy of El Cajon Police Department, California.)

to the murder of the husband and rape against his wife. Under the law *at the time of the murder* in 1965, Wilkerson could only be sentenced to 7 years to life in prison. The other charges were not pursued as he would receive no additional prison time and would most likely die in prison for this offense.

CONTINUING THE INVESTIGATION—THE INTERNET

The investigation into Wilkerson's decades-long crime spree did not end with his arrest and return to San Diego. Detective Robert Anderson believed that Wilkerson was responsible for more murders and set out to identify other unsolved cases that fit Wilkerson's M.O. when he was not in custody. Such is the mark of a true detective. Wilkerson was already suspect in another unsolved San Diego homicide from July 1965, as well as a 1954 Los Angeles area murder and attempted murder.

On his own time, from his home computer, Detective Anderson began to search the internet and the web pages of law enforcement agencies and unsolved homicides. He discovered that the Tulsa, Oklahoma, Police Department had an unsolved rape-homicide of a junior college student from

Figure 4.16 Low-budget meth lab. Officers recovered this setup at the time of Wilkerson's arrest. (Courtesy of Det. Anderson, El Cajon Police Department, California.)

February 1975. The victim had been abducted from the parking lot of her downtown campus, and her body was found 3 weeks later in a vacant apartment. She had been raped and strangled. The victim suffered numerous facial injuries due to blunt force trauma and both nipples and areolas had been amputated postmortem, with one each inserted into her vagina. The official cause of death was ligature strangulation. The victim's clothes, jewelry, purse, checkbook, and other identification were missing. A day after the victim was reported missing, a white male cashed one of her checks and attempted to use one of her credit cards in the Tulsa area. Evidence seized from the crime scene provided a DNA profile of the offender.

Anderson contacted the Oklahoma agency, and because of his diligence and tenacity, the authorities there re-opened their unsolved case. DNA linked Wilkerson to this crime, and on April 28, 2004, Clyde Carl Wilkerson pled guilty to the Oklahoma crime and was sentenced to life in prison. His prison time was to run concurrently with his California sentence. Under the California law at the time of the offense, Wilkerson was eligible for parole after 6 years, and after 20 years in Oklahoma. Wilkerson died in prison in 2016.

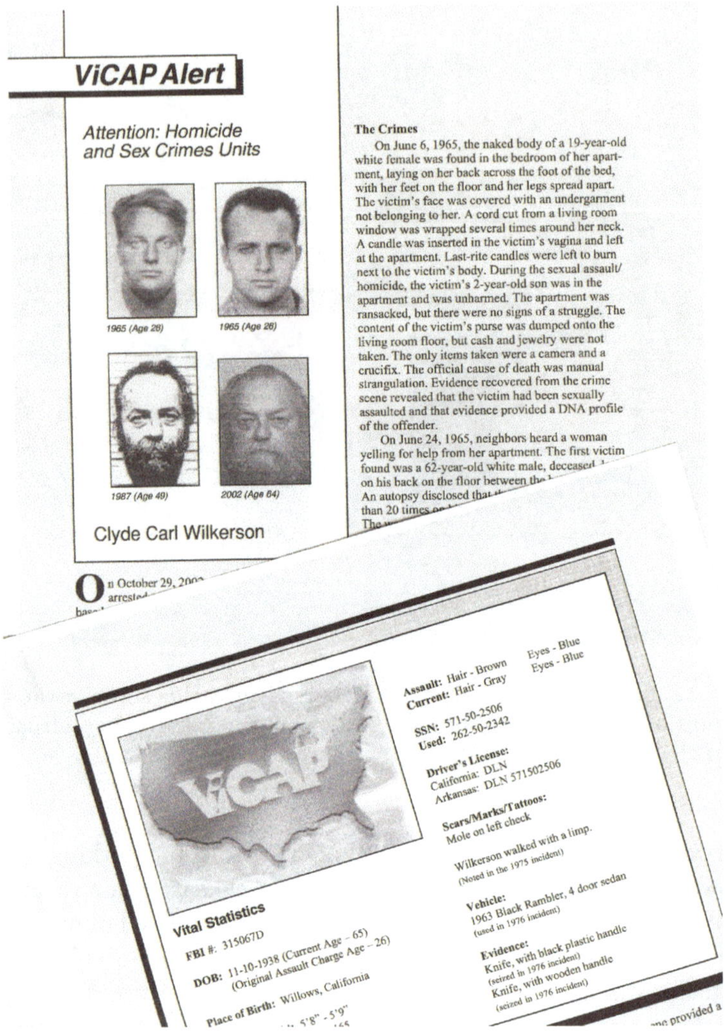

Figure 4.17 ViCAP Alert for Clyde Carl Wilkerson. Wilkerson is a poster child for the need of this agency and similar state programs. The more law enforcement learns about people like this, and communicates this knowledge, the better the chances that killers such as Wilkerson will be identified and removed from society. (Picture from author's file from ViCAP Alert in FBI Law Enforcement Bulletin.)

Due to the serious crimes and his interstate movements, Wilkerson was the subject of a Violent Criminal Apprehension Program (ViCAP) Alert in the FBI Law Enforcement Bulletin in August 2003 (Figure 4.17). This notice to the nation's law enforcement community detailed events of his numerous crimes, including method of operation, personal identifying information, known vehicles, and evidence. It was disseminated to alert law enforcement to Wilkerson's existence so that local agencies could review any unsolved homicides or other crimes in light of what was now known about him.

The ViCAP Alert provided additional detail regarding Wilkerson's M.O., and further information may be obtained from the FBI's ViCAP. Wilkerson's DNA profile has been entered into CODIS.

Conclusion

The means and methods of cold case homicide investigation are based upon the crime, evidence, original investigation, and subsequent events. Each cold case must be weighed and evaluated on its own merits. *How to* proceed is based upon the experience, training, and best investigative plan as conceived by the investigator or investigative team. Different cases call for different tactics and there can be no one "best way." The investigation of these cases exploits the advantage of time as it is primarily revealed through changes in relationships and changes in technology. Various tools are at the disposal of the cold case investigator, and the combination of these factors has allowed some cold cases to be solved. Not all will be solved, however, and many will be re-shelved as unsolved, cold case homicides.

We wish to express our deepest gratitude and appreciation to Captain Joseph Hartshorne and the late Sergeant Richard Longshore of the Los Angeles County Sheriff's Department as well as Detective Tim Marcia (Ret.) and Detective Rick Jackson (Ret.) of the Cold Case Unit of the Robbery-Homicide Division of the Lost Angeles Police Department for sharing their thoughts and experiences and suggestions for this chapter. In addition, we wish to also recognize and extend our deepest gratitude to former Texas Ranger Lieutenant Tony Leal for sharing his thoughts and perspectives on cold case homicide investigation.

The investigation of Clyde Wilkerson by Detectives Anderson and Wooddell exemplifies the highest abilities of cold case investigators. Their teamwork with Criminalist Connie Milton, Deputy District Attorney Dan Lamborn, the FBI, and others exemplifies the results of team effort applied to cold case investigation. In addition, we wish to acknowledge the leadership of the ECPD for their proactive efforts in identifying and re-investigating unsolved, cold case homicides.

The case history was compiled by extensive interviews with Detectives Anderson and Wooddell and Criminalist Milton, and review of case records. In addition, we wish to acknowledge Mr. Paul Levikov of the San Diego county District Attorney's Office and his report "How a Thermos Helped Catch a Killer" in the Winter-Spring 2003–2004 edition of *Law Enforcement Quarterly*.

Suggested Reading

Anonymous. (2002). *Cold case homicide.* Sacramento, CA, C.P.T. Network, Commission on Peace Officer Standards and Training.

Anonymous. (August 2003). ViCAP alert. *FBI Law Enforcement Bulletin.* Vol. 72, No. 8.

Eliopulos, L. N. (2003). *Death investigator's handbook: Expanded and updated edition.* Boulder, CO, Paladin Press.

Geberth, V. (1996). *Practical homicide investigation: Tactics, procedures, and forensic techniques.* (3rd Ed.). New York, CRC Press.

Jackson, I. M. (October 30, 2002). 1965 crime spree may be solved. *San Diego Union.* Vol. A1, p. 9.

Jackson, I. M. (March 18, 2003). Plea is guilty in '65 rape, murder. *San Diego Union-Tribune*, March 18, 2003, Section B, p. B-3.

Johnson, R. S. (1995). *How to locate anyone who is or has been in the military.* San Antonio, TX, MIE Publishing.

Lee, H. C., Palmbach, T., and Miller, M. (2001). *Henry Lee's crime scene handbook.* New York, Academic Press.

Levikow, P. (2003–2004). Special report: How a thermos helped catch a killer. *Law Enforcement Quarterly.*

Newcombe, B. (1990). *Paper trails: A guide to public records in California.* Oakland, CA, Center for Investigative Reporting, California Newspaper Publisher's Association.

Nyberg, R. (October, 2004). Justice served cold. Police. *The Law Enforcement Magazine*. Vol. 28, No. 10. p. 44.

Poole, H., and Jurovics, S. (March, 1993). MUST: A team for unsolved homicides. *FBI Law Enforcement Bulletin*. Vol. 62, No. 3, pp. 1–4.

Ray, D. (1995). *California investigator's handbook: A public records primer.* (6th Ed.). Burbank, CA, ENG Press.

Spraggs, D. (May, 2003). How to open a cold case. *Policemag.com.*

Turner, R., and Kosa, R. (July, 2003). *Cold case squads: Leaving no stone unturned.* Bulletin NCJ 199781. Washington, DC, Bureau of Justice Assistance.

Westvear, A. (unknown). *Death investigation.* Washington, DC, Federal Bureau of Investigation.

The Role of the Medical Examiner

5

LOUIS N. ELIOPULOS

Throughout their careers, investigators may have been exposed to working on cases with only a single pathologist. Depending on the investigator, some medical expertise may be somewhat limited; thus, they heavily rely on the information provided by the pathologist. Additionally, some investigators may hold the view that the education acquired by the pathologist in becoming a Doctor of Medicine supersedes any investigative expertise they have gained. Questioning a pathologist's findings is never seen as an option.

In this country, a limited number of certified pathologists are available for many vacant certified forensic pathologist positions. Like any other profession, many certified forensic pathologists are exceptionally qualified. However, some may be incompetent. Due to the many unfilled forensic pathologist positions, certain pathologists who have been found unqualified or have faced other issues resulting in their dismissal often return to practicing in another jurisdiction.

Medical examiners and coroners perform similar or overlapping roles, but have different histories, training, and qualification standards today.

Coroners investigate the cause and manner of death, often completing the death certificate. Across the U.S., coroners are typically elected laypeople who may or may not have medical training, depending on local laws. They may also be appointed and hold additional roles, such as law enforcement officers or prosecuting attorneys. Since coroners are often not pathologists, they must hire a forensic pathologist, usually through a contract, for autopsies and medical expertise to assist in their investigations.

A forensic autopsy is conducted under state laws to protect citizens, requiring authorization from the state. Generally, state statutes involve a medical examiner or coroner in investigating the following types of deaths:

- Deaths that occurred without medical supervision or when a physician is unable to determine the cause of death.
- Violent fatalities, including suicides, homicides, or accidents.
- Deaths that raise concerns of criminal activity.
- Deaths occurring while in police or correctional custody.
- Deaths that pose public health concerns or involve contagious diseases.

DOI: 10.4324/9781003415633-7

A forensic autopsy is performed for several reasons, including:

- To determine the cause and manner of death.
- To estimate the time of death.
- To identify, collect, and preserve evidence.
- To provide information to relevant parties.
- To protect the innocent and assist in the prosecution or defense of an individual for an action resulting in the death of an individual.
- To generate a factual, objective, and legal report involving the death of an individual.

The forensic pathologist will perform preliminary steps in preparation for the forensic autopsy. These steps will include:

- An examination of the body will be conducted before removing any clothing.
- The clothing, body, and hands will be protected against contamination.
- The pathologist will observe and assess the general condition of the body.
- A search for trace evidence before cleaning the body will be conducted.
- The pathologist will document any birthmarks, tattoos, bruises, and injuries, using an alternate light source if necessary.
- The autopsy examination should be properly documented through photography.
- Following crime scene photography protocols, photographs will be taken of all collected evidence before it is removed.

You will never appreciate a good forensic pathologist until you encounter a bad one! For this reason, a cold case investigator must be able to trust or question the medical and toxicological evidence presented in the case. If qualified and experienced, the investigator can assess the medical information as inadequate, incomplete, or incorrect. If the previous medical details are believed to be dubious, then the investigator must seek a trusted, reliable, and competent source to review the information and provide a more accurate assessment.

In a cold case investigation, the original pathologist may no longer be available for consultation due to retirement, disability, or death. In such cases, the current pathologist who has assumed responsibility for the same jurisdictional cases may offer updated guidance and opinions after thoroughly reviewing the file. The cold case detective may also choose to consult an outside pathologist or other experts to seek investigative advice.

Detectives and medical examiners frequently collaborate, especially in criminal investigations involving suspicious deaths or homicides. This partnership is essential for several reasons:

- *Gathering evidence*: Detectives depend on the insights of medical examiners concerning the cause and manner of death, which can significantly assist the investigation. The findings from the medical examiner may direct detectives to vital evidence or potential witnesses.
- *Autopsy reports*: Medical examiners conduct autopsies to establish the cause of death, offering crucial information for detectives. This involves identifying injuries, analyzing toxicology results, and determining the time of death.
- *Legal proceedings*: Both detectives and medical examiners can be involved in court cases. The medical examiner typically testifies as an expert witness regarding their findings, while detectives provide evidence and investigate the circumstances surrounding the death.
- *Crime scene analysis*: Detectives often collaborate with medical examiners at crime scenes to understand how the circumstances of the death relate to the larger context of the investigation. This teamwork is crucial for thoroughly understanding the case and ensuring justice is served.

The opportunity to commit a murder may bring out the importance of determining the postmortem interval or the time frame of death. Estimations based upon the cadaver's examination may assist investigators in refuting or corroborating the alibi of a person of interest. The time of death estimation, based upon scientific research, will usually include the following:

- Development of rigor mortis.
- Development of livor mortis.
- Temperature of the viscera.
- Digestive state of stomach contents.
- Condition of decomposition.
- Presence of insect activity.
- Evidence of plant growth on the remains.

Pathologists must understand the significance of the relevant details when estimating the time of death. For example, if entomological evidence is utilized, they must conduct or have performed the correct documenting and photographing of the insect activity on the body before collecting any specimens. Once completed, they should gather live and deceased insects, along with their casings, while documenting their locations and the specific areas of the body.

In addition to insect activity (Anthropophagy), the pathologist's examination of the remains should also include a description of postmortem artifacts, including:

- Artifacts of decomposition.
- Third-party artifacts.
- Animal activity (Anthropophagy).
- Medical treatment.
- Deliberate mutilation (dismemberment).
- Artifacts of the environment.
- Postmortem burning.
- Postmortem corrosion.
- Postmortem maceration.

The investigator should be aware of proper autopsy procedure. An appropriate and complete autopsy report should begin with the forensic pathologist conducting an external examination of the body. This should include the following information:

- Note the time and place of the autopsy examination.
    - apparent age,
    - height and weight,
    - state of nutrition,
    - scars,
    - tattoos,
    - color of eyes and hair,
    - state of dentition,
    - muscular development,
    - abnormalities,
    - deformities,
    - marks of hospitalization.
- Perform a detailed examination of injuries, noting size, shape, location, pattern, and relationship to anatomic landmarks.

At the direction of, or by the pathologist, photographs should be taken:

- To identify the deceased.
- To document injuries and their location (include a scale for comparison).
- To show the relationship between external and internal injuries.
- To demonstrate pathologic processes other than those of traumatic origins.

At the direction of, or by the pathologist, X-ray examination should be conducted:

- To locate bullets or other radiopaque objects.
- To identify victims.
- To document old and recent fractures, anatomic deformities, metallic foreign bodies, plates, nails, and screws from surgical procedures.

After the external examination is completed, the pathologist begins the internal examination of the remains, which consists of:

- A general examination of the head, neck, spine, thorax, and abdomen.
- The pathologist notes the course and direction of wound tracks within the body.
- The pathologist observes the relationship and conditions of the viscera.
- The pathologist initiates collecting and preserving any evidence, in addition to recovering and identifying foreign objects. All collected items should be labeled and properly preserved. The preserved specimens should be collected in appropriate containers under suitable conditions.
- The pathologist establishes the chain of evidence for all the collected items.

The decedent's clothing may require forensic examination prior to removal and following the autopsy examination. The standard protocol for this examination typically correlates defects in the clothing with bodily injuries and identifies areas of blood spatter. The pathologist or staff under the pathologist's direction will then secure the clothing in a protected and uncontaminated area and allow it to air-dry, if wet, before packaging it in suitable evidence collection bags.

The autopsy report should be organized as follows:

- External description.
- Evidence of injury, to include:
    - External injury.
    - Internal injury.
- Systems and organs.
- Special dissections and examinations.
- Brain and other organs.
- Microscopic examinations.
- Findings (diagnosis).
- Opinion as to the manner of death.
- Pathologist performing the autopsy examination signature.

Some Common Errors Made by Forensic Pathologists

If forced to provide investigators with an instant analysis while visiting a scene, the pathologist may provide incorrect information. Instead, the pathologist should wait until the completion of the autopsy before combining the information obtained from the scene visit to provide conclusive or definitive information. Scene visits should be utilized to establish basic information to assist the pathologist with the medical conclusions they may be responsible for providing in the investigation.

The pathologist should not assume the cause of death before the actual completion of the autopsy.

The pathologist should not confuse the time of death with the time of infliction of the fatal injury.

Interaction with Homicide Investigators

Whether investigating a current or cold case, homicide detectives must cultivate a strong working relationship with the forensic pathologist. In many jurisdictions, this collaboration can be facilitated through the involvement of medico-legal death investigators, who are highly trained professionals in this field. However, in those coroner or medical examiner jurisdictions that do not have these investigators available, the detective must take a more proactive role and provide guidance based on the case's specific needs. Ultimately, the responsibility to provide information concerning a case to the medical examiner or coroner rests with the detective.

Before the autopsy, the homicide investigator should share current details regarding the scene and investigation with the pathologist. This information should encompass photographs and videos of the scene, the deceased, and any other pertinent information related to the cause of death, manner of death, weapon involved, identification of the decedent, time frame of death, next of kin details, and any relevant information concerning the application of injuries and their effects on the scene, the victim, or the perpetrator.

The homicide investigator should also be prepared to discuss the results of witness interviews with the pathologist.

Any additional equipment that may aid in advancing the investigation of the victim's death should be communicated to the pathologist. Crime scene investigators may offer tools that could enhance or reveal probative evidence during the autopsy examination, including alternate light sources, sexual assault kits, specialized photography applications, and fingerprint acquisition techniques.

Ensure that the homicide investigator and the pathologist collaborate by sharing the complete body X-ray or magnetic resonance imaging (MRI) results for cases where it is warranted.

The homicide investigator should document all individuals at the autopsy in their notes. When preparing the homicide report, exercise caution when recording the comments made by the pathologist during the autopsy examination, as these remarks may be based on preliminary information and could evolve upon further review of all completed tests. The final written autopsy report should be regarded as the definitive findings from the pathologist of record.

Medical examiners play a crucial role in cold case investigations. They utilize their expertise in forensic pathology to re-examine cases, analyze evidence, and potentially identify victims or perpetrators using advanced techniques like DNA analysis.

Requesting the On-Call Pathologist at the Death Scene

Depending on the jurisdiction, some pathologists may request notification of certain cases and have the opportunity to respond to a death scene. This may provide more clarity and enhance understanding of the circumstances surrounding a death from medical and criminal investigative perspectives. The following list outlines types of cases or circumstances in which a visit to the death scene may benefit the investigative agency and medical examiner, coroner, forensic pathologist, or any other individual responsible for establishing the cause and manner of death.

- *Major scenes*: High-profile cases in which some population segment and media representatives will heavily scrutinize every decision, non-decision, and action.
- Deaths involving prominent people.
- Sensational activity causing the death of one or more people.
- *Multiple deaths*: Scenes with multiple fatalities may necessitate the pathologist's assistance in investigating the incident sequence, reconstructing the scene, and identifying the fatalities.
- *Identification of the weapon*: In cases where it may be highly critical to identify or eliminate a possible weapon that may have been used to inflict injuries on a decedent. This initial inspection may have ramifications as to not only the manner of death but may implicate or exonerate a particular suspect from consideration. The item may be a common household item that may be easily overlooked.

- *Reconstruction of the scene*: In complicated scenes, it may be essential to analyze and reconstruct the events leading up to the death of the decedent(s). For example:
  - Identification of the suspect and the victim in a homicide/suicide scene.
  - The sequence of events in which the incident may have involved a prolonged activity and multiple weapons.
  - Was the apparent movement of the injured person prior to death consistent with the evidence present and witness statements concerning the incident?
  - To assist in distinguishing which version may be closer to the truth in conflicting statements.
  - To assist in determining if a suspect may have been injured and bleeding when he was at a death scene.

Recovery of skeletal remains.

- The pathologist may be called upon to supervise the collection of all bones, teeth, and other artifacts necessary to identify the remains and establish the cause and manner of death.
- Evidence collection may also become important. The technician processing the scene may not readily identify these items; therefore, crucial items may go uncollected.
- The pathologist may be called on to distinguish the following while at the scene:
  - Whether the bones are human or animal in origin.
  - Whether the bones are modern.
  - Race, sex, approximate age, and how long the remains may have been there.

Recovery of remains from a fire scene:

- The pathologist may supervise the collection of all bones, teeth, and other artifacts necessary to identify the remains. In a fire scene, these items may not be readily identifiable by the technician processing the scene and therefore may go uncollected.
- The pathologist's presence at the scene of the fire can facilitate the immediate collection of clothing fragments to ensure hydrocarbon preservation for future testing for accelerants.

Undetermined deaths:

- The pathologist may be requested at the scene where initial information concerning the manner of death may be essential in determining what steps are initiated or are contemplated being initiated, based on preliminary information that the pathologist may provide.

Establishing the time of death:

- In cases where it may be critical to establish the time of death, the pathologist should be requested at the scene to begin collecting information, which will be used to arrive at a general conclusion.

Unusual or educational:

- In any case, the activity, method, type of weapon, and circumstances appear rare and may serve a purpose in future investigations by educating others.

(Police) officer-involved or correctional custody deaths:

- These cases are critical. Community activist groups and media reporters categorize any variation in protocol involving the processing of the scene, handling of the decedent, interviewing of witnesses, and handling or processing of evidence as cover-up activities of the investigative agencies involved.

Buried remains:

- Supervise the collection of all artifacts necessary to identify the remains and establish the cause and manner of death. Evidence collection may also become important. Items associated with the burial, such as plastic bags buried with the remains, may become critical in establishing a suspect.
- The pathologist may be called on to distinguish the race, sex, approximate age, and the length of time the remains were at this location.

Airplane or helicopter crash:

- It may involve multiple fatalities. The cause of the crash and evidence associated with that determination may become critically important.

Identification cases (multiple):

- The investigator should request the pathologist's presence in cases involving multiple decedents where identification could become confused.

In any scene, the investigating agency feels they would be more comfortable or need the pathologist's support:

Role in Cold Case Investigations

- *Re-examining cases*: Medical examiners can be brought in to re-examine cases previously deemed cold, using new technologies and techniques to analyze evidence that may have been overlooked or unavailable in the past.
- *Identifying unidentified remains*: Medical examiners are often involved in identifying unidentified remains, using techniques like DNA analysis and comparing dental records, fingerprints, and other identifying features.
- *Analyzing evidence*: They can examine evidence, such as tissue samples, bone fragments, and other biological materials, to determine the cause and manner of death, which can be crucial in solving cold cases.
- *Providing expert testimony*: Medical examiners can provide expert testimony in court, helping to present evidence and interpret findings related to the cause and manner of death.

Techniques Used

A forensic pathologist may be utilized in cold case investigations. They may assist with the following:

- *DNA analysis*: Advances in DNA technology, including genetic genealogy, have allowed medical examiners to identify unidentified remains and even link them to perpetrators of violent crimes.
- *Forensic pathology*: Medical examiners use their expertise in forensic pathology to conduct autopsies, analyze tissue samples, and determine the cause and manner of death.
- *Other forensic techniques*: Forensic experts may also use different techniques to identify victims and gather evidence, such as fingerprint analysis, dental record comparison, and toxicology testing.

Examples of Cold Cases Solved with Medical Examiner Help

- *Unidentified remains*: Medical examiners have successfully identified unidentified remains, providing closure to families and potentially leading to the apprehension of perpetrators.
- *Cold case homicides*: Medical examiners have played a crucial role in solving cold case homicides by re-examining evidence, analyzing DNA samples, and providing expert testimony.
- *Terrorist attacks*: Medical examiners have been involved in identifying victims of terrorist attacks, such as the 2001 attacks on the World Trade Center, using advanced techniques to analyze remains and identify individuals.

Contamination Issues That May Be Encountered Affecting the Case Investigation

Former and, in some cases, current practices and procedures may be responsible for problems that arise in the cold case investigation. Chasing down an unknown DNA specimen may not relate to the case. Contamination issues linked to inadequate evidence collection and preservation practices may be associated with the following problems:

- *Shared body bags*: Body bags used in transporting the remains may be used in numerous cases, with or without proper cleaning between uses.
- *Shared transport sheets*: Transport sheets used in transporting the remains may have been used in multiple cases, with or without proper cleaning between uses.
- *Shared autopsy tables*: Autopsy tables used in the examination may have been used in multiple cases, with or without proper cleaning between uses.
- Contamination of the body/evidence by morgue staff due to the non-use of personal protection equipment (PPE).
- Lack of sterilization between uses of autopsy equipment.

Exhumations

The widespread use of Investigative Genetic Genealogy in generating investigative leads for violent crimes and unidentified human remains has led to a higher demand for exhumations to obtain DNA material for comparison purposes. A forensic pathologist is usually required to examine the remains recovered during an exhumation.

In cold case investigations involving exhumations, key considerations include obtaining proper authorizations, meticulously documenting the process, preserving evidence, and employing forensic techniques to analyze remains and the surrounding soil for clues that may have been overlooked or unavailable during the initial investigation. This may involve the original pathologist, the current pathologist assuming the former cases of a retired or deceased pathologist, or a subject matter expert pathologist hired to perform a secondary autopsy examination. This pathologist may assume additional responsibilities associated with an exhumation or be considerate of other issues that may arise from a planned exhumation, including:

- *Legal and ethical considerations and obtaining authorizations*: Exhumation requires legal authorization, often involving court orders and consent from the deceased's next of kin or legal representatives. The responsible pathologist must ensure all procedures adhere to relevant laws and regulations regarding exhumation and handling of human remains.
- *Respect for the deceased and families*: The process must be handled with sensitivity and respect for the deceased and their families, acknowledging the emotional impact of exhumation.

Documentation and preservation of every step of the exhumation process, from the initial site inspection to the removal of remains, must be meticulously documented with photographs, diagrams, and detailed notes.

To prevent contamination or degradation, the pathologist must properly collect, package, and preserve all evidence, including soil samples, clothing, and other relevant items. To ensure the integrity and admissibility of all evidence collected during the exhumation and subsequent examination, the chain of custody must be established and maintained.

Considerations must be given to the possibility of not having accurate information regarding the previous burial site of the individual being the subject of the exhumation. Locating the body previously buried may become difficult, and in some cases, impossible. Various cemeteries employ different methods, protocols, and practices for burials and selecting grave sites. Some burial records are meticulously maintained, while others can be quite haphazard. It is not uncommon for the wrong body to be exhumed. The longer the period between interment and exhumation, the higher the likelihood of complications that exhumation may cause.

Exhumations are often linked to unidentified and unclaimed bodies. The jurisdiction investigating the death may have selected the original grave site. A funeral home might have handled the disposition of the remains, and the cemetery involved with the original burial may have been selected as a result of a lowest-bidder contract. The quality of embalming, casket, and vault selection, and cemetery space may not guarantee optimal conditions for providing investigators with the necessary information to generate additional leads and clarify details.

The condition of the remains expected upon exhumation depends on several factors, including:

- *Time since burial.* Obviously, the longer a body has been buried, the more decomposed the remains are likely to be.
- Embalming of the corpse may affect its decomposition. An embalmed corpse is expected to decompose more slowly than an unembalmed corpse.
- Environmental factors such as soil composition, temperature, and moisture levels can affect the condition of the remains upon discovery. The area's water levels and the soil's drainage capacity may eventually compromise protective vaults and caskets, exposing the once-protected remains.
- The composition and sealing condition of a casket may affect the condition of the remains. The sturdiness of the casket to resist collapse may be influenced by whether or not the casket was placed into a burial vault. Incursion of the casket by water and soil may greatly influence the condition of the exhumed corpse.
- State and local government statutes may require the casket to be placed in a burial vault before being placed in the grave. The strength, composition, and seal capabilities of a burial vault may profoundly affect the integrity of the grave, resisting any water or soil incursion into the vault and protecting the casket. The weight of the soil, water in the grave, or the material decay of the vault and/or casket may eventually cause the collapse of the material used in protecting the remains from the natural elements. It is not unusual to find remnants of the vault, casket, and dirt mixed in with the remains during an exhumation.
- *Clothing.* If the body is clothed, some clothing fibers may resist decomposing. Clothing consisting of natural fibers will disintegrate much quicker than man-made fibers.

During an exhumation, a forensic pathologist, or a person working under their direction, may be responsible for ultimately conducting a forensic analysis associated with:

- *Soil sampling*: Soil samples should be collected from various locations around the grave, including above, below, and to the sides of the coffin, to analyze for trace evidence.

- *Sifting the grave fill in a collapsed grave*: The grave fill should be sifted to search for any missed evidence, such as small objects, bullets, bones, or other items that may be missed because it is mixed with other soil or soil debris.
- *Forensic anthropology*: At the direction of the forensic pathologist, forensic anthropologists may be utilized to recover and analyze skeletal remains. They may assist the forensic pathologist in the determination of age, sex, stature, and potential causes of death or injuries.

Forensic toxicology:

- Toxicological analysis of tissues and fluids can help determine the presence of drugs or poisons that may have been missed during the initial examination.

DNA analysis:

- DNA specimens may be collected and compared to other samples to identify the deceased or to compare the DNA profile with potential suspects.

For the cold case investigator, understanding the role of the medical examiner or coroner's forensic pathologist who conducted the autopsy and assessing the competency of the previous work completed on the case is critical for advancing the investigation. Evaluating the conclusions regarding the cause of death, manner of death, time frame associated with the death, and the identification of the decedent may be essential components associated with any homicide cold case investigation.

Generally, medical examiners and coroners are special and dedicated to their jobs, which involve "talking for the dead." They serve as the last resort in determining the cause of death and classifying it as a homicide, suicide, accident, or natural. Many of them are extremely competent, while a few others may be grossly incompetent. The cold case investigator must be able to distinguish between the two when assessing the medical information associated with the case.

End

Louis N. Eliopulos
PO Box 837
Occoquan, VA. 22125
904 423-6433
deathhandbook@gmail.com

Death Certificate, Obituary, & Coroner's Inquest

6

RACHEL H. WALTON

A number of documents not normally encountered in the unsolved homicide investigation case file may provide investigative direction to cold case homicide investigators. These documents may be especially valuable when, in the perception of the investigator(s), the case file is incomplete or lacking in some material areas, or as a guide for investigating and determining relationships. Among these documents are

- Certificate of death
- Application and permit for disposition of human remains
- Physician/coroner's amendment
- Obituary
- Coroner's inquest

This section examines the foregoing and their relevance during the course of a cold case homicide investigation.

Death Certificate

Interestingly enough, in my experience, it is not uncommon or unusual to find the certificate of death, also called the *death certificate*, absent when reviewing a case file that has been inactive. During the course of the initial homicide investigation, obtaining this document for the file may not have been a high priority due to the course of the investigation and other duties encountered by the original investigators. As the case was not forwarded to the district attorney for prosecution, obtaining this document for the murder book, as it was, did not get done.

With the reactivation of a cold case, obtaining and reviewing this document is an important course of action. The information in the certificate of death is compiled and constructed by officials involved in the course of establishing death and disposition of the remains. Unlike the obituary, this document is not directly compiled by family members, although some information on the death certificate may originate with a family member or close friends.

DOI: 10.4324/9781003415633-8

There is no national system of death investigation in the United States, nor is there a uniform system for recording the information on a certificate of death. There is, however, some information that is consistent across the nation. This includes basic information identifying the deceased and other individuals, and information surrounding the cause and manner of death. All states provide for a permanent and compulsory vital registration system. This system, however, depends upon the willingness and cooperation of those involved with the decedent, including physicians, hospitals, coroners or medical examiners, and funeral directors, to prepare and certify necessary information.

In some states, vital statistic information relating to births, deaths, or fetal deaths may be mandated for direct reporting to the state vital statistics unit by the primary source. This may include hospitals, coroners and/or medical examiners, and funeral directors. Some, but not all, states are divided into registration districts in furtherance of collecting vital statistic information and utilize a local registrar system. These districts may be a county, city, or other geographical or political subdivision, or a combination of these. In these states, this office collects the necessary information for transmittal to the state bureau or office of vital statistics. The local registrar is required to ensure that a complete certificate for each of these events is filed. In some states, this official also issues burial and transportation permits for deceased persons.

Not uncommonly, the certificate of death is initiated by the mortuary. The mortuary obtains vital information from the family (as the legal representative) as well as the attending physician. It prepares the document and forwards it to the physician for signature. After this signing, the document is returned to the mortuary and then forwarded to the registrar for assignment of a file number and permit for disposition. A sign of the times—in some locales, mortuaries are now prohibited from keeping copies of death certificates in their case files due to identity theft concerns and post-9/11 concerns (Figure 6.1).

It is suggested that review of the death certificate be completed in the earliest stages of the reinvestigation of a cold case homicide. In those cases in which the identity of the victim is known yet the case must be reconstructed from scratch, that is, with little or no information in file, this document provides a jump-off point for numerous avenues of investigation. These include

- Identification of dates for newspaper review and subsequent identification of persons and reported events
- Dates and time frames for review of agency archives and document search
- Names of relatives
- Mortuary records or other disposition information, which may contain more detailed information

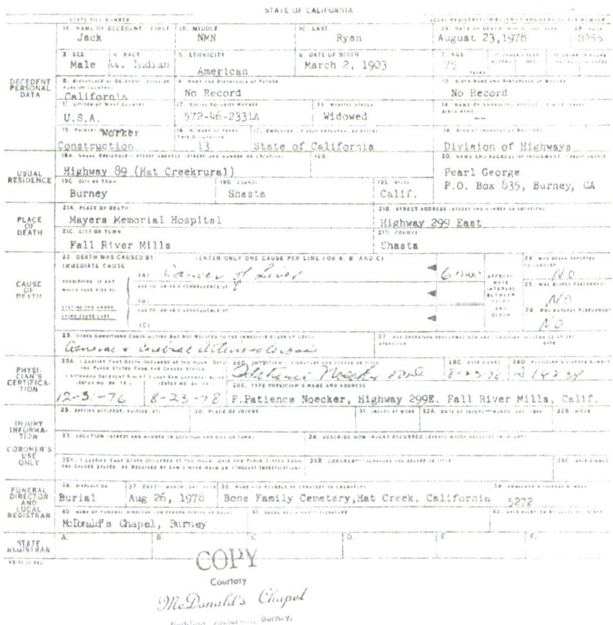
STATE OF CALIFORNIA

DECEDENT PERSONAL DATA: Jack | NMN | Ryan | August 23, 1978 | Male | Am. Indian | American | March 2, 1903 | 75 | California | No Record | No Record | U.S.A. | 572-46-2331A | Widowed | Worker Construction | 13 | State of California | Division of Highways

USUAL RESIDENCE: Highway 89 (Hat Creekrural) | Burney | Shasta | Calif. | Pearl George P.O. Box 835, Burney, CA

PLACE OF DEATH: Mayers Memorial Hospital | Highway 299 East | Fall River Mills | Shasta

CAUSE OF DEATH: Cancer of Liver | 6 mos | NO | NO | NO

PHYSICIAN'S CERTIFICATION: 12-3-76 | 8-23-78 | F.Patience Noecker, Highway 299E, Fall River Mills, Calif.

FUNERAL DIRECTOR AND LOCAL REGISTRAR: Burial | Aug 26, 1978 | Bone Family Cemetery,Hat Creek, California | 5272 | McDonald's Chapel, Burney

COPY
Courtesy
McDonald's Chapel
Redding, Anderson, Burney

Figure 6.1 Ryan death certificate (1978). The format of death certificates has changed over the years, but the core information has not. (Author's file.)

At the outset of the cold case investigation, the certificate of death identifies significant information about the deceased as well as time and circumstances surrounding death, informant information, as well as physician and coroner/medical examiner certifications and mortuary/disposition information.

As a result, this document provides specific information as officially recorded. This information, or portions of this information, may be lacking in the present case file, and this document offers investigators potential sources for investigative information as well as, in some circumstances, potential sources to recover missing or uncollected evidence. That the death was ruled a homicide is important for investigation and prosecution, although cold case investigations can, and have, gone forward when the death certificate has initially ruled the case as accidental, suicide, or undetermined (Figure 6.2).

At the forefront of the investigation, the death certificate informs the cold case investigators as to the medical opinion rendered at the time of the autopsy (if there was an autopsy). While required in homicide cases, they may not have been performed, depending upon the medical, legal, or—sadly—political climate at the time.

According to the National Centers for Disease Control and Prevention (CDC), two types of autopsies are performed in the United States. These are either "(a) hospital or clinical autopsy which family or physicians request to

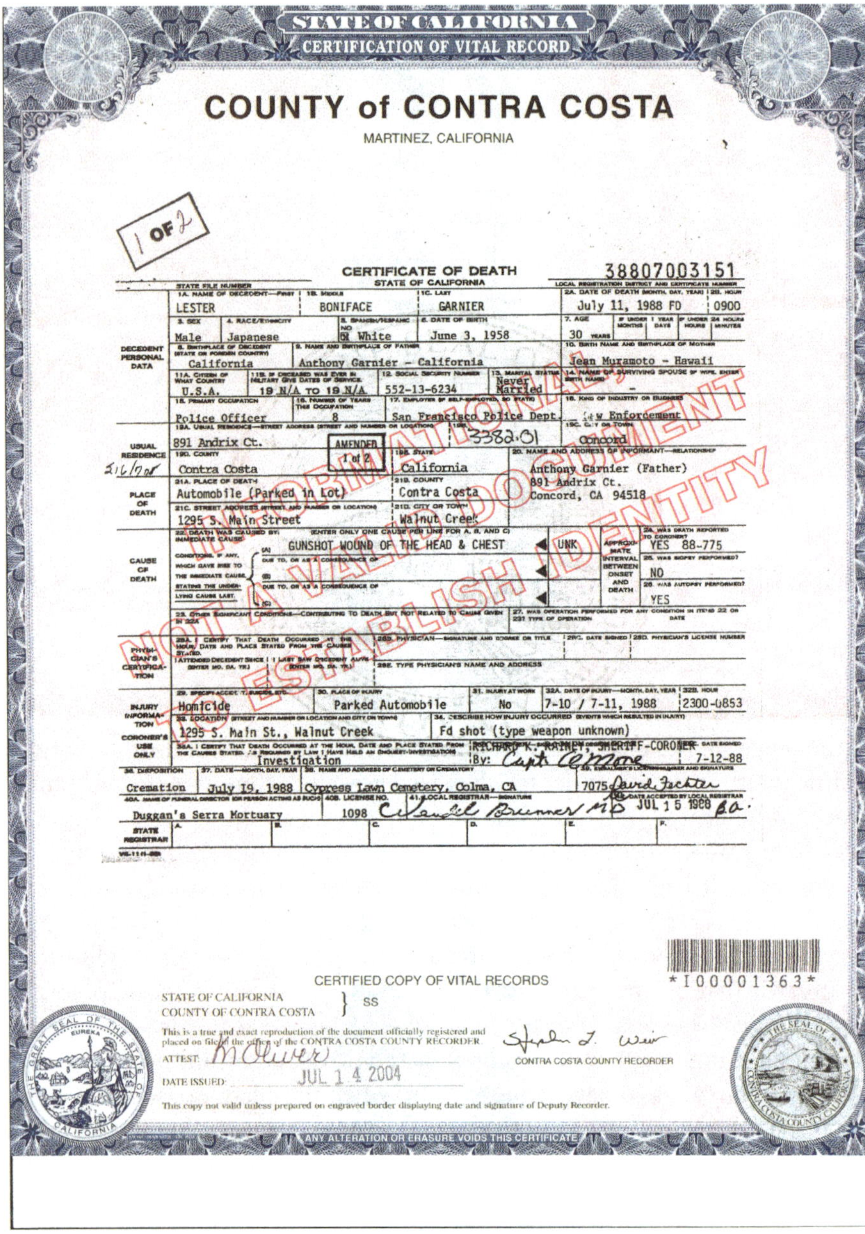
STATE OF CALIFORNIA
CERTIFICATION OF VITAL RECORD

COUNTY of CONTRA COSTA
MARTINEZ, CALIFORNIA

1 OF 2

CERTIFICATE OF DEATH
STATE OF CALIFORNIA
38807003151

DECEDENT PERSONAL DATA
1A. NAME OF DECEDENT—FIRST: LESTER | 1B. MIDDLE: BONIFACE | 1C. LAST: GARNIER
2A. DATE OF DEATH (MONTH, DAY, YEAR): July 11, 1988 FD | 2B. HOUR: 0900
3. SEX: Male | 4. RACE/ETHNICITY: Japanese | 5. SPANISH/HISPANIC: NO White | 6. DATE OF BIRTH: June 3, 1958 | 7. AGE: 30 YEARS
8. BIRTHPLACE OF DECEDENT: California | 9. NAME AND BIRTHPLACE OF FATHER: Anthony Garnier - California | 10. BIRTH NAME AND BIRTHPLACE OF MOTHER: Jean Muramoto - Hawaii
11A. CITIZEN OF WHAT COUNTRY: U.S.A. | 11B. IF DECEASED WAS EVER IN MILITARY GIVE DATES OF SERVICE: 19 N/A TO 19 N/A | 12. SOCIAL SECURITY NUMBER: 552-13-6234 | 13. MARITAL STATUS: Never Married | 14. NAME OF SURVIVING SPOUSE: –
15. PRIMARY OCCUPATION: Police Officer | 16. NUMBER OF YEARS THIS OCCUPATION: 8 | 17. EMPLOYER: San Francisco Police Dept. | 18. KIND OF INDUSTRY OR BUSINESS: Law Enforcement

USUAL RESIDENCE
19A. USUAL RESIDENCE: 891 Andrix Ct. | AMENDED 1 of 2 | 3382.01 | 19C. CITY OR TOWN: Concord
19D. COUNTY: Contra Costa | 19E. STATE: California | 20. NAME AND ADDRESS OF INFORMANT—RELATIONSHIP: Anthony Garnier (Father) 891 Andrix Ct. Concord, CA 94518

PLACE OF DEATH
21A. PLACE OF DEATH: Automobile (Parked in Lot) | 21B. COUNTY: Contra Costa
21C. STREET ADDRESS: 1295 S. Main Street | 21D. CITY OR TOWN: Walnut Creek

CAUSE OF DEATH
22. DEATH WAS CAUSED BY: (A) IMMEDIATE CAUSE: GUNSHOT WOUND OF THE HEAD & CHEST | APPROXIMATE INTERVAL BETWEEN ONSET AND DEATH: UNK
24. WAS DEATH REPORTED TO CORONER? YES 88-775
25. WAS BIOPSY PERFORMED? NO
26. WAS AUTOPSY PERFORMED? YES
23. OTHER SIGNIFICANT CONDITIONS CONTRIBUTING TO DEATH BUT NOT RELATED TO CAUSE GIVEN IN 22A
27. WAS OPERATION PERFORMED FOR ANY CONDITION IN ITEM 22 OR 23?

PHYSICIAN'S CERTIFICATION
28A. I CERTIFY THAT DEATH OCCURRED AT THE HOUR, DATE AND PLACE STATED FROM THE CAUSES STATED. | 28B. PHYSICIAN—SIGNATURE AND DEGREE OR TITLE | 28C. DATE SIGNED | 28D. PHYSICIAN'S LICENSE NUMBER
28E. TYPE PHYSICIAN'S NAME AND ADDRESS

INJURY INFORMATION
29. SPECIFY ACCIDENT, SUICIDE, ETC.: Homicide | 30. PLACE OF INJURY: Parked Automobile | 31. INJURY AT WORK: No | 32A. DATE OF INJURY: 7-10 / 7-11, 1988 | 32B. HOUR: 2300-0853
33. LOCATION: 1295 S. Main St., Walnut Creek | 34. DESCRIBE HOW INJURY OCCURRED: Fd shot (type weapon unknown)

CORONER'S USE ONLY
35A. I CERTIFY THAT DEATH OCCURRED AT THE HOUR, DATE AND PLACE STATED FROM THE CAUSES STATED: Investigation | RICHARD K. RAINEY, SHERIFF-CORONER By: Capt [signature] | 7-12-88

36. DISPOSITION: Cremation | 37. DATE: July 19, 1988 | 38. NAME AND ADDRESS OF CEMETERY OR CREMATORY: Cypress Lawn Cemetery, Colma, CA | 39. EMBALMER'S LICENSE NUMBER AND SIGNATURE: 7075 [signature]
40A. NAME OF FUNERAL DIRECTOR: Duggan's Serra Mortuary | 40B. LICENSE NO.: 1098 | 41. LOCAL REGISTRAR—SIGNATURE: [signature] MD | 42. DATE ACCEPTED BY LOCAL REGISTRAR: JUL 15 1988

NOT A VALID DOCUMENT TO ESTABLISH IDENTITY
INFORMATIONAL

CERTIFIED COPY OF VITAL RECORDS
STATE OF CALIFORNIA } SS
COUNTY OF CONTRA COSTA

I00001363

This is a true and exact reproduction of the document officially registered and placed on file in the office of the CONTRA COSTA COUNTY RECORDER.
ATTEST: M Oliver
DATE ISSUED: JUL 14 2004
[signature] CONTRA COSTA COUNTY RECORDER
This copy not valid unless prepared on engraved border displaying date and signature of Deputy Recorder.
ANY ALTERATION OR ERASURE VOIDS THIS CERTIFICATE

Figure 6.2 Informational death certificate. Due to increasing concerns for identity theft and terrorism, access to copies of death certificates is increasingly more restricted. For non–family members or other nonofficial purposes, copies of more recent death certificates may be marked as "informational" so as to identify them as being issued to third parties. (Author's file.)

clarify cause of death or assess care, or (b) medicolegal autopsies which legal officials order to further investigate the circumstances surrounding a death." The CDC has also reported, "Autopsy rates declined more than 50 percent from 1972 through 2007… In 1972, almost 1 out of 5 deaths were autopsied. From 1972 through 2003, however, the autopsy rate dropped 58 percent from 19.3 percent to 8.1 percent" (CDC). The agency noted that "while the autopsy rate increased slightly since 2003, … fewer than 1 out of 10 deaths, were autopsied in 2007" (CDC). It is important for cold case investigators to be aware that cases exhibiting external causes were more likely to be determined by autopsy than deaths due to diseases or ill-defined conditions, according to the CDC, and autopsy rates declined with increasing age after ages 15–24 years (CDC). This raises the serious issue of how many criminal homicides went undetected due to lack of autopsy.

Death certificates are issued for the known death of any human being. Death certificates are normally issued only in the county and state in which the death occurred, excluding a death at sea. A *regular* state death certificate is issued for any person who has breathed on his/her own. A *fetal* death certificate may be issued for the death of a fetus. If a fetus took one breath of air on his/her own, a birth certificate would be issued and then a death certificate.

A legal document, the certificate of death is a certification of vital record and is issued in the name of the state. It may indicate the manner of death as natural, accidental, suicide, homicide, or undetermined.

Death certificates may be *amended* when erroneous information has been found to have been included on the original death certificate (Figure 6.3). Normally, this change is at the behest of the physician or coroner. In this case, an affidavit to amend a record or similar procedure may be filed to correct the error, and the certificate of death will subsequently reflect these changes as well as noting that this change process occurred. Only a physician can amend those portions of the certificate of death pertaining to medical aspects of the document. If a typo or other change needs to be made, the mortuary may process the amendment. When obtaining a certificate of death for a cold case homicide, investigators may seek to determine whether any subsequent corrections and amendments had occurred.

Information Found on the Death Certificate

In addition to the autopsy report, inspection of the death certificate may reflect detailed information that includes

- Decedent personal data
    - First, middle, last name
    - Date of death (month/day/year)

STATE OF CALIFORNIA
CERTIFICATION OF VITAL RECORD

COUNTY of CONTRA COSTA
MARTINEZ, CALIFORNIA

AFFIDAVIT TO AMEND A RECORD

STATE CERTIFICATE NUMBER

☐ BIRTH ☒ DEATH ☐ FETAL DEATH ☐ MARRIAGE

38807003151
LOCAL REGISTRATION DISTRICT AND CERTIFICATE NUMBER

PART I INFORMATION AS REPORTED ON THE ORIGINAL REGISTERED CERTIFICATE

TYPE OR PRINT IN BLACK INK ONLY

1A. FIRST NAME	1B. MIDDLE NAME	1C. LAST NAME
Lester	Boniface	Garnier

2. SEX	3. DATE OF EVENT	4. PLACE OF OCCURRENCE—CITY AND COUNTY
Male	July 11, 1988	Walnut Creek - Contra Costa

5. NAME OF FATHER	6. BIRTH NAME OF MOTHER
Anthony Garnier	Jean Muramoto

2 of 2

PART II STATEMENT OF CORRECTIONS

2/6/709
LIST ONE ITEM PER LINE

7. ITEM NUMBER	8A. ERRONEOUS INFORMATION AS STATED ON THE ORIGINAL RECORD	8B. CORRECT INFORMATION THAT SHOULD HAVE BEEN STATED ON THE ORIGINAL RECORD AT THE TIME OF OCCURRENCE
5	X - White	No

REASON FOR CORRECTION: 9. to correct the record

PART III SUPPORTING AFFIDAVITS

FIRST SUPPORTING AFFIDAVIT

I hereby certify under penalty of perjury that I have personal knowledge of the above facts and that the information given above is true and correct.

10. SIGNATURE OF PERSON COMPLETING THE AFFIDAVIT: Billie Jo Ecke
11. RELATIONSHIP TO PERSON WHOSE NAME IS ENTERED IN ITEM 1: Funeral Director
12. AGE OF PERSON COMPLETING THE AFFIDAVIT: 28
13. DATE SIGNED: July 27, 1988
14. ADDRESS OF PERSON COMPLETING THE AFFIDAVIT (STREET, CITY, STATE): 500 Westlake Ave., Daly City, CA 94014

SECOND SUPPORTING AFFIDAVIT

I hereby certify under penalty of perjury that I have personal knowledge of the above facts and that the information given above is true and correct.

15. SIGNATURE OF PERSON COMPLETING THE AFFIDAVIT
16. RELATIONSHIP TO PERSON WHOSE NAME IS ENTERED IN ITEM 1: Funeral Director
17. AGE OF PERSON COMPLETING THE AFFIDAVIT: 51
18. DATE SIGNED: July 27, 1988
19. ADDRESS OF PERSON COMPLETING THE AFFIDAVIT (STREET, CITY, STATE): 500 Westlake Ave., Daly City, CA 94014

STATE OR LOCAL REGISTRAR USE ONLY
20. DATE ACCEPTED: JUL 28 1988
21. OFFICE OF THE STATE OR LOCAL REGISTRAR: Wendell Brunner MD

STATE OF CALIFORNIA, DEPARTMENT OF HEALTH SERVICES, OFFICE OF THE STATE REGISTRAR OF VITAL STATISTICS (REV. 7-88) Form VR-9A

NOT A VALID DOCUMENT TO ESTABLISH IDENTITY

INFORMATIONAL,

CERTIFIED COPY OF VITAL RECORDS

I00001364

STATE OF CALIFORNIA
COUNTY OF CONTRA COSTA } SS

This is a true and exact reproduction of the document officially registered and placed on file in the office of the CONTRA COSTA COUNTY RECORDER.

ATTEST: M Oliver

DATE ISSUED: JUL 14 2004

Stephen L. Weir
CONTRA COSTA COUNTY RECORDER

This copy not valid unless prepared on engraved border displaying date and signature of Deputy Recorder.

ANY ALTERATION OR ERASURE VOIDS THIS CERTIFICATE

Figure 6.3 Amendment to death certificate. (Author's file.)

- Estimated hour of death
- Sex
- Race/ethnicity
- Date of birth

  - Age at time of death
  - Birthplace
  - Name and birthplace of father
  - Birth name and birthplace of mother
  - Country of citizenship
  - Dates of military service
  - Social Security number
  - Marital status
  - Name of surviving spouse
  - Occupation
  - Number of years in occupation
  - Employer
  - Nature of business or industry
- Residence information
  - Usual residence (street and address or location)
  - Town or city
  - County
  - State
- Place of death
  - Physical location of death (inside automobile in a parking lot, etc.)
  - Nearest street address
  - City
  - County
- Name and address of informant (and relationship)
  - Normally the legal next of kin (which goes in order from wife, adult children, parents, etc.) who provides needed information for the certificate. An exception could be a person with a medical durable power of attorney or the public administrator.
- Cause of death
  - That which caused *immediate* death
  - Conditions, if any, that gave rise to the immediate cause of death
  - Underlying cause of death
  - Other significant conditions contributing to death but not related to cause given
- Approximate interval between onset and death
  - Was death reported to the coroner/medical examiner (and case number)?
  - Was biopsy performed?
  - Was autopsy performed?
- Physician's certification
  - Certification by physician that death occurred as described

    - Certification of attending physician, if applicable, for time period prior to death
    - Physician signature and title
    - Date signed
    - Physician's name and address (typed)
    - Physician's license number
- Injury information
    - Specific injury type (accident, suicide, etc.)
    - Place of injury (parked automobile, etc.)
    - Location of injury (street or other address)
    - Description of how injury occurred or events resulting in injury ("found shot, type of weapon unknown")
    - Whether work related
    - Date of injury (month/day/year)
    - Hour of death
- Disposition of remains
    - Type of disposition
    - Date (month/day/year)
    - Name and address of cemetery
    - Embalmer's name and license number
    - Name of funeral director or person acting as such
    - License number
- Other information
    - Coroner's investigation
    - Coroner's inquest
    - Signature of coroner or medical examiner certifying the document and events
    - Date of signature

Certificate of Fetal Death

When the deceased is a fetus, a certificate of fetal death may be substituted for a regular state certificate of death. While the specific definition for this purpose may vary, for example, in California, a fetus for this purpose would be defined as one 21 weeks of age or older and who has not breathed air on his/her own. In this state, if the fetus is less than 21 weeks of age, no death certificate is required. In some circumstances, if the fetus is less than 21 weeks, a letter from an attending physician attesting to gestation may only be necessary, and the fetus may be buried or otherwise disposed of with no formal certificate or permit. Due to the nature of the victim in these cases, and apparent statistical reporting purposes, additional information is required on the certificate (see Figure 6.4).

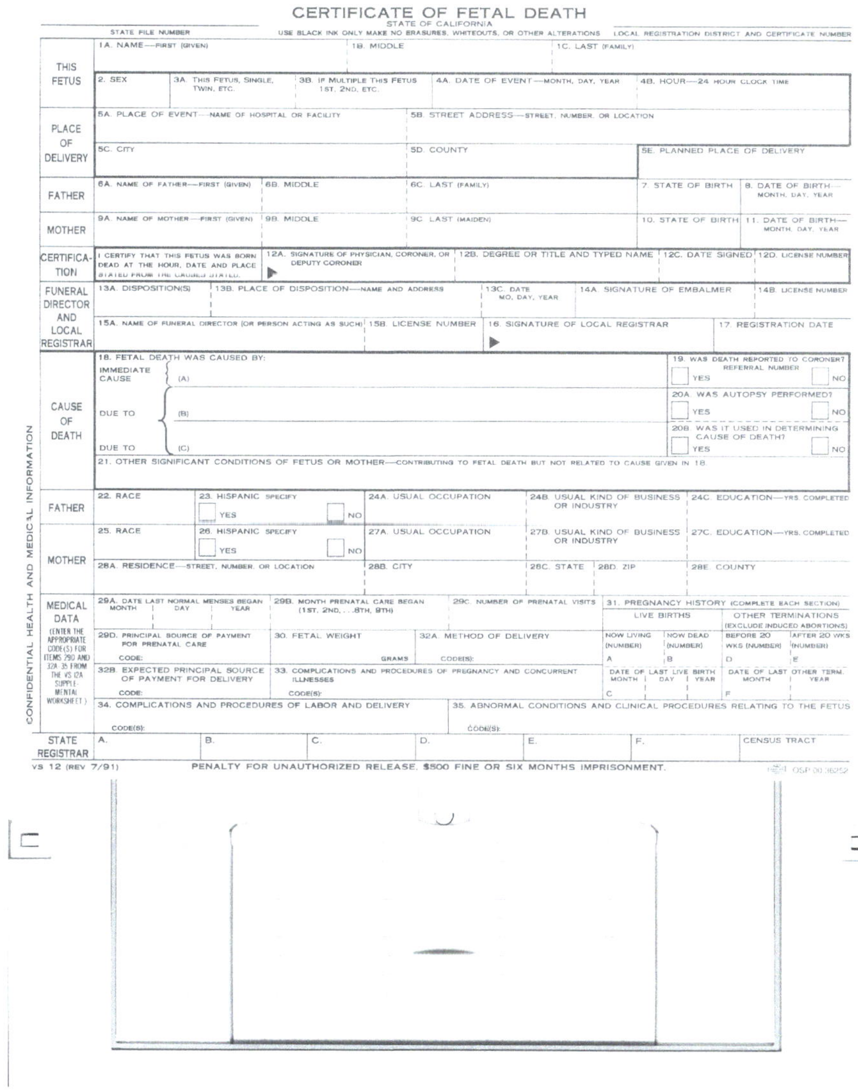

CERTIFICATE OF FETAL DEATH
STATE OF CALIFORNIA
USE BLACK INK ONLY MAKE NO ERASURES, WHITEOUTS, OR OTHER ALTERATIONS

STATE FILE NUMBER — LOCAL REGISTRATION DISTRICT AND CERTIFICATE NUMBER

THIS FETUS: 1A. NAME—FIRST (GIVEN) | 1B. MIDDLE | 1C. LAST (FAMILY) | 2. SEX | 3A. THIS FETUS, SINGLE, TWIN, ETC. | 3B. IF MULTIPLE THIS FETUS 1ST, 2ND, ETC. | 4A. DATE OF EVENT—MONTH, DAY, YEAR | 4B. HOUR—24 HOUR CLOCK TIME

PLACE OF DELIVERY: 5A. PLACE OF EVENT—NAME OF HOSPITAL OR FACILITY | 5B. STREET ADDRESS—STREET, NUMBER, OR LOCATION | 5C. CITY | 5D. COUNTY | 5E. PLANNED PLACE OF DELIVERY

FATHER: 6A. NAME OF FATHER—FIRST (GIVEN) | 6B. MIDDLE | 6C. LAST (FAMILY) | 7. STATE OF BIRTH | 8. DATE OF BIRTH—MONTH, DAY, YEAR

MOTHER: 9A. NAME OF MOTHER—FIRST (GIVEN) | 9B. MIDDLE | 9C. LAST (MAIDEN) | 10. STATE OF BIRTH | 11. DATE OF BIRTH—MONTH, DAY, YEAR

CERTIFICATION: I CERTIFY THAT THIS FETUS WAS BORN DEAD AT THE HOUR, DATE AND PLACE STATED FROM THE CAUSES STATED. | 12A. SIGNATURE OF PHYSICIAN, CORONER, OR DEPUTY CORONER | 12B. DEGREE OR TITLE AND TYPED NAME | 12C. DATE SIGNED | 12D. LICENSE NUMBER

FUNERAL DIRECTOR AND LOCAL REGISTRAR: 13A. DISPOSITION(S) | 13B. PLACE OF DISPOSITION—NAME AND ADDRESS | 13C. DATE MO, DAY, YEAR | 14A. SIGNATURE OF EMBALMER | 14B. LICENSE NUMBER | 15A. NAME OF FUNERAL DIRECTOR (OR PERSON ACTING AS SUCH) | 15B. LICENSE NUMBER | 16. SIGNATURE OF LOCAL REGISTRAR | 17. REGISTRATION DATE

CAUSE OF DEATH: 18. FETAL DEATH WAS CAUSED BY: IMMEDIATE CAUSE (A) | DUE TO (B) | DUE TO (C) | 19. WAS DEATH REPORTED TO CORONER? REFERRAL NUMBER YES NO | 20A. WAS AUTOPSY PERFORMED? YES NO | 20B. WAS IT USED IN DETERMINING CAUSE OF DEATH? YES NO | 21. OTHER SIGNIFICANT CONDITIONS OF FETUS OR MOTHER—CONTRIBUTING TO FETAL DEATH BUT NOT RELATED TO CAUSE GIVEN IN 18

CONFIDENTIAL HEALTH AND MEDICAL INFORMATION

FATHER: 22. RACE | 23. HISPANIC SPECIFY YES NO | 24A. USUAL OCCUPATION | 24B. USUAL KIND OF BUSINESS OR INDUSTRY | 24C. EDUCATION—YRS. COMPLETED

MOTHER: 25. RACE | 26. HISPANIC SPECIFY YES NO | 27A. USUAL OCCUPATION | 27B. USUAL KIND OF BUSINESS OR INDUSTRY | 27C. EDUCATION—YRS. COMPLETED | 28A. RESIDENCE—STREET, NUMBER, OR LOCATION | 28B. CITY | 28C. STATE | 28D. ZIP | 28E. COUNTY

MEDICAL DATA (ENTER THE APPROPRIATE CODE(S) FOR ITEMS 29D AND 32A–35 FROM THE VS 12A SUPPLEMENTAL WORKSHEET): 29A. DATE LAST NORMAL MENSES BEGAN MONTH DAY YEAR | 29B. MONTH PRENATAL CARE BEGAN (1ST, 2ND, ...8TH, 9TH) | 29C. NUMBER OF PRENATAL VISITS | 29D. PRINCIPAL SOURCE OF PAYMENT FOR PRENATAL CARE CODE: | 30. FETAL WEIGHT GRAMS | 32A. METHOD OF DELIVERY CODE(S): | 32B. EXPECTED PRINCIPAL SOURCE OF PAYMENT FOR DELIVERY CODE: | 33. COMPLICATIONS AND PROCEDURES OF PREGNANCY AND CONCURRENT ILLNESSES CODE(S): | 31. PREGNANCY HISTORY (COMPLETE EACH SECTION) LIVE BIRTHS: NOW LIVING (NUMBER) A, NOW DEAD (NUMBER) B, DATE OF LAST LIVE BIRTH MONTH DAY YEAR C | OTHER TERMINATIONS (EXCLUDE INDUCED ABORTIONS): BEFORE 20 WKS (NUMBER) D, AFTER 20 WKS (NUMBER) E, DATE OF LAST OTHER TERM. MONTH YEAR F | 34. COMPLICATIONS AND PROCEDURES OF LABOR AND DELIVERY CODE(S): | 35. ABNORMAL CONDITIONS AND CLINICAL PROCEDURES RELATING TO THE FETUS CODE(S):

STATE REGISTRAR: A. | B. | C. | D. | E. | F. | CENSUS TRACT

VS 12 (REV 7/91) PENALTY FOR UNAUTHORIZED RELEASE, $500 FINE OR SIX MONTHS IMPRISONMENT.

Figure 6.4 Certificate of fetal death. This form of death certificate reveals more information about mother, father, and other births. (Author's file.)

This certificate may indicate information relative to

- This fetus
  - First (given), middle, last (family) name
  - Sex
  - Single, twin, etc.
  - If multiple birth, whether this fetus is first, second, etc.

    - Date of event (month/day/year)
    - Hour
    - Place of delivery
- Place of event
    - Address
    - City
    - County
    - Planned place of delivery
- Father
    - Full name
    - State of birth
    - Date of birth
- Mother
    - First, middle, last (maiden) name
    - State of birth
    - Date of birth
- Certification by physician, coroner, or deputy coroner
    - Degree or title and typed name
    - Date signed
    - License number
- Funeral director and local registrar
    - Disposition
    - Place of disposition
    - Date
    - Signature of embalmer
    - License number
    - Name of funeral director or person acting as such
    - License number
    - Signature of local registrar
    - Registration date
- Cause of death
    - Immediate cause
    - Whether death was reported to coroner and referral number
    - Was autopsy performed
    - Whether it was used in determining cause of death
    - Other significant conditions of fetus or mother contributing to fetal death but not previously given
- Father
    - Race
    - Ethnicity
    - Usual occupation
    - Usual kind of business
    - Education

- Mother
    - Race
    - Ethnicity
    - Usual occupation
    - Usual kind of business
    - Education
    - Residence address
    - City, state, and zip code
    - Country
- Medical data
    - Date last normal menses began
    - Month prenatal care began
    - Number of prenatal visits
    - Principal source of payment for prenatal care
    - Expected principal source of payment for delivery
    - Complications and procedures of pregnancy and concurrent illnesses
    - Complications and procedures of labor and delivery
    - Abnormal conditions and clinical procedures relating to the fetus
    - Fetal weight
    - Method of delivery
    - Pregnancy history
        - Live births
            - Now living (number)
            - Now dead (number)
            - Date of last live birth
        - Other terminations
            - Before 20 weeks
            - After 20 weeks
            - Date of last other term

Application and Permit for Disposition of Human Remains

Normally, a permit from local health authorities is required to transport human remains. This permit may offer additional information to cold case investigators regarding the decedent, death, and disposition of the remains. This permit may be required at all stages of the handling of human remains, including the forensic exhumation (see Chapter 22). This application and permit may be issued by the city or county registrar or other designated official, including the health department. Among the information to be found on this document may be found

- Decedent's full name
- Date of birth
- Date of death
- Sex
- City of death
- County of death
- Name, relationship, and address of informant
- Name and address of funeral director or those acting on his/her behalf
- Signature and date of applicant for permit

Types of Disposition of Human Remains

There are a number of options available for the disposition of human remains:

- Burial (including entombment)
- Temporary envaultment
- Cremation
- Disposition of cremated remains other than in a cemetery
- Scientific use
- Transit
- Scattering or burial at sea or disposition other than in a cemetery

While a review of this application and permit denotes the disposition of the remains, it may also indicate:

- Name and address of the cemetery of burial, including
    - Date buried
    - Signature of person in charge of burial
- Cremation
    - Name and address of crematory
    - Date cremated
    - Signature of person in charge of cremation
- Scientific use
    - Name and address of facility receiving remains
    - Date received
    - Signature of person in charge of facility
- Transit
    - Name and address in receiving state or country where remains or cremated remains are to be shipped
    - Date shipped
    - Address and signature of person in charge of placing with the carrier

- Scattering, including burial at sea or disposition other than in a cemetery
  - Address, nearest point on shoreline, or other description sufficient to identify final place. If burial at sea, latitude and longitude
  - If a full-body burial at sea by a military service, the name of the branch of service is given

Other Mortuary and Funeral Home Resources

Although local and regional customs may vary, cold case investigators may consider visiting the funeral home or mortuary to seek further information. Among those records that may be of interest is the *case file*. Review or copying of such records may require a search warrant or subpoena. This contains most of the records pertinent to the individual deceased's case. It may include

- Cemetery records.
- Copies of any checks written for funeral and internment expenses.
- Work sheets.
- Burial record or record of funeral.
- Logs of family conversations, or any problems experienced during the handling and internment or disposition of the remains.
- Embalming report. (The embalming process tends to bring out bruises that may not have been previously noticed, especially with children.)
- *Removal sheet*: This is the document(s) that cemetery personnel fill out when picking up a body for transport. It will note the date, times, and vital information of the decedent such as Social Security numbers, when the deceased last seen by a physician, time of death, next of kin, and list of personal effects on the body.
- *Hospital sheet*: Similar to the removal sheet, vital information, Social Security numbers, date of birth, etc.
- *Clothing sheet*: Clothing brought in by the family for dressing the decedent.

Mortuary or funeral home personnel that who possess information of interest to the investigation may include:

- *Case arranger*: This is generally the person responsible for overseeing the process.
- *Funeral director*: Handles the funeral as set up by the arranger. On the mortuary side, handles the arrangement, and on the cemetery side, handles markers, internment, etc.
- *Super director*: In some locales, this person handles both mortuary and cemetery sides, but this practice varies from place to place.

Visitor's Log

A visitor's log is often present at the time of viewing of the deceased through the internment. These names may be of interest to cold case investigators in some situations. These are normally returned to the family at the conclusion of the service. The case file may reflect to whom the log was given after the service.

Obituary

The obituary is a voluntary, unofficial public announcement by the family or friends of the deceased pronouncing their passing. It is published in the local newspaper, typically in a dedicated "Notices" section of the paper, pursuant to that media's rules and policies. In most cases, it is published within a week and runs for a number of days, depending upon the arrangement between the family or author and newspaper.

The obituary often attests to the deceased's birth, youth, career, hobbies, military or other service, and other interests. It commonly closes by listing the names of relatives—to the grandchild level—and friends, as well as to where contributions in their memory may be sent. In cold case investigations, these obituaries may offer information of interest that includes:

- Date of death
- Age at death
- Residence community
- Names of parents, siblings, and other relatives
- Names of close friends and associates
- Relationships
- Deceased children or siblings
- Residence locations and history
- Employment and military history
- Other biographical information and hobbies or interests
- Mortuary or funeral home
- Dates and location of services
- Location of internment
- Casket bearers

Coroner and Medical Examiner Operations

The American medicolegal system of death investigation was founded in the English coroner system and was brought to the United States by the early colonists. In this founding period, the positions of sheriff and coroner were usually combined in one office and person, and the earliest reported coroner's inquest was held in the colony of New Plymouth, New England, in 1635. In the late 1800s, pathology began to become an important role in death investigation, and in 1915, New York City eliminated the coroner's office and instituted a medical examiner's system. The first statewide medical examiner system was instituted in Maryland in 1939. This system has grown and expanded in the ensuing decades.

Three primary systems are in use today. These systems may vary from county to county within a state, and understanding the type and background of their system may be of value to cold case investigators. These are the county coroner, the sheriff–coroner, and the medical examiner.

The roles and duties of these offices may often be found in the government code or other codified sources of agency authority. Cold case investigators, when seeking to identify what material may be, or has been, present in coroner's inquest files, may attempt to find the appropriate codes from the time of the homicide under investigation in an attempt to learn what may or may not have been done. A coroner's inquest record may be a very informative resource during a cold case homicide investigation.

County Coroner

The county coroner is usually an elected official and normally does *not* need to be a licensed and trained physician. As such, he/she is not authorized or permitted to physically open human remains. Not infrequently, the minimum qualifications are to be 18 years of age or over and a resident of the county or district. There is no minimum qualification for education and training in the forensic sciences. These persons usually have primary jurisdiction within their county or district. An additional qualification is, and has always been, that they need to win a popular vote. In some jurisdictions, the coroner may have additional duties, such as acting as the public administrator. This office may be part-time, full-time, or on an as-needed basis. In the past, coroner's fee schedules may have been based upon the findings they officially rendered.

In my experience, especially in smaller, more rural counties, recordkeeping systems varied, and record retention for periods dating to the 1980s and before may be hit or miss. The writing of reports and file organization and maintenance were at the discretion of the office holder. A search for coroner's records by investigators in older cold cases may entail identifying previous coroners and their assistant coroners and attempting to locate these individuals and make inquiry into possible retention of records from their tenure. Similarly, identifying their secretaries or other clerical personnel may yield helpful information. Smaller agencies are not alone in this, however, and larger coroner's offices have been known to lose files, bones, and other remains, property, or evidence.

During the course of their duties, the coroner or staff may have consulted with local medical personnel or have employed qualified forensic pathologists to conduct autopsies. In decades past, in some instances, autopsies were not always conducted by the most qualified of medical personnel. Their education in forensic matters may have been minimal, and ultimately, however, the coroner made the conclusion reflected upon the death certificate regarding cause and manner of death. I recall one report decades ago in which the part-time coroner, a hotel owner, held a .25-caliber rifle bullet to an entrance wound and proclaimed it as the fatal projectile as opposed to a .32 pistol bullet as it most closely matched the entrance wound!

Investigators may consider conducting a forensic exhumation for a secondary autopsy. See Chapter 22.

Coroners may be required by law to keep a coroner's register. This record contains:

- Name or alias of the deceased
- Description necessary for identification
- Property taken from person or premises
- Disposition of money or property
- Cause of death
- Information as to disposition of remains
- Persons notified of the death as well as notations of any unsuccessful attempts at notification

Sheriff–Coroner

A variation of the coroner system is the office of sheriff–coroner. This practice is less common but still in use today in some areas. In addition to other prescribed law enforcement duties, the sheriff of the county is also mandated to perform the duties of the coroner. As such, deputy sheriffs may also be empowered as deputy coroners. In these jurisdictions, a search for records may begin within the county sheriff's office.

Medical Examiner

The medical examiner may have county, district, or statewide jurisdiction. These persons must be licensed physicians and are generally forensically trained pathologists. They are usually appointed and serve at the discretion of the appointing authority, and traditionally have been encountered in more metropolitan areas or larger population bases.

For the purposes of this segment, the term *coroner* is used synonymously as reference to the medicolegal authority responsible for conducting the death investigation.

Despite the variations in these systems, their responsibility was, and is, to take charge of the body when notified of the death; make identification; and inquire into circumstances, manner, and means of death. Classification of deaths requiring inquiry was mandated by the state in which the jurisdiction rested. Not uncommonly, the duty of the coroner, past and present, would include inquiry and determination into the circumstances and manner of:

- All violent, sudden, or unusual deaths, unattended deaths, or deceased not attended by physician within the past 20 days before death and deaths related to or suspected to be self-induced or resulting from criminal abortion
- Deaths known or suspect homicide, suicide, or accidental poisoning
- Deaths due to accident, injury, drowning, fire, hanging, gunshot, stabbing, cutting, exposure, starvation, acute alcoholism, drug addiction, strangulation, aspiration
- Death in whole or in part occasioned by criminal means; deaths associated with a known or alleged rape or crime against nature; deaths in prison or while under sentence
- Deaths under such circumstances as to afford a reasonable ground to suspect that the death was caused by the criminal act of another

These duties were separate from those performed by other law enforcement agencies. Review of older unsolved cases has shown a joint coroner–law enforcement participation in those cases that ultimately became cold cases. Other qualifying deaths may include those situations in which there is a possible threat to public health. In all events, the medicolegal investigation sought to learn the following:

- Who died?
- How and why?
- Who did it (when applicable)?

Coroner's Inquest

To answer these questions, coroner officials in past decades, as well as medical examiners, have utilized a process called the coroner's inquest. This centuries-old system was once more prevalent than it is today, although it is still in occasional use. Documentation that this inquest occurred may or may not be found in the cold case file but, rather, in review of coroner's or newspaper files.

A primary purpose of a coroner's inquest was to provide a means for the prompt securing of information for the use of those charged with the detection and prosecution of crime. In this manner, people were subpoenaed to the inquest and questioned under oath, and a transcript was made of the proceedings. Knowledge of this process and the record systems it produced may provide investigators with information in those cold cases in which this process was utilized.

These may be valuable investigative sources. While variations may occur in different states, this synopsis provides an overview of the manners and methods of coroner's inquests as may be encountered in practical cold case investigation. Issues identified with the coroner's inquest include

- Discretion of the coroner or medical examiner to hold an inquest
- Jurisdiction and venue of the inquest
- Juror qualifications to serve on a coroner's inquest
- Oath and duties of the juror
- Inquest process
- Verdict or decision and findings

Unlike a grand jury process, there was and is no confidentiality or secrecy barrier.

For cold case investigators, decades after a coroner's inquest, there is no legal barrier to identifying and attempting to contact former members of the coroner's inquest, or coroner's jury, when and where possible. As in any other cold case interview, ask about any notes or other documents or photos. Until you ask the question, you never know what might turn up.

Discretion

The decision to hold a coroner's inquest rested with the coroner or medical examiner and was *discretionary* at their pleasure and if circumstances warranted it. These circumstances could range from mystery surrounding the death to political considerations. An inquest could be held using a coroner's jury or with the coroner acting as the sole inquisitor and official, at the discretion of the coroner. The coroner only needed a reasonable ground to suspect the possibility of death at the hands of another or through the instrumentality of some other person. The coroner did not need the consent or permission of the family to hold an inquest. These inquests were open to the public and, especially in more sensational investigations, attended and reported by the local media.

Such an inquest may have been mandatory, however, when requested by the sheriff or chief of police, district attorney, or attorney general. In those circumstances in which the coroner conducted the inquiry, the coroner or a deputy would personally sign the certificate of death. If the death appeared to have occurred under natural circumstances, and the inquiry determined that the physician of record possessed sufficient knowledge to state that death occurred under natural circumstances, a coroner could authorize that physician to sign the certificate of death.

Jurisdiction and Venue

The inquest was limited to conduct inquiry into death in the county where the death occurred (rather than the county where the deceased may have resided). The coroner or his/her authorized deputy or a hearing officer would conduct the inquest. In addition, the coroner had the right to exhume the body of a deceased person when necessary to discharge his/her duties as prescribed by law. Depending upon authority and location, the coroner or his/her deputy may have exercised peace officer power. Although coroners usually did not have power to subpoena witnesses from outside their county, they have had authority to travel outside the jurisdiction to obtain information.

Juror Qualifications

No one was exempt for jury service except at the discretion of the coroner. Inquest jurors were not subject to challenge by any party. Exemptions were noted, however, and included those persons:

- Related to the decedent
- Charged or suspected with the killing of the decedent
- Prejudiced for or against the deceased

Oath and Duties

Upon selection, the jurors participating in a coroner's inquest took an oath in which they were sworn to inquire into who the person was; when, where, and by what means the person came to his/her death; and circumstances attending his/her death; and render a verdict according to the evidence offered or arising from inspection of the body.

Inquest Process

Upon notification that a death had occurred and the coroner determined that an inquest was to be conducted, the coroner decided whether to conduct the inquest himself/herself or to use a coroner's inquest jury. The coroner was authorized by law to summon a number of jurors to serve as coroner's inquest jurors, and the number varied among different jurisdictions. For instance in California, the coroner

> ...shall summon, or cause to be summoned by any sheriff, constable, or policeman, not less than nine nor more than 15 persons qualified by law to serve as jurors, to appear before him forthwith, either at the place where the body of the deceased is or at some other convenient place within the county designated by him, or at the request of the district attorney, to inquire into the cause of the death.

In the "Boulder Jane Doe" case cited in Chapter 22, the recovered records indicated that the coroner's inquest jury numbered six persons. The inquest did not have to be held at the coroner's office or in a government facility. Such inquests could be, and have been, held at the site where the deceased died or other locations.

Jurors could be summoned orally or in writing. A summons was that, a command to a person to appear at a given time and place to meet. Coroner's inquest jurors were residents of the county in which the inquest was to be held. Coroner's jury members were compensated at a schedule set by the county.

During the proceedings, coroner's inquest jurors were often required to view the body as a necessary part of the identification process.

Witnesses were subpoenaed to attend a coroner's inquest in a manner similar to being summoned to appear in a regular court. Upon being called, a witness would step forward and be administered an oath. Questions would be directed toward the witness by the coroner, or in some instances, by members of the coroner's jury. In some situations, witnesses also viewed the body (most often to establish the identity of the deceased). Among those summoned to a coroner's inquest would include:

- Person who discovered the body
- Law enforcement personnel
- Medical personnel
- Expert witnesses (who may provide opinion as to cause of death)
- Family members of the victim
- Friends, associates, and coworkers of the victim
- Spouse, boyfriend, or girlfriend of the victim
- Others thought to have knowledge pertinent to the investigation

Transcripts and Records

A court reporter or stenographer made a transcript of testimony taken at coroner's inquests. Beginning around the late 1940s, a mechanical device could be used to make a recording of the inquest process in lieu of a written record in some locales. Upon completion of the proceedings, the transcript or tape recording was filed with the coroner, or county clerk, usually within a specified time period. I have seen coroner inquest files that include original stenographic notepads. Transcriptions may or may not have been made.

Verdict or Finding

Upon completion of their duty, coroner's inquest jurors were to render a verdict or finding based upon what they heard and saw. This verdict, *inadmissible* as evidence in civil or criminal proceedings, was set forth without regard to civil or criminal responsibility:

- Name of the deceased
- Time and place of death
- Medical cause of death and whether by
  - Natural causes
  - Suicide
  - Accident
  - Hands of another other than by accident
  - Undetermined

When the findings of the coroner's jury suggested that death came at the hands of another, the coroner would also transmit his written findings to the district attorney and/or police agency for the jurisdiction in which the body was recovered.

In addition, I have viewed a number of coroner's inquest verdicts in which the jurors provided additional detail, including:

- State or country of origin (birth)
- Age
- Occupation
- Marital status
- The name of the person who inflicted the fatal injuries upon the victim

Suggested Readings and Bibliography

Center for Disease Control. https://www.cdc.gov/nchs/data/databriefs/db67.pdf. Retrieved June 11, 2015.

Hoyert, D. (2001). The autopsy, medicine, and mortality statistics. National Center for Health Statistics. *Vital Health Stat* 3(32), 1–42.

7 Long-Term Missing Persons & No-Body Cold Case Investigations

THOMAS A. DIBIASE AND
RACHEL H. WALTON

Criminal homicide investigations generally begin with the response of officers to the finding of a body and a crime scene. From this, investigators develop leads, evidence, and cases, identifying and interviewing witnesses and others. Notes, reports, sketches, and photographs become the case file. Due to the severity of criminal homicide/murder, most agencies traditionally spared little expense to solve the case. Similarly, reports of missing persons begin in much the same way, but given exigent circumstances such as large-scale publicity or public status of the missing person, large-scale devotion of agency resources and investigative follow-through have often been minimal, or lacking.

When investigators identified a perpetrator in a homicide and compiled the evidence that allowed prosecutors to file appropriate criminal charges, the police agency moved the case status from *open* to *closed* in their records. If they were unable to do so, the case remained open and *unsolved*. As new cases arrived and department priorities shifted, these unsolved cases became cold case homicides with little, if any, proactive effort. Similarly, missing-persons cases were handled in much the same way but often in a much abbreviated form. This has been the traditional paradigm.

Sometimes, however, there is no body. Indeed, there is no evidence that a criminal homicide has occurred. The person has just disappeared. In decades past, such circumstances did not necessarily attract much departmental interest or effort, especially with missing adults. In 2021, there were 521,000 reported missing and only 12% were adult females. In recent years, about 80% of missing people are under 21 years old. This was evidenced by only minimal documentation and little if any follow-up investigative effort. As a young new officer in the late 1960s, one of the authors observed that, not uncommonly, agencies often mandated a 24-hour waiting period before they would take a missing-persons report. With young persons, departments sometimes surmised that they were willful disappearances/runaways and would return in a day or so. Today, research and statistics suggest that three-quarters of

 DOI: 10.4324/9781003415633-9

abducted children that are killed are murdered within the first three hours (Brown et al. 2006).

In the past, the investigation of missing persons was minimal, and documentation the same. As a result, two things happened. The persons never were seen again, and the paperwork was eventually archived or destroyed, or disappeared. These and other issues plague, and confront, investigators who reinvestigate both types of unsolved cases today, often many decades later. The application of cold case homicide investigative methodologies and techniques, as they can be applied to long-time missing persons (LTMP), may assist in the reinvestigation of these cases. Like their homicide counterparts, shoe-leather detective work and forensic advances may help resolve these cases. Too often, sadly, the LTMP are murder victims. They just were not investigated as homicides. A study in England showed that 1 in 7,400 missing-persons cases ends in homicide but 1 of 34 homicides starts as a missing-persons case.[1] Obviously, not every missing-persons case turns into a homicide case; indeed, the vast majority do not.[2] But many homicide cases start off as missing-persons cases, and in any case where there is a suspicion that a person may be dead and not just missing, err on the side of treating it as a homicide case. It is better to have your missing person turn up alive during a homicide investigation than to learn your victim is dead during a missing-persons investigation.

See the case history regarding Russell Jordan in Chapter 12.

Long-Term Missing Persons Defined

As in cold case homicides, the definition is that which the individual agency designates such to be, and there is no universally accepted designation. Some consider them "long-*time* missing persons," while others denote them as "long-*term* missing persons." As utilized by the New Jersey State Police, a long-*term* missing person is "any person that has remained the subject of a missing person investigation for over thirty (30) days" (New Jersey State Police 2007).

The California Peace Officer Standards and Training (POST) guidelines for investigating such cases suggest nine categories and definitions. These are (1) *catastrophic missing*, a child or adult reported missing and assumed to be a victim of natural or man-made disaster; (2) *dependent adult*, an adult reported missing and who has physical or mental limitations, such as Alzheimer's disease; (3) *lost*, a child or adult reported to have strayed away and whose whereabouts is unknown; (4) *parent/family abduction*; (5) *runaway*, a child under 18 years of age who is reported missing but has left of his/her own free will or was rejected by his/her family; (6) *stranger abduction*; (7) *suspicious circumstances*, a child or adult reported missing and circumstances give rise to the belief that foul play may be involved, or the person is a danger to his/herself, due to physical/mental/emotional conditions, or the disappearance is out of character for the individual and no known reasons can be determined; (8) *unknown*, a child or adult reported missing but insufficient facts to determine circumstances; and (9) *voluntary missing adult*, an adult reported missing but has left of his/her own free will. Each of these categories will entail individualized investigative methodologies, but identifying the LTMP within a category may suggest or guide the investigative response (California Commission on Peace Officer Standards and Training 2011).

Case Reactivation, Locating Original Documentation, and File Reconstruction

While these issues are covered in depth in Chapters 2 through 4, these same procedures may assist in facilitating resolution of LTMP cases. Whatever the reason for reactivating a long-time missing-persons case, as in cold case homicides, basic steps must be considered. These include locating and reviewing the original case file and evidence, preliminary file review and development of an investigative plan, and investigation (including forensic review). An LTMP case can often take many years to solve. It can take so long that the original detectives on the case retire or move into other assignments and the case, now maybe years old, is assigned to a brand new set of eyes. The benefit of new eyes is that they look at the file with no preconceived notions about the case. Another advantage of a new set of eyes is the ability of a new investigator to have a more comprehensive overview of the entire case file. Whereas the original investigators may have been working the case for years and, as a result, fail to recall certain aspects of a case file, a new investigator can typically get his or her arms around a file within a matter of days or weeks. Every piece of paper in the file must be carefully reviewed to see if any lead was missed or not completely investigated. Remember that very often, the murderer's name is in the file, and the key is finding out which name it is.

Agency size, history, protocols, and plain human behavior may make this relatively easy or an investigative task on its own. Past patterns and practices affect file retention. While some agencies may have retained files in an orderly and retrievable manner over the decades, others routinely destroyed paperwork after a designated period of time. Current and archived record storage facilities, both on and off premises, should be checked as well. It is also critical to check for any associated or overlooked forensic evidence since technology changes may make it easier to extract helpful information from evidence now than in the past.

When searching for files that are not readily available, investigators may seek to identify and contact prior personnel, active or retired, who may have knowledge of the case, and have even retained copies. Secretaries and clerks are often a treasure trove of knowledge. With the advent of computers and their usage by law enforcement beginning in the late 1970s and early 1980s, some agencies were slow to incorporate this new technology. Depending upon the age of the missing-persons case, file documentation may have incorporated computerized records, paper documentation, or a combination of both. As technology has continued to expand, agencies discarded generations of hardware and software. As a result, if technology such as 5.25-inch floppy disks or older operating systems is encountered, it is recommended that investigators seek appropriate technology support.

Absent finding the original file, such information may be reconstructed beginning with the name of the missing person and date of disappearance, if known. Identification information may or may not be learned by running the victim through available databases, including the National Center for Missing and Exploited Children (NCMEC) and National Crime Information Center (NCIC). Investigators may review news media (including both print and film/video of the period regarding the disappearance and investigation) to begin reconstructing what was reported. Investigators are encouraged to identify each person interviewed by media, as well as their statements (to be compared with statements when reinterviewed). These sources may be maintained in libraries and universities, newspaper "morgues" or broadcast facilities, websites such as Newspapers.com, and media archives found on the internet. As the investigation progresses, and these persons are located and reinterviewed, it may be important to note, and account for, discrepancies or variations between past and current statements. Additionally, social media has been around long enough that reviewing it can often lead to helpful information. There are also websites such as the CharleyProject.org that contain a wealth of well-curated information on missing-persons cases.

In addition to the evidence review, examine any photographs that may be in the file and understand their purpose. These photos may be of assistance in reconstructing a neighborhood canvas. Are there pictures of:

- The missing person? What is the similarity of their likeness in the photo to when they disappeared?
- Identified and unidentified persons?
- Places and locations relative to the disappearance?

Attacking a cold case no-body murder file

You just inherited a cold no-body murder case, how do you attack it? Outlined below is one system that can be used by all investigators on no-body murder cold cases.

First, you must make sure you get the entire file. All the paperwork, physical evidence, crime scene photographs, cellphone records, recorded or videotaped interviews, everything. That's because you want a fresh set of eyes on the entire file and because by having everything at your disposal in real time you may be able to make connections in the evidence that an investigator, who may have worked on the case for years, may have missed because he or she forgot what was in there.

Second, you have to commit to reviewing all the material. This is no time for skimming or not going through every single piece of evidence in an organized fashion. It is important to keep meticulous notes on what you've reviewed and when you stop, where you left off. Reviewing old physical evidence is particularly critical. What do you have that you can subject to new forensic technology that didn't exist previously? Can you do DNA testing on something that was from a time before DNA? Can you re-submit evidence to a different lab that has different/better techniques? Talk to your forensic folks to find out what's new in their world that may be able to help you. Genealogical profiling is a new technique that many police departments are now using and someone was the first to bring it into criminal cases.

From the first "touch" on a case to when everything is reviewed, you should record everything in a Word document that will ultimately be a report on the case. You can use a standard format like the one below with the following topic headings:

- List of all detectives, investigators, officers, and prosecutors, either listed in the file or assigned to the case, you want to know every official person who touched the case.
- A final analysis of the case, strengths, weaknesses, and the chances of arrest/prosecution, sometimes we have to make choices about where to put law enforcement resources and having an honest assessment of the solvability of the case is essential.
- General case information including quick summary of time and place of disappearance, basic victim biographical facts, and same for suspect if any.
- *Timeline*: This is crucial. Missing-persons/no-body murder cases often involve investigations over many years or, even if over a short period, many important events occur in that time, some of which are occurring at the same time. It's important to have a "go-to" chronology or timeline of what happened when, to place events in a broader context and make it easier when questioning witnesses to know what happened when.
- *Player's list*: This is essential, a listing of individuals in the file no matter how obscure their connection to the case. List them in

alphabetical order for later ease of reference and include their date of birth, address, and cellphone number. Write their role/connection to the case and include a summary of any interviews they have done in the case. Also list any relation to any other "player" on the list. This list is one of the most important parts of a case review. Being able to make connections between folks over the years and knowing exactly what they said will lead to other people to interview or do follow-up interviews, i.e., "I spoke to your mom who said you didn't come home on the night in question but you said you did." One thing one of the authors has found doing case consults is investigators understandably losing track of what people said early in the investigation that may later prove either not to be true or may be more valuable information when combined with later discovered information. The use of a player's list enables you to look at everything at one time when you have been through the entire file. The big advantage of a review by new eyes on a case is the more immediate access and recall of key facts that the original case detective may not have possessed due to the passage of time.

- *Defendant's statements*: Often overlooked are the importance of using a defendant's statements/lies against him or her. Having everything the suspect/defendant ever said about the case in one place makes it easy to see contradictions and will enable the prosecutor to impeach the defendant at trial if he or she takes the stand. Be sure to include exact time and date of statement to see the evolution of what the suspect has said.
- *Notes*: Use this section to list random facts that stand out as you go through the file and that do not quite fit elsewhere, e.g., victim missed a doctor's appointment around the time of her disappearance, victim had no benefits from Social Security, etc.
- *Questions*: Use this section to write down questions you have about the case or questions to ask the investigators. Sometimes you may answer your own questions as you finish the review of the file but keep the question and answer in the report in case you forget the answer or if someone else asks the same question. These questions also form a natural To-Do list for the new investigator.

When writing this report, which can take many weeks or months depending on the size of the case file, you must note where you got each piece of evidence from. There's no worse feeling than realizing you found a connection between two pieces of evidence but are not able to put your fingers on where you found. Every entry on your report should be footnoted as to where it came from, "folder marked Defendant's statement January 3, 2021."

Think about getting help. One of the most daunting tasks in any investigation is going through phone records. Reading pages of incoming and outgoing calls, looking at call time lengths and frequency of calls can be a challenge to organize. This is where interns, retired detectives, citizens groups, or college students studying criminology can all help. Setting up individual projects that you can oversee and reap a report from is a perfect ask for these groups, often eager to help and often with time on their hands. (Not to mention that young people have far superior computer skills than us oldsters and can often do a task (such as reviewing cellphone records or GPS data) much more quickly and efficiently than we can.) Don't be shy!

When your review is done and you have your report, what's the next step? It's to … think. Having accumulated all of this information in one place the best next step is to figure out how strong of a case you have, what the next investigative steps might be, and how to implement those steps. It is also the time to share what you have with other investigators in your office and really brainstorm on next steps. With any luck, you're on your way to an arrest and possibly a trial.

Investigative Plan

During this review, the investigator attempts to understand what was known, and what needs to be learned as the investigation moves forward. As in a cold case homicide, the investigator seeks to learn the *who/what/how/why/when/where* aspects of the case, as well as *MOM*—who had *motive-opportunity-means*?

- *Who*: Who is my LTMP? My suspect? Witnesses? Are unidentified others not previously contacted? Learning as much about the LTMP as possible may open avenues of investigation heretofore unknown.
- *What*: What happened to my LTMP? What evidence do I have?
- *Why*: Why did it happen? Is my LTMP's disappearance voluntary or involuntary?
- *When*: When did it happen?
- *How*: How did it happen? Did my LTMP disappear voluntarily, or is this a case of foul play?
- *Where*: Where did my LTMP disappear from? Where was my victim last seen? By who and under what circumstances?

Police must think outside the box. In one case, the family had not heard from the missing victim for some time but was receiving letters allegedly written by the victim. The family, suspicious that the victim was actually dead, wrote back and reminded the victim to send the money he owed to another family member and to not forget that same family member's birthday. A few days later, a birthday card arrived along with a check for $25. Of course, the victim did not owe that family member any money, and it was not his birthday, so the family knew that it was not the victim writing the letters. This is just one example of police and a family thinking creatively to ensnare a killer.

In addition, the investigator needs to learn, and confirm, the following:

- Who reported my LTMP missing? During the investigation, it is prudent to recontact this person(s) as well as others involved in the original investigation. Current statements should be analyzed and compared to the original statements and any discrepancies noted and investigated.
- Date and time reported? Date and time last seen? By whom? Where? Relationship?
- Where was the LTMP reported missing from?
- Exactly what were original officers told?

The most frequently asked question at the outset in a cold case homicide investigation is, "Do we notify the victim's family?" As have families of cold case homicide victims, families of these LTMPs have ridden an emotional roller coaster since the event. However, and depending upon circumstances, contact with the family is suggested to ensure that the missing person did not return home or was otherwise accounted for, without the reporting party ever notifying law enforcement. It has happened!

While such contact may also open the floodgates of emotion, it is important to ascertain if family members heard or became aware of anything in the subsequent years that investigators may not be aware of, and to confirm that which is already known or to learn new information about the LTMP or others. It is important to stay close to the family because they hear things about the case. People who would never go to the police with information often go to the family instead. Even if the family is frustrated with the pace or results of the investigation to date, and they often are, it is imperative to try to maintain cordial relationships with them so that you can both get information from them and have them assist you in sifting any new information or leads. If the LTMP had younger siblings or friends, were they interviewed? When and where, and in the presence of whom? It is worth noting that with the passage of time, and potential maturity and growth, these siblings or other young persons may now reveal information that they were previously afraid to disclose. Family reputation or fear of disclosure may have inhibited revealing to original investigators information that might have been important to the investigation. Such might include family dynamics that involved sexual abuse.

Go back to reinterview witnesses and suspects. As years pass, people's memory changes, and it is always good to keep memories fresh by having witnesses repeat what they have previously said (which you duly recorded in some fashion the first time they told you), see if they have any new memories, and keep the word out there that the case has not languished. Interviewing suspects also tells them you're not going away either. Guilt is a powerful emotion, and you would be surprised at how it eats away at some people and can lead to a confession years later. Also, you never know what new witnesses you might find to whom the suspect confessed because he/she felt safe so many years after the murder. Always be alert for new friends/girlfriends/boyfriends of the suspect whom you can interview. The number one rule of both cold cases and LTMP cases is simple:

NEVER, NEVER, NEVER GIVE UP.

Investigation

If known (or ascertained from the family), the investigator may revisit the location where the missing person was last seen. Over time, the scene may have altered (but do not necessarily assume that it has), and people come and go. By visiting the location, the investigator may identify possible locations of witnesses and potential locations for disposal of human remains. Investigators should keep in mind and not overlook that many persons often live in their same locations for many decades.

If the neighborhood has changed significantly during the interlude between the LTMP's disappearance and the reactivation of the investigation, investigators may reconstruct the neighborhood or location by consulting records of building and planning departments, water and other civic services, and police/fire departments, and other reconstructive methods as shown in Chapter 4. This method should certainly include accessing current and prior versions of Google Earth and Apple Maps. In addition, investigators may consider a neighborhood canvas.

By reconstructing who lived where at the time the LTMP went missing, investigators may locate and interview persons who might offer investigative leads. Not uncommonly, if a canvas was done at the time of the LTMP and no one was home at the time the officer knocked on the door, no follow-up occurred, and the potential witness went without contact.

In LTMP cases, the following is suggested:

- Identify, locate, and reinterview all investigators and personnel involved in the original investigation. During this, investigators should attempt to learn if these personnel have any documents or other evidence pertaining to the case and any information that they may not have reduced to written documentation.

- Identify and review similar homicide or missing-persons cases within the area and the region to try to establish links between cases.
- Consider geographic profiling.
- Identify and explore individuals arrested or convicted for offenses both before and after the critical time period that may suggest potential involvement.
- Consult the National Missing and Unidentified Persons System (NamUs). Do not assume that unidentified remains have been entered into NamUs. Check local coroner and medical examiners (MEs) in this jurisdiction as well as surrounding jurisdictions for unidentified human remains discovered since/about time the LTMP went missing. Do they retain DNA samples as well as dental or skeletal X-rays, and fingerprints?
- Does the jurisdiction have access to, or is there in existence of, a state or national registry for missing persons?
- Is there familial DNA on file? Has a family reference sample kit been obtained?
- Was the missing person's effects examined for DNA? Sources of such might include clothing, toothbrush, and hairbrush. If not, the LTMP's family may have retained such items, and investigators are urged to explore this avenue of investigation.

Other avenues for investigation include a search for indications of the following:

- Bank account activity.
- Arrest or police contacts.
- Social Security activity.
- Requests for high school or college transcripts.
- Driver's license or identification card activity.
- Who gained financially from the LTMP's disappearance?
- Did anyone obtain a legal finding of death?
- Did anyone move away shortly after the victim disappeared?
- Did anyone exhibit unusual or strange behavior after the victim disappeared?
- Social media.
    - Obtain the passwords to all social media used by the victim through either a search warrant or the family's cooperation. You will be able to view stored messages and the victim's postings on Facebook, X, Tumblr, or other media. Given the ubiquity of social media, it is essential that any interviews of friends and families include questions about what social media the victim used. It is also essential that, if you are not conversant with

these technologies, you find someone who is. The face of social media changes rapidly as shown by the rise and fall of sites such as Myspace. As of this writing, Facebook, X, and Instagram reign supreme. However, a year from now, the popular sites could be completely different. Do not let any tech phobia you may have hinder your investigation. Get help if needed.

- It is critical that you have a skilled forensic examiner review the victim's or suspect's computer history. This is important not only so you do not miss any important clues but also so that your search is preserved and can be provided to the defense in the event of a trial.
- You should also consider whether using social media in an undercover capacity could further your investigation. Can you reach out to the suspect through Facebook, establish a friendship, and insert an undercover that could get him/her to talk? Meeting online is so common today that it might be the best way to draw out a suspect, and people tend to let down their guard more readily online. Do not overlook blogs, social media, and other new media as a way to keep the case in people's minds. The more people who are aware of the case, the greater the chances of getting a breakthrough via a previously unknown witness and of keeping the pressure on the defendant.
- Using social media is also a way for the family to stay involved. Setting up a Facebook page or X feed about the case serves to keep the case alive, keeps family and friends productively involved, and may even lead to your killer. Once the media has been online for some time, obtain a list of the IP addresses that have viewed the site. If you have a suspect's IP address (you can use sites such as maxmind.com and protonvpn.com to obtain IP addresses), you can see how often he/she is accessing the site and often track down who the suspect is through sites such as whois.net. See Chapter 4.
- In his 2020 book *Chase Darkness with Me*, journalist Billy Jensen details how he uses the power of social media to solve cold cases. Jensen's secret sauce is that he posts videos of unsolved murders on social media, typically Facebook and Twitter, but targets the posting to be shown in the exact location of the murder. In a nutshell, through his knowledge of how social media works and geotargeting, Jensen is able to target the video evidence to the people the most likely to have information about that particular murder: the people who live and work nearby. It's a fascinating technique and it does cost money and a level of expertise that

many detectives may not have, but it works and is well worth investigating as a modern investigative technique since the footage can now reach hundreds or thousands of a targeted audience. Obviously, the footage does not have to be of the murder itself, it can be the last known sighting of the victim (who was she with?) or to identify someone with the victim. A powerful new technique.

- Finally, using social media in cold cases can also often involve an investigator looking at websites that focus on so-called citizen detectives solving cases such as Reddit and Websleuths. Using these sites can be a double-edged sword. On the one hand, reviewing these sites for information/leads can be productive, particularly if you are just lurking and not revealing who you are. The downsides are the risk of wasting time chasing down crazy theories or misinformation posted on the site. Worse still is if "citizen detectives" interfere in an investigation or alert suspects that they are suspects. (In the Boston Marathon bombing case, Reddit users infamously posted photographs of a "suspect" who was not involved in the crime at all.) It is best to start off slowly and tread carefully. Certainly, many cold cases have benefited from the involvement of social media and unofficial sleuths and the reach of the internet is difficult to beat, but actively working with citizen detectives who do not have the same rules as government investigators can be risky.

Searches

One of the biggest challenges in a LTMP case is the decision about whether to search for a body. In most no-body murder investigations, there is an emphasis early in the investigation on searching for a body. As time goes on, however, the chances of finding a body decrease both because the more obvious places have been searched to no avail and a body decomposes at a fairly steady rate. Thus, in any cold case missing-persons case/homicide, a number of factors need to be considered when determining whether to continue to conduct searches. First, were there prior searches? How many and how well-organized were they? Searches by professional search teams with canine assistance are obviously preferable to all-volunteer searches by friends and family. What areas were searched? Is there new evidence that points to possible new search areas? How soon after the person was reported missing did the searches commence? Searches begun soon after disappearance that were well-conducted yet fruitless may mean trying to do additional searches years later are unlikely to yield positive results. The single most important factor to consider is the potential location of the body. Any body left outdoors or placed into water is going to be exceedingly hard to find given the passage of even a few years. Other than very cool climates where the decomposition of a body may be greatly slowed (think Alaska), two to three years is likely all that is needed to make an outdoor body very difficult to find and recover (other than maybe clothing). Passage of time, climate, and possible location must be the primary consideration in determining whether to spend resources to conduct searches for a body.

Research by one of the authors has shown that putting a body into water is the most common method of hiding a body. Of the 576 no-body murder trials analyzed in the book *No-Body Homicide Cases*, we know where the body was allegedly disposed of (either through confession of the defendant or other evidence in the case) for about 231 cases. Of those 231 cases, 94 involved disposal of water with another 84 being buried; 58 more were disposed of in a dump or landfill while another 53 were simply dumped outdoors. Therefore, if your victim is missing in an area where water burial or burying or dumping into the earth is possible or likely, you need to take steps to determine if this is a possibility. Remember: even if you do not find a body, it is important to show a jury what steps were taken to find a body and thus prove the victim is actually dead. You do not want to be on the witness stand being cross-examined about all the things you might have done to find a body and not be able to give any examples of what steps you took to find the body.

Determine if there are ways to get into the air to survey the area and look for recent disturbances in the earth. Can you get a local pilot to fly you over the area if you are looking in a rural or suburban area? Is it winter, and any disturbance to the earth is going to be very noticeable? Talk to those who go out into the woods, such as hikers, hunters, and trail runners. Ask them if they've seen anything out of the ordinary or recently disturbed areas.

As a person of interest or suspect is developed, investigate what hobbies they have to help determine where he/she might go to bury a body. Is he/she hunter? Where does he/she hunt? A bird-watcher? Camper? Cross-country skier? As always, put yourself in his/her shoes and ask yourself, *If I need to get rid of a body and needed some time to do it, where would I go?* It is unlikely you would go somewhere you did not know well and risk detection since you would not know the potential traffic at the location.

When bodies are found in LTMP cases, they are often found in locations either near or familiar to the murderer. Search warrants or consent searches should be executed on any suspect's car, home, or workplace. When disposing of a body, a murderer will try not to be too obvious. Thus, while he/she may have murdered the victim in his/her own home, he/she will not necessarily hide the body there. It is still critical to search his/her home for clues to the murder, but you must also search areas outside his/her home: his/her property and nearby properties, particularly if they are wooded or belong to entities other than private citizens, such as government-owned property or property owned by commercial interests such as factories, farms, etc. Concealing a body on private property can be dangerous because a suspect will stand out while on the property and will be afraid that someone else may discover the body by accident. Burying a body on his/her own land, land owned by an absentee owner, or land that is unoccupied at night is a much safer bet.

In connection with burying, it is common to see bodies dismembered as well. A thorough search of the suspect's house must be conducted for signs of this grisly process. Because of the time and effort involved in cutting up a body, it is often conducted indoors, and needless to say, it is messy. Drains in sinks, bathtubs, and washing machines must be removed and checked for signs of blood. Basements and crawl spaces are common places to both cut up the body as well as hide the tools used to do so. It is also extremely common to see signs of a cleanup throughout a house, and often, this is the best evidence not only that a murder did occur but also of where it took place. Evidence of a cleanup can include finding cleaning products such as bleach and carpet cleaners; the removal of carpets, rugs, or furniture; and even the running of fans to get rid of a smell. Consider blood enhancement, as noted in Chapter 26.

Instruments that could have been used to cut up a body must be searched for, and with LTMP cases, what is missing is often as important as what is present. Are knives missing from the house? Saws or other cutting implements? Family members and friends are often familiar with what was in a house, apartment, or toolbox. In a case in Massachusetts, the evidence against the defendant included flesh and bone recovered from a power saw.[3] One of the first cases that brought forensic criminologist Henry Lee to fame was a Connecticut case where the defendant fed his wife through a wood chipper during a snowstorm. Pieces of her bone and hair were recovered, which helped lead to Richard Crafts' conviction.[4]

As the nation becomes more urbanized, disposing of bodies in dumpsters, which then go to landfills, or landfills themselves has become increasingly common. Obviously, in any urban location, nearby dumpsters must be carefully checked, not just for a body or body part but also for evidence of a cleanup or evidence of the victim's clothes or other possessions being disposed of. Once the dumpster has been removed to the landfill, however, it becomes much more difficult to search for a body, but it can be done. Searching a landfill is not only difficult; it can be extremely dangerous due to hazardous materials and the buildup of dangerous gases from the decay of waste such as methane and carbon dioxide. There are actually experts on conducting landfill searches, and consulting with such an expert and working closely with the landfill owners or operators are essential.[5] Landfills often track where trash came from and where it is placed in the landfill, so having close cooperation from the landfill owners, whether private or public, is critical.[6] In any event, searching a landfill can be extremely expensive and even cost too much given the difficulties of finding anything. In a case in the District of Columbia, the police and prosecutors opposed a defendant's request to search a landfill even though the defendant had confessed to putting the body into a dumpster that was delivered to the landfill, because of the prohibitive cost and low probability of recovering a body. Apparently, the defense hoped that recovery of the body would lead to evidence that would show that the defendant had not committed the murder or that the lack of a body would show that the confession was false.[7]

Recent advances in geophysical tools may lead to a greater ability to search landfills and other places where bodies might be buried. According to an article in *Science Live*, British researchers are conducting experiments with buried pigs to test ground-penetrating radars and other geophysical methods. (Pig skin is very similar to human skin.) Although their research is in the early stages, these techniques could prove to be a real boon to investigators searching for a missing body.[8]

Searches for the body are often conducted by private citizens. These private searches are often a good way for the family and friends of the victim to get involved in a positive and productive way. While it is preferable that a member of the investigative team go along on these searches, in all cases, the searches performed should be maintained in a logbook keeping track of when the search occurred, the location and areas searched, the resources used, and man-hours spent searching. All of this can be very useful at trial to demonstrate the immense effort that went into finding the victim.

It is also essential that any unidentified bodies in the area are carefully checked to make sure that an ME's office does not have your victim's body but just does not know who it is. Statistics from the Department of Justice show that every year, ME's offices nationwide will receive 4,400 unidentified bodies (Driscoll 2013). Of those 4,400 bodies, an average of 1,000 remain unidentified after 1 year (Driscoll 2013). One of the best ways to identify a body is by using NamUs. NamUs "assists law enforcement in their investigations of missing and unidentified person cases."[9] NamUs has three databases: the Missing Persons Database, the Unidentified Persons System, and the Unclaimed Persons Database. The Missing Persons Database contains information on missing persons entered by law enforcement. The information is verified before being entered into the system. The Unidentified Persons System contains information entered by MEs and coroners on unidentified bodies. The Unclaimed Persons Database contains information entered by MEs and coroners about persons who have been identified but not claimed by family. See Chapter 17.

NamUs also provides a number of free forensic services including DNA testing and anthropology and odontology services. NamUs provides analytical services that assist law enforcement with solving missing and unidentified cases. Analysts have access to multiple law enforcement databases including Accurint for Law Enforcement and Consolidated Lead Evaluation and Reporting (CLEAR). The NamUs analysts can also research the NCIC database. Additionally, NamUs analysts are experts in using social media to search for missing people, something critical in a no-body murder. They can review sites such as Facebook, Spokeo, Google, and Ancestry.com to determine whether the missing person is posting information. This evidence (or lack thereof) can prove critical to proving a person is not missing but is actually dead. It is important to exhaustively search both government and private databases to ensure both yourself and a jury that the victim is not somehow secretly living somewhere else.

If you have the victim's DNA, it should be entered into the Federal Bureau of Investigation's (FBI's) Combined DNA Index System (CODIS). CODIS contains DNA from persons convicted of crimes, DNA profiles taken from crime scenes, profiles from unidentified human remains, and DNA samples from the families of missing persons.[10]

Behavioral Analysis

During the investigation, investigators may seek experienced assistance in understanding behavioral aspects of both the LTMP as well as any persons of interest who may be developed. In the United States, many state criminal justice agencies as well as federal law enforcement agencies include personnel specifically trained and experienced in behavioral analysis as exhibited at the crime scene, or in individual behavior. Do not hesitate to ask for help. Many police departments in the United States have fewer than 10 officers.[11] Few if any departments of under 100 officers could reasonably handle a major case without help. Besides, the help is free, so why not use it, even of it is only to run down the bogus leads that come in any no-body murder investigation? The FBI's Behavioral Analysis Unit (BAU) does a great job at both profiling who the possible killer might be as well as suggesting approaches to a suspect during an interview or interrogation. As noted previously, the Naval Criminal Investigative Services (NCIS) does the same, although they are typically looking for a naval or armed forces connection.

Learning as much about the LTMP as possible is important in these investigations, and investigators may consider a *victimology assessment.* This may initially be undertaken by an experienced investigator to help identify whether this was a voluntary disappearance or any of the nine categories previously noted by the California POST report types. As in cold case homicides, investigators seek to identify who might have had MOM, and assessment of the LTMP might also include inquiry into their:

- Financial situation
- Marital/sexual relationship
- Family issues (including custody)
- Business concerns and pressures
- Emotional issues and mental state
- High-risk lifestyle, including prostitution, alcohol, and drugs
- Health issues

The National Center for Analysis of Violent Crime (NCAVC) unit at the FBI Academy assists local agencies in reviewing circumstances of these cases, analysis of behavioral characteristics, as well as consideration of investigative plans.

In any LTMP investigation, the victimology, that is, what type of person this victim is, is essential in solving the case. An investigation of a known street prostitute or drug addict is much different than the investigation of a hardworking mother of three. (Note that we did not say that one investigation is more important than the other. All LTMP cases deserve the same level of investigation, resources, and dedication no matter who they were or what their stature was in life.) Knowledge of victimology is critical to keeping your investigation on the right track. In an LTMP case, victimology is even more important because, again, your investigation focuses on not only who committed the murder but also proving that a murder occurred.

Your victim's victimology assessment can make proving the fact of his/her murder more difficult. A missing drug addict is much more likely to be thought of as dying from an overdose or simply disappearing than a young mother with no history of drug abuse. By studying and knowing your victim's victimology, you will know what types of evidence will persuade a jury that your victim is indeed dead. Remember that every victim has a victimology that can help prove he/she is dead. While it is easy to prove the death of most individuals who have a well-worn path of obligations such as families, jobs, friends, etc., even the most downtrodden victim has habits and patterns, family and friends. The absence of these patterns can demonstrate just as conclusively that a person is dead as someone missing work or an important family milestone. In one no-body murder case in the District of Columbia, the victim was an alcoholic and possible drug user who was not employed. The initial detective assigned to the case even dismissed her sister as a "crack-head" in a written report. In fact, she had five children for whom she cared deeply, and at trial, it was demonstrated that she had missed their birthdays and holidays when she had never done so before. This was proof to a jury that she was dead. One of the most poignant moments of the trial was the testimony of the victim's 12-year-old daughter, who testified that her mother had never missed her birthday or Christmas until after she went missing.

The fact that the person is presumed dead and not merely missing can also lead to your pool of suspects. As a matter of logic, an LTMP case does not lead itself to a certain type of defendant. A burglar who breaks into a home and is surprised by the owner, who he then shoots and kills, is not going to hang around to dispose of the body. Disposing of a body takes time, and that is not something an accidental killer, such as a burglar, robber, or carjacker, is typically willing to risk. There are certainly stranger-on-stranger no-body murders, but those cases typically involve the murderer deliberately seeking a victim for the thrill of the killing such child predators. He/she wants to cover up his/her crimes in order to get away with them. In cases of accidental murders where the body is hidden, there is almost always a preexisting relationship between the killer and his/her victim. A classic example is a coworker killing another coworker over a work dispute or two business associates having a falling out when one kills the other. These types of murders occur on familiar grounds for the killer, often the workplace, and the murderer can take the time to dispose of the body, safe in the knowledge that no one is likely to surprise him/her at the workplace. Since a no-body murder requires time and effort, by far, the most common suspect is a person known to the victim.

If the missing person had a computer, tablet, or other such device, and it was never analyzed, and is perhaps still in the possession of family members or others, a forensic examination is suggested. Cold case homicide and LTMP investigations involve teamwork and cooperation among many disciplines and knowledge of available resources to complement the investigation. Among these are government resources for LTMP and cold case homicides as well as nongovernment sponsored organizations.

Interagency Cooperation

With the growth and expansion of police agencies, organizational practices often lead to specialized units, sometimes physically distant. These specialized units can include missing persons, in addition to homicide, robbery, sexual assault, and more. As a result, case resolution can suffer due to lack of communication. In larger agencies, those tasked with missing-persons investigations do not always receive the same allocation of resources, or perhaps prestige, as those charged with homicide investigations.

As previously noted, LTMPs are not uncommonly homicide cases. Recognizing that their physical and organizational practices inhibited efficiency in this regard, homicide and missing-persons administrators in the Los Angeles Police Department, California, facilitated a solution to help minimize these deficiencies. At their regular meetings and reviews of missing-persons cases, experienced homicide investigators became part of the review team and were given authority to assume responsibility for the investigation of long-time missing-persons cases when, in their opinions, the case circumstances warranted homicide levels of expertise and investigation. This practice has proven successful.

Federal Agencies and Databases

Federal Bureau of Investigation

This agency maintains numerous programs and databases, which may assist in these investigations. Included in these are NCIC, NCVAC, NGI, the Integrated Automated Fingerprint Identification System (IAFIS), CODIS, and the Violent Criminal Apprehension Program (ViCAP). Each of these is discussed in detail in following, separate chapters.

The National Crime Information Center

The NCIC is a computerized nationwide information system supporting criminal justice agencies and is available to law enforcement 24 hours a day, 365 days a year. It consists of a series of specialized files, including those on property and persons. An archive of entries is also kept in an offline system. See Chapter 8 regarding offline searches. While all file indices may be of assistance during the course of these investigations, the Missing Person File was originated in 1975, using defined criteria. These include whether the missing person is a juvenile, endangered, or disabled, or the disappearance is involuntary or due to catastrophic circumstances or other factors. In addition, NCIC has also maintained the Unidentified Person File since 1983 and the national Sex Offender Registry File since 1999. The IAFIS was introduced in July 1999. These systems incorporate data held at state levels as well as federal levels. See Chapter 8.

The Combined DNA Index System

CODIS became operational in October 1998. This tiered system is the national DNA database into which are entered DNA profiles from (1) forensic unknowns at crime scenes; (2) convicted offenders who are required to provide such samples; (3) missing persons; (4) unidentified human remains; and (5) relatives of missing persons. See Chapter 18.

National Center for the Analysis of Violent Crime

This unit provides behavioral-based investigative support for local, state, national, and international law enforcement. It consists of different units, including those units tasked with providing behavioral analysis for crimes against children and crimes against adults. Within this center is ViCAP. It consists of a database and tools available to law enforcement for investigation and linkage of missing-persons and unidentified-human-remains cases as well as homicides and other offenses. These sources enable law enforcement to associate cases that are dispersed geographically and might not otherwise appear to be connected. See Chapter 7.

Next-Generation Identification (NGI)/Automated Fingerprint Identification System (AFIS)

Implemented in 1999 and upgraded, this electronic database is the national fingerprint and criminal history record system of criminal arrests and civil fingerprint filings. It provides automated fingerprint searches, latent search capabilities, electronic image storage, and electronic exchanges of fingerprints. It is available and responds to inquiries and requests 24 hours a day, 365 days of the year. See Chapter 14.

National Center for Missing and Exploited Children

This organization is a partnership between public and private entities. It works with law enforcement on issues related to long-time missing, missing, and sexually exploited children. (Children are defined as those under 21 years old.) Founded in 1984, it provides investigators with a number of resources. In addition to a national toll-free hotline and assistance in current case investigations, this partnership offers numerous resources to law enforcement.

Acknowledgments

We wish to express our deepest appreciation to former Assistant U.S. Attorney Thomas A. (Tad) DiBiase for his lead-authorship in this chapter. Tad has both tried a no-body homicide case during his career as a homicide prosecutor and consulted across the country on more than 50 additional no-body murder cases. He lectures on the topic to police and prosecutors and blogs on these cases at http://www.nobodymurdercases.com. He is considered the nation's leading expert on no-body murders.

Notes

1 Centrex, Developing Policing Excellence, NCOF, Operational Support Section, Missing Persons, Suggested Lines of Enquiry in Suspicious Missing Person Investigations, Version 3, September 2003.

2 Also note that 40% of missing person cases are of missing minorities, a percentage higher than the minority population of the United States (currently 36.7%). Bui, L., "How Many Other Relishas Are There?," *Washington Post*, March 1, 2015; http://usnews.nbcnews.com/_news/2013/06/13/18934111-census-white-majority-in-us-gone-by-2043, accessed March 1, 2015.

3 http://mercuryservices.hubpages.com/video/No-Body-Trials-Locking-Up-Murderers-When-the-Victims-Corpse-Is-Missing. Last accessed March 9, 2013.

4 http://www.trutv.com/library/crime/notorious_murders/family/woodchipper_murder/10.html. Last accessed March 9, 2013.

5 See http://www.policechiefmagazine.org/magazine/index.cfm?fuseaction=display&article_id=2270&issue_id=122010, which profiles Ron Olive of the Naval Criminal Investigative Services (NCIS) and his expertise in searching landfills. Last accessed March 17, 2013.

6 http://www.letsk9professionals.org/landfills.html. Last accessed March 17, 2013.

7 http://homicidewatch.org/2011/04/27/judge-wont-compel-search-for-latisha-fraziers-body/. Last accessed on March 17, 2013.

8 Hidden Graves Revealed with Geophysical Tools, http://www.livescience.com/31982-hidden-bodies-found-using-geophysics.html. Last accessed May 17, 2013.

9 See Driscoll (2013). All of the information in this paragraph and the next is from this article. See also http://www.namus.gov.

10 Behavioral Analysis Unit, National Center for the Analysis of Violent Crime, "Serial Murder, Multi-Disciplinary Perspectives for Investigators" at 37.

11 https://web.archive.org/web/*/http://www.fop.net/labor/icpra/3TheFutureofLawEnforcementintheUnitedStatesofAmerica.pdf. Last accessed January 20, 2014.

Suggested Readings and Bibliography

Brown, K.M., Keppel, R.D., Weis, J.G., and Skeen, M.E. (2006). Investigative Case Management for Missing Children Homicides: Report II. https://www.ncjrs.gov/pdffiles1/Archive/218936NCJRS.pdf, accessed December 29, 2014.

California Commission on Peace Officer Standards and Training. (2011). Missing Persons Investigations: Guidelines & Curriculum. https://post.ca.gov/Portals/0/Publications/Missing_Persons_Investigations.pdf?ver=2019-07-12-131131-303, accessed May 20, 2016.

DiBiase, T.A. (2023). *No-Body Homicide Cases: A Practical Guide to Investigating, Prosecuting and Winning a Case When the Victim's Body is Missing*. 2nd ed. CRC Press, Boca Raton, FL.

Driscoll, D. (2013). Resolving Missing and Unidentified Person Cases Using Today's Technology, *The Police Chief*, May.

New Jersey State Police. (2007). Missing Persons Investigative Best Practices Protocol. https://www.njsp.org, accessed May 20, 2016.

Pettem, S. (2009). *Someone's Daughter: In Search of Justice for Jane Doe*. Taylor Trade, Lanham, MD.

Pettem, S. (2013). *Cold Case Research: Resources for Unidentified, Missing and Cold Case Homicides*. CRC Press, Boca Raton, FL.

Regensburger, D. (2011). Law Enforcement Volunteers: An Essential Tool in the Investigation of Cold Case Homicides. *Sheriff Magazine*. May–June. Vol 63, Issue 3, pp. 22–23.

The Prosecution of Cold Case Homicides

8

ANNE MARIE SCHUBERT

Introduction

On May 7, 1977, 15-year-old Penny Parker went out to collect money for her paper route with the *Sacramento Bee* newspaper. She never returned home. Two days later, Penny's body was found in a rural field in Sacramento County. She had been sexually assaulted and stabbed to death. For 25 years, her murder remained unsolved despite diligent and persistent efforts of law enforcement to find her killer while Penny's family waited for justice. Finally, in 2002, as a result of Sacramento County's Cold Case Prosecution Program, Penny's murderer was identified and charged with her murder (Figure 8.1).

Cold case murders present unique and interesting challenges for both investigators and prosecutors. Unlike active homicide cases, there are many legal and evidentiary issues that would never arise in a fresh homicide that must be addressed in both the investigation and the prosecution in order to effectively present an old murder case to a jury.

Figure 8.1 Penny Parker.

 DOI: 10.4324/9781003415633-10

The most significant factor in the investigation and prosecution of cold cases is—not surprisingly—the passage of time. The passage of time can both help and hinder a cold case. While time clearly has an adverse impact on the memories of witnesses, it also may become an ally if once-reluctant witnesses become forthright and cooperative. While some investigative leads can be lost with time—perhaps because physical evidence was lost or destroyed or because witnesses have died or become disabled—other avenues may open up. In the last 25 years, DNA has revolutionized the ability of investigators to evaluate physical evidence. DNA has, in essence, become the silent witness to the truth.

While the investigation of a cold case presents distinctive challenges, so too does the prosecution. In addition to learning and briefing legal issues that must be mastered in many ordinary murder trials, the prosecutor in a cold murder trial may also have to deal with legal issues arising from sometimes extensive pretrial delay, which will be governed by the statute of limitations and constitutional standards of due process.

Additionally, the prosecutor must master the facts and, in doing so, take into account the expectations of the jury. With the introduction of cold cases in television media, jurors expect scientific evidence on par with what television writers and producers have presented to them. Satisfying these expectations in any murder case, let alone an old one, can be very difficult.

Early Involvement of a Prosecutor

Due to the legal, evidentiary, and modern-day challenges presented by cold cases, it is critical for law enforcement and the prosecution to work together at the earliest phase of the investigation. This should be done as soon as the cold case is reopened. Through this team approach, the investigator and prosecutor can effectively anticipate and prepare for any legal or evidentiary challenges that may arise in court once an individual is charged. Coordination and cooperation may involve discussing the necessity and sufficiency of search warrants, photographic or live lineups, and the chain of custody for forensic evidence. It may also involve discussing what scientific tests should be used, as well as what defenses may be raised. Through this coordination and cooperation during the investigative stage, the likelihood of a successful prosecution will increase dramatically.

Additionally, many of these cold cases will involve hundreds, if not thousands, of pages of police reports. This may be due to several reasons: the case was initially investigated by law enforcement at the time of the murder; the investigation may have continued over several years by many different investigators; and the case was ultimately solved. Further, once the perpetrator is identified, police reports will be generated not only connecting the suspect to the crime but also detailing his/her criminal background. If the defendant is charged with capital murder, a thorough review of his/her background will be required for the penalty phase. Obtaining and organizing these materials in a manner sufficient to justify arrest, conviction, and perhaps even the imposition of the death penalty requires prosecutorial involvement—and the sooner, the better.

Due to the complexity of cold cases, the involvement of a local prosecutor during the investigation will assist in the organization of the case and the presentation of evidence to a jury.

Prosecuting the Cold Case Murder

Charging Cold Case Murders

There are several considerations that must be taken into account when charging a cold case murder.

1. *Statute of limitations:* In many murder cases, additional crimes have been committed along with the homicide. In both the homicide charge and the other offenses, the prosecutor must determine the appropriate statute of limitations for all charges.

   In general, there is no statute of limitations for murder. There can be exceptions to the general rule, however, depending on the jurisdiction and the date of the offense. For instance, in October of 2000, Michael Skakel was charged by the state of Connecticut with the 1975 murder of 15-year-old Martha Moxley. At the time of his arrest, Skakel was 39 years old—he was barely 15 years old at the time of the crime. Numerous legal motions were filed by the defense seeking a dismissal based upon the statute of limitations. In particular, the defense claimed that the prosecution of the murder was time barred by a 5-year statute of limitations in effect in Connecticut in 1975. While the trial court denied the motion to dismiss, the claim was the defendant's primary contention on appeal.

   In addition to the statute of limitations for murder, the prosecution must also become familiar with the statute of limitations for any lesser and included offenses to murder (such as manslaughter), and for any other crimes that were connected to the murder. These statutes will vary according to the jurisdiction. As a result, in many jurisdictions, the charging document may be limited to the murder charge alone.

However, even if the statute of limitations precludes the charging of related offenses, in many jurisdictions, the prosecution can still allege special circumstances that may qualify the defendant for capital punishment. For instance, a murder case from 1981 may involve the kidnap, rape, and murder of a young female. While the statute of limitations may bar the filing of kidnap and rape as separate counts, it may not bar the filing of kidnap and rape as *special circumstances* attached to the count of murder.

2. *Law of murder:* One of the most important issues that must be confronted when charging a cold case murder is determining what the law of murder was at the time of the crime. This includes the degree of murder and any lesser included offense to the crime of murder, such as manslaughter. The simplest means of determining this is to consult the penal code for the year of the crime. Additionally, the prosecutor must determine what jury instructions will be provided to the jury at trial. This may require finding jury instructions that were in use at the time of the crime and determining whether those jury instructions or some more modern variant must be used.
3. *Law of special circumstances:* In jurisdictions that have capital punishment, it is imperative to know what special circumstances existed at the time of the crime. In many jurisdictions, the list of special circumstances has been expanded over the years. For instance, if a murder occurred in 1982 and involved a kidnapping and carjacking, it is necessary to know if the kidnapping and carjacking were on the list of special circumstances law in 1982. If they were not, but some related charge was (such as robbery), the prosecutor might be able to allege robbery as an alternative special circumstance in the charging document.

   Additionally, even if the death penalty was authorized under the penal code at the time of the murder, there are jurisdictions where court rulings nullified those statutes, finding that the law was unconstitutional. In such jurisdictions, the death penalty cannot be sought for offenses committed before the court ruling. For instance, the California Supreme Court found the death penalty statute of that state unconstitutional in August 1977. As a result, no defendant in California who committed murder before August 1977 can be put to death, and in fact, they face a maximum term of 7 years to life in prison. Thus, in Penny Parker's murder, the prosecution was precluded from seeking the death penalty because the crime occurred in May 1977.

Clearly, the potential charges and sentence will have a significant impact on both the investigation and prosecution of a cold case. Understanding the laws that existed at the time of the murder is critical.

4. *Proper court for filing charges:* In some murder cases, the defendant may have been a juvenile at the time of the murder. In those instances, the prosecutor must determine whether his/her jurisdiction requires that charges first be filed in juvenile court or adult court. The determination of whether a juvenile defendant may be tried in adult court presents many complex issues that must be fully explored by the prosecutor.

Necessary Elements of the Investigation

The successful prosecution of a cold murder case is dependent upon the investigation conducted by law enforcement. From a prosecutor's perspective, there are several key elements to a successful cold case investigation. These include the following:

Thorough Review of Case File

A thorough review of the case file is necessary to effectively investigate and prosecute a cold case. From an investigator's point of view, this is necessary to complete the investigation. From a prosecutor's perspective, this review is necessary not only for an effective prosecution but also to ensure compliance with the rules of discovery, which in most jurisdictions impose upon the prosecutor an ethical obligation to provide all reports associated with the case file to the defense.

In this case review, the following steps should be taken:

- Obtain all reports, including the following:
  - *Police reports*: This includes reports in the original case file as well as those maintained in the police records division. It is not uncommon for reports in the original case file not to have been submitted to the records division. It is highly recommended that the prosecutor personally review the original police file to verify that all records have been obtained.
  - Autopsy reports.
  - *Laboratory reports*: This includes all final reports as well as laboratory notes generated or relied upon by the laboratory analyst.
  - Medical records.

    - Psychological records.
    - *Records in possession of prosecution*: In some instances, the prosecutor's office may have a copy of the case file. This may be due to several reasons. The case may have been filed and later dismissed, or the case may have been submitted for filing but rejected by a prosecutor. In many instances, the prior prosecutor may have obtained records that were never seen by the original investigator.
- *Locate all photographs, videotapes, audiotapes, and composites*: These include those from the following agencies:
    - *Law enforcement*: These items should be in the records division. As noted previously, however, items sometimes do not make it from the original case file to the records division. This can include original reports, photographs, tapes, composites, or Polaroid photographs of suspects and/or vehicles.
    - *Medical examiner's/coroner's office*: The original autopsy photographs should also be obtained. While the law enforcement agency may also have taken photographs at the autopsy, the photographs taken by the medical examiner may be more comprehensive. In particular, the medical examiner may have taken photographs depicting the collection of evidence and the internal examination of the victim. Many times, these photographs will become critical for the prosecution in demonstrating the proper chain of custody in the collection of evidence or for identifying particular wound patterns for the victim.
    - *Hospital photographs*: In some instances, a hospital may have taken photographs of injuries of the victim prior to or after death.
    - *Other sources of photographs*: The investigator and prosecutor should also determine if other individuals have photographs relevant to the investigation. These include media sources (TV or newspapers) or those in the possession of civilian witnesses. For instance, it may be necessary to obtain photographs from the victim or suspect's family demonstrating events around the time of the homicide.

Thorough Review and Analysis of Physical Evidence

One of the most critical steps in the investigation and prosecution of a cold case involves review of the physical evidence. In many cases, the identity of the suspect is determined through forensic evidence. In particular, the introduction of forensic DNA testing and the use of convicted-offender DNA databanks have allowed investigators to identify suspects in cases that may otherwise remain unsolved. As such, it is important that both the investigator and the prosecutor understand how to handle and evaluate physical evidence. In many cases, the reliability of the evidence testing and the chain of custody will be aggressively attacked by the defense. As such, it is imperative that this review be thorough and that all necessary and relevant items of evidence be analyzed.

In reviewing the state of the physical evidence, the following steps should be taken:

- Consider all possible locations where the evidence may be located. This may include the following locations:
  - Law enforcement property room.
  - *Coroner's office*: In many jurisdictions, the coroner's office provides the autopsy kit to either the crime laboratory or police agency at the time of the autopsy. However, in some jurisdictions, the coroner's office keeps additional biological samples (such as smears of biological fluids placed on slides) in its own possession. Additionally, the coroner's office may have tissue samples from the victim. These autopsy and tissue samples may become vital to the investigation of the case. This is particularly true where the law enforcement autopsy kit has been either lost or destroyed.

    For instance, in Penny Parker's murder, the law enforcement agency was unable to locate the autopsy kit taken in 1977. However, the Sacramento County Coroner's Office retained autopsy samples in its possession. These samples became the vital piece of evidence for identifying Penny's killer.
  - *Crime laboratory or specific laboratory analyst's possession*: This should include all laboratories that have conducted analyses in the case. In many cases, several laboratories may have conducted analyses over many years. It is vital to determine if any of these laboratories have retained any evidence in the case.
  - Prosecutor's office.
  - Previous investigator's possession.
  - Court file.

Additionally, in reviewing the physical evidence, both the investigator and the prosecutor should consider the following:

- Do not assume evidence is lost or destroyed.

  It is not uncommon for investigators to be told that the evidence is lost or destroyed when, in fact, it isn't. The evidence may have been misplaced, or the property clerk may not know where to find it. The investigator should personally seek to find the evidence by going to all the possible locations it may be stored. A diligent and meticulous search for the evidence can oftentimes result in locating the critical items of evidence.

- Seek the assistance of an expert when conducting an inventory and review of the evidence.

    To fully understand the significance of physical evidence in a cold case, an expert will need to be consulted. The analysts employed in law enforcement crime labs will likely be able to either provide this expertise personally or know someone who can. The expert can also evaluate whether potential defenses are scientifically viable. For instance, in many cold case murders, the defendant may claim that he had consensual sex with the victim prior to her death but did not kill her. This defense, however, may be undermined by an understanding of the significance of the physical evidence that only an expert can provide. If a large amount of semen belonging to the defendant is found in the victim's body, the expert may understand that this indicates recent sexual relations, thereby possibly defeating a consent defense.

- Reevaluate old lab reports.

    Forensic science has changed dramatically over the last 20–30 years. Tests, particularly of biological substances, are much more definitive and reliable than they once were. For instance, some of the following factors should be considered in reviewing forensic testing performed in a cold case:

    - If a lab report indicates "no semen or sperm" was *found*, do not automatically assume that no semen or sperm was present. It may be that the laboratory only performed a *presumptive* test (such as acid phosphatase) at the time. In many cases, the lack of a positive response on this presumptive test does not mean there is no semen or sperm present. The investigator and/or prosecutor should confirm this through a microscopic analysis by the laboratory.

        In the Penny Parker case, for example, the victim's underwear was analyzed in 1977, and at that time, the laboratory reported that no seminal fluid was detected on the underwear (Figure 8.2).

        A review of the analysis revealed that this conclusion was based solely on a presumptive test. In 2002, the laboratory performed a microscopic analysis of the underwear, which had a large amount of sperm. DNA testing of the sperm conclusively identified the individual later charged with Penny's murder.

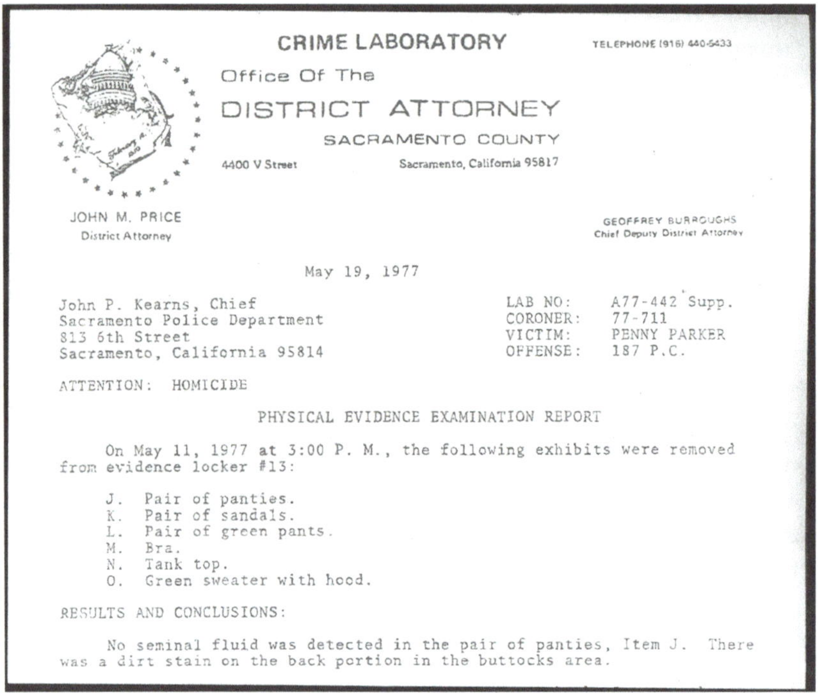

CRIME LABORATORY TELEPHONE (916) 440-5433

Office Of The

DISTRICT ATTORNEY

SACRAMENTO COUNTY

4400 V Street Sacramento, California 95817

JOHN M. PRICE
District Attorney

GEOFFREY BURROUGHS
Chief Deputy District Attorney

May 19, 1977

John P. Kearns, Chief
Sacramento Police Department
813 6th Street
Sacramento, California 95814

LAB NO: A77-442 Supp.
CORONER: 77-711
VICTIM: PENNY PARKER
OFFENSE: 187 P.C.

ATTENTION: HOMICIDE

PHYSICAL EVIDENCE EXAMINATION REPORT

On May 11, 1977 at 3:00 P. M., the following exhibits were removed from evidence locker #13:

J. Pair of panties.
K. Pair of sandals.
L. Pair of green pants.
M. Bra.
N. Tank top.
O. Green sweater with hood.

RESULTS AND CONCLUSIONS:

No seminal fluid was detected in the pair of panties, Item J. There was a dirt stain on the back portion in the buttocks area.

Figure 8.2 1977 laboratory report.

- Do not rely exclusively on the autopsy and/or medical sexual assault examination to determine whether sperm is present. In many old cases, the method of evidence collection by the medical examiner may have precluded the observation of sperm. While the autopsy report may indicate "no sperm" *found*, this does not necessarily mean that there is no sperm *present* or there was no sexual assault. Thus, the autopsy kit may well have to be retested using current forensic technology.

- View and photograph the condition of the existing evidence.

By viewing the evidence in person, both the investigator and prosecutor can better understand the significance of items that either were not photographed before or cannot be adequately portrayed in photographs. This may provide a better understanding of the circumstances surrounding the crime.

Additionally, viewing and photographing the evidence can assist in determining the chain of custody. In many cold cases, the chain of custody is difficult to establish. In some instances, property sheets may have been lost or destroyed—if they were ever prepared at all. By viewing the evidence in person, the investigator and prosecutor can see what documentation relating to the chain of custody was maintained with the evidence itself. Photographing these items as well as documentation relating to the chain of custody will often help the prosecution in court proceedings.

- Determine whether additional forensic testing is available and advisable.

  Both law enforcement and the prosecution should consult about whether additional testing is possible and is needed in a particular cold case. For instance, further analysis may reveal that additional sexual acts were committed against the victim. As a result, it may be possible to allege additional special circumstances against the defendant.

  Furthermore, additional testing may provide greater insight into the circumstances surrounding the crime and the defendant's connection to it. This could provide useful information when the case is presented to a jury.

Reconstruct the Crime and the Defendant's Connection to the Crime

One of the most challenging aspects in both the investigation and prosecution of a cold case murder is reconstructing the crime and the defendant's connection to it. Presenting a cold case homicide to a jury presents unique challenges because many jurors expect that even an investigation conducted years ago will meet the latest scientific standards. Defense attorneys are sure to contrast modern standards with those that were actually used at the time. One way to address this issue is for the investigator and prosecutor to reconstruct the crime as fully as possible.

There are several ways that a cold case homicide can be reconstructed for a successful prosecution. These include the following:

- Reconstruct the crime scene. This can be accomplished in several ways:
  - Original crime scene photographs.
  - Aerial photographs taken at or near the time (often by a government planning department or private aerial photography company).
  - Maps drawn at or near the time of the crime. This can be from the original investigation or by obtaining plot maps from private or public agencies.
  - Revisit the crime scene. In some instances, the scene has changed very little, if at all. As such, current photographs may provide useful information that may not have been photographed in the original investigation. In some instances, the original photographs

taken may have been lost or destroyed. As a result, current photographs will be all the investigator or prosecutor can get.
- *Video footage*: In many instances, video footage was taken at the time by either law enforcement or the news media. If possible, this footage should be obtained. If the footage is unavailable, new video photography may be useful.

- Reconstruct the circumstances surrounding the crime.

  Understanding *why* the homicide occurred is a question that every jury wants answered. While a prosecutor technically does not have to establish that a motive exists, because motive is not an element of the crime of murder, the *absence* of motive may present a viable defense to the crime. In reconstructing the circumstances of the homicide, a prosecutor may therefore want the following investigations conducted:
  - A thorough analysis of the victim's background (*victimology*)
  - Interviews of the original investigators and medical examiners
  - Current background investigation and interviews with witnesses interviewed at the time of the crime (if possible)
  - Reanalysis of all forensic evidence
  - A complete background investigation of the defendant
- Background investigation of the defendant.

  In cold cases, as in all murder cases, the defendant must be connected to both the victim and the crime scene. This is particularly true in "cold hit" cases, where the primary evidence will typically be a DNA match between biological samples obtained from the victim's body and a reference sample taken from the suspect. While it might be tempting for resource-strapped investigators and prosecutors to conclude that that is all the jury *needs*, that may not be all the evidence they *want*. In presenting a cold case to a jury, a complete background investigation of the defendant will provide the jury with a thorough understanding of the defendant's connection to the murder. Sources of information that should be considered in obtaining a complete background of the defendant include the following:
  - Interviews with the defendant's family, friends, coworkers, and previous sexual partners.
  - Police reports of all crimes committed by or involving the defendant.
  - Field identification (FI) cards on the defendant. This may assist in determining the whereabouts of the defendant around the time of the murder.
  - Registration cards, such as sexual offender, drug, or arson registration cards.

- Records relating to the defendant, including medical, mental health, and employment records.
- A complete copy of the defendant's prison file. This should include:
  - Visitation logs
  - Information regarding addresses used for parole or family members
  - Family history
  - Old prison photos (particularly those near the time of the murder)
  - Psychological reports

Special Considerations in DNA Cold Hit Cases

In cold cases that are solved through a DNA cold hit, the defendant is identified through the use of an offender database, where the DNA from crime scene evidence is linked to the defendant's DNA. In these cases, there are several factors that should be considered. This includes the following:

- Once the hit is made, the most critical concern is a determination of whether the suspect is in or out of custody. Clearly, if out of custody, the law enforcement agency will need to expedite the investigation. If, however, the suspect is in custody, law enforcement will have more time and can more effectively and thoroughly prepare the case for prosecution.
- Once a hit is made, law enforcement should obtain and test an additional DNA sample from the defendant. This will confirm the analysis conducted in the case. In addition, it will allow the local DNA laboratory that conducted testing on the crime scene evidence to provide all the necessary testimony in court.
- Prior to filing criminal charges, law enforcement and the prosecution should also determine whether additional DNA testing should be conducted. If additional items of evidence will be consumed through DNA testing, the prosecutor must also determine whether this testing should be done before or after criminal charges are filed. If the testing is done after, the prosecutor should be aware that the defense may have a right to be present during the testing analysis.

Preparation for Penalty Phase

In many cold cases, the defendant may be facing capital punishment. Because many of the solved cold case murders involve sexual assault, the prosecution may seek the death penalty against the defendant. Like many other death cases, preparation for the penalty phase is critical. One benefit for the prosecution in cold cases is that, where the defendant is already in custody for other offenses, much of this preparation can be done before the murder charges are even filed. This may be very beneficial since some witnesses—particularly the defendant's family and friends—may be more cooperative before the charges are filed.

In preparation for the penalty phase, the following avenues of investigation should be considered:

- *Interview family and friends of the defendant*: While the family and friends of the defendant will often resist providing law enforcement any helpful information, this is not always the case. Some may cooperate because they dislike the defendant or dislike what he/she has done. Others may try to limit disclosures to innocuous information but, because they don't know all the facts (particularly before charges are filed), may in fact provide information of great value. These individuals may be able to provide relevant information for the guilt phase of the trial—information that may connect the defendant to the murder. They may also provide useful information regarding the defendant's background, childhood, and any mental health issues. Once the defendant is charged, the defense will conduct an extensive background of the defendant's life in an effort to avoid the death penalty. In cold cases, having these individuals interviewed *prior* to the filing of charges may provide useful information that can be later used at trial.
- *Interview other victims*: In all death penalty cases, it is imperative to locate and interview every person victimized by the defendant who survived encounters with him. These other crimes may be relevant in the guilt phase as evidence of such facts as common modus operandi or intent and will certainly be relevant during the penalty phase as the jury weighs the appropriate verdict. In cold cases, it is suggested that these witnesses be identified and contacted in person at the earliest possible time. It should be anticipated that this contact may be emotionally traumatic for them.
- *Obtain all necessary records*: In preparation for the penalty phase, the prosecution should obtain all records pertaining to the defendant. In cold cases, this can be very challenging given the age of the case and the fact that many businesses or agencies have destroyed records over the years. The following types of records should be obtained, if possible:
    - Prison and jail records
    - School records
    - Employment records

- Military records
- Medical records
- Mental health records
- Police records

Legal Issues in Cold Cases

There are several legal issues that may be present in cold cases that are rarely seen in other homicide cases, including the following:

1. *John Doe warrants*: John Doe warrants—which identify the defendants by their physical characteristics, rather than by name—are rare but have been used for over a century. In the California case *People v. Montoya* (1967) 255 Cal.App.2d 137, for example, the court of appeals said that it was legal to issue a warrant describing the defendant as "John Doe, white male, dark hair, medium build, 30–35."

   With the introduction of DNA tests in criminal cases, John Doe warrants have been revived, with a twist. Instead of providing a physical description of the defendant in a traditional sense, these warrants have spelled out the defendant's "type" at specific genetic locations. This has proved to be a useful tool in tolling the statute of limitations. The first John Doe DNA warrant was filed in 1999 by Norm Gahn, a prosecutor in the Milwaukee County District Attorney's Office. Since that time, numerous jurisdictions have filed these warrants. Several courts have upheld the use of John Doe DNA warrants reasoning that while an individual can readily change his/her identity, name, address, or even physical appearance, a person cannot change his/her DNA. As such, there is no better way to describe a defendant than by his/her genetic code.
2. *DNA admissibility hearings*: In cold cases that are based primarily on the use of DNA evidence, the defense may challenge the admissibility on the ground that the technology is new or novel. In some jurisdictions, the court must find that such scientific technique is "generally accepted" in the relevant scientific community.[1] In other jurisdictions, the court must first find that the DNA testing was reliable.[2] Even if these hurdles are overcome, the defense may argue that there are problems with the testing so grave that no jury should hear the results.

   When a cold case is filed, the prosecutor must be aware of the possibility of a pretrial challenge to the DNA evidence. In particular, the defense may challenge the strength of the evidence where a cold hit is made. The prosecution must be prepared for the testimony of expert witnesses retained by the defense.

3. *Evidentiary issues in cold cases*: Cold cases present several potential evidentiary issues for the prosecution. Because these issues may have significant impact on the outcome of the case, the prosecution and investigation team should work closely throughout the investigation and prosecution of the case. The following are potential evidentiary issues that may arise in a cold case:
   - *Chain of custody*: One of the most common concerns in cold case homicides is the chain of custody. In many instances, items of evidence were packaged or stored inappropriately. Additionally, there is often an incomplete log detailing the chain of custody. In some cases, items of evidence were removed from law enforcement's possession without any record of it. In other cases, witnesses integral to the chain of custody are unavailable or deceased. While an improper chain of custody should not result in the exclusion of evidence, it may present defense claims that the integrity of the evidence has been compromised. As such, the prosecution must be prepared to address this with a jury.
   - *Loss or destruction of evidence*: In many cold cases, evidence may be lost or destroyed. While this presents obvious challenges for the investigator, it also presents challenges for the prosecution. If items of evidence have been destroyed, the defense may seek sanctions against the prosecution, alleging a due process violation. In some instances, the defense may seek dismissal of the charges. In order for the defendant to win this motion, however, it must demonstrate that the evidence both possessed an exculpatory value that was apparent before the evidence was destroyed and was of such a nature that the defendant would be unable to obtain comparable evidence by other reasonably available means.[3] While it is rare that a defendant can succeed in dismissal of charges on these grounds, both the investigator and the prosecutor should be prepared to litigate the motion when it is made.
   - *Use of hypnosis*: In many cold cases, the investigators relied upon hypnosis to develop information from witnesses. While this practice may have aided the investigation, it will create problems for the prosecution in many states. If a prosecutor has hypnosis evidence in his/her case, it is imperative to consult the rules of evidence regarding that evidence. For instance, in California, the testimony of a witness who has been previously hypnotized is limited to events that the witness "recalled and related prior to the hypnotic session."[4] Clearly, such limitations on admissibility

of such evidence can have a significant and adverse impact on the prosecution's case.

- *Insufficient memories of witnesses*: One of the most common concerns in cold cases is the inability of witnesses to recall the events surrounding the homicide. In most cases, witnesses can refresh their memories by reviewing the statements they gave to law enforcement. However, in cold cases, there may be little, or no memory left to refresh, and reviewing the police report will do little or no good.

  In cases where a witness gave a prior statement to law enforcement but no longer recalls that statement, the contents of the written statement itself may nevertheless be admissible through an exception to the hearsay rule called *past recollection recorded.*[5] Through this exception, the investigator may be allowed to read the witness's statement into evidence if certain factors have been proved. Most notably, if the prosecution can show that the statement of the witness was made at or near the time of the events and the events were still fresh in the witness's mind at the time of the statement, then the statement should be admissible.

  The older the case, the more likely that witness memories will fail, and the more likely that the prosecutor will have to rely on the past recollection recorded hearsay exception at trial. The investigator must therefore anticipate this issue and determine whether the facts necessary to prove this exception can be met as he/she meets and reinterviews witnesses so that the prosecutor can later prove to the court that all the requirements of this exception have been met.

- *Admissibility of prior/post crime evidence*: In many cold cases, the defendant has a criminal history that includes similar crimes that occurred either before or even after the homicide. This type of evidence, particularly in sexually motivated homicide cases, can play a decisive role in the prosecution's case if it demonstrates the defendant's modus operandi. In some jurisdictions, the prosecution may use evidence of other sexual assaults to demonstrate that the defendant has a propensity to commit such crimes.[6]

  In a cold case prosecution, a complete background investigation of the defendant's criminal behavior, whether reported to law enforcement or not, is vital. This background investigation should include not only reports made to law enforcement but also interviews with family and friends of the defendant. In many instances, the defendant may have committed crimes against family or friends, but it was never reported to law enforcement.

The use of prior/post criminal behavior not only may be used during the guilt phase of the prosecution's case but may also play a significant role in the penalty phase of a capital murder case.

4. *Defense motion to dismiss for precomplaint delay*: In many cold cases, years pass before the defendant is ever arrested and/or charged with the murder. In that time, evidence may have been lost or destroyed, memories have faded, and some witnesses may have died.

   A prearrest or prefiling delay in prosecution may constitute a denial of the defendant's right to a fair trial and to due process under the state and federal constitutions.[7] If the defense moves to dismiss charges for such delay, the court will likely undertake a three-step analysis to determine whether the delay violated the defendant's due process rights to a fair trial: (1) The defendant must show that he/she has been prejudiced by the delay. (2) If prejudice is established, then the burden shifts to the prosecution to justify the delay. (3) Finally, the court balances the prejudice to the defendant caused by the delay against the justification for that delay.[8] In addition, in order for the defendant to make a claim of a due process violation under the federal constitution, he/she must show that the delay was undertaken to gain a tactical advantage over the defendant.[9]

   In cold cases, the prosecution must be prepared for a motion to dismiss for delay in prosecution. The prosecutor should be prepared to present evidence at a pretrial hearing to justify any delay in prosecution. In many cold cases, the prosecutor will need to establish that the charges could not have been filed without the use of new scientific tests. Further, the prosecution may also need to determine whether potential defense witnesses are unavailable or *material* to the defense. In doing so, the prosecution can demonstrate to the court that the defendant has not been prejudiced by the delay.

Discovery Issues in Cold Cases

The prosecution has a legal and ethical duty to disclose evidence favorable to a defendant.[10] With this ethical obligation, it is imperative that all discovery be provided or made available to the defense once a defendant is charged in a cold case murder. In many cold cases, because of the passage of time, it may be very difficult to find all the documents related to the investigation. In some instances, reports, photographs, or tapes have been lost or destroyed. In some cases, reports were never written at all; rather, notes from the original investigator may be found in the original investigation file.

In order to comply with the prosecution's obligation under *Brady*, the following suggestions are made:

- *Obtain and copy original "murder book"*: In most cold cases, the police agency maintains an original murder book, which was the working copy of the homicide detective. While the records maintained in this file should have been given to the police agency's records division, in some instances, they were not. It is highly recommended that the prosecutor obtain, review, and copy the original file. This file will oftentimes contain such items as investigator notes, phone logs, suspect lead information, Polaroid photographs, and composites.
- *Record keeping for the prosecutor*: Cold cases can often involve hundreds, if not thousands, of pages of documents. As a result, it is important for the prosecutor to organize these documents for trial in a logical format. In addition to an organized file, it may be helpful for the prosecutor to keep a "master discovery" file that documents exactly what items have been discovered or made available to the defense. This practice will ensure that all discovery obligations have been satisfied.

Sentencing in Cold Cases

In cold cases, the defendant will be sentenced according to the law at the time of the crime. Therefore, while a first-degree murder conviction may currently result in a 25-year to life sentence, it may be significantly different for a first-degree murder that occurred 25 years ago. Thus, in Penny Parker's murder, if the defendant were convicted of first-degree murder, his resulting sentence would have been 7 years to life.

Recent Advancements in Forensic Investigative Genetic Genealogy

The Golden State Killer (GSK) wreaked havoc on communities across California during the 1970–1980s. Over that period, the GSK murdered 13 people, raped approximately 50 women, burglarized over 100 homes, and terrorized entire communities throughout Northern, Central, and Southern California. For over 40 years, law enforcement worked tirelessly to identify this sadistic serial rapist and killer. Over a dozen law enforcement agencies dedicated detectives and others to identifying the person responsible for these crimes. Beginning in the late 1990s, DNA linked many of the crimes together. By 2001, the Northern California crimes were linked to the Southern California murders. For decades the DNA profile of the GSK was routinely searched in California's DNA Databank of convicted offenders. No matches were ever made. Task forces were created throughout the years to seek new leads and solve this horrific crime spree. Thousands of people were considered "persons of interest." Hundreds had their DNA collected; all were eliminated as the perpetrator.

In the fall of 2017, Contra Costa District Attorney Investigator Paul Holes sought out my assistance in utilizing forensic investigative genetic genealogy (FIGG) to identify potential family members of the GSK. Paul Holes and I had known each other for nearly 20 years as we both worked on cold cases and collaborated on the GSK case.

With a small team of investigators, including a genealogist providing advice, the team undertook advanced DNA testing to develop an extensive DNA profile of the killer that thereby allowed investigators to identify relatives of the GSK through traditional genealogy research. This technique later became known as FIGG. By building family trees, and using traditional law enforcement resources, the team was able to identify Joseph DeAngelo, a former police officer, as the GSK. DeAngelo later pled guilty to all crimes and was sentenced to life without parole.

The use of FIGG to identify the GSK has revolutionized law enforcement's ability to solve violent crimes with DNA. Scientific studies suggest that this new tool has the potential to solve 90% of violent crimes with DNA. Not only has FIGG solved crimes that have remained unsolved for years, but it has exonerated the innocent and identified human remains.

With the use of FIGG comes responsibility and the critical need for public trust. To utilize publicly available genealogy databases, such as GedMatch and Family Tree DNA, the public must trust that law enforcement will use it responsibly. Terms of service outline law enforcement's use of these databases. Additionally, various states have adopted legislation to establish best practices. The US Department of Justice has established guidelines on its use as well. It is critical that investigators understand the rules and laws relating to the use of FIGG.

It is highly suggested that investigators consult with prosecutors prior to utilizing FIGG on cold cases. This approach ensures that both the investigator and prosecutor are fully informed of legal considerations, including the jurisdictional laws, use of warrants, discovery obligations, and trial tactics where FIGG was utilized.

FIGG is a historic and exciting advancement in cold case investigations. Case that would *never* have been solved with traditional DNA and law enforcement investigations are now being solved around the world. With the power of this new tool to solve crime, it is incumbent upon police and prosecutors to make FIGG a standard practice in their investigations. Making FIGG a standard practice, however, requires adequate funding and dedicated personnel. The coming years will reveal the commitment of funding and resources needed to advance these cases. In this quest, we must always remember that behind each cold case is a victim, family, and countless people who have been devastated by these crimes. We owe it to them to do everything in our power to provide answers and perhaps some form of justice for victims and their loved ones.

Conclusion

Cold cases are exciting and challenging cases to investigate and prosecute. Law enforcement and prosecutors have an obligation to the families of murder victims to thoroughly investigate and prosecute those responsible for these crimes. With an effective investigation and prosecution, justice—while delayed—will be served.

The advent of DNA testing in particular has revolutionized murder investigations. Not only are more fresh murder cases being solved, but also cases that have long languished for lack of leads are being resurrected. The window of opportunity to reopen these cold cases, however, is closing; time continues to exact its toll on surviving evidence, witnesses, and memories. At some point, courts will find that further delay in investigating and prosecuting these cases is inexcusable.

Penny Parker's family had to wait a quarter of a century for answers, but in the end, they got them. With the suicide of Penny's murderer, a painful chapter in their lives could be closed. Penny mattered to the officers charged with solving her murder, and they did not allow her to be forgotten. Today, there are literally thousands of families just like Penny's all over the country. They, too, deserve answers.

Notes

1 See *Frye v. United States* (D.C. Cir. 1923) 293 Fed. 1013.
2 See *Daubert v. Merrell* (1993) 509 U.S. 579.
3 See *California v. Trombetta* (1984) 467 U.S. 479.
4 See *People v. Hayes* (1989) 49 Cal.3d 1260, 1263, 1270–73.
5 See *Federal Rules of Evidence* section 803.
6 See *California Evidence Code* section 1108.
7 See *People v. Caitlin* (2001) 26 Cal.4th 81, 108; see also *United States v. Marion* (1971) 401 U.S. 307.
8 See *United States v. Lovasco* (1977) 431 U.S. 783, 789–790.
9 See *United States v. Lovasco* (1977) 431 U.S. 795.
10 See *Brady v. Maryland* (1963) 373 U.S. 83.

Criminal Investigative Analysis

9

SHARON PAGALING HAGAN

> In solving a problem of this sort, the grand thing is to be able to reason backward. That is a very useful accomplishment, and a very easy one, but people do not practice it much. In the everyday affairs of life it is more useful to reason forward, and so the other comes to be neglected… Let me see if I can make it clearer. Most people, if you describe a train of events to them, will tell you what the result would be. They can put those events together in their minds, and argue from them that something will come to pass. There are few people, however, who, if you told them a result, would be able to evolve from their own inner consciousness what the steps were which led up to that result. This power is what I mean when I talk of reasoning backward, or analytically.
>
> —**Sherlock Holmes**
>
> *From A Study in Scarlet, by Sir Arthur Conan Doyle*

Homicide cases often remain unsolved because pertinent information or evidence was either overlooked or misinterpreted. Upon close inspection and analysis of an unsolved case, investigators sometimes discover that theories originally pursued regarding the motive, the manner in which the crime was committed, and the primary suspect(s) are inconsistent with the crime scene, the physical and/or trace evidence, and wound pathology. These common pitfalls are magnified with the passage of time.

The purpose of this chapter is to provide investigators with an introduction to the analysis of a cold homicide from a behavioral perspective. The degree to which an investigator understands human behavior, and is able to apply such understanding to a crime scene, is directly related to their ability to be successful in homicide investigation. Unfortunately, over time, homicide investigation has become increasingly focused upon forensic analysis of trace and biological evidence to solve cases, while the behavioral component has been neglected.

Criminal investigative analysis is a behavioral analytic process that integrates information regarding the victim, the initial crime scene investigation, physical and trace evidence, wound patterns, toxicological examination results, geographical information (including demographics and crime patterns), witness accounts, and an indirect personality assessment of any potential suspects.

 DOI: 10.4324/9781003415633-11

Investigators tasked with a cold homicide investigation can benefit from the process of criminal investigative analysis in:

- Organizing old case files
- Prioritizing cases based upon solvability factors
- Identifying elements of the original investigation that require follow-up
- Providing new focus to the investigation by integrating a prediction of human behavior with the most recent advancements in forensic science

Historical Perspective

Criminal investigative analysis is an investigative tool developed by the Federal Bureau of Investigation's Behavioral Science Unit. During the 1970s, special agents assigned to the unit believed that a detailed understanding of the behaviors exhibited by an offender during the commission of a violent crime could assist investigators in the identification, investigation, and successful prosecution of the subject. The agents began conducting research on violent offenders to identify commonalities and behavioral patterns that could assist police investigators in the detection of such offenders.

Robert Ressler, Ann Burgess, and John Douglas provided an early example of such research in *Sexual Homicide* (Ressler et al. 1988), which compiled information obtained from interviews and background investigations of 36 sexual killers. Ressler and Douglas identified commonalities shared by the offenders, including the habitual use of violent pornography from an early age, dysfunctional relationships with their parents, and social isolation from peers. Although their study gathered data from a relatively small number of subjects, the information offered clinicians and criminal justice professionals insight into the behavioral traits, personality characteristics, and patterns of social interaction, which might assist the criminal justice system in the identification and management of such individuals.

Although criminal investigative analysis, commonly termed "psychological or criminal profiling," has received much attention from the media and has been popularized in television, movies, and books, the potential benefits of this investigative tool continue to be misunderstood. The most common misconception is that criminal profiling is identical to criminal investigative analysis; in fact, profiling is only one element of criminal investigative analysis. A behavioral profile, or description of an unidentified offender's personality and lifestyle, may assist investigators in the identification of an offender by narrowing the focus of an investigation to a more restricted pool of potential suspects. A profile may be particularly useful in cases in which a potential suspect is not identified during the initial investigation, because the profile can then be used to reevaluate those people who have already been contacted that bear similarity to the profile. However, while such a description may be useful to investigators during their search for the offender, profiles have rarely if ever led to the actual identification of an offender. Further, "profiling" information is not admissible in court to prove the guilt or innocence of a defendant.[1]

Criminal investigative analysis refers to a range of functions related to the behavioral analysis of violent crimes and the perpetrators who commit such crimes. The types of analytical services available to investigators and prosecutors include:

- Crime scene analysis and reconstruction
- Indirect personality assessment
- Threat assessment
- Interview and interrogation strategies
- Crime linkage analysis
- Equivocal death investigation
- Trial and cross-examination strategy
- Expert testimony[2]

Criminal investigative analysis is currently conducted by a small group of highly skilled crime analysts who are trained in numerous disciplines including the psychology of persons who commit violent crimes, forensic science disciplines such as DNA analysis, comparative analysis, trace evidence, toxicology, bloodstain interpretation, wound pathology, threat assessment, interview and interrogation, crime scene analysis, and crime scene reconstruction. These analysts, who are sworn or retired law enforcement professionals, have completed a structured training and certification program under the supervision of the International Criminal Investigative Analysis Fellowship (ICIAF). Investigative assistance and expertise are available from members of the ICIAF to requesting investigators and/or prosecutors within the United States, Canada, Australia, and several European countries, often at no expense to the requesting agency.

Investigative Role

Criminal investigative analysis can assist investigators to organize existing case materials, identify "good" cold cases, prioritize cases based upon solvability factors, and identify issues that require additional investigative follow-up. Although advances in forensic science have enabled law enforcement agencies to solve crimes through biological evidence that identifies the perpetrator, investigators still need help to accurately interpret crime scenes that reveal such evidence.

Investigators who are confronted with the task of reactivating an unsolved homicide investigation typically face a variety of challenges resulting from the passage of time. Such challenges include the retirement and/or death of the original investigators; missing or deteriorated physical evidence; misplaced or lost case notes; incomplete or partial case files; poor documentation of previous investigative efforts; photographs that are of poor quality and/or insufficient quantity; and the death or unknown location of key witnesses.

A thorough and fresh evaluation of the case by newly assigned detectives who have no prior commitment or loyalty to the theories that were originally developed regarding the motive or responsible person(s) has proven instrumental in solving many cold homicides. However, recontacting and establishing a positive relationship with the original investigators can be helpful. It is essential that the newly assigned investigators not criticize the original investigation or point out any investigative errors that may have been identified by reactivation of the investigation. The original investigators may have saved their investigative notes, know the whereabouts of missing case materials, and/or recall information pertinent to the crime that was not documented in reports.

The passage of time has also proven beneficial to the successful resolution of many unsolved homicide cases by offering investigators the opportunity to reinterview potential witnesses, persons associated with the victim, and any potential suspects for pertinent information that developed after the initial investigation was concluded. Likewise, deteriorated relationships may allow investigators to access information withheld by witnesses who were originally motivated by loyalty or fear.

Investigative Materials

Ideally, before a comprehensive analysis of the crime is initiated, investigators should compile as much of the following materials as possible:

- Complete historical information regarding the victim(s)
- Natural/candid photographs of victim(s) in life
- Initial and follow-up investigative reports
- Media accounts, including newspaper clippings and videotapes of television news

- Geographical information, including map(s), crime rates, and similar crimes committed during that period of time
- Narrative description(s) of crime scene(s)
- Photographs of crime scene(s)
- Photographs of decedent(s) at scene
- Crime scene diagram(s)
- Laboratory reports and analyses
- Autopsy report(s), diagrams, and photographs

Victimology

Criminal investigative analysis begins with an in-depth study of the victim's personality and lifestyle. To this end, a thorough background investigation of the victim is essential to shed light on such questions that may help focus the investigation. For example: Why was it "necessary" for this particular person to die? Did someone perceive them as an obstacle? What was their risk level of becoming the victim of a violent crime? Was the victim "specifically selected" by the offender, or was his or her interaction with the offender the result of opportunity and circumstance? Did the geographic location where the crime was committed effect the victim's risk level? Was the victim "security conscious," or did he or she feel comfortable leaving windows and doors unlocked? Did lifestyle place the victim in contact with persons who potentially posed a physical threat? Had the victim previously been the victim of a violent crime or expressed concern regarding their safety? Had the victim ever discussed how they planned to defend themselves if they were threatened or assaulted? What was the victim's medical and psychological history? Was the victim involved in any high-risk behaviors such as drug or alcohol abuse, domestic violence, extramarital sexual encounters, sexual deviation(s), or criminal enterprise?

Experience has shown that most homicides are the result of interpersonal conflict, and the offender can be found in the victim's family, social network, or work environment. Homicides that are motivated by interpersonal conflict are an attempt by the perpetrator to "solve a problem" he or she is experiencing with the victim. As such, consideration of any potential problems and conflicts that may have either been present in the victim's personal life, or perceived as a problem or conflict by a potential offender, is often effective in narrowing the search for the perpetrator. Experience has shown that with the passage of time, persons who had close personal relationships with the victim become more willing to divulge sensitive or unflattering information regarding the victim's lifestyle and activities.

Investigators should make every effort to obtain an understanding of the victim's background, personality, lifestyle, and interpersonal relationships, with particular attention to compilation of a detailed timeline of the victim's activities and contacts with other persons during the last 72 hours of life. Investigators should produce a detailed timeline of everyone the victim had contact with during this 72-hour window that precedes the murder, including telephone conversations and written messages. In most cases, the decision to commit a murder is made within a relatively short period of time prior to initiation of the assault. As a result, the perpetrator can typically be found within the group of persons who had contact with the victim within the last few days, hours, and sometimes minutes that preceded the murder.

Geographic Information

Information regarding the geographic location, accessibility, and the area surrounding the crime scene(s) is important to the analysis. How and where did the offender encounter the victim? What types of crimes were common to the area during that period of time, and were there any crimes that bore resemblance to the behaviors the offender displayed during the murder of the victim? Information should be accumulated regarding traffic patterns, accessibility to and from major thoroughfares, lighting conditions, and environmental factors including weather. Was the victim vulnerable to an assault by a stranger, or could the victim have only been contacted in that particular location, at that particular time, by someone familiar?

Geographic analysis can assist in narrowing the search for an offender responsible for a crime or a series of crimes that involve multiple locations. If possible, investigators should consult with a geographic profiler to identify the most probable area the offender may be found in. Because offenders can often be found a short distance from the crime scene, a less formal technique involves marking the areas on a map that approximates a one-half mile radius around each location, and then concentrating the search for the offender in any areas that overlap and are therefore geographically common to the scenes.

Crime Scene Analysis

Crime scenes depict the final outcome of the behavioral interaction between the offender(s) and the victim(s). Unfortunately, this simple truth is complicated by the fact that the locations are typically not sterile environments prior to initiation of the murder and therefore contain various evidence items not related to the crime. Consequently, in order to most effectively filter out such misleading items and identify only those pertinent to the homicide investigation, investigators must make a concerted effort to determine the preexisting condition of the crime scene. As specific information is often unavailable regarding the condition of the crime location on a particular day and time, investigators may be limited to whatever information they can obtain regarding the "normal" appearance of the scene. This process is essential since many homicide investigators rely heavily upon forensic examination of biological and physical evidence recovered from the scene to identify the perpetrator. Scientific testing of items that are not associated with the murder, and which erroneously identify innocent persons, will confuse the investigation and may even exonerate the responsible party.

Physical evidence from a crime scene is the product of behaviors that were exhibited by an offender(s) and a victim(s). A crime scene (cs) may be represented by the equation: cs=o (offender)+v (victim). Analysis of a crime scene from this perspective encourages investigators to more fully consider the contribution the victim's behavior likely had on the crime scene, which is essential in order to avoid the all-too-frequent error of attributing the scene solely to behaviors exhibited by the offender. Further, analysis from this perspective allows investigators to acquire an accurate assessment of the manner in which the offender behaved by acquainting themselves with the victim's personality and behavioral patterns, and "subtracting," so to speak, the victim's behavior from the crime scene. This concept can be represented as follows: o=cs−v. Theoretically, once the victim's behavior is subtracted from the scene, the behavioral evidence that remains can more appropriately be attributed to the offender. The following case description illustrates the importance of understanding the "preexisting" condition of the crime scene, as well as the behavioral patterns of the victim.

Case Study

Investigators responded to a single-family residence located in a new housing development at approximately noon on a weekday regarding the homicide of a 38-year-old pregnant female. The victim's husband told detectives he had discovered his wife's body several minutes earlier when he came home to drive her to a counseling appointment. The residence was in significant disarray. Furniture was overturned, drawers were emptied, and the contents scattered. A waterbed had been punctured and was leaking onto the carpet, and a large entertainment center situated in the living room had been overturned. Many household items were scattered in the backyard, including several televisions, the dining room chairs, and the contents of the kitchen cabinets and refrigerator. All of the upholstered living room furniture had been cut and were heavily stained with the victim's blood. A blood trail led from the living room into the master bathroom. The victim was located in the bathtub in the master bathroom, covered by a plastic jug, which was partially filled with coins, and a laundry hamper. The body was in a semi-seated position, and the victim was wearing a dress, bra, panties, and a wristwatch. Although there was no water in the bathtub, a bloody bathtub ring was visible in the tub, and blood spatter was visible on the adjacent wall. Chemical burns were present over portions of the right side of the victim's body and both shoulders; her hair appeared to have been bleached, and a small portion of her hair had been shaved above her right forehead. Barber shears, scissors, tweezers, and a bloodstained towel were found beneath her body. A racial slur was written on the bathroom mirror in toothpaste. The victim's cause of death was manual strangulation; however, she also suffered five stab wounds to her right back and buttocks and blunt force trauma to her head, left breast, face, and left leg. She suffered fractures to her nose and two ribs and had many bruises and abrasions to her arms and legs, and there was no evidence of defense-style injuries. During the course of the investigation, detectives learned the victim had a volatile temper and on a previous occasion had slashed the furniture after becoming angry. The couple had a limited history of domestic violence and had argued repeatedly during the preceding days. According to a female friend of the victim who had visited the residence on the morning of the murder, the victim had admitted causing nearly all of the damage to the home after her husband left for work. Interviews of the couple's neighbors revealed the victim's husband had arrived at the residence approximately 15 minutes prior to the time he had given to the investigators. He was subsequently arrested and convicted of the murders of his wife and unborn child.

As illustrated by this case, essential information regarding the behavioral sequence that occurred during the crime, the probable motive for the crime, the type of relationship the victim likely had with the perpetrator, and the type of person most likely to have committed the crime can be garnered through analysis of the crime scene and victimology. This information can also be useful during the interview or interrogation of suspects, and by prosecutors to distinguish between planned and impulsive homicides.

Information regarding the sequence of behaviors that occurred at the scene may be obtained through careful consideration and integration of the crime scene characteristics with the physical evidence. These characteristics may include, but are not limited to,

- The amount of risk the offender accepted to commit the crime
- The manner in which the offender approached the victim
- The size of the crime scene
- Bloodstain patterns

- Items taken or left behind
- Positioning and disposition of the body
- Wound patterns
- Indications of postmortem activity at the crime scene
- Indications of sexual activity

Some murders involve multiple crime scenes, which may include a point of abduction, initial assault, murder, body storage, and body and evidence disposal sites. When multiple crime scenes are involved, it is typically more difficult for investigators to locate pertinent physical evidence and information regarding the behavioral interaction of the offender and the victim.

Offender Risk

The offender determines the time, place, and circumstances under which the murder occurs. Since the offender is in control of these factors, investigators can learn a great deal by examining the environmental factors (location, time, lighting conditions, and traffic patterns in the area where the crime occurred) and assessing the amount of risk the offender was willing to accept in order to commit the crime.

Regardless of the time or location the offender selects for the murder, the offender cannot be absolutely certain he or she will not be seen by witnesses. An offender may reduce that risk by altering their appearance or committing the murder during late night or early morning hours. In general, however, the anxiety an offender has regarding the possibility of being seen by witnesses depends on several factors: the type of relationship the offender has with the victim; the extent to which the offender "belongs" at the location where the crime will occur; and the number of potential witnesses the offender believes will likely be present in the vicinity when the crime is committed.

An offender who has a close personal relationship with his or her victim often has less concern about being seen by other persons while either with the victim or at the location. An offender who "belongs" at a location, because he or she resides in, works in, or frequently visits the area, is often unconcerned that his or her presence at the scene will be noticed and considered unusual by potential witnesses. Persons who have a legitimate reason for being in the area (e.g., service workers) are often not reported to investigators during the neighborhood canvasses that are typically conducted in the hours immediately following discovery of the victim's body and during the subsequent investigation. Potential witnesses are not usually asked questions regarding *all persons* seen in the area, but rather are primarily focused on persons who were perceived as being somehow *unusual*.

Offenders who are strangers to the victim and do not frequent the area where the crime occurs also tend to be less concerned that other persons will be able to accurately identify them to law enforcement as potential suspects. These offenders are often careful not to return to the area of the crime in order to avoid being recognized.

Another type of risk an offender likely considers both before and after commission of the murder is the likelihood that he or she will eventually be identified as the person responsible for the victim's death. Criminally sophisticated offenders may take precautions to either reduce or eliminate physical and trace evidence from the scene by wearing gloves, using condoms, cleaning the crime scene after the murder, and removing items from the scene they believe might reveal their identity. However, given the dramatic strides in forensic science, even the most knowledgeable and criminally sophisticated offenders can no longer be confident that they did not leave potentially incriminating evidence at the scene.

Prior to the commission of a planned homicide, and frequently during the commission of a more spontaneous killing, offenders consider the likelihood they will be interrupted during the commission of the crime by unexpected persons or events. Unexpected visitors, the premature arrival of other residents to the location, mail delivery, or even incoming unanswered telephone calls may sharply curtail the amount of time the offender is willing to spend at the scene. Offenders may take precautions to reduce the number of potential interruptions, including familiarizing themselves with the victim's schedule and routine behaviors, unplugging or disabling telephones, and extinguishing all interior and exterior lights.

If the murder involved prior planning, the offender may have taken precautions to facilitate his or her escape from the scene in order to avoid being apprehended. In these instances, offenders may plan their escape route, prop windows and doors open, and position a vehicle, bicycle, or other means of transportation in a location that is out of view but easily accessible.

Method of Approach

Analysis of the manner in which an offender likely gained access to the victim often supplies investigators with valuable insight regarding the offender's perception of his/her own talents and weaknesses, as well as identification of behaviors he or she is willing to exhibit. Although homicide scenes frequently lack conclusive evidence regarding the exact manner in which the offender was able to access the victim, criminal justice professionals are frequently able to accurately theorize the method that was employed through an analysis of the crime scene, the victim's personality, lifestyle and circumstances, and the "process of elimination."

Hazelwood and Warren (2001) suggest sexually motivated offenders employ three methods to approach victims: the con, the blitz, and the surprise. Offenders who are confident in the strength and persuasiveness of their interpersonal skills prefer the con approach. These offenders attempt to literally talk their victims into positions of vulnerability and/or persuade them to accompany them to locations that afford the offender a sufficient degree of privacy in order to perpetrate the crime. The blitz-style approach is the immediate application of debilitating force against the victim in order to incapacitate and render them incapable of physically resisting. Offenders who select the surprise approach use their physical strength to quickly gain control of the victim. Offenders who are more confident of their physical prowess than their social skills prefer the surprise approach. The correct identification of the method of approach an offender uses during the commission of a violent crime can help identify and facilitate the interview and prosecution of the perpetrator.

Few crime scenes exhibit evidence of forced entry. Because most homicides are the result of interpersonal conflict, it is common for victims to have admitted the offender to the location or willingly spent time with the offender immediately before the murder. Knowledge of the victim's habits is often helpful in determining whether other persons would have had access to the crime scene location, whether the victim routinely left doors and/or windows open or unlocked, or would have answered the door to an unexpected visitor or stranger.

Size of the Crime Scene

A crime scene that is littered with overturned furniture is behaviorally quite different from a small, contained scene that is limited to the location of the body. Expanded crime scenes may result from several scenarios, including recognition by the victim that the offender posed a significant threat prior to initiation of the assault; a substantial attempt by the victim to defend him/herself; an inability by the offender to effectively control the victim during the assault; and/or the possibility there was an escalation of violence, from a verbal argument to a physical assault. Expanded crime scenes are also more likely to be found in homicides that were not carefully planned by the offender, and in cases where the victim and the offender were of comparable size and strength. Conversely, smaller, more contained scenes are more likely to be found in premeditated murders, or cases where the offender is either significantly larger and/or stronger than the victim, or was able to exert and maintain effective control of the victim throughout the assault.

Bloodstain Patterns and Deposits

Accurate analysis of the bloodstain patterns and deposits found at the crime scene may provide police investigators with extremely valuable information regarding the physical movements of the offender and the victim during the murder. Conversely, misinterpretation of bloodstain patterns may cause a homicide to remain unsolved. Analysis of bloodstain patterns from an unsolved homicide depends upon the quality and quantity of photographs taken of the crime scene.

It is important when inferring behavior from bloodstain patterns to differentiate between blood from the victim and blood from the offender. In some cases, careful analysis has enabled investigators to discover that blood previously assumed to have come from the victim was actually deposited by the perpetrator. Investigators are encouraged to seek an informed opinion regarding any blood deposits associated with an unsolved murder in order to obtain an enhanced understanding of the behaviors that likely occurred at the scene.

Items Taken or Left Behind

Did the offender use items he or she found at the scene to facilitate the murder, or did the offender bring all of the items to the scene for the specific purpose of perpetrating the crime? What, if anything, is missing from the scene? Were there any items left at the scene that do not belong?

There are several possible explanations as to why an offender may have utilized items available at the crime scene, such as knives and heavy objects as weapons, or clothing items as bindings. These include (1) a murder that involved little or no prior planning; (2) a murder in which the offender was familiar with the location where the crime was committed and was confident the items could be found there; or (3) the offender was not willing to risk being found in possession of weapons, tools, or binding materials as he or she approached or left the crime scene.

Offenders who choose to bring specific objects to the scene may do so because they are routinely in possession of the item (e.g., a pocket knife, handgun), the crime involves a significant degree of prior planning, or the items utilized by the offender are of special significance to him/her.

Offenders who are criminally sophisticated—or who are forensically knowledgeable—are hesitant to leave transportable items behind that could lead to their identification. Homicides committed by such an offender may show evidence that the offender attempted to "clean up" prior to departing the scene, and any incriminating evidence was taken and discarded a safe distance away. In contrast, offenders who utilize weapons, bindings, or other items that have special meaning or significance (e.g., linked to their sexual fantasy) are often unwilling to discard them, and choose to retain possession of them so they can use them again. In these instances, investigators are often able to recover the items from the offender's possessions months or even years after the crime was committed.

Positioning and Disposition of the Body

The manner in which the victim's body was left often provides investigators with valuable information regarding the relationship, if any, the offender had with the victim, the emotional state of the offender immediately following the murder, and any logistical problems that the offender perceived following the murder.

Offenders can choose among numerous options once they are satisfied the victim is dead. They may choose to leave the victim's body at the crime scene without any further manipulation, transport the body to another location, or conceal or cover the body, or in rare instances, the perpetrator may position and "display" the body in a manner that will likely be particularly provocative or shocking to the person who finds the body.

In most instances, offenders are anxious to distance themselves from the crime scene and the victim's body shortly after the commission of the murder. They are aware that continued association with the victim's body increases their risk of being discovered. Consequently, only offenders who have serious/severe mental impairments, are driven by a specific need (usually sexual), or believe they must alter the death scene somehow in order to avoid detection will remain in contact with the body.

Offenders who are confident that other persons are not aware of their association with the victim are more likely to leave the body at the crime scene. However, offenders who had a close personal relationship with the victim, or who believed their association with the victim near the time of death was witnessed or known by others, may attempt to transport or conceal the body in hopes of either delaying or preventing discovery of the murder.

The amount of time and contact an offender has with the victim's body following the murder is a function, at least in part, of the offender's personality and ability to function under pressure. Offenders who had a close personal relationship with the victim or who cannot tolerate touching a deceased person may have more difficulty controlling their emotions sufficiently in order to move or manipulate the deceased. Crime scenes sometimes reflect evidence that the offender "changed their mind" and aborted an attempt to move or transport the victim's body.

The offender's ability to transport the victim's body is influenced by such factors as physical strength, access to a vehicle, and a sufficient opportunity. Disposition of the body is influenced by the physical strength of the offender, a significant disparity in size between the victim and the offender, the physical layout of the murder scene, the degree of privacy the murder scene affords the offender, and the offender's ability to easily and covertly access an appropriate means of transportation. For instance, did the residence where the crime was committed have an attached garage, or could the vehicle only be parked in an open area in view of potential witnesses? How many persons were present and active in the area during the time immediately following the murder? Was there any indication the offender remained at the murder scene for an extended period after the death, waiting for nightfall? Were window coverings manipulated; did the offender engage in extensive cleanup; and/or did the offender eat, sleep, launder clothing, or bathe at the crime scene?

Cause of Death and Wound Patterns

Significant information regarding the sequence of events at the crime scene is available by examination and assessment of the victim's wounds. Factors that are often relevant to the behavioral analysis of a murder include the presence of blunt force trauma, the presence or absence of defense-style injuries, identification of patterned injuries, analysis of the lethality of multiple wounds, estimation of the time period during which the wounds were inflicted, the cause of death, and postmortem activity. It is essential that the wounds be considered within the context of the scene, and background information regarding the victim's personality, history of drug and alcohol use, medical history, and lifestyle. In some instances, a thorough analysis may reveal the death was not the result of homicide. This was illustrated by the following case, which was initially suspected to be a homicide.

Case Study

The 20-year-old male college student resided in a private room on the second floor of a fraternity house, which was located in a low crime-rate area. He was academically successful, had an active social life, had a steady girlfriend, and had a positive relationship with his family. He had a minor criminal history, resulting from several incidents during which he had been drinking alcoholic beverages. He had no reported enemies, and no history of physical or psychological problems. Shortly before his death, his parents said he had been anxious regarding his course of study, and had suffered bouts of insomnia. Two fraternity house roommates told investigators they last saw him at approximately 1 a.m. when he retired to his room, following a quiet evening of television. During the next 2 days, his roommates said they knocked on the deceased's door and called his name; however, when they got no answer, they assumed he was visiting friends.

His roommates obtained a key to his room from the company that managed the house and discovered the deceased in bed, partially covered by a comforter. The room was dark, music was playing, and the deceased was wearing earplugs. Bloodstains were apparent on three walls, the rug, desk, and bedding. His shirt, shorts, and sock bottoms were bloodstained. His shirt had numerous defects, which corresponded to numerous of his 25 stab wounds and 4 incised wounds to his face, scalp, neck, chest, and wrists. He had also suffered fatal stab wounds to his chest, which penetrated both lungs and his heart, a fatal 4-inch-deep incised wound across his neck, and moderately deep horizontal incised wounds to both wrists. There was no evidence of blunt force trauma, broken bones, torture, bindings, or sexual assault. Several minor abrasions and cuts were found on the fingers of his right hand; however, there was no indication of defense-style injuries. A toxicological examination revealed no traces of alcohol or drugs. A bloodstained knife was found on the bed, and all of the fingerprints on the knife were matched to the decedent. There was no indication of forced entry or a struggle involving a second person. None of the deceased's roommates reported hearing any sounds emanating from the deceased's bedroom or finding any evidence that an intruder had been present in the house.

Analysis of the deceased's wounds revealed that all of the stab wounds were uniform and had no jagged edges (which would be consistent with a struggle); many were superficial and all of the wounds were located within his reach. Although stabbing is the least common method of suicide, experience has shown that suicide cannot be eliminated from consideration based upon the severity of the wounds. Since the deceased had no history of suicidal ideation, his family and friends, as well as numerous investigators, were reluctant to accept a finding of suicide. However, an integrative analysis of his personality, wounds, and the physical evidence brought perspective to the case and convinced all parties he had committed suicide.

Detectives involved in a cold homicide investigation should carefully review the postmortem medical examination report and photographs, and consult with a forensic pathologist to obtain a thorough understanding of the victim's wounds, the manner and mode of death, and an estimate of the time the victim could have remained ambulatory before succumbing to such wounds. Investigators are often reluctant to thoroughly review the autopsy report and photographs because they have little or no training in wound pathology, and find the medical terminology used in the autopsy report difficult to understand. Consequently, after determining the victim's cause of death, they do not adequately consider the implications of any other injuries.

Minor injuries such as bruising to the victim's face are important to the analysis of a homicide because they may indicate that an escalation of violence occurred. Murders motivated by interpersonal conflict often begin as verbal arguments that escalate to physical assaults. The possibility that the victim exchanged blows with the offender should be considered. The presence of defense-style injuries or bruising to the victim's body is also consistent with the possibility that an argument and physical struggle preceded the murder. Recognition of these types of wounds may be an indication that the offender did not originally approach the victim with the intent to kill. In such cases, the offender may have had a personal but problematic relationship with the victim, and he/she may have rationalized the murder as justifiable.

Offenders intent on ensuring the victim's death often inflict multiple potentially fatal injuries. Infliction of serious injury that does not cause immediate death may motivate the offender to resort to another mode of attack (e.g., manual strangulation followed by a gunshot wound; a gunshot wound followed by throat slashing; stomping of the abdominal region followed by stabbing injuries). A pathologist is usually able to estimate the amount of time necessary for the victim to succumb to each of the potentially fatal injuries. The following case summary is an example of a homicide that involved multiple fatal injuries.

Case Study

The 22-year-old female was last seen entering her apartment with her two-year-old child at approximately 1 a.m. after playing cards at her next-door female neighbor's apartment. Residents in the complex told investigators they had been awakened several hours later by loud noises, including voices arguing, a baby crying, and several loud "thumps." The victim was found dead in her locked apartment approximately 36 hours later, when the apartment manager went to the victim's apartment to investigate the source of water leaking into the unit immediately below.

Evidence at the scene indicated a struggle had occurred in the living room; the victim's body had been dragged into the bedroom and then partially covered with newspaper. She was dressed in her normal sleeping attire; however, her bra had been pushed up, exposing her right breast. The child was unharmed. The victim's cause of death was listed as internal hemorrhage due to blunt force trauma to her abdomen. A patterned bruise was faintly visible on the victim's abdomen. She suffered blunt force injury to her head and neck, and all of the injuries were consistent with stomping and kicking injuries. She had numerous bruises on her face, left knee, and left elbow. She had facial suffusion, conjunctival hemorrhages, and scalp edema, caused by mechanical compression of her neck. The victim had a stab wound to her neck, which occurred prior to death, and five additional stab wounds to her abdomen, which were inflicted between the perimortem and postmortem states. There were no injuries to the victim's hands, no evidence of binding, or sexual assault. The victim had a trace amount of alcohol in her system; however, no drugs were found. A knife stained with the victim's blood was found stored with other knives in a butcher block on the kitchen counter. After a prolonged investigation, the boyfriend of the victim's next-door neighbor was eventually identified as the perpetrator. He told investigators he had gone to the victim's apartment for sexual purposes. She had refused him and he became enraged. He admitted taking the victim's door key, returning to her apartment the day following the murder, and turning the water on in order to ensure the safety of the child.

Analysis of this case provided investigators with valuable information regarding the sequence of events that led up to the victim's death. The analysis was used to narrow the focus of the investigation to persons who were known to the victim, and later provided investigators with information that was useful during the interview and subsequent prosecution of the offender.

Sexual Activity

A thorough understanding of the crime scene is necessary before investigators can efficiently search for and identify trace evidence left by an offender. While some crime scenes contain obvious indications the offender had sexual contact with the victim close to the time of the murder, evidence of sexual activity is often difficult to identify. Various types of sexual activity may occur during a homicide, including masturbation by the offender onto the victim's body, oral copulation, penile vaginal penetration, and/or penetration with a foreign object. Sexual activity may occur prior to, during, or following the victim's death.

Sexual activity by the offender can offer investigators an opportunity to identify the perpetrator of an unsolved homicide. Although it is relatively common for sexually motivated offenders to experience sexual dysfunction, recent advances in forensic science have enabled scientists to identify and retest extremely small deposits of trace evidence. In cold case investigations, detectives should request forensic scientists review all physical evidence to determine the utility of conducting further laboratory tests for identifiable material. Items that have been previously analyzed using older, less sensitive and/or discriminating forensic techniques, or evidence not previously analyzed, should be carefully evaluated.

Experience has shown that serology DNA test results are often misinterpreted. Even experienced investigators are prone to misinterpreting the conclusions drawn from test results. For instance, are the test results consistent with sexual contact? Are any of the samples tested inconsistent with the victim? How many donors contributed to the sample(s) that were tested? Was the victim's consensual sexual partner(s) excluded? Have all potentially relevant samples been tested? Investigators should consult with forensic scientists to thoroughly review all of the biological and trace evidence associated with the crime to gain a thorough understanding of the meaning of the test results and determine whether further testing is feasible. See Chapters 15 and 16.

The following case was submitted for analysis to determine whether the victim's death was the result of sexual misadventure, as the defendant claimed, or homicide.

Case Study

The 55-year-old male victim was a successful businessman, lived alone, and was openly homosexual. He drank excessively and frequented several local bars where he flashed significant amounts of money and enjoyed giving others the impression he was wealthy. The victim was described as security conscious and routinely locked and secured his doors and windows. His neighbor said the residence had appeared secure at 5:30 p.m.; however, at 7:45 p.m., the garage door was standing open and the victim's car was gone. When she was unable to contact the victim by telephone, the neighbor called the police.

The police entered the residence through an unlocked garage door that led into the kitchen and observed an empty liquor bottle on the table. The telephone had been unplugged. The victim's nude body was lying on his bed in the unlit master bedroom. An electrical cord had been wrapped around the victim's neck five times, and the lamp to which it was attached was hanging down toward the floor. Minor lacerations were visible on the victim's face, chin, and chest. Semen that did not match the victim's DNA profile was recovered from the victim's chest and a towel that was lying near the corner of the bed. The victim's DNA and the unidentified DNA profile were recovered from an empty glass on the bedside table. A dresser drawer had been overturned near the foot of the bed, and several items were missing from the residence, including the victim's vehicle, a briefcase, a gold ring, a jewelry box, and the victim's wallet, which contained his identification and credit cards. The vehicle was recovered the following day in a residential area where it had been abandoned, and bloodhounds trailed to a nearby bus stop. A latent fingerprint was located on the base of the lamp. The fingerprint was matched to a young married man approximately 1 year later, following his arrest for theft.

The analysis integrated information regarding the victim's lifestyle and sexual habits with the victim's wound patterns and physical evidence found at the scene. Investigation of the victim's behavioral patterns showed that he had no history of using ligatures or other devices to restrict his breathing during sexual activity, and no information was found to indicate the victim had any suicidal intent. The wound patterns found on the victim's face, chin, and chest were consistent with the base of the lamp that was found attached to his neck, suggesting the item had likely not been applied with the victim's consent. The prosecutors used the analysis to effectively refute the defendant's claim of consensual sexual misadventure, and the defendant was convicted of murder.

Staged Crime Scenes

The Crime Classification Manual defines staging as the alteration of the death scene in order to either direct the investigation away from the perpetrator or to protect the deceased or their family from potential embarrassment (Douglas et al. 1992). In homicides, staging involves a variety of behaviors that may be exhibited at the scene following a death, including alteration of the scene so that it appears to have been financially or sexually motivated, or reporting the victim to law enforcement authorities as a missing person. When a death scene is staged, it is nearly always accomplished by a person who had a close personal relationship to the deceased.

One of the most common instances in which staging is encountered is in a domestic homicide in which a spouse is murdered at their shared residence. In these cases, the perpetrator is aware that if the spouse's body is discovered at the unaltered scene, he or she will immediately become the primary suspect. The perpetrator will therefore attempt to rearrange the scene to suggest an alternative motive for the crime, provide misleading statements to investigators, and/or clean the scene, hide the body, and report the victim as a missing person.

Staged scenes are often recognizable because the circumstances surrounding the victim's death or disappearance are inconsistent with the physical evidence and victimology. Domestic homicides are typically committed by offenders who are criminally inexperienced and who are therefore unaware of the appearance of a genuine crime scene. Their inexperience, combined with the likelihood they attempted to alter the crime scene while agitated and/or in a highly emotional state, inhibits their ability to think clearly. As a result, individuals who stage scenes often make unintended errors, termed "red flags," that reveal that the scene is inconsistent with an actual burglary, sexual assault, kidnapping, or missing person case (Douglas et al. 1992).

Criminal investigative analysts can assist investigators and prosecutors in the identification of the sometimes-minute inconsistencies reflected in the scene or in problematic statements made to the investigators. The case example that follows illustrates numerous crime scene indicators often found in a staged domestic homicide.

Case Study

The victim was an attractive, physically fit middle-aged woman who resided with her husband of 30 years. Their home was located in an upscale neighborhood that had a low rate of violent crime. The victim had many friends, was socially active, and was a part-time teacher. On the day of her death, the victim taught a morning class, and then purchased coffee and a pastry before returning to her residence to prepare for an afternoon lesson. At approximately 1:40 p.m., the victim's husband returned to the residence in the company of two of the couple's friends and found the front door standing open. He found the victim's body lying head first near the bottom of the basement stairs fully dressed, with the exception of one of her shoes, which was located on a step above her body. After summoning his friends and asking them to telephone for help, the victim's husband pulled her body onto the cement basement floor and attempted resuscitation. Emergency personnel who responded to the scene were unable to revive the victim and she was pronounced dead at the scene.

The victim's husband tearfully told investigators he had warned the victim the shoes she had been wearing that day were not appropriate for the basement stairs and that she had slipped before. There was no sign of forced entry; however, the couple was not security conscious and had often left doors and windows unlocked. None of the neighbors reported seeing any strangers in the area, heard any dogs barking, or heard loud voices or screams in the time period during which the victim died. There was no evidence of ransacking or theft, although many items of value were openly displayed. Examination of the residence with luminol revealed the presence of blood on a kitchen chair, on the kitchen floor through the main hallway to the area at the top of the basement stairs, and bloody drag marks on the last seven steps in the basement. Blood had been cleaned from the kitchen floor, the hallway, and the area at the top of the basement stairs, and the blood was matched to the victim.

The postmortem examination revealed the victim's cause of death was massive head injury and manual strangulation. She suffered multiple lacerations to the back of her head, her skull was fractured, and she had numerous bruises and lacerations to her forehead, left cheek, eyes, lips, and jawline. She had defense-style injuries to her left arm and wrist. During the investigation, detectives discovered the victim's husband had uncharacteristically removed vegetation from a back gate, making it operational, several days before her death. A financial investigation revealed the couple had depleted most of their financial assets during the preceding several years. A search of the vehicle operated by the victim's husband produced a shirt and shoes stained with the victim's blood, which had been hidden beneath the driver's seat. Analyses of his cellular telephone records were inconsistent with the locations he claimed to have visited during the time his wife was killed.

In order to obtain a better understanding of this murder, the assigned investigators requested the assistance of a criminal investigative analyst shortly after this crime was committed. Following a careful review of the victimology, physical evidence, witness statements, and wound pathology, the analyst prepared a detailed written report that delineated the "red flags" that were present in the crime scene. During the trial of the victim's husband, the prosecutor consulted with the analyst during cross-examination of the defendant and used the report to effectively describe the elements of staging during his closing statement to the jury. The defendant was convicted.

Evaluation of Eyewitness Evidence

Detectives involved in cold homicide investigations often rely heavily upon the accuracy of eyewitness accounts, particularly in cases with no physical or biological evidence.

Since the 1970s, researchers have been studying the causes of eyewitness errors (Loftus 1979). The unreliability of eyewitness accounts and identifications has been dramatically illustrated by recent court cases in which DNA evidence exonerated individuals wrongfully convicted of violent crimes. Many wrongful convictions have been based almost exclusively on testimony from eyewitnesses who remained convinced that their identifications were accurate. Despite the fallibility of such evidence, testimony from eyewitnesses is often perceived as the most compelling trial evidence.

Misconceptions regarding the manner in which human memory functions and the factors that influence an eyewitness's ability to accurately make an identification are common not only in the general population but also throughout the criminal justice system. Historically, criminal investigators have routinely relied upon statements from witnesses to develop investigative leads, identify perpetrators, and exonerate the innocent. Additionally, criminal prosecutions have frequently been based exclusively upon identifications by individuals who claim to have seen either the victim or suspect engaged in normal noncriminal behaviors prior to the commission of the crime. DNA evidence, on the other hand, is often difficult for jurors to understand (Ainsworth 1998).

Despite belief to the contrary, the identification process does not operate like a videotape recording system. Scientific research has shown that several cognitive processes are involved in "identification memory," which enables a person to accurately select a person from a photographic or live presentation. These processes, which consist of encoding, storage, and retrieval, operate separately; however, each is essential to the identification process. Identification memory is a complicated process that is vulnerable to alteration by numerous factors, including the nature of the instructions given to the eyewitness regarding identification, the amount of time between the witnessed event and identification, the presentation format, the emotional state of the eyewitness, environmental factors such as lighting and duration of the event, and the degree of familiarity the eyewitness had with the potential suspect. As a result, memories are vulnerable to change by internal and external conditions, interactions with other persons, and exposure to additional information.

One of the most prevalent techniques used within the criminal justice system to evaluate the accuracy of eyewitness statements is an assessment of the level of confidence the witness reports. Although it has been popularly assumed that confidence is predictive of accuracy, researchers have found a relatively weak correlation, which would likely be functionally worthless in real-life settings (Wells & Loftus 1984; Sporer et al. 1995). Research has confirmed that a witness's confidence level is affected by factors unrelated to accuracy, such as receiving affirmative feedback, which confirms the accuracy of their identification (Wells & Bradfield 1998, 1999). This finding has important implications for homicide investigations. It is common for investigators to solicit a self-confidence rating from the witness regarding the accuracy of their identification, and to use their confidence level as a basis for prioritization of leads. Investigators and prosecutors also use the witness's confidence level to make a determination of whether there is sufficient probable cause to make an arrest and/or file charges.

Another misperception is that an eyewitness who was highly emotional at the time of the event is a more reliable and accurate witness. It is assumed that a witness or victim will not forget a person they saw during a violent or threatening encounter and that human memory regarding this type of event is essentially unaffected by the passage of time. Researchers have determined that high levels of stress actually interfere with a person's ability to encode information, and that people who are only moderately aroused are more likely to make accurate identifications (Deffenbacher 1983; Christianson 1992).

The role that familiarity plays in accurate identification is another issue that is frequently misunderstood. Higher rates of misidentification have been found with persons who had previously been seen than for total strangers; however, higher confidence ratings were reported in identifications of persons rated as familiar (Read 1994). Researchers believe witnesses are often unable to distinguish between two or more memories, possibly because they perceive them to be similar in quality, content, or characteristics. Accurate identification requires that the person recall the exact context in which he or she saw the person, and not base identification on exposure to media accounts, viewing mug shots, or conversations with other persons (Reed 2004). This finding has significant implications during assessment of statements from neighbors or persons who regularly saw the person they identified, and for identifications that followed publicity of the crime. Research by Shapiro and Penrod (1986) found that the only characteristic predictive of identification accuracy was distinctiveness of appearance.

Detectives should carefully review the procedures utilized and the circumstances under which eyewitnesses made identifications. Close scrutiny should be given to any witness who became more confident over time regarding the accuracy of their report; reported details or events they could not have witnessed due to distance, impaired eyesight, insufficient lighting, or position; or reported new details or modification of their account following exposure to other witnesses or media coverage.

Witnesses who were young children at the time of the event require special consideration. Criminal justice professionals should review *Children Who Witness Homicide and Other Violent Crimes* (Boychuk-Spears 2002) for recommendations regarding appropriate interviewing procedures and analyses of statements given by children.

Unfortunately, procedures utilized by police investigators regarding eyewitness identifications have not comprehensively integrated the findings of psychological researchers. Although a collaboration of researchers and criminal justice professionals in 1999 produced the U.S. Department of Justice's publication, *Eyewitness Evidence: A Guide for Law Enforcement* (Technical Working Group for Eyewitness Evidence 1999), their recommendations regarding double-blind testing and sequential presentation format have not been commonly adopted (Wells et al. 2000).

Conclusion

Criminal investigative analysis is a valuable tool that can bring fresh focus to the investigation of a cold case by providing a comprehensive understanding of the manner in which the crime was committed. The technique integrates information regarding the victim, the initial crime scene investigation, physical and trace evidence, wound patterns, toxicological examination results, geography, witness accounts, and an indirect personality assessment of potential suspects. This comprehensive analysis process can serve as a means of organizing numerous sources of investigative information from a cold case file that might otherwise remain dormant for many years. The passage of time is both an enemy and ally with regard to a cold homicide case. New insights spawned by a comprehensive analysis of the case are possible through integration of all available information, including behavioral analysis of the interaction of the victim and offender, forensic evidence, and a determination of the feasibility of conducting scientific tests on evidentiary items that may have been overlooked or misinterpreted. Criminal investigative analysis is available to investigators and prosecutors upon their request from members of the ICIAF.

Acknowledgments

I wish to express my deepest gratitude and appreciation to Sharon Pagaling Hagan for her authorship and contribution of this chapter. Hagan is a clinical psychologist and retired Special Agent Supervisor of the California Department of Justice's Violent Crime Profiling Unit. She studied criminal investigative profiling and crime scene analysis in conjunction with the ICIAF and the Federal Bureau of Investigation's (FBI's) National Center for the Analysis of Violent Crime, and has provided investigative assistance to law enforcement agencies and prosecutors throughout California and nationally regarding homicide, sexual assault, threat assessment, and child abduction cases.

Notes

1. Testimony regarding behavioral profiles of offenders who commit various types of crimes has been ruled to be potentially prejudicial and/or of limited probative value in the determination of the facts relevant to a specific crime or defendant.
2. Expert testimony has been allowed regarding crime scene analysis, crime scene reconstruction, and staging.

Suggested Readings and Bibliography

Ainsworth, P. B. (1998). *Psychology, Law and Eyewitness Testimony*. West Sussex, England: John Wiley & Sons, Inc.

Boychuk-Spears, T. (2002). *Children Who Witness Homicide and Other Violent Crimes* (pp. 91–115). San Diego, CA: Specialized Training Services.

Christianson, S. A. (1992). Emotional stress and eyewitness memory: A critical review. *Psychological Bulletin, 112,* 284–309.

Deffenbacher, K. (1983). The influence of arousal on reliability of testimony. In S. M. A. Lloyd-Bostock & B. R. Clifford (Eds.), *Evaluating Witness Evidence: Recent Psychological Research and New Perspectives* (pp. 235–251). Chichester, England: Wiley.

Douglas, J. E., Burgess, A. W., Burgess, A. G. & Ressler, R. K. (1992). *Crime Classification Manual* (pp. 249–258). New York: Lexington Books.

Hazelwood, R. R. & Burgess, A. W. (2001). The behavioral-oriented interview of rape victims: The key to profiling. In Hazelwood, R. R. & Burgess, A. W. (Eds.), *Practical Aspects of Rape Investigation: A Multidisciplinary Approach,* Second Edition (pp. 118–119). Boca Raton, FL: CRC Press.

Loftus, E. F. (1979). *Eyewitness Testimony.* Cambridge, MA: Harvard University Press.

Read, J. D. (1994). Understanding bystander misidentifications: The role of familiarity and contextual knowledge. In D. F. Ross, J. D. Read & M. P. Toglia (Eds.), *Adult Eyewitness Testimony: Current Trends and Developments* (pp. 56–79). New York: Cambridge University Press.

Reed, S. K. (2004). *Cognition: Theory and Applications* (pp. 111–115). Belmont, CA: Wadsworth/Thomson Learning.

Ressler, R. K., Burgess, A. W. & Douglas, J. E. (1988). *Sexual Homicide: Patterns and Motives.* New York: Lexington Books.

Shapiro, P. N. & Penrod, S. D. (1986). Meta-analysis of facial identification studies. *Psychological Bulletin, 100,* 139–156.

Sporer, S., Penrod, S., Read, D. & Cutler, B. L. (1995). Choosing, confidence and accuracy: A meta-analysis of the confidence-accuracy relation in eyewitness identification studies. *Psychological Bulletin, 118,* 315–327.

Technical Working Group for Eyewitness Evidence. (1999). *Eyewitness Evidence: A Guide for Law Enforcement* (Booklet). Washington, DC: United States Department of Justice, Office of Justice Programs.

Wells, G. L. & Bradfield, A. L. (1998). "Good, you identified the suspect": Feedback to eyewitnesses distorts their reports of the witnessing experience. *Journal of Applied Psychology, 83,* 360–376.

Wells, G. L. & Bradfield, A. L. (1999). Distortions in eyewitnesses' recollections: Can the post identification feedback effect be moderated? *Psychological Science, 10,* 138–144.

Wells, G. L. & Loftus, E. F. (1984). *Eyewitness Testimony: Psychological Perspectives.* Cambridge, MA: Cambridge University Press.

Wells, G. L., Malpass, R. S., Lindsay, R. C. L., Fisher, R. P., Turtle, J. W. & Fulero, S. M. (2000). From the lab to the police station. *American Psychologist, 55*(6), 581–598.

Interviewing in Cold Cases
Evidence-Based Best Practices for Extracting Long-Term Memories

10

HEATHER PRICE, KIRK LUTHER, WAYNE THOMAS, FIONA GABBERT, AND LORRAINE HOPE

> Our memories are constructive. They're reconstructive. Memory works a little bit more like a Wikipedia page. You can go in there and change it, but so can other people.
>
> —**Elizabeth Loftus,** *NPR TED Radio Hour*

In recent decades, violent crime clearance rates have declined across Canada (Statistics Canada, 2022), the USA (Federal Bureau of Investigation, 2017), and the UK (Home Office, 2021), resulting in a growing number of unsolved cases, often referred to as "cold" cases. There has also been a surge of public interest in cold cases, fueled by popular media, public inquiries into historical wrongdoings, and advancements in DNA and investigative genetic genealogy technology that have led to the resolution of high-profile cases (e.g., the Golden State Killer; St. John, 2020). While such advances represent a significant milestone for cold cases, properly stored DNA evidence is often unavailable in most cold cases (Davis et al., 2021). Investigators, therefore, often have to turn to other methods, particularly re-interviewing previous witnesses and suspects as well as identifying new ones, to bring these cases to resolution.

Solving cold cases offers numerous societal benefits, such as preventing perpetrators from committing further crimes, providing peace and closure for victims and their loved ones, and reassuring living victims that they are not forgotten. Crucially, the discovery of new evidence, especially witness evidence, is the primary factor leading to the re-opening of a cold case for active investigation (Davis et al., 2011, 2014). However, cold cases present unique challenges beyond those of typical investigations. The passage of substantial time inherently weakens witness memory and makes it more susceptible to interference or distortion from a range of sources, including conversations with others or leading questions from the media or even investigators.

DOI: 10.4324/9781003415633-12

This chapter focuses on providing practical, evidence-based strategies for investigators to effectively elicit long-term memory evidence in cold cases. We will explore how an understanding of memory processes can directly inform investigative interviewing techniques. Our aim is to equip cold case investigators with useful tools derived from current psychological research, highlighting the critical importance of effective witness engagement strategies. We will dive into specific, actionable methods for eliciting autobiographical memory and discuss practical considerations for person identification within the unique context of investigations relying on information recalled after significant delays.

Understanding Long-Term Memory: Practical Implications for Investigators

When working cold cases, investigators are fundamentally dealing with long-term memory, a process that is far from a perfect recording of past events. Instead, memory retrieval is a subjective and reconstructive process (Howe et al., 2018), meaning that what someone remembers and reports is influenced by many factors, including what they attended to, their emotional state, how often they thought about the event, any subsequent conversations or information they encountered about the event, and how they are interviewed. Understanding this reconstructive nature of memory is crucial for investigators to adjust their expectations and approach when interviewing in cold case investigations.

The Effects of Delay (Forgetting Over Time)

One of the most predictable consequences of the passage of time is *forgetting*. As the period between an event and its recall increases, the amount of information remembered generally decreases (Ebbinghaus, 2013; Rubin & Wenzel, 1996). We forget things over time partly due to the weakening of our memory trace, making information less accessible over time (Anderson, 1983). Memories can also become more "gist-like" or general, as fine-grained details are forgotten more rapidly than coarse-grain information (Goldsmith et al., 2005). For instance, reports provided after a delay were found to be less detailed than those given immediately (Chevroulet et al., 2021; Fisher, 1996; Lifanov et al., 2021).

Investigator takeaway: Investigators should anticipate that witnesses *may* not be able to recall past events in full detail, especially if a significant amount of time has passed. Investigators should therefore temper expectations and recognize that a witness who is only able to provide few details after a long delay is demonstrating a natural memory phenomenon of memory decay, and the lack of detail is not necessarily an indication of unreliability or deception. Despite this natural forgetting over time, it is important to remember that many details *can* be retained and remain available for retrieval (Fisher, 1996), especially if certain memory mechanisms (e.g., rehearsal) have offered some protection, and/or if interviewers are skilled in providing retrieval support. The approach taken by the investigator is also likely to play a significant role in the outcome of retrieval attempts, including skill in providing retrieval support and effective use of techniques designed to support retrieval.

Co-witness Influences on Memory

Crimes are often witnessed by more than one person, and these co-witnesses frequently "debrief" or discuss the event informally. These discussions can lead to the co-witness suggestibility effect, where details from one witness's account are integrated into another's, potentially distorting their original memory (Gabbert & Wheeler, 2018; Ito et al., 2019).

A witness is especially vulnerable to co-witness influences when their memory is weak (e.g., due to age or time delay), when the co-witness provides details that fill gaps (though this can enhance accuracy if the co-witness information is correct), when the other witness appears confident or more reliable, or when the co-witness is familiar to the witness (e.g., family member; Allan et al., 2012; Hope et al., 2008). These influences are frequently observed after short delays (days to weeks) and are likely amplified in the context of cold cases due to the extended delay between the event and recall. While there may be benefits to co-witness discussion, such as correcting errors, investigators must be aware of the potential for memory distortion.

Investigator takeaway: Investigators should be mindful that witnesses in cold cases may have discussed the event with others. These interactions can subtly, or overtly, alter their memory and recollection for events. While direct empirical evidence for co-witness effects after very long delays is still needed, the principles suggest a heightened risk for introducing memory errors.

Memory Contamination and Interference

The presence of a significant delay provides opportunities for one's memory to become contaminated or subjected to interference from various sources. Interference can come from both internal and external sources during the encoding, storage, and retrieval of one's memories. Weaker memories, which are characteristic of witnesses in cold cases due to the passage of time, are particularly vulnerable to these external influences. Research shows that witnesses are prone to interference effects after a delay, as they are less likely to notice discrepancies between their original memories and any post-event information they encountered (Ridley et al., 2013).

One significant aspect of this vulnerability to memory interference is something known as *source monitoring errors*. That is, people struggle to discriminate whether they experienced an event firsthand or learned information about the event from another source (and later adopted it as their own memory; Johnson et al., 1992, Johnson, 1997). In cold cases, where witness evidence may be critical for re-opening a case or generating new leads, knowing the true origin of a memory is key.

Investigator takeaway: To protect against source monitoring errors and memory contamination, investigators should implement specific practices, including:

i. *Providing warnings*: Inform witnesses about the potential for exposure to misinformation. Since memories in cold cases are likely to be weaker, witnesses are particularly prone to interference effects and less likely to notice discrepancies between their original memories and any post-event information they encountered. A clear warning at the outset, such as "People can hear information from various sources like friends, family, or the media. It's important for us to know what you remember from that day, and to let us know whether you think that information came from someone else," may help inoculate against such influences (Blank & Launay, 2014).

ii. *Critically appraising memory*: Encourage witnesses to evaluate their memories and their origins by prompting them to consider *how* they know a piece of information. For instance, an investigator might ask, "How do you know it happened during the summer?" This type of question can help witnesses distinguish between personally experienced events and information acquired from other sources.

iii. *Avoiding suggestive interviewing practices*: Crucially, investigators must avoid suggestive questions and interviewing practices, as these can easily distort weakened long-term memories. For example, instead of asking "Did you see the suspect wearing a dark jacket?," which implies both a jacket and a dark color, a non-suggestive question would be, "Describe what the person was wearing." Adhering to open-ended questioning and avoiding leading language minimizes the risk of inadvertently planting inaccurate information.

Impact of Poor Initial Interviews on Long-Term Memory

The science of investigative interviewing has evolved considerably over the past few decades. Witnesses in cold cases may have been initially interviewed using methods now known to be problematic (e.g., agenda-driven questioning, use of leading or suggestive techniques, failure to build rapport). The quality of that initial interview can have a substantive influence on a witness's ability to recall past events. There is evidence to suggest that a high-quality initial interview can actually enhance information provided at a delayed recall (Hashtroudi et al., 1993; Hope et al., 2014; Marsh et al., 2005). However, the long-term impact of a poor initial interview on a later, high-quality interview has been less explored; some research suggests that even a suggestive initial interview may not substantively impact accuracy for certain types of memories after decades (Goldfarb et al., 2019).

Investigator takeaway: When reviewing witness evidence collected many years ago, investigators should carefully consider the context and quality of the original interview. A witness who previously provided little detail may actually be able to recall significantly more information with modern memory retrieval techniques and appropriate interviewing practices. Conversely, investigators should be aware that suggested details from a poor initial interview might still be retained in a witness's memory. Thus, investigators should develop a strategic re-interviewing approach that acknowledges the past while focusing on best practices for current retrieval.

Essential Interviewing Techniques for Cold Case Investigators

While the passage of time can weaken memories, there are tools available for investigators working on cold cases. Applying evidence-based interviewing techniques, which are crucial in timely investigations, arguably becomes even *more* critical when memories are weaker and more vulnerable to external influences. Interviewer skill in delayed cases is therefore paramount for ensuring the best chances of success.

Regardless of the delay between experiencing an event and being questioned about it, certain core principles of interviewing remain essential. Investigators should always aim to build rapport with the witness and actively encourage elaborate and effortful retrieval. Equally important is for investigators to avoid practices that can interfere with the retrieval of a potentially weakened memory, such as interrupting, over-talking, or asking too many closed-ended or suggestive questions. Many existing interviewing tools and techniques, though not always extensively tested after very long delays, offer theoretical promise for cold case investigations. We review several of these tools and techniques next.

The Cognitive Interview

The Cognitive Interview (CI) is a comprehensive and well-established protocol designed to elicit detailed narrative descriptions of experienced events (Fisher & Geiselman, 1992). Extensively tested over decades, the CI has consistently been shown to generate more information and more precise responses than standard free recall interviews (Memon et al., 2010). Crucially for cold cases, the benefits of the CI have been demonstrated even after delays of up to 21 months and even up to 35 years (Dodier et al., 2021; Fisher et al., 2000). Certain CI mnemonics may be particularly useful for delayed interviews.

Mental Reinstatement of Context (MRC): This technique involves helping the witness mentally recreate the encoding context of the target event. Investigators can guide witnesses to focus on sensory details such as sounds, smells, feelings, and people present at the time and place of interest, which can then trigger memories for other related details. MRC has been shown to increase the amount and accuracy of recall, even at delays of weeks to months (Dietze et al., 2012; Drohan-Jennings et al., 2010; Emmett et al., 2003; Hershkowitz et al., 2001). For cold witnesses, providing a range of temporal and contextual cues can assist in retrieving older, weaker memories. In some promising cases, physical context reinstatement—that is, taking the witness back to the scene of the crime—can facilitate retrieval by reinstating the encoding context, particularly after a long period of not thinking about the event (Wong & Read, 2011). However, investigators must consider that environments may have significantly changed over time (potentially leading to memory errors), and the potential negative emotional impacts for the witness.

Sketching: This technique involves asking an interviewee to draw details of a witnessed event (e.g., locations, movements, people) and then use their sketch as a reference to provide a verbal account (Dando et al., 2011). Sketching is believed to help an interviewee recreate the spatial cues present during encoding of the event that facilitate recall. Further, sketching can reduce cognitive load by externalizing memory cues, preventing working memory from being overloaded

(Middendorf & Macan, 2002). Several studies have shown that sketching increases the amount of detailed and accurate information obtained from both children and older adults (Dando, 2013; Dando et al., 2009, 2020; Eastwood et al., 2018, 2019; Mattison et al., 2015, 2018) as well as helps the interviewer better understand the interviewee's account (Luther et al., 2022). For cold witnesses, reducing working memory load can provide critical support for recalling their accounts.

Memory Cuing and Structure Reporting

Memory Jogs: Memory jogs are essentially nudges designed to help people access and retrieve information by encouraging them to think about what they are trying to recall in different ways (Fisher & Geiselman, 2010; Heidt et al., 2015). Memory jogs can be useful when a witness is struggling to recall a specific detail, providing alternative routes into their memory. For instance, to help with the retrieval of a name, an interviewer could ask them if the name was common or unusual, or short or long. Similarly, if a witness is trying to recall a vehicle, they might be asked about its color, make, body style, or whether it had any distinguishing features. The goal is to encourage retrieval by presenting various, non-suggestive attributes of the target memory, allowing the witness to initiate a new search through their weakened or fragmented long-term memory. This technique is likely valuable to cold cases because it helps overcome retrieval blocks without introducing external, potentially contaminating information (Fisher & Geiselman, 1992).

Self-Generated Cues (SGCs): Unlike generic cues provided by an interviewer, SGCs are memory cues that are personalized based on the individual's representation of the target event (Kontogianni et al., 2018; Wheeler & Gabbert, 2017). These cues are particularly salient and distinctive, optimizing the activation of relevant memory networks to facilitate successful retrieval. An example in an interview context is asking a witness to note down the first six things that come to mind when thinking about the event, and then using those "cues" to prompt more focused recall. SGCs have proven successful for retrieving detailed and accurate memories of target events (Kontogianni et al., 2018) and autobiographical memories (Harris & O'Connor, 2022; Uzer & Brown, 2017). Theoretically, SGCs are promising for cold cases as the cues are self-generated, minimizing the risk of contamination from interviewer suggestions.

The Timeline Technique: Developed for complex or extended events where a witness has a large amount of information, the Timeline

Technique (Hope et al., 2013) uses a visual "timeline" to structure recall. This technique allows witnesses to report and organize information as they remember it, rather than being restricted to a linear narrative. Witnesses are provided with a physical timeline and use individual cards or notes to add details about people and actions, linking specific individuals to specific actions. Witnesses can start at any point and freely re-order or revise information for accuracy. This technique has been shown to elicit more information (including person descriptions, actions, and sequence details) without compromising accuracy (Gabbert & Hope, 2023). It also facilitates recall of criminal conversations and repeated events. Its self-administered nature helps reduce contamination risk from leading questions or interviewer assumptions. Reports of use in the field include use to obtain detailed accounts of historical and extended events.

The Self-Administered Interview (SAI): The SAI (Gabbert et al., 2009) is a standardized protocol designed to elicit witness accounts efficiently, without requiring an investigator to conduct an immediate interview. It incorporates clear instructions, CI mnemonics, and best-practice open-ended questions. A meta-analysis (i.e., a study that pools together the results of many studies) found that compared to other recall methods, the SAI significantly increased the number of correct details reported (Horry et al., 2021). Critically for cold cases, completing an SAI (compared to no initial retrieval attempt) improved the accuracy and completeness of subsequent memory reports after delays of longer than 1 week. The SAI may be particularly useful for cold case investigators who need to make broad calls for witnesses in cases where specific individuals with information may not be known or readily available.

To illustrate, a witness completing an SAI begins with an MRC, which guides them in mentally revisiting the event. They are prompted to focus on sensory and contextual details relevant for remembering the target event (such as where they were, what they could see, hear, and feel at the time) and encouraged to close their eyes to aid concentration. This is followed by an open-ended "Report Everything" instruction, which encourages comprehensive recall while avoiding speculation. Later sections of the SAI focus on eliciting detailed descriptions of persons involved, using non-leading prompts, and include space for a sketch of the scene to capture spatial information and movement. Individuals are also asked about other potential sources of information, vehicles present, and viewing conditions (e.g., lighting, weather, obstructions).

A particularly relevant adaptation for cold cases is the SAI-MISSING, developed for use in missing-persons investigations (Gabbert et al., 2020). This adapted form uses the same principles as the standard SAI, but incorporates additional retrieval support, such as mental context reinstatement instructions for the physical description of the person. When tested against a standard missing-persons form without retrieval support, the SAI-MISSING resulted in significantly more details regarding physical descriptions, personal effects, and clothing, and these reports were also more accurate. These findings demonstrate the SAI-MISSING's ability to effectively trigger thorough recall of an experienced event and its practical utility for missing-person investigations.

Reporting Information about Networks and Groups (RING) Task: The RING task (Hope et al., 2019) was developed to improve recall and reporting of information about people and their associates, such as friends, family, or members of criminal networks. Based on the associative nature of memory and visual representation, the RING task prompts witnesses to think about individuals and their links, facilitating recall of other relevant people and promoting a more comprehensive retrieval of information. Investigators can instruct witnesses to create a paper-and-pen diagram of the network, providing a non-suggestive way to elicit details about individuals, their relationships, and the strength of those relationships. This format offers significant potential for probing unrehearsed semantic information relevant to cold cases particularly pertaining to groups of people and how they associated with each other.

Person Identification in Cold Cases: Practical Considerations for Images

Beyond eliciting narrative accounts of events, investigators in cold cases are often keenly interested in person-specific evidence—particularly information about the identity or actions of individuals. While extracting descriptions of prior events sometimes yields information about people, there are many instances where investigators must directly target person identification.

The large body of eyewitness identification research indicates that making an accurate identification of a previously seen person (e.g., from a photographic, live, or video lineup) is often very difficult, even after a short delay of minutes or hours (Wells et al., 2020). Thus, our "people recognition" ability for those who are unfamiliar to us may not be the most promising avenue for generating leads in cold cases, particularly because the task is likely to become even more difficult after a long delay. However, when an individual has had a meaningful interaction with a target person, or possesses some level of familiarity, the likelihood of obtaining valuable information from a potential witness increases.

Person memory can play at least two significant roles in cold case investigations. First, investigators may seek retrospective recall of prior encounters or activities of a person of interest (a victim, suspect, or witness) before or during the crime. Second, investigators may request the public's assistance in identifying or locating a missing person, which involves a prospective memory task.

Retrospective Recall: Remembering a Person's Actions

Investigators frequently ask witnesses to recall sightings of a person or information about their activities prior to or during an event, which involves recalling both events and accurately attributing those events and actions to the correct person.

There is a growing body of literature on alibi provision, which offers insights into recalling one's own or another's past actions (Behl & Kienzle, 2022). An alibi is a statement of where a person was at a particular time on a particular day, typically provided to police to demonstrate they could not have been involved in a crime. An alibi witness is someone who corroborates this statement. Research consistently shows that providing accurate alibis poses a considerable challenge: it is difficult to remember both our own and others' past actions, especially when the time frame is narrow (Culhane et al., 2008; Olson & Charman, 2012; Olson & Wells, 2004). For example, one study asked participants to recall their whereabouts from a six-hour period three weeks earlier; almost half (44%) were inconsistent on the timing of their activities, and 19% were inconsistent on their actions (Strange et al., 2014).

Most alibi research has focused on delays of hours, days, or a few weeks. Naturally, this task becomes even more challenging after the many years typical of cold cases. For instance, participants were more likely to be mistaken for distant alibis (up to 14 weeks prior) than for more recent ones (Olson & Charman, 2012). While alibi research has not extended to delays of many years, the general literature on remembering past experiences indicates that recalling the precise time and location of events from years ago, particularly if they were not encoded as notable at the time (e.g., Harvey et al., 2025), will be exceptionally challenging.

Recalling actions of familiar others: While much alibi research focuses on recalling one's own activities, cold cases often involve recalling the actions of a person who was familiar (but not necessarily well known) to the witness. Recalling the actions of a familiar other may be simpler than recalling a stranger's actions as it bypasses the initial person identification challenge, but it also introduces the complexity of sorting through repeated exposures to the same person over time. While research on the identification of familiar people after relatively short delays exists, less is known about the fading of familiarity over very long periods. Despite this knowledge gap, some evidence suggests that identifications of familiar individuals (e.g., former teachers) are not devalued even after a year, perhaps due to the inherent familiarity (Pica et al., 2018). However, the long-term dynamics of "fading familiarity" remain largely unexplored.

Prospective Person Identification: Searching for a Missing Person

The second key area for person identification in cold cases is when public assistance is sought to locate a missing person. This active search is a prospective memory task, uniquely challenging in cold cases because the target person's appearance has likely changed significantly over time. Even under optimal recognition conditions where a person is directly in front of us and we are trying to match an image, people tend to make a high rate of identification errors. For example, grocery store clerks showed an error rate of over 30% when trying to match faces to photo identification (Kemp et al., 1997). In another study, accuracy for matching a live person to a photo lineup was only 70% (Megreya & Burton, 2008). Not surprisingly, the selection of images influences matching accuracy, with higher accuracy when the lineup image closely matches the current target appearance. Accuracy is even worse when the image to match the person is no longer available (i.e., a person has seen a photo of the target, but it is not currently in front of them during the identification task), as is common with missing-persons posters. In one study, fewer than 5% of students accurately identified a target man they had studied a photograph of two days earlier, even when offered a substantial reward (Lampinen et al., 2009). This finding highlights the inherent difficulty in the task, even with motivation.

Investigator takeaways: In cold cases, where images are dated and the target person has aged considerably, investigators face additional complexities. The witness's encoded image of a suspect or missing person will be from a long time ago, and the person's current appearance may no longer match that original memory. This disconnect creates three main strategies for presenting images to potential witnesses or the public: (1) a dated image of the target, (2) an updated image (if available) of the target, and (3) an age-progressed image of the target (using technology and/or forensic artists). Which strategy an investigator chooses depends on the available resources and nature of the case.

For identifying a suspect in a cold case where a lineup is created for eyewitness identification, investigators must decide between using a dated suspect image (with dated filler images) or an updated suspect image (with updated fillers). Eyewitness identification research has not definitively answered which is more effective for long delays. However, research suggests that the closer the match between the witness's encoded memory and the retrieval image, the more likely successful retrieval will be (Tulving & Thomson, 1973); thus, presenting a dated image would likely be most effective. Most lineup identification research has focused on very short delays, leaving much longer delays largely unexplored (Dysart & Lindsay, 2007).

For locating a person who has been missing for a long time via public appeals, the decision is whether a dated or an age-progressed image would be most effective. Investigators may commission an age-progressed image to approximate what the missing person might look like now, years after their disappearance. While the missing person may have been familiar to many at the time of disappearance (e.g., a child well known in the community), the age-progressed image is an unfamiliar representation of the now-older person. This process blurs the lines between memory for familiar and unfamiliar people. While releasing an age-progressed image can generate new media attention and interest, the primary question for investigators is its usefulness for recognition accuracy.

Age-Progressed Images: A Realistic Assessment

Age progression is a set of techniques, including computer simulation (altering a dated photo) or hand drawings by a forensic artist (Yang et al., 2019). These progressions consider typical growth patterns based on demographic norms and often supplement this with images of parents or other relatives. The accuracy of such images is influenced by the person's adherence to average growth, as well as lifestyle factors like sun exposure, weight, and health problems. Ultimately, there is substantial variability in how aging affects appearance.

For age-progressed images to be useful, they should lead to more accurate identifications than dated photos, without incurring a commensurate cost. So, how accurate are they? Research exploring age-progressed images created by trained forensic artists found that while they were rated as more similar to real images than description-matched foils, the overall similarity was only moderate, and there was significant variability between artists (Lampinen et al., 2015). A series of studies on the added value of age-progressed images to public appeals found that, although identification sometimes exceeded chance, recognition accuracy was generally not better than dated images alone, and in one case, was even worse. Thus, their accuracy appears variable, modest, and not superior to dated images (Lampinen et al., 2012a,b).

While age-progressed images did not consistently increase recognition accuracy in Lampinen and colleagues' studies, they also did not impede the ability to recognize a target. This finding suggests that any additional benefits (e.g., generating public interest in the case) might justify their use. However, some research indicates that adding an age-progressed image to a dated image may actually impair the ability to identify a target, possibly by changing observers' decision strategies to consider a wider range of images plausible (Charman & Carol, 2012).

If age-progressed images can interfere with accurate recognition when a dated image is available, a critical question arises: How well can people be recognized from dated images alone? If the baseline recognition from dated images is very low, the risk of introducing an age-progressed image might be worth taking for other case-related advantages. Existing evidence suggests that people are reasonably accurate in recognizing individuals who have aged since a photo was taken (Charman & Carol, 2012; Lampinen et al., 2012a). However, the substantial variability in the accuracy of age-progressed images means more work is needed to fully assess this cost benefit balance.

Avoiding Pitfalls and Biases: Critical Practices for Cold Case Investigators

Investigators working on cold cases inherit a "chain of decisions" from the initial investigation that necessitates a fresh, unbiased review (Roach, 2017). It is imperative that investigators consider the possibility that individual pieces of evidence may have been influenced by the investigative theories prevalent at the time of the original investigation. This potential for influence introduces significant pitfalls and biases that can undermine the accuracy and objectivity of a re-investigation.

One critical concern is the way bias can propagate through the justice system, creating the illusion of converging evidence; this phenomenon is known as *bias cascade* and *bias snowball* effects (Dror, 2025). Rather than evaluating each piece of evidence independently, earlier information (e.g., a suspect's confession) can bias the interpretation of subsequent evidence such as eyewitness accounts or forensic findings. As bias cascades from one individual to another, it can lead to multiple elements of a case appearing to support the same conclusion, when in reality they are all influenced by the same initial bias. This interaction creates an exaggerated perception of evidentiary strength, because what seems to be independent corroboration is actually a byproduct of shared cognitive contamination.

Another prevalent bias to be aware of is investigator skepticism regarding changing alibis. Despite evidence suggesting that some investigators are aware that alibi errors may be normative and not indicative of deceit, investigators tend to be skeptical of alibis that change over time. For instance, one survey found that 81% of law enforcement officers believed that if a suspect's alibi story changed over time, it likely indicated they lied to police (Dysart & Strange, 2012). This finding highlights a disconnect between the genuine difficulty people have recalling precise, time-specific details about their own or others' actions, and the assumptions investigators may make about their honesty or general credibility when they struggle to do so.

To mitigate biases and work toward an objective re-investigation, specific strategic practices are recommended:

- *Independent evidence review*: A useful approach to avoid the influence of prior confirmation bias or "tunnel vision" is for investigators to avoid talking with original investigators until all of the evidence from the original investigation has undergone an initial, independent review.
- *Strategic case rethinking protocol*: A structured protocol for reviewing unsolved cases can significantly limit bias. Rossmo (2016) outlined four stages for "rethinking" an unsolved case, which helps to minimize the influence of previous investigative decisions (Rossmo, 2016):
    - i. *Identify the evidence*: Focus solely on the evidence itself, not existing theories, assumptions, or inferences about the case.
    - ii. *Interpret the evidence*: Draw only reasonable conclusions that can be directly derived from the identified evidence.
    - iii. *Look for patterns*: Search for connections and patterns across the entire constellation of evidence.
    - iv. *Generate and analyze investigative hypotheses*: Use the evidence to develop and evaluate investigative hypotheses, prioritizing diagnostic evidence that can help distinguish between different theories.

Ultimately, conducting interviews in an open-ended manner whenever possible and adhering to evidence-based practices will naturally work against the influence of unintentional bias.

Warning against Pseudoscience and "Last-Ditch" Efforts

When leads are scarce in cold cases, there can be a strong temptation to resort to pseudoscientific or unconventional memory retrieval strategies. However, the desire to obtain a larger volume of information must always be balanced against the significant cost of obtaining inaccurate information that could waste substantial resources. Unfortunately, unproven, pseudoscientific practices that lack an evidence base, such as hypnotizing witnesses or using other suggestive or unorthodox methods, pose severe risks. Such efforts can ultimately corrupt the witness's memory, rendering any future attempts at retrieval unsuccessful, risking credibility issues in future court proceedings, and wasting valuable resources that could be used more productively elsewhere. Investigators must prioritize evidence-based methods to ensure the integrity of the investigation and the reliability of any recovered information.

Empowering Cold Case Investigators

Cold case investigations, by their very nature, present immense challenges, primarily due to the inherent fragility and susceptibility of long-term memory to decay and interference. Yet, with significant advances in our understanding of memory processes and the development of evidence-based interviewing techniques, there is an opportunity to revisit these cases with updated strategies and potentially uncover new evidence.

Our goal with the chapter was to outline practical tools and considerations for investigators tasked with eliciting long-term memory evidence. By understanding that memory is reconstructive rather than a perfect recording, and by acknowledging the impact of time, interference, and even prior problematic interviews, investigators can adjust their expectations and approach witnesses more effectively. Techniques such as the CI and structured reporting formats offer powerful, non-suggestive methods for maximizing detailed and accurate recall from witnesses in cold cases. Even in the complex area of person identification, a nuanced understanding of dated versus age-progressed images, coupled with the encoding specificity principle, can guide optimal public appeals and lineup construction.

Empowering cold case investigators means equipping them to actively combat cognitive biases like corroboration inflation and tunnel vision. Adopting structured review protocols and maintaining an independent perspective are crucial to ensure that investigations proceed without being unduly influenced by past assumptions or errors. A stern warning against pseudoscientific memory retrieval strategies is also paramount, as such practices risk contaminating fragile memories, undermining credibility, and wasting precious resources.

Ultimately, the key to empowering cold case investigators lies in continuous specialized training that is unique to the particular challenges of such investigations. Investigators should be provided training on advanced memory retrieval options as well as fostering a deeper understanding of memory itself and the various pitfalls that can arise when dealing with long-term recall. Researchers have a significant role to play in this empowerment, requiring sustained efforts to collaborate with law enforcement, translate theoretical findings into practical applications, and conduct further research into currently neglected areas. By bridging the gap between cutting-edge psychological science and investigative practice, we can provide cold case investigators with the robust tools necessary to bring resolution to some of society's most challenging unsolved crimes.

References

Allan, K., Midjord, J. P., Martin D., & Gabbert, F. (2012). Memory conformity and the perceived accuracy of self versus other. *Memory & Cognition, 40,* 280–286.

Anderson, J. R. (1983). A spreading activation theory of memory. *Journal of Verbal Learning and Verbal Behavior, 22*(34), 261–295. https://doi.org/10.1016/s0022-5371(83)90201-3

Behl, J. D., & Kienzle, M. R. (2022). *Alibis and Corroborators: Psychological, Criminological, and Legal Perspectives*. Springer.

Blank, H., & Launay, C. (2014). How to protect eyewitness memory against the misinformation effect: A meta-analysis of post-warning studies. *Journal of Applied Research in Memory and Cognition, 3*(2), 77–88. https://doi.org/10.1037/h0101798

Charman, S. D., & Carol, R. N. (2012). Age-progressed images may harm recognition of missing children by increasing the number of plausible targets. *Journal of Applied Research in Memory and Cognition, 1*(3), 171–178. https://doi.org/10.1016/j.jarmac.2012.07.008

Chevroulet, C., Paterson, H. M., Yu, A., Chew, E., & Kemp, R. I. (2021). The impact of recall timing on the preservation of eyewitness memory. *Psychiatry, Psychology and Law, 29*(3), 471–486. https://doi.org/10.1080/13218719.2021.1926366

Culhane, S. E., Hosch, H. M., & Kehn, A. (2008). Alibi generation: Data from US Hispanics and US non-Hispanic whites. *Journal of Ethnicity in Criminal Justice, 6*(3), 177–199. https://doi.org/10.1080/15377930802243395

Dando, C. (2013). Drawing to remember: External support of older adults' eyewitness performance. *PloS One, 8,* e69937. https://doi.org/10.1371/journal.pone.0069937

Dando, C. J., Gabbert, F. & Hope, L. (2020). Supporting older eyewitnesses' episodic memory: the self-administered interview and sketch reinstatement of context. *Memory, 28(6)*, 712–723. https://doi.org/10.1080/09658211.2020.1757718

Dando, C. J., Wilcock, R., Behnkle, C., & Milne, R. (2011). Modifying the cognitive interview: Countenancing forensic application by enhancing practicability. *Psychology, Crime & Law, 17*(6), 491–511. https://doi.org/10.1080/10683160903334212

Dando, C., Wilcock, R., Milne, R., & Henry, L. (2009). A modified cognitive interview procedure for frontline police investigators. *Applied Cognitive Psychology, 23*(5), 698–716. https://doi.org/10.1002/acp.1501

Davis, R. C., Jensen, C., & Kitchens, K. E. (2011). *Cold-Case Investigations: An Analysis of Current Practices and Factors Associated with Successful Outcomes.* RAND Corporation.

Davis, R. C., Jensen, C. J., III, Burgette, L., & Burnett, K. (2014). Working smarter on cold cases: Identifying factors associated with successful cold case investigations. *Journal of Forensic Science, 59*(2), 375–382. https://doi.org/10.1111/1556-4029.12384

Davis, R. C., Jurek, A., Wells, W., & Shadwick, J. T. (2021). Investigative Outcomes of CODIS Matches in Previously Untested Sexual Assault Kits. *Criminal Justice Policy Review, 32*(8), 841–864.

Dietze, P., Powell, M. B., & Thomson, D. M. (2012). Examination of the effect of mental reinstatement of context across developmental level, retention interval and type of mnemonic instruction. *Psychiatry, Psychology and Law, 19*(1), 89–103. https://doi.org/10.1080/13218719.2010.543410

Dodier, O., Ginet, M., Teissedre, F., Verkampt, F., & Fisher, R. P. (2021). Using the Cognitive Interview to recall real-world emotionally stressful experiences: Road accidents. *Applied Cognitive Psychology, 35*(4), 1099–1105. https://doi.org/10.1002/acp.3828

Drohan-Jennings, D. M., Roberts, K. P., & Powell, M. B. (2010). Mental context reinstatement increases resistance to false suggestions after children have experienced a repeated event. *Psychiatry, Psychology and Law, 17*(4), 594–606. https://doi.org/10.1080/13218711003739110

Dror, I. E. (2025). Biased and biasing: The hidden bias cascade and bias snowball effects. *Behavioral Sciences, 15*(4), 490. https://doi.org/10.3390/bs15040490

Dysart, J. E., & Lindsay, R. C. L. (2007). The effect of delay on eyewitness identification accuracy: Should we be concerned?. In R. C. L. Lindsay, D. F. Ross, J. Don Read, & M. P. Toglia (Eds.), The Handbook of Eyewitness Psychology: *Vol. 2: Memory for People* (pp. 137–154). Lawrence Erlbaum Associates Publishers.

Dysart, J. E., & Strange, D. (2012). Beliefs about alibis and alibi investigations: A survey of law enforcement. *Psychology Crime & Law, 18*(1), 11–25. https://doi.org/10.1080/1068316x.2011.562867

Eastwood, J., Snook, B., & Luther, K. (2019). Establishing the most effective way to deliver the sketch procedure to enhance interviewee free recall. *Psychology, Crime and Law, 25*(5), 482–493. https://doi.org/10.1080/1068316X.2018.1538416

Eastwood, J., Snook, B., & Luther, K. (2018). Measuring the effectiveness of the sketch procedure for recalling details of a live interactive event. *Applied Cognitive Psychology, 32*(6), 747–754. https://doi.org/10.1002/acp.3454

Ebbinghaus, H. (2013). Memory: A contribution to experimental psychology. *Annals of Neurosciences*. https://doi.org/10.5214/ans.0972.7531.200408

Emmett, D., Clifford, B. R., & Gwyer, P. (2003). An investigation of the interaction between cognitive style and context reinstatement on the memory performance of eyewitnesses. *Personality and Individual Differences, 34*(8), 1495–1508. https://doi.org/10.1016/s0191-8869(02)00131-9

Federal Bureau of Investigation. (2017). *Clearances*. https://ucr.fbi.gov/crime-in-the-u.s/2017/crime-in-the-u.s.-2017/topic-pages/clearances

Fisher, R. P. (1996). Implications of output-bound measures for laboratory and field research in memory. *Behavioral and Brain Sciences, 19*(2), 197. https://doi.org/10.1017/s0140525x00042229

Fisher, R. P., Falkner, K. L., Trevisan, M., & McCauley, M. R. (2000). Adapting the cognitive interview to enhance long term recall of physical activities. *Journal of Applied Psychology, 85*(2), 180–89. https://doi.org/10.1037/0021-9010.85.2.180

Fisher, R. P., & Geiselman, R. E. (2010). The cognitive interview method of conducting police interviews: Eliciting extensive information and promoting therapeutic jurisprudence. *International Journal of Law and Psychiatry*, *33*(5–6), 321–328. https://doi.org/10.1016/j.ijlp.2010.09.004

Fisher, R. P., & Geiselman, R. E. (1992). *Memory-Enhancing Techniques for Investigative Interviewing: The Cognitive Interview*. Charles C. Thomas.

Gabbert, F., & Hope, L. (2023). The self-administered interview. In G. Oxburgh, T. Myklebust, M. Fallon, & M. Hartwig (Eds.), *Interviewing and Interrogation: A Review of Research and Practice Since World War II* (pp. 413–430). Torkel Opsahl Academic EPublisher.

Gabbert, F., Hope, L., & Fisher, R. P. (2009). Protecting eyewitness evidence: Examining the efficacy of a self-administered interview tool. *Law and Human Behavior, 33*(4), 298–307. https://doi.org/10.1007/s10979-008-9146-8

Gabbert, F., Tamonyte, D., Apps, J., Caso, A., Woolnough, P., Hope, L., Handscomb, M., & Waterworth, G. (2020). Examining the efficacy of a self-administered report form in missing person investigations. *Legal and Criminological Psychology, 25*(1), 1–16. https://doi.org/10.1111/lcrp.12163

Gabbert, F., & Wheeler, R. (2018). Memory conformity following collaborative remembering. In M. L. Meade, C. B. Harris, P. Van Bergen, J. Sutton, & A. J. Barnier (Eds.), *Collaborative Remembering: Theories, Research, and Applications* (pp. 100–112). Oxford University Press.

Goldfarb, D., Goodman, G. S., Larson, R. P., Eisen, M. L., & Qin, J. (2019). Long-term memory in adults exposed to childhood violence: Remembering genital contact nearly 20 years later. *Clinical Psychological Science, 7*(2), 381–396. https://doi.org/10.1177/2167702618805742

Goldsmith, M., Koriat, A., & Pansky, A. (2005). Strategic regulation of grain size in memory reporting over time. *Journal of Memory and Language, 52*(4), 505–525. https://doi.org/10.1016/j.jml.2005.01.010

Harvey, M. B., Price, H. L., & Luther, K. (2025). What happened that day? Recall for events of a day that later became important. *Journal of Criminal Psychology.* https://doi.org/10.1108/JCP-06-2023-0040

Harris, C. B., & O'Connor, A. R. (2022). On the same wavelength: The impact of other-generated cues on the reported retrieval processes and qualities of autobiographical memories. *Journal of Applied Research in Memory and Cognition, 12*(1), 82–93. https://doi.org/10.1037/mac0000030

Hashtroudi, S., Johnson, M. K., Vnek, N., & Ferguson, S. A. (1993). Aging and the effects of affective and factual focus on source monitoring and recall. *Psychology and Aging, 9*(1), 160–170. https://doi.org/10.1037/0882-7974.9.1.160

Heidt, C. T., Arbuthnott, K. D., & Price, H. L. (2015). The effects of distributed learning on enhanced cognitive interview training. *Psychiatry Psychology and Law, 23*(1), 47–61. https://doi.org/10.1080/13218719.2015.1032950

Hershkowitz, I., Orbach, Y., Lamb, M. E., Sternberg, K. J., & Horowitz, D. (2001). The effects of mental context reinstatement on children's accounts of sexual abuse. *Applied Cognitive Psychology, 15*(3), 235–248. https://doi.org/10.1002/acp.699

Home Office. (2021). *Crime Outcomes in England and Wales 2020 to 2021*. National Office of Statistics.

Hope, L., Gabbert, F., Fisher, R. P., & Jamieson, K. (2014). Protecting and enhancing eyewitness memory: The impact of an initial recall attempt on performance in an investigative interview. *Applied Cognitive Psychology, 28*, 304–313. https://doi.org/10.1002/acp.2984

Hope, L., Kontogianni, F., Geyer, K., & Thomas, W. (2019). Development of the Reporting Information about Networks and Groups (RING) task: A method for eliciting information from memory about associates, groups, and networks. *Journal of Forensic Practice, 21*(4), 240–247. https://doi.org/10.1108/JFP-04-2019-0011

Hope, L., Ost, J., Gabbert, F., Healey, S., & Lenton, E. (2008). "With a little help from my friends. . .": The role of co-witness relationship in susceptibility to misinformation. *Acta Psychologica, 127*(2), 476–484. https://doi.org/10.1016/j.actpsy.2007.08.010

Hope, L., Mullis, R., & Gabbert, F. (2013). Who? What? When? Using a timeline technique to facilitate recall of a complex event. *Journal of Applied Research in Memory and Cognition, 2*(1), 20–24. https://doi.org/10.1016/j.jarmac.2013.01.002

Horry, R., Hughes, C. M., Sharma, A., Gabbert, F., & Hope, L. (2021). A meta-analytic review of the Self-Administered Interview©: Quantity and accuracy of details reported on initial and subsequent retrieval attempts. *Applied Cognitive Psychology, 35*(2), 428–444. https://doi.org/10.1002/acp.3753

Howe, J. L., Knott, L. M. & Conway, M. A. (2018). *Memory and Miscarriages of Justice*. Routledge/Taylor & Francis Group.

Ito, H., Barzykowski, K., Grzesik, M., Gülgöz, S., Gürdere, C., Janssen, S. M. J., Khor, J., Rowthorn, H., Wade, K. A., Luna, K., Albuquerque, P. B., Kumar, D., Singh, A., Cecconello, W. W., Cadavid, S., Laird, N. C., Baldassari, M. J., Lindsay, D. S., & Mori, K. (2019). Eyewitness memory distortion following co-witness discussion: A replication of Garry, French, Kinzett, and Mori (2008) in ten countries. *Journal of Applied Research in Memory and Cognition, 8*(1), 68–77. https://doi.org/10.1016/j.jarmac.2018.09.004

Johnson, M. K., Hashtroudi, S., & Lindsay, D. S. (1992). Source monitoring. *Psychological Bulletin, 114*(1), 3–28. https://doi.org/10.1037/0033-2909.114.1.3

Johnson, M. K. (1997). Source monitoring and memory distortion. *Philosophical Transactions of the Royal Society B, 352*(1362), 1733–1745. https://doi.org/10.1098/rstb.1997.0156

Kemp, R., Towell, N., & Pike, G. (1997). When seeing should not be believing: Photographs, credit cards and fraud. *Applied Cognitive Psychology, 11*(3), 211 222.

Kontogianni, F., Hope, L., Taylor, P., Vrij, A., & Gabbert, F. (2018). The benefits of a self-generated cue mnemonic for timeline interviewing. *Journal of Applied Research in Memory and Cognition, 7*, 454–461.

Lampinen, J. M., Arnal, J. D., & Hicks, J. L. (2009). The effectiveness of supermarket posters in helping to find missing children. *Applied Cognitive Psychology, 23*(3), 407–423.

Lampinen, J. M., Arnal, J., Adams, K., Courtney, J. L., & Hicks, J. L. (2012a). Forensic age progression and the search for missing children. *Psychology Crime Law, 18*(4), 405–415, https://doi.org/10.1080/1068316X.2010.499873

Lampinen, J. M., Erickson, W., Frowd, C. D., & Mahoney, G. (2015). Mighty morphin' age progression: How artist, age range, and morphing influences the similarity of forensic age progressions to target individuals. *Psychology Crime & Law, 21*(10), 952–967. https://doi.org/10.1080/1068316x.2015.1077245

Lampinen, J. M., Miller, J. T., Dehon, H. (2012b). Depicting the missing: Prospective and retrospective person memory for age progressed images. *Applied Cognitive Psychology, 26*(2), 167–173, https://dx. doi.org/10.1002/acp.1819

Lifanov, J., Linde-Domingo, J., & Wimber, M. (2021). Feature-specific reaction times reveal a semanticisation of memories over time and with repeated remembering. *Nature Communications, 12*(1). https://doi.org/10.1038/s41467-021-23288-5

Luther, K., Snook, B., Eastwood, J., & Fisher, R. P. (2022). Sketching: The effect of a dual-modality technique on recall performance. *Journal of Police and Criminal Psychology*. https://doi.org/10.1007/s11896-022-09544-4

Marsh, E. J., Tversky, B., & Hutson, M. A. (2005). How eyewitnesses talk about events: Implications for memory. *Applied Cognitive Psychology, 19*(5), 531–544. https://doi.org/10.1002/acp.1095

Mattison, M. L. A., Dando, C. J., & Ormerod, T. C. (2018). Drawing the answers: Sketching to support free and probed recall by child witnesses and victims with autism spectrum disorder. *Autism, 22*(2), 181–194. https://doi.org/10.1177/1362361316669088

Mattison, M. L. A., Dando, C. J., & Ormerod, T. C. (2015). Sketching to remember: Episodic free recall task support for child witnesses and victims with Autism Spectrum Disorder. *Journal of Autism and Developmental Disorders, 45*(6), 1751–1765. https://doi.org/10.1007/s10803-014-2335-z

Megreya, A. M., and Burton, A. M. (2008). Matching Faces to Photographs: Poor Performance in Eyewitness Memory (Without the Memory). *Journal of Experimental Psychology: Applied, 14*(4), 364–372.

Memon, A., Meissner, C. A., & Fraser, J. (2010). The cognitive interview: A meta-analytic review and study space analysis of the past 25 years. *Psychology, Public Policy, and Law, 16*(4), 40–372. https://doi.org/10.1037/a0020518

Middendorf, C. H., & Macan, T. H. (2002). Note-taking in the employment interview: Effects on recall and judgments. *Journal of Applied Psychology, 87*(2), 293–303. https://doi.org/10.1037/0021-9010.87.2.293

Olson, E. S., & Charman, S. D. (2012). "But can you prove it?"—examining the quality of innocent suspects' alibis. *Psychology Crime & Law, 18*(5), 453–471. https://doi.org/10.1080/1068316x.2010.505567

Olson, E. S., & Wells, G. L. (2004). What makes a good alibi? A proposed taxonomy. *Law and Human Behavior, 28*(2), 157–176. https://doi.org/10.1023/b:lahu.0000022320.47112.d3

Pica, E., Sheahan, C., & Pozzulo, J. (2018). I know him!: Does witness–defendant familiarity impact mock jurors across different aged witnesses and types of crime? *Applied Psychology in Criminal Justice, 15*(2), 177–195.

Ridley, A. M., Gabbert, F., & La Rooy, D. J. (2013). Suggestibility in legal contexts: What do we know. In A. M. Ridley, F. Gabbert, & D. J. La Rooy (Eds.), *Suggestibility in Legal Contexts: Psychological Research and Forensic Implications* (pp. 217–228). John Wiley & Sons Ltd.

Roach, J. (2017). The retrospective detective. Cognitive bias and the cold case homicide investigator. *Papers from the British Criminology Conference, 17*. https://www.britsoccrim.org/wp-content/uploads/2017/12/The-Retrospective-Detective.pdf?utm_source=chatgpt.com

Rossmo, D. K. (2016). Case rethinking: A protocol for reviewing criminal investigations. *Police Practice and Research, 17*(3), 212–228. https://doi.org/10.1080/15614263.2014.978320

Rubin, D. T., & Wenzel, A. (1996). One hundred years of forgetting: A quantitative description of retention. *Psychological Review, 103*(4), 734–760. https://doi.org/10.1037/0033 295x.103.4.734

Statistics Canada. (2022, August 2). *Crime Severity Index and Weighted Clearance Rates, Canada, Provinces, Territories and Census Metropolitan Areas*. https://www150.statcan.gc.ca/t1/tbl1/en/tv.action?pid=3510002601

St. John, P. (2020, December 8). The untold story of how the Golden State Killer was found: A covert operation and private DNA. *Los Angeles Times*. https://www.latimes.com/california/story/2020-12-08/man-in-the-window

Strange, D., Dysart, J. E., & Loftus, E. F. (2014). Why errors in alibis are not necessarily evidence of guilt. *Zeitschrift Fur Psychologie, 222*(2), 82–89. https://doi.org/10.1027/2151-2604

Tulving, E., & Thomson, D. M. (1973). Encoding specificity and retrieval processes in episodic memory. *Psychological Review, 80*(5), 352–373. https://doi.org/10.1037/h0020071

Uzer, T., & Brown, N. R. (2017). The effect of cue content on retrieval from autobiographical memory. *Acta Psychologica, 172*, 84–91. https://doi.org/10.1016/j.actpsy.2016.11.012

Wells, G. L., Kovera, M. B., Douglass, A. B., Brewer, N., Meissner, C. A., & Wixted, J. T. (2020). Policy and procedure recommendations for the collection and preservation of eyewitness identification evidence. *Law and Human Behavior, 44*(1), 3–36. https://doi.org/10.1037/lhb0000359

Wheeler, R. S., & Gabbert, F. (2017). Using self-generated cues to facilitate recall: A narrative review. *Frontiers in Psychology, 8*, 1830. https://doi.org/10.3389/fpsyg.2017.01830

Wong, C. A., & Read, J. D. (2011). Positive and negative effects of physical context reinstatement on eyewitness recall and identification. *Applied Cognitive Psychology, 25*(1), 2–11. https://doi.org/10.1002/acp.1605

Yang, H., Huang, D., Wang, Y., & Jain, A. K. (2019). Learning continuous face age progression: A pyramid of GANs. *IEEE Transactions on Pattern Analysis and Machine Intelligence, 43*(2), 499 515. https://doi.org/10.1109/tpami.2019.2930985

Technology

II

11 The Role of the Crime Lab

DAVID MACNEIL

Section 1: Introduction

In every cold case investigation I've worked on, the crime lab has either created a turning point or represented the final frontier. Traditional leads may dry up, but science, especially DNA, does not forget. Over the past two decades, advances in forensic science have transformed how we approach these long-dormant homicides. From short tandem repeat (STR) DNA testing to forensic genealogy, today's lab is more than a testing facility; it's an investigative partner.

DNA submission standards are now universally guided by protocols set by the Scientific Working Group on DNA Analysis Methods (SWGDAM, 2020). NIST is a main player in these investigations—National Institute Standards and Technology—(took over for SWG). These standards ensure consistency and reliability across jurisdictions. Agencies like the Federal Bureau of Investigations (FBI) Laboratory provide a broad range of forensic services to support local cold case investigations, including DNA, ballistics, trace, and latent print analysis (FBI, 2022). Yet despite these resources, investigators often fail to leverage them due to backlog issues, miscommunication, or lack of awareness of new technologies.

What we need is not just better technology but better case strategy and inter-agency collaboration. Agencies and resources talking and working together is going to be the game changer in all of this—no more "Close to the Vest" thinking—if the cases are just sitting—why can't we work them together—forget credit—let's just solve the case! This chapter breaks down those issues through my experience, experiences learned while working alongside some of the country's best success stories, and the evolving landscape of forensic tools.

Section 2: Historical Perspective and Crime Lab Overview

When I started law enforcement in the mid-1980s, the "crime lab" was often viewed as a place where we sent evidence and hoped something came back. DNA wasn't mainstream, and the backlog of latent prints could take months. Ballistics was mostly done through manual comparison microscopes, and

DOI: 10.4324/9781003415633-14

cross-jurisdictional information sharing was almost non-existent. The crime lab was considered a reactive component, not a strategic partner.

Fast forward to today, we now have forensic intelligence units embedded in many major agencies. These labs don't just wait for evidence—they help prioritize cases, provide investigative leads, and often generate actionable intelligence from previously ignored or misunderstood materials (Houck, 2015; NIJ, 2021).

One of the most pivotal shifts came with the establishment of CODIS (Combined DNA Index System), which changed everything. Cold cases that had sat idle for decades were now connected to unknown offenders—or linked to other cases—through DNA profiles that didn't exist when the crimes occurred (FBI, 2023). Similar developments followed with the National Integrated Ballistic Information Network (NIBIN) for ballistics (ATF, 2023), and the National Missing and Unidentified Persons System (NamUs) for unidentified remains (NamUs, 2023).

Understanding how the role of the lab has changed over time helps us appreciate what it offers today—and what it might offer tomorrow. We've gone from "evidence storage" to dynamic digital ecosystems that tie together DNA, fingerprints, ballistics, and even digital and cyber evidence across state and international boundaries (Interpol, 2021).

But this evolution didn't happen evenly across the board. Some agencies are still stuck using processes from two decades ago. Unfortunately, this is the process often—I teach crime scene investigation classes across the country and this—still—seems to be "the norm:" Others are partnering with private labs and using forensic genealogy and whole-genome sequencing (WGS) (Butler, 2011; Kayser & de Knijff, 2011). This section isn't just about rewarding celebrating progress—it's about reminding investigators that the "cold" in cold case doesn't have to mean "dead end" or "There's no chance!"

Section 3: The Crime Lab—An Overview

Cold case investigations would be nearly impossible to resolve without the resources and expertise of modern forensic laboratories. While crime labs may vary in size, scope, and capabilities, the fundamentals of their structure and their role in unsolved homicide investigations remain consistent across jurisdictions. Understanding how labs are organized and what each division can offer is essential for any detective, prosecutor, or advocate working on long-dormant cases.

Structure and Organization of Modern Crime Labs

At their core, modern crime labs are divided into specialized scientific units, each designed to analyze a specific type of evidence. A **fully equipped forensic laboratory** typically includes the following sections:

- *DNA analysis*: Processes biological samples such as blood, saliva, semen, and touch DNA, often subdivided into STR profiling, Y-chromosomal STR (Y-STR) analysis, and mitochondrial DNA. In cold cases, this is often the most valuable unit (Butler, 2011; SWGDAM, 2020).
- *Fingerprint analysis (latent print unit)*: Responsible for the identification and comparison of latent prints from crime scenes. Automated systems like **AFIS** (Automated Fingerprint Identification System) allow national and regional searching (James et al., 2014).
- *Ballistics/firearms examination*: Examines bullets, casings, and firearms to determine matches. This unit often participates in NIBIN run by the Bureau of Alcohol, Tobacco, Firearms and Explosives (ATF), which can link cases across jurisdictions (ATF, 2023).
- *Trace evidence*: Analyzes fibers, hairs, glass, paint, and other small particles. Though often underutilized, trace can corroborate victim-suspect contact or support reconstruction theories (Houck, 2015).
- *Toxicology*: Identifies drugs, alcohol, and poisons in biological samples.
- *Digital evidence/multimedia analysis*: Recovers, authenticates, and analyzes data from mobile phones, surveillance video, and computers—an area increasingly vital in modern cold cases (NIJ, 2022).
- *Serology*: Screens evidence for the presence of blood, semen, and other bodily fluids prior to DNA extraction.

Many public labs also offer forensic anthropology, odontology, entomology, and pathology consultation—particularly in homicide and unidentified remains cases.

Local vs. State Crime Labs

In the United States, **local crime labs** typically operate within large city or county police departments and handle day-to-day forensic needs. However, their capacity is often limited—especially when it comes to advanced or specialized testing like mitochondrial DNA or forensic genealogy. Many small to mid-sized departments have designated areas—sometimes just a spare room or closet—to process evidence. Although their capabilities are gradually improving, they still rely on state or private crime labs for DNA typing and other advanced analyses.

State crime labs, such as those operated by the state's Department of Public Safety, often provide broader services. They are typically accredited, centralized, and can receive evidence from multiple jurisdictions. However, state labs often face **backlogs** due to volume and prioritize active or time-sensitive cases, potentially delaying cold case testing (NIJ, 2021).

Federal Crime Labs: FBI, Secret Service, ATF

Federal labs offer some of the most advanced forensic services in the world:

- *FBI laboratory (Quantico, VA)*: Provides free forensic services to state and local agencies upon request. The FBI lab includes the **CODIS Unit** (for DNA), the **Trace Evidence Unit**, and the **Evidence Response Team Unit (ERT)**, among others. However, they prioritize **national security and federal investigations** unless a local case has strategic significance (FBI, 2023).
- *ATF crime lab*: Specializes in ballistics and explosives, managing the NIBIN system to connect shell casings and firearms nationwide. They may accept local cases that involve gun crime patterns or links to broader investigations (ATF, 2023).
- *Secret Service laboratory*: Primarily handles document forgery, counterfeit currency, and threats to protected persons. While not usually involved in cold case homicides, they offer expertise in handwriting and ink analysis that could be relevant in some unique cases (James et al., 2014). Note: Secret Service labs have been very helpful to local police even in smaller level cases—great resource!

Staffing and Expertise Required in a Crime Lab

Crime labs are staffed by civilian scientists, not usually sworn officers. A fully operational forensic lab relies on **forensic analysts, biologists, chemists, digital examiners, firearms examiners**, and **toxicologists**, among others. Most require at least a bachelor's degree in a natural or forensic science; many senior analysts or technical leads hold master's or doctoral degrees.

- Lab personnel must meet **accreditation and proficiency testing standards**, such as those established by **ANSI National Accreditation Board (ANAB)** or **ISO/IEC 17025** standards (SWGDAM, 2023).
- Analysts must also testify in court, meaning they require training in legal standards such as **Daubert** or **Frye**, depending on the jurisdiction.

Ultimately, knowing which lab is capable of what—and how to properly submit evidence—can make or break a cold case. A misrouted form or an improperly sealed envelope can delay results for months or exclude evidence from trial. Lab directors have access to training and resources through "American Society of Crime Lab Directors" (ASCLD) conferences—updated training, etc.

Section 4: Forensic Techniques in Cold Case Investigations

In cold case homicide investigations, time can be both a curse and a blessing. While years or decades may have passed, the preservation of evidence—when done right—allows modern forensic tools to uncover what was previously undetectable. Just because it's old does not mean it is not good or worthless.

DNA Analysis and Reanalysis

DNA remains the single most powerful tool in solving cold cases. Initially, many cases only had serological testing or no biological analysis at all. Today, evidence can be reexamined using techniques like STR analysis, mitochondrial DNA typing, and Y-STR for male-specific DNA—methods that didn't exist or weren't widely available at the time of the original crime (Butler, 2011; SWGDAM, 2023). We've also seen success with low copy number DNA and enhanced touch DNA protocols, especially in cases involving ligatures, clothing, or intimate contact (NIJ, 2022).

Forensic Genetic Genealogy

More recently, forensic genetic genealogy (FGG) has changed the game. While not without its legal and ethical debates, FGG or sometimes called IGG (Investigative Genetic Genealogy) or FIGG (Forensic Investigative Genetic Genealogy) allows for identification of unknown suspects or remains through familial DNA matches on public genealogy databases (Mitchell, 2022). In one of my own cases, we were able to get an investigative lead on a decades-old homicide through a second cousin match, leading to an arrest and conviction.

Latent Fingerprint Re-examination

Latent prints that yielded no hits decades ago can now be reprocessed with updated algorithms and compared against much larger and more complete databases. Today's AFIS are not only faster but far more accurate than the early systems (James et al., 2014). Note: Additionally, the systems now do 360 degrees searching on latent prints—for years, the orientation of a latent may have been a holdup on an identification, depending on the examiner.

Ballistics and Firearms Evidence

The NIBIN system has allowed shell casings and bullet striations from decades-old shootings to be compared across jurisdictions. Many cold case shootings are now solved because shell casings from one scene are linked to another crime where a suspect was arrested and the firearm was recovered (ATF, 2023).

Digital and Multimedia Forensics

In some more recent cold cases—particularly from the 2000s—old flip phones, CDs, floppy disks, and even early DVR systems are being revisited. The evolution of digital forensics means that obsolete devices can sometimes be read or recovered using specialized labs or tools. Surveillance footage once thought to be "too blurry" can now be clarified using AI-based enhancement tools (Interpol, 2021).

Each of these forensic techniques not only reopens the door for evidence that was previously considered unusable, it also brings new expectations. As investigators, we have a duty to revisit evidence with modern capabilities in mind, not just with the tools we had at the time of the original investigation.

Section 5: Case Management and Prioritization

Reopening a cold case isn't just about grabbing a file off the shelf and re-running DNA. Strategic case management is critical to success, especially when a department has dozens—or even hundreds—of unresolved homicides. In my experience, the best outcomes happen when agencies adopt structured, criteria-driven methods to determine where limited resources should go first.

Prioritization Frameworks

Many departments now use formalized scoring systems to prioritize cold cases based on solvability factors. These can include:

- Availability and condition of physical evidence.
- Existence of known suspects.
- Witness cooperation or re-interview potential.
- Availability of forensic testing not previously used.
- Public interest or prosecutorial support.

Some agencies use the **Cold Case Review Matrix** developed through NIJ-funded research, which assigns a weight to each factor and helps rank cases for reinvestigation (NIJ, 2021). This is particularly useful when pitching a case for grant funding or lab resources.

Case Review Teams

Multi-disciplinary review teams often include homicide detectives, forensic scientists, prosecutors, victim advocates, and sometimes medical examiners (MEs).

Regular case review sessions—monthly or quarterly—keep momentum going and help agencies avoid the trap of reopening a case only to let it stall again. These teams also identify new testing opportunities that frontline investigators may not be aware of.

Evidence Tracking and Preservation

Before anything can be retested, you need to ensure the evidence still exists and has been preserved properly. Chain of custody records, property room audits, and lab submission logs are often the first thing I look at when beginning a cold case consultation.

In many older cases, you find boxes labeled only "Homicide—1987." Inside, you might discover a cigarette butt with blood transfer, or a ligature improperly stored in plastic. The condition of that evidence—and whether it was ever tested or documented thoroughly—will determine what modern tools can be applied.

Data Centralization and Management Software

The rise of digital case management tools—such as Violent Criminal Apprehension Program (ViCAP), Case Explorer, and agency-specific cold case databases—has made it easier to track test results, case notes, and pending lab work. In my own work, I often hear of agencies who implement these tools to streamline communication with labs and avoid duplication of effort. Ultimately, the difference between a successful cold case resolution and another ten years of silence often comes down to whether the case was managed with intention and structure.

Section 6: Challenges and Limitations

Cold case investigations often suffer an exaggerated perception—TV shows make it seem like a fingerprint, or a hair is all it takes to close the case. Working a cold case homicide is a battle against time, contamination, legal restrictions, and human error. As a detective, I've seen firsthand the challenges that frustrate even the most determined teams.

Evidence Degradation and Loss

Physical evidence deteriorates. DNA breaks down. Biological samples may no longer meet the threshold for testing, especially if they are improperly stored. I've opened boxes containing moldy evidence, degraded lift cards that lost all ridge detail because they were stored in high humidity for 30 years. Sometimes key evidence was discarded entirely due to space constraints, policy gaps, or a simple lack of understanding at the time of its value.

Even when evidence exists, it may have been contaminated during the original investigation—crime scenes weren't always processed with gloves, and packaging standards were far looser in the 1970s or 1980s.

Legal Barriers and Statutes

Cold cases come with their own legal issues. Search warrants may no longer be valid. Witnesses may have died or become incompetent to testify. Statutes of limitations may apply for lesser charges. And even when a suspect is identified, prosecutors may hesitate to move forward without rock-solid evidence due to the time lapse and potential credibility issues.

Lack of Resources

Crime labs face serious backlogs. According to NIJ (2022), some public labs take months or even years to process complex DNA mixtures. Even with grant funding, cold cases compete for space with active investigations. This often forces agencies to rely on private labs—which can cost thousands of dollars per sample, putting pressure on already very thin budgets.

Technological Constraints

Not all labs have access to the latest tools. For example, while forensic genealogy has solved numerous high-profile cases, not every lab is equipped for it. Complex DNA mixtures may be too degraded or low quantity for STR analysis or even Y-STR targeting. Advanced tools like M-Vac DNA collection, next-generation sequencing (NGS), or proteomic analysis may be out of reach entirely.

Investigative Gaps

One of the most frustrating limitations is the human factor, a very big player in all of this. Key case notes may be missing. Retired detectives may not be available to interview, either being unable to locate or having passed away, etc. Original witnesses may be reluctant, relocated, or have passed away. And in some cases, there may have been tunnel vision or misconduct in the original investigation—something that complicates modern review efforts and can put a chill on reinvestigation.

Working a cold case requires tackling challenges directly, thinking creatively, and reassessing assumptions. The top investigators combine technical skill with resilience, humility, and flexibility.

Section 7: Inter-Agency Collaboration

No single agency solves a cold case alone. That's the lesson I learned early in my career—and one that's only grown truer with time. Collaboration isn't optional in this work; it's essential. The evidence may sit in one jurisdiction, the suspect in another, and the lab in a third. When we don't talk to each other, cases stall. If you have credit issues or the one who needs all the glory—do not work cold cases—this is about solving a case for victims and their families—not personal award or credit.

FBI and Federal Partnerships

The FBI Laboratory offers critical support to local agencies through services like CODIS, mitochondrial DNA testing, digital forensics, and forensic genealogy assessments (FBI, 2022). In several cases, the FBI's resources—not just scientific, but also behavioral analysis and victimology—were what turned stalled leads into active ones.

Similarly, ATF's NIBIN allows local departments to compare ballistic evidence with hits from across the country. In one Massachusetts case, a fire arm recovered during a routine traffic stop turned out to be linked to an unsolved homicide multiple states away.

State Crime Labs and Regional Units

State forensic laboratories, including those in Massachusetts and neighboring states, provide DNA testing, toxicology, firearm examinations, and latent print analysis. Their role is central—but without coordinated scheduling, reporting, and shared goals between lab and investigators, it's easy for evidence to sit unprocessed.

I've found that proactive relationships—calling your lab analyst before submission, attending case triage meetings, and understanding their queue—go a long way in aligning priorities. It really is a "must" to have a great "rapport" and relationship with your lab and their staff.

Private Laboratories

Private labs like Othram, Bode Technology, and Parabon Nanolabs are becoming vital allies. Many offer advanced services such as WGS, proteomic profiling, and forensic genealogy analysis (Kayser & de Knijff, 2011). These labs often respond faster than public ones, especially when funding or advocacy groups are involved.

For example, in a 1985 cold case I reviewed, we partnered with a private lab to extract DNA from degraded remains. Their enhanced touch DNA recovery and genealogy matching led us to a distant relative, and eventually, to a suspect who had eluded us for decades.

Medical Examiner's Offices and Coroners

ME offices are often overlooked in cold case collaboration. Yet they hold critical autopsy reports, evidence swabs, and photographs that can be reanalyzed. I would make it a point to re-interview forensic pathologists, even years later, when feasible. Their insights—especially if we're considering exhumation or alternative causes of death—can make or break a reinvestigation.

Victim Advocacy and Public Engagement

Families are more than stakeholders—they're often sources of new leads. I've seen parents and siblings collect records, suggest suspects, and even track down witnesses on social media. Advocacy organizations like Project: Cold Case, Cold Case Initiative, and the Doe Network also amplify unsolved cases through national exposure.

Cold case review teams that include victim advocates not only support families, and they also help investigators stay focused on victim-centered justice.

Working together across agencies doesn't just increase efficiency—it brings new energy to long-dormant cases. Collaboration builds momentum, and in cold case work, momentum is everything.

Section 8: Technological Advancements and the Future of Forensics

In my early years, cold case work often meant dusty boxes of evidence and typewritten reports. Now, the tools available to us feel like science fiction has come to life. Technology has changed everything—not just in how we solve cases, but in how we think about solvability itself.

DNA Analysis: Beyond the Swab

Traditional STR analysis laid the groundwork, but new methods like **NGS** and **WGS** allow labs to recover usable DNA from degraded or trace evidence (Butler, 2011). These techniques are especially helpful in older cases where only partial profiles or contaminated samples remain.

Advanced techniques such as **probabilistic genotyping software** (e.g., STRmix, TrueAllele) are now able to interpret complex mixtures that were previously uninterpretable. These tools, once controversial, are now widely accepted in courts across the country (NIJ, 2022).

Forensic Genetic Genealogy

FGG has cracked open thousands of cases once considered unsolvable. Using open-source genealogy databases like GEDmatch and FamilyTreeDNA, investigators can identify relatives of unknown suspects and build family trees to reverse-engineer the perpetrator's identity.

In one case I assisted on, a DNA sample from a decades-old sexual homicide was uploaded to a genealogy database. Within weeks, a distant relative match helped us identify the suspect—a man who had never been in CODIS.

This method is particularly valuable when the suspect has no prior criminal record and would otherwise never trigger a CODIS hit (Mitchell, 2022).

3D Imaging and Reconstruction

Modern imaging techniques allow for facial reconstructions from skeletal remains using both manual artistry and AI-enhanced rendering. These visuals, when shared publicly, have led to identifications in long-unidentified cases (NamUs, 2023).

Ballistics and Toolmark Databases

ATF's **NIBIN** system and newer AI-driven comparison tools help identify patterns in fired bullets and shell casings. These links often reveal serial shooters or weapons used across multiple jurisdictions (ATF, 2023).

Digital Evidence and AI Integration

The explosion of **digital forensics**—phones, hard drives, cloud data—means cold case detectives now routinely revisit tech that didn't even exist at the time of the crime. AI is increasingly used to scan large datasets, detect anomaly patterns in suspect behavior, and assist in image and voice recognition. Interpol (2021) reports significant growth in machine learning tools designed to match fingerprints, ballistics, and digital footprints more efficiently and accurately.

Alternative Light Sources and Chemical Reagents

New portable alternate light source (ALS) technology now detects latent prints, fluids, and trace evidence in ways that were previously confined to high-end labs. These tools have found critical stains, smudges, and evidence that were missed in the original investigation. For years, this process was thought to be only used by highly trained technicians, Chemists etc. Now enhanced police training makes it more widely used and as a great aid in cases.

The future of forensic technology is not just in what it can find, but in how it empowers us to go back and reexamine what was always there—waiting for the right tools, the right eyes, and the right moment. Remember: "What I see, you don't and what you see I don't."

Section 9: Case Studies and Lessons Learned

I've always believed that a cold case is not a hopeless case. It's a case waiting for new eyes, new tools—or simply someone who refuses to let it go. Below are *anonymized case examples* that reflect the intersection of traditional detective work and modern forensic science.

Case Example 1: Touch DNA on a Ligature

An elderly woman was strangled in her home in the early 2000s. The ligature—a cord from a set of blinds—had been tested previously with no result. When we revisited the case in 2020, the crime lab employed **enhanced touch DNA recovery** using a wet-vacuum system (e.g., M-Vac®). A partial profile was developed from the inner knot fibers. That DNA, when submitted to the FBI's CODIS database, generated a familial match that led to the victim's former home health aide's adult son. He later confessed. This case reminded me that overlooked evidence isn't always bad evidence—it may simply need new techniques.

Case Example 2: Cold Hit from NIBIN Leads to Interstate Confession

In 2007, a homeless man was shot execution-style and left behind a strip mall. Despite interviews, canvassing, and surveillance review, the case went cold. In 2022, a new firearm entered the NIBIN system after being seized in a domestic violence arrest in one state. That gun's shell casings matched those found at another state's scene.

With this lead, they tracked down the gun's origin, which led to an individual who had never been a suspect. Faced with the ballistic match and additional forensic evidence, he confessed. This case underscored how **inter-jurisdictional cooperation and database integration** can solve what once seemed unsolvable.

Case Example 3: Genealogy + Ground Truth

One of the most emotional cases I've been involved in is the murder of a teenager, found in a wooded area in the 1980s. A degraded semen sample had previously produced only an inconclusive STR profile. Through a partnership with a private lab specializing in **forensic genealogy**, the evidence was reprocessed using SNP-based testing and uploaded to GEDmatch.

Within three months, a family tree was built that led us to an elderly suspect—now living quietly in the same area. His niece unknowingly provided a buccal swab during a routine ancestry test that created the match. With the help of a forensic anthropologist, they recreated the scene and timeline. The case was charged, and the family—after 40 years—finally got a name.

Lessons Learned

Across all these cases, the common thread wasn't luck. It was **persistence, technology, and collaboration**. Cold case work demands a willingness to re-question old assumptions, dig through forgotten reports, and forge new partnerships—especially with crime labs.

One of the most difficult but valuable lessons I've learned is to **let the evidence lead**, even when it points in a direction you don't expect.

Confidentiality and Professional Disclaimer

The case examples above in this chapter have been **anonymized and modified** to protect the identities of victims, suspects, and agencies involved. Details such as dates, locations, and relationships have been changed or generalized for confidentiality. These examples are **composite narratives** drawn from multiple cases across a 38-year law enforcement career. Any resemblance to actual cases is purely coincidental unless publicly documented.

This chapter reflects my **personal professional experiences and opinions** and does not represent official statements from any agency, laboratory, or investigative body. Readers are encouraged to verify all methods and practices through accredited forensic and legal sources.

Section 10: The Future of Crime Labs in Cold Case Investigations

The future of cold case investigations will depend not only on technological breakthroughs but on how well crime labs are integrated, funded, and understood by the law enforcement and legal communities they serve. While past decades have seen dramatic improvements in forensic tools, many cold cases still sit idle due to evidence backlogs, staffing shortages, and limited access to specialized testing. As we look ahead, the evolution of the modern crime lab will be central to closing long-unsolved homicides and delivering long-overdue justice.

Predictions and Future Directions

Over the next decade, several key trends are expected to redefine the capabilities of forensic laboratories:

- *Rapid DNA and mobile forensics*: Advances in rapid DNA technology will enable on-site or near-site DNA analysis, allowing investigators to generate preliminary profiles in hours rather than weeks. This technology is already being piloted in booking stations and large urban departments and will likely expand to cold case units seeking to reprocess stored evidence (NIJ, 2022).
- *AI and machine learning integration*: Artificial intelligence will increasingly be used to assist in the analysis of latent prints, firearm toolmarks, and mixed DNA profiles. These systems can flag potential matches, identify degraded samples worth retesting, and streamline the triage of digital evidence—all critical for backlogged cold case files (Interpol, 2021; Mitchell, 2022).
- *Forensic genealogy and data linking*: The use of **FIGG** will become more standardized, especially in conjunction with databases such as GEDmatch and FamilyTreeDNA. Combined with AI-driven data mining of CODIS, NIBIN, and NamUs, these tools will allow labs to connect seemingly unrelated cases across state lines and decades (Mitchell, 2022; NIJ, 2021).
- *Miniaturization of lab technology*: Portable spectrometers, microfluidic DNA chips, and mobile toxicology labs will allow field teams to perform triage testing that previously required full lab submission. This decentralization may relieve pressure on state crime labs and speed up the resolution timeline for cold cases (NIJ, 2022; SWGDAM, 2023).

Enhancing the Effectiveness of Crime Labs

To fully leverage new technologies, future crime labs must also become more **collaborative, interdisciplinary, and strategically aligned** with investigators.

- *Cross-training between scientists and detectives*: Detectives should understand the capabilities and limitations of lab tests, while scientists must be trained in investigative priorities. Programs that embed forensic advisors within major case units or establish regular inter-agency briefings can significantly improve results (James et al., 2014).
- *Streamlined evidence submission systems*: Cloud-based evidence tracking, real-time status updates, and automated notification systems can reduce the communication gaps that often stall cold case progress.
- *Shared national lab resources*: A central, federally supported database of accredited private labs and their specialties could allow small or under-resourced departments to access high-end services such as **NGS** or ultra-sensitive touch DNA testing (SWGDAM, 2023).

Policy Recommendations and Funding Needs

Despite these innovations, crime labs remain chronically underfunded and understaffed. To address this, national and state-level policies should include:

- *Dedicated cold case forensics grants*: Just as agencies receive separate funding for body cameras or school security, targeted grants should be established for the forensic testing of cold case evidence. These could fund private lab outsourcing, genealogy analysts, or backlog reduction staff (NIJ, 2021).
- *Mandated cold case testing review cycles*: Every major crime lab should conduct **biennial reviews** of stored homicide evidence for new testing opportunities, especially considering emerging technologies. Legislation could standardize this process across jurisdictions.
- *Investment in lab infrastructure and salaries*: Many labs operate with outdated instruments and high turnover. Improving facilities, offering competitive salaries, and funding continued education for forensic analysts will pay dividends in solving cases that once seemed unsolvable (FBI, 2023; Interpol, 2021).
- *Public-private partnerships*: Government-funded contracts with accredited private labs have proven cost-effective and efficient.

Policies that encourage these partnerships—while preserving evidence integrity and chain of custody—will continue to be critical in addressing forensic bottlenecks.

In summary, the future of crime labs in cold case investigations is promising but hinges on more than just tools—it requires **policy alignment, investment, and inter-agency collaboration**. With the right funding and strategic approach, labs can move from passive processors of evidence to **active engines of justice** in solving society's most difficult cases.

Section 11: Conclusion

Cold case homicides remain among the most complex, emotionally resonant, and publicly scrutinized investigations in criminal justice. While they often begin with limited leads and deteriorated evidence, the evolution of forensic science has rewritten what is possible. This chapter has explored how the modern crime lab—through advancements in DNA analysis, fingerprint reprocessing, ballistics databases, forensic genealogy, and inter-agency collaboration—has become a critical partner in the renewed pursuit of justice. Despite incredible breakthroughs, the effective use of forensic labs in cold case investigations still requires proper evidence handling, realistic expectations, strategic case prioritization, and communication between investigators and lab personnel. Public-private partnerships, increased funding, and policy support can further strengthen these efforts. Ultimately, the power of the crime lab lies not just in its technology, but in its integration into a larger investigative strategy—one that centers families, upholds ethical standards, and never stops asking difficult questions. Every victim deserves to be found. Every case deserves to be heard. And every family deserves answers—no matter how much time has passed.

References

ATF (Bureau of Alcohol, Tobacco, Firearms and Explosives). (2023). *National Integrated Ballistic Information Network (NIBIN)*. https://www.atf.gov/resource-center/nibin

Butler, J. M. (2011). *Advanced Topics in Forensic DNA Typing: Methodology*. Academic Press.

Federal Bureau of Investigation. (2022). *FBI Laboratory Services*. https://www.fbi.gov/services/laboratory

Federal Bureau of Investigation. (2023). *CODIS and Crime Laboratory Services*. https://www.fbi.gov/services/laboratory

Houck, M. M. (Ed.). (2015). *Forensic Science: Modern Methods of Solving Crime*. Praeger.

Interpol. (2021). *Artificial Intelligence and Machine Learning in Global Forensic Systems*. https://www.interpol.int/en/How-we-work/Innovation/Artificial-Intelligence-Toolkit

James, S. H., Nordby, J. J., & Bell, S. (2014). *Forensic Science: An Introduction to Scientific and Investigative Techniques* (4th ed.). CRC Press.

Kayser, M., & de Knijff, P. (2011). Improving human forensics through advances in genetics, genomics, and molecular biology. *Nature Reviews Genetics*, 12(3), 179–192.

Mitchell, K. (2022). The rise of forensic genetic genealogy. *Forensic Science International: Reports*, 6, 100223.

National Institute of Justice. (2021). *Cold Case Investigations: Resources for Law Enforcement*. https://nij.ojp.gov

National Institute of Justice. (2022). *Rapid DNA Technology and the Future of Forensics*. https://nij.ojp.gov/library/publications/rapid-dna-technology-and-future-forensics

National Missing and Unidentified Persons System (NamUs). (2023). https://www.namus.gov

Project: Cold Case. (2023). *Advocacy and Awareness for Unsolved Homicides*. https://www.projectcoldcase.org

SWGDAM (Scientific Working Group on DNA Analysis Methods). (2020). *Guidelines*. https://www.swgdam.org

SWGDAM. (2023). *Emerging Forensic Methods in Public-Private Collaboration*. https://www.swgdam.org

Trace Evidence 12

JAY W. HENRY

> Never give in, never give in, never, never, never, never—in nothing, great or small, large or petty—never give in except to convictions of honor and good sense.
>
> **—Winston Churchill**

Introduction

It was the week before Memorial Day 2005 when the investigator received the call. The laboratory had some unbelievable news. There was a Combined DNA Index System (CODIS) hit to some newly tested trace evidence. This "new" sample had previously been tested multiple times with older technology, but this was the first time that it would provide useful information. Originally, the item had been submitted in the 1980s as a bloodstain sample on U.S. currency; however, so much testing had been done that there was no longer anything visible. From everyone's perspective, further testing seemed bleak.

At the crime laboratory, the forensic scientist's quandary was, "Do I swab where the stain used to be or try another approach?" The many years of testing had consumed most of the visible blood sample. The evidence had essentially transitioned from a DNA to a trace submission, and a standard test didn't seem quite adequate. In a moment of inspiration, she decided to soak the sample, and that strategy produced enough DNA for a profile. The result: a critical first lead for the agency in over 20 years. The determination and perseverance of the investigator and laboratory had finally paid off.

Why the crime laboratory was performing another test on an otherwise overtested sample is interesting. For over two decades, many items on this case had already been tested and substantial resources expended. Discouraged, the case had even been closed by the agency until a motivated detective reopened it. Further, because of the constant resource drain of this one case, agency relations with the state crime laboratory were strained. However, the lead detective was undaunted. By using constant, personal communication supported with thoughtful probative logic, he managed to convince a poorly resourced laboratory to run one more test. That strategy ultimately tied a previously unknown individual to the scene.

 DOI: 10.4324/9781003415633-15

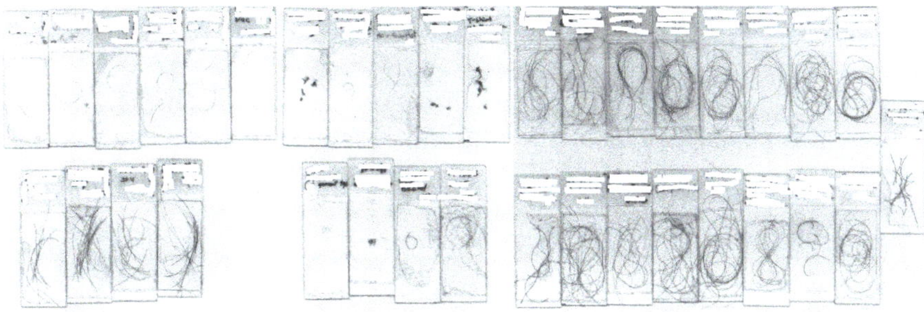

Figure 12.1 Fight scene and reference standard hair mounts. (Courtesy of Pilar Shortsleeve, Utah Department of Public Safety [DPS].)

The lab heard nothing more until a year later, when the agency and prosecutor requested additional testing due to a new theory, which, if proved true by the evidence, would strongly bolster their case. They believed that the suspect may have shed some hairs in an area of the crime scene referred to as the "fight area." This area of the scene was located on the floor of a dirty convenience store and probably had years of accumulated hairs and such. Additionally, the crime laboratory had already performed conventional DNA testing on the hair root of many of those same hairs, and that had yielded no results (Figure 12.1). Now, the agency wanted to send some of those hairs to a vendor laboratory for mitochondrial DNA (mtDNA) testing. Based on their many years of experience, the laboratory scientists felt that there was little chance of a positive result. In addition, outsourced DNA testing was expensive, and the lab could not and would not cover the cost. They advised the prosecutor to take the original trace results and move forward with the resolution of the case. The prosecutor felt otherwise.

The case was at an impasse until the legal team convinced local officials to provide funding to test nine of the evidence hairs. The laboratory, still believing it was a poor use of resources, nonetheless did their best to assist them in selecting samples. Using microscopy, the laboratory eliminated the candidate hairs that were least likely to give a result (e.g., hairs similar to the victim, animal hairs) and selected nine dissimilar hairs to send to the vendor laboratory.

The results that came back were significant. Much to the amazement of the investigative team, three of the hairs were associated back to the suspect, proving once again that a never-give-in attitude, coupled with a substantial resource investment, can make the difference in a case. The defendant was ultimately convicted and received a sentence of life without parole.

Trace Evidence—The Last Resort for Physical Evidence?

Frequently, the person that finds himself/herself reading the chapter on trace evidence has exhausted all of the traditional forensic science choices (e.g., DNA, latent prints) and may be looking for anything trace related to provide a lead or establish an association.

Thus, the purpose of this chapter is to provide an overview of the concept of trace evidence:

- What is trace evidence?
- What is its *value* in a cold case criminal investigation?
- What are its *limitations* in cold case investigations?

As illustrated in the previous case example, it is not necessarily uncommon that investigators, prosecutors, and laboratory personnel have strong differences of opinion regarding case issues. Mutual understanding of these concepts, however, will enhance the teamwork aspect these cases require, as well as foster better communications and relations among all concerned.

While the glue that binds a successful cold case investigation together is the law enforcement investigator, it is critical that other team members understand these concepts involving trace evidence. The focus of this chapter is to provide a basic understanding to all involved in the investigation and prosecution of cold case homicides on the applicability of physical evidence and how to leverage it to provide case fact information.

Redefining Trace Evidence

The scope of what type of physical evidence constitutes "trace" is immense and does not fit a strict definition. Within the crime laboratory, the term trace has referred to evidence consisting of hair, fibers, paint, glass, soil, gunshot residue (GSR—primer residues), etc. However, the investigator should use a broader definition and think of it as "any evidence in small amounts," which includes DNA.

A principle of trace evidence is its mechanism of transference, and this is known as the Locard exchange principle. Locard was an early-twentieth-century French scientist who first proposed the idea of evidence moving back and forth across a contact boundary. This means evidence is transferred from the suspect to the victim or to the crime scene, and vice versa. In essence, a criminal brings something of himself/herself to the crime scene and takes something away, thus connecting each to the other.

Early crime laboratory technology methods could only detect evidence that fit into the traditional categories (e.g., hair, fibers). However, with scientific enhancements such as DNA, alternate light sources, and more, forensic scientists are now able to better study and find evidence that crosses that contact boundary. Scientists can do more with the traditional categories of trace evidence, such as expanding the analysis of hairs to include the root (e.g., short tandem repeat [STR] and Y-chromosomal short tandem repeat [Y-STR] DNA) and the shaft (e.g., mtDNA). (See Chapter 15.)

Technology has also made possible greater discrimination for fiber, paint, and glass evidence; however, a full description of those innovations is beyond the scope of this chapter. It is sufficient for the investigator and other cold case team members to understand that those technologies exist and for them to rely upon the laboratory to guide them through the various analytical options.

With regard to any forensic investigation, a concerted effort to maintain a spirit of teamwork cannot be overemphasized. Interpretation of forensic evidence can be complicated, and it is common for misunderstandings to occur among team members. Thus, all parties must work in conjunction with—not against—the laboratory.

Advantages and Challenges with Trace Evidence

The appeal of trace evidence is its pervasiveness. It has a wider range of applicability (compared to other disciplines) and can assume multiple forms (e.g., soil/dust to hairs/fibers). Because of its ubiquitous presence, it can be argued that trace evidence can be found in all crime scenes. No other physical evidence has this attribute; however, it does have some potential limitations.

One challenge with trace evidence can be determining its associative value. There is little debate about the significance of a DNA profile hit in the CODIS database. For instance, a comparison between a full DNA crime scene profile to a suspect's reference standard can result in a random-match probability in the quadrillions (1,000,000,000,000,000), which leaves little doubt with regard to whose sample was left at the scene. Contrasting against the strength and individuality of the DNA profile is the sample(s) recovered from trace evidence. What is the value or significance of a single fiber or glass fragment comparison? This question is difficult to answer since most of this type of evidence is based on class features.

Class characteristics are those aspects that a certain group of items have in common. An example would be two fibers that share the same color, cross-sectional shape, and chemical composition. Each of the listed physical properties (e.g., color, shape) is not in itself unique or, even if combined, sufficient to suggest they are unique to each other. This type of evidence is *associative* in manner but not normally sufficient to convey uniqueness. In layman's terms, a fiber "match" probably does not equate to a full DNA profile match, because currently, there is no commonly accepted manner in which to provide a statistical weight to a single fiber.

Table 12.1 Common Types and Properties of Trace Evidence

Types of Trace Evidence	Some Common Physical Associative Properties (Nonunique)	Some Potentially Individualizing Factors
Hair evaluation	Type: human versus animal/ body origin/presence or absence of root	Root=STR or Y-STR DNA Shaft (body)=mitochondrial DNA
Fiber	Type, color, shape	
Glass	Type, color, refractive index	Fracture match
Paint	Type, color, layer structure	Fracture match/layer structure
Soil	Type, color, composition	

The associative power of trace evidence can be enhanced by evaluating additional physical properties of, for example, the examined fiber from above; looking for additional different types of fibers on the same evidence; or searching for other types of trace such as glass, paint, and building materials (Table 12.1). Furthermore, the forensic scientist is often able to offer an expert opinion regarding the rarity of class characteristics (e.g., orange automotive paint on victim's pants versus white) based on his/her case-working experience, training, and peer-reviewed published studies that address these issues.

Combining multiple types of associative evidence is a strategy that can be used to strengthen investigative facts. While it may not have the discriminating power of a fingerprint, DNA, or firearms identification, it can still provide powerful information. For instance, it would be a challenge for someone to explain how a homicide victim's body, which was discarded alongside the highway, came to "coincidentally" have five different carpet fiber types on his/her clothing that happen to be consistent with the flooring from the suspect's house. This is especially true if the suspect denies any involvement or knowledge of the victim.

Trace Evidence Types

Hair

Over the past 10–15 years, the discipline of hair comparison has been under considerable scientific and legal scrutiny, resulting in confusion and doubt about its evidentiary usefulness. For decades, forensic scientists used microscopic hair comparison techniques to compare physical hair attributes (e.g., color, texture, modulation). It was understood by most practicing forensic scientists that this process was not uniquely sufficient to provide individualization to the exclusion of all others. A laboratory report might read, "The hair from defendant X was found to be consistent in color, texture, and modulation to the hair recovered from the crime scene." Unfortunately, this approach probably left too much interpretation to nonscientists.

Perhaps the issue is not necessarily the comparative science of hair microscopy but a combination of factors. The wording of the laboratory report and the limitations of the technique combined with an adversarial legal system in which scientists are pressed to describe nonquantifiable similarities could easily create confusion, instead of clarity. Of more recent concern, regrettably, the testimony of some "experts" possibly went beyond the science involved, potentially contributing to wrongful convictions. Furthermore, when scientific reports are used without an adequate explanation of the limitations such as interpretation by law enforcement on the witness stand or use by attorneys in closing arguments, then misunderstandings can occur. Nevertheless, some laboratories still offer microscopic comparative hair analysis, a practice that is still acceptable; *however*, appropriate limitations to the technique must be understood by all entities evaluating that evidence. It is crucial that the investigator understand the difference between a microscopic hair comparison and a hair evaluation for potential DNA testing. The latter is the subject for this section's discussion.

Hair Evaluation for DNA

Most crime scenes contain too many hairs to practically test all of them. Indeed, depending on the collection method, hundreds to thousands of potential hairs can be collected. From a fiscal point of view, it is not possible to test each hair. There are not enough resources, and the math doesn't add up. Making a quick, conservative back-of-the-envelope calculation can show the sizable financial obligation of a *test-all* policy: 50 hairs × \$150 screening test per hair + 50 hairs × \$400 DNA test per hair (average contracted standard STR test) = \$27,500. No forensic provider could routinely afford to offer this level of service for testing on all potential hair roots for every crime scene. mtDNA testing of the hair shaft is even more costly, and with that same calculation and service, the cost approaches six figures.

An alternative to the test-all method is for the investigator and laboratory scientist to take a thoughtful, intelligent approach in assessing the crime scene hairs. Several steps are involved in this process.

- Step 1 is limiting the selection to the most useful, probative hairs that are most likely to provide investigative direction. Some examples are those hairs located in the victim's orifices, in areas of struggle, near defense wounds, or on the victim that are dissimilar to the victim's own hair.
- Step 2 is microscopic evaluation of the hair to determine suitability for further testing (Figure 12.2). Questions that the laboratory forensic scientist will attempt to determine in this screening assessment are as follows:

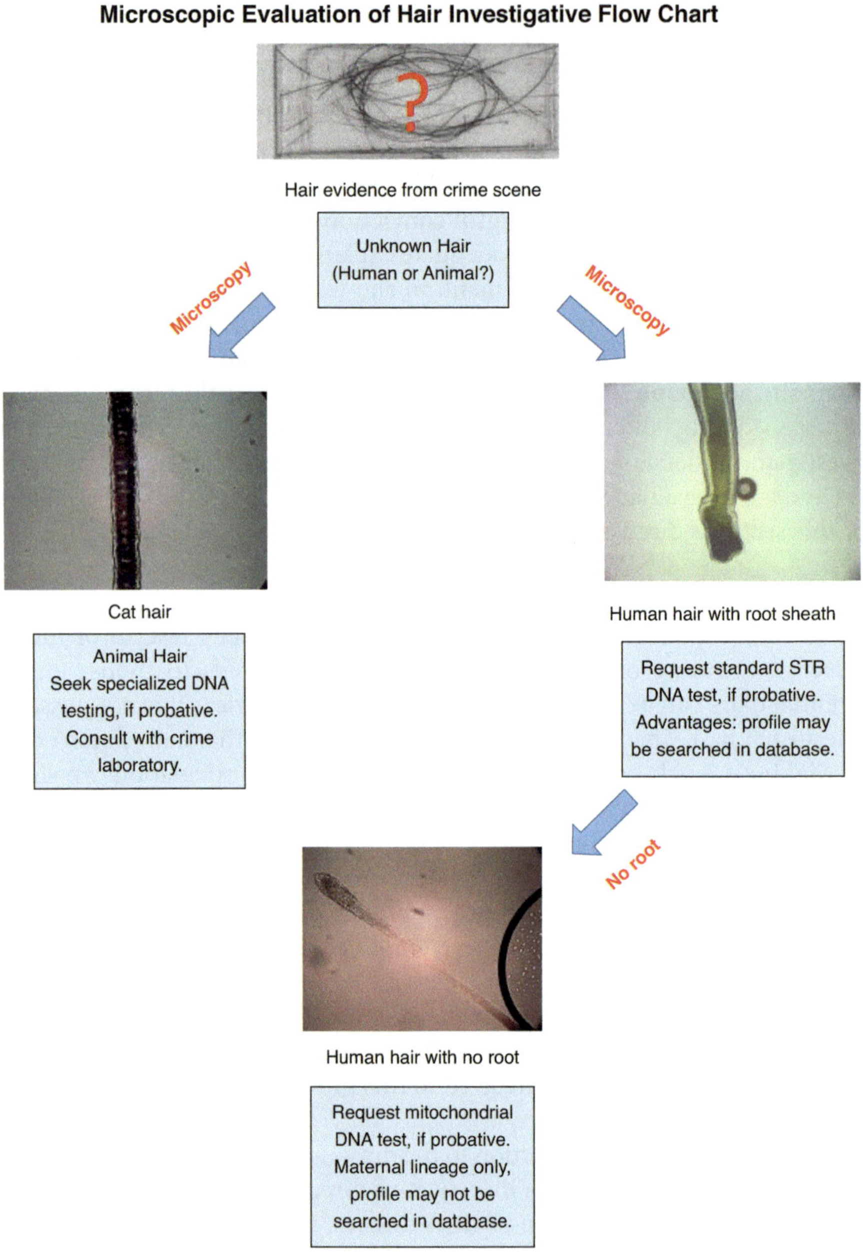

Figure 12.2 Hair flowchart. (Courtesy of Bryan Holden, Utah DPS.)

- *Is the hair animal or human?*

  Depending on the crime scene, hair from multiple species may be collected. Thus, to find the probative hair for DNA analysis, the microscopist must determine the species of the compared

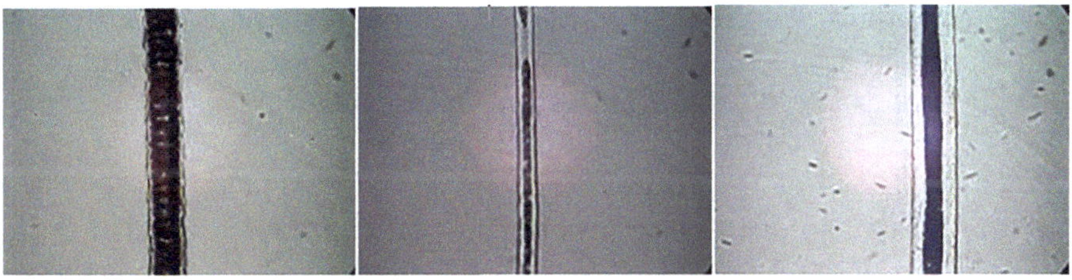

Figure 12.3 Cat, rabbit, and alpaca hair (left to right). (Courtesy of Bryan Holden, Utah DPS.)

hair. He/she does this by comparing the microscopic features within the hair itself (Figure 12.3).

For most crime scenes, the probative value of analysis is the testing of human hair (e.g., associating a human to the crime scene). However, there have been cases that place value in associating an animal (e.g., cat or dog) to a person or crime scene. This is done by identifying the type of animal hair and then conducting the appropriate DNA test applicable to that species type. The majority of public crime laboratories are set up to perform human DNA testing only and do not have capability to test multiple species. As such, specialty laboratories such as the U.S. Fish and Wildlife Service Forensic Laboratory and other vendors have developed specialized DNA methods to individualize animals. If a cold case requires such analysis, the investigator should work closely with his/her crime laboratory to locate an appropriate vendor.

- *Does the hair contain a root tag of skin suitable for potential DNA testing?*

  The most crucial feature to maximize the value of a hair is the presence of a root sheath or tag of skin. This structure contains the nucleated cells that will provide the DNA for standard STR. (See Chapter 15.) If there is sufficient sample to develop a full DNA profile, then it may be eligible for entry into CODIS. This is the best solution for most cases.

- *Should mtDNA testing be considered?*

  Assuming that a hair was not amenable to STR testing, the next best option would be mtDNA testing. Mitochondria are cellular structures that are located within the shaft of the hair. While there are many more copies of this type of DNA available, which makes the test more sensitive with a greater likelihood of obtaining a result, it is less informative than the standard STR DNA test. Thus, it is not useful for a CODIS database search and can only be used as a direct comparison to a suspect or victim standard. Additionally, mitochondria are maternally inherited, which means that multiple individuals may have the same mitochondrial type, thus diminishing its uniqueness.

Reference Samples for Hair Evidence

For comparisons to distinguish between suspect and/or victim hair for the prioritization of DNA testing, reference hair must be collected and submitted to the laboratory along with the unknown hair. For head hair collections, representative hairs should be pulled from the parietal (sides), occipital (rear), and frontal areas of the scalp. For pubic hair, several representative groups of hair should be pulled from the pubic region. Be sure to consult with your laboratory for the number of samples to collect.

For DNA testing, a buccal (oral) swab or blood reference sample is sufficient.

Fibers

Often referred to synonymously with hairs, fibers are collected at the same time as hair evidence. Fibers do not have the potential for DNA testing; however, depending on case circumstances, they can provide very strong associative inference. The more like fibers found on the evidence, the stronger the association.

Similar to a hair analysis, the microscopist will evaluate trace evidence collections to determine the class characteristics of the recovered fibers to include type, color, shape, and chemical composition. (See examples of fiber shape in Figure 12.4.) These will then be compared to the submitted reference samples.

Reference Samples for Fiber Evidence

A known sample should be submitted with each unknown item. If the reference sample is clothing (e.g., a sweater), then the entire item should be submitted. If it is a larger item such as carpeting from a room or an automobile seat, then a representative cutting may be substituted (Figure 12.5).

Figure 12.4 Cross sections of some common fibers. (Courtesy of Bryan Holden, Utah DPS.)

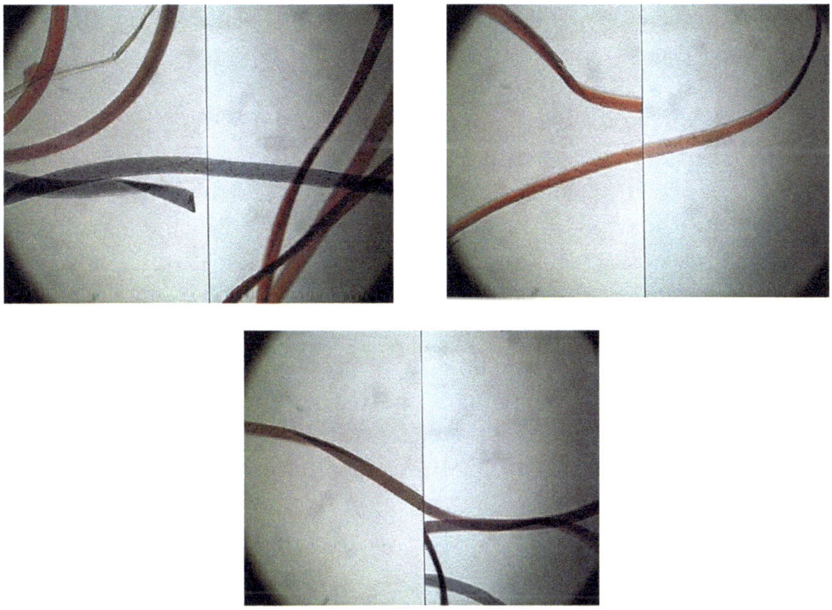

Figure 12.5 Unusual fibers from residence linked to suspect's vehicle. (Courtesy of Bryan Holden, Utah DPS.)

Paint

Paint evidence has been used in a variety of ways to prove association. Typically, it is encountered with hit-and-run and burglary cases as microscopic fragments or smears left behind after some type of contact. Like other forms of trace evidence, it can easily be overlooked and requires that the cold case investigator apply substantive thought to make the most of its potential value.

In the laboratory, an analyst will begin his/her analysis by examining vehicles, clothing, or tools for evidence of contact. He/she will collect any fragment or smears of paint and begin comparing them to submitted reference samples. There are two types of comparisons.

- *Paint layer comparison*: Paint may be composed of multiple coatings, each with a potentially different composition. The more the layers in the evidence, the greater the uniqueness and the stronger the association. Most analyses of this type resulting in a positive comparative report may describe many class features (e.g., color, chemical composition) but still not be sufficient to convey uniqueness.
- *Fracture match*: Paint evidence associations can sometimes be unique. Similar to fitting a missing piece into a jigsaw puzzle, a paint fragment can be physically matched to a common origin. The caveat is that the evidence must be sufficiently large with enough detail for the laboratory analyst to perform the comparison.

Paint Data Query Database

The Paint Data Query (PDQ) database is a unique effort within the trace discipline to maintain a reference set of automobile paint samples. Managed by the Royal Canadian Mounted Police (RCMP), the PDQ database is an international, collaborative effort by forensic laboratories to use a database to provide automobile make/model information from paint evidence fragments to law enforcement. Not all laboratories participate in this effort; thus, cold case investigators are encouraged to work with their provider to identify a laboratory willing to assist them. Most forensic providers work in a spirit of mutual cooperation and are more than willing to assist other agencies.

Reference Samples for Paint Evidence

For cases involving automobiles, known samples should be collected nearest the point of suspected contact or where damage is evident but not within the area of damage itself. With respect to cold cases, the damage may have been repaired with new paint applied. In these situations, the investigator should be aware that the collection and comparison of case samples can be challenging and may require extra collaborative effort. All standards should be rigorously recorded by the investigator with both notes and photographs. This is necessary due to the variation in paint application processes on vehicles (e.g., automotive paint on metal parts is chemically different from paint on plastic parts), and the potential to collect a sample that may not be appropriate. Additional reference samples may need to be collected.

With regard to paint transfer from tools, the entire item should be submitted, if practical (Figures 12.6 and 12.7).

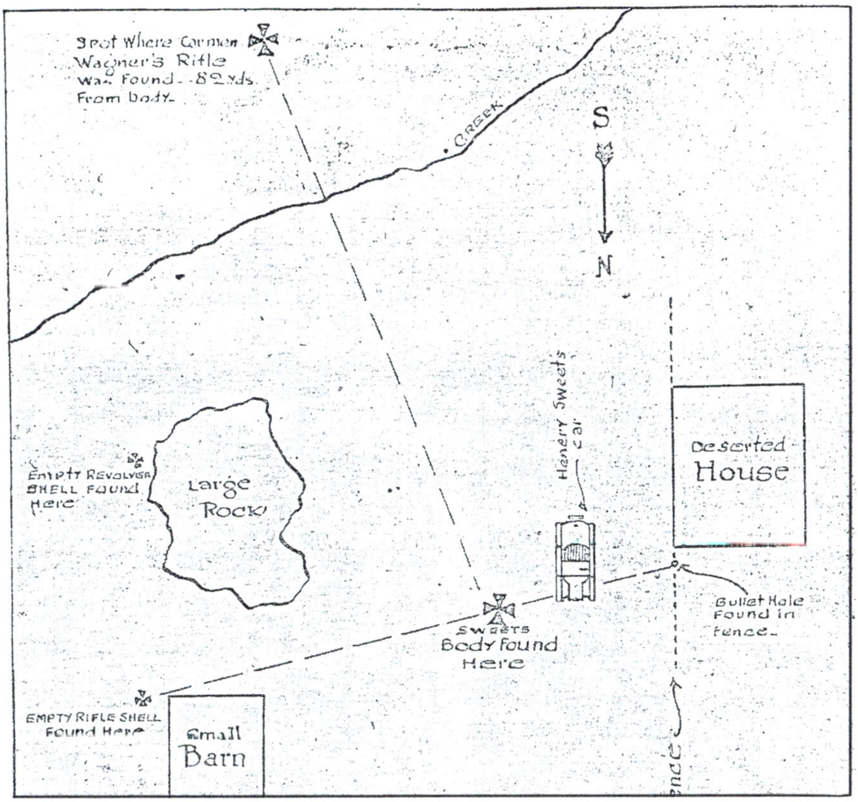

Figure 12.6 Paint fragments and physical match of zip tie in hit-and-run homicide. (Courtesy of Jennifer McNair, Utah DPS.)

Glass

Glass fragments may be transferred to clothing and footwear and have a practical potential for adherence and retention to those items. If the case facts suggest a glass fragmentation event (e.g., broken window, display case), then it may worthwhile to have the laboratory examine the clothing, automobile, or other items for the presence of fragments.

The analyst may begin their analyses by looking in the pockets and the surface of outerwear or soles of shoes for embedded fragments and collecting those items for testing. Somewhat similar to paint, there are two types of comparisons.

- *Glass fragment comparison*: Glass fragments are distinguished by their optical properties and chemical compositions. An analyst will measure each fragment's refractive index and evaluate its chemical makeup to determine consistency with submitted standards. Similar to other trace disciplines, most analyses of this type resulting in a

Trace Cold Case Feature: Guarded Secrets

Courtesy of Bill Schneck, Microvision Northwest

In 1991, Bryan Ruff, a security guard at Kennecott Copper Mine near Salt Lake City went missing from his guard shack one evening. A search of the shack revealed no foul play. Dale Bradley was another security guard that often worked with Brian. Dale Bradley became a suspect when investigators learned Brian was having an affair with Dale's wife. Dales 1974 orange-red Camaro was searched for GSR and blood and came up negative. When Dale later passed a lie detector test he was no longer a suspect. One year latter hikers discovered the remains of Brian Ruff 50 miles from the mine. An autopsy determined Bryan had been shot 5 times in the back with a.22 caliber handgun and buried in a shallow grave. Approximately 200 yards from the body search dogs found a cowboy boot that was identified as Brian's. Fourteen years later a Salt Lake County cold case detective received a call from a neighboring county's Sheriff's Office stating that Todd Bradley was a suspect in yet another murder. Dale was once again a suspect in the murder of Brian Ruff. Dale's wife mentioned in an interview that Dale cleaned out his Camaro one day after the murder of Brian Ruff, an uncommon event. The Salt Lake County detective examined the boot and observed a reddish smear on the bottom and remembered that Dales car was of a similar color. Schneck was hired to determine if Camaros were painted in the trunk with the same color as the exterior of the vehicle and if the smear on the boot could have originated from the truck of the Camaro where it was believed Brian may have been placed. Unfortunately the Camaro was sold as scrap in 1993. During the original search of the Camaro an officer also collected red paint samples from the car. The red smear on the boot was compared to the control paint samples for the 1991 Camaro and a known reference paint sample from a 1991 Camaro acquired from NIST. Schneck identified orange-red lead chromate paint of similar color and chemical composition in all three samples using polarized light microscopy, scanning electron microscopy- energy dispersive spectroscopy and infra-red spectroscopy. Brian Ruff likely was in the trunk of Dale Bradley's Camaro and as he tried to kick the trunk open, some of the red paint transferred to his boot. This case was featured in Forensic Files, Episode 324, Guarded Secrets.

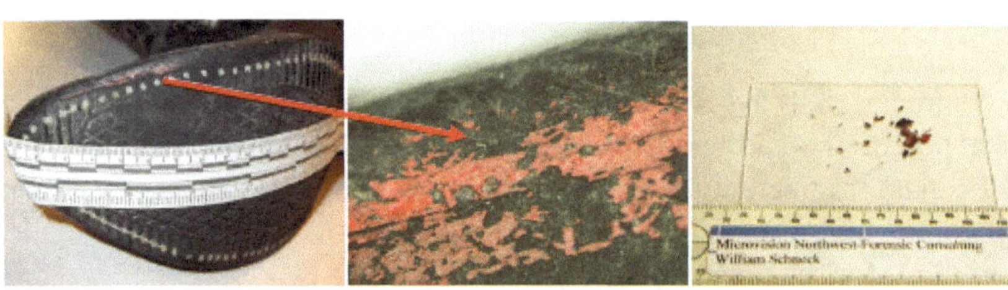

Boot | Close-up of boot | Paint from Bradley's Camaro

Figure 12.7 Paint cold case. (Courtesy of Bill Schneck, Microvision Northwest.)

positive comparative report may describe consistency in refractive index and elemental composition but still not be sufficient to convey uniqueness.

- *Fracture match*: Similar to paint, a glass comparison can sometimes be unique. A glass fragment of sufficient size and detail may have the potential to be physically matched to show that the two compared items originally were one.

Reference Samples for Glass Evidence

Glass reference samples should have been taken of the area nearest the breakage event.

Other Forms of Trace Evidence

The aforementioned trace evidence disciplines represent the most common laboratory requests. However, as mentioned at the beginning of this chapter, there is no strict definition of what type of evidence is considered trace. Thus, cold case investigators are encouraged to not limit themselves to just the typical discipline requests but to carefully consider the facts of each case, consult with their local forensic provider, and think deeply about the evidence in their case. Some additional considerations are cosmetics, soil, pollen, seeds, wood, and building materials, among others. The variation of physical evidence can be substantial and may not fit a traditional comparison category (Figure 12.8).

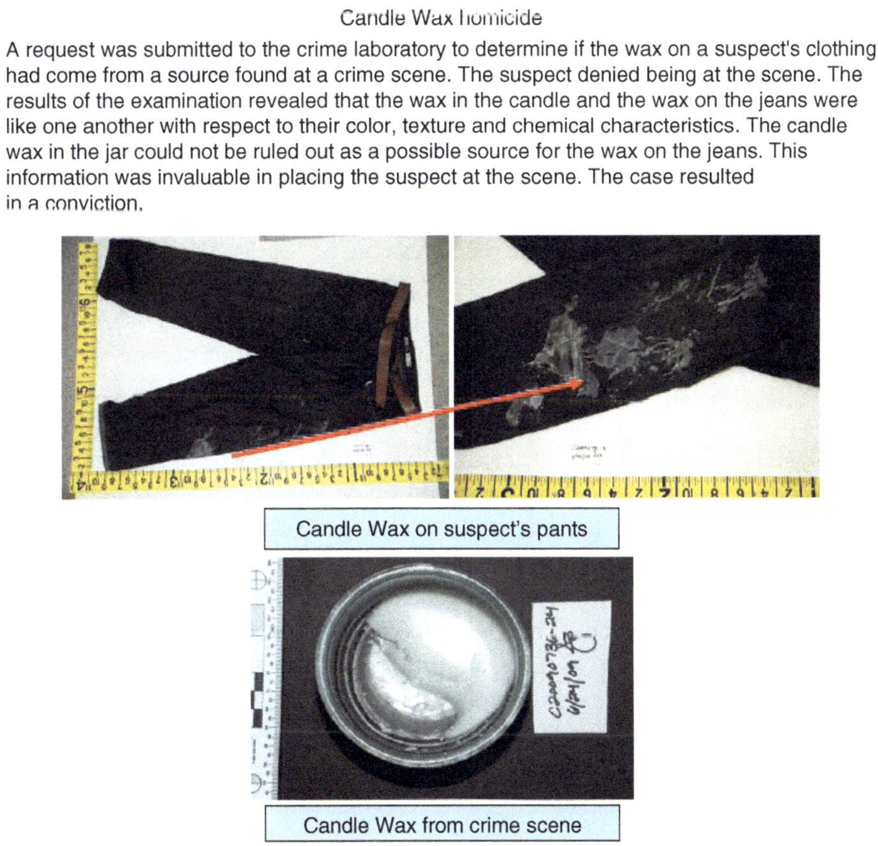

Figure 12.8 Candle-wax homicide. (Courtesy of Justin Bechaver, Utah DPS.)

Where Is It Now?

As with law enforcement agencies, the evidence retention practices and policies of forensic providers vary greatly, and there is no national, standardized procedure. Hence, finding cold case trace evidence can be a challenge. The following represents some additional thoughts beyond what has already been discussed in previous chapters.

- *DNA swabs/cuttings*: Some laboratories adopted a practice of retaining biological evidence on all positive cases. Inquiries should be made regarding the location of those samples. Many cases have been solved with samples that have been stored in long-term evidence freezers or rooms. A not-uncommon practice has been for medical examiners to make two sets of swabs: one would be furnished to the law enforcement agency and the other maintained by the medical examiner. Although the agency's evidence may not be available, investigators should check with the medical examiner to ascertain their retention of any evidence.
- *Hair/fiber lifts*: Many providers have used water-soluble lift tape to process clothing and other items for hair and fiber evidence. Prior to accreditation of forensic laboratories, these lifts were sometimes stored on plastic sheets within the original case file itself. After a certain retention period, those case files may have been transferred to a long-term archives building.
- *Hair/fiber microscope slides*: In the laboratory, forensic scientists would conduct their comparison analyses using microscope slides. For convenience, the slide, along with the potential evidence, was kept within the crime laboratory in a slide holder or in the case file itself. There may be a chance that those slides are still in the laboratory or in a long-term archives building.
- *Bullets*: Often overlooked, projectiles (e.g., jacketed hollow points) are excellent collectors of evidence such as fibers, DNA, and building materials. A continuing practice of law enforcement is to rush to request the comparison of the bullets to the firearm in question but neglect considering the applicability of any trace evidence.
- *Autopsy and/or rape kits*: Autopsy and rape kits are a great source of a variety of evidence. A review of each kit between the investigator and laboratory personnel is a great starting point. Most commercial kits contain packets labeled for trace evidence.

Acknowledgments

I wish to extend my deepest appreciation to Jay W. Henry, laboratory director for the Utah Department of Public Safety, for his contribution of this chapter. The case studies provide much insight into the experiences of team members in cold case investigations and lessons to be learned from the close cooperation of laboratory, investigative, and legal personnel. He was assisted in this endeavor by laboratory team members of the Utah Department of Public Safety—Bureau of Forensic Services, including Pilar Shortsleeve, Bryan Holden, Jennifer McNair, and Justin Bechaver, and to each, I also extend my deepest appreciation.

Forensic Anthropology 13

ERIN H. KIMMERLE

Understanding the Cold Case Problem

Cold cases fascinate the public, but they represent a growing crisis. Nationwide, unresolved violent crime is a significant problem despite advanced technology with forensic applications and modern investigative strategies. While the number of open homicides is unknown, we do know that the national homicide clearance rate has fallen to its lowest level. Some have estimated there are more than 280,000 unsolved homicides since 1980, and thousands more will be added to that total each year. There is also a growing concern over the number of unidentified decedents and missing persons in the United States, with more than 84,000 reported missing persons in the National Crime Information Center (NCIC) and over 600,000 additional people reported missing annually. It is also estimated that there are more than 40,000 unidentified bodies, most of whom represent open homicides or equivocal deaths. For the stats that are reported, we know these are low numbers because many agencies do not self-report their crime statistics. Further, when it comes to long-term open cases, many have been mishandled, erroneously closed, or reports were not taken. A big part of doing cold case investigations is trying to figure out what cases exist and whether evidence and the case files are still accessible. This problem has been called "The Nation's Silent Mass Disaster" (Ritter 2007). The result is that justice is stalled until *The Missing* are found, *The Unknown* are identified, and their homicide investigations are closed.

The amount of time and resources that any agency in the medico-legal community puts into long-term missing and unsolved cases is voluntary and varies widely across jurisdictions. Each "case" represents grieving friends and family who exist in limbo, not knowing what happened to their loved one or where to turn for help. For example, a lot of long-term homicides are not investigated as they are considered *just a missing person* because the body has not yet been recovered. Families find themselves without support because their cases are designated as "non-crimes."

For the past fifteen years, my goal has been simple: to help increase the number of long-term open cases getting solved through technical assistance, policy recommendations, legislation, public awareness, and education. Forensic anthropology has a lot to offer homicide investigations, whether the murder was yesterday or 20 years ago. This chapter discusses the many tools and processes available

 DOI: 10.4324/9781003415633-16

to homicide investigators from the field of forensic anthropology and draws on case examples and programming from the Forensic Anthropology Laboratory at the University of South Florida (USF-FAL). The following chapter draws on research and programming done through this program. The purpose of the Florida Unidentified Remains & Homicide Cold Case Program, later renamed the USF Cold Case Initiative, was initially created in 2010 to seek funding and to collaborate with scientific experts from diverse technical fields to find innovative solutions for long-term case resolution. This turned into a statewide program to help law enforcement and medical examiners solve cold cases (unsolved homicides, long-term missing persons, and unknown decedents) in Florida and more recently resulted in a new statewide program for the Commonwealth of Pennsylvania. This effort is a multi-disciplinary, multi-jurisdictional effort to pool resources and apply modern science to long-term unsolved cases. A significant portion of these cases include missing, endangered, and unidentified people. It is estimated that fewer than 20% of agencies have protocols to manage and re-investigate long-term open cases (Davis et al. 2011). Our Cold Case Initiative has aided agencies around the country with very successful outcomes. A planned policy approach to managing resources for open cases, combined with scientific innovation and new tools that can be applied to older cases, has shown very positive results. The program seeks to help bring forensic and investigative resources to the wider pool of law enforcement, medico-legal, and coroner communities. It is vital to solve such cases for the families and victims who have been denied justice for so many years.

Developing a Model for Cold Case Management with the Inclusion of Forensic Anthropology

There are many ways in which forensic anthropology contributes to homicide and cold case investigations (Figure 13.1). These tools range from the crime scene to the laboratory and morgue and even go so far as to include public engagement and a variety of public events designed for missing person cases.

At its core, forensic anthropology is the study of the human skeleton and human biology. The way in which forensic anthropologists apply that knowledge, training, and skills to open investigations includes technical assistance ranging from the field to the lab. Not all forensic anthropologists are trained the same and so not all of them offer all the services discussed in this chapter, but this range demonstrates the plethora of services, skills, and tools available throughout the course of highly diverse and complex investigations. Forensic anthropologists are hired by either the law enforcement agency, medical examiner, coroner, or prosecutor, and serve as scientific expert witnesses in cases that bring criminal charges, including testifying at trial.

The first step in developing a cold case model and a working protocol is to know who the experts are that can bring scientific value and expertise

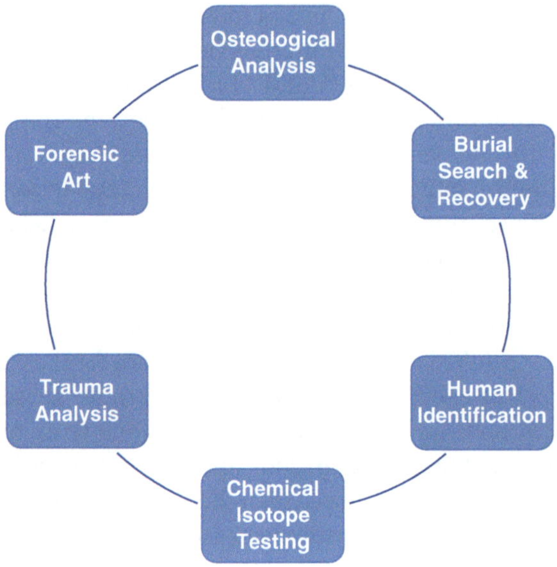

Figure 13.1 Forensic anthropology contributes to homicide and cold case investigations in many ways from the crime scene to the morgue.

from each area and to understand why it is that so many homicides have remained unsolved. To resolve many of the cases that have been open for decades, it is necessary to go back to the beginning of the case and evaluate each aspect of it. That means redoing things that have been done and adding new methods and technologies where innovation and science have progressed. We call this *bringing the case up to current investigative standards,* and it means questioning everything from the autopsy conclusions to any testing that was completed or, in some cases, not done and reworking the case from the beginning. Because there are many factors that have led to cases remaining open (Table 13.1), there are a lot of different solutions that can be applied to try and tackle a large caseload, beyond funding, such as creating a system for evaluating and classifying cases that have different likelihoods of being solved (i.e., death of offenders). Other solutions have included the use of forensic art and public programming to reach out to the public for leads, reference DNA samples, and inter-agency collaboration and are discussed in more detail at the end of the chapter.

Human Identification

Human identification is usually one of the first and most critical questions that bones can help answer, but there are a number of areas within an investigation that may benefit from forensic anthropology. Table 13.2 summarizes

Table 13.1 Factors Leading to a High Rate of Unsolved Cases

1. Inconsistency among agencies in how unresolved cases are counted and handled.
2. Lead-driven vs. intelligence-driven cold case policies within an agency.
3. Statistics not maintained and no statewide or federal agencies tracks this problem.
4. High personnel turn-over rate.
5. Lack of case management systems.
6. Lack of responsibility, "Not my problem" mentality.
7. Missing evidence including bodies of John/Jane Does or key body parts.
8. Unidentified victims.
9. Developing but inconsistent standards and protocols.
10. Errors in the cause and manner of death.
11. Case priority.
12. Lack of training—keeping up with innovative forensic science.
13. Human error.

Table 13.2 Questions That Can Be Addressed through Forensic Anthropology

IS THIS CASE FORENSIC?

- Many times human remains come through the medico-legal system that are actually from historic cemeteries, archaeological sites or burial mounds, or anaotmical supply companies.

WHO WAS THIS PERSON?

- Basic data about individuals such as age, sex, and ancestry creates a Biological Profile.
- Chemical Isotope testing can give leads about the general regions the individual lived and can be useful to generate leads when the person came from a different part of the county or from a foreign country.
- Radiographs of teeth for living juveniles and young adults can also estimate the age of a living person whose identity may be questionable.

ARE THERE INJURIES?

- Analysis of bone defects, fractures, and fracture lines inform about the timing of the injury, the mechanism of force, the number of injuries, and the general category of a weapon.

How long has this person been dead?

- Data on burial factors, taphonomic processes, the post-mortem interval, and basic crime scene data provide information about the context and timing..

What did this person look like?

- Forensic artists use the biological profile estimated from skeletal remains and the underlying boney architechture of the face to create facial approximations.
- Anthropoloigsts can further inform the artist about asyemmetries, healed facial trauma, deviated septums, and other facial features that effect the soft tissues for a more realistic approximation.

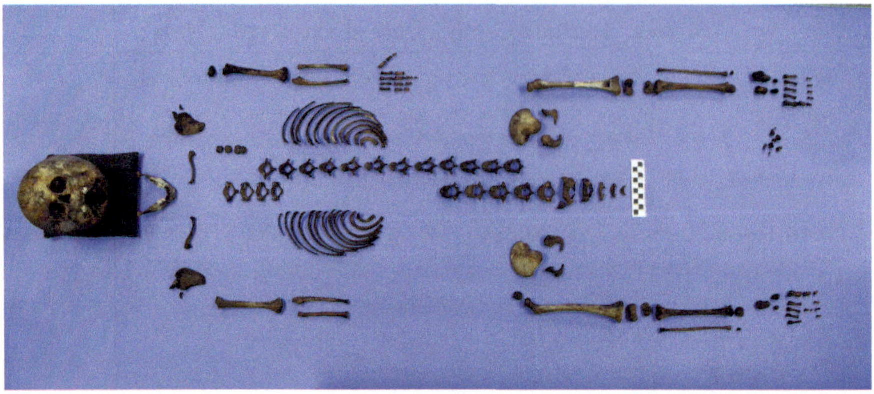

Figure 13.2 Juvenile bones are shown to be laid out in anatomical order.

the critical questions answered through forensic anthropology about the context, time since death, and cause of death. The methods and techniques available to estimate individual characteristics about a person from skeletal remains and trauma analysis based on bone are the areas that set forensic anthropology apart from forensic pathology (Figures 13.2 and 13.3).

Forensic anthropologists use osteological methods for the purpose of individual identification and trauma analysis. First, they construct a biological profile. Biological profiles are estimated from skeletal and dental data. The completeness of the profile depends on what data is available due to recovery and/or preservation. To begin, a skeletal inventory must be made of all elements present. Depending on whether the decedent is immediately identified or not, the biological parameters for identity (i.e., age at death, sex, stature, ancestry, etc.) may be made available to the public and entered in different local, state, and federal databases. Some of these databases are for law enforcement use only (i.e., NCIC), while others are available to the public (NamUs.org). Depending on the goals of investigators, many biological parameters can be narrowed or widened to be more or less inclusive. At various stages in the identification process, it may be advantageous to be more inclusive. Therefore, investigators must decide what information or level of details to provide the medico-legal community and to the public.

Classification Types of Identification

Presumptive Identification

- The possible identity of an individual is based on information that is consistent with individuality but that is not mutually exclusive to only one person. All the initial parameters for identification are used here, such as age, sex, ancestry, stature, unique skeletal markers, skeletal pathology, and antemortem trauma.

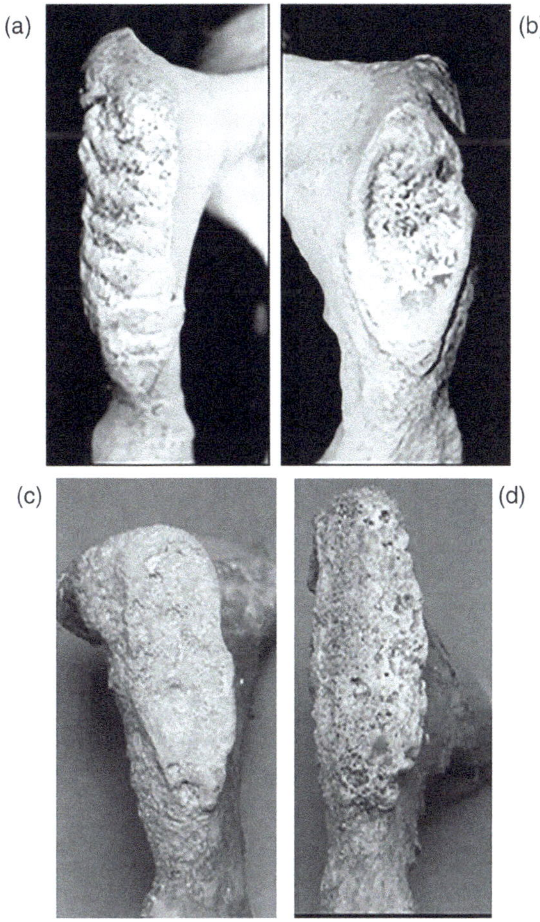

Figure 13.3 The pubic symphysis (a feature on the pelvic bone used for aging adults) is shown for four different individuals: (a) male, age 18 years; (b) male, age 75 years; (c) male, age 84 years; and (d) female, age 84 years. The morphology of this bone changes relatively consistently throughout life, enabling age estimation. But significant differences are present between males and female among older aged adults, note how different the shape, texture, and appearance are among the two individuals at age 84. This is largely the result of osteoporosis and the significant amount of bone loss females experience as they age.

Positive Identification

- The positive identification of an individual is established through information that is exclusive to only that individual (i.e., DNA, fingerprints, unique skeletal or dental morphology, or sinus patterns) and is derived by comparisons of ante- and postmortem information that are unique to a particular individual.

Collective Identification

- The identification of an individual into a particular cultural, demographic, religious, or ethnic group may estimate a collective identity. General descriptive characteristics about the individual place him/her within a particular group. For example, the age, sex, or ethnicity of the individual may demonstrate group membership derived from biological factors or other physical evidence associated with the decedent (i.e., clothing or jewelry depicting religious affiliations).

Contextual Identification

- For an individual or group of individuals, contextual identification is like a collective identity but can be applied at the individual or group level. This form of identification serves to inform about the status and context of the individual, such as "Foreign born individuals," Migrant workers," or "Homeless." In this context, the characteristics about an individual are consistent with certain population characteristics but limited to strict "group" membership. Increasingly this category is useful along Border States in the United States where many of our unknown, unidentified decedents fall to categories such as migrant workers, transients, or victims of human trafficking.

Chemical Isotope Testing for Generating Leads in Human Identification

The chemical analysis of human remains may provide scientific information on food, water, and other elements that were consumed during an individual's life and in what quantities, during the period that each structure was growing or forming in an individual's life, such as oxygen or lead. Since the elements are linked to geography, this type of testing gives investigators a broad geographic reference and can show mobility from different samples in the same individual that represent different geographic regions. In other words, the bones, teeth, and hair in a person's body serve like a time capsule and timeline from when those structures formed. By looking at elements in each structure, a pattern of where the person has lived throughout the course of their life is constructed. This testing does not give investigators individual identification, but it can provide a critical lead when a person dies in one place but was born in another such as across the country or in a foreign country.

Since isotopic and elemental values in the air, home, plants, and animals are passed on to their consumers, tooth samples inform about diet at the time they formed (prenatally or during the first 12 years of life); bone samples provide the average diet over the last 7–10 years of an individual's life; and hair root samples provide information about recent diet in the months or few years prior to death (depending on the length of hair).

Bone (and tooth root) collagen mainly represents dietary protein, while bone and tooth root apatite (and tooth enamel) represent the whole diet. These analyses can be used to address annual and seasonal dietary patterns, changes since childhood, and human mobility. More specifically, stable carbon isotopes vary based on different plant photosynthetic pathways (e.g., maize is quite different from wheat and rice) and between terrestrial and marine foods, with these foods varying considerably in availability in different parts of the world; nitrogen isotopes inform us about the importance of meat and fish in the diet, as well as the use of plant fertilizers; and oxygen isotopes help identify specific geographic locations based on distance from the sea, temperature, and altitude. Trace element analysis of barium and strontium also may be used to assess the importance of seafood in the diet along with geographic locations. These methods complement strontium isotope analysis in addressing human mobility and identification.

Strontium (Sr) and lead (Pb) are metals that readily substitute for calcium (Ca) and so accumulate in body tissues and bones in vivo. In contrast to Ca, which has relatively uniform isotopic composition, Sr and Pb isotopic compositions can vary widely depending on local geological and environmental factors. Therefore, we can use the Sr and Pb isotope composition of skeletal material to determine the birthplace and geographic mobility of a given person or remains (Figure 13.4).

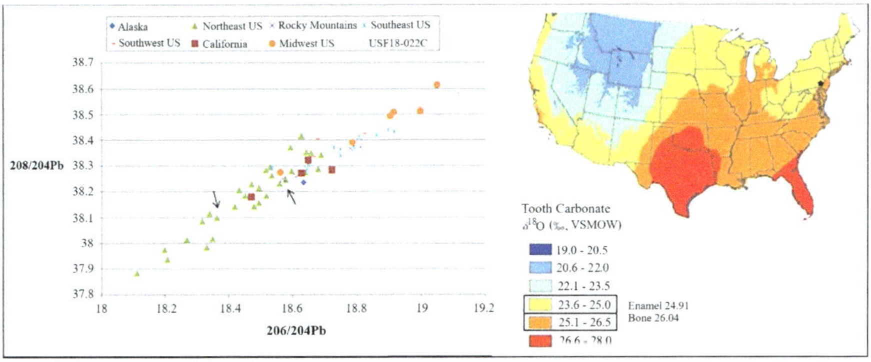

Figure 13.4 An example of an oxygen isotope map showing where human remains were recovered in Philadelphia, Pennsylvania, in 1973. The 206/204 lead versus 208/204 lead isotope values of the unknown juvenile male were plotted against known samples from different regions within the United States and illustrated the juvenile was likely born in the same general region where his remains were recovered. He had been missing for approximately 42 years and was identified through familial genealogical testing after being exhumed from an unmarked grave in 2016. The decedent was in fact from Philadelphia. The oxygen isotope map shown here was adapted from Meier-Augenstein (2018).

What Is the Context? Is This a Missing Person, Historic Burial, or Some Other Artifact?

Establishing the Context

Human remains are often recovered in a variety of contexts such as storage units, dumped in public spaces, or found through the course of other criminal investigations. The first question in these types of cases has to do with whether the remains are of medico-legal significance. Is this a forensic case? Does the bone come from someone who recently died, or is it from an historic burial or an anatomical specimen? The conundrum is that even in cases of grave robbing, this once was a person, and the medical examiner and coroner systems are not consistent or clear on how to handle such cases. Forensic anthropology methods can be used to evaluate the context of the skeletal remains and provide an assessment for the general timing and context to some degree. For example, in some cases there may be clothing, artifacts, or dental implants that suggest they came from a historic burial. Cranial metric analysis can be used to determine if the skeletal remains are archaeological or come from indigenous Native American groups. In cases that are less clear, the default is always to treat the case as if it is of forensic significance until otherwise proven otherwise.

Establishing the Time Since Death or Postmortem Interval

Given the number of variables and range of factors that influence the postmortem interval (PMI), the PMI estimation usually ranges from several days to months or years. This body of research comes largely from facilities that focus on human donations for forensic science research such as the USF-FORT (Facility for Outdoor Research and Training) or the Forensic Anthropology Center at the University of Tennessee, which are otherwise known as *Body Farms.*

There are various interpretations, models, and definitions regarding decomposition, taphonomy, and taphonomy processes as they relate to interpretations of the postmortem modification and the length of the PMI. The general stages of decomposition and their characteristics are listed in Table 13.3. For more research on this subject refer to Bass (1997), Clark et al. (1997), and Galloway et al. (1989).

Taphonomy refers to the multiple processes that effect human remains following death. Careful documentation of observations made at the crime scene, burial variables, and modifications to skeletal remains is needed. Collectively, this information will enable interpretations about the PMI and the differentiation between perimortem trauma and postmortem damage.

Table 13.3 Characteristics of the Decomposition Process

Stage	Characteristics	General Timeline
Fresh	Egg masses may start to form. *Algor mortis*, *rigor mortis*, and *livor mortis* set in. Slight discoloration of body tissues due to *putrefaction*.	24 hours
Early decomposition/ bloat	Body tissues bloat and increase in size. Skin slippage begins to occur. Marbling of the vascular system becomes pronounced. Body fluids purge from the mouth, nose, and eyes. Purging of body fluids will often kill nearby vegetation and stain the soil a dark color.	~1+ week
Advanced decomposition	Facial bones and hands become skeletonized before the torso and limbs. The body is no longer bloated, the gases have purged, body mass appears much reduced. Soft tissues continue to break down.	Weeks–months
Mummification (wet or dry)	Adipocere forms in wet environments, either in water or in wet graves. Embalmed bodies that have been buried in a wet grave often resemble a wet mummy with significant tissue preservation. Dry mummification will occur in a cool or dry environment this is often seen also when bodies are left in structures shielded from scavengers and a lot of heat and humidity such as abandoned buildings.	~1+ year
Skeletonization	Soft tissues become completely desiccated and dry or absent, leaving only skeletonized remains. Remains may be disarticulated due to animal and bird scavenging. Bones become stained from sun bleaching, decaying vegetation, or the chemical properties of the soil.	~1 year
Skeletal decomposition	Over time, the cortex of bone begins to show cracking and erosion. The bone itself may disintegrate and become extremely fragile or powder-like upon excavation.	Years–decades

The single largest factors in variable rates of decay are temperature and access by scavengers to the remains. For example, human remains left outdoors on the ground surface in Florida in July without the use of any container can be skeletonized in one week. When a cage is placed over the remains limiting access by scavengers (or any other type of container), vultures in particular, the soft tissues may remain for a year and even become mummified.

The skeletonization of a complete body within a week is virtually unheard of in most regions of the United States.

To standardize how PMI is calculated and discussed, it is recommended that Accumulated Degree Days (ADD) are used. ADD is calculated by adding the average daily temperature over a given period. Since temperature is one of the most influential factors in the rate of decomposition, using ADD provides a standard scale that can be applied to any location. For example, for a body to decompose to the point where bloating occurs, it may take an average of 285 ADD. In Alaska, where average temperatures are 65°F, this may equal 4.5 days, whereas in Florida, with average temperatures of 95°F it may take only 3 days. In this example, the time since death may vary by as much as 1.5 days, depending on the temperature and geographical location (Vass et al. 1992). Figure 13.5 shows early and advanced states of decomposition. Figure 13.6 illustrates damage to bone caused by vultures that mimics an injury.

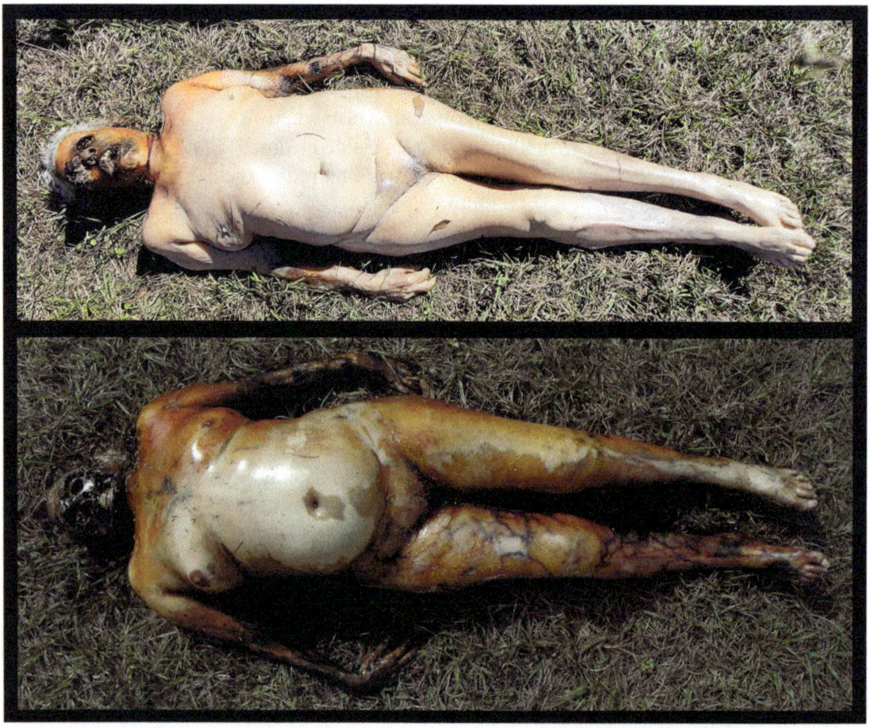

Figure 13.5 Comparison of a human donor at the USF-FORT facility in early and advanced stages of decomposition. Placement of the donor at the facility is shown at 9 days (top figure) and 14 days (bottom figure).

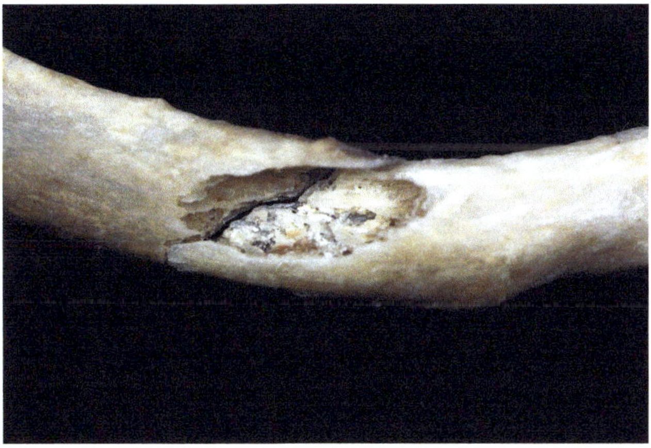

Figure 13.6 Vulture damage on a human rib mimics trauma.

Trauma Analysis

The reconstruction of skeletal fractures is imperative for determining the mechanisms of injury as well as the circumstances, cause, and manner of death. The morphology of skeletal injuries is shaped by internal factors (e.g., the type of bone affected and age of victim), extrinsic factors (e.g., the type of weapon), and contextual factors (e.g., trauma resulting from act of volition or the position of the victim). Refer to Kimmerle and Baraybar (2008) for a complete discussion on how to identify skeletal injuries.

The morphology of wounds, defects, and fracture patterns provides information on the mechanism of injury. Table 13.4 lists the different mechanisms of injury that can be determined from skeletal analysis including: gunfire, blunt force, sharp force, blasting, thermal, and chronic abuse. In other words, fractures that result at the time of death and may have contributed to the death have to be differentiated from animal scavenging, warping due to ground pressure for buried remains, or excavation damage.

All deaths resulting from traumatic injuries benefit from the direct study of skeletal trauma (Figures 13.7–13.9). While once considered the exclusive domain of forensic pathologists, the use of forensic anthropologists in the evaluation of injuries is now widely prevalent and includes cases ranging from fresh autopsies to cold case reviews, occurring years or decades after the remains were found. On an individual level, ante- and perimortem injuries provide details about a person's life and death. The healed injuries reflect events that occurred throughout a person's life and may be relevant for human identification or establishing a pattern of abuse or neglect. In contrast, the

Table 13.4 Mechanisms of Injury and Skeletal Traits of Injury

Gunfire injuries	The class of weapon, distance of shot, number, and sequence of injuries can often be determined from skeletal analysis. Skeletal defects and fracture lines will reflect the general shape and size of the projectile, number, and direction of shot(s).
Blunt trauma	An object that crushes tissue. Object may strike the individual or the decedent may have been expelled toward an object. This category is differentiated from other mechanisms of crushing injuries such as projectile trauma. Did an object strike the individual or did the individual strike a stationary object? Skeletal defects often display plastic deformation, displacement, bending, fragmentation, and defects that mimic the shape of the impacting object.
Sharp trauma	A penetrating object that cuts tissues and bone. Wounds may consist of incisions, punctures, sawing, and cut marks. Skeletal defects or cuts may have smooth, notched, or chipped edges.
Sharp-blunt trauma	A penetrating object that cuts tissues and bone but due to its size, force, or way in which weapon is used also causes significant crushing blunt injury. This can include a combination of crushing defects, fractures and fracture lines, incisions, punctures, and cut marks. Typically, this category results from hacking types of tools like a machete or hatchet.
Blast injuries	Explosive injuries create thermal, blunt, sharp, and penetrating trauma including dismemberment. Shrapnel creates irregular-shaped penetrating defects in skeletal tissue and may become embedded in bone. Injuries are largely affected by extrinsic factors such as the type of explosive, location of the incident (i.e., in an enclosed space), or the type of surrounding materials.
Thermal injuries	Thermal injuries due to fire cause discoloration, bone fractures, bone shrinkage, and dismemberment. Trauma inflicted prior to burning is still evident even after severe burning. Color and fracture patterns may indicate if burning occurred when bone was fleshed, opposed to postmortem burning that occurs after soft tissues decomposed. Burning may result from incident at the time of death, such as an automobile accident or explosion. Burning may also be used postmortem to hide or destroy evidence.

injuries occurring in association with the death event speaks to the cause and manner of death.

The diagnosis of inflicted trauma in cases where a false report of a traumatic event or a suicide occurred (e.g., equivocal deaths) can change the outcome of a case. Equivocal deaths are those inquiries that are open to interpretation. There may be two or more meanings, and the case may present as either a homicide or a suicide depending upon the circumstances. The facts are purposefully vague or misleading as in the case of a "staged crime scene" (Practical Homicide Investigations). Cases of equivocal deaths often include infants, small children, or elder abuse cases in which the parent or caregiver provides false statements to the police or homicide cases staged to appear as something else.

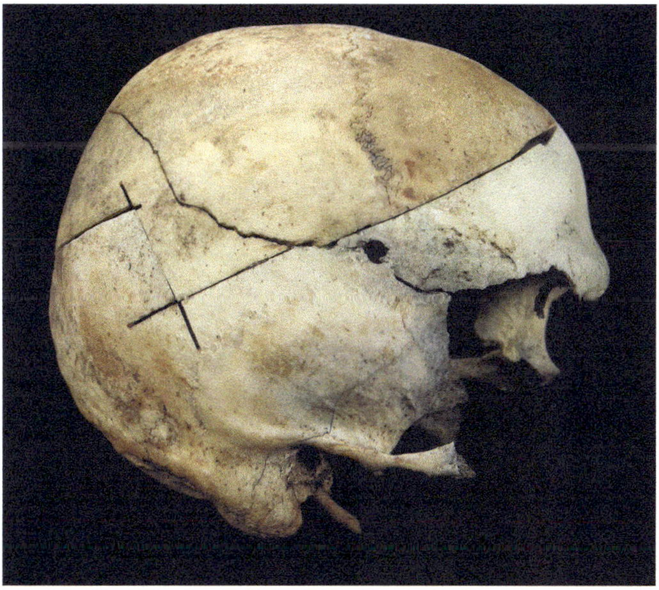

Figure 13.7 Gunshot injury. Entrance wound to the right temporal bone, this was a through and through shot, from right to left. Self-inflicted injury at near contact range.

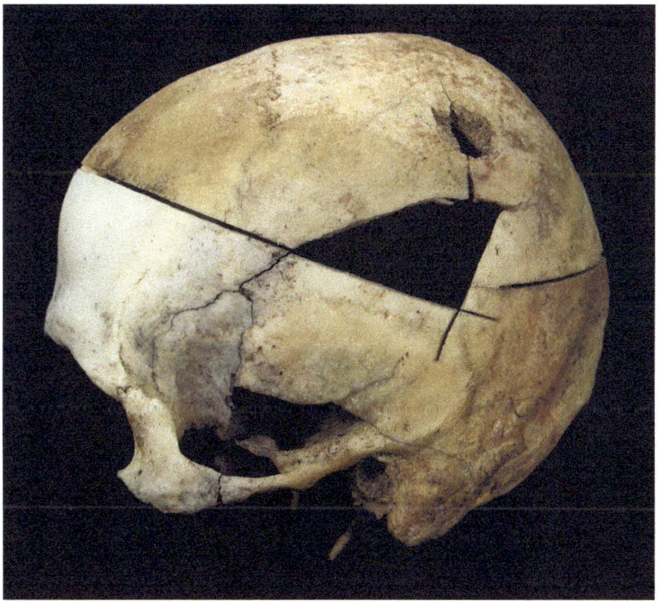

Figure 13.8 Corresponding gunshot injury to Figure 13.7. Exit wound to the left temporal bone. The defect is larger than the entry wound defect, with multiple radiating fractures and fragmentation.

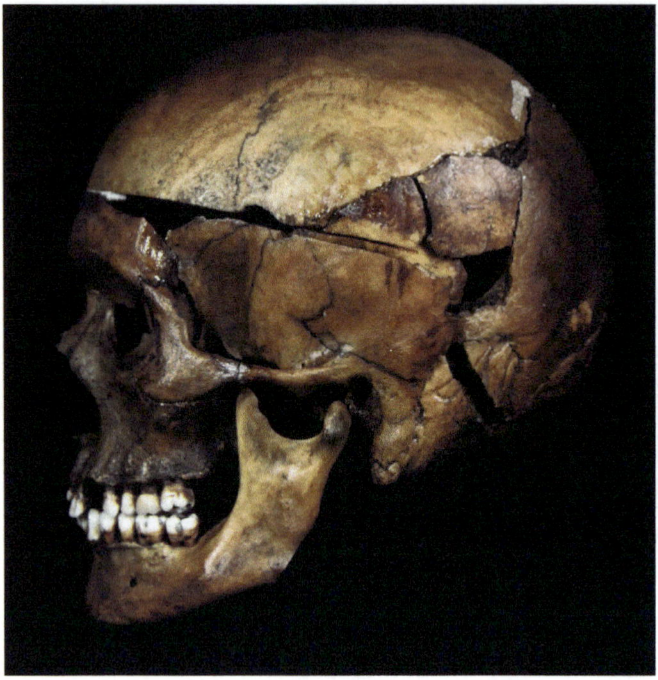

Figure 13.9 Example of a blunt injury with significant fragmentation to the skull.

Chronic Abuse as Commonly Observed in Children and Elders

Chronic abuse and neglect are approached as both the intentional infliction of physical harm and/or the denial of food, medicine, or necessary medical care. Cases of child and elder abuse or neglect are commonly encountered. In cold cases involving the deaths of children or the elderly, establishing patterns of abuse or neglect prior to death can be critical for bringing criminal charges. Therefore, it is important to know the ways in which skeletal remains can help inform about abuse and neglect.

Abuse cases often include multiple injuries that occur over time and so there may be a temporal component to injuries. In other words, there may be numerous healed injuries as well as those that contributed to the cause of death. Such examples include a wide selection of any possible trauma form, injuries in various stages of healing, and pathological and nutritional conditions arising from malnutrition. Malnutrition and vitamin deficiencies leave specific markers on bone that can be seen by examining the bone directly and through radiographic methods that enable the evaluation of trabecular bone or generalized bone density. Skeletal manifestations of abuse and neglect can include multiple fractures in various stages of healing, nutritional deficiencies, malnutrition or starvation, untreated medical conditions, failure to thrive, or insufficient dental care.

Understanding Hyoid Fractures

In cases of manual strangulation, the hyoid is often analyzed for evidence of trauma. Examination of the hyoid becomes especially important in cases where skeletal remains are found and were dumped as often seen among female homicide victims. In those contexts, many have been strangled. Careful excavation of the scene can lead to good recovery, including the hyoid, if done properly. In such cases, it is important to consider that the ossification of the hyoid bone occurs slowly over time and is more likely to fracture when fused. The bone forms from three separate parts in young adults and may fuse into one bone later in life. As the greater cornua fuses with the hyoid body, the chances of traumatic injuries increase (Pollanen & Chiasson 1996). The challenge for investigators is that wide variation exists in the unilateral and bilateral fusion patterns of the hyoid bone. Unilateral fusion has been observed as early as 8 years of age, while the earliest bilateral fusion for the hyoid was reportedly visible in a 23-year-old. In some cases, the hyoid bones never fuse; therefore, asking questions at autopsy is imperative for understanding what if any effect strangulation may have had in producing fractures when present.

Anthropological Methods for the Crime Scene

Forensic anthropologists contribute to law enforcement investigations at the scene in several ways. In some cases, anthropologists are called to help search for a clandestine burial, using a combination of methods such as remote sensing, historic imagery, and archaeological field methods to create a search strategy and/or narrow the search location down to the highest probability areas. From there more specific methods can be used to try and establish whether a burial is present and its boundaries.

Locating Clandestine Burials

In many long-term missing person cases, authorities may obtain information about a possible dump site or burial location based on various leads or tips that need to be searched (Figure 13.10). Although this niche is a small percentage of all homicide investigations, the cases tend to be especially difficult to resolve, highly public, expensive, and rely heavily on forensic anthropologists to assist with remote sensing and archaeological search methods (Table 13.5).

It is also worth pointing out that in many cases where John, Jane, or Baby Doe graves were created when unidentified remains were buried by coroners and medical examiners, the burial plot information is not included in the case files. So a good proportion of the bodies that were buried are now

Figure 13.10 Heavy equipment can be useful for clearing large tracts of land in search of a clandestine burial, so long as a qualified and experienced anthropologist is able to direct the machinery operator and watch for features or changes in the soil stratigraphy to indicate unmarked burials.

missing. Approaching the John Doe grave as a clandestine burial within the cemetery context can provide useful results and the body may be located in spite of a lack of records. Success depends on what is available in terms of a plot map, cemetery records, other historic or case information, and the specific context. If it is a matter of graves shifting over time, something like ground penetrating radar (GPR) may be useful to reestablish the boundaries of a grave or row of graves, but if it's an unmarked grave within a larger cemetery where there are many unmarked burials, it may not be possible to know which grave is the one in question. It is worth nothing that almost every cemetery has unmarked burials, sometimes these represent unidentified human remains, but they also represent unclaimed bodies buried in the county, or older graves in which headstones no longer exist.

Table 13.5 Methods for Locating Clandestine Burials

Discipline	Method Examples	Factors That May Indicate a Burial
Archaeological	Pedestrian survey/line search Landscape topography Probe Shovel testing Soil chemistry Heavy equipment	Evidence of ground disturbance, sunken depression (useful if located in a cemetery but not in the woods or natural landscape) Changes in soil density Changes in soil stratigraphy Changes in pH level, fatty acids, or phosphates Changes in soil stratigraphy
Environmental	Vegetation Entomology Soil staining	More or less vegetation depending on time since death Increased insect activity Staining from body fluids
Geophysical	Ground penetrating radar Metal detector Electromagnetics LIDAR Thermal imaging	Underground disturbances in soil Near surface metal objects Useful for shallow burials/metal objects
Aerial	Aerial photography (present day and historic), GIS site analysis Satellite images	Changes to the landscape Modifications to land use over time such as old roads or absent structures

John/Jane Doe Grave Exhumation

There are many reasons for cold case exhumations—typically it is done to obtain samples needed for the identification of the victim. Other reasons include obtaining DNA of a deceased offender or suspect, re-evaluation of trauma analysis for the victim, the documentation and visualization of injuries, or to answer other questions about equivocal deaths or a questionable manner of death.

It is not uncommon to exhume numerous graves to locate the correct body in cases where graves are misaligned or burial information is incomplete. Remote sensing such as GPR can be very useful for determining the location and boundaries of burials within existing cemeteries. As a rule, expect remains to be very well preserved due to embalming, the use of body bags, and that processing in a wet lab or morgue will need to occur prior to analysis of the bones themselves (Figures 13.11 and 13.12). Table 13.6 provides a checklist for investigators preparing for an exhumation. Other best practices recommendations include the following:

- Radiograph and photograph human remains prior to processing.
- Cut DNA samples prior to processing or cleaning to avoid damaging samples through washing or heat.

Figure 13.11 The excavation of human remains from a single sub-surface burial. Note the "step-like" feature on the right side of the image. Excavation methods included using a flat shovel to remove the layer of topsoil, then trowels were used to hand excavate the feature. This is what created the step-like appearance of the grave. The burial feature was identified by a stain in the soil. The anthropologists used the method known as *excavating the feature* to follow the original burial outline. The pit in which the body was placed was roughly oval shape. By removing only the soil that was backfilled into the grave, careful excavation revealed the original outline of the burial and tool marks. This method is very different from how most crime scene technicians are taught to excavate through police training, where establishing a grid and excavating within each unit is the commonly used method. In this case, using the grid method would have obliterated the original burial shape and tool marks.

- Use only hot water, dish detergent, and non-corrosive elements for processing.
- Do not overheat the remains during processing.
- Process each hand and foot separately to maintain anatomical association of corresponding phalanges.

Public Engagement

A victim-centered approach to cold case investigations utilizes public engagement. Raising public consciousness about the problem of unsolved violent crimes, including homicides, sexual assaults, and the long-term missing persons and

Figure 13.12 Example of tomb filled with water and the coroner's body bag exposed for the exhumation of a Jane Doe.

Table 13.6 Checklist for Cemetery Exhumation

1. Obtain a court order for exhumation and the necessary burial and transport permits.
2. If the grave is not marked, obtain copy of plot map and burial log from funeral home and/or cemetery company to have on hand at the time of exhumation.

(Continued)

Table 13.6 (*Continued*) Checklist for Cemetery Exhumation

3. The initial removal of topsoil can be completed with the use of heavy equipment. Equipment may also be needed if there is a vault and/or modern casket.
4. Have a plan in place for what will be done with the burial plot and coffin hardware and/or vault lid. Will the remains be reburied?
5. Bring copies of the original crime scene photographs, autopsy, crime scene reports, and photographs to ensure that the body exhumed is the current individual. A graveside comparison is to ensure the right body is exhumed.
6. Wet vacuums are often needed for water removal in cases with a concrete vault.
7. John/Jane Does in the United States are typically buried in a body bag, which may have been placed in a casket or coffin of varied types (i.e., metal, particle board, wood, etc.).
8. Establish ahead of time if the remains were embalmed, and type of burial container. But expect surprises, burial records are rarely accurate.

unidentified human remains, provokes action toward helping to solve more cases. Public engagement through the media, public events for families of the missing, and DNA drives help advocate for the victims and their families. Although it may feel intrinsically odd for criminal investigators to share information, there is always a part of the victim's story, and the hurdles investigators are facing that can be shared. The USF-FAL has offered one or more of these events annually since 2015 and each one has resulted in one or more cases getting resolved. It is recommended that agencies work in collaboration with one another and other partners in this area to reach out to the public, especially in cases involving unidentified human remains and missing persons (Figures 13.13 and 13.14).

The Art of Forensics

Forensic art can play a vital role in sharing the face of an unknown person, their clothing, jewelry, or other artifacts about a story with the public. In cases of missing persons and unidentified human remains, it is imperative that the public engage with investigators to file a missing person report, share DNA reference samples, and help identify those who are unknown. The purpose of forensic art is to trigger memory, through a likeness of what the person may have looked like based on their skeletal anatomy and other contextual variables such as their clothing and the context in which they are found.

Facial reconstructions or approximations may be created through a variety of techniques, including clay reconstructions, drawings and illustrations, or digital composites. These images may be based on postmortem or autopsy photographs or reconstructed from skeletal remains. Information generated for the biological profile (sex, age, ancestry, stature, and build) is used

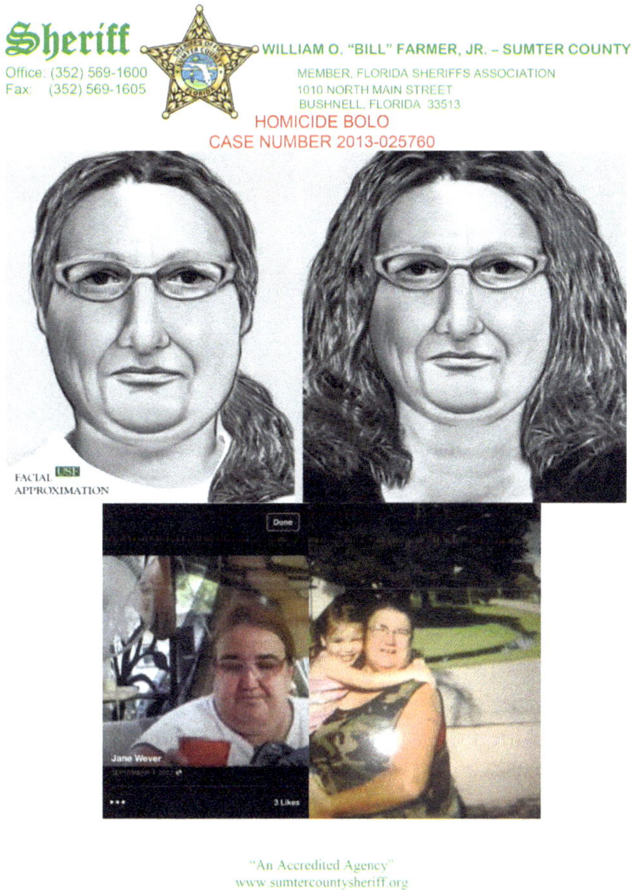

Figure 13.13 This is an updated law enforcement BOLO created when Jane Doe was identified. The image shows the facial reconstructions created from skeletal remains, utilizing pictures of the actual clothing and eyeglasses recovered at the scene. The image was created through drawing a digital composite by the author of this chapter. Actual photographs of the identified victim are also shown next to the reconstructions. In this case, her family recognized the image put out to the public through media releases and online and called authorities.

in combination with the unique bony architecture of the skull. Photographic reconstructions of clothing, jewelry, artifacts, or teeth are also possible and recommended as the more that can be shared, the chance that someone recognizes some element of the individual or their story increases.

Ancestry estimation based on cranial bones and combined with contextual information about mobility, birth origins, and burial factors creates an integrated biological profile of the decedent. Using these data combined with images of the skull, a facial reconstruction or approximation can be completed for public viewing. These images are given to law enforcement.

Figure 13.14 Example of unidentified persons cases featured at the 2023 Missing in Florida Day hosted by USF-FAL in Tampa, Florida.

The images are shown to the public through police bulletins and press releases. Forensic imaging such as facial approximations is not used for positive identification of the victim, but rather to create a likeness of the individual which should help trigger the memory of a family member or witness who may recognize the photograph. The recognition of even one facial feature can trigger memory and thereby lead witnesses to come forward and provide law enforcement agencies with new information about a case.

The *Art of Forensics* first developed as a program organized by USF-FAL in 2015 for professional artists and anthropologists to learn how to create facial reconstructions of unknown homicide victims, using actual open cases to aid in their investigation. Following the success of teaching methods to aspiring new artists using actual cases, it was decided to create an event combining art and science to try and identify more of the Jane and John Doe cases. This workshop grew into a series of annual events that to date has featured 75+ cases, with many successfully identified. Another important outcome of this programming is that it has helped change the dialogue about the marginalization of many victims and their families among partnering agencies. The events are designed to engage the public to learn about the problem of the missing, for families to have safe access to report missing loved ones and provide DNA samples for identification, and to solve more cases so that unknown remains can be returned to families of the missing.

Missing Persons' Days

Many states have begun to adapt some form of a *Missing Person's Day.* While each event and jurisdiction run their programming a little bit differently, the common goal is to host a DNA drive to obtain more family reference

DNA samples for comparison to unknown persons, and to raise awareness about the problem of missing persons. Typically, it is a day-long event where the public is invited to attend. It is a great event to boost the relationship among law enforcement with diverse communities that are most affected by violent crime. The events that the USF-FAL hosted were unlike other "missing person" events in Florida because they were focused on entering new case reports and reaching those who have fallen through the cracks in the system over the years. In later years, we also combined the *Art of Forensics Event* with the *Missing in Florida Day*. For these events, partnering law enforcement agencies from around the state came together to help collect new case information from anyone who wanted to report it. This included some individuals who even flew from out of state to report missing loved ones, because agencies in their area were unable to assist them. In such cases, the local agency may not have jurisdiction or believe that the person went missing within their jurisdiction. During these public events, no one is turned away, rather another police agency takes the report as an agency assist. The participating law enforcement agencies later followed up with the correct jurisdictions to ensure a smooth transition of the case to the appropriate authorities, but because the problem of jurisdiction has been one of the greatest obstacles in past cases, these events are designed to help victims and their families circumvent this common problem. Collectively, the goals of the event were to:

- Educate the public about the problem of missing and unidentified persons.
- Share prevention measures and resources for families of the missing and the medico-legal community.
- Highlight and feature long-term unidentified human remains cases with facial reconstructions.
- Families were encouraged to attend so DNA reference samples could be collected, as well as other identifiers or biological data about the missing person such as dental records, fingerprints, and photographs.
- The public was encouraged to file missing person reports and law enforcement is on hand to facilitate this, so that jurisdiction is not a barrier for families to find support.
- Media attention brought new light to many long-term cases.
- Victims and families were given a platform to interact and connect with the medico-legal community, which is otherwise a very closed system to them.
- Families were offered a private meeting/support group where they could express the unique pain of having a missing loved one.
- Law enforcement provided educational information on missing persons and the issues surrounding featured cases.

Conclusion

Forensic anthropology contributes to homicide and cold case investigations in a myriad of ways that are becoming more routine. Many jurisdictions do not have access to a FAL, and as a result, many of the larger programs across the country, such as USF-FAL, provide technical assistance nationwide. Forensic anthropology services range from the crime scene to the laboratory. Increasingly, public engagement efforts among collaborating agencies are also utilizing the unique role and skill sets that anthropologists can provide when working with diverse and marginalized communities. Forensic anthropology is an applied science that brings a lot of tools and methods into modern criminal investigations. This chapter discussed the need for establishing cold case investigative models and working protocols that include scientific experts such as anthropologists and how analyzing older cases as if starting at the beginning can be crucial for adding new methods and technologies where innovation and science have progressed. *Bringing the case up to current investigative standards* means questioning everything that was done prior and past conclusions, including the cause and manner of death in some cases. This methodology and cold case protocol has resulted in many successful outcomes including human identification, the repatriation of long-term missing persons, and homicide convictions in cases that had been open for decades.

References

Bass, W.M. 1997. Outdoor decomposition rates in Tennessee. In Haglund, W. D. and Sorg, M. H. (Eds.). *Forensic taphonomy: the postmortem fate of human remains.* Boca Raton, FL: CRC Press, pp. 181–186.

Clark, M.A., Worrell, M.B., and Pless, J.E. 1997. Postmortem changes in soft tissues. In Haglund, W. D. and Sorg, M. H. (Eds.). *Forensic taphonomy: the postmortem fate of human remains.* Boca Raton, FL: CRC Press, pp. 151–164.

Davis, R.C., Jensen, C., and Kitchens, K.E. 2011. *Cold case investigations: an analysis of current practices and factors associated with successful outcomes.* Santa Monica, CA: RAND Center on Quality Policing. National Institute of Justice.

Galloway, A., Birkby, W.H., Jones, A.M., Henry, T.E., and Parks, B.O. 1989. Decay rates of human remains in an arid environment. *J. Forensic Sci.* 34(3): 607–616.

Kimmerle, E.H. and Baraybar, J.P. 2008. *Skeletal trauma: identification of injuries resulting from human rights abuse and armed conflict.* Boca Raton, FL: CRC Press, 493 pp.

Meier-Augenstein, W. 2018. *Stable isotope forensics: methods and forensic applications of stable isotope analysis.* Chichester, UK: John Wiley & Sons, 512 pp.

Pollanen, M. S., & Chiasson, D. A. (1996). Fracture of the hyoid bone in strangulation. *J. Forensic Sci.* 41(1), 110–114.

Ritter, N. 2007. Missing persons and unidentified remains: the nation's silent mass disaster. *Natl. Justice J.* 256(7): 2–7.

Vass, A.A., Bass, W.M., Wolt, J.D., Foss, J.E., and Ammons, J.T. 1992. Time since death determinations of human cadavers using soil solution. *J. Forensic Sci.* 37(5): 1236–1253.

14 Forensic Dentistry

NORMAN D. SPERBER AND
ANTHONY R. CARDOZA

Introduction

Cold cases are solved using a variety of means and methods. Modern technological developments are a leading factor, especially in the area of genetics (DNA). The discipline of forensic odontology (forensic dentistry) can assist cold case homicide investigators in a variety of situations. This chapter presents the practical use of forensic odontology in cold case homicide investigation through its use in the identification process and the role of bite mark analysis.

Dental Identification

Since approximately 1980, several advances have occurred in this field. The states of California, Texas, and Washington developed data processing that linked missing persons' *dental* information with that of unidentified deceased individuals, including unidentified living persons. Comparisons with *reported missing individuals* eliminated the necessity for impractical, expensive, and complex procedures, which would have required the entry of dental information from *all* living persons. Following California's success in the positive identification of dozens of individuals employing a central clearinghouse supervised by the Department of Justice, Sacramento, Missing and Unidentified Unit, the U.S. government developed a computerized dental identification system through the National Crime Information Center (NCIC) for the identification of human remains. Dr. Irvin Sopher has excellently addressed the rationale for dental identification as follows:

> The individuality or specificity of the dentition is based upon the multiple points of comparison inherent in a variable combination of events, which alter the status of a given set of thirty-two teeth, each comprising five anatomic surfaces. Such events include (1) hereditary, congenital, or developmental alterations; (2) acquired, natural, or traumatic alterations; (3) the presence or absence in multiple combinations of one, many, or most of the thirty-two units; and (4) the combinations and permutations in the variable construction, constitution, and morphology of a various array of restorable procedures, materials, and prosthetic devices employed by the dental profession. In addition, the innumerable features of the dental and jaw structure, as revealed by the

 DOI: 10.4324/9781003415633-17

roentgenogram, further enhance the criterion of individuality. The instance where chronologic age exercises a role in the identification, the added dimension of time and its effect on the teeth is introduced as a measurable criterion.

More concisely put, the presence of 160 available dental surfaces (32 teeth times 5 surfaces) subject to alteration by decay and restoration, the latter process including numerous materials of varying shape and size, as well as the innumerable combinations of one or more missing teeth at variable locations, impart uniqueness or specificity to the dental medium.

Indeed, a basic premise of dental identification is that no two mouths are identical. Theoretically, this may represent a true statement; however, in actuality the reliability of this statement depends upon the number of points of specificity available for the comparison between the ante-mortem and the post-mortem data in any particular case. The greater the number of quantitative and qualitative points of comparison, the more reliable is the comparison and the more nearly one approaches the axiom. Computer models have shown that there are more than 2.5 million possibilities in charting the human mouth. Much effort is currently being expended in evaluating the efficacy of computerized dental charts as a means of classifying mass identification data.

(Sopher 1976, p. 58)

Cold Case Identification of Unknown Persons through Dental X-Rays

Positive identification of an individual who cannot be recognized by the usual means, such as viewing the body, fingerprints, scars, marks, tattoos, personal possessions, or identification papers, is often successfully accomplished through dental means. The dentition (teeth, soft tissue, and the supporting bone) is unique for every individual. This identification can be accomplished years, even decades, after death (Figure 14.1).

Dental records usually denote X-rays and written records. These records are now typically created and stored electronically, so the term *written* will be used versus *electronic*. Since written records are sometimes inaccurate, most experts in the field will agree that X-rays are by far the most important and reliable method because they readily demonstrate the morphology (shape) of existing restorations (fillings) or crowns, fixed bridges, root canal procedures, implants, and missing teeth (Figure 14.2). In addition, forensic dentists can observe the shape of the roots, the shape of the crowns (portion of the tooth visible above the gingiva [gum]), the relationship of the roots to anatomical landmarks such as the maxillary sinus to adjacent teeth, as well as the shape of the nutrient canals (trabecular bone patterns) within the jawbones. These relationships become exceptionally important when an individual has no dental restorations in place. In some states, labeling of removable full

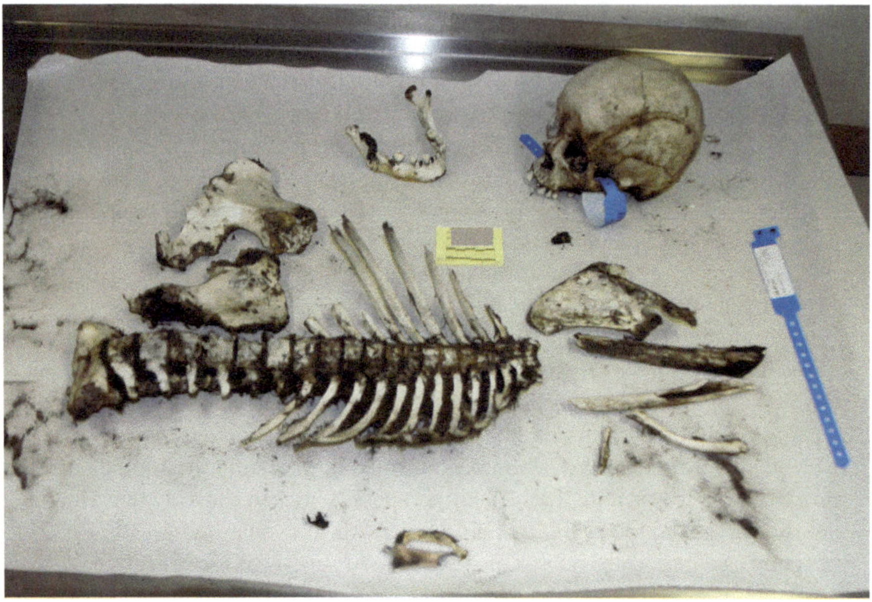

Figure 14.1 Skeletonized remains of a John Doe. (Courtesy of Dr. Anthony R. Cardoza.)

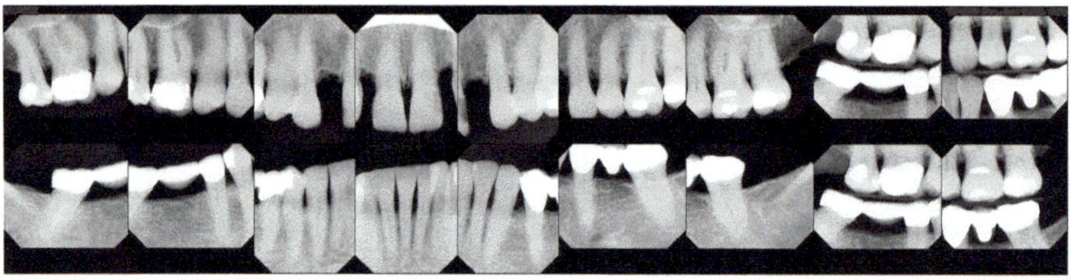

Figure 14.2 Postmortem full-mouth dental radiographs. (Courtesy of Dr. Anthony R. Cardoza.)

dentures and partial dentures is required. However, an unmarked denture found near a body can be linked to the body if the forensic dentist is convinced that the denture "fits" in all respects. This facet can be determined if little or no decomposition has occurred (Figure 14.3).

If the identification of the decedent is unknown in a cold case investigation, several steps can be considered by the investigator(s):

1. Have dental records been created (full-mouth X-rays of all remaining teeth)?
2. What agency (federal, state, or local) has custody of said X-rays?
3. If this evidence has not been collected, is exhumation of the body possible, or has the body been cremated?

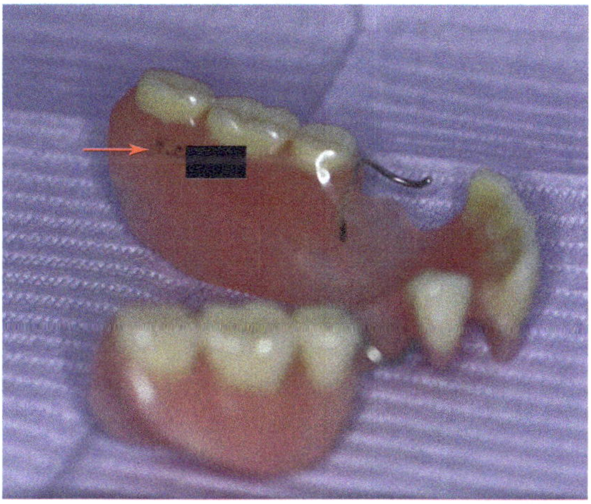

Figure 14.3 Mandibular partial denture recovered on an unidentified decedent. The denture led to the identification of the individual. (Courtesy of Dr. Anthony R. Cardoza.)

4. If the dental X-rays exist, has the information therein *been distributed to local, state, or federal systems*?
5. Have there been recent submissions or inquiries to the agencies listed previously?
6. Are there existing antemortem X-rays in the possession of investigators?
7. If antemortem and postmortem records are available, has a certified forensic dentist compared them? A list of such individuals is available online by visiting the website of the American Board of Forensic Odontology.

Thus, when case circumstances are such that investigators have an unknown decedent with dentition (teeth present), check with the following:

1. Your state coroner's office or state medical examiner's office if there is such an agency.
2. In California, the Department of Justice's Missing and Unidentified Persons System (MUPS), which includes the Unidentified Persons System (UPS) and the Missing Persons System (MPS). Their telephone number is 916-227-3290.
3. Federal Bureau of Investigation (FBI)/NCIC (unidentified dental files established in 1983, updated in 2004).
4. National Dental Image/Information Repository (NDIR), established in 2006.
5. National Missing and Unidentified Persons System (NamUs), established in 2007.

Possible Sources for Antemortem X-Rays

1. Private dental sources (private dental offices, dental schools)
2. Union sources if the employment of the individual is known
3. Insurance companies
4. Federal sources (military records, NCIC, NamUs, NDIR)
5. Custodial (prisons or jails)

NCIC Missing Person and Unidentified Person Files

Cold case investigations may be stalled, often for years, due to the inability to recover the body and learn what it can tell us. Cases that begin as a missing-persons report not uncommonly become a homicide case, but until the body is located, the case may languish in a state of limbo. Sadly, this is all too common for reported missing children. Not infrequently, bodies or their parts may repose in the medical examiner's office in one jurisdiction and other parts from the same body in the coroner's office in another jurisdiction.

In an effort to unite information between those agencies that recover unidentified bodies or body parts and those agencies that hold missing-persons reports, the NCIC has set up a system for data entry by these agencies in efforts to obtain a match between the two databases. This may offer a significant resource to cold case investigators. However, investigators are reminded that the information in the computer is only as reliable and accurate as what was entered into the data system. The system is not perfect. If information is miscoded on the entry forms, or if erroneous information due to error on the part of the person filling out the forms occurs, a match between these two databases may not occur.

NCIC Missing Person File

This file inputs data through a Missing Person Packet. Entry of a missing person into this index is accomplished by the completion of a form and its submission to NCIC by the responsible agency. This packet seeks information that includes

- Initial report completed by the reporting officer and entered into NCIC immediately.
- Personal descriptors. Information completed by parent, legal guardian, or next of kin and returned to the police agency that completed the initial report.
- Jewelry description.
- Medical/optical information.
- Medical release forms.

See Figures 14.4 and 14.5.

NCIC Missing Person File
Data Collection Entry Guide

Agency Case #________________

NCIC Initial Entry Report

Message Key **(MKE)** (*See Categories, page 2*) Disability (EMD) · Catastrophe Victim (EMV) · Other (EMO) Juvenile (EMJ) · Involuntary (EMI) Endangered (EME) · Caution	Date Reporting Agency **(ORI)**
Name of Missing Person **(NAM)**	Sex **(SEX)** Male (M) Female (F)
Aliases	
Race **(RAC)** Asian or Pacific Islander (A) · American Indian/Alaskan Native (I) · Black (B) · White (W) · Unknown (U)	Place of Birth **(POB)** · Date of Birth **(DOB)**
Date of Emancipation **(DOE)** · Height **(HGT)** · Weight **(WGT)**	Eye Color **(EYE)** Black (BLK) · Blue (BLU) · Brown (BRO) · Gray (GRY) · Green (GRN) · Hazel (HAZ) · Maroon (MAR) · Pink (PNK) · Unknown (XXX) · Multicolored (MUL)
Hair Color **(HAI)** Brown (BRO) · Black (BLK) · White (WHT) · Sandy (SDY) · Gray or Partially Gray (GRY) · Red/Auburn (RED) · Blond/Strawberry (BLN) · Blue (BLU) · Green (GRE) · Orange (ONG) · Pink (PNK) · Purple (PLE) · Unknown or Completely Bald (XXX)	FBI Number **(FBI)**
Skin Tone **(SKN)** Albino (ALB) · Black (BLK) · Dark (DRK) · Yellow (YEL) · Dk. Brown (DBR) · Fair (FAR) · Light (LGT) · Lt. Brown (LBR) · Medium (MED) · Medium Brown (MBR) · Olive (OLV) · Ruddy (RUD) · Sallow (SAL)	Scars, Marks, Tattoos, and Other Characteristics **(SMT)** (*See Checklist, page 8*)
Has the missing person ever been fingerprinted? No · Yes, by whom?________ · Other Identifying Numbers **(MNU)**	
Fingerprint Classification **(FPC)***	
Social Security Number **(SOC)** · Operator's License Number **(OLN)**	Operator's License State **(OLS)** · License Expiration **(OLY)**
Missing Person **(MNP)** Missing Person (MP) · Catastrophe Victim (DV) · Child Abduction (CA) · AMBER Alert (AA) · Date of Last Contact **(DLC)**	Originating Agency Case Number **(OCA)**
Miscellaneous **(MIS)** Information such as build, handedness, any illness or diseases, clothing description, hair description, should be included. If more space is needed, attach additional sheet.**	Missing Person Circumstances **(MPC)** Abducted By Stranger (S) · Runaway (R) · Abducted By Non-custodial Parent (N)
License Plate Number **(LIC)** · State **(LIS)** · Year Expires **(LIY)**	License Plate Type **(LIT)**
Vehicle Identification Number **(VIN)**	Year **(VYR)**
Make **(VMA)** · Model **(VMO)** · Style **(VST)**	Color **(VCO)**

Rev 2/06 * Fingerprints, if available, may be submitted electronically via the CJIS Wide Area Network or in hard copy to the FBI, CJIS Division, Post Office Box 4142, Clarksburg, West Virginia 26302-9929.
** All dental information should be recorded on the NCIC Missing Person Dental Report and entered into NCIC as supplemental information. 4

Figure 14.4 NCIC initial entry form, missing persons, page 1. (Courtesy of Dr. Anthony R. Cardoza.)

In addition, a list of personal descriptors is offered to investigators to further define a missing person. These descriptors include:

- Artificial body parts and legs
- Eye disorders
- Deafness
- Deformities

NCIC Missing Person File
Data Collection Entry Guide

Agency Case #________________

Caution and Medical Conditions **(CMC)**

Code	Description	Code	Description	Code	Description
00 ☐	Armed and dangerous	25 ☐	Escape risk	65 ☐	Epilepsy
05 ☐	Violent tendencies	30 ☐	Sexually violent predator - contact ORI for detailed information	70 ☐	Suicidal
10 ☐	Martial arts expert			80 ☐	Medication required
15 ☐	Explosives expertise	50 ☐	Heart condition	85 ☐	Hemophiliac
20 ☐	Known to abuse drugs	55 ☐	Alcoholic	90 ☐	Diabetic
		60 ☐	Allergies	01 ☐	Other

Has the missing person ever donated blood? **(MIS)** ☐ Yes ☐ No

Blood Type **(BLT)**
☐ A Positive (APOS) ☐ A Negative (ANEG) ☐ A Unknown (AUNK)
☐ B Positive (BPOS) ☐ B Negative (BNEG) ☐ B Unknown (BUNK)
☐ AB Positive (ABPOS) ☐ AB Negative (ABNEG) ☐ AB Unknown (ABUNK)
☐ O Positive (OPOS) ☐ O Negative (ONEG) ☐ O Unknown (OUNK)
☐ Unknown (UNKWN)

Circumcision? **(CRC)** ☐ Was (C) ☐ Was Not (N) ☐ Unknown (U)

Footprints available? **(FPA)** ☐ Yes (Y) ☐ No (N)

Body X-Rays? **(BXR)** ☐ Full (F) ☐ Partial (P) ☐ None (N)

Does the missing person have corrected vision? **(SMT)** ☐ Yes ☐ No ☐ Glasses ☐ Con Lenses

Corrective Vision Prescription **(VRX)**

Jewelry Type **(JWT)** *(See Checklist, page 20)*

Jewelry Description **(JWL)** *(See Checklist, page 20)*

DNA Profile Indicator **(DNA)** ☐ Yes (Y) ☐ No (N)

DNA Location **(DLO)**

Complainant's Name

Complainant's Address

Complainant's Telephone Number

Relationship of Complainant to Missing Person

Missing Person's Occupation **(MIS)**

Missing Person's Address

Close friends/relatives

Places Missing Person Frequented **(MIS)**

Possible destination **(MIS)**

Reporting Officer

Reporting Agency Telephone Number

Investigating Officer and Telephone Number **(MIS)**

Complainant's Signature

Date

NCIC Number **(NIC)**

Rev 2/06 5

Figure 14.5 NCIC initial entry form, missing persons, page 2. (Courtesy of Dr. Anthony R. Cardoza.)

- Fractured bones
- Medical devices
- Missing body parts/organs
- Moles
- Needle or "track" marks
- Other physical characteristics

- Scars, marks, tattoos
- Skin discolorations
- Medical conditions and diseases
- Drugs of abuse
- Therapeutic drugs

Dental History Information

Dental characteristics are a significant feature in the Missing Person File. A packet of forms detailing requested information is provided by NCIC for data entry. The information supplied in this packet is designed to be completed by a *dentist* familiar with the missing person as his/her patient or as a previous patient. The dental report is extremely comprehensive and was designed for entry into the NCIC for comparison with dental data of unidentified individuals. This format has changed over the years, however. While information sought through these descriptors is best supplied by a trained dentist, in some instances, these forms have been filled out by the patrol officer taking a missing-persons report or by investigators. The result has been less than satisfactory in many instances. Certainly, a law enforcement officer, unless he/she is a dentist, should not fill out dental forms. In addition to patient information, information sought includes:

- Date of last patient treatment
- Charting dentist contact information
- Whether X-rays are available
- Date last X-rays were taken
- Whether dental models are available
- Whether photographs of teeth are available
- Whether all 32 teeth are present without decay, restoration, or any unusual characteristics
- Tooth restorations including caries and types of fillings and crowns and combinations
- Dentures/partial dentures and replacement teeth
- Other forensic odontological descriptors

See Figure 14.6.

NCIC Unidentified Person File

The Unidentified Person Packet is used for initial and immediate data entry into the NCIC system. Criteria for entry into the NCIC Unidentified Person File are as follows:

- *Unidentified deceased*: Any unidentified deceased person and/or body parts when a body has been dismembered.

NCIC Missing Person File
Data Collection Entry Guide

Agency Case # ____________

NCIC Missing Person Dental Report

SECTION 1
Patient's Name: ____________ Age at Disappearance: ______ NCIC #: ____________
Completed by: ____________ Date Completed: ____________
Address: ____________
Telephone #: ____________ Email Address: ____________
X-Rays Available? ☐ Yes ☐ No Dental Models Available? ☐ Yes ☐ No Dental Photographs Available? ☐ Yes ☐ No

Section 2 *DENTAL CHARACTERISTICS*

Upper Right		Lower Right
01 (18)____	(Numbers in parentheses represent FDI system.)	32 (48)____
02 (17)____		31 (47)____
03 (16)____		30 (46)____
04 (15)____(A)		29 (45)____(T)
05 (14)____(B)		28 (44)____(S)
06 (13)____(C)		27 (43)____(R)
07 (12)____(D)		26 (42)____(Q)
08 (11)____(E)		25 (41)____(P)
Upper Left	(Letters in parentheses represent deciduous dentition.)	**Lower Left**
09 (21)____(F)		24 (31)____(O)
10 (22)____(G)		23 (32)____(N)
11 (23)____(H)		22 (33)____(M)
12 (24)____(I)		21 (34)____(L)
13 (25)____(J)		20 (35)____(K)
14 (26)____		19 (36)____
15 (27)____		18 (37)____
16 (28)____		17 (38)____

SECTION 3 *DENTAL CODES*

X = Tooth has been removed or did not develop
V = Tooth is unrestored or no information (Default Code)
M = Mesial Surface Restored
O = Occlusal/Incisal Surface Restored
D = Distal Surface Restored
F = Facial or Buccal Surface Restored
L = Lingual Surface Restored
C = Lab Processed or Prefabricated Restoration
R = Endodontic Treatment
/ = Tooth present but clinical crown missing (i.e., fractured)*

(*The codes V and / are used differently in the Missing Person Dental Report than in the Unidentified Person Dental Report.)

SECTION 4 *DENTAL REMARKS*

☐ **ALL** (All 32 teeth are present and unrestored) ☐ **UNK** (No dental information available)

(Rev 11/08) 30

Figure 14.6 NCIC missing-persons dental report form. (Courtesy of Dr. Anthony R. Cardoza.)

- *Unidentified living person*: A living person of any age who is unable to ascertain his/her identity. This can include those with amnesia, victims, infants, etc. There may be consent issues involved in this category.
- *Unidentified catastrophe victim*: Any unidentified victim or body parts dismembered as a result of a disaster.

See Figures 14.7 and 14.8.

NCIC Unidentified Person File
Data Collection Entry Guide

Agency Case #________________

NCIC Initial Entry Report

Message Key **(MKE)** *(See Categories, page 2)*
☐ Unidentified Deceased (EUD) ☐ Unidentified Living (EUL)
☐ Unidentified Catastrophe Victim (EUV)

Date

Reporting Agency **(ORI)**

Body Parts Status **(BPS)**
☐ All 15 parts recovered - fresh **(ALF)**
☐ All 15 parts recovered - decomposed **(ALD)**
☐ All 15 parts recovered - skeletal **(SKL)**

Body Parts Status **(BPS)** if incomplete body or skeleton, see body diagram page 7 for coding corresponding parts
N - Not Recovered D - Recovered Decomposed F - Recovered Fresh S - Skeletal
☐ ☐ ☐ ☐ ☐ ☐ ☐ ☐ ☐ ☐ ☐ ☐ ☐ ☐ ☐
1 2 3 4 5 6 7 8 9 10 11 12 13 14 15

Sex **(SEX)**
☐ Male (M) ☐ Female (F)
☐ Unknown (U)

Race **(RAC)**
☐ Asian or Pacific Islander (A) ☐ American Indian/Alaskan Native (I) ☐ Unknown (U)
☐ Black (B) ☐ White (W)

Estimated Year of Birth Range **(EYB)** ☐☐☐☐-☐☐☐☐

Estimated Date of Death **(EDD)** ☐☐-☐☐-☐☐☐☐

Date Body Found **(DBF)** ☐☐-☐☐-☐☐☐☐

Approximate Height Range **(HGT)** ☐☐☐-☐☐☐

Approximate Weight Range **(WGT)** ☐☐☐-☐☐☐

Eye Color **(EYE)**
☐ Black (BLK) ☐ Green (GRN) ☐ Unknown (XXX)
☐ Blue (BLU) ☐ Hazel (HAZ) Multicolored (MUL)
☐ Brown (BRO) ☐ Maroon (MAR)
☐ Gray (GRY) Pink (PNK)

Hair Color **(HAI)**
☐ Brown (BRO) ☐ Sandy (SDY) ☐ Blue (BLU) ☐ Purple (PLE)
☐ Black (BLK) ☐ Gray or Partially Gray (GRY) Green (GRE) ☐ Unknown or
☐ White (WHT) ☐ Red/Auburn (RED) Orange (ONG) Completely Bald
Blond/Strawberry (BLN) Pink (PNK) (XXX)

Scars, Marks, Tattoos, and other Characteristics **(SMT)** *(See Checklist, page 8)*

Fingerprint Classification **(FPC)***
☐ ☐ ☐ ☐ ☐
☐ ☐ ☐ ☐ ☐

Originating Agency Case Number **(OCA)**

Miscellaneous **(MIS)** Information such as build, handedness, clothing description, hair description, weather conditions at the time of death, place where the individual was found, should be included. If more space is needed, attach additional sheet.**

* Fingerprints, if available, may be submitted electronically via the CJIS Wide Area Network or in hard copy to the FBI, CJIS Division, Post Office Box 4142, Clarksburg, West Virginia 26302-9929.
** All dental information should be recorded on the NCIC Unidentified Person Dental Report and entered into NCIC as supplemental information.

Rev 2/06 4

Figure 14./ NCIC initial entry form, unidentified persons, page 1. (Courtesy of Dr. Anthony R. Cardoza.)

Antemortem personal descriptors in this file include those designed to correspond to the MPS, including:

- Artificial body parts and aids
- Eye disorders
- Deafness
- Deformities

NCIC Unidentified Person File
Data Collection Entry Guide

Agency Case #________________

Blood Type **(BLT)**

A Positive (APOS)	B Positive (BPOS)	AB Positive (ABPOS)	O Positive (OPOS)	Unknown (UNKWN)
A Negative (ANEG)	B Negative (BNEG)	AB Negative (ABNEG)	O Negative (ONEG)	
A Unknown (AUNK)	B Unknown (BUNK)	AB Unknown (ABUNK)	O Unknown (OUNK)	

Circumcision? **(CRC)**	Footprints available? **(FPA)**	Body X-Rays available? **(BXR)**	Does the Unidentified Person have corrected vision? **(SMT)**	Corrective Vision Prescription **(VRX)**
Was	Yes	Full (F)	Yes ☐ Glasses	
Was Not	No	Partial (P)	No ☐ Con Lenses	
Unknown		None (N)		

Manner and cause of Death **(CDA)**	Describe
Natural Causes (N) Suicide (S) Accidental (A) Unknown (U) Homicide (H)	

Jewelry Type **(JWT)** *(See Checklist, page 20)*	Jewelry Description **(JWL)** *(See Checklist, page 20)*

DNA Profile Indicator **(DNA)**	DNA Location **(DLO)**
Yes No	

Medical Examiner/Coroner Agency Name and Case Number **(MAN)**	Medical Examiner/Coroner Locality **(MAL)**
Medical Examiner/Coroner Telephone Number **(MAT)**	Investigating Officer and Telephone Number **(MIS)**
NCIC Number **(NIC)**	

Rev 2/06 5

Figure 14.8 NCIC initial entry form, unidentified persons, page 2. (Courtesy of Dr. Anthony R. Cardoza.)

- Fractured bones
- Medical devices
- Missing body parts/organs
- Moles
- Needle track marks

- Other physical characteristics
- Scars
- Tattoos
- Skin discoloration
- Medical conditions and diseases
- Drugs of abuse
- Therapeutic drugs
- Jewelry type
- Optic information

Dental information includes:

- Coroner/medical examiner case number
- Charting dentist's name and address
- Whether X-rays are available
- Date last X-rays were taken
- Whether dental models are available
- Whether photographs of teeth are available
- Whether all 32 teeth are present without decay, restoration, or any unusual characteristics
- Tooth restoration including caries and types of fillings and crowns and restorations
- Dentures/partial dentures and replacement teeth
- Other forensic odontological descriptors

See Figure 14.9.

National Dental Image Repository

NDIR is a supplement to NCIC to be used by forensic dentists. It is found on the Law Enforcement Online (LEO) CJIS website, and it contains the missing/unidentified (MUP) wanted-person form, the digitized copy of the NCIC record, the digitized copy of the dental condition worksheet, and the digitized dental radiographs.

National Missing and Unidentified Persons System

NamUs was created in 2007 as the first online repository for missing persons and unidentified remains when the National Missing Persons Task Force, through the National Institute of Justice, identified the need to improve access to database information by people who can help solve cases of missing

NCIC Unidentified Person File
Data Collection Entry Guide

Agency Case # ______________

NCIC Unidentified Person Dental Report

SECTION 1

ME/Coroner Case #: ______________ NCIC #: ______________

Completed by: ______________ Date Completed: ______________

Address: ______________

Telephone #: ______________ Email Address: ______________

X-Rays Available? ☐ Yes ☐ No Dental Models Available? ☐ Yes ☐ No Dental Photographs Available? ☐ Yes ☐ No

SECTION 2 ***DENTAL CHARACTERISTICS***

Upper Right		**Lower Right**
01 (18) ______		32 (48) ______
02 (17) ______		31 (47) ______
03 (16) ______		30 (46) ______
04 (15) ______ (A)	(Numbers in parentheses represent FDI System.)	29 (45) ______ (T)
05 (14) ______ (B)		28 (44) ______ (S)
06 (13) ______ (C)		27 (43) ______ (R)
07 (12) ______ (D)		26 (42) ______ (Q)
08 (11) ______ (E)		25 (41) ______ (P)
Upper Left		**Lower Left**
09 (21) ______ (F)	(Letters in parentheses represent deciduous dentition.)	24 (31) ______ (O)
10 (22) ______ (G)		23 (32) ______ (N)
11 (23) ______ (H)		22 (33) ______ (M)
12 (24) ______ (I)		21 (34) ______ (L)
13 (25) ______ (J)		20 (35) ______ (K)
14 (26) ______		19 (36) ______
15 (27) ______		18 (37) ______
16 (28) ______		17 (38) ______

SECTION 3 ***DENTAL CODES***

X = Tooth has been removed or did not develop
V = Tooth is present and unrestored
M = Mesial Surface Restored
O = Occlusal/Incisal Surface Restored
D = Distal Surface Restored
F = Facial or Buccal Surface Restored
L = Lingual Surface Restored
C = Lab Processed or Prefabricated Restoration
R = Endodontic Treatment
/ = Postmortem Missing or Not Recovered (Default Code)

(*The codes V and /are used differently in the Unidentified Person Report than in the Missing Person Dental Report.)

SECTION 4 ***DENTAL REMARKS***

☐ **ALL** (All 32 teeth are present and unrestored) ☐ **UNK** (No dental information available)

Rev 2/06 30

Figure 14.9 NCIC unidentified-persons dental report form. (Courtesy of Dr. Anthony R. Cardoza.)

and unidentified deceased persons. It brings together two innovative programs and their online, searchable databases: https://namus.nij.ojp.gov/ (for information on unidentified human remains) and http://www.findthemissing.org (for information on missing persons). NamUs allows the general public to actively participate in providing access to resources, information, and nationwide tools for missing adults (Figure 14.10).

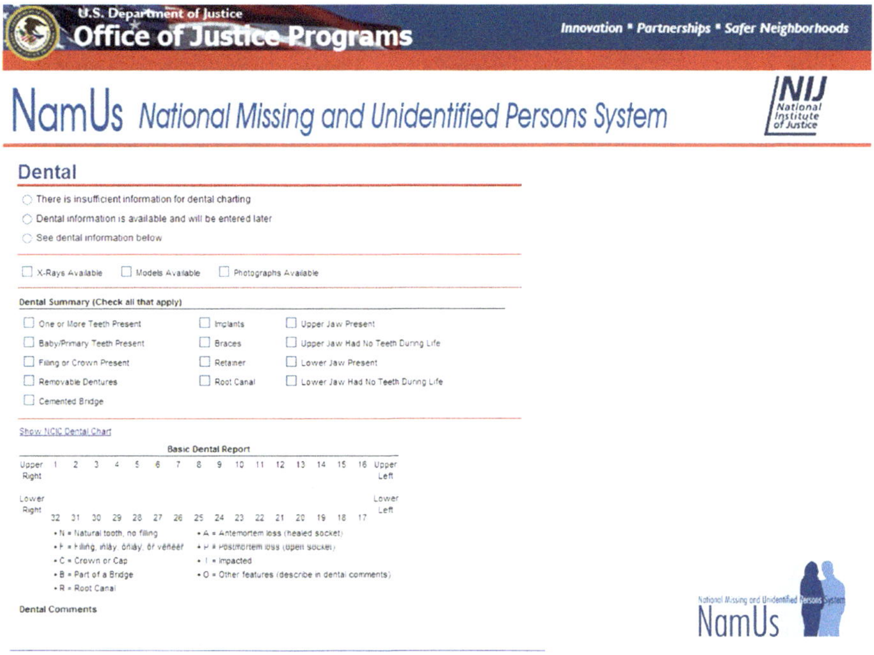
U.S. Department of Justice
Office of Justice Programs
Innovation • Partnerships • Safer Neighborhoods

NamUs National Missing and Unidentified Persons System

NIJ National Institute of Justice

Dental

- ○ There is insufficient information for dental charting
- ○ Dental information is available and will be entered later
- ○ See dental information below

☐ X-Rays Available ☐ Models Available ☐ Photographs Available

Dental Summary (Check all that apply)

☐ One or More Teeth Present	☐ Implants	☐ Upper Jaw Present
☐ Baby/Primary Teeth Present	☐ Braces	☐ Upper Jaw Had No Teeth During Life
☐ Filling or Crown Present	☐ Retainer	☐ Lower Jaw Present
☐ Removable Dentures	☐ Root Canal	☐ Lower Jaw Had No Teeth During Life
☐ Cemented Bridge		

Show NCIC Dental Chart

Basic Dental Report

Upper Right	1	2	3	4	5	6	7	8	9	10	11	12	13	14	15	16	Upper Left
Lower Right	32	31	30	29	28	27	26	25	24	23	22	21	20	19	18	17	Lower Left

- N = Natural tooth, no filling
- F = Filling, inlay, onlay, or veneer
- C = Crown or Cap
- B = Part of a Bridge
- R = Root Canal
- A = Antemortem loss (healed socket)
- P = Postmortem loss (open socket)
- I = Impacted
- O = Other features (describe in dental comments)

Dental Comments

National Missing and Unidentified Persons System NamUs

Figure 14.10 NamUs unidentified-persons dental report form. (Courtesy of Dr. Anthony R. Cardoza.)

Bite Marks on Victims or Perpetrators

Bite mark evidence in felony crimes such as homicide, child abuse, and sex crimes has been recognized by the courts in numerous jurisdictions for several decades. When properly preserved and protected, these marks may provide an important link between a victim and his/her assailant. While bite marks on victims are seemingly the most commonly encountered during law enforcement investigations, equally incriminating may be those inflicted by the victim on the assailant (Figure 14.11).

Analysis of bite marks on perpetrators and victims is one of the responsibilities of modern forensic dentistry (Figure 14.12). Bite mark analysis is more *interpretive* and less objective than, for example, toxicology or DNA procedures. In fact, several cases of positive comparisons logged by a number of odontologists have been reversed by DNA analysis. (As of 2016, there have been 27 cases nationally that have been reversed where bite mark testimony was used as a contributor to the original conviction.) There have been far too many criticisms of existing procedures in legal literature. Bite mark analysis has been termed a "junk science." Some experts in the field believe that it is not a science at all, especially when lesions occurring during resuscitative attempts by medical personnel or insect marks found on the body have

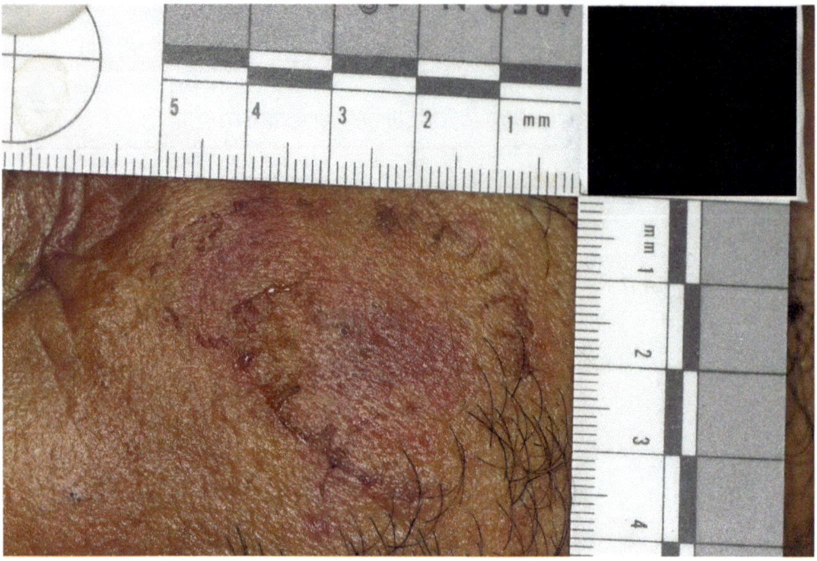

Figure 14.11 Closeup view of a human bite mark found on the face of a decedent. Note that a scale is in place. (Courtesy of Dr. Anthony R. Cardoza.)

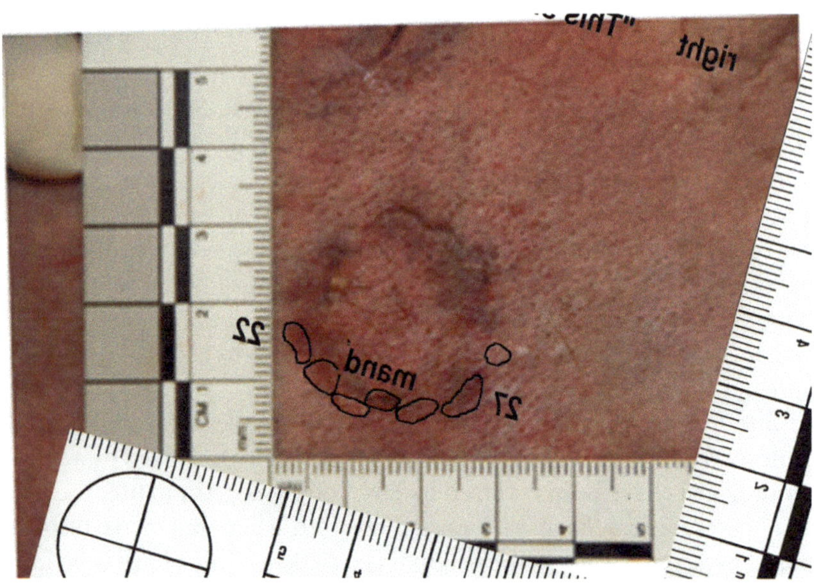

Figure 14.12 Human bite mark pattern with suspect bite overlay in place for comparison. Note that scales on both images correspond to a 1:1 size orientation. (Courtesy of Dr. Anthony R. Cardoza.)

been falsely identified as bite marks. The field of odontology has always urged the collection of saliva for DNA analysis and now considers the collection of trace salivary evidence on a suspected bite mark to be the *critical step* in bite mark analysis.

Not uncommonly, case or file review will reveal the presence of bite marks on either the victim or a suspect. Investigators should consider the following:

- Were swabbings of the alleged bite mark accomplished (critical step)?
  - What swabbing procedure was used (dual-swab technique)?
  - Have these swabbings been located?
  - Is there an original DNA report?
  - Have the swabbings been reexamined?
  - What were the results?
- Is clothing that was over the bite mark available for DNA testing?
- If DNA results were obtained, were they entered into the Combined DNA Index System (CODIS)?
- Were salivary specimens secured from the victim or suspect?
- If photographs are available, were they examined by a certified forensic dentist?

In these instances, cold case investigators should consult with a qualified forensic odontologist.

Bite Mark Photography

A number of issues may confront cold case investigators when reviewing past photographs of purported bite marks. These photographs may be valuable evidence, but a number of factors may affect their usefulness and reliability. Camera angle and scale placement (if any) may be important considerations in evaluating the reliability of these photographs. In reviewing the photographs and this record, investigators should consider the following:

- How long after the crime were the photographs taken?
- What was the distance from the camera to the bite mark?
- Is this record sufficiently documented?
  - Date
  - Time
  - Photographer
- Are there both black-and-white and color photos available? Black-and-white photographs cannot differentiate between, for example, freckles and an actual bite mark.
- At what camera angles were the photographs taken? Right-angle photography eliminates distortion.

- Were the photographs taken before or after the autopsy?
- *Was a ruler or scale placed next to the alleged bite mark during photography (critical photographic step)?* (Other objects such as a coin may be used if a scale is not available.)
- Who took the photographs?
    - Is this photographer still available?
    - Does he/she have any notes, records, or other photographs?

If the photography is distorted, a forensic dentist may be able to use Adobe Photoshop software to correct this problem.

Bite Mark Impressions

Similar considerations as in conditions of swabbings or photography should be taken into account when reviewing bite mark impressions. In addition, cold case investigators need to know the following:

- Were they taken by a forensic odontologist, dentist, or experienced lab technician?
- What materials were used?
- What procedures were used or followed during this process?

It is also important to point out that in some cases, tooth marks have been found in objects such as chewing gum, apples, cheese, duct tape, Styrofoam, weather stripping, etc.

Standard procedures in evaluating bite mark cases are as follows:

1. Orientation photographs
2. Swab for DNA evidence (dual-swab technique)
3. Closeup photography
4. Impressions of bite mark if perforations are noted

Exhumations of Embalmed Bodies with Bite Marks

Usually at autopsies, photographs of suspected bite marks are taken by pathologists. On occasion, these bite mark lesions may not be recognized at the time of autopsy. If this is the case, an exhumation may result in the completion of better photographic images with corresponding rulers in place. It should be understood that the embalming process is not always effective and the lesion may not be as obvious or objective as the original preautopsy photographs might have been had they been collected at that time. Also, collecting bite mark evidence postautopsy can result in a distorted bite mark due to the surgical manipulation of the body during autopsy.

Qualified forensic dentists may be located through the following:

American Board of Forensic Odontology
http://www.abfo.org
American Academy of Forensic Sciences
PO Box 669
Colorado Springs, Colorado 80901
1-719-636-1100
(http://www.aafs.org)

For further information:

Anthony R. Cardoza, DDS
Diplomate, American Board of Forensic Odontology
9530 Cuyamaca Street, Suite 101
Santee, California 92071

Acknowledgments

I wish to extend my deepest appreciation and gratitude to Dr. Norman D. "Skip" Sperber for his authorship of this chapter. Dr. Sperber has been repeatedly acknowledged as perhaps the world's leading forensic odontologist, and his leadership efforts in this field have contributed greatly to the betterment of the forensic and law enforcement spectrum for over 50 years. Prior to his graduation from the New York University College of Dentistry in 1954, Dr. Sperber worked for the New York Chief Medical Examiner's Office in New York City. After passing his board exams in New York and California, he practiced in his field and served 10 years as a dental officer in the U.S. Navy. In 1963, Dr. Sperber was appointed the forensic dentist for the San Diego County Coroner's Office, California (later medical examiner), and has served continually since.

Dr. Sperber has instructed law enforcement officers in aspects of forensic dentistry for over 30 years. In 1983, he attended and completed, on his own time, the San Diego Police and Sheriff's Reserve Academy and became a reserve police officer.

Dr. Sperber helped devise the first civilian dental identification computer system in the United States in 1978, one used extensively to identify over 100 of 144 victims from a midair collision over San Diego the following year. As a result of a U.S. congressional appointment, he devised the dental section of the NCIC computer relating unidentified-persons data to missing-persons data, and he continues today as a consultant in that capacity. This was the first national dental identification system in the history of the United States. He has testified in over 215 trials, including the first U.S. court-martial bite mark case, and as a primary forensic bite mark expert in the cases against Ted Bundy and Jeffrey Dahmer.

Dr. Sperber has served as director of the American Board of Forensic Odontology, in addition to chair positions and other duties and accomplishments. He has served as vice president of the American Academy of Forensic Sciences (AAFS) and as chair of the Odontology Section of this highly respected organization. In 2000, he and a codentist were named the first distinguished fellows from the dental section of the AAFS. He was one of three dentists to design the first state system (California) for body identification and continues to the present as chief forensic dentist for the California Department of Justice's statewide identification system.

I further wish to recognize and extend my deepest gratitude to Anthony R. Cardoza, DDS, D-ABFO, for his contributions to this chapter. Dr. Cardoza is a 1985 graduate of the Northwestern University Dental School and maintains a general dental practice in Santee (San Diego County, California). He began his affiliation with the San Diego County Medical Examiner in 1992 under the mentorship of Dr. Norman Sperber. Dr. Cardoza is a diplomate of the American Board of Forensic Odontology (ABFO), a fellow of the AAFS, and a member of the American Society of Forensic Odontology (ASFO) and the California Society of Forensic Dentistry (CSFD). Dr. Cardoza serves as a forensic dental consultant for the Office of the Medical Examiner, County of San Diego; Office of the Coroner, County of Imperial; Office of the Coroner, County of Riverside; Department of Justice, Sacramento; the San Diego Police Department; and the San Diego County Sheriff's Department, California. He is also a member of the California Dental Identification Team (CalDIT) and the California Office of Emergency Services (CalOES).

Dr. Cardoza maintains a busy forensic caseload due to the proximity of the San Diego and Imperial Counties to the Mexican border. He has performed numerous postmortem dental examinations, comparisons, and identifications and most recently was involved with the identifications of victims of the Southern California wildfire disasters.

Suggested Readings and Bibliography

Bowers, C. M. 2010. *Forensic Dental Evidence*. Second Edition. Burlington, MA: Elsevier.

Senn, D. R. and R. A. Weems. 2013. *Manual of Forensic Odontology*. Fifth Edition. Boca Raton, FL: American Society of Forensic Odontology.

Sopher, I. M. 1976. *Forensic Dentistry*. Springfield, IL: Charles C Thomas.

Investigative Genetic Genealogy

15

JENNIFER MOORE AND
ASHLEY LINK

Investigative genetic genealogy (IGG), also known as "forensic genetic genealogy," is still a new tool available for law enforcement, with the first successful case receiving media attention in 2018. The infamous "Gold State Killer" case, which went unsolved for 42 years until this new technique, opened the door up to law enforcement to reexamine cold case homicides and other violent crimes. Eight years later, over 650 criminal cases have been solved with the assistance of forensic genetic genealogy.[1]

This chapter will examine, among other things, an overview of DNA and its uses in law enforcement, the testing methods used for IGG, when IGG is appropriate for a case and how it is used, and the Department of Justice's guidelines regarding best practices for IGG use in the law enforcement fields.

BOX 15.1 THE GOLDEN STATE KILLER

During the 1970s and 1980s, California was struck with a stream of serial rapes and murders across multiple counties. Early on, the crimes began as burglaries, shootings, and quickly turned with the suspect tying his victims up and committing sexual assaults. A sketch of the suspect was shared across the nation in hopes of catching him. On April 24, 2018, after decades of remaining cold, Joseph James DeAngelo, a former police officer, was arrested and the fascination with IGG began.

Using forensic samples from the crime scene, law enforcement and court documents explained how they were able to crack the case by using FamilyTreeDNA and GedMatch, two genealogy websites in creating family trees which led them to DeAngelo. After retrieving a sample of his DNA and comparing it to the forensic samples from the cases, they received a positive match.

On June 29, 2020, DeAngelo pled guilty to 13 counts of first-degree murder. During the court hearing, he admitted to victimizing a total of 87 individuals at 53 separate crime scenes. He received multiple life sentences without the possibility of parole.[2]

DOI: 10.4324/9781003415633-18

Understanding Human DNA

The human body is made up of trillions of cells that form the tissues, skin, and all other organs and parts of the human body. A most recent study suggests adult males have more than 36 trillion cells, adult females 28 trillion, and a 10-year-old child has close to 17 trillion.[3] Inside each cell is the "nucleus" which contains the cell's chromosomes and all the cell's genetic material. The chromosomes are made up of protein and deoxyribonucleic acid, or in simplest terms, "DNA" (Figure 15.1).

Each strand of DNA is made up into a structure known as a "double helix" which gives the DNA its intertwining look. On each strand, there are four types of molecules or "bases" attached to a sugar-phosphate backbone. These four bases are: adenine (A), cytosine (C), guanine (G), and thymine (T). These four bases will only pair a certain way when going across the two strands of the helix, with adenine pairing with thymine and cytosine pairing with guanine.

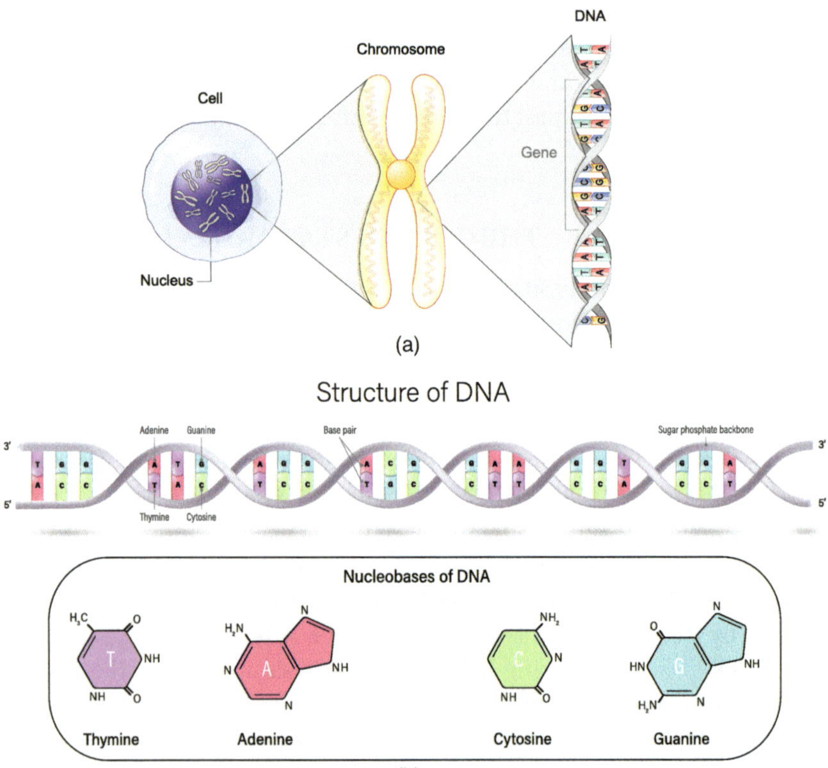

Figure 15.1 (a) The structure of the cell, chromosomes, and genomic sequence. (b) The structure and nucleobases of DNA. (Source: Both images used courtesy and with permission Shutterstock.com.)

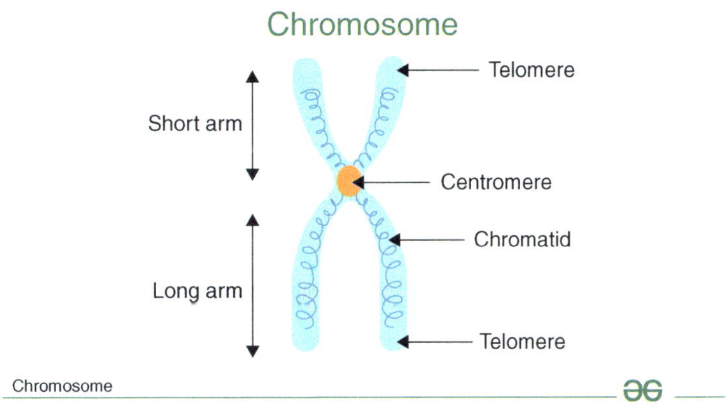

Figure 15.2 Illustration showing parts of chromosome.

Each human has 23 pairs of chromosomes, making a total of 46. The first 22 of the 23 pairs are known as "autosomal chromosomes." The last pair are sex chromosomes and as the name suggests determines if a person is born a male or female using the "Y" and "X" chromosomes. A person born as a male will have both a "Y" and "X" chromosome while a person born as a female will have two "X" chromosomes. Autosomal chromosomes do not participate in the determination of the sex of a person at all.

One copy of each chromosome in a pair is inherited from each parent. The genes a human inherits from their parents are within these chromosomes. The chromosome is further divided up into strands (or "arms") by a center known as a "centromere" and each strand is protected by a "telomere." It is within these stands DNA is found (Figure 15.2).

Autosomal chromosomes can be broken down even further depending on placement of the centromere, lengths of the arms, and abnormalities within the chromosome. The autosomal chromosomes become a vital part in IGG.

Humans share over 99% of the same DNA sequences as each other. The remaining 1% is what makes each individual person unique including their eye color, hair color, skin tone, and other hereditary and genetic factors inherited by both their paternal and maternal sides. It's this 1% investigative genetic genealogist use in their investigations.

Overview of DNA in Law Enforcement

Combined DNA Index System

CODIS, the Combined DNA Index System, was implemented to connect local, state, and federal agencies along with forensic laboratories as a way to exchange forensic profiles electronically with one another. The CODIS system allows these agencies to upload forensic samples and compare matches to create leads with one another if a positive match is created.

The Federal Bureau of Investigation (FBI) first began the pilot project CODIS in 1990. Through the DNA Identification Act of 1994, the FBI was authorized to establish a National DNA Index System (NDIS) for law enforcement purposes and is used in conjunction with CODIS. In 2005, the DNA Fingerprint Act allowed the FBI to increase the number of profiles added into NDIS and what could be used into CODIS. As of today, over 190 public law enforcement laboratories participate in NDIS across the United States and 90 law enforcement laboratories in over 50 countries.[4]

When a forensic sample is uploaded into CODIS, the DNA analysis used to examine the sample is known as "short tandem repeat" (STR). STR describes the examinations of the bases (adenine (A), cytosine (C), guanine (G), and thymine (T)). One example might be looking for the sequence "GCCT," which is created in multiple copies in a certain sequence that would be unique across certain individuals. Thirteen autosomal STR bases or "loci" were used when CODIS first began (see chart) but the list has now expanded with 20 as of 2017 to increase the accuracy of results (Figure 15.3).

Rapid DNA

The Rapid DNA Act of 2017 allowed the FBI to create standards and procedures regarding a technique which could generate quicker leads than CODIS but still came with its own limitations. Unlike CODIS, rapid DNA uses forensic samples collected through buccal swabs, not samples collected directly from crime scenes. Once a swab is collected, the DNA profile is uploaded

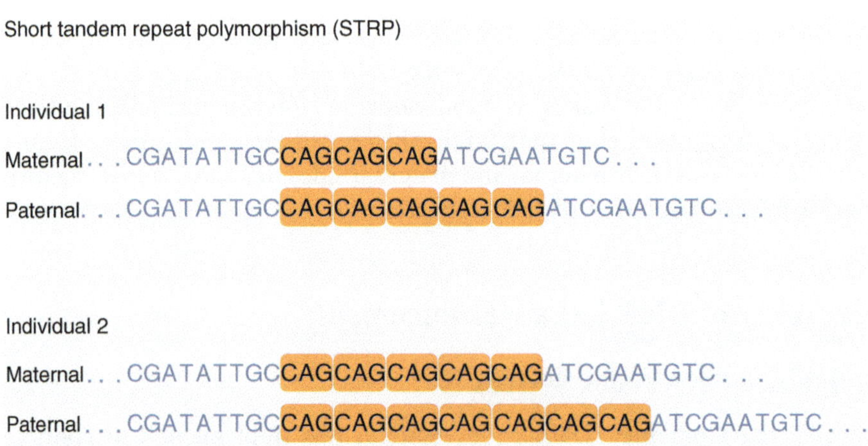

Figure 15.3 Illustration examining bases using short tandem repeat method.

and compared. While generating leads and results from CODIS can typically take days or weeks, the rapid DNA system is able to provide a hit sometimes within as little as an hour. Agencies who have rapid DNA readily available to them have machines dedicated to the collection and upload of these samples. Some machines are even mobile and can be taken straight to an individual whose sample needs to be collected which can be quite useful if a potential suspect is still on the crime scene. However, just like CODIS, only a lead is generated and STR testing is still used.

IGG Overview

Traditionally, genealogists look at three different types of sources of DNA when conducting genealogy research: Y-DNA, mtDNA, and atDNA. Y-DNA is Y-chromosomal DNA and is only present in male samples; it can only provide information from a patrilineal line. Mitochondrial DNA, or mtDNA, is present in both males and females and gives information on matrilineal lines. Autosomal DNA or atDNA, comes from the autosomal chromosomes and provides information from both the paternal and maternal lines of the family tree. atDNA provides the biggest advantage as it can identify several generations.

BOX 15.2 THE STORY OF PRINCESS DOE

On July 15, 1982, in Blairstown Township, New Jersey, a body of a young female was found in a cemetery. Her face had been beaten so badly she was unrecognizable. She became known as "Princess Doe" as her story went across the nation over media outlets and even on America's Most Wanted in hopes someone would recognize her due to the distinct clothing she was wearing.

Princess Doe would become the first unidentified persons case entered into the National Crime Information Center (NCIC). She was also posted on the National Center for Missing & Exploited Children website and with their help in 2021, two samples, *an eyelash and a molar*, were sent to a lab to be extracted and create the single nucleotide polymorphisms (SNP) profiles needed to conduct IGG. Through these two small samples, Princess Doe's identity became known. Dawn Olanick was only 17 years old at the time of her death. Law enforcement was also able to charge Arthur Kinlaw with first-degree murder with her death, who was already serving a life sentence for another killing of an unidentified woman from 1984.[5]

The Use of "SNP"

IGG has a huge advantage over CODIS. While CODIS is limited to looking at only a select few markers through the STR testing method, IGG uses what's called the "SNP" or single-nucleotide polymorphism method. "SNPs" simply are the most common genetic variation among people, with millions being present across the human genome. "SNPs" represent the difference in the nucleotides or "bases" across DNA. For example, adenine may replace thymine in a certain stretch of DNA. When a mutation occurs through a SNP, it remains present throughout the descendants. It's these changes in the SNPs that are helpful to genealogists when creating family trees and also in many other fields including in the field of medicine (Figure 15.4).

A forensic sample entered into CODIS for STR testing will not be able to be automatically used for IGG. Instead, the forensic sample must go through what's known as "whole-genome sequencing." As of the writing of this book, only a handful of labs across the United States can properly prepare a sample for IGG using this process. The process of whole-genome sequencing literally takes the sample and looks at the entirety of the "bases" or nucleotides of the DNA sequence across the organism's genome. It then pinpoints those mutations and markers to create the SNP profile that is needed to be uploaded into the databases investigative genetic genealogists need to begin their research.

Samples used to create the SNP profiles are the same samples used by law enforcement for other types of DNA analysis including tissue, bone, semen, saliva, hair, and teeth. Another benefit of using a SNP profile is that the sample may have a higher chance of creating a profile for analysis even if the forensic sample has experienced degradation due to the enormous amount of markers the SNP profile is able to produce on examination. If there are a limited number of samples available for extraction from a case for IGG, law enforcement should seek a consultation with the lab and approval from the prosecution. Depending on the type of sample and the amount needed for extraction, the

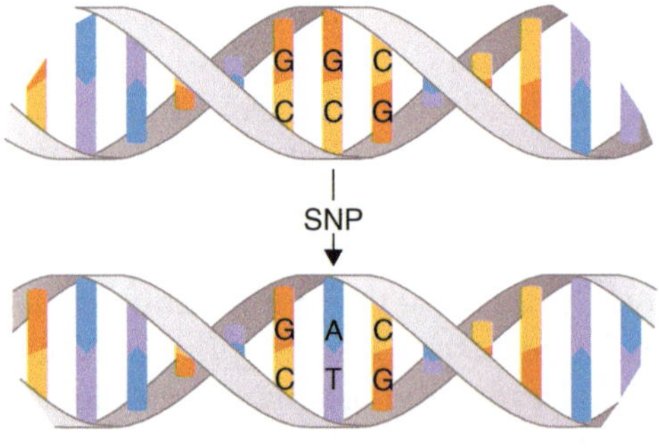

Figure 15.4 Illustration examining bases using the "SNP" technique.

sample can be consumed in its entirety for testing. Talking with an experienced lab consultant and investigative genetic genealogist will help ensure the sample is not submitted unless there is a chance IGG will be able to assist.

Databases Used

Only two genetic genealogy databases allow law enforcement and its agents to use its services for law enforcement purposes: FamilyTreeDNA and GedMatch. Both websites allow users to upload SNP profiles into their databases and compare their results among others in order to do genealogical research. The websites will further bring down a person's ethnic origins by percentage and rank matches by highest match, or highest kinship. However, for law enforcement to use these websites, there are some caveats.

BOX 15.3 THE CASE OF BRIAN AVIS

In 2022, Brian L. Avis was sentenced for aggravated sexual assault of a ten-year-old girl in 1996 and child endangerment of a five-year-old girl in 2003. In 1996, the Brigantine Police Department responded to a report of a sexual assault of a ten-year-old girl. It was reported a male suspect had broken into the home while the young girl was sleeping, sexually assaulted her, and then fled once she woke up. After going cold with no leads and no hits after uploads into CODIS, the City of Brigantine and New Jersey State Police reopened the case from 1996. To further the investigation and to generate higher matches on the IGG front, the New Jersey State Police used reference samples. The lead of Brian L. Avis was then generated and a search warrant to obtain his DNA was then obtained. Upon his arrest for the 1996 crime, his fingerprints were collected and at that point were confirmed as a hit for the 2003 crime that occurred in Galloway, New Jersey. [6]

First, law enforcement must acknowledge when creating their profiles that the profile is for law enforcement purposes. Second, law enforcement and any third-party agents who are using the profile can only use the users on the websites who have "opted in" to participate in assisting law enforcement in IGG matching. Third, it is strongly encouraged if third-party agents of law enforcement are being used, these agents do not contact any of the matches directly for fear of interference with the investigation. If a law enforcement agency decides to hire a genetic genealogist company to assist them with this research, ensure that they will not be contacting the matches, and the agency maintains full access to all match lists and work product as necessary for future discovery purposes if needed.

Using Trees to Generate the Lead

Once the SNP profile has been uploaded into FamilyTreeDNA and GedMatch, both sites generate "match list" which shows the relationship between the sample uploaded and other users in the database. Investigative genetic genealogists use this match list to create family trees based on "genetic networks." Genetic networks are made up of a group of people who share common ancestors with each other, each with their own lineage or descendants. The goal is to find an intersecting connection, such as a marriage, between descendants of two separate genetic networks, but evaluated by "centimorgans" which shows the probability of a genetic relationship to the match (Figure 15.5).

Investigative genetic genealogists get to the examination of these networks by analyzing "centimorgans" which is also provided within the match lists of FamilyTreeDNA and GedMatch. In the simplest terms, a centimorgan is a unit that can measure the genetic linkage between the two matches. The higher the number of centimorgans the sample has with a match provided in these online databases, the closer the genetic link will be (see the chart below). Investigative genetic genealogists are able to work off these matches to build their trees and can even find leads from a sample through comparison of the matches with as little as 200 centimorgans in common through other investigative tools (Table 15.1).

Reference Samples

To ensure the investigative genetic genealogist is on the right track, to create a better lead, or to eliminate certain parts of the ancestral tree, the genealogist may request the agency collect a "reference sample." A reference sample can be very beneficial in building up the family tree and creating more matches for the sample with higher centimorgans. Reference samples are collected through buccal swabs and can be sent directly to FamilyTreeDNA or GedMatch for uploading into the databases without having to go to the lab first.

When a reference sample is collected, it's important to collect as much information as possible on the potential person the sample is being collected from including closeness to the potential suspect or victim sample, criminal background, and location. Law enforcement agencies should be the one contacting and collecting the samples. Samples should also be collected with the consent of the person when possible, in case the sample provides a link to the suspect that leads to an arrest. This will help with any challenges defense may raise at a trial.

Challenges Faced by IGG

When creating ancestral trees and examining matches, numerous things can occur which can lead to the incorrect building of lineages, misidentification

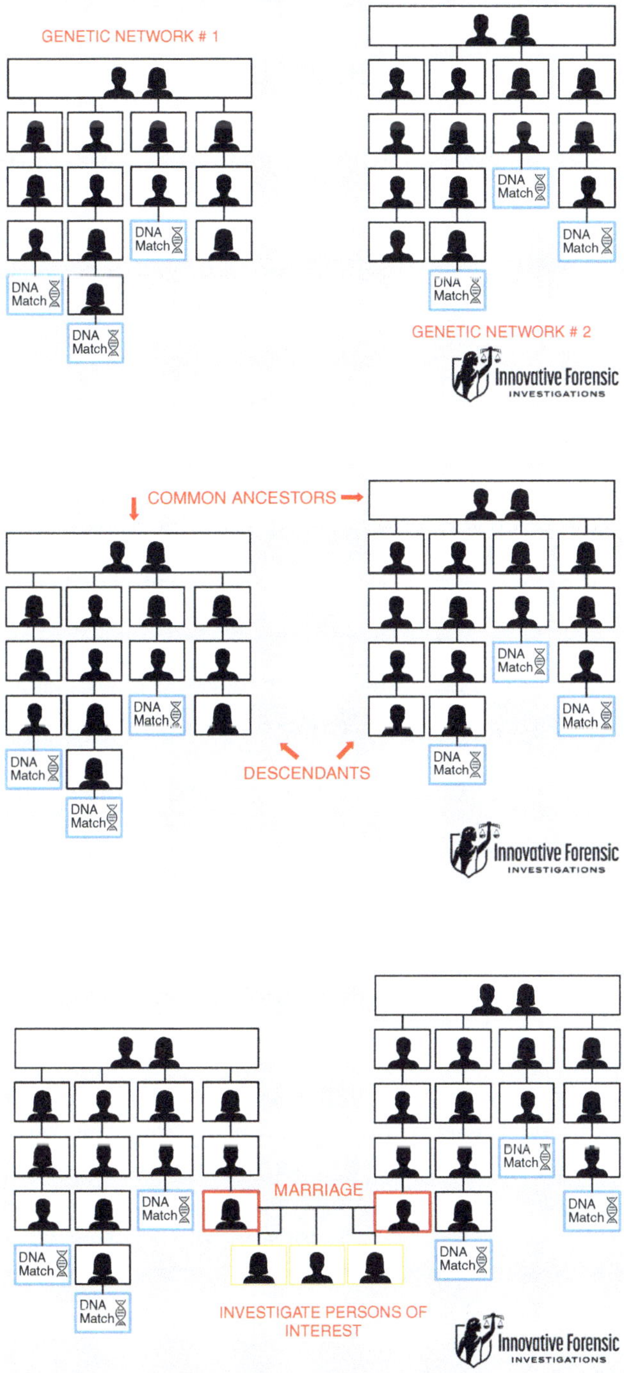

Figure 15.5 Shared centimorgan relationship chart.

Table 15.1 The structure of the cell, chromosomes, and genomic sequence. The structure and nucleobases of DNA.

Shared Centimorgan Relationship Chart

Average shared cM	Average Percentage shared DNA	Relationship	Range of shared cM*
3,400	50%	Parent/Child	2,376-3,720
2,550	50%	Full Sibling	1,613-3,488
1,700	25%	Half Sibling Aunt/Uncle/Niece/Nephew Grandparent/Grandchild	1,160-2,436 1,201-2,282 984-2462
850	12.50%	First Cousin Half Aunt/-Uncle/-Niece/-Nephew Great Grandparent/Grandchild Great Aunt/Uncle/Niece/Nephew	396-1,397 492-1,315 485-1,486 330-1,467
425	6.25%	First Cousin Once Removed Half First Cousin Half Great Aunt/Uncle/Niece/Nephew	102-980 156-979 184-668
212.5	3.125%	Second Cousin First Cousin Twice Removed Half First Cousin Once Removed	41-592 33-471 62-469
106.25	1.56%	Second Cousin Once Removed Half Second Cousin First Cousin Three Times Removed Half First Cousin Twice Removed	14-353 10-325 25-328 16-269
53.13	0.78%	Third Cousin Second Cousin Twice Removed	0-234 0-244
26.56	0.391%	Third Cousin Once Removed	0-192

*range of shared centimorgans are estimates and may vary slightly

of relatives, and overall inaccuracies with matches. When this happens, a trained investigative genetic genealogist will have to research in other ways besides just looking at the centimorgans of the matches in order to ensure the tree is accurate, and the correct lead is provided.

Adoptions can cause complications while trying to create family trees because an individual who is adopted and not biologically related will not share centimorgans in common with others being built into the tree. A non-paternal event shares similar problems as an adoption because the match will show it shares a parent–child relationship with someone when, in fact, it does not. False positives in matches may also occur due to shared ancestry, database, or lab errors.

Regarding shared ancestry, investigative genetic genealogists come across different types: pedigree collapses and endogamy. A pedigree collapse happens when two individuals who share a common ancestor reproduce together; this makes the common ancestor show up multiple times within the genetic network and can look like an error at first glance on the genealogists' behalf. Endogamy takes a pedigree collapse even further as it is essentially a pedigree collapse happening over and over within the ancestral lineage.

United States Department of Justice Interim Policy Regarding IGG

On November 1, 2019, the United States Department of Justice released an Interim Policy which includes certain guidelines regarding the use of IGG for the Department, federal agencies, and any other federal, state, local, tribunal, or contractual agencies conducting criminal investigations receiving sources of funding or grants from the Department.[7] To receive funding and/or grants, agencies, departments, and contractors must agree to abide by the policy in its entirety as a condition if IGG is used.

The Department is quick to emphasize the technique as a "lead" as already stressed in this chapter and certain requirements that must be met prior to the use of IGG on a criminal case. First, the case must be one involving an "unsolved violent crime." The Department defines "violent crime" in a number of ways including any homicide or sex crime case, and for the purpose of attempting to identify the remains of what the investigators reasonably believe to be a suspected homicide victim. A "violent crime" can also be determined by the genetic genealogy service company providing services to the law enforcement agency for investigative purposes.[8] A prosecutor may also authorize IGG be used for a violent crime or an attempt to commit a violent crime in accordance with the policy other than those described. However, for the prosecution to authorize its use, such violent crime or attempted crime must present a substantial and ongoing threat to public safety or national security for this scenario to be triggered.[9]

The second criterion regards the collection of the forensic sample. Forensic samples collected must only be from a putative perpetrator or from unidentified human remains in the case of a suspected homicide victim. Third, the investigative agency must have pursued all reasonable investigative leads available to the agency to solve the case or in identifying the unidentified human remains.

Lastly, if the forensic sample was from a putative perpetrator, the sample must have been uploaded into CODIS and subsequent CODIS searches must have failed to produce a confirmed DNA match. Where appropriate, case information must also have been uploaded into the National Missing and Unidentified Persons System (NamUs) and the Violent Criminal Apprehension Program ("ViCAP") national databases.[10] Only after these criteria are met can the case be ripe for IGG per the guidelines. Any agency receiving federal funding through the Department should read the policy in its entirety to ensure compliance with all grant and funding requirements.

Other Things to Consider When Using IGG

The Chain of Custody of Forensic Sample

Ensure your agency maintains control of the forensic sample being used to create the "SNP" profile for IGG. The agency should send the sample(s) off to the lab and ensure any sample sent is returned directly to the agency. Any investigative genetic genealogist company never needs to have the physical sample to assist you in your research in creating a lead unless the company is also providing the lab services. The labs that create the SNP profile typically creates a zip file format to the investigative genetic genealogist to upload into the database on the agency's behalf once the sample has been processed.

Finding the Right Investigative Genetic Genealogist

There are many companies and independent contractors out there today who claim to be "experienced" in this line of work but have only just begun or are interested in doing it because of the media attention they receive. When consulting with an investigative genetic genealogist, here are some of the things to consider if you are working with a qualified individual.

Type of Genealogical Work Prior to Beginning IGG

Many of the best investigative genetic genealogists first solved hundreds and thousands of adoption cases, not just finding hereditary background for their family and friends. Adoption cases have their own challenges just as IGG work as both require extra research and investigation into finding out an individual's identity and not just examining the list of matches and limited information provided by them.

Some colleges now provide degrees or certificates in IGG, although many candidates of these programs have very little practical experience.

The Different Types of Ethnicities Researched and Solved by the Genealogist

As one can imagine based on historical discrimination, certain ethnicities are wary of uploading their genetic profiles into the websites due to concerns of abuse and the government's involvement. The majority of uploads into FamilyTreeDNA and GedMatch are of Caucasian ancestry, making samples with other ethnic backgrounds more difficult to solve. An experienced investigative genetic genealogist should be able to answer in the affirmative of solving cases across all ethnicity backgrounds and how they were able to overcome these challenges during tree building and investigative research.

Genealogist Contacting Matches

An investigative genetic genealogist should never contact any match within the databases and there are no exceptions. An investigative genetic genealogist who tries to provide explanations to the contrary is a red flag. The agency should have full control of contacting matches. It's the agency who knows the case in and out and has the experience of what to say and not to say to potential matches or individuals needed for reference samples. If for some reason the investigative genetic genealogist needs assistance with getting more identifying information without using sources available to them, the genealogist should request assistance from the agency.

Ensure the Genealogist or Their Company Provides Reports and Access to Data

Due to the various discovery laws throughout the United States and what the defense may or may not be entitled to, it is vital the agency receives reports from the investigative genetic genealogist documenting in detail the work conducted creating the agency's lead. Further, any request from the agency to have access to the match lists regarding the lead should be provided to the agency without hesitation if access has not already been granted. The agency should ensure that once the work is completed by the investigative genetic genealogist, the genealogist does not delete anything until completion of trial, and that the IGG does not delete it but saves it until the completion of trial just in case a judge does decide to entertain any pretrial motions by the defense or testimony is needed.

Testifying at Trial

Any IGG who says they will not testify is a red flag. Due to IGG still being so new and not regulated throughout the states, many defense attorneys are attempting to challenge its use in cases. It doesn't matter if IGG is only used as a lead; a judge may still entertain any pretrial motions by the defense or require testimony at trial. When challenged, you will need someone to explain how IGG works and explain the work done on your case. This also wraps back around to the training and experience of the investigative genetic genealogist because in order to qualify as an expert, they will have to overcome the standards set by your particular state. If the genealogist or the company has a policy about not testifying, find someone else.

Publishing Cases over Media Outlets

This can become problematic if your agency has strict press release policies, or your prosecutor has ethical guidelines to abide by regarding commenting on ongoing investigations. If your agency and the prosecutor wish to remain out of the public eye ensure the genealogist or company you are working with are on the same page. If your agency is fine with releasing certain case information to the public, make sure your agency and the genealogist and their company work together in sharing the same information and all information is accurate.

Notes

1. https://www.genealogyexplained.com/igg-cases/
2. https://variety.com/2020/tv/news/golden-state-killer-joseph-james-deangelo-sentenced-to-life-in-prison-1234743710/
   https://www.latimes.com/california/story/2020-12-08/man-in-the-window
   Golden State Killer: Where the case stands one year after suspect's arrest | CNN
   https://abcnews.go.com/US/inside-timeline-crimes-golden-state-killer/story?id=54744307
3. https://www.livescience.com/health/anatomy/how-many-cells-are-in-the-human-body-new-study-provides-an-answer
4. https://le.fbi.gov/science-and-lab/biometrics-and-fingerprints/codis-2#:~:text=The%20Combined%20DNA%20Index%20System,other%20and%20to%20known%20offenders
5. https://www.missingkids.org/blog/2022/after-40-years-princess-doe-identified
6. https://www.fox29.com/news/egg-harbor-city-man-sentenced-on-sex-assault-and-endangerment-of-2-children
   https://www.forbes.com/sites/instituteforjustice/2024/06/10/state-insists-it-can-keep-babies-blood-without-parental-consent/
   https://www.nj.gov/njsp/news/2021/20210917.shtml
7. https://www.justice.gov/olp/page/file/1204386/dl
8. https://www.justice.gov/olp/page/file/1204386/dl
9. https://www.justice.gov/olp/page/file/1204386/dl
10. https://www.justice.gov/olp/page/file/1204386/dl

Linguistic Analysis for Cold Case Homicides

16

STEVE JOHNSON

The obvious problem with cold case homicides is that the critical information needed to solve the case is missing. I remember how I often felt that the information I needed was very close, or perhaps hidden somewhere within the case file, and I was simply missing it. Another scenario we often encounter is that the witnesses and suspects seem to be withholding information. They may be talking, but you have a sense that there is more information in their mind that they are not sharing. If you are an investigator, I'm sure you have encountered similar scenarios whether you've been working a cold case or working a current case.

Fortunately, you have a powerful tool at your disposal that will allow you to obtain critical information stored in the minds of those involved in your cases. Looking back now, I wish I could revisit several cases, armed with the information that I am going to share with you in this chapter. You see, the missing pieces of information needed to solve many cold cases are often right under your nose, inside the case files!

The answer to solving many of your cold cases is not in obtaining additional information, it is simply ***recognizing the latent information*** that is already in the files. All you need are the skills to recognize that information when you see it in the interview transcripts and written statements, or when you hear it in the recorded interviews. More times than not, the suspects and witnesses in your cases have the information you need. What they don't realize is that their brain will literally leak information to you whenever they speak or write. It is latent information that is hiding in plain sight, right in front of you. Once you learn how to mine that information from their own words, it will likely forever change the way you view a case and conduct an interview.

There are different terms for this skill set such as Statement Analysis, Statement Profiling, Forensic Linguistics, and Forensic Statement Analysis. Call it what you will, they are all intertwined. All of them involve an analysis of linguistics based on human nature.

When analyzing the language, we ask questions to guide us.

- Why did the subject use this word or phrase at this particular time and in this context?

DOI: 10.4324/9781003415633-19

- *What was going on inside their brain that produced those words, or caused them to* ***omit*** *certain words?*

Their brain has the information we need, which will be exposed through their own words. When you mine that information by analyzing their words, in essence you will be able to use their words to paint a picture of the incident.

The principles contained in this chapter are effective. They have proven themselves time and time again, in thousands of statements, and in many languages. They are effective when applied to cold cases and equally effective when applied to fresh cases.

Let's start by asking what it is that makes a story believable?

The answer is linguistic evidence.

In a courtroom, evidence is presented with the end goal of persuading the judge or jury to believe one side or the other. The evidence is weighed, and a determination made.

The same thing occurs when we:

- Hear a version of *what happened* from a suspect or witness.
- Read a social media post.
- Listen to a news interview.
- Read an employment application.
- Investigate a workplace injury complaint or sexual harassment complaint.
- Evaluate a business contract.
- And the list goes on and on.

We weigh the linguistic evidence of veracity versus the linguistic evidence of deception and make our determination. It sounds pretty straightforward, doesn't it? If only that were the case! The truth is, there are many factors that inhibit our ability to accurately weigh the linguistic evidence, or in some cases, to even recognize the evidence at all! The more knowledge you have regarding this process, it will not only help you recognize linguistic evidence you might have missed, but also allow you to accurately analyze it and come to an accurate conclusion.

You will find several core principles in this chapter that will guide you to the truth of any statement. If you tether yourself to the principles, you will come to an accurate conclusion every time.

The Foundational Truths

Human nature is fascinating. It has been predictable and consistent since the beginning of time. Yet, despite its predictability, we consistently fall prey to the foibles of human nature. This is certainly true when it comes to how we listen to others. It applies to what we hear them say, and conversely to what they may have communicated, ***but we did not hear or recognize***. I'm referring to the latent, or unapparent information contained within the words.

There is always more information within the words than is readily apparent. There is critical information beneath the surface that is crucial for investigators to recognize.

There are two foundational truths that all the forthcoming principles are based upon:

1. The brain was designed to communicate.
2. The brain default setting is to tell the truth.

The Brain Was Designed to Communicate

As human beings, when we open our mouths to speak or take a moment to write our thoughts, we cannot help but reveal information stored in our brain. Our brain will reveal information about our experiences, background, personality, and of course information that it might want to keep secret.

Human beings are programmed to communicate. We need to communicate. As such, it is difficult for most people to remain silent, even when it is in their best interest, such as during an interview with the police. During my 28-year law enforcement career, it never ceased to amaze me that suspects talked after they had committed a crime. They spoke to friends, girlfriends, family members, cellmates, and quite often to the investigators. Sometimes they were bragging, other times they were seeking advice. Sometimes they tried to manipulate the situation and the outcome. And of course, sometimes they talked to simply unburden themselves from the conflict in their mind. Whatever the reason, they all felt compelled to talk to someone. It is human nature to communicate; we were designed to communicate. We thrive on human interaction.

A scientist friend recently shared an interesting bit of information. He said there are pockets of centenarians around the world, that is, people that have reached 100 years of age. He said there have been various studies seeking to find the commonality between these groups. However, they really do not have much in common except for one thing. The one common factor is that each of these groups regularly socializes with friends. I'm talking about face-to-face communication and human interaction.

Human beings were designed to communicate. With that in mind, consider that ***it is more difficult to withhold what we know to be true than it is to talk openly about it***. That brings us to the next truth, which is that the human brain was designed to tell the truth. We thrive on it.

The Brain's Default Setting Is to Tell the Truth

Deception is stressful on the brain and physiologically stressful on the body. Thus, when someone speaks from *experiential memory* the process is smooth because it is truthful.

When we experience an event, all our senses are engaged—what we see, hear, smell, taste, and feel, both emotionally and physically. All this information is sent to the brain, causing thousands of neurons to connect and chemicals to be released into our body. If it is a pleasant event, that chemical might be serotonin, dopamine, or endorphins. If it is a stressful or traumatic event, we might experience a release of cortisol or an elevated hormonal response such as an adrenaline dump. It is an intricate process that occurs in a split second. Thus, when truthfully recounting an event, it is easy to do. Not only does our brain remember, but so does our physical body.

Conversely, when experiential memory is disengaged and replaced by deception, that is, inventing or fabricating reality or deliberately withholding information, there is a mental and physiological reaction in the body. The brain not only knows what is true, but it was designed to tell the truth. This means that deliberate deception creates conflict within the brain, a cognitive dissonance. The person who is deliberately deceptive feels the stress caused by a *disruption* in the powerfully speedy process of their brain. That stress creates physiological responses that can be measured by lie detection machines such as the Polygraph and the Voice Stress Analyzer.

The fascinating thing about the stress from deception is that it also creates anomalies in speech. You see, the brain does not like to operate contrary to how it was created. It will attempt to protect itself from that stress by using language that minimizes, explains, or justifies their deception. Once you understand how the psychological stress from deception is manifested linguistically, you will realize that guilty people will unknowingly teach you where you should focus your investigation. They also teach you where they are feeling the most stress and sensitivity, which is where you should focus your questions in an interview.

Their words will betray them because their words reflect what they know in their mind, including the information they are trying to hide or disguise. They reveal not only when stress and sensitivity are felt, but also when they would like to distance themselves psychologically.

Recognizing and exploiting these linguistic anomalies is a skill used by the best interviewers and the best investigators. It is one thing to believe that someone is lying, it is quite another to articulate *how* that person is lying and exactly what part of their story might be deceptive. Keep in mind, the best deception is cloaked in truthful information, which makes it more difficult to recognize and articulate.

The fact is, we are not all equipped with the natural ability to detect deception. In any given interview or review of the transcript, you might think that what you are hearing or reading is *likely* deceptive. The real skill is to articulate exactly *how* the person is deceptive. Criminal investigators should be able to identify what part of the story is deceptive and what part of the story is actually true. Perhaps the entire statement is truthful. How do we recognize a truthful statement from a deceptive statement? Or more difficult yet, is there deception found within a technically truthful statement?

These are all questions that this chapter will provide the answers to.

The Core Principles

Since our brain was designed to tell the truth, it makes sense that most deception is simply in the form of withholding information. In fact, most deceptive statements contain a large amount of truthful information. Some deceptive statements are entirely true, yet deceptive due to the information left out, or the way the statement is structured or skewed. It is easier on the brain to provide partial or skewed truths than it is to tell an outright lie. This is why it is imperative for investigators to understand the varied ways in which deception is manifested.

There are several linguistic indicators we look for to determine if a person is skirting the truth.

Here are a few that we will discuss in this chapter:

- *Unsolicited explanations*: Providing a reason why something happened when they were not asked for an explanation.
- *Normalizing*: Describing what normally happens rather than saying what actually occurred. Believe it or not, the majority of people, including investigators, fall for this.
- *Psychological commitment*: Using language that is psychologically distancing and non-committal.
- Missing time, which is missing information.

Unsolicited Explanations

When someone is asked to tell us what happened, it is easy for them to do when they are telling the truth.

As we have already learned, deception creates mental and physiological stress within us. However, some people are so good at controlling their stress that they can pass a polygraph test. It's as if they are not affected by the stress that betrays the rest of us if we tell a lie. I once watched a federal agent conduct an interview and accuse the suspect of lying. The suspect offered to take a polygraph test, which he was allowed to do. A polygraphist administered the test and the suspect passed! That was the end of the interview, no follow-up was conducted.

The problem with this is that the suspect displayed elevated sensitivity within his language during the interview. In fact, it was enough to indicate that he was not being entirely truthful. The interviewer missed it. Or if he did recognize it, he disregarded it once the polygraph was passed. Sadly, this same scenario has been played out over and over again. Months later, that suspect later confessed and admitted that he had lied during the polygraph. Had the federal agent known how to recognize the sensitivity, there is a good chance he would have had a successful interview.

There are several linguistic indicators we look for to determine if a person is skirting the truth. One of the most effective, yet overlooked indicators is the unsolicited explanation. This is when the subject provides a reason why something happened but was not asked to do so. These unnecessary and unsolicited explanations are easy to overlook because we hear them and speak them almost daily. However, the context in which they are used makes a big difference. In the context of an investigatory interview, these types of explanations are unnecessary and take more cognitive effort. If you understand their importance and focus on them, they will shed a huge amount of light on your interviews and your investigations.

When someone speaks truthfully from experiential memory, their words are concise, simple, and to the point. There is no need for unnecessary wording or extra cognitive energy. However, when there is any form of deception involved, the stress from that deception will often appear in the form of heightened sensitivity. In other words, they will offer explanations for the portion of their story that is manufactured. If their story was de facto true, no explanation would be necessary. However, if the story is not entirely true, an explanation is often necessary (*in their mind*) to make the story believable.

Listening and looking for clusters of unsolicited explanations will identify those with guilty knowledge. When you ask follow-up questions focused around those areas of heightened sensitivity, it sends a message to the deceptive subject that you are not fooled by his deception. This will naturally elevate their level of stress. Answers provided in response to the follow-up questions will typically manifest additional stress and sensitivity.

Many current and cold cases could be solved by simply recognizing the unsolicited explanations provided by those being interviewed. Take, for example, the Lina Reyes Geddes case. Lina's disappearance was a mystery for over 20 years. Her husband, Edward Geddes, told investigators that the last time he saw Lina was when he dropped her off at the airport in Pittsburg.

He said that she took a flight to Mexico to visit her family. However, Lina never arrived in Mexico and there was no known trace of her anywhere.

A cursory interview was conducted with Edward after Lina's family reported her missing. The interview was five months after Lina allegedly flew to Mexico. Edward's interview contains classic examples of how unsolicited explanations reveal stress and sensitivity within the brain.

Below is a portion of Edward's interview transcript in which he is describing the morning he took Lina to the airport. You will see several areas highlighted, which are the unsolicited explanations. The areas in **bold font** are the important points that are being explained and therefore most important. Simply by following the sensitivity in Edward's language, key pieces of this investigation are exposed. It's too bad the interviewing detective did not have the same training you are receiving; this case might have been solved 20 years ago!

Edward Geddes Interview Transcript

EDWARD: *OK on, um, Wednesday morning April 8th, we left ah, I would have to guess at 6:45 am. Ah our place in Austintown, ah, we had Cheekies, the dog with us, OK and ah she had packed cosmetic case, a suitcase, um, I think a hang-up bag, ah and,* ***she had a, ah, ah, a sleeping bag****. OK, ah, which was ah, going to be a present for one of her little cousins. You know he always liked to go out into the backyard, um, you know and play camp. He had a little hut and things like that.*

DETECTIVE: So, she had a sleeping bag?

EDWARD: ***She had the sleeping bag.*** *I had rolled the sum bitch up tight. Ha-ha. That's an odd combination to carry.*

DETECTIVE: OK.

EDWARD: *ah, it was going to be a present for ah Paco.*

DETECTIVE: What color was the sleeping bag?

EDWARD: *Blue, the outside, I guess it was a light color on the inside. I think, yeah. Oh, man, now you are testing my memory.*

DETECTIVE: That's in case we, who knows, if we find something down there. You know find a sleeping bag.

EDWARD: *Since I talked to you, I'm going to ah, say one thing. We ought to enter it here. I might have told you this before, because it didn't come to mind or until about a month or so ago. Um, she got up pretty early that morning, cause she had long hair. And she went shampoo and it took a while to dry her hair.* And so, *I was lying in bed watching her you know. But so, the first thing she would do she would come out of the shower. She would have the towel wrapped around her thing.*

And she came out nude. She would put on a pair of underpants and bra. OK, then she would you know start working with her hair.

I can, **I can tell you what underpants and bra she had on**. Ah, she they were white cotton, and the bra, the reason that I remember, it's it was my favorite pants and bra. Ah, it was white cotton with pictures of apples and maybe bananas on it. OK, little pictures like this, like the size of a nickel.

DETECTIVE: OK.

EDWARD: And the bra had the same pattern.

DETECTIVE: Apples and what?

EDWARD: I think Apples and bananas.

DETECTIVE: Bananas.

EDWARD: Unusual. OK. They left, ahh, about 6:45. Austintown we went down to the Pittsburgh Airport. Ah, I pulled up to the check in, the U.S. Air check in, she didn't have a ticket, so the skycap cannot check something just on your word, you have to have a ticket. So, I gave him $10.00 bucks, and said OK you now take care of all her baggage, make sure she gets to where she is going. Okay, and ah, you know **I didn't come into the airport** because I had Cheekies in, in the car. And, ah we hadn't really broken Cheekies of keeping her in the car. Okay, ah, we hadn't taught her how to stay in the car and not go pee pee.

Ah, so you know **we kissed**, I was out of the car, **we kissed**, ah, skycap picked up all the stuff and went into the Pittsburgh Airport. That's the last time I saw her.

As you can see, the key areas that Edward taught us to focus on are:

1. The sleeping bag.

   Edward expended an unusual and unexpected amount of effort to explain why Lina had the sleeping bag with her. Excessive explaining is a key indicator that he has an acute need to explain something that we probably would not have thought to be that important. Excessive explaining tells us that we better focus on that topic, which in this case is the sleeping bag. For some reason, that sleeping bag is very sensitive to Edward.
2. The bra and underpants Lina was wearing.

   This area of excessive explanation was a little more difficult to recognize. He expended a lot of cognitive energy to tell the story, which purpose we learned was to explain why he knew what bra and underpants Lina was wearing. He could have simply stated, "by the way, I remembered what bra and underpants Lina was wearing. They were white cotton with apples and bananas." Instead, Edward spent a lot of time explaining *how* he knew what bra and underpants Lina was wearing. He even added an additional explanation, which was that he remembered because they were his favorite. Edward's excessive explanation taught us that the bra and underpants that Lina was wearing are going to be a key part of this case.

There is one more thing to note while we are analyzing this portion of Edward's interview. Note how he described what Lina did after she came out of the shower. He stated that Lina *would have a towel wrapped around her thing*. The word "thing" is a stark contrast from the word "head." This is an indication that he has depersonalized Lina. This will end up being a key part of this investigation, which I'll reveal to you later.

3. Edward not going into the airport.

   Edward tripled down on his explanations as to why he didn't go into the airport.

   a. "…because I had Cheekies in, in the car."
   b. "And ah, we hadn't really broken Cheekies of keeping her in the car."
   c. "Okay, ah, we hadn't taught her how to stay in the car and not go pee pee."

   Edward's sensitivity displayed by his excessive explanations taught us that we should ask why he was so sensitive about not going into the airport. The reason is that he never took Lina to the airport. One of the reasons we know this from the statement alone is that the first part of his description does not make sense. Edward stated that Lina did not have a ticket, and the sky cap could not check her in without a ticket. Yet, he gave the sky cap $10 and told him to take Lina and her luggage and make sure she got to where she was going. The interviewer should have definitely asked follow-up questions regarding this part of his story. One of the reasons that Edward needed to explain why he didn't go into the airport was because there are cameras in the airport. He knew that he would not be seen on the cameras because he was never there.

4. His portrayal that he was such a good husband that he kissed her goodbye.

   Most everyone kisses their loved one goodbye when they drop them off at an airport. It is one of those things that does not need to be explained. We frequently witness goodbye kisses whenever we go to the airport. The goodbye kiss is one of those things that is so mundane that most people do not feel the need to mention it. Similarly, most people will not mention that they told their loved one "goodbye" or "good night" or "I love you." It is just something that most everyone does. The fact that Edward took the time to tell the detective, "we kissed," is an indication that he has a need to portray the relationship as a good one. This observation is backed up by the fact that Edward had to explain that he was out of the car, which is how they were able to kiss.

The unnecessary explanation of him being out of the car and able to kiss Lina goodbye indicates that the kiss is very sensitive to Edward. If we had no other unnecessary explanations prior to this, we could determine that the kiss is sensitive because it was his last one with Lina. However, the context in this case is different. His unnecessary portrayal of him being a good husband indicates that he is likely not a very good husband or has done something wrong. Also, this part of his story is a continuation of his persuasion that he was at the airport.

Unfortunately, these key areas were not recognized by the interviewer and therefore not exploited. Had the interviewer recognized the sensitivity and known how to exploit it, this case might have been solved 20 years ago. Imagine what would have happened if the interviewer had simply let Edward give his version of events, and then revisited the sensitive areas manifested in Edward's own words. To exploit the sensitivity, the investigator should have focused on questions surrounding those sensitive areas and asked follow-up questions similar to the following:

- *Edward, you stated that Lina had a sleeping bag and that you tied the sum bitch up tight. Describe that to me… Tell me more about that… What did that look like?*
- *Edward, thank you for all your help and the information you've given us so far. You said that you dropped Lina off at the airport. Tell me about your last conversation with Lina…what did you talk about on the way to the airport… at the airport… what is your last memory of her… describe that in more detail.*

By focusing on the sensitivity in Edward's own words, his stress level will automatically be elevated. His responses will reveal additional points of sensitivity that should then be exploited in a similar manner. When Edward answers those follow-up questions, his stress levels will elevate even more. All you need to do is focus your questions on the sensitive areas!

When you are reviewing interview transcripts in a cold case, take note of these sensitive areas. They will reveal not only deception but key pieces of the investigation that you should focus on. Here is how those sensitive areas played out in the Lina Reyes Geddes disappearance.

The rest of the story:

Lina never made it to the airport. Her body was actually dumped near Lake Powell in Utah, a few weeks after she went missing. However, her identity was unknown for close to 20 years. She had been shot in the back of her head. Her fingers were cut off and she was wrapped up in… you guessed it, the blue sleeping bag that was so sensitive to Edward. She was also wearing the same bra and underpants he had described. In fact, that is all she was wearing. Lina's body was also frozen solid.

Remember how Edward depersonalized Lina by saying that she had a towel wrapped around "her thing" instead of her head? When Lina was found, her entire head was wrapped in duct tape. It was as if her killer did not want her face to be seen, or perhaps he did not want to look at her face. The sensitivity surrounding the airport story and Edward not going inside was due to the fact that he manufactured that story. He was never at the airport on the day he said he dropped Lina off.

Edward told investigators that a couple weeks after Lina disappeared, he drove a van to the El Paso area in an attempt to find Lina. He told them that he mostly used cash on that trip, and that he took "another sleeping bag" with him and slept in the van. Of course, that means his exact whereabouts could not be tracked by credit card usage.

The sleeping bag Lina was found in was tied up with ropes and several knots. Recent advancements in DNA technology helped identify Edward's DNA on those ropes. He really did tie it up tight—that part was actually true! Sadly, Edward shot himself about three years after Lina was killed. He will never get to serve his time in prison. Obviously, he was not a good husband like he made himself out to be (Figures 16.1–16.6)!

As you conduct your cold case investigations and interviews, remember that people will teach you where you should focus your questions in the interview, and where to focus your investigation. If you no longer have the opportunity to interview a potential suspect, such as in the Lina Reyes Geddes case, simply listening for the sensitive information will provide critical information you might have missed otherwise. Recognizing and focusing on the areas of elevated sensitivity will put you way ahead of the game!

Normalizing

Normalizing is a common tactic used by those with guilty knowledge. When a person is presented with a question regarding the crime, we expect them to answer with language that is experiential. That is, language that includes past tense reference to what they experienced. When someone responds to the investigator's question with language describing what they normally or usually do, take note. They are avoiding a description of what actually occurred. It is a way of being deceptive without the stress of telling an outright lie. In fact, when people describe what normally or usually happens, it is often a true statement. At the same time, it is deceptive because it allows them to withhold factual information.

Figure 16.1 Edward and Lina Reyes Geddes.

Figure 16.2 Unknown female body (Lina) found in Garfield County, Utah.

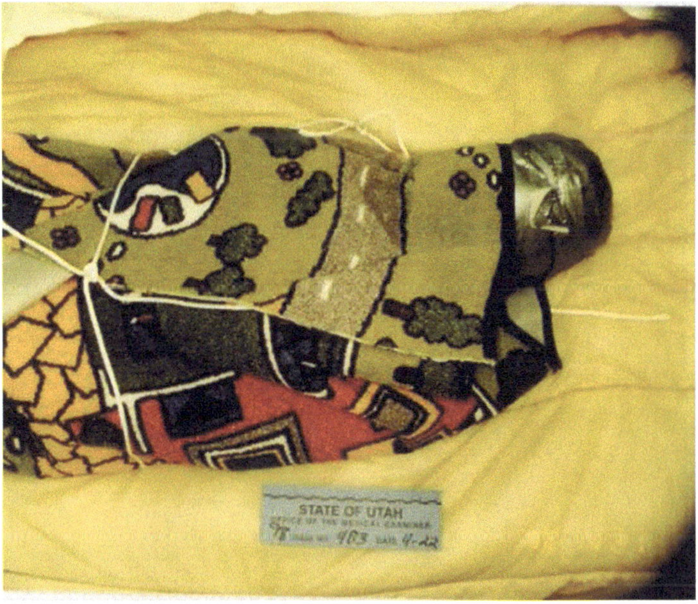

Figure 16.3 Lina's head wrapped in a garbage bag and duct tape.

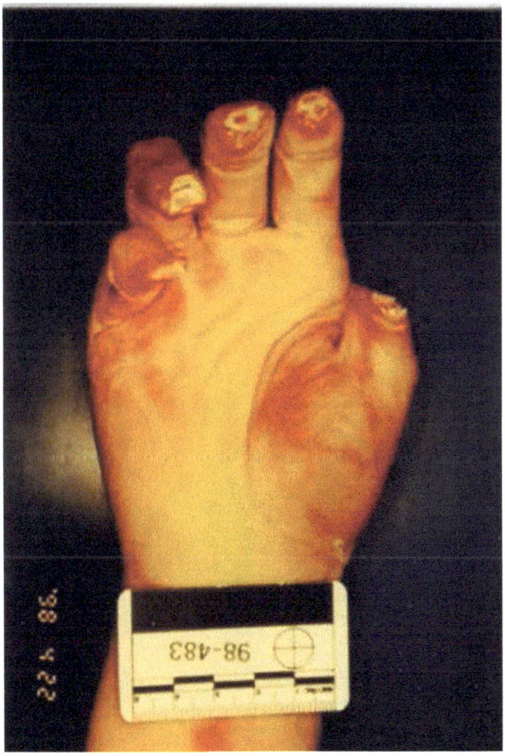

Figure 16.4 Lina's fingertips cut off.

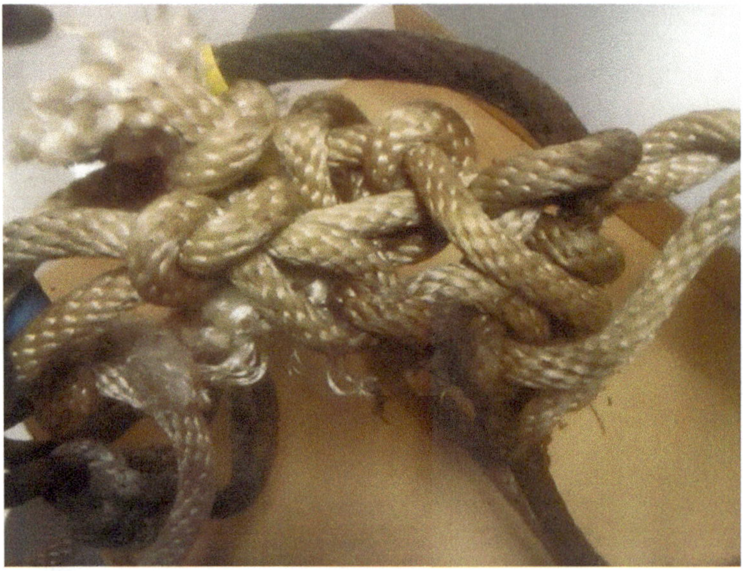

Figure 16.5 Rope that was used to tie Lina up.

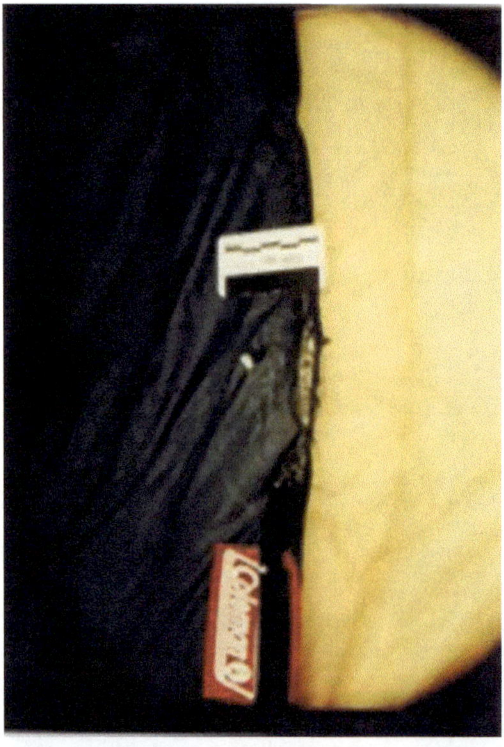

Figure 16.6 Sleeping bag Lina was tied up in.

In addition to the unsolicited explanations that Edward gave, did you notice that his description of what Lina did that morning was not experiential? Note that he did not state what Lina actually did, but rather what Lina usually does:

> ***But so, the first thing she would do she would come out of the shower. She would have the towel wrapped around her thing. And she came out nude. She would put on a pair of underpants and bra. OK, then she would you know start working with her hair.***

When language is used that explains what usually happens, or what one *would* do, rather than what they actually *did*, it is a good indication that the subject does not want to tell you what actually occurred at that particular time. By using language that describes what would normally occur, they are relying on the listener to interpret their words and assume that the same thing occurred that day. They want the listener to say it for them, which relieves them of the psychological stress of lying about the actual events.

Let's take a look at another cold case that demonstrates the use of normalizing language. This case centers around the disappearance of an adult female. She is married to a college professor, and they have two sons. One of her sons is away at college and the other is in middle school, living at home. Our victim works at a local hotel and loves her job. Her co-workers are among her best friends, and she often vacations with them. If she is going to miss work, they know about it.

One day our victim did not show up for work, but she did not call in to notify her employer. The co-workers found this very troubling and called her husband. He told them that she had left for work that morning as usual, and he had not heard from her since. He suggested that maybe she decided to take some time for herself and that they should not worry. The co-workers eventually called the police to report her missing. Since she was an adult, nothing was investigated for several days. After about a week, the husband was called in for a cursory interview. At the time of the interview, he was not a suspect in his wife's disappearance.

Below is a small portion of his interview transcript. If this was your case, it would benefit you to recognize that his response contains critical information about the case. He is an educated college professor, yet he cannot withhold what his brain knows. He is unaware that his response reveals that he is withholding information about what occurred the morning his wife disappeared.

DETECTIVE: Ok and that morning was there anything that you noticed unusual about her behavior or anything?

HUSBAND: *"No, she, she, we get up at, the youngest son gets up at about twenty to six, ahh the older one isn't at home. The youngest son got up about*

> *twenty to six. You always know he's up cause you hear the shower start and he's thirteen going to be fourteen so he's one of the probably sixteen to seventeen minute shower people, you know, where most people probably take a shower in five to six minutes.*
>
> *And then she gets up at six and I get up at six and I go down and usually walking, watching CNN and doing, doing, sit-ups in the family room. And she got up as usual and, brushing teeth and ironing cloths and, and, a bath, and then left the house at about a quarter to seven as usual."*

Take note of the question and ask yourself what the appropriate response would be if given by a de facto innocent person. The innocent response would likely be something similar to, "No, I didn't notice anything unusual that morning." A truthful and innocent response is typically short, concise, and does not need any persuasive language. Wordy responses like the one above are typically convincing in nature. Wordy responses often reveal that the subject knows something that he would rather conceal.

Let's see what information we can glean from the husband's statement above.

First of all, we have to note that he spent the majority of his answer talking about the youngest son taking a shower. More specifically, it was the timing of his shower.

1. The time the youngest son gets up: "...about twenty to six."
2. Why everyone always knows he's up: "...because you hear the shower start."
3. How long he is in the shower: "sixteen to seventeen minute shower people."
4. Why he takes so long in the shower: "He's thirteen going to be fourteen... where most people probably take a shower in five to six minutes."

Obviously, the timing of the son's shower was a significant factor the morning his wife went missing. His brain just taught us that. He likely just gave us a time frame for when his wife met her demise.

Next, the husband spoke about he and his wife getting up that morning. However, if you are paying attention, you will notice that most of what he said was not actually about that particular morning. It was about every other morning, or more specifically, their usual routine.

"And then she gets up at six and I get up at six..." He did not use past tense, experiential language. Also note that he did not use the pronoun "we," even though they get up at the same time. In his perception of reality, they are separated each morning. It could mean that they are emotionally separated and do not have a good relationship. It could also mean that they are physically separated by sleeping in separate bedrooms.

"...and I go down and usually walking, watching CNN and doing, doing, sit-ups in the family room." He is not saying what he did that morning. He is counting on the interviewer to interpret or assume that because he does this every morning, that is what he did that morning.

"And she got up as usual and, brushing teeth and ironing cloths and, and, a bath, and then left the house at about a quarter to seven as usual." Again, almost everything stated about her morning is what she usually does rather than what she actually did.

The only thing you can really count on in his statement is the time frame, the time the youngest son was in the shower. Everything else is what normally or usually occurs, and as such, you cannot assume that it happened that morning.

As of this writing, this particular case is still an open investigation. However, I can tell you that the wife's body was later found in the desert. It was severely decomposed. The husband and wife had a rocky relationship, and they slept in separate bedrooms and was talking about divorce. You can probably surmise the rest of the story... After all, his own words are painting a pretty vivid picture.

Psychological Commitment

One of the amazing aspects of our brain is that it is designed to protect us. In moments of physical danger, it will shut down all unnecessary bodily functions and turn up those functions that are necessary for survival. This is commonly referred to as the fight or flight response. A similar phenomenon occurs linguistically. Since our brain's default setting is to tell the truth, telling an outright lie creates a stressful physiological response. The brain views this stress in the same way as if we were in a physically dangerous situation. To mitigate this stress, the brain will often alter our words in ways that remove psychological commitment, which avoids the stress of telling an outright lie. The end result is usually a phrase that requires some level of interpretation or assumption on the part of the listener. This is often so subtle that most people do not notice it. The deceptive person relies on the listener to interpret what they said and fill in the linguistic gap. This tactic works time and time again because most people will actually interpret what was stated. It's as if the listener's mind is thinking, *oh, I know what they meant so I'll just fix it.* Whenever we fall prey to this tactic, we unintentionally become complicit in the deception.

Here is a good rule of thumb; if the subject did not actually say it happened, do not assume it did happen or could have happened.

Let's look at a few examples that illustrate the different ways psychological commitment is removed in language.

The first example comes from the Edward Geddes interview, during which he employed the ***element of intention***. Language of intention is often interpreted as something that actually occurred. It is an effective tool for those that are deceptive.

During Edward's interview, he described the last morning he was with Lina, which is the morning when he allegedly took her to the Pittsburg airport. During this part of the interview, he stressed that Lina used cash for all her transactions during her trip to Mexico. Of course, this would ensure that no paper trail existed.

At the beginning of Edward's interview, the detective asked him how Lina paid for her airline ticket. Here is a portion of that interview transcript:

DETECTIVE: Let ah me ask a question, when she made the reservations from Pittsburgh, she made it from the house, she called?

EDWARD: *Yea.*

DETECTIVE: Do you know what flight? What Flight company? What Plane?

EDWARD: *I thought it was the U.S. Air flight that I gave you.*

DETECTIVE: U.S. Air. Now at that point, she makes a reservation, does she pay for the ticket? *How did she pay for the ticket?*

EDWARD: ***She was going to pay cash for the ticket at the airport.***

DETECTIVE: Okay now, okay so, you made the reservation and then…

EDWARD: *I told her to take the credit card, but she wouldn't take the credit card.*

DETECTIVE: Okay then, Okay let's go back to what you were saying.

Note that the question was direct and pertinent, "How did she pay for the ticket?" If you knew that your spouse actually bought the ticket at the airport and paid cash for it, how would you respond to this question? You would likely say, *she paid cash for the ticket at the airport.* That response includes the appropriate past tense verb, "paid." Utilizing past tense verbiage is one element of experiential language.

Edward phrased his response in a way that only reflects Lina's *intention* to pay cash for the ticket. For some reason, he is not able to commit, or does not want to commit that she actually bought the ticket. Remember, his words reflect the way he perceived or experienced the alleged event. Since he is not committing, you should not commit for him. Stating Lina's intention to buy the ticket sounds believable and is definitely less stressful than telling an outright lie. There is also a high probability that this type of response will be interpreted by the listener as factual. In this particular case, the detective bought into Edward's deception and assumed that Lina actually paid cash for a ticket. This detective should have focused on this area of Edward's story and asked for more details. It's too bad he didn't know what to listen for.

The next example of psychological commitment involves the use of ***pronouns***. We are going to look at a missing person case from 1989. The victim, who was a wife and mother, disappeared one night and has never been located. The victim's husband was interviewed and described the last night he saw his wife. In this excerpt from his interview, there is a lot of deceptive language. However, I will focus on his psychological commitment. More specifically, how he removes that commitment by removing the appropriate pronouns that either refer to himself or his wife.

You might ask yourself why a missing pronoun is such a big deal? Well, here is why pronouns are so important. Pronouns are one of those small words with big implications. They are one of the first words we learn to speak, and we use them hundreds of times each day. They are important and powerful words because they are instinctive. We do not have to think about which pronoun is appropriate to use in any particular situation. We automatically refer to ourselves or someone else with a pronoun that matches our perception of any given situation. The way a person uses a pronoun often reflects the nature of their relationship to others within their statement at that particular time.

Here is an example that demonstrates how the pronouns reflect the nature of a relationship. A Sergeant I worked with approached me one day and asked me to look after his squad the following week. I asked him where he was going. He said, "I'm going on vacation with my wife and kids." I noted how he referred to himself and then his wife and kids separately. He is at the beginning of the sentence, and the wife and kids are at the opposite end. By the way he phrased that sentence, I knew something was wrong. It could have been something small such as he wanted to do something else, or it could have been something significantly wrong in the family relationship. I simply made a statement to find out, "Vacation huh? That sounds fun." His response provided the answer I was seeking. He said, "Yea, my wife wants to go to San Francisco and visit all the tourist sites. That's just not my thing. I'd rather go up to the mountains and ride quads and go fishing." There it was. The reason for the separation in his language was simply that he did not want to go to San Francisco.

Once he returned to work, I asked him how his vacation was. He responded, "we had a great time." The pronoun "we" is small but powerful. His use of the pronoun "we" told me that unity was restored in their relationship.

Since pronouns are instinctive, consider that it actually ***takes more effort to not use a pronoun*** when it should be used. It is as if they are psychologically ejecting themselves, or someone else, out of their statement at that particular time. When someone does not commit with the appropriate pronoun, there is a reason why and it should not be overlooked.

Here is a portion of the husband's statement regarding the last time he saw his wife. Pay close attention to those areas in which he should have used a pronoun but didn't.

DETECTIVE: Could you for my purposes, could you just tell me what happened Friday night, in your own words?

HUSBAND: *"Uh, Friday, we talked about the kids and me going to Tucson, Saturday morning and uh getting some clothes for school. She wanted uh, a stuffed pepper for lunch, and I went to Jordan's to go get that stuffed pepper, couldn't find it, couldn't find one, so I come back, talked about it, told her I couldn't find one.*

She packed her lunch, put it by the door, uh, she put it by the door. I did, anyway, uh, she got her lunch ready uh, she was telling me about she would still need time and space, and uh, time to herself, and I went to, went up to my mom's or went, went and drove up the street, and went up to my mom's and I was just up there a few minutes.

The weekend, the weekend before, we, I'd stayed the weekend before. I had stayed up at mom's a couple days and I just, I just, I just couldn't stay away from the kids, and uh, so I come back and that's when I, I seen her lying on the couch, and uh, she stirred and, when I come in, she's a pretty light sleeper, but uh, and I went to bed, the lights were out, you guys asked me about that, I went to bed, and that was right, sometime after nine, I wasn't much, I wasn't only gone a couple of minutes, and uh, I went, like I said I went to bed, and that is the last time I seen her."

When you notice a pronoun is missing, it sometimes helps to mark that spot with a large (**X**). If you have a red pen available or a digital copy, make a red (**X**) so that it stands out.

Here is the first half of the same statement with X's added where the pronouns are missing.

Uh, Friday, we talked about the kids and me going to Tucson, Saturday morning and uh getting some clothes for school. She wanted uh, a stuffed pepper for lunch, and I went to the market to go get that stuffed pepper, (X) couldn't find it, (X) couldn't find one, so I come back, (X) talked about it, (X) told her I couldn't find one.

She packed her lunch, (X) put it by the door, uh, she put it by the door. I did, anyway, uh, she got her lunch ready uh, she was telling me about she would still need time and space, and uh, time to herself, and I went to, went up to my mom's or went, went and drove up the street, and went up to my mom's and I was just up there a few minutes.

This guy obviously knows how to use pronouns and he used a lot of them in this short statement. Why then did he suddenly eject his psychological presence by dropping the pronoun in certain areas? In this case, the dropped pronouns centered around three things:

1. The husband himself, going to the store to get a stuffed pepper, but not being able to find one.
2. The subsequent conversation about the stuffed pepper and telling her he couldn't find one.
3. Putting his wife's lunch by the door.

Because he removed his psychological commitment at those times, there is a high probability that the events did not happen the way he is portraying them, or they did not happen at all. His brain is protecting him from the stress of telling an outright lie by removing his psychological commitment. For his story to make any sense, you would have to interpret what he meant and insert the appropriate pronouns where he left them out. However, doing so would be a critical mistake. Since pronouns are instinctive, we know that it took more effort for him to remove them. There is a reason why he did not include them. He purposely created psychological distance at those particular times. If you were to fill in the blanks for him, you would be playing into his deception.

You likely noted that in addition to the pronouns being dropped, there are incongruencies in his story. He cannot maintain consistency, which collaborates with his lack of psychological commitment noted with the dropped pronouns. That makes this area of time very sensitive to him, and therefore extra important for you the investigator. That area of time is critical in the context of his wife disappearing, or more likely being murdered and her body disposed of.

Let's break his statement down a bit more and see what he revealed. The first two missing pronouns are seen here:

> ***Uh, Friday, we talked about the kids and me going to Tucson, Saturday morning and uh getting some clothes for school. She wanted uh, a stuffed pepper for lunch, and I went to the market to go get that stuffed pepper, (X) couldn't find it, (X) couldn't find one...***

Out of all the things he likely did and talked about on Friday night, the only thing he mentioned was that there was a conversation about him and the kids going to Tucson and getting some school clothes. Since he did not say anything else about the evening's activities and conversations, it makes this one sentence very important. Note that this sentence provided a reason for going to Tucson, which in this case was an hour drive through the desert. He just drew our attention to the area between his town and the city of Tucson. By the way, that area happens to be a perfect place to dispose of a body.

We know from his next sentence that she wanted a stuffed pepper for lunch, and he went to go get that stuffed pepper.

> ***She wanted uh, a stuffed pepper for lunch, and I went to the market to go get that stuffed pepper, (X) couldn't find it, (X) couldn't find one…***

Note that he did two things here:

1. He painted himself as a good husband that went to get her that stuffed pepper. Everyone wants to be seen in a good light, but most of us do not tell the world that we are a good person. If you remember, Edward Geddes did the same thing when he said "we kissed" at the airport. In the context of a missing wife, this becomes even more important. In the context of describing your day when a loved one disappeared, who needs to describe themselves as a good person? It is typically the person that knows they have done something wrong, or they are not a good person. Their brain is sending the signal to rehab their character and build themselves up. This is a red flag.
2. He gave a *reason why* he left the house. Earlier in this chapter we learned how important these unsolicited explanations are. For some reason, he had to provide a reason for leaving the house. That elevates the importance of that block of time.

I believe he left the house. However, by following his language, we cannot say that he even tried to find her a stuffed pepper. Since he cannot commit to it, you should not assume it for him.

In the next sentence, he said:

> ***… so I come back, (X) talked about it, (X) told her I couldn't find one.***

By following his language, you know that he is not committing to talking about the stuffed pepper or telling her that he couldn't find one. Remember that it took more effort to not use an instinctive pronoun. Because he did not use the appropriate pronouns, you know that the conversation he is alluding to likely did not occur.

> ***She packed her lunch, (X) put it by the door, uh, she put it by the door. I did, anyway, uh, she got her lunch ready uh,***

Her lunch is packed, but initially there is no commitment as to who put it by the door. In fact, he then stated she put it by the door, but then contradicted himself and stated that he did it. That tells us that there is stress in the brain, which in this case is caused by deception.

Another thing that we commonly see in deceptive statements is the person going out of chronological order. That is exactly what this subject did. After expending a lot of cognitive energy regarding the lunch being packed and put by the door, he also went out of chronological order by stating that she packed her lunch, put it by the door, and then later stating that she packed her lunch again. Regarding the lunch, we have a lot of mental energy being exerted, dropped pronouns, contradiction, and confusion in the order of events. His language tells us that he is experiencing stress and sensitivity, which means this is critical to the investigation. In this particular case, when the husband reported her missing, the investigators noted that her lunch was in fact sitting by the door. With all that we noted in his language, we have to consider that her lunch was put by the door in order to make things appear normal. In other words, it was staged.

> ***...she was telling me about she would still need time and space, and uh, time to herself.***

The word "still" tells us that this discord in their relationship was not new. It was an ongoing part of their relationship. We know that she either wanted to leave or she wanted him to leave.

> ***...and I went to, went up to my mom's or went, went and drove up the street, and went up to my mom's and I was just up there a few minutes.***

Note that the word "went" is repeated five times. Anytime a word is repeated, the sensitivity surrounding it is elevated. Also note that there is a distinct separation in "went to, went up to my mom's" and "drove up the street." He added the word "or" between the two thoughts. Also, he cannot go to his mom's without driving up the street, which makes part of that sentence unnecessary to say. Unnecessary wording is often what gives liars away. If he is not lying about it, it is an area of elevated sensitivity and should be explored. The need to include extra wording not only reveals sensitivity, but often a need to persuade.

Speaking of persuasion, he also stated, "I was just up there a few minutes." He has already told us that she wanted time and space to herself. She wanted him to leave. Why then was he only gone for a few minutes? His need to persuade makes us question whether he actually went anywhere at that time. This isn't the end of his persuasion, look what comes next.

> ***The weekend, the weekend before, we, I'd stayed the weekend before. I had stayed up at mom's a couple days...***

This sentence is a continuation of his persuasion. In other words, it is his way of saying, *you must believe I went to my mom's because I stayed there the weekend before and furthermore, I stayed there a couple days.* This is a convincing statement to bolster what he previously stated. Why is he putting so much mental energy into convincing us? Because something else occurred at that time. This is a form of deception.

> ***...and I just, I just, I just couldn't stay away from the kids, and uh, so I come back and that's when I, I seen her lying on the couch, and uh, she stirred and, when I come in, she's a pretty light sleeper, but uh, and I went to bed, the lights were out, you guys asked me about that, I went to bed, and that was right, sometime after nine, I wasn't much, I wasn't only gone a couple of minutes, and uh, I went, like I said I went to bed, and that is the last time, I seen her.***

By now, you might have sensed that there is a huge amount of time missing from his story. Whenever time is missing, information is also missing. With all the persuasion, sensitivity, lack of commitment, and deception we have noted, it is not surprising that he has skipped over information. It is easier to simply skip over the information than it is to lie about it. He has not told us very much about what occurred on Friday night. If the investigators are able to reinterview this guy, they need to ask him for details of Friday evening. Focusing on the missing time will send a subtle message to him that the investigators know more than he would like them to.

From his version of events, we noted the lack of commitment and deception surrounding her lunch and going to find the stuffed pepper. He then said that she needed time and space and so he drove up the street or went to his mom's. He stated that he was only gone a few minutes and returned because he couldn't stay away from the kids. Does that even make sense? If he was leaving because of relationship problems, why would he return within a few minutes? This might indicate that he knew there was no possibility of an argument or friction.

He reports that when he returned, he saw *her lying on the couch.* Note that she was not sleeping but lying on the couch. There is a difference. Also of note is that she is on the couch, not in her bed. If she wanted him gone and thought he went to his mom's house, why would she not be sleeping in her bed? Again, his language reveals that he is not concerned about their relationship issues at this time.

What comes next is interesting. He states:

> ***She stirred and, when I come in, she's a pretty light sleeper...***

This is subtle and might be missed by most investigators. However, it is critical to recognize what is going on in his language.

Remember that he did not say that she was sleeping but lying on the couch. We also questioned why she was not in her own bed. If he could not say that she was sleeping, why did he make the effort to say that ***she stirred?*** That in and of itself raises questions, but then he gave us a *reason why* she stirred: "she's a pretty light sleeper." It would have sufficed if he could have simply stated that she was sleeping on the couch. However, by explaining *why* he saw her stir, his brain has exposed his acute sensitivity.

Another way to phrase what is going on in his mind is this. *You should believe me that she stirred when I come in, because she is a pretty light sleeper.* This is a convincing statement at a critical juncture in his story. He is attempting to convince us that his wife was still alive at this time. In essence he is saying that you should believe his story because she is a light sleeper and he saw her stir as she was lying on the couch.

As you can see, analyzing the language is like peering into the mind. If there was any doubt before that this husband has guilty knowledge of his wife's disappearance, there shouldn't be now. The latent information in his mind has been exposed.

There are many other ways in which psychological commitment is linguistically omitted. Read and listen carefully to what others are saying.

The rule of thumb is this: If they are not committed, there is a reason why. Do not interpret for them and do not commit for them. If you do, you unwittingly become complicit in their deception.

Missing Time—Missing Information

Truthful statements are given in chronological order, one event following another. As such, any wording that spans over time indicates an unnecessary pause of some form. In fact, it means that the subject has not only paused, but also ejected information out of their statement.

Words that span time are called a *Temporal Lacunae*. Many people use an easier term and simply refer to them as a *time gap*. A temporal lacuna or time gap does not, by itself, indicate deception. It simply means that information has been left out. It is either information the subject does not consider important, or the subject knows it is important and has left it out on purpose.

Since telling an outright lie is stressful, one of the most common forms of deception is to simply withhold information. This is where the time gap comes into play. It is often employed when one desires to withhold or skip over the information, they do not want others to know. Although skipping over a period of time does not necessarily indicate deception, time gaps are often found in deceptive statements.

In the previous section, the husband's version of the night his wife disappeared was obviously missing time and information. He simply did not include enough details and only included that which he wanted the investigator to know.

When a person wishes to verbally skip over time, they will often do so by using words such as the following:

"Finally"
"Later on"
"Eventually"
"Afterwards"
"From there"
"After a while"
"Shortly thereafter"
"A short time later"
"A few minutes later"
"The next thing I know"
"The next thing I remember"

Be aware of words and phrases that span over a period of time. Focusing on those areas will be very beneficial during your interview and during your overall investigation.

In 2008, Jodi Arias murdered her ex-boyfriend, Travis, while he was in the shower. Travis sustained 27 stab wounds, a slit throat, and a single gunshot to the forehead. Jodi also took pictures of Travis, and then left the memory card in the washer. When Jodi was eventually interviewed, she had a few different versions of what happened to Travis. One version was that they were both victims of a home invasion while at Travis's home. Eventually, Jodi testified at her trial that she killed Travis in self-defense. The jury did not buy into her story, and Jodi was convicted of murder. She is now serving a life sentence without the possibility of parole.

During Jodi's interview with the homicide investigator, she often used words that spanned time. Knowing about the injuries that Travis sustained, the time gaps are significant.

This is one of the statements she made while telling the home invasion version of what happened:

I heard… ah, really loud pop, and the next thing I remember, I was lying next to the bathtub and Travis was, um… screaming.

The interesting thing about made-up stories is that they often contain a lot of factual information, or details that actually occurred. The subject simply alters the context a bit to fit their deceptive narrative. I believe that Jodi's sentence above is a de facto truthful sentence. At the same time, it is also a deceptive statement in that she withheld critical information. She used details that she experienced, but also used the words "and the next thing I remember" to skip over the critical details of stabbing Travis 27 times, slitting his throat, and shooting him in the head. I believe that Jodi was lying on the floor next to Travis as he screamed and suffered. Knowing Jodi's personality and knowing that people will use details they actually experienced, it is likely she was taunting him at that time, and perhaps taking pictures.

In Jodi's statement above, the phrase, "and the next thing I remember", is not only an unnecessary connection, but it is a long pause that took more effort to formulate. She devoted five words to skipping over the critical information she did not want the detective to know. In other words, more cognitive energy was required to purposely skip over that period of time and the information surrounding it.

Remember, you cannot withhold information that you do not have. Thus, gaps in time create questions:

- ***What is missing here?***
- ***Why is the subject withholding information here?***

Here is the rule of thumb:

Flag any passing of time and make a note to visit it in the interview.

- ***You said, "the next thing I know;" tell me about that.***
    - "I don't remember."

Do not accept this type of response. Follow up with:

- ***Please take a moment and think about what happened.***
- Then follow up on their answer with, ***what happened just before that?***

Continue to ask questions using vague and open language that is non-accusatory.

If you hear a temporal lacunae phrase such as "and then later on" and also encounter a missing pronoun, you are likely at the place where the event took place, and likely speaking to the person responsible for the crime. Since pronouns give us ownership, and the guilty person does not want to take ownership of the missing time and information, they will often omit the pronoun. This results in language that spans time and removes psychological ownership.

Conclusion

Moving forward, as you conduct your cold case investigations and interviews, remember that people will unknowingly teach you where you should focus your questions in the interview, and where to focus your investigation.

Here are the guidelines:

- Recognize the areas in which sensitivity manifests in their language. Remember, sensitivity is manifested by:
  - Providing an explanation that was not asked of them.
  - Removing themselves psychologically from their own statement—removing psychological commitment.
  - Describing a past event as something that they normally do, which is most often stated in present tense language.
  - Temporal lacunae's—words and phrases that span over a period of time and information.
- If you have the opportunity of doing a live interview, exploit their sensitivity by asking for details and other non-confrontational questions that surround the areas in which the sensitivity was manifested. Focusing on those areas will send a subtle message that you know more than they want you to. This in turn will elevate their stress, which in turn weakens them psychologically and physiologically. Once they break down psychologically, utterances, admissions, and confessions will naturally follow.
- Their brain has the information you need to solve your case. Follow their language and let it paint the scene for you.

The Role of the Crime Analyst

17

KATHY MACKAY

Introduction to Cold Case Homicide Analysis

In 2018, Utah enacted a law mandating that all cold cases be entered into a Law Enforcement Cold Case Database, as outlined in Utah Statute Code Section 53-10-115. When the database was launched, the Department of Public Safety (DPS) created an analyst position to oversee its management. I was hired for this role as the state's cold case homicide analyst. My primary responsibility was to ensure that all law enforcement agencies entered their cold cases into this database and supplied the necessary information to be entered into a separate website for the victims' families and the public to access. I also assisted the agencies with their cold cases, helping them to advance their investigations.

The information presented in this chapter will showcase my journey from having no experience with cold cases to collaborating with all law enforcement agencies in Utah that deal with them, through over seven years of trial and error, and by consulting numerous experts. I have learned how to be a valuable cold case homicide analyst.

A cold case homicide analyst serves as a crucial bridge between unsolved crimes of the past and modern investigative capabilities, breathing new life into cases that might otherwise remain forever unresolved. These specialized professionals assist in applying advanced analytical techniques, cutting-edge forensic technologies, and fresh investigative perspectives to cases that have grown cold due to the passage of time, lack of leads, or resource constraints. By systematically reviewing evidence, identifying previously overlooked connections, and leveraging contemporary tools such as DNA analysis and digital databases, cold case crime analysts not only help provide resolution to grieving families but also enhance public safety by assisting in the potential identification of active offenders and preventing future crimes. Their meticulous work transforms what were once dead ends into renewed opportunities for justice, ensuring that the passage of time does not diminish society's commitment to accountability and that no victim is forgotten.

Cold case homicide analysis involves re-examining unsolved criminal investigations, often related to serious offenses such as homicide, sexual assault, missing persons, and the identification of unidentified human remains (UHR). A case is deemed "cold" when all viable leads have been

DOI: 10.4324/9781003415633-20

exhausted and active investigative efforts have ceased. The classification of when a case is considered "cold" varies by agency or state. In Utah, cases are recognized as cold after remaining unsolved for three years or more.

However, advancements in forensic science, data analytics, and investigative techniques have equipped law enforcement agencies with new tools to revisit and potentially solve these cases.

The significance of cold case investigations extends beyond individual cases; they play a broader role in delivering justice, restoring public trust, and preventing future crimes. Unsolved cases leave victims' families in prolonged uncertainty and grief, with unanswered questions about their loved ones' fates. By reopening these cases, cold case analysts can play an essential role in bringing hope to victims' families, providing justice for the victim, and helping to find answers to cases that have been dormant, regardless of how much time has passed.

Additionally, solving cold cases can help prevent future crimes by identifying repeat offenders who may have evaded capture for years. Many violent criminals, particularly serial offenders, remain at large, posing an ongoing threat to public safety. Cold case analysts can uncover new leads, connect cases across jurisdictions, and provide long-awaited closure to victims and resolution to their families by employing modern investigative techniques, such as DNA genealogy, digital forensics, and law enforcement collaboration.

Role of a Cold Case Crime Analyst

A cold case analyst plays a vital role in reviewing, analyzing, and investigating unsolved criminal cases, including unsolved homicides, missing persons, UHR, and sexual assaults. They work closely with law enforcement to overcome barriers to sharing case information between agencies. I have had to reach out to other law enforcement agencies when I found valuable information on a case I was handling. In this example, a person of interest owned various vehicles and was possibly involved in the murders of two females. I wanted to determine if there were any other potential victims in the state of Utah. I sent an email to specific law enforcement agencies with cold cases involving a female victim who went missing or was murdered. I was trying to determine if a specific car and color were involved in their cases. I received several replies, but none matched any vehicles. One agency was hesitant to respond, so I spoke directly with the detective and explained the information I was seeking and its purpose. After our discussion, the detective was open to sharing details about his case. Unfortunately, I did not find any connections with the cases from the other agencies.

Sometimes I receive anonymous tips that contain a large amount of information but lack details about the crime's location. I'm unsure which agency they pertain to. In such cases, I will email all the agencies in our state to request any information regarding a possible connection to the tip I received. This presents an opportunity for agencies to communicate and share information with each other, especially when they have been reluctant to do so in the past.

The cold case analyst's secondary mission is to rekindle interest in cold case files, bringing new life and hope to them. They continually research new tools that may help advance these cases. Working as a cold case homicide analyst is highly proactive, time-consuming, and often frustrating. The frustration stems from learning that working these cases does not yield answers as quickly as they do on TV. There is a considerable amount of waiting for results from DNA testing. Additionally, there is a growing awareness of how law enforcement officers must balance their caseload, with cold cases sometimes taking a back seat. As an analyst, you want to jump in any way to try to help them make progress on the higher-priority case, so they can return to addressing the cold cases that are always waiting for advancement. Perhaps the most difficult aspect of cold case work is confronting the reality that, despite exhaustive investigation, some cases may never be resolved. Sometimes, for example, you encounter a case where the victim's remains were cremated in the past, and there is no way of getting a positive identification.

Another example is when you start assisting in a case and discover that either the evidence was not stored in proper containers and has developed mold, or the evidence was accidentally destroyed. It can be so aggravating knowing that the family members of this loved one will probably never get the answers they are seeking about what happened to their loved one.

Just knowing that not all cold cases can be solved with the specific tools that are readily available is frustrating. For instance, a cold case that has ashes instead of the victim's bones highlights this issue. Knowing that DNA technology cannot be used to identify someone through their ashes brings the frustration of having to set a case aside until the necessary DNA technology is developed.

However, it becomes immensely rewarding when answers are uncovered, cases are solved and closed, and victims receive justice while their families find the resolution they have long awaited. It creates powerful emotions when imagining how long these families have been waiting for answers, whether it is knowing that their loved one has been found, or at least an explanation of what happened to their loved one and possibly why. The joy in their hearts and the tears on their faces represent the reward of working together with law enforcement and never giving up in finding those answers.

Responsibilities of a Cold Case Homicide Analyst

Case File Review and Reconstruction

Analysts play a vital role in reviving old cases that have not been opened or examined for more than 60 years, sometimes even longer. The case file contains outdated police reports, crime scene photos, autopsy records, witness statements, correspondence, and notes on previous actions taken regarding the case. This is when the analyst can rejuvenate the investigation by reorganizing, creating timelines of events, charting associations, and linking the individuals involved in a visual chart that conveys the case story more swiftly than reviewing everything and rereading it.

The Importance of Charts in Cold Cases

Charts are essential tools that help bring cold cases into perspective. They save time for the case agent, allowing them to avoid spending too much work sifting through the details of the case. A timeline chart can illustrate what has been accomplished in a case. The analyst can gather all the information from the case and arrange it chronologically, showing what has been done from beginning to end, identifying where work needs to be completed and where gaps exist. Charts provide the case agent with an understanding of what is present in the case, what is missing, and what remains to be finalized.

One timeline chart I created visualized the cases of missing and unidentified human remains throughout Utah's history. On this chart, I displayed the names of missing individuals in Utah from every agency at the top of the timeline. I included victims' photos, names, dates they went missing, and descriptive information such as height, weight, hair color, eye color, clothing, and any distinguishing features, including scars or tattoos. At the bottom of the timeline, I listed the cases of UHR. For these cases, I did not include a photo of the victim; instead, I provided images of boots, clothing, tattoos, or any other details that might capture someone's attention while viewing this timeline. I also included the date when the body or bones were found, the law enforcement agency involved, the case number, and relevant descriptive details.

This chart is highly beneficial for each agency to have in their office. When a body is found or a person goes missing in their area, law enforcement officers gain a clearer understanding of related cases involving missing and unidentified human remains that they may not have previously been aware of. They can verify who is missing if a UHR is discovered in their region. The agency and case numbers are included with each entry, allowing the agencies to contact one another and discuss possible similarities.

Another valuable chart is the association chart, which allows the cold case homicide analyst to make sense of the individuals in the case and gather vital information about them. Who is the victim, and what are the family dynamics? This is also an ideal time to research updated information on family members. Are they alive? Have they moved away? What is their most recent contact information?

This information will be valuable for the case agent to reach out to and re-interview potential witnesses, because time has lapsed.

Link charts help visualize the possible suspects and victim information, illustrating their relationships or connections. They effectively demonstrate how the witnesses are connected to the crime. Who has been interviewed, and who needs to be re-interviewed?

As a cold case homicide analyst, I have encountered several instances that involved creating charts, one of which related to a case involving a missing teenage boy. The family dynamics appeared confusing in the report, with multiple divorces and deaths in the family. The officer assigned to the case requested a visual that clarified the family structure, which included stepfamilies, aunts, and uncles. It showed how family members were associated, who had passed away, and the number of divorces. By creating an association chart to provide perspective on the family dynamics, it becomes clear who the boy was living with at specific times in his life. The officer gained a better understanding of the family dynamics, allowing him to organize who and how he wanted to interview according to their connections.

Forensic and DNA Records

As an analyst, gathering all forensic testing and DNA records in the case file is essential. Develop a checklist of completed tasks. The crime lab and medical examiner reports are valuable resources for this purpose. Compile a list of the dates and tests conducted, along with their results. This will assist the officer assigned to the case by providing readily available information. It will also clarify which information needs to be discussed or requested from the lab or the medical examiner's office.

As an analyst working with cold cases, it is essential to understand DNA testing and the fundamentals of DNA. Seek training that will enhance your comprehension of these concepts. It is crucial to determine whether testing has been completed on the case, given the ongoing advancements in DNA technology. Many items in the case can and should be retested using the latest DNA techniques. Therefore, it is important to gather information from the previous testing that has been conducted. The officer assigned to the case can meet with the local crime lab to discuss what testing has occurred and what might benefit from being retested.

In Utah, law enforcement agencies can schedule a case review meeting with the crime lab, which includes its forensic specialists. Personnel from the medical examiner's office provide any available information about the case. The agency presents a brief overview, detailing the victim, information on the crime, crime scene photos, what was collected at the scene, and what was tested in the crime lab. After the presentation, the crime lab reviews its records regarding the evidence received, the tests conducted, and any results obtained. From there, the agency and the crime lab discuss what can be retested using DNA technology and what has yet to be tested.

For example, if there are fingernail clippings in the evidence, the fingernails can be swabbed to collect trace evidence that may contain DNA from either the victim or the perpetrator. If a piece of the victim's clothing is tested at the lab, and it reveals that the victim's DNA is present along with DNA from an unknown subject, further testing is conducted to identify the unknown DNA. A game plan outlining the testing that can be conducted and the locations where it can be performed is developed to obtain further answers for advancing the case.

Family Trees Created for DNA Collection Purposes

This task is typically requested after a meeting with the crime lab to determine the best plan for DNA collection. As an analyst, obituaries are highly valuable in this process. In some cases I have assisted with, the most common family tree requested includes the males in the family, often starting with the grandfather and continuing down the tree to the required line. You will need to obtain contact information, addresses, and indicate whether each person is still living. These trees can encompass possible suspects or victims, depending on which DNA they intend to collect and test. If there are no living males, the request will be for the maternal lineage. Ultimately, this depends on the case and the decisions made by experts in the forensic field.

Witness and Suspect Information

Collecting information from witnesses and about suspects is essential to the case. Analysts need to organize interviews and obtain updated contact details for each witness, as well as any new information for individuals mentioned by the witnesses. The officer will likely want to re-interview those involved in the case. Additionally, the suspect information must be updated. The suspect's status and location are crucial as the case progresses. An updated profile on the suspect will assist the officer in determining the necessary actions as the case unfolds.

As I work on a case, I like to create written timelines for the suspect that include their addresses and the dates they lived at those locations. I also note their criminal record, detailing when they were arrested and the reasons behind those arrests. If they were interviewed, I record when and why, any vehicles they owned, and newspaper articles published about them or the crime at hand. On this specific timeline, I highlight the crime itself. Witness interviews may be included with this timeline or kept separate, depending on the agent's case preference.

Utilization of Databases and SITES

Open-Source Intelligence (OSINT) refers to the process of gathering, analyzing, and disseminating information from publicly available sources, including Google, Facebook, Instagram, news media, and newspaper archives. Numerous websites facilitate research and the collection of information that helps bridge gaps in a case. Law enforcement databases are also accessible to analysts as they investigate information about the ongoing case.

Many law enforcement agencies provide their analysts with access to databases to assist in the identification and research of individuals.

I won't go into detail about these sites, but I use them regularly. Dr. Rachel Walton has written extensively on databases used in investigations in previous chapters. I want to discuss my favorite go-to sites for working on cold cases.

The best resource you'll find is the newspaper archives. There are various sites available to the public through a subscription, and it's well worth the investment. This is a gold mine for cold cases, where you can discover articles published to help piece together family dynamics, media reports on cases, information on arrests, old phone numbers, and addresses.

Every case contains unique information—the actual events reported by law enforcement. Then, there is the media aspect of the story. In the past, the media would include everything in their reports, leaving nothing out. However, they do not do that today. Another way to familiarize yourself with a case is to search old newspaper articles. Some cases received extensive coverage when the crime happened, while others might have only one article or none at all. Either way, these articles are invaluable for inclusion in the case file. For every case I assist with, I gather all the published newspaper articles and include them in the file.

Law enforcement agencies appreciate this information. In cold cases, sometimes there is nothing left in the case file due to floods, fires, or accidental loss of information. For instance, in Utah, an unsolved homicide involving a female serves as a perfect example of the value that newspaper articles bring to such cases. The officer assigned to the case could only rely on newspaper articles because the case file was lost. He was able to build a case, arrest a suspect, and close the case.

The Polk City Directories are another valuable research tool I have found. The Polk City Directory was the old white and yellow pages delivered yearly in a large paper book. These thick books contained address information and phone numbers, sometimes indicating the person's profession. I understood the significance of these pages in a case I assisted with that took place in the early 1970s. As a cold case homicide analyst, one must be willing to be creative and think outside the box. Developing methods to locate individuals mentioned in an interview can be challenging. I discovered that the local library held the City Polk Records.

In this specific case, I aimed to identify the tenants who had lived in a house that had been converted into a fourplex. I was trying to locate a female with a young son who supposedly lived in one of the units. I spent hours at the local library with a coworker, trying to determine who lived at the four different addresses associated with the fourplexes. I managed to compile a list of possible tenants. With this list, the officer on the case asked me to gather the most current information on each tenant so they could reach out and interview them about a female and a boy seen at the fourplex. Another search for the same case involved finding a babysitter who lived around the corner and was mentioned in an interview.

Social media includes many sites that can help advance a case. At times, the age of the case may influence the value of social media though. Google and other platforms can be gold mines for newer cold cases. This is because everyone shares so much about their lives on social media, making it a treasure trove of helpful information.

Collaboration with Law Enforcement

Collaboration with law enforcement is essential for a successful analyst. Providing support is one of the best ways to build trust and establish a strong working relationship with police officers. It's important to understand that each law enforcement agency has its own priorities regarding how cases are handled. Cold cases are typically at the bottom of the priority list. This is not intentional; with crime rising in the United States and the constant turnover in police agencies, cases must be prioritized. The most recent ones are usually the top priority for finding answers, as the information is new and fresh. This sometimes forces cold cases to be set aside temporarily to address newer crimes. Some agencies have a designated cold case detective or unit solely assigned to cold cases, allowing them to work on older cases continually. The cold case analyst will work closely with homicide detectives, forensic specialists, Sexual Assault Kit Initiative (SAKI) agents, and legal professionals to develop new investigative strategies. They also cooperate with federal partners, such as the Federal Bureau of Investigation (FBI), and utilize national databases, including CODIS (Combined DNA Index System) and NCIC (National Crime Information Center), to compare evidence or gather information for reports.

Collaboration with National and International Sites

When I started as a cold case homicide analyst, I was unaware of some valuable resources that would have been beneficial to me. One of those was NamUs (National Missing and Unidentified Persons System). Dr. Walton has covered important information on this site in previous chapters. I will share my experience and discuss the value of the website. When word spread in 2018 that Utah was mandating the entry of cold cases into a law enforcement database and making other information available on a public site for family and public awareness, the NamUs representative from Utah contacted me, leading to a collaboration. We worked closely together to ensure that I was informed about all missing and unidentified person cases that had been entered into that site. In return, NamUs would keep track of the cases submitted to the Utah Public Cold Case Site, which helped us bring some organization to these cases. By being proactive and communicating constantly about the cases, I was always aware of any new cases added to the NamUs site. Conversely, the representative from NamUs was aware of which new cold cases had been entered into the database. I reached out to local agencies and requested that they submit their cold cases to the LE Cold Case Database, which is housed within a secure Utah state facility, with access limited to Utah law enforcement. The public can visit a website (https://bci.utah.gov/coldcases/) to view the entries added to the LE database, which contains non-LES information.

Another valuable resource is the Doe Network, a national and international database for missing and unidentified person cases. The representative for Utah, who volunteers to keep this site updated, began sending me emails that included information about a case featured on the Doe Network, along with newspaper clippings, obituaries, and cemetery records. I must give credit to the representative for sharing so many cases I was previously unaware of. I would take the shared information and email it to the relevant agency. Often, the agency was not aware of the case. These cases included newspaper clippings and other materials that helped the agency research their records and locate the case file for that specific instance. In return, this enabled me to engage in discussions about moving forward and entering the case into the LE Cold Case Database.

This collaboration with the Doe Network has proven to be invaluable in helping to collect cold cases in Utah. Other websites I am aware of include the "National Center for Missing & Exploited Children (NCMEC)" and "The Charley Project." These sites play a crucial role in the investigation of cold cases within each local agency. Nowadays, with numerous crime shows on

TV and podcasts discussing the latest solved cold cases and their resolutions, there is a growing interest in cold cases, leading to the development of more websites. I have my favorites, as well as those that have benefited Utah the most.

Research New Tools That Can Help with Moving Cold Cases Forward

Another important aspect of being a cold case homicide analyst is learning about other new and innovative tools that are available for cold cases. Numerous training opportunities focus on specific DNA technologies, such as investigative genetic genealogy (IGG)—a forensic technique that combines DNA analysis with traditional genealogy to solve crimes and identify UHR. An analyst can assist with basic genealogy or help build family trees. I became more familiar with the technique by reaching out to law enforcement agencies that had closed cases utilizing it and requesting their lab reports. Those reports yielded potential family matches for individuals needing identification. I practiced constructing the family trees to align with the information in the reports. It resembles a large puzzle; your job is to piece together the family connections to unveil a person of significance to the case. This process can be time-consuming and may become addictive if you enjoy such challenges. Be prepared to search for individuals who emerge during the research process for reference testing. This happens when the genealogist identifies a potential person of interest or reaches an impasse and requires a reference DNA test to steer them in the right direction.

Search for tools that help solve cold cases in other areas by reading news reports or watching documentaries, such as Forensic Files, which discuss the techniques used in various cases throughout the U.S. Find training for yourself and the case agents you work with that will benefit you and help you understand the new tools and techniques that are available. Learn as much as you can about DNA because it helps to solve many cold cases every day. It is essential to always find and share information on the latest techniques with other agencies.

A great example of this is the first case I assisted with as a cold case homicide analyst, which was a 1979 case in Garfield County, Utah, involving a female victim who was found bound and wrapped up in a sleeping bag. All the evidence in this case, including rope, duct tape, child's play carpet, and other items, had been tested three times at the local crime lab, with no other DNA coming back except for the victim. Interestingly, before assisting on this case, I attended a local homicide school training that is held annually. I spent a week learning all the different types of death that officers see every day. Between sessions, Jared Bradley, the owner of M-VAC Systems, took 15 minutes to discuss his company's most valuable tool, a commercial DNA vacuum. I found it interesting and beneficial. I didn't think much about it after that. Until one day, the case agent and I were discussing the case, and he was trying to decide on the next move. He was frustrated with not getting any valuable DNA from the ropes and duct tape that were used to bind the victim. Up to that point, there was nothing else that could be done with the evidence because every test had been performed repeatedly with negative results. At that time, the M-VAC came to mind, and I inquired if he had heard or seen this tool. The case agent had not. I told him that I remembered it was great at pulling DNA off ropes and duct tape. The case agent was interested in learning more about the tool. He arranged for a demonstration of the M-VAC at his office. This M-VAC, being a last-resort DNA collection tool, ultimately led the case agent to the suspect, who was ultimately identified as the husband. This is an excellent example of why it is essential for a cold case homicide analyst to stay informed and educated on the latest techniques that identify suspects in cases and provide unknown identities.

Collaboration with the Crime Lab and the Medical Examiner's Office

As a cold case homicide analyst, if you have not stepped foot into the crime lab or medical examiner's office, make an appointment to take a tour. Get to know the personnel and the processes that are carried out at these facilities.

In Utah, we have a collaborative relationship with our crime lab and the medical examiner's office, which began when I requested a tour. I informed everyone I met about my job, which involves assisting with cold cases. I learned about the Automated Fingerprint Identification System (AFIS), which utilizes computer technology to compare fingerprints. It works by converting fingerprint images into digital codes that are stored in a database, allowing for quick searches to identify possible matches. I also learned about the National Integrated Ballistic Information Network (NIBIN) process for matching spent casings fired from various guns and how they can determine if a shell casing matches a specific firearm and if it was used at different crime scenes. All of this is fascinating and valuable.

One of the most important relationships I have developed in my job is with the medical examiner's office. I have been working with the investigator who oversees all the bone cases there. Utah is fortunate to have such dedicated individuals working to identify our UHR cases. As an analyst, you can find out how many of these UHR cases they have. Familiarize yourself with those cases. The Office of Medical Examiner (OME) investigator we collaborate with has conducted an inventory of all the bone cases at the OME. We have collaborated to create a spreadsheet containing basic information for each case, including the agency responsible for gender, case number, and other relevant details. I have reached out to agencies to inform them of cases involving UHR that could be tested for DNA. There have been instances where the agency was unaware it had a case at the OME. When we started collaborating with the OME, there were more than 30 cases in the bone room. As of this writing, approximately 10 cases remain, with some out for DNA testing. That exemplifies collaboration. As a cold case homicide analyst, you can build these relationships whether you have one case or many. The value of collaboration is repeatedly demonstrated as cold cases are resolved.

Collaboration with the SAKI Program and Agents Regarding Cold Cases

I work closely with the SAKI investigators based in the Utah State Bureau of Investigation (SBI) Office. They play a vital role in addressing unsolved homicides involving sexual assault and UHR. The investigators I collaborate with have written multiple grants that include federal Community Project Funding (CPF), which covers cases not funded by the SAKI grant, such as violent felonies, UHR, and missing persons cases. Another grant being utilized in Utah is the Byrnes JAG Community Project Funding (CPF) 2023, titled the "Utah Forensic Genetic Genealogy DNA Testing Initiative."

Without their efforts and dedication to grant writing, many of these cases would still be gathering dust on the shelves, as the testing required to find answers is often unattainable. If you are part of a single agency, it is crucial to reach out to the SAKI investigators in your state and inform them of any cases you have that might qualify for funded grants. The SAKI investigators will travel to engage with each agency to inventory their cases and offer assistance on each one. This collaborative effort underscores the importance of teamwork. In my experience, the SAKI investigators help many agencies with their cold case inventories and inform them about the resources available when collaborating with a cold case homicide analyst.

Other Effective Ideas a Cold Case Crime Analyst Can Assist, Create, and Suggest

Create a spreadsheet of cold case victims in your state. Then, research potential suspects linked to any sexual assault, murder, or assault in your state. I was able to enlist interns to assist with this project. The spreadsheet should list the names of victims, their ages, races, crime dates, suspects, where the bodies were found, MOs, how the bodies were discovered, suspect charges, sources of information, and an additional detail column for any follow-up notes. The purpose of this spreadsheet is to fill in the gaps regarding which crimes or suspects were present before and after each cold case. It can provide suspect information that the investigation hasn't yet explored. I've included information on any serial killers and their victims in Utah, which may aid ongoing investigations into finding possible additional victims. I highlight any row that has a suspect who is deemed a serial killer.

Another important feature this can offer is the ability to search for suspects after DNA testing is completed and a surname is provided. The spreadsheet can be referenced for suspects whose last names match the provided surname. This project is time-consuming, but it will serve as a valuable investigative tool you can share with local law enforcement agencies as they work on their cases.

Propose the creation of a cold case review board. Anyone working with law enforcement can draft a proposal and submit it to the relevant authority. I dedicate this suggestion to Professor Rachel Walton. Without her, the Utah Cold Case Review Board would never have come to fruition. With her experience with the Vidocq Society, a national cold case review board, Professor Walton guided me in creating the best one-stop shop for cold cases. She also provided me with a copy of the National Institute of Justice's National Best Practices for Implementing and Sustaining a Cold Case Investigation Unit (https://www.ojp.gov/pdffiles1/nij/252016.pdf), which Professor Walton co-authored.

In Utah, we hold the presentations at the same facility every month on the third Thursday. We meet for nine months each year, taking a break during the months of June, July, and August. This year, we held one presentation in a rural county, making it easier for surrounding rural agencies to participate without the need for extensive travel. Our board consists of 30 members with diverse experiences:

- The Bureau of Forensic Services or Crime Lab
- OME
- Experienced cold case investigators
- SAKI investigators
- Prosecutors and district attorneys
- Crime scene specialist
- Retired Officer/professor teaches forensic/cold case
- Cold case analyst
- Forensic psychologist
- Invite a representative from NamUs or the Doe Network

The only requirement is to have everyone attending each meeting sign a confidentiality agreement. Avoid being judgmental about how a case was handled or any mistakes that may have been made. Show respect for board members and presenters. No cell phone use or computer use is allowed unless necessary. The board members are there to give their full attention to the presenting agency; bringing work to do or catching up on phone calls is not allowed. We have the board members step out if they get a phone call that needs to be addressed. Additionally, refrain from seeking notoriety; any information released to the media will be managed by the presenter and/or the respective agency.

Establish goals for the board, such as:

- To help the presenting agencies find justice for cold case victims.
- To establish open communication with each agency to foster future assistance and build relationships.
- To provide support, not recognition.
- To offer hope and resources to law enforcement agencies.
- To unite a diverse group of seasoned investigators and specialists with expertise across various disciplines to assist with unsolved cases.

From there, contact law enforcement agencies with cold cases and invite them to present them. They should prepare a PowerPoint presentation that closely follows the guidelines of the Vidocq Society, available at https://vidocq.org/.

The Utah Cold Case Review Board has successfully assisted law enforcement agencies with their cold cases. In the past five years, 23 different agencies have utilized this tool in 50 cases, resulting in the resolution of four of those cases.

Working as a cold case homicide analyst has been a valuable experience in fostering communication and collaboration among law enforcement agencies and their partners. I have witnessed a growing passion to bring resolution to these cases, instilling hope in investigations that once had none. I have acquired new skills and discovered tools to support these cases. Being surrounded by remarkable individuals with extensive experience in various fields plays an important role in advancing cases that have exhausted all leads, opening the possibility of new hope and ideas. I play a crucial part in the process of organizing, researching, and collaborating with others who are also committed to perseverance and maintaining hope in seeing these cold cases through from start to finish.

My takeaway for anyone considering a career as a cold case homicide analyst is that you will grow as a person, knowing that you have played an essential role in piecing together parts of a puzzle while working alongside some of the finest individuals. You will become a valued person to the families who have waited so long for answers. I have developed friendships with some family members who trusted me and just needed someone to talk to about their loved ones when they felt unheard. I have learned to think outside the box more in finding answers as these cases move forward. You learn to be proactive, always considering ways to better serve the agencies you work with. Most importantly, you learn to ask questions; there are never too many questions. That is how you will learn the processes and techniques, as well as how conclusions are made. I used to be afraid to ask questions until I realized that this is how I will learn to be the best analyst I can be.

Thank you, Professor Rachel Walton, for guiding me in helping law enforcement and for inspiring me to make this job as a cold case homicide analyst as rewarding and successful as possible. You were my rock when I stood still, not knowing which direction to go. You believed in me when I did not believe in myself. I dedicate the Utah Cold Case Review Board and this chapter to you and all the success it brings.

Open Source Intelligence (OSINT) 18

TODD VANCANTFORT

Managing Expectations

Before we jump into this prose, I believe a few thoughts on managing expectations are warranted. I have spent over 40 years of my professional life in law enforcement, various local, state, and federal, criminal investigations including homicides, and cold case reviews. I have also managed and led public safety, national security, and criminal intelligence organizations from mid-management to executive levels. So, as you would imagine, I do not presume to be an expert in the field of Open Source Intelligence (OSINT) nor the world of cold case investigations or really much of anything else. Likewise, should anyone else hold themselves up as such be very dubious of their value to your investigation. As we work through the key topics of this chapter, you will quickly learn just how vast and deep the OSINT waters run and how utterly complex most cold case investigations can be. There is simply no way any one person or even small team can fully know, let alone leverage every source and tool available within the OSINT domain or within the realm of paradoxical investigations. With one exception on this last point, that of the case you have been stuck with and doggedly pursued.

While it may seem daunting, don't get too overwhelmed by the topic, or avoid leveraging the power of OSINT to help solve case(s). It is understandable to be put off at first, but the reality is you already employ elements of OSINT in your investigations as well as your everyday life. You leverage the power of the internet through google searches along with public and proprietary government records searches, and through a variety of data search and management resellers. These are often referred to as closed sources of information, but more on that later.

Regardless of the web access companies your agency contracts through some broad licensing that provides you with investigative management tools, none will serve all your needs. I would argue they actually provide you very little that will advance your case, a large part of why many cases go cold in the first place. A dearth of critical information needed to either identify the victim, the suspect, viable witnesses, or sufficient evidence to facilitate a successful resolution of the case is the norm with homicide cold cases.[1] Be it through prosecution or closure as a result of the confirmed death of the perpetrator,

 DOI: 10.4324/9781003415633-21

or even evidence changing the manner of death from homicide to suicide, accidental death, or maybe even an alien abduction, current statistics put murder case closures near an all-time low in most jurisdictions.[2] Ok, so before I devolve too far down that quirky rabbit hole, suffice to say the challenge we've all faced in these investigations is the lack of concrete information that we can understand, effectively link to some element of our case, and prove beyond the reasonable doubt test in court. Or, in that last circumstance, to the level of risk tolerance of the prosecutor's office(s) with jurisdiction over the case.

Finally, it would be impossible for this little confabulation to provide you enough enlightenment to miraculously solve your most perplexing challenges or effortlessly find those missing pieces to your *WWWHWW* puzzles. My objective here is to provide you with an understanding of OSINT and its many, *MANY* layers. And, to help demystify the world of open source information so you can move past the ominous sound of it all and dive in. Or at least dip your toe in the shallow end of the kiddie pool as you acclimate yourself. All while skirting the tsunami of information overwhelming you while trying to bring justice to the victims and closing your case.

The Lay of the Land

Ok, now that we have set the stage and hopefully put you a bit more at ease with the topic, let's start with the fundamentals. Terminology, acronyms, OSINT's place within the world of "INTs" and why it matters to some, but not really much to you as a cold case investigator or supervisor. Or, more aptly described, as masters of triage as you try to fix what broke while managing the seemingly impossible.

As to terminology, there's much that's standardized since the term itself, *OSINT*, is obviously an acronym that immediately makes one believe it belongs entirely within the traditional intelligence professional space. Such a belief though is flawed for two reasons that come to mind. One, that open source information has generally been seen as nothing more than what an investigator or intelligence operative can learn through everyday observation of information available to anyone with rudimentary access to the same sources. And, as such, the concept was not really recognized as a form of tradecraft until the modern period of the internet. And, as that nest of snakes proliferated, the ubiquity of information availability. The second reason is the notion of leveraging openly available information requires advanced skills only available to the traditional intelligence community which is, well, wrongheaded and, if claimed, someone's pure egotistical bluster.

To be clear, while the application of OSINT information is not rocket surgery, it is far more complicated and intricate an undertaking than simply searching for something through your preferred internet browser search tools. There are many commonsense elements, however, anyone that is going to apply OSINT as a means of finding, assessing, analyzing, and ultimately attributing information gleaned must understand the fundamentals of information research. That includes ensuring they check their personal prejudices, assumptions, and presumptions prior to even sitting down at the computer. The risk of just looking for proof, or to disprove a belief or a finding guarantees bias and failure. Experience, extensive training, and the correct mindset of disbelief along with a robustly dubious outlook are critical to ensuring your case is not compromised or your evidence skewed. After all, an oft-quoted rumination attributed to the big man himself, Abraham Lincoln, notes: *The Problem With Quotes Found On The Internet Is, That They Are Often Not True.* We all know the consequences of such approaches and see it in headlines all the time when our cases are obliterated in court or in the media due to myopic or single focused searches for evidence simply to prove one's suspicions or conjectures in solving the *WWWHWW* riddle.

Now, back to the point of this section: taxonomy, meanings, and relevance. While OSINT is an exercise in gleaning somewhat hidden or obscured information shrouded in lots of noise, it has been in existence since long before we bothered to put a label, let alone a ring on it. The purposeful binning of the information with the intent of isolating open source information from the other means of intelligence collection really is fairly nascent.[3] Of the six current disciplines of intelligence as defined by the Office of the Director of National Intelligence (ODNI), OSINT is the newest recognized.[4] Again, I wish to emphasize the point such information sources have been around long before the internet or the acceptance by the national security intelligence organizations. As common sense will tell you, OSINT even predates the agencies' existence as well. But I don't think a history lesson is what you're looking for and, since the point is made, I won't dwell here any longer.

OSINT is a recognized discipline, and frankly critical as a tool of intelligence *AND* investigative information, to national security agencies, your agency, the courts; the public should and do expect you to leverage those tools and the insights they bring to light. I also proffer, should you choose not to apply these tools, you're doing your case and your victims an inexcusable injustice while making your investigation astronomically more difficult, *and* less credible and defensible in court.

What OSINT Is and Is Not

In the context of criminal investigations, and, in particular, active and "cold case" homicide investigations, OSINT is simply an officialized term representing the "publicly available" sources of information leveraged and compiled in the advancement of your investigation. I stress publicly available in quotations to reflect, in part, what OSINT is not. OSINT, though it could be, is not necessarily information obtained through a warrant, subpoena, or other form of court order or compulsory collection method.

OSINT has two basic recognized categories, arguably they are somewhat informal and more important to professional "INT" practitioners and source clarification than they are to practical investigative application. The "Open" within the OSINT name is also often construed as "free". In this case meaning no fee or membership or access limitations other than a means to leverage the information through basic internet service providers (ISPs). Though such a caveat is a misnomer in that such a "paywall" or membership or access to many forms of information do exist. But still, they do not restrict access via a formal limitation for access to the general public, or, by extension to you as an investigator/crime analyst. There are often "terms of use"; however, such terms do not constitute public servant, investigative, or privacy constraints since the very existence of the information has been published for public consumption.[5] That said, some genealogy databases have taken the extraordinary step of calling out law enforcement investigative use as a violation of their corporate terms of use. I remind you though, such terms are not a violation of any law, nor should you allow them to be proscriptive in any way, and they should not deter you from, within the bindings of your local policies, finding and leveraging every source of information to resolve your unknowns and your case.

The distinction though between free and membership-based sources should be non-existent in the relevance of information gained when the only limitation is agreement to terms of use and fees for service/access. Such distinctions are often confused by some as being "closed sources", which is the second category of OSINT information. These systems are often argued by the ill-informed or simply obstinate as proscriptive and therefore off limits, presumptively requiring a warrant or subpoena for access. Such a distinction is ignorant and, put plainly, bollocks. The sole requirement of membership or a fee for access is not a limitation, nor should it be construed as such if any other member of society is free to join or pay the same fee. That said, you must understand and comport to your local and state agency guidelines as they relate to leveraging OSINT that crosses into the Personally Identifiable Information (PII) realm. An important resource for you to leverage, all of which really boils down to common sense guidelines, is the federally published Real-Time and Open Source Analysis (ROSA) Resource Guide which includes the Fair Information Practice Principles (FIPPs), which are most relevant to this topic.[6]

So then, what is OSINT *not*? Well being captain obvious for a bit, it is not a silver bullet to solving your case or finding all your unknowns. And, while I started out with the quip of a mixed metaphor, of OSINT not being rocket surgery, it is not easy to leverage or navigate. It is also not easy to know where to begin, where to hunt, or to keep up with every new aggregator of information or sites that can lead you down the most fruitful yellow brick road. You will invariably cross some dark forests and some dead ends in some wonderfully distracting poppy fields. While some of them can be entertaining, they are not going to help you find your answers. We will explore this proverbial bridge over the information abyss more later, as we get into the topic of resources, both tools and personnel.

OSINT is also only a form of intelligence if you choose to define it as such. Leveraging legally and openly available information within the investigative context *is not*, at least in my mind, defined as "intelligence". That distinction is important both as a talking point and as a way to disabuse the public, open-records-act hunters. Intelligence is defined in how the information gleaned is used, not how it is obtained. As an investigator, or investigative analyst, you are not using the information to focus enforcement actions against a community, group, neighborhood, or a specific area within your jurisdiction. You are also not using it to focus on a specific group for investigative action outside the scope of your purposes. Only to solve your case. That is really only important when discussions of policy come into play and what I have seen in some jurisdictions on the use or reliance on any form of intelligence within police agencies. For validation of that point, I point you back to the BJA OSINT resource guide cited earlier.

Policy Considerations

Now for the fun part. Yes, I am being facetious, but this topic is critical to keep you, your team, and your agency out of hot water. And just like the parable of the frog in the slowly increasingly hot water, ignorance and minor transgressions can and will build up to a boiling point that could sideline your investigation, create a potential civil rights nightmare, or get your evidence tossed in court. Oh, and of course potentially get you fired. All really bad outcomes that will, and by all rights, should lead to career roadblocks at a minimum. As you will quickly deduce, OSINT policy leans heavily toward common sense applications. Know what not to do, how to preserve and document the information you seek and obtain, and stay within your lanes. Ensure your analysts do not stray into areas that are not explicitly related to the case and what they are working on. While the research on cold cases shows there is no single reason for a case to go cold, sloppy, incomplete, or poorly executed investigative actions have a significant impact leading to such consequences.[7] Also, for a more daunting point, as a cold case investigator or analyst, compromising your training or your ethics would be adding salt to an already excruciating wound borne by the family and the justice unserved for the victim(s).

Moving on, if you're going into the world of the Onion sites, known better as the dark web, you really need to know what you're diving into. In fact, I would advise only your most seasoned OSINT analyst be allowed to operate in that muddy, shark-infested sludge, and world of scary beasts. The TOR network is full of really good and unique information, but it's also fraught with the worst graphically obscene criminal and violent material. It is also very easy to stumble into the worst on there as well as into other much bigger and broader international investigations.

I think, this is a good place to touch on the topic of pseudonyms, usually referred to as personas or "sock puppets". Depending on the type of work your most seasoned analysts and investigators undertake within their OSINT duties, they may need to develop and manage a number of personas. This is NOT necessary for general case research and investigation processes. Such tools are only necessary if your team will be actively seeking out engagement with potential suspects or sources. Additionally, this could be necessary if they are going to delve into the more involved activities of monitoring servers such as Telegram, WhatsApp, Discord, KIK, and similar places where peer-to-peer (P2P) activity takes place along with postings similar to less exclusive sites like Facebook, Instagram, Pinterest, and so on. This topic will need its own rules of engagement, monitoring, and management. It requires additional skill sets since it is also often an active means of collection and not just capturing historical or static information. They may and will often directly seek out information or engage others within the spaces they operate. They will also need additional tools we will get into in the next section. In most cases, this work should also be reserved for commissioned officers and not civilian analysts due to the nature of the activities and the intentional misdirection through the use of pseudonyms.

A core element of any Agency OSINT policy must emphasize the critical requirement to safeguard sensitive law enforcement information. Such information is codified in federal as well as many state and local laws as Law Enforcement Sensitive (LES) information, and in the federal realm is categorized as Sensitive but Unclassified (SBU). Unauthorized release or compromise of such information carries both criminal and civil liabilities. Not only is LES information at risk but in most cases PII is often at play, and at risk. Should an individual intentionally or even unintentionally compromise PII, they are subject to additional criminal and/or civil penalties. This is an important point for not only investigators but should also be emphasized and written into any agreement for employment, volunteer work, or any other means of participation where a person may be granted access to investigative information. In addition, when students from local universities or colleges are allowed to work with cold case units, they should also include not only criminal and civil liability but also warnings of educational consequences through the higher education centers governing student and faculty integrity processes. They should include the most significant consequences such as expulsion and permanent debarment from attendance and, if permissible, the denial or transfer of any earned course credits prior to the violation.

Now that you are thoroughly disinclined to venture into the spooky world of OSINT, let's pull you a bit further into the riptide: the core of your agency policy and the intent you want to keep in mind.

As I noted previously, you will want to ensure those working in OSINT need to fully understand the lanes they are operating in, and the perils of violating the rules and policy of the agency and the unit. Violating those policies will put them at risk, both personally and professionally for civil rights violations, compromising the case outcome, and, in some cases, criminal culpability. They need to fully understand their role in the investigations, the information they are targeting, and why. They also need to understand the criticality of documenting what they were looking for, why they were looking where they were, and what results they obtained at each site, including null or negatively impacting results. In other words, they need to adhere to strict evidence collection, citation/source reporting, and retention. These chain of custody records must be airtight, just like all other forms of evidence. Not just those that validate existing or presumptive case information, but also any information that might shed additional light or even raise doubt or refute other information. Such practices are critical for case integrity and preventing civil as well as criminal consequences for the agency, analyst, and investigators for potential civil rights and privacy abuse claims.

For model policy documents, I would start with your state or major city fusion center, though remember too, they may not have the mandate you do, and their model generally follows the federal intelligence approach, which is far more proscriptive than what yours should be. You will often have criminal investigatory authorities the fusion center analysts may not, so don't bind your hands unnecessarily out of too much of an error on the side of caution. Additionally, other agencies have already been down the road you are now venturing. Reach out to them for copies of their policy documents and plagiarize the hell out of them. Especially if they have already shown to save that agencies' bacon in the past. Then of course run them past your own legal office, civil rights office, and leadership to ensure you have full buy-in and Cover Your Ass (CYA).

What Equipment and Skills You're Going to Need

Now that we have covered the basics, let's get into the tools and the technology you're going to need to get the job done. By now you've probably realized the scale of the mountain you're about to climb. The reality is there's just *way* too much information out there to even begin to make sense of it all without a clearly established methodology. Even then, the scope and scale of all the information is just unmanageable, let alone useful if you can't get through all the noise the important data is buried within. A great synthesis of this dilemma is spelled out in a Harvard paper focused on the enormity and challenge faced by intelligence analysts today, and by extension cold case investigators who must find ways to apply the most cutting-edge and modern techniques and tools to solve sometimes decades-old challenges and, yes, failures.[8]

Starting with technology since that's a bit less in-depth a discussion. You're going to prefer computers that are not connected to your internal networks or databases. Especially if you're going to venture into the dark TOR world of dirty deeds and dirty trolls. If they are though, or your IT gurus insist on it, they will need to be firewalled and able to have unfettered (dirty IT word there) access to the internet without the usual security or "not safe for work" (NSFW) constraints. This is important because you are going to want your analysts to have the fastest possible internet speeds which most shared internal systems are not capable of providing. And, regardless of whether you get a dedicated outside internet feed or are forced into the agency wide network, every terminal should, by default, operate through a high-end virtual private network (VPN). This will help shield the team from outside sources, including the ISP from having access to your operations or where your team goes. It will also ensure your Internet Protocol (IP) address does not reflect your agency, which is visible, easy for anyone to check, and leads directly back to your agency by name. I say high-end VPN because free or discounted VPNs are not always as secure and also tend to cause lag and slow down your internet feeds. Also note a warning in what I just pointed out here, VPNs are not going to fully keep your identity secret or stop the most ardent tracker from finding your IP address. Simply put, if the government can compromise the security of the VPN network, so can the more accomplished hackers.[9] I would add one other option that could keep you within the agency network but provide a significant barrier to systems compromise and that is a cloud-based platform like Silo.[10] I have not fully explored them, but they offer a single pane of glass dashboard for all things OSINT searching while providing you more than just a VPN separation. There are, I am sure, more companies beyond Silo; however, it is an example worth exploring. The bad guys would naturally revel in compromising your case, exposing your operations, or reverse-engineering their way back and attempting to collect, disrupt, deny, degrade, or destroy your information system resources or the information within. This would constitute a bad day in the office, isn't it?

Now that you have your first introduction in communications security (COMSEC) here, and undoubtedly this is not your first rodeo on the topic, let's get back to the tech talk. The desktops or laptops you obtain need to be able to manage graphics and, if it is laptops you are considering, make sure there are docking stations allowing them to leverage multiple monitors. In the "bloody hell, mate" category of examples, I have seen setups with a large screen along with four to six normal size monitors. The uninitiated would ask why so many and why so big, until they were asked to manage, sometimes dozens of sources of disparate information simultaneously. Keeping it all binned for their easy reference and transfer to other documents, and immediate access, all while not going blind trying to squint at small text over the period of several hours a day. Day by day, week after week, ad nauseum. I would recommend no less than three 27- to 32-inch monitors per station. That also means your graphic cards will need to also be able to manage multiple monitors. High resolution and high amounts of RAM are also critical when they are looking for or managing geographic intelligence information (GEOINT), images or video. Most laptops are simply not capable of such high-resolution work, nor are most off-the-shelf desktops. Find a gamer or web developer in your midst. Anyone between the age of 12 and 20 will do, and they can help you spec out the top-of-the-line setup. Then when you're ready to pitch that to your leadership, *AND* they stop laughing at you, *certainly not with you*, you have a starting point to scale down to a minimally acceptable setup.

While I pointed out the value of maintaining an isolated system, that does create a fundamental problem with the need to maintain oversight as well as the need to keep all the work effectively managed and tracked. I know this is a 180° turn; however, what may be ideal for some is not going to be the reality for most. Smaller agencies without the robust network will benefit from the one-off setup, whereas the larger agencies shouldn't have to. In addition you will need to keep all that work integrated with the rest of the case management within the records management/case management systems you currently use. That will, of course, ensure you have all your chain of evidence tracked properly. That will just lead to you really getting a dedicated pipeline into the network with fewer shared servers exposed to the outside world. And again, make sure there are robust firewalls to keep the internet sewer backflow from entering your networks.

Peripheral equipment such as scanners, printers, and additional storage capability all have to be factored in as well, but the most current technology is more than adequate there. Just remember to think in terabytes and not megabytes of data storage, or even investing in a server to hold as much data and separate backup for that data. Backups should be in secure spaces and not on the desktop/laptop where the risk of corruption, loss, or compromise is the greatest. All systems whether stand-alone or networked must of course be encrypted. And that includes forwarding evidence/case information in any format. All must be encrypted to avoid loss or theft. While we are on the topic of information sharing, don't forget the environment. Office setups for different approaches (open vs isolation), quiet space, not public area, etc., all need to be part of your consideration.

Next on the list, yes there is much more, is the software needed. You're going to get very little accomplished with Google or Bing or Duck-Duck-Go alone. There are currently many one-off or specialized search engines out there along with the most common ones. I'll share what will be an obsolete link in the end notes to a great source as of this writing.[11] But, be warned much like the technology you buy, the source I provide will be outdated as soon as it's published. To stay current, and to start learning what you don't know, I would strongly encourage you to join the Reddit OSINT sub-reddit, which is a running message board on the topic with lots of questions and answers and some pretty good practitioners sharing what they know and how.

As you build your team, that is, if you can fund a team, you're going to want to ensure each has the software and search tools that are focused on their unique area of talent and investigative scope. Remember at the very beginning, I pointed out there are no OSINT experts, but there are narrow subject matter experts (SMEs) that will evolve in the various niches of the OSINT enterprise. Before I get into a couple of the more specialized areas due to their sheer volume of resources and steep learning curves, all of your analysts need to be proficient in Google Dorking.[12] This is a fundamental tool they must know how to use before any other, to ensure you can leverage the information you need while avoiding as much of the white noise, that is the internet, as you can. This will ensure your analysts are not sifting through mountain-high silos, or searching the stars for the guy holding the bow, that would be constellation Orion if you were about to google that like I just did.

You'll find some people adept at finding everything and anything in the geospatial arena (GEOINT) and you will find them an invaluable resource for cold case reviews and investigations. They are your experts on weather, atmospheric conditions, and geological topics that may help you predict where evidence might be located. Imagine trying to dig a grave in hard rock, or a mountain range. What was the weather really like at the time and on the date of the crime? And how does that information mesh with witness reports? What about timelines, could they do it, or not, within the time and spaces allotted to the subject/witness, victims. This obviously also applies to the cover stories, alibies, or scenarios proffered. Geographic and geological realities are hard to contemplate but with the current technology and resources, you'll find them invaluable to assessing your multi-location scenes and testimonial evidence. There are a slew of tools for this, starting with Google Earth and Esri and branching out from there with specialty tools that will cost license fees.

Next area of high value when searching for people, validating information, or getting good profiling information is of course social media. For that I would encourage you to consider younger analysts, those that are fully active in the most current applications (Apps) and sites, which are constantly evolving, and shifting in demography and popularity. These are all critical in knowing not only the people of interest but all their friends and associations, and what they all have to say, hang out, and gossip about. Knowing the demographic of each social media outlet is an important means to target and focus your investigative resources. Likewise, I promise you the obvious, most discussed media outlets are not necessarily going to be your most target-rich sources. As a running joke in OSINT goes, even bad guys order pizza, which is true but they spend most of their time not on Facebook or TikTok, but most commonly on the more obscure sites. Currently sites like TOR Boards, VKontakte (VK) which is a Russian Facebook where the extreme white supremacist now like to congregate, Discord, 8chan, Telegram, Signal, KiK, and others with some degree of presumed anonymity are where they migrate to play in the mud.

Your GEOINT guru may or may not be a great asset for image searching. This too is going to be critical in your investigation as you try to locate or identify a specific car, location, or where an image might have been captured with reverse image lookups such as Google Image and Tineye. All your members should be proficient in this space as it is important to all investigations. They should also be familiar with the possibility of image steganography, which is the imbedding of coded data within the lines of code that make up a digital image. But only peripherally in that it requires advanced software and is impossible to identify through sight or observation alone.

Next up on the list would be your Human Intelligence (HUMINT) analysts. While you would think any investigator could manage this, you would be mistaken. It's one thing to talk with people and do some digging to get a general feel. It's a wholly different exercise to find everything there is to know about someone. To dig into every aspect of who they are, what makes them tick, why they do what they do, who their friends are, their acquaintances, where they hang out, where they stay vs where they live, and the potential leverage you can use to make them squeal, or better yet, source them. There are a hundred other questions you will want answered if they are witnesses, potential suspects, or victims where you have yet to sleuth out potential suspects. That all requires a wholly different skill set and that's where your HUMINT analyst will come in. They'll be able to build your links analysis based on all those aspects and help identify your target's vulnerabilities, strengths, and potential for approaches, to include *effective* interrogation, through an expanded psych profile. Your psychological pathologists and profilers will love you if you can give them that kind of information when ruling suspects in or out. Your HUMINT analyst will also be one of the consumers of your social media analysts while they find more information on your UNSUBs. This position must be someone qualified and authorized to access your internal databases as well as National Crime Information Center (NCIC), National Law Enforcement Telecommunications System (NLETS), and the data aggregators like Whooster, LexisNexis, Clear, TLO, etc.

Stepping back at this point, I would argue the very first billet you will want to fill out should be your first priority, and your most critical position: that of the "all-source" analyst. This person is essentially a jack of all trades, yet a master of none. This may seem to be a pejorative way to look at the role, but it's one you, yourself, really should aspire to. Should you lack the regular need, the resources, or the command support to fill out a fully realized team of OSINT SMEs, well tag—you're it! The person you'll want to seek out needs to have the intellectual capacity to fully understand, and respect each role, each OSINT specialty's nuances, and their unique requirements. They'll also need to possess exceptional communications and report writing skills. And the ability to bring together all the knowledge and finished reporting from the rest of the team. And ensure the information was obtained properly, cross-checked, *ALL* sources validated, and answer all the questions posed in a cohesive manner. They must be able to tie it all back to the case and ensure the team are not chasing rabbits down the wrong holes. They would also be the aggregators and need the gap analysis skill to see where information is still missing. Additionally, they will need to have a broad understanding of the methodology to help figure out how and where to find the missing pieces. Essentially, they must be able to normalize data so you can trust the distillation of that data along with the need for the layering of all the disparate information in order to make a case and identify links between the knowns and unknowns.

This nearly impossible person to find would also generally serve as the team lead/supervisor that is delegated the authority to coordinate with outside support or resources. They are the guardian that can help avoid the curse of knowledge. They can translate between the detectives and the analysts to make sure analysts understand unique colloquial sayings or other things they (detectives) think are obvious. The analysts may not, based on their life experience and where they grew up, lived, etc., that is different, and they won't see what is needed to be seen and comprehend. Am I the only one visualizing some really cheesy comic book cover with someone standing looking off into the distance with a cape flapping behind them?

Back on topic. Additionally, your all-source analyst is your primary liaison and can coordinate your grad student volunteers or other means of outsourcing the information collection efforts as well as resolve challenges or hurdles to success of the SMEs. Naturally they would also be the coordinator and manager/gate keeper for SME taskings since the really good SMEs are quickly sought out and can become overwhelmed with requests/requirements. They would naturally need good "managing" skills. In other words, you will find to fill this position requires the existence of unicorns. Or at least the one in a million golden goose, once discovered, you never want to risk losing.

If you're still with me at this point, and not totally demoralized at the notion of how heavy a lift an OSINT team would be for an agency, what I have outlined is a bare bones, basic OSINT capability and larger operations could build out the bench strength to further refine their teams with an even greater depth of SMEs in each skill set based on your agency's requirements and workload. I also recognize the far majority of agencies have no resources to build such a team. That's where creative problem solving comes in handy, along with strategic partnerships. There are ways to share resources between agencies, as well as working with task forces, the fusion centers, and even volunteers for select/limited functions. And, of course, there are skills you could try and develop yourself where you see a frequent use. But you will quickly find the learning curve for each area unrealistic and inordinately steep. Plus, the amount of time you would have to spend would burn you out quickly, even before you actually got to a point of confidence or success. And being captain obvious again, it would sideline you for quite some time and naturally interfere with the traditional investigative steps you need to focus on as well.

Training, Skills Development, and Management

By now, I think I've stressed the high value placed on OSINT skills. It takes a unique personality and work ethic for someone to not only engage in the tasks related to OSINT but also the need for a dubious mindset is just one aspect in the professional constitution of a high-performing OSINT analyst. As a Senior Intelligence Officer and manager with the U.S. Department of Homeland Security Office of Intelligence and Analysis (DHS-I&A), I managed the work of dozens of analysts, set collection requirements and priorities based on the mission scope of the teams I was assigned to. I also led joint federal, state, local, and tribal law enforcement and intelligence agency teams focused on global and domestic terrorism as well as critical infrastructure sector-specific vulnerability and direct threats globally and domestically. In my earlier years, I also served as a U.S. Air Force (USAF) Office of Special Investigation (AFOSI) Agent trained at the Defense Intelligence Agency (DIA) as an advanced counterterrorism analyst and assigned as an AFOSI reservist, to the only USAF Antiterrorism Specialty Team (AST) in existence at that time. As a result, while working as a Houston homicide investigator with one of only two major assault squads in a city with roughly four million people, I was ordered back on active duty. I was ordered back while the horrific fires were still burning in New York, Arlington Virginia, and Pennsylvania. In those early positions, I performed and led a number of intelligence analytic efforts focused on everything from pre-operational planning for a NEO in Africa during the Sierra Leone Embassy evacuations as well as for the NORAD Air Defense command for over a year after the 9–11 attacks, fusing traditional intelligence with LES information to assess active, real-time aviation-born and targeted threats throughout the United

States. I was also assigned as the Special Agent in Charge at a remote site in Pakistan focused on the counterintelligence, and force protection threat for deployed U.S. forces, aircraft, and air operations at my deployed location. There, I was also responsible for sifting through and reporting on classified felony level criminal and terrorist threats facing the supply chain between the Port of Karachi and the Afghan border, where the handoff of responsibility was transferred to the Joint Intelligence group operating at Bagram, Afghanistan. I point out my background only to give you some perspective of both my high stakes operational/collections requirement experience all the way to my national-level criminal, violent extremist, and terrorist threat intelligence collections, reporting, and analysis scope of responsibilities. What I found in those years was how incredibly capable and competent the analysts I interacted with and learned from were. In these positions, I had to craft and fight for our budgets which taught me how incredibly expensive top-shelf analysts and their resources can be. Yet, how critical it is for the individual competencies and personalities to mesh with the work each was expected to carry out. Every segment of the intelligence cycle required a broad understanding of why information was needed as much as what information was being required to ensure we delivered precise, accurate, and validated critical decision-making reporting. Oh, and that nagging little birdy reminding us that failure involved the lives of many others who were trusting and counting on us to get it all right. All these increasing positions of responsibility led at one point or another to the production of reporting required for tactical operators, governors, national fusion centers, and major metropolitan police chiefs, all the way to the Secretary of Homeland Security and National Security Council members, sub-committees, and directorates.

Why does this devolution into my own past lives matter? How is it relevant here? Well, if you're like me, the first question you might have asked yourself is if you should pay any heed to what I'm selling and what you're reading. Is this guy even remotely qualified to proffer his opinions on the matter of OSINT and how all this knowledge should be applied? Those are valid considerations, only you can answer for yourself, now that you're armed with the knowledge of my lengthy, yet not uncommon background. I learned early on, there was no room for error but also no one size fits all in the information priorities, requirements, or analysis intended as actionable intelligence products. I also learned how critical every "INT" was in the identification and following the trail of disparate and almost always obscure hints of critical information. Knowledge that often led to the development of the threat information necessary to thwart attacks or mitigate the impact of attack indicators we collectively missed.

The way to ensure you and your team are capable of serving the needs of your agency and your cases by leveraging OSINT information is of course to ensure you obtain the best knowledge and training to build the base for solid experiential learning. There are some free training opportunities available to sworn and non-sworn law enforcement personnel through the Department of Homeland Security, Department of Justice, and for those that are also in the military reserve, the Department of Defense (DoD). Actually, on that note, I was able to enroll some of our civilian agency analysts into DoD training based on their security clearance level and my certification of their need for the assignment. Something to keep in mind if you have analysts that are also in the military reserve or national guard. There is also some exceptional training available through an organization I would strongly recommend you and your team join: Law Enforcement Intelligence Units (LEIU) and the International Association of Law Enforcement Intelligence Analysts (IALEIA).[13] Both offer annual training and are an invaluable resource for you and your analysts to create and maintain a network of top-shelf professionals to support you and often coordinate where you have mutual interests or cases crossing jurisdictional boundaries.

All of the DHS intelligence courses you and your folks can take are free and are approved by the Federal Emergency Management Agency (FEMA) so that you can apply through your state to pay for travel and lodging, etc.[14] These courses will build a certification portfolio for your folks and ensure they learn the rules and the methods to ensure the information is obtained, stored, analyzed, and applied within the law and to ensure airtight cases for court.

There are also some incredibly valuable training opportunities through the Department of Justice that will add great value and focus regardless of where you and your people start. I encourage you to put your people through as much training from as many legitimate sources as possible to ensure you avoid group think and that they are well rounded and not biased by one approach over another. And never forget, self-fulfilled, valued, and appreciated analysts with a clear path for increased knowledge and advancement will stick around. Those you fail to support will take that hard-bought and hard-earned knowledge elsewhere. And I promise you in this world, those skills they hone are worth far more than your agency will ever be able to pay them. So you had better find and ensure the tangible benefits are there even when the financial resources are lacking. See the link in the footnote for a current list of frequently updated Department of Justice-sponsored training, again all these courses are free to law enforcement personnel.[15] Now that you have the sources to get the ball rolling, the obvious needs to be stated. You and your team can not sit on the knowledge they gain early on, they must continue to learn, collaborate, and evolve or they will cease to be of value and will in fact become a detriment to your cases and your team's value to the agency and the community.

Practical Applications

OK, now this is where we can burn down the house of metaphors as we get to gettin'. First, though this is another time where I feel the need to manage expectations, this section is not going to be a deep dive, nor will it prepare you to become the OSINT guru you always dreamt of becoming. And while in the Debby downer arena, nor are you going to be able to read this section, then jump online and solve your case, or even for that matter navigate your way to that gold nugget you were looking for. That dog just ain't gonna' hunt.

What I can do is provide a fundamental understanding of how the analysts will approach their work. The types of sources they may choose and how to get yourself and them out of the starting gate. It's still a massive and dark forest they will be entering, and the more light you can shed on your requirements, the information needs you have and the priorities, if any, you need them to focus on, the more they will be able to help you. As with any other work, they need to understand what you're looking for to ensure they have the greatest chance of success. Again, let's remember the curse of knowledge—don't leave them with the need to assume what you mean or try to decipher your colloquialisms. Keep the request as clear as you can without being so specific they miss searching for critical information even you may have overlooked.

Let's start by breaking down some of the leading challenges in many cold cases. Yes every case has unique characteristics, and yes no two are ever alike. But, having worked enough cases of all types over the decades and having become the voluntold sap on more occasions than I care to remember to take over a daunting case with a dearth of tangible evidence, some information types tend to be quite common.

The first item of interest is always the who, yes? We may or may not know the name of the victim in which case your "Doe" case has to start there. Assuming you've already gone through the normal drudgery of missing persons cases matching your victim and finding none. If you were able to get prints, and there are no results, and you worked with the media on a sketch or likeness, all to no avail. Let's then assume you have the decomposed body which would still lead to some decent DNA samples that can be sent off. Now you are going to have to jump into the investigative genetic genealogy (IGG) world. This is not a time to let your buddy's girlfriend that dabbles in family tree exploration step in. The information you need and methodology are very complex and quite rigorous. It's also a realm fraught with misleading and often just bad information from armature sleuths linking dubious records with little or no validation. Your analyst will have to start with the *GenMatch*[16] tools as they delve into standard sites such as *GEDMATCH*, *Ansestry.com*, *Family Tree*,[17] and others, some of which are tailored to specific ethnic categories. This is a lengthy process where many IGG analysts get stuck or simply can't find enough familial links to associate and identify the victim's potential familial linkages. This is often the case with people of African, Middle Eastern, and Asian decent where DNA testing and historical documentation are lacking. I would strongly encourage you to contract with an IGG specialized company with a proven track record in your victim's ethnicity because the most marketed and best known companies tend not to be very successful in identifying the family connections in immigrant and African descendant subjects. If a lab is trying to be the source for all the stages and steps of DNA testing and IGG, I would be very dubious of their capacity to serve all areas as top in class. Further, you risk what may be your only shot at solving your case if you have little DNA left for testing. Also, if they are chasing your cases and promising you free services without a clear and transparent funding source, be very, VERY wary. There are stories of petty games involving the withholding of test and IGG results, should they be stuck, and you opt to move your case to another vendor. Still others suffer from poor management, lack law enforcement and criminal investigative experience. There is no free ride and DNA testing as well as IGG experience is very expensive and incredibly time consuming to obtain. Do your homework and if you can ensure you have the right vendor, try, if at all possible, to not let the acquisition/contracting officers make the final decisions, even if you have to have the chief step in. Many cases sit dormant, or evidence lost due to such catastrophic failures. Again, don't believe me—I encourage you to just look at the news, search for issues such as contamination of evidence, lost evidence, or infighting between professionals in social media over methodology. Those playing in are what I would consider armatures at best and mercenaries out for what they see as easy money at worst.

Once you have the DNA profile—IF, you have the DNA profile, and familial possibles from the IGG team, you'll need to track down the surviving family members with the closest possible link to your test subject(s). That will require a deep dive into skip tracing and the traditional methods of locating the correct people. These are tools like LexisNexis, TLO, Clear, and Whooster. All are only available to law enforcement agencies and licensed private investigators that must certify as their searches are related to specific allowable applications under federal privacy and information laws. All the aggregators have their benefits and limitations. While I am biased based on my own experience over the years, I would encourage you to check out Whooster, if you have the option in that they have the most up-to-date information and a wealth of resources that are "live" such as phone and address data as well as historical records, such as phones going back a few decades. Additionally they have expanded their information to hacked/exploited information that can lead to email and phone information otherwise not available. All of this combined would give you more bang for your very limited buck in reducing the time it takes to dig up not only the next of kin, but other family relations based on shared addresses and phone information. They can even point to co-habitation partners that can lead you closer to your goal with the fewest vendors and least expense. This is also where you'll be diving into the social media sites to identify familial links and associations. It's also here where you'll do a lot of research on the victims, as well as subjects, and potential witnesses' social media and life patterns. You'll very quickly find the sheer number of social media tools in themselves overwhelming, and many specializing on one particular platform. You will hear or learn about some of these tools being free. As with my previous warning, these too will be red herrings. Don't take the bait. The good search tools are pricy in general and again, while there are some that claim to be free, you will get very frustrated with those very quickly. You will find them to be inaccurate, full of white noise, and exhaustively time consuming as well as requiring coding or script writers to make work.

Social media search and aggregator tools such as *Maltego* are highly effective and relatively cheap in the grand scheme of things. At this writing a single "Pro" seat is about US$1,200.[18] There are other commercial brands such as Shadow Dragon, Voyager Labs, and others that will cover not only social media but also have modules for dark and deep web, which you will often want and need and again require a whole different skill set to navigate. But fair warning, they are all pricy options, nonetheless, options you may need. It's here where data breach information is found and hugely helpful in identifying unknown or intentionally unreported emails and phone numbers associated with individuals related to your case.

Once you located your potential familial matches, you have to go to them and convince them to provide a DNA sample to validate the IGG results. Or, if you are pursuing a potential criminal suspect, it may be necessary to obtain the DNA surreptitiously. A whole different topic for a different chapter written by someone else. No doubt all of you understand the concept of dumpster diving, more appropriately termed "trash pulls".

For even more on IGG, there are a number of resources to get smart and understand this area of specialty. It is critical here that every step in this chain is captured, tracked, and properly recorded to preserve the chain of information and sources as evidence for trial. One misstep can derail your whole case.

Now let's move onto the crime scene topics. If you've inherited an older case, GEOINT is going to be a tough challenge as well. Understand the lay of the land, literally, the topography, involved in your crime scene. Important issues such as geological makeup can simplify your search for evidence such as can they dig? Would it be washed out? How far would they have to carry a heavy body? Roads, rivers, creeks, and washouts all naturally impact your scene. No pun intended there. But you get it, the art of the realistic and the possible in body/evidence disposal and helping to limit search areas. Also in this vein are meteorological conditions at the times before, during, and after your crime, and those impacts on evidence that may not have been covered in the original case file. For this area you're going to dive into resources such as *World Imagery Wayback*, *Google Earth Time-lapse*, *Zoom Earth*, *Google lens*, and *Overpass Turbo* as just a few. These types of data sets will also help you prepare questions for potential or purported witnesses. Could they have seen what they did where and when they did? How long does it take to get from point "A" to point "B" and during the environmental conditions at the time of the crime? I think you get it.

Along with all this, there is the basic deep web search for newspapers, graves, and secure or restricted group sharing and chat sources such as *Tor Channels*, *Discord*, *Reddit*, *8chan*, *KiK*, *Telegram*, *WickrMe*, *Signal*, *WhatsApp*, and others that will no doubt be around in the future as they all come and eventually go. These sites can be invaluable in identifying behaviors and patterns of life of your subjects and possibly your victims if they are engaged in fringe or criminal activities.

I could continue for a hundred pages or more just on each of the different sources of information and the myriad of tools available for each. Many require basic programming or scripting skills, while others are fee based and some are both. I encourage you to use the links in the endnotes to launch your exploration. In them you will find not only specific citations and links to narrow the lanes of data, but you will also find documents that have hyperlinks expanding out to several dozen different sources of OSINT tools. Again, this is just the beginning of your journey and I have not even given you the full drop in your bottomless bucket of needs.

Good luck and again, remember there really are incredibly talented OSINT operators and analysts, genuinely interested in helping you succeed. The place to start, and the best place to find them is your state and major city fusion center or real crime center. Also the FBI and DHS resources will not lead you astray and have some of the absolute best practitioners in the world, bar none. I would also encourage you to poach the hell out of the federal analysts any time you have the opportunity. I promise you they will be scouting yours and they usually pay a hell of a lot more than your agency can.

Notes

1 Ortiz, Claudia Yvette, "What Factors Contribute to a Murder Case Being Designated as a Cold Case?"
(2021). Theses and Dissertations. 131. https://rio.tamiu.edu/etds/131

2 Murder.org, Accessed March 2024; https://public.tableau.com/views/ClearanceRates/ClearanceRate_1?:increment_view_count=no&:embed=y&:sid=&:loadOrderID=0&:display_count=y&:showTabs=y&:origin=viz_share_link

3 Janes.com Podcast, Episode 80, Published June 8, 2023, Accessed March 2024; https://www.janes.com/intelligence-resources/open-source-intelligence-podcasts/podcast-details/optimising-osint-for-the-intelligence-community
4 ODNI Official Website, Accessed March 2024; https://www.dni.gov/index.php/what-we-do/what-is-intelligence
5 Ghioni R, Taddeo M, Floridi L. Open source intelligence and AI: a systematic review of the GELSI literature. *AI Soc.* (2023):1–16. doi: 10.1007/s00146-023-01628-x.
6 Bureau of Justice Assistance Publication, "Real-Time and Open Source Analysis Resource Guide", Published July 2017, Accessed March 2024; https://bja.ojp.gov/sites/g/files/xyckuh186/files/media/document/rosa_resource_guide.pdf
7 Wellman AP, Meitl MB. Exploring cold case homicide survivors' perceptions of and relationships with law enforcement. *Journal of Interpersonal Violence* 36(23–24) (2021):11553–11575. doi:10.1177/0886260519897327
8 Alex Young, *Too Much Information: Ineffective Intelligence Collection*, Originally published in the HIR Summer 2013 Issue, Harvard International Review, Accessed April 2024, https://hir.harvard.edu/too-much-information/
9 "Can a VPN be Hacked," Miklos Zoltan, Privacy Affairs website, Published January 2024, Accessed March 2024, https://www.privacyaffairs.com/can-vpn-be-hacked/
10 Silo web isolation platform, Authentic8 website, Accessed March 2024, https://authentic8.com/products/silo-web-isolation-platform
11 OSINT Framework web site, Accessed March 2024, https://osintframework.com/
12 "Google Dorking Cheat Sheet", Tutorials Freek Website, Accessed March 2024, https://www.tutorialsfreak.com/ethical-hacking-tutorial/google-dorking-cheat-sheet
13 LEIU and IALEIA Websites, Accessed April 2024 https://leiu.org/default.aspx?MenuItemID=4&MenuGroup=Public+Home and https://www.ialeia.org/
14 FEMA Catalogue of available intelligence courses, Accessed April 2024, https://www.dhs.gov/fema-approved-intelligence-analyst-training-courses
15 DOJ Law Enforcement Partner Intelligence Training Program bulletin posted December 2023 and Accessed April 2024, https://leb.fbi.gov/articles/focus/focus-on-training-law-enforcement-partner-intelligence-training-program#:~:text=At%20its%20core%2C%20the%20intelligence,and%20other%20public%20safety%20components
16 Noah Greifer, *Genetic Matching, from the Ground Up*, published on Github, October 8 2022, Accessed April 2024, https://ngreifer.github.io/blog/genetic-matching/
17 International Society of Genetic Genealogy, *Investigative genetic genealogy FAQs*, Accessed April 2024, https://isogg.org/wiki/Investigative_genetic_genealogy_FAQs#GEDMATCH
18 Maltego Website, Accessed April 2024, https://buy.maltego.com/shop/default

The Print Media

19

RACHEL H. WALTON
AND FRANK P. TONA

Introduction

Despite the sometimes-rancorous relationship between members of law enforcement and the media—misunderstanding on both sides—the news media plays an integral role in the function of a free society. The media, through print mediums such as newspaper and magazines and through video and the Internet, informs the public of local, regional, and national news and events. In this manner, they serve to inform, and to help safeguard, the public. Agency news releases, publication of the FBI's Top Ten wanted fugitive list, and television shows such as *America's Most Wanted* utilize different forms of media to alert the public to wanted persons and regularly result in their apprehension as a direct outcome of public involvement.

Crime and politics are chief among those events that have been regularly reported since news reporting began. The public is fascinated with crime, and this interest has long been noticed by those who report crime, those who investigate crime, and those who study various aspects of crime and public interest. In the investigation of cold case homicides, the media has taken on a new, and valuable, role in its mission to inform and safeguard the public. The media serves as an *information resource* for cold case homicide investigation, and in some instances, may be the only repository of information cold case investigators have when they seek to build a case from scratch. In addition, the media at times may assist in the furtherance of a cold case investigation. The role of social media is addressed elsewhere in Chapters 4 and 5.

This chapter presents the role of the media in cold case investigation. This role is presented in three major categories: (1) information base, (2) generating public interest and assistance, and (3) reporting successful conclusion and resulting public perception and increased affirmation of agency mission: positive public relations.

The Print Media as Information Resource

During the initial review of a cold case file, and subsequent in-depth familiarization with the case, investigators become immersed in the facts of the

 DOI: 10.4324/9781003415633-22

case. These facts encompass people, places, dates and times, relationships, and more. Media records with potential information about the crime may include:

- Newspaper reporting at the time of the crime and thereafter
- "Sunday Supplement" and other reviews in subsequent years and decades
- Magazine articles, books, or other literary publications
- Old video clips and sometimes movies

Review of available newspaper and other media reports of the cold case under investigation is suggested during the early stages of a cold case investigation. These accounts may yield information not necessarily found in the case reports. Of importance in this review is to determine what facts and information regarding the case are to be found in the media sources. Among these may be:

- Nature and location of injuries
- Weapon used
- Property taken
- Ingress and egress to the crime scene
- Other information known only to the killer

This may become an issue later during suspect development or at defense when someone says "Well, I read about it in the papers."

This source may be especially more valuable in older, sketchier, and seemingly uninformative or incomplete case files. In my experience, the older the homicide case becomes, the more detailed, and voluminous, the written media reporting *may* be. This reporting, however, may have been influenced by several other factors at the time, including:

- Victim status. Prostitute versus young child of prominent citizen
- Other newsworthy events at the time
- Bizarre or more unusual elements of the crime
- Mystery surrounding the crime or lack thereof
- Political links or ramifications
- Relationship to other crimes
- Personal or professional interest of the editor
- "Newsworthiness"

Keep in mind that while the media serves as an unofficial record of events, it does serve as a record. In this regard, the media may serve as a basis to turn a once unofficial record into the official record. These issues may become a major source of information in those cases in which files are missing, or non-existent, and provide the basis for crime scene reconstruction and identification of those involved in the case as victims, suspects, investigators, etc. However, the information in media accounts is only as reliable as the sources of information, the interpretation and repetition of the information, and any self-serving motives of those providing information. Just like in a police investigation.

Newspapers

Print media was the standard for decades of how Americans received their news. In the age before radio, and later television, it was *the* primary news medium. Newspapers were the daily format for news, and magazines and short story booklets or magazine articles also recorded people, stories, and events. In prior decades, it was not unusual for towns and cities to have multiple, competing print news media. These may have operated on a morning daily schedule, an afternoon basis, sometimes a semiweekly or weekly schedule, or variations of these. When newspapers competed with one another, it might not be unusual to find one paper hitting the streets in the morning hours, while the competition came out in the afternoon. Over the past two decades, however, many major dailies have closed their doors. In addition to closing, some have been bought out by other news organizations or merged with other media interests.

For cold case investigators, this is relevant as a review of both editions may be valuable, as well as the awareness of potential other sources of news reporting. Due to deadlines for reporters' stories, what one newspaper printed in detail may have been only lightly touched by the competitor, which instead perhaps concentrated on an aspect of the story totally neglected by the competition. And that's what reporting was: *competition.*

Then, like now, the media sought to solicit readership and to sell advertising. Crime stories could mean additional sales. On occasions, and in response to intense public interest, newspapers would rush to press urgent breaking news stories—often to "scoop" the competition—known as "extras." These might be exemplified by the word "Extra" in color at the top of the first page. The addition of this color, and an extra edition, often was more expensive to produce and is found usually in the most sensational of cases (see Figure 19.1).

Where to Find Newspapers

Historically, the newspaper companies themselves kept back copies of their editions. This served not only as a record of their business but also, in the pre-computer age, as an in-house source of background information on persons, events, places, and other items of report. These repositories of back issues were called the newspaper *morgue.* This is *not* to be confused with the coroner's repository of the deceased by the same name.

EXTRA

Humboldt Standard

FIND CARMEN DEAD

HEARING IS DATED FOR NEXT WEEK

WOMAN'S THIRST FOR FINE DUDS CAUSES THEFTS

BULGARIA STILL HOT FOR BLOWS

KELLOGG HAS AROUSED NEW RUMPUS OVER COMMUNISTS

Two Members Of Posse Locate Bodies Of Girl And Her Pet Dog "Pronto"

BODY IS DISCOVERED BURIED IN SHALLOW GRAVE ALONG CREEK NEAR FORT BAKER

COYOTE FLAT,. Oct. 23. (Via Standard's Wireless) – Carmen Wagner was found dead today a few feet from Baker Creek near Fort Baker, buried in a shallow grave. Fifteen feet away lay her dog Pronto, shot to death.

The discovery was made by Sidney Pixton and Kenneth Buck who first discovered the dog Pronto. Led on by the finding of the body of the dog, the man searched the neighborhood carefully, and soon came upon a human arm projecting from a shallow grave. A little exhuming soon uncovered the body of Carmen.

The body was lying in a piece of ground between a large rock and the river bank, where it had been carefully covered with loose earth, driftwood and rock.

The right arm was lying on the breast, and the left elbow was crushed and sticking above the surface. This led to the discovery. It had not been ascertained yet if she was shot, but the condition of the dog has pretty well demonstrated that she was killed in that way.

BITTER LEGAL BATTLE IS ON OVER RAILWAY BOOZE MOVING

SEAPLANE SHATTERED BY TUMBLE

ITALIAN MACHINE FAILS

LODGE SAYS LEAGUE HAS NO POWER TO END CONFLICT

Convicts Moved To Another Sanctuary

SAVE with SAFETY at your Rexall DRUG STORE

GEORGIA ROSE BODY POWDER

$1.00 a package

Atkinson & Woods

STOP These Coughs and Colds GODFREY'S LUNG BALSM will cure them. It gets the germs. 40c and 75c

HEMSTITCHING STAMPING ART NEEDLEWORK SUPPLIES

Figure 19.1 Humboldt Standard EXTRA newspaper 1925. Review of newspapers is necessary to identify witnesses and information not found in the file as well as what information is found in the public domain. Older newspapers may furnish more detail than more recent. (Author's file.)

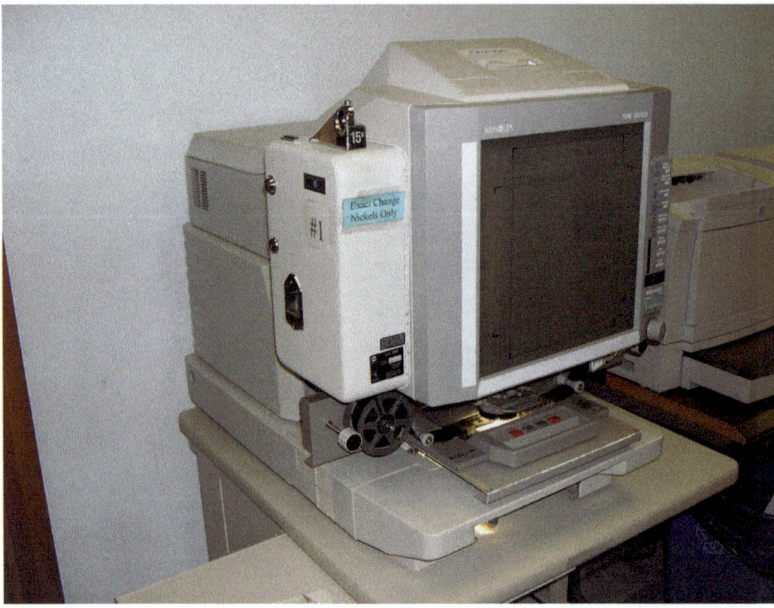

Figure 19.2 Photo of microfilm reader. Cold case investigators may spend hours reading microfilm, a tactic not encountered in normal homicide investigations. (Author's file.)

In the past quarter century, however, some newspapers have eliminated the storage costs and other accompanying problems and issues by getting rid of their original hard copies of back editions. Computerized data systems and other techno-advances have eliminated the need to maintain hard copies of daily editions. Decades of back issues took up a lot of space. After copying these to microfilm, many news organizations have simply destroyed the original copies or donated them to universities or research facilities that have room to store them (see Figure 19.2). In some instances, media companies may retain hard copies for a set period of time before copying them to microfilm and destroying or otherwise discarding these.

For cold case investigators seeking to locate back issues of local newspapers, whether original hard copy or microfilm style copies, there are a number of places to explore. Among these are:

- The local newspaper publishing company (if still in business locally). When this source is contacted, however, keep in mind that good reporters sense stories. If known detectives start asking questions about cold cases, so might a reporter.
- Local library. May possess original or microfilm copies.

Figure 19.3 Photo of San Diego Public Library building. Libraries may be a source of a number of investigative aids in cold case investigation, including newspapers, city directories, and telephone books. (Author's file.)

- Local college or university. Most often possesses microfilm copies (see Figures 19.3 and 19.4), but may have originals.
- Other college- or university-operated libraries or research facilities.
- Local historical society. May possess older, original newspapers as a result of donation by the newspaper publisher.
- State archives or repositories.

What May Be Found in the Newspapers

> Killed by two savage blows on the forehead, the lifeless body of Mrs. Pearl Martin, 55, was discovered yesterday afternoon lying at the bottom of steps, which connected the Martin garage with the family living quarters at 2926 E Street…Mrs. Hazel Skipper, 16 West Trinity St., on her way to an appointment with Mrs. Martin, discovered the crime and notified police at about 2 p.m. when she looked through the half-open garage doors at the Martin residence.

This was the lead story reporting a homicide in the Eureka, California *Humboldt Times* newspaper on December 11, 1946, and reported in a story on cold case homicides in the *Times-Standard* newspaper in Eureka, California, 58 years later. The information revealed in these few passages is not untypical

WOMEN'S NEWS
MEXICO ROUNDUP
SAN DIEGO COUNTY

The San Diego Union

LOCAL NEWS

SAN DIEGO, CALIFORNIA, MONDAY MORNING, JUNE 7, 1965

Ferryboats Whistling A Parting Tune

OF THE SEA

Short Trip Is Lure To Thousands Daily

23 Receive Law Degrees In Colorful Rite

POLITICAL SNARL

Love Out Of Reach For Giraffe

Teen Divorcee Is Found Slain

An attractive, 19 year-old divorcee was found strangled in her El Cajon apartment yesterday.

The nude body of Mrs. Cheryl Burnett, a drapery cord around the neck, was found by a neighbor at 9:30 a.m. in the bedroom of Mrs. Burnett's ground-floor apartment at 932 Leslie Road, El Cajon.

Her 2 year-old son, Todd, also was found in the apartment, unharmed.

CHERYL BURNETT
. . . called "Cinderella"

NYLON ROPE

Figure 19.4 Microfilm homicide report San Diego Union front page June 7, 1965. (Courtesy of El Cajon Police Department.)

reporting, even today. Cold case investigators reviewing this case would immediately note that in just these few sentences, information is found.

- Identifying the name of the victim
- Identifying the age of the victim
- Identifying the victim's address
- Identifying the location where the body was found

- Identifying the name of the person who discovered the crime
- Identifying the name of the person reporting the crime
- Reporting the manner of death
- Reporting the location of potential fatal wounds to the victim
- Describing the scene of the crime
- Reporting the date and time the crime was reported to police
- Reporting the circumstances by which the victim was discovered

In this and subsequent reports, the newspaper reported that she was a victim of a robbery and that approximately $300 in cash, jewelry, and a handgun were reported missing. Thus, information perhaps known to the suspect is now in the public domain.

Initial and subsequent newspaper reports regularly report information of interest in a cold case investigation. In addition to the topics, newspaper reports not uncommonly provide information including:

- Names and addresses of witnesses
- Names and addresses of friends and associates of the victim
- Names and addresses of relatives and coworkers of the victim
- Employment information regarding the victim
- Victim marital status
- Victim's past or ongoing relationships
- Identities of those last known to have seen the victim
- Names of responding law enforcement officers and investigators
- Identities of initial coroner/medical examiner personnel
- Identity as to where the remains were transported
- Other circumstances surrounding discovery of the body
- The victim's activities prior to disappearance and/or commission of crime
- Reported relationships of the victim, including possible suspects
- Suppositions and theories of those who knew the victim
- Other similar crimes in the neighborhood or time span
- Political or time and circumstances potentially relevant to the crime
- Identities of persons of interest
- Statements by friends, associates, and others
- Name of the author of the article
- Description or discussion of the weapon used
- Description of victim injuries
- Description of evidence seen by others
- Discussion of evidence or property seized by law enforcement investigators
- Coroner or medical examiner findings

In some, especially more notorious or sensational cases, suspects have mailed letters or items belonging to the victim to local news media. In most cases, these have been turned over to the police. Cold case investigators may keep the possibility of this in mind during interviews and conversations with media representatives. If so, do they *still* possess any of these items?

Searching the Newspapers

Depending upon the source location, newspaper contents may be indexed or catalogued as to allow searching for specific news stories, or they may not be catalogued. In either case, investigators should query the custodian of these newspapers or files to ascertain what retrieval options exist.

- Catalog systems may be indexed by card index files in which articles between a given time are referenced by type, i.e., "crime" or "murder," by individual names, or a variety of other methods (see Figure 19.5). Investigators will need to identify what, if any, information retrieval systems exist and work with the custodian of the newspapers to maximize efforts to retrieve all relevant items. In other instances, they may be computerized back to a certain date, and these systems may more readily facilitate item retrieval.

Figure 19.5 Library newspaper file index system. Not all libraries have index systems, and the only way to research information about cold cases is to begin with the initial reporting and review subsequent issues. (Author's file.)

- Noncatalogued. In this situation, the newspapers are usually filed and maintained by year on shelves or stacks, or on microfilm. Investigators will need to know a starting date or period to begin a review. In my experience, homicide cases are usually found within the first few pages, if not the first page, depending upon the time period, size of the newspaper, perceived public interest, and other editing factors. If the date of the homicide is not known, and the identity of the victim is, the death certificate may provide a starting date for a newspaper search. These searches will be very time consuming.

Keep in mind that as the case grew "cold," so did media interest. Stories that once occupied front page, consecutive issues became smaller references, often weeks or months later, and ultimately nothing more than brief mention that detectives were still following up on leads. As fresh cases overtake ongoing investigations and consume law enforcement resources, the news media experiences a similar situation. Their business is to report the news and, for the most part, they do not go back on a story unless there is a "newsy" element. As a consequence, media reporting of a homicide may trail off after a day or two, a week, or a month.

In either case, however, it may be prudent to check newspaper accounts on anniversaries of crimes and for a month or two afterward for any mention.

- Internet. Investigators may search online for newspaper articles, and some search engines may allow searching for specific news items. My experience in doing this has suggested that searching the local newspaper as well as searching the nearest large city newspaper may prove beneficial. In some instances, expand your search for other large newspapers of national scale. These may include the *Los Angeles Times*, the *Washington Post*, *New York Times*, and others. Some newspapers, however, do not put stories prior to 2000 on the World Wide Web due to legal concerns addressing copyright and royalty issues for authors of articles. I have not found this to be a uniform practice, however. In addition, local universities or colleges may have research facilities that may assist investigator efforts in this regard

Utilizing College and University Library Systems

Using college and university libraries during a cold case homicide investigation can be a treasure trove of information. These institutions often house decades' worth of archived materials, including microfiche collections and expansive newspaper databases that contain local and national coverage—sometimes including forgotten details or overlooked leads. Newspaper archives such as NewsBank, ProQuest Historical Newspapers, and America's News can help investigators track down articles, obituaries, crime reports, or public notices that never made it into official case files. Librarians—often the unsung heroes of research—are incredibly helpful in guiding access to these resources, offering support in person or through convenient online chat features. Investigators can also access a wide array of scholarly and legal databases, including JSTOR, LexisNexis, and specialized forensic journals. In an era where digital sleuthing meets old-school gumshoe work, academic libraries serve as critical allies in the pursuit of long-delayed justice.

The Photographic Record

Newspaper reports were, and are, often illustrated with photographs and diagrams or sketches of the scene of the crime (see Figure 19.6). These photos may be of the exterior of the building of a crime scene, interior shots,

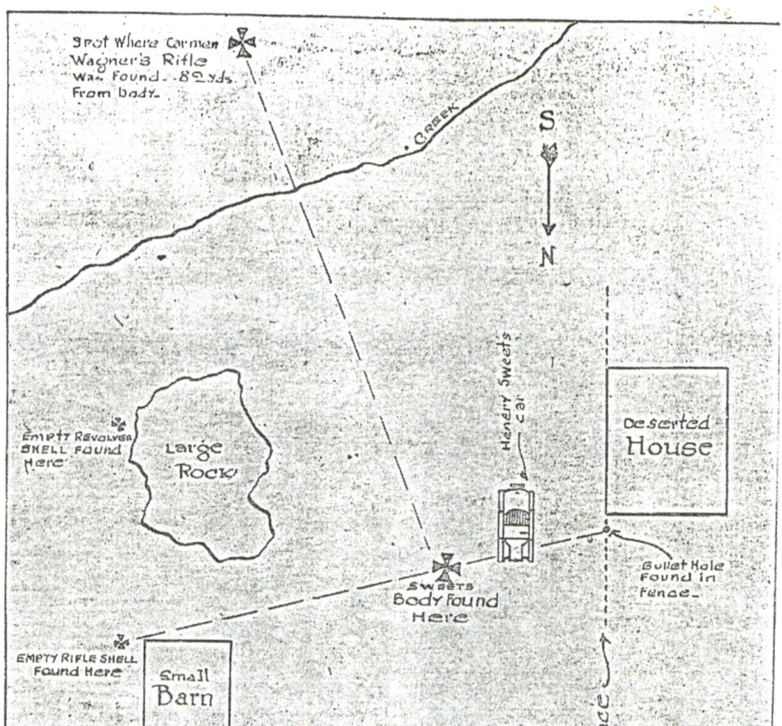

Figure 19.6 Sketch of crime scene 1925. While perhaps more common many decades ago, media crime scene sketches are to be found in reporting today as well. They can serve to orient the reader. Not the specific distance and orientation of evidence. (Courtesy of Humboldt Standard Newspaper.)

neighborhood shots, or a combination of these. Additional photos to be found in review of newspapers in the course of a cold case investigation may be of:

- Other persons connected to the victim or the crime, often identifying them by name and occupation, and address
- Weapons
- Scene of the crime
- Persons present *within* the crime scene
- Surroundings of the crime scene
- Potential witnesses or suspects (in crowd scenes)

In the past, in some jurisdictions, *private photographers* responded to crime scenes to take the pictures for the law enforcement agencies. For other purposes, including financial gain, other persons may also have taken photos of the crime scene or related locations or persons or items and sold or otherwise furnished these to the media. During the review of the newspaper photos, cold case investigators may seek to ascertain *who* took the photographs. This source information is often noted at the bottom of the picture. In cases of private photographers, cold case investigators may seek to locate them to ascertain if they have other photographs remaining of the case and to attempt to obtain copies. In those instances, in which the photographer is determined to be deceased, attempts may be made to

- Identify the descendants of the photographer or
- Determine the disposition of photographs remaining in the individual's estate

In situations where the local photographer was a professional and operated a business, inquiry to determine who bought the business may seek to learn whether they also bought any photographic collections. Other sources of potential photographs may be:

- Local private photograph collections
- Historical society photograph collections
- Local or state archives

When reviewing newspaper accounts, it was not uncommon to see a photograph of the victim's face with the article. *Who* furnished the picture? *Where* did it come from?

Keep in mind that a reporter's information was only as good as their sources.

Film and Audio Media

With the growth of television in the 1950s, and later cable news networks in the early 1980s, written media began to be usurped by these mediums. In decades past, many stations were individually owned and affiliated with major news organizations, ABC, NBC, or CBS. In later periods, many of these stations began to be bought by other media concerns, and it would not be uncommon to find a station in one city owned by a company that owns similar media in other cities and states. Newspaper and film stories and photographs were carried and transmitted nationally and internationally by the Associated Press (AP) and United Press International (UPI), including photos. These two organizations also transmitted photos for the newspaper media for many decades.

Local camera crews (not uncommonly one person) recorded information in the field for nightly broadcast. After shooting the event, the camera crew brought the film back to the studio where it was edited for broadcast. It was up to the discretion of the editor to preserve and broadcast what suited their purpose. Material that was not broadcast often wound up on the proverbial "cutting room floor" and was discarded.

Film and video taken in the field are described in the media jargon as "raw material" or "raw footage." The material that is broadcast is "aired material" or "air cuts." This distinction is important for cold case investigators to understand. Raw material is all the film or footage that was shot, including the snippets that found their way onto the air. This material was normally discarded, unless, perhaps, the case was high profile. Investigators should ask if the station retains any raw footage. However, news media will *only* release to law enforcement, even under subpoena, that material that was aired and will not normally release unaired footage. This material may be protected under the shield laws that govern media disclosure of sources or other material.

Aired material is that portion of the raw material that was broadcast by the medium. This is the material normally retained by the news facility. For cold case investigators, it may be significant to understand that, in older cases, it was not uncommon for news cameras and reporters to conduct an interview with a witness or other person at length and shoot perhaps 20 minutes of footage. However, by the time editing was complete, perhaps two-minute footage was aired, and partial statements—*sound bites*—were broadcast. It would not be unusual for a reporter's three-minute interview to be reduced to a 15-second sound bite. In older broadcasts, it might not be uncommon to view a lengthier interview than later, or present, practices and constraints allow.

Consequently for cold case investigators, ease of media review and access to this material is somewhat more difficult. In my opinion, written media no longer reports in detail to the degree as was once common. One of the many advantages of assigning senior, veteran investigators to cold case homicide investigation is their grounding in the local community. This experience includes knowledge of media, newspapers, and audio-video, and changes in media ownership or broadcast initials as well as potential personal contacts.

When reviewing and investigating cold cases, do not *assume* anything! This includes the assumption that the film media has nothing remaining decades later. You don't know until you inquire, and it is not to be unexpected that local media may still possess film footage many decades old. This was the experience of El Cajon, California, cold case investigators Robert Anderson and Jon Wooddell during their investigation of the 1965 homicide and other crimes committed by serial killer Clyde Wilkerson (discussed in Chapter 4). Investigators determined that San Diego television channel KFMB had retained footage of their coverage of the case, which the station converted to videotape and provided to detectives.

Not uncommonly, news stations have video footage dating to their origins. In the case of KFMB, they retain film video dating to the late 1950s and early 1960s. The earliest format was 16 mm film, and a transition from film to video began in the 1970s. This format was originally a three-quarter inch Sony Beta formatted tape with a different encoding from the Home Beta format. The three-quarter inch format later changed to a one-half inch format and to a mix of one-half inch Beta and digital. The current trend is to all digital formats.

Elements of a Newscast

Depending upon the time period and type of newscast, these elements made up the dissemination of the news event:

- Film or videotape of the event
- Written script of what was aired in the media
- Anchor's script of what was aired regarding the story

Depending upon age, film footage may not have had sound on the same reel. Sound came later with the addition of a sound stripe. Film with audio was sometimes accompanied by a separate sound track containing the reporter's narration of the story. In addition, the media had a "reporter package" where the narration is put on the story and the anchor would make reference to the reporter, whose narration is on one track and field footage is on another track.

Further, in stories where there was no reporter in the footage and the anchor speaks over it, there might have been an original reporter, but three to four days later, they may have pulled the footage from the crime scene or topic and the anchor would now say "Now for an update..." and reuse this footage, imposing later dialogue over earlier footage as the anchor narrated it on air.

Contacting the Media

Any contact with the media offers a potential for making law enforcement's cold case effort public. As with some prosecutors and judges, there are misconceptions about what cold case investigation is and how it is conducted. Cold case investigators can go a long way by educating those in the media of some of the aspects of cold case investigation and how it differs from hot case investigation. Among these differences is maintaining a lack of publicity until the right time. Responsible journalists may understand this, but ask that they be notified when the case breaks. This is not unreasonable and may facilitate obtaining the desired footage and information, as well as promoting relations for future cooperation.

When seeking this information, it is suggested that investigators first approach the station management. Contact may be made with the manager or a "special projects" person. In some instances, the station may request a subpoena. This is one reason why a prosecutor should be brought on board as early as possible in the investigation. Keep in mind that the degree of cooperation and speed of cooperation vary on a case-by-case basis, depending upon station personnel, resources, and policies.

Media Retrieval

Media stations have different filing systems, and like those in law enforcement, these have changed and evolved over the years and decades. Once common card files have been replaced by computerized databases, and on occasions, some stations still maintain both. Card index files were common pre-computer, and this requires a manual search. In some instances, these were later transferred to a computer program, but that program may have become history with software advances and the data may no longer be retrievable. Many stations, as do some law enforcement agencies, maintain off-site storage facilities, and it may require some time and effort on the part of station personnel for them to cross-check records in available databases. Remember: the information on card files was only as good as the person who filled it out, and information retrieval may well depend upon the ability to cross-check information between cards.

When contacting media, date of the crime, discovery of the body, or when the story aired is important for their search. Knowing this date allows them to more quickly identify and retrieve the film. Since the advent of computers, however, software for newsrooms allows them to search national as well as local stories.

When attempting to locate the film, also attempt to locate the written script. The *written script* is what is said on the air; it may also include what the reporter *did* during the broadcast of the story and may include narration and text of the sound bite. The written script is not uncommonly transcribed and filed. If it is one read by an anchor, what the anchor says is also in the script. Names in sound bites and scripts may be searchable in databases and, in older instances, card files, depending upon how the story was catalogued by the local station.

Maintenance of scripts may vary from station to station, depending upon their policies, and may be searchable depending upon their filing systems or databases. Usually, however, what is saved is only that which was aired. Also ask if they have still pictures, "stills," from old interviews.

When reviewing older footage, do not be surprised to see camera crews in the heart of the crime scene, or officers handling evidence in front of the camera. It happened.

During review of footage, investigators should note what is revealed about people, the scene, and other revelations by the footage, in particular:

- Names. Cold case investigators should cross-check to be sure that persons interviewed by the media had been interviewed by law enforcement. These investigative statements should be cross-checked to their media accounts.
- Dates and times. These should be compared to the case file and may assist in timeline preparation and/or enhance or discredit statements of concerned persons.
- Scene and analysis of what the footage shows and compared to case photos.

Film Degradation and Acuity

Film is subject to degradation, depending upon storage conditions and exposure to heat and humidity. Normally, film does not readily show detail like blood spatter and holes unless a zoom lens was used. In addition, film footage is usually not of the quality of later videotape. In certain cases, cold case investigators may wish to have a forensic specialist examine the film for possible enhancement of frames or images. Investigators may consider consultation with local law enforcement or state laboratory personnel or other specialists.

Magazines and Other Literature

When reviewing cold cases, keep in mind that these may have been written up in magazines or books. During the course of investigation, officers from the time period of the case, friends or family of the victim, or other witnesses may have knowledge whether, and when, the story was reported in news magazines or literary magazines or books.

In previous decades, magazines such as *True Detective* and similar works regularly published true-crime stories submitted by law enforcement authors (see Figure 19.7). These reports may detail names, events, and other matters concerning the crime, as well as photographs. It may be prudent to ascertain if any such publication occurred. Keep in mind that many of these accounts

Figure 19.7 *True Detective* 1958. This issue carried detailed reporting and pictures to be found nowhere else when cold case investigators revisited the 1957 murders of two El Segundo Police officers in 2003. (Courtesy of El Segundo Police Department.)

may or may not be "enhanced" or embellished. When direct knowledge of the existence of a specific article or crime report is not known, cold case investigators may attempt to use Internet resources such as https://www.ebay.com/ to identify and locate these articles.

During the course of a cold case investigation, it may prove valuable to ascertain if any persons connected to, or known to, the original or subsequent investigation authored any published material or unpublished manuscripts. Comparison of what is revealed in this material to the case file may be of interest in the cold case investigation.

In one extreme example, a fire of suspicious origin in South Pasadena, California, in 1984 claimed the lives of four persons, including a 2½-year-old boy. It was initially ruled "accidental," although some fire investigators did not agree with this conclusion by law enforcement investigators. The fire case was closed and remained this way for over a decade.

Among those involved in the earliest stages of the investigation was Glendale, California, fire department arson investigator John Orr. Orr was considered an expert arson investigator by his peers and highly respected. In 1998, Orr was convicted of setting the fatal fire, one in a series the esteemed fire marshal had set over the years. During the course of their investigation, investigators discovered that Orr had authored an *unpublished manuscript* detailing people and events in a fatal arson. The revelations contained in this document became a pivotal point during the investigation and ultimate conviction of Orr for the murders. This is represented in Figure 19.8.

Other Media Sources for Information

Ever wonder how or where the media obtains information for broadcast today on something that happened years, or decades, ago? Complete with footage and pictures? Go to http://www.footage.net. This website links numerous archives of footage dating to 1896, including dash cam or caught-on-tape, amateur surveillance videos, and more. This news footage network offers the media the ability to rapidly find previous news reports and archival footage. This site links to stock footage houses with access to footage, news reports, and more. After checking with your local media, this may be a good place to start when searching for footage and pictures. Links are provided to numerous sources of historical clips, images, and footage. And don't forget to check "YouTube."

Case Study

The following case history is drawn only from four newspaper accounts and the death certificate. The information presented is retrieved from post-initial reporting articles in the *Los Angeles Times* newspaper, January 5, 1989, and

POINTS OF ORIGIN

by

John L. Orr

It flared up much quicker than he expected. He had planted the device only seven minutes earlier and already the paper bag was on fire. The blossoming flames quickly spread to a weathered cardboard box, then began eating away at the side of a discarded sofa next to it. He lowered himself in the driver's seat and squinted through binoculars for a better view. It was a moonless night and the flickering light from the fire looked obscenely out of place, scarring the otherwise serene August evening. Beyond the carport where the fire was burning, he saw the HOLLYWOOD sign lighting up the horizon above the deteriorating city.

Figure 19.8 Manuscript of John Orr paper. Cold case investigators should inquire if anyone connected with a cold case authored any papers, stories, or other literature on the case. This front page of a text authored by former Glendale, California, arson investigator John Orr helped to convict him for setting a series of fires, including one that killed four people. His descriptions of "fictional" events were too close to factual to be considered fictional by investigators, and the jury agreed. (Courtesy of Special Agent Mike Matassa, ATF.)

the *San Francisco Chronicle* newspaper from July 9, 1991, and May 20 and 21, 1998. The subject was the unsolved murder of San Francisco Police Officer Lester Garnier (Figure 19.9). The purpose of this is to illustrate the *detailed* information that *may* be uncovered in a cold case newspaper review and to explore possible avenues of investigation due to the passage of time in light of changes in relationships and technology.

Figure 19.9 San Francisco Police Officer Lester Garnier was murdered in Walnut Creek, California, in 1988. His murder remains unsolved. (Courtesy of Lt. John Hennessey, San Francisco Police Department.)

It will appear that there is information in these reports that many investigators would prefer not to see in the press. These reports reflect the depths of investigation and variety of sources utilized in news reporting. By use of this case example, I intend in no manner or design to criticize, demean, or impugn the character or reputations of the victim or of any personnel involved in the investigation, nor of the law enforcement agencies. In cold case investigation, best results are obtained not by looking back and saying "why didn't they do this?" or "why did they do this?" but rather by objective, systematic study of the facts and evidence and moving forward in a cooperative manner with the objective of solving the case.

What happened in the past is in the past...move forward.

The Initial Investigation

The Crime Scene

Police Officer Lester Garnier was found shot to death, slumped behind the wheel of his blue 1984 Corvette, in a parking lot of a shopping mall in Walnut Creek, California, on July 11, 1998. The general location is a suburb of homes and office complexes on the east side of San Francisco Bay.

The vehicle was angled across three spaces near a group of upscale department stores. This was a position a police lieutenant would later state indicated that he was making a "meet." The same lieutenant stated that the murder had to be work related, as his car was placed so that no one could surprise him.

Garnier was found by workers approximately around 7:30 a.m., the vehicle being reported as having been there all night. The car still had its parking lights on, the doors were unlocked, and the driver's window was down. He apparently had no gun or any money with him at the time of his death.

The victim's face was streaked with dry blood, and blood stained his long-sleeved white sweatshirt and Levi pants. The victim's badge was inside one of the car's storage compartments.

Upon report of the crime, eight officers from the 78-member Walnut Creek Police Department, which usually experienced perhaps one murder a year, responded to the scene.

Reported Witness Statements

1. A workman in the shopping center reported hearing several gunfire-like noises approximately around 11:30 p.m. but paid no attention as it was near July 4. This witness later observed two women walking in the parking lot area. This may be the same witness as #3 reported below.
2. Another witness told of seeing a woman exit the passenger's side of Garnier's vehicle. Police used a hypnotist with this witness in an attempt to create a composite drawing of the woman. The woman was described as being approximately 28 years old, blonde, 5 feet 6 inches to 5 feet 8 inches, weight approximately 110 pounds. Neither woman had been identified as of July 9, 1991, despite repeated requests by police to the public for information. This may be the same as #4 below.
3. Approximately 11:15 p.m., a man laying carpet at a store near the Ross Dress for Less Parking lot heard what appeared to be two or three gunshots coming from the vicinity of the parking lot. A few minutes later, he saw two women walking through the lot. One woman was described as in "…her mid-30s, tall and slender with blond hair below her shoulders." The other was described as being in her 20s and had shoulder-length blond hair and a medium build. The witness stated he observed the taller woman drive away in a faded blue Toyota, while the other drove away in a Toyota or Datsun with white or gray oxidized paint.
4. Another witness reported driving through the parking lot around 11:30 p.m. and observed a "slim, blond[e] woman get out of the passenger's door of Garnier's Corvette." The witness said the woman circled the car and appeared to look in the driver's window before she walked away. None of the women was ever located.

The Investigation

These news accounts further reported that within approximately three years of the homicide, the Walnut Creek Police Department had "…interviewed more than 600 persons and traveled hundreds of miles in search of clues." During this, they had used hypnosis on a key witness and also consulted a psychic. In addition, "…every time a similar gun was used in a crime elsewhere," investigators "discussed it" with law enforcement representatives of that agency.

The investigation into Garnier's personal and professional life is reported in the news accounts. The media also stated that investigators had spoken to "several hundred prostitutes" Garnier had arrested in the course of his undercover work. Other information found in these reports includes the following.

1. **Evidence**

According to media reports, little physical evidence was recovered at the scene. However, the reporting in these articles indicates that fingerprints and a spent bullet were recovered. According to the media, "Fingerprints in the car didn't produce a suspect."

The news reports further stated that "…police recovered one copper jacketed bullet from inside Garnier's sweatshirt and tested it against similar guns owned by eight San Francisco police officers, finding no matches." In a report by the *Los Angeles Times* in 1989, the media review suggested deeper elements of the investigation, noting that the "revolvers" of 10 San Francisco police officers had been reportedly checked by Walnut Creek detectives.

In my experience, the media and others have not, infrequently in the past, lumped the term "revolver" as identifying *all* handguns, including semiautomatics, which is not correct. According to the chief of San Francisco Police Department (SFPD), this was done "merely to cover all the bases." The chief is further reported as saying he had no knowledge of a police officer as a suspect in this case. By this and other news reports, it was suggested that a strong rift had occurred between the SFPD and the agency of primary jurisdiction, the Walnut Creek Police Department. Senior officers and investigators of the SFPD are identified and quoted at length in these accounts regarding their lack of participation in the initial investigation.

The *San Francisco Chronicle* in 1991 further reported similarly that

> In addition, they ran innumerable fingerprint checks and test-fired the weapons of eight officers in the San Francisco Police Department who owned guns similar to the murder weapon. In at least one instance, a San Francisco officer submitted to a lie detector test.

This brings to mind the question, why were the guns and fingerprints of fellow officers examined? The answer to this would be found in the review of later news reports.

> Within the San Francisco department, rumors have circulated that an officer killed Garnier and that Walnut Creek did not trust San Francisco police to help find the killer. Some San Francisco officers are angry that their detectives were not summoned to the murder scene immediately.

Senior SFPD officers are quoted regarding their perception of the Walnut Creek investigation. In response, Walnut Creek police are reported as responding that they tested the officers' weapons "'to cover potential defense issues at a later time' and that they came up with no ballistic matches." Walnut Creek police were reported as saying the suspect could be, or could not be, a police officer. This area of investigation had not been eliminated.

2. **The Victim**

Garnier's life was reportedly examined in detail by investigating detectives, and published in the press. He was held in high esteem by his colleagues and known as a very cautious man. According to the press, Garnier "...was extremely particular about who he let into his car, but apparently allowed his assailant to get into his vehicle and sit next to him without evidence of a struggle." On the night of the homicide, he apparently left his 9 mm and .357 caliber handguns at home.

The media, and investigation, explored his past. Garnier was born in the local Mission District of San Francisco and attended Mission Dolores Elementary School and Riordan High School. Described by a classmate as a "solid B student," the victim was further described as "street smart." After school he would stay around the Boys and Girls Club. Garnier was named Boy of the Year and Regional Boy of the year, and earned a trip to Washington, District of Columbia, to meet President Gerald Ford. Those who knew him advised they had never heard anyone say anything bad about him.

Beginning in 1980, Garnier worked for the Broadmoor Police Department, a suburb near San Francisco. He joined the SFPD that same year and spent four years as a patrol officer at the Northern Station in the Fillmore District. He arrested three gunmen holding up a restaurant on a main city street in 1981, and in 1983, helped capture an attempted murderer. He was twice decorated for bravery. In 1984, he transferred to the vice unit and worked there until his own murder. During this time, he had arrested hundreds of prostitutes. Prior to his assignment to the unit, a series of scandals and allegations of corruption had been levied against the SFPD. These were reported in the media as centering on the vice unit amid allegations of officers using and selling drugs, hiring prostitutes, and providing favors for bookies, drug dealers, and pimps.

When he was off-duty, Garnier worked three part-time jobs (other accounts state four part-time jobs), and reports indicated that he was further thinking of opening up a small business—a hot dog stand. He bought the Corvette and had a cell phone. The latter was not yet common at that time. Garnier liked nice clothes, worked out, and had dated a number of women.

According to these reports, Garnier purchased a home with a pool in nearby Concord and lived there with his parents shortly before his death. Other reports say he helped his parents purchase the home.

Garnier was reportedly a quiet person and did not often speak about his job with his family. He did, as was reported, once say that "There are good policemen and bad policemen, just like anything else."

3. **Victim's Movements on the Night of the Homicide**

   On the night of the homicide, Garnier ate a roast beef dinner with his family and left his home at approximately 8:45 p.m. At approximately 9 p.m., he called his "best friend," the owner of a San Francisco gas station. The two had spoken of going to see the movie *Bull Durham*, but Garnier said he was behind schedule and could not make it. His best friend later reported that he tried to call Garnier back but that the phone just kept ringing.

4. **The Weapon**

   The weapon used in the slaying was an AMT .380 caliber semiautomatic pistol. It has never been recovered.

5. **Motive**

   No motive has been identified in this crime.

6. **Suspect**

   No suspect has been identified in this crime.

7. **The Wounds**

   The victim was shot twice at close range, once in the right temple and once in the right side.

8. **The Political and Investigative Environment**

   Not unheard of in hot homicide cases, political and other elements are thrust into homicide investigations. Cold case investigations are no different. By 1991, according to press reports, police had no reported motive or suspect. The two lead detectives on the case are identified and quoted during the news reports. Detectives reportedly had eliminated motives that included robbery, revenge, a casual pick-up, girlfriend, or prostitutes that Garnier had arrested. At this time, police discounted any relationship of this crime to a series of political scandals within San Francisco City Hall. Press reports offer insight into elements that cold case investigators may need to examine in depth for relevance to the murder of Officer Garnier.

Not long before his murder, Officer Garnier was assigned to surveillance duty on a brothel that reportedly specialized in underage girls. This was part of an investigation into the activities of the brothel and that led to the indictment of the city's chief administrative officer, a San Francisco police officer, and numerous others for patronizing the brothel. The investigation stemmed from an informant's letter, and a follow-up letter advising of the brothel, and a second letter notifying the SFPD of possible officer patronage of the brothel. Later reports of a friend of Office Garnier note that Garnier told his friend he was working on a case that had high-level political ramifications. Subsequently the brothel was raided on April 30, 1988, but the two named "ringleaders" got away. Officials were later reported as saying the suspects were tipped off in advance of the raid. When one *timelines* the events reflected in news accounts, this was almost a year after the initial reports of the existence of the brothel yet slightly over two months *before* Officer Garnier's murder.

Garnier's surveillance activities were reportedly documented in his logs. The newspaper reports detail statements of other "authorities" relating to past "police bachelor parties" attended by officers from other jurisdictions in which young prostitutes were alleged to have attended by invitation of the indicted officer. The indicted officer's lawyer is quoted in the articles suggesting that Garnier may have attended one of these "stag parties" while a reserve officer, and perhaps known some of the girls in the brothel he was staking out. In addition, the indicted officer had previously served as a reserve officer in the same agency as Officer Garnier. According to the press accounts, the SFPD could not verify this information and the former officer "could not be reached for comment." According to the news accounts, the SFPD officer was fired from the force after pleading to one count of unlawful sex with a minor in which he received a suspended sentence, fine, and probation. The city official also pleaded guilty to patronizing the brothel, was fined $100,000, and "performed six months of community service picking up trash in the city." The chief of police at the time of the murder was reported as saying Officer Garnier's murder was not connected to the prostitution ring and in 1998 reportedly said that while he could not recall saying this, assumed it was the result of information from subordinate officers.

The news media often timelines events in accounts of reporting of events and, in this instance, provided summaries detailing, in part, the careers of the dismissed officer and murder victim Garnier as well as other events:

- Garnier served as a reserve officer in 1980. During this period, the dismissed officer was employed for a private security service at an apartment complex near Broadmoor, had friends on that force, and may have known Garnier.
- Garnier joined the SFPD in 1980 and the dismissed officer in mid-1982.
- One of the brothel ringleaders attended bachelor parties also attended by members of the Broadmoor Police Department and other agencies. The dismissed officer allegedly invited prostitutes to these parties.
- In May 1987, SFPD receives an anonymous letter regarding the brothel. A second letter follows two months later.
- On April 30, 1988, the brothel is raided.
- Capture of one of the brothel owner suspects in Oklahoma on July 9, 1988.
- Officer Garnier was murdered the next day.
- Presence of a grand jury investigation of a prostitution ring specializing in underage girls.
- Capture of the second brothel owner suspect in South Carolina on July 19, 1989, after the case is aired on the television show *America's Most Wanted*.
- Walnut Creek police were reported as interviewing an SFPD narcotics officer who had filed an unsuccessful lawsuit alleging that he had been punished for "blowing the whistle" on corruption within the department.
- In early 1998, SFPD reopens a new investigation as a result of discovery of an internal memorandum in a vice unit file suggesting the presence of a corrupt officer within the unit about the time Garnier was murdered. The SFPD pledges to follow this investigation to wherever it leads.

According to newspaper reports, police were unable to find any link between the death of Officer Garnier and the prostitution ring. In addition, the news reports announce that the SFPD had launched a new investigation in early 1998 into the murder of Officer Garnier. Interestingly enough, the news accounts do not report how well Garnier and the dismissed officer knew each other, and noted that this relationship was one that was being investigated.

These accounts reflect concern and anger by SFPD police officials and investigators about their lack of participation in the initial homicide investigation. This decision not to conduct a formal investigation into the death of one of their "own" is reported as a decision that "…still rankles officers in the department," although it occurred in another agency's jurisdiction. These accounts further suggest that Walnut Creek police "…tried with little success" to establish a link between the murder and allegations of corruption or scandals within the SFPD of the period.

According to press reports in 1998, the FBI confirmed that Walnut Creek investigators had requested the Bureau to reopen an investigation into allegations of corruption involving SFPD officers that had been conducted in the mid-1980s. An FBI agent is quoted as saying that Walnut Creek police were interested in knowing if someone from within the SFPD was involved in the murder of Officer Garnier. The request had been denied due to lack of new information.

Based upon review of these four newspaper reports only, and assuming the validity as written, cold case investigators would seek to apply the advantages to be gained from exploiting (1) advanced technology and (2) changes in relationships.

- Changes in technology
    - Automated fingerprint identification system (*AFIS*). Rerun all fingerprints and utilize updated databanks and techniques. Also run them in other local, state, and national databanks.
    - National Integrated Ballistic Information Network (*NIBIN*). Input and run the bullet through updated data banks, despite the age of the case. In addition, due to the growth of laboratories in the region, update publicizing this bullet to local crime laboratories and police agencies. The news reports do not indicate that the shell casings were recovered; however, this avenue would also be explored.
- Changes in relationships
    - It appears from the news media reports that hundreds of persons, including those arrested by the victim, were interviewed against a possible background of corruption and a prostitution ring. These included suspects in the brothel investigation as well as friends and coworkers of the victim. Cold case investigators may seek to identify those for re-contact and interview in light of the intervening years and changes in relationships, as well as to update information they may have "heard" over the years. Among these would be those close to or associated with named principals, and personal or professional relationships.
    - Reinterview those close to the victim for additional statements after passage of time.

The news accounts further suggest exploration and a review of:

- Cell phone records (if existent and obtained) and residence or work telephone records of the victim and others. Cell phones were coming of age at this time and were not the compact devices we have today. The carriers have changed many times since this time period, and if these records were not obtained during the initial investigation, they may or may not be available now. How he came to be where he was when reportedly going to a movie with a friend is of interest. In addition:
  - Phone records of the two fugitives and communications before the murder
  - Known associates of the two fugitives just before and after the murder
- Parallel duty assignments that might have brought the victim and the deceased officer into possible frequent contacts. Reinterview of coworkers, friends, and associates of each.

These ideas are but a few that may be suggested from review of these media reports. A full, in-depth identification and review of all media accounts may provide further detail for possible exploration. This example is used for illustrative purposes only.

Media Assistance in Cold Case Investigation

Unlike hot homicide investigation, there is no fresh crime scene to which the media responds and begins to take pictures and conduct interviews. In cold cases, the press doesn't know when a cold case is reactivated, and does not learn of it until the case is solved and a news conference is called or a news release is generated by the agency. In the course of cold case investigations, investigators may seek to maintain a low profile to further their efforts until the suspect has been identified and taken into custody. The element of surprise may be a consideration in many of these cases.

In some instances, however, and as an investigation progresses, investigators may decide whether to release information to the public. These situations may include:

- Law enforcement efforts to seek new witnesses and tips
- Publishing or running stories on anniversaries of a crime or other significant dates
- Law enforcement attempts to identify property associated with unknown or known victims
- Law enforcement attempts to locate suspects or others

Law enforcement efforts may utilize more proactive methods, depending upon the circumstances of the case. These may include:

- National media or special reenactments of crimes and information wanted such as *America's Most Wanted*
- National law enforcement media resources such as the FBI *Law Enforcement Bulletin*
- Written flyers and posters, widespread or localized
- Local televised or radio broadcasts
- Newspaper announcements
- Local magazine or other publications

Consideration of media resources in furtherance of cold case investigation should not be limited to just newspapers, radio, or television (see Figure 19.10). Seeking information through other forms of media may include Internet websites such as:

Figure 19.10 Billboard—Use of media to solicit public information. On June 19, 1991, this young girl apparently answered the doorbell at her family residence in a condominium complex shortly after 9 p.m. A short time later, her family noticed her missing, and her shoes by the door. The next morning, her body was found by workers at a nearby business complex, still wearing the pajamas she had worn when she disappeared. She had been hacked to death. A billboard was utilized to seek information about the case. The murder went unsolved. In October 2003, the DNA Laboratory of the San Diego (California) Police Department discovered a perfect DNA profile match between oral swabs and fingernail material collected from the victim, and the DNA profile of a neighbor, a convicted felon. (Courtesy of Detective Bob Conrad, Chula Vista Police Department.)

- Agency World Wide Web site.
- Social media.
- Special focus websites such as http://doenetwork.org. This volunteer organization assists law enforcement concerning unexplained disappearances and unidentified victims from North America, Australia, and Europe (see Chapter 31).

Case Study

On May 28, 1982, 16-year-old Los Gatos, California, high school student Russell Jordan vanished without a trace. A missing persons report was taken by the Santa Cruz County Sheriff's Office, Jordan's official county of residence. The student disappeared, however, in neighboring Santa Clara County, where he attended school. During the investigation, it was discovered that he had cleaned out his high school locker a month before he disappeared and many presumed the youth was a runaway juvenile. In April 1995, a transient found some bones in Los Gatos Creek not far from the boy's high school. Determined to assist police, the homeless person picked up some bones and carried them to the front counter of the police department.

Responding officers returned to the scene and conducted a detailed search in which they applied anthropological recovery techniques and recovered more remains. Winter rains and wildlife activity had affected the site, however. The skull and other parts were missing and could not be located. Among the items recovered, however, was a distinctive belt buckle. Investigators were aware of the missing juvenile from 13 years before, and believed that this might be the missing boy. The belt buckle was identified as very similar to the one he was last known to be wearing, but could not be considered conclusive proof of identity, however. The remains were turned over to the county coroner. Although the case was treated as a homicide by the police department, they were unable to identify the remains. *Forensic anthropology* examination suggested that the remains were of the same description as the missing boy, but identification was inconclusive.

In late 1999, advances in DNA technology presented the Los Gatos Police Department with the opportunity for further investigative possibility. The remains were sent to the FBI mitochondrial DNA unit. In 2003, this specialized unit of the FBI Laboratory affirmed the identity through *mitochondrial DNA* comparison to the victim's mother.

In March of 2003, the results of the DNA examination were published in the newspapers with a request for information. As a result of this newspaper story, a former classmate of the youth came forward to admit that the missing boy was not a runaway juvenile but in fact had been murdered by another classmate.

Sergeant Tim Morgan and Officer Randy Bishop of the Los Gatos Police Department moved quickly on the investigation. The investigators learned that after Jordan was reported as a runaway, Jordan's friend, Sean Viehweg, had told others that he was not a runaway and admitted that he had killed the boy. Thus, other *classmates* knew but had kept quiet over the decades. Investigators began to interview others in Jordan's close circle of friends, and as a result, obtained the names of two other classmates with knowledge of the murder. In the course of this investigation, officers of this smaller police agency encountered what many in cold case investigation have discovered is not unusual—the need to travel and the extra unbudgeted expense of this particular investigation.

One of the witnesses to the admission still lived locally, but another now lived many miles away in Eureka, in northern California. Morgan and Bishop located and interviewed the second witness, who admitted to helping Viehweg dispose of the body the day after the murder. As a result, investigators obtained an arrest warrant for Viehweg.

Investigation revealed that Viehweg, now 38 years old, lived near Klamath Falls, a small farming community in southern Oregon. In my experience, it is not unusual that suspects in cold case homicides have often moved out of the state in which they committed their crimes. Viehweg was now married and had a family. In the course of planning their strategy for the investigation, the investigators contacted detectives in the Los Angeles Police Department to draw upon their experiences and expertise in this phase of the investigation. This was an excellent tactic on the part of the Los Gatos investigators.

The investigators contacted law enforcement in the jurisdiction where Viehweg now lived, and strategized their investigative plan. In this phase of the investigation, there are no clear-cut rules to define what cold case investigators should do or not do. Each case, and circumstance, is different. Investigators consider the suspect's background and the life he or she has led in the period since the homicide. *Is the suspect a career criminal? Is the suspect a serial killer? Is this the suspect's only crime?* The investigators had checked Viehweg's background. Viehweg had served honorably in the military, including duty in Somalia, Panama, the Persian Gulf, and elsewhere for eight years. Nothing suggested a serious criminal history. Officers were aware, however, that at this phase of the investigation, suspect contact offers a number of options. These may be (1) fight, (2) flight, or (3) admission and/or confession.

Individual investigators have different methods that have worked for them, and here is where experience and training pay off. Sgt. Morgan and

Officer Bishop, assisted by officers from the local jurisdiction, contacted Viehweg, in a low-key approach at home. At this initial contact, cold case investigators should note, and record, the *immediate* reaction of a suspect when confronted about the past crime or advised of the investigator's jurisdiction. Observe their *immediate* reaction and record their *exact* words at this initial confrontation with their past. Viehweg turned "white." He agreed to accompany officers to the local law enforcement facility for an interview and Viehweg was arrested on May 17, 2003. He ultimately waived extradition to return to California, and offered a defense that he killed the victim when the victim assaulted him with a knife. The suspect subsequently pleaded no contest on December 18, 2003, to one count of voluntary manslaughter.

Identified cold case issues

- Initial report as missing juvenile
- Knowledge, and silence, by peer group (classmates)
- Recovery of suspected remains but inability to confirm identity
- DNA advances that allow for positive identification of the remains
- News media information and request for information from the public
- Previously silent witness coming forward
- Identification of other witnesses and accomplices
- Suspect out-of-state residence and arrest by local law enforcement agency from another jurisdiction
- Legal considerations of prosecution as juvenile or adult
- Suspect's life style and law-abiding status since the murder
- Age of the case and lack of witnesses to the act

Media and Reporting of Solved Cold Cases

Announcement to the public via the news media of the successful conclusion of a cold case investigation serves a number of purposes. Among these are as follows:

- Announces the identification and arrest of an alleged murderer
- Advises the public that law enforcement has not forgotten these cases, as exemplified by this case solution
- May stimulate others with knowledge of unsolved homicides to come forward with information
- Recognizes the role of the dedicated persons and investigators who made this possible
- Reaffirms the commitment of the police agency to serve and protect the community

Other Guidelines

Prior to the news release or new conference, the victim's family or other concerned persons should be notified. It would not be unusual for the media to locate and contact relatives of the victim and the suspect after the announcement. Efforts to provide victim assistance resources should be made available to the victim's family members as soon as possible upon arrest of the suspect and prior to news release (see Chapter 31).

In cold cases where the victim was a member of a minority community, the agency may consider news or press release to be disseminated to any media groups that focus or are dedicated to that community. As an example, if the victim was a member of a Korean community and that community has a community newspaper or radio or television station, be sure that these entities are notified of the arrest and case developments (see Figure 19.11).

Conclusion

Freedom of the press is a hallmark of democracy and a necessary component of our society. The press, like law enforcement, helps to safeguard the public and to expose wrongdoing. For cold case homicide investigations, the press may serve as an information base, providing a record of persons and events sometimes not retained, or found, in the original case file. These records may offer additional avenues of investigation for cold case investigators through reporting of persons, events, and other information pertaining to the crime and related events. In addition, the media may serve to generate public interest and assistance for cold case investigations, and ultimately serve to broadcast the successes of cold case investigations. These successes reflect positively on the law enforcement agency and serve to remind the public, and those who have killed and not yet been caught, that law enforcement does not forget.

Acknowledgments

I wish to recognize and extend my deepest gratitude and appreciation to David Gotfredson of KFMB in San Diego, California. Gotfredson is a veteran newsman and editor and contributed much of the material used as a basis in this chapter. In addition, I wish to also acknowledge and express my deepest gratitude to David Browning for his material, input, and thoughtful review of this chapter. Browning is a veteran producer of news and documentaries for CBS News, covering stories such as the RFK assassination, the Manson murders, the Patty Hearst kidnapping and trial, as well as natural disasters, political conventions, and Hollywood frivolities. In the 1990s, he served in the *CBS*

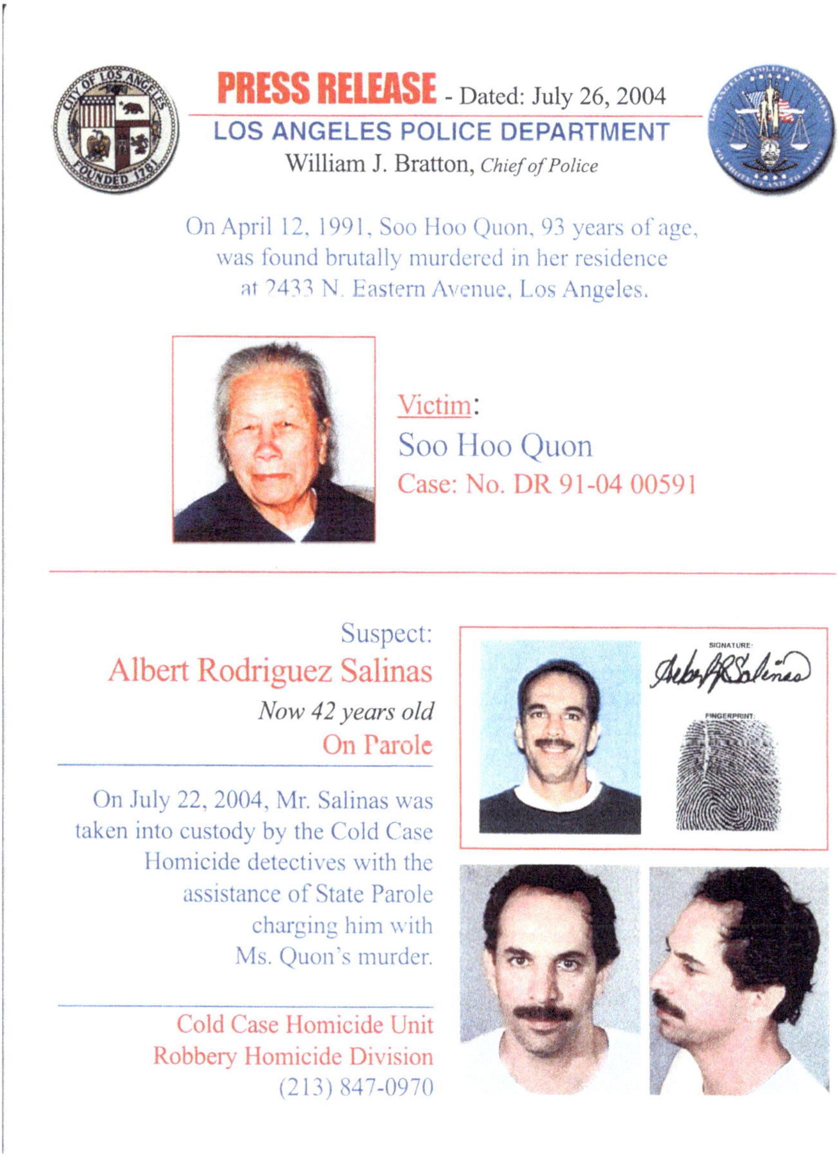

PRESS RELEASE - Dated: July 26, 2004

LOS ANGELES POLICE DEPARTMENT

William J. Bratton, *Chief of Police*

On April 12, 1991, Soo Hoo Quon, 93 years of age, was found brutally murdered in her residence at 2433 N. Eastern Avenue, Los Angeles.

Victim:
Soo Hoo Quon
Case: No. DR 91-04 00591

Suspect:
Albert Rodriguez Salinas
Now 42 years old
On Parole

SIGNATURE:
FINGERPRINT:

On July 22, 2004, Mr. Salinas was taken into custody by the Cold Case Homicide detectives with the assistance of State Parole charging him with Ms. Quon's murder.

Cold Case Homicide Unit
Robbery Homicide Division
(213) 847-0970

Figure 19.11 Press release to announce a solved cold case homicide. Cold case homicides are the most difficult to solve. When they are, it is incumbent that law enforcement blow its own horn. There can be no better use of resources than to clear an old, unsolved murder. This reassures the public that these victims are not forgotten, and that the law enforcement agency is committed to solving these crimes. In cases involving the member of a minority community and that community has local media, press releases should be brought to their attention in addition to regular press outlets. In this case, the LAPD solved a 13-year-old homicide of an elderly woman. It is no surprise that the offender was a parolee. (Courtesy of Detective Rick Jackson, Los Angeles Police Department Robbery-Homicide, Cold Case Unit.)

Reports documentary unit, writing and producing the television memoirs of Walter Cronkite and Mike Wallace, and has worked in recent years primarily for *60 Minutes* as well as occasional production duties for *48 Hours*.

Suggested Readings and Bibliography

Anonymous. (1989). The state: Metro desk. Los Angeles Times, p. 2 (January 5, 1989). Los Angeles, CA.

Durant, C. (2005). Humboldt County's cold cases: Can these crimes be solved? Times-Standard (May 29, 2005). Eureka, CA.

Gathright, A. (2003). Others knew of killing, D.A. says: Los Gatos students remained silent about 1982 death. San Francisco Chronicle (May 10, 2003). San Francisco.

Ryan, K. (2003). No contest plea in '82 killing of teen. *San Francisco Chronicle* (December 19, 2003). San Francisco.

Stannard, M. (2003). Arrest in 1982 Los Gatos Killing: Oregon man accused in death of classmate in high school years. *San Francisco Chronicle* (May 9, 2002). San Francisco.

Stannard, M.B. (2003). Dad says his son admitted to killing: Self-defense claim in 1982 death of Los Gatos classmate. *San Francisco Chronicle* (May 12, 2003). San Francisco.

Sward, S. and Wallace, B. (1998). Still no suspect, motive in '88 killing of sf cop: '88 slaying stumps Walnut Creek police. San Francisco Chronicle (July 9, 1991 Final Edition). San Francisco.

Sward, S. and Wallace, B. (1991). New probe of s.f. cop's '88 slaying. *San Francisco Chronicle* (May 20, 1998 Final Edition). San Francisco.

Sward, S. and Wallace, B. (1991). How trail grew cold in '88 s.f. cop killing. *San Francisco Chronicle* (May 21, 1998 Final Edition). San Francisco.

Wambaugh, J. (2002). *Fire Lover: A True Story*. New York: Avon Books.

Using Social Media Platforms & the Broadcast Media 20

PAUL WAGNER

In the early morning hours of October 23, 1988, Tammy Thorpe drove her 1986 Pontiac Grand Am through a car wash in the Fauquier County town of Warrenton, Virginia.

It was around 3:00 am.

The 20-year-old was following the direction of Fauquier County Sheriff's Deputy Bob Mosier who told her to get it washed and then bring the car to the sheriff's office the next day.

Earlier that night Tammy had been at a dance in Marshall, Virginia, where her car had been slightly damaged as Deputy Mosier tried to handcuff a man he was trying to arrest.

But what happened after Tammy left the car wash has remained a mystery for 36 years.

Her gold Grand Am was found in a parking lot adjacent to the car wash.

It was unlocked with Tammy's purse still inside. The driver's seat was in a position for someone much taller than Tammy who was 5′5″.

A few hours later and about a mile away Tammy Thorpe's body was found on a gravel lane off Route 17. She had been shot in the face with a small caliber handgun.

Although a motive has never been established, FBI profilers told investigators they believe Tammy knew her killer.

For years investigators worked the case interviewing dozens of people, but it wasn't until 2004 when detectives got the break they were hoping for.

It came in a tip after a story about the murder was broadcast by Fox 5 (WTTG-TV) in Washington, DC.

Two nurses working at the Winchester Medical Center in Winchester, Virginia, saw the story and remembered a man they said had confessed to the crime in the early 1990s. In fact, they told detectives it had been documented in medical records.

The man's name was Duane Mecham.

The detective assigned to the case, Ray Acors, who had been featured in the television story, then filed a search warrant for the records.

DOI: 10.4324/9781003415633-23

It took some time, but Acors eventually got the file and after reviewing what was written and documented he secured a search warrant for Mecham's home in Culpeper County, Virginia.

The search failed to turn up anything that would lead to an indictment but Mecham, who knew Tammy Thorpe, became a person of interest.

The case has taken many twists and turns since 2004. Mecham, whose wife was a Canadian citizen, left the country for Canada shortly after the search where they stayed for several years until the couple divorced.

When Fauquier County detectives learned Mecham had moved back to the United States they filed another search warrant for his fingerprints. The investigators had hoped they could match a partial set of prints found inside Tammy's car. But those hopes were dashed when the examiner determined the evidence and Mecham's fingerprints could not be linked.

I have reported on this story many times since 2004.

Years ago, while the couple were living in Canada I interviewed them over the phone. Duane Mecham told me he had nothing to do with the crime, and he has always maintained his innocence.

Tammy's family has never stopped looking for answers and I have stayed in touch with them for more than 20 years.

I can say the same for the Fauquier County Sheriff's Office.

From the day I got the call to see if I would be willing to profile Tammy's case until the last story I filed in 2021, I have worked closely with the investigators.

For me, the story worked because I was allowed to interview the lead detective and as I recall (it was more than 20 years ago) we sat in a room at headquarters going over photos and documents.

I listened as the investigators briefed me on the evidence they had and what they thought would be helpful to include in the story. I had full editorial control, but I was willing to include the facts the detectives thought might be most helpful.

The other part of the story was the family. I have always thought that having an emotional angle to a cold case story was essential. It draws the viewers in.

I interviewed Tammy's mother and father and her sister Lisa.

Over the years I have interviewed members of the family multiple times.

In 2019 the sheriff's office contacted me again and asked if I would come out to Warrenton for a meeting with the Commonwealth's Attorney and Sheriff Bob Mosier. (Yes, the same Bob Mosier who told Tammy to take the car through the car wash that night.)

They told me investigators had some evidence they wanted to test and asked me to do the story.

(Those fingerprints I mentioned.)

I write all of this to say a collaboration with the reporter is essential with cold case stories. The reporter must have editorial control and report the facts but there is nothing wrong with making sure the elements of the case the investigators want mentioned make it into the piece.

A cold case story has several benefits. It gets the facts of the case out into the public eye and lets the community know the investigators are still working on it. The family gets the satisfaction of knowing their loved one hasn't been forgotten while at the same time hopeful a new tip or lead may come in.

One story I reported for Fox 5 in Washington, DC resulted in a closure. An administrative closure.

On June 3, 1998, Mary Alice Pratt was found beaten to death inside her home on Emerald Street NE in Washington, DC. A distinctive ring with a unique design was taken from one of her fingers. When we broadcast the story in the early 2000s someone came forward with a tip that ultimately led to a closure. The lead detective with the Metropolitan Police, Mitch Credle, told me the information was good enough to close the case without making an arrest. The suspect was no longer a threat.

(I had hopes of having more information on the case for this chapter but when I contacted Detective Credle, now retired, he could not remember if the suspect was dead or serving a long prison term.)

Since the case was closed administratively there is no public record.

During my time at Fox 5 the cold cases mainly aired on Saturday nights and they were what we would call one and done. Meaning, unless the viewers at home were recording on a VCR or a TIVO there was no chance the pieces would be seen again. They were rarely rebroadcast and Fox management at the time did not believe in putting its content on the internet.

I was always of the opinion the stories should be rebroadcast in hopes of hitting a larger audience.

After 2010 changes were made and the management at Fox decided it could no longer keep the stations and the network's content off the internet. All the other broadcast and cable networks were doing it. So now, stories could be shared on the World Wide Web. They could be put in links and shared on social media like Facebook and Twitter and Instagram.

The stories that aired just once could now be seen by a much larger audience.

Fox 5 management in DC also came up with a new plan. Instead of airing cold case stories only on Saturday nights they would air instead on the station's regularly scheduled weekday broadcasts at 5, 6, and 10 p.m. They were also renamed. Station management called the stories "Rewind to the Crime".

Once a month or so I would put together a story that would be four to five minutes in length and include the elements I thought were essential. Interviews with the lead detective and members of the victim's family. A visit to the crime scene would be included along with photos or video. If possible, we would reveal a detail that had previously not been disclosed to the public. It's what we would call "the hook".

A way to reel viewers in rather than broadcast a "rehash" of the crime.

In two of the stories we produced during that time detectives closed the cases with an arrest.

Because of the internet and the worldwide reach of social media the details of a cold case are seen by a much larger audience than ever before.

If you have a cold case that you and your investigators think could be helped by a news story here are some suggestions.

If you have a new piece of evidence and want to get the word out, call a news conference.

For broadcast, the best time is 11 a.m. That gives the reporter plenty of time to produce a nicely edited "package". If you can, have photos blown up and put on easels. They should also be available electronically.

Reporters want to hear from the lead investigator, not the department's public information officer. If possible, include a member of the victim's family.

Provide that "hook" we are all looking for. Release a piece of information that will be the lead in every story. Be it on television, radio, a website, or in print.

You could also "pitch" the story to the news outlet of your choice.

Sometimes a cold case story is best told in print where visuals may be unavailable. A newspaper (or a website) can get far deeper into the facts of the case if the editor is willing to give the reporter space for a long feature. The story can, as we say, "breathe".

TV reporters working on a "day turn" are rarely given any more than two minutes. It is a good length of time, but nothing beats having four or five minutes.

For television, in order to let the story "breathe" five minutes is about right.

So, let's say you would rather have a well-told television story that is not a "day turn". That is, a story that must be shot, edited, and broadcast on the same day.

How do you get that done?

Pitch it to the reporter or station of your choice. Here is how it works.

Most news outlets have three shifts, and a conference call will usually precede all three.

During those calls reporters pitch story ideas before producers and assignment desk managers join in.

If you (the detective or public information officer) pitches an idea for a story to a particular reporter or assignment desk manager the pitch will be discussed during the meeting. Sometimes the story idea is so good a manager will approve it on the spot.

Keep in mind a five-minute television story will take more time to produce. Usually a day to "shoot" it and a day to write and edit.

The time commitment is what sometimes gets in the way. These days staffing levels are not what they once were, and managers are hard pressed to get that "day turn" rather than one that could take two days to produce.

Social Media

When I first started telling cold case stories for Fox 5 in the early 2000s they would only air once on Saturday nights. It wasn't ideal if you were trying to capture a large audience and so many of those stories were as we say, "one and done".

These days the internet will share your story over and over again. A simple search on a browser and there it is. Available to copy and email.

Links can also be shared on the app or website of your choice. Facebook, X, Bluesky, Instagram, TikTok, and YouTube.

Once a cold case story is aired on the station, newspaper or website will undoubtedly share it on the internet or link it to one of its social media sites.

To capitalize on the attention, your department, sheriff's office, or agency should do the same on your own accounts. Photos and videos will get way more attention than just posting a press release. Social media consumers love to watch videos and everyone loves a mystery.

Podcasts

Another way to get your case noticed is with a podcast. "Your Own Backyard" is a podcast that helped solve the 1996 disappearance and murder of Cal Poly student Kristen Smart. It is one of the best cold case podcasts I have ever listened to.

It was produced by an amateur sleuth who had no experience other than his own curiosity.

It renewed interest in the case and helped investigators with new tips and leads. Detectives finally made an arrest in 2021.

A podcast series is a bit easier to produce because the creator is only interested in audio but for police it's a bigger investment in time.

In the summer of 2020, I began work on a podcast about the January 1998 unsolved murder of Sherry Crandell, a nurse who was raped and killed inside her office at the Prince George's Hospital Center in Cheverly, Maryland.

I first reached out to Sherry's three children. I had previously interviewed Tiffany, the oldest child, and I wanted to see if she and her brothers would be interested in taking part. One of her brothers, a police officer, was initially against the idea. He was concerned a re-telling of the story in such a format might invite unwelcome comments about his mom on social media. But after talking it over with his siblings he agreed to take part and agreed to an interview.

The negative comments never came.

In order to tell a complete story, I also needed the full cooperation of the Prince George's County Police Department and the lead detective in the case, Bernie Nelson. He was initially skeptical, having never listened to a podcast, but he eventually came around after I explained the benefits of a podcast and its broad reach.

During the months we worked together I called Detective Nelson numerous times to fact check what I was writing.

I also learned something new about the case. A detail the police had kept to themselves for more than 20 years.

There was a witness to the murder. A woman on the cleaning crew saw Sherry being assaulted but was too afraid to immediately speak up. Nelson described the woman, Edna Brown, as being mentally challenged. The nurse's body was eventually discovered by another member of the cleaning crew.

Detective Nelson had a videotaped interview with Brown that had been sitting in a box for decades. It was on a VHS tape that he then copied to DVD. He gave it to me so that I could use it in the podcast.

It was an angle to the story that made news when the episode was released.

Bringing new attention to the case which was the intention all along.

The eight-episode podcast series was produced along with WTOP News radio and launched by Podcast One.

It became a hit within days of its debut. Rising into the top 25 of the true crime podcasts available at the time.

(As of this writing, May 2025, the case is still unsolved. Detective Nelson has retired from the force but the investigation using genetic genealogy continues.)

I produced a second podcast series with WTOP titled "Unknown Subject".

A series that detailed the investigation into a predator known as the Potomac River Rapist who terrorized women in Washington, DC and Montgomery County, Maryland, in the mid- to late 1990s.

Raping and beating multiple women before killing Christine Mirzayan in Georgetown in the summer of 1998.

The case went unsolved until 2019 when detectives began searching for the man using genetic genealogy. They built a family tree and discovered a close relative living in Prince George's County, Maryland.

After multiple interviews with family members on that tree detectives came up with a prime suspect. Giles Warrick had lived for years in Montgomery County, Maryland, but his name had never surfaced in the investigation.

Detectives discovered he had recently moved to South Carolina and decided to pay him a visit.

Detectives Todd Williams with the DC Police Department and Alyson Dupouy with the Montgomery County, Maryland Police knocked on Warrick's door in Horry County early one morning in November of 2019.

Dupouy had a tape recorder hidden in her pocket and turned it on before Warrick opened the door.

The detectives had a warrant for Warrick's DNA but never had to use it. He voluntarily agreed to give them a sample.

After it was rushed to the lab in Maryland the detectives were told it was a match, and Warrick was arrested the very next morning as he attempted to flee.

During an in-custody interview Warrick denied having anything to do with the murder and rapes and maintained his innocence. He never had his day in court. He died by suicide in the DC Jail just weeks before his trial was set to begin.

The tapes of those two interviews were played during pretrial hearings in DC Superior Court and because of that I was able to get copies and use them in the podcast.

I write all of this as an example. If you have audio or video evidence that can be used in a cold case story and it will not jeopardize your case, it could make a huge difference in the story.

The recorded interviews were fascinating. Until then no one had heard Warrick's voice, and it took listeners inside an unfolding investigation.

I want to end this chapter with a success story.

In March of 2024, Megan McGrath with News4 (WRC-TV) in Washington, DC got a call from the Sheriff's Office in Charles County, Maryland.

The veteran reporter was told detectives had positively identified the victim of a 1998 murder and it was all thanks to her and a story she had put together nine months earlier.

The following comes directly from a press release:

On June 18, 2023, the 25th anniversary of the date Jane Doe was discovered, reporter Megan McGrath from NBC News 4 Washington, met with detectives and members of the Forensic Science Section to air another story, providing as many facts as could be released. That news coverage generated a lead.

On the very night the story aired, Deputy Director Noelle Gehrman of the Forensic Science Section received a tip from a family member, indicating they had just watched the story on television and that Jane Doe might be their relative. "We have received tips in the past and had our hopes up, but DNA ruled those potential relatives out", said Gehrman. "But when this tip came in, everything the caller conveyed just fit. I felt we now had a direction to move forward and a solid lead to pursue", said Gehrman.

The family member sent photos of their relative to investigators who immediately noted a similarity in the sketch used to try to identify Jane Doe in 1998. Through further investigation, detectives located potential siblings of Jane Doe and in 2023, one of her siblings provided a DNA sample for comparison.

On October 12, 2023, the DNA analysis report from Bode Technology confirmed that Jane Doe's mtDNA profile could not be eliminated from her sibling's profile, meaning she was related to the sibling.

On October 25, 2023, officials met with the victim's family and confirmed Jane Doe's identity. Williams' last residence was in S.E. Washington, DC. The case is being investigated as a homicide and detectives are pursuing leads.

Megan Mcgrath told me in an interview,

> As a reporter you are often wondering if people are paying attention or whether your stories are having the intended impact or effect and when you get word back that something you've done actually brought about a break in the case I mean it is tremendously satisfying.

Megan went on to say, "and you also think about the family, I mean for 25 years this person has been missing and because she was unidentified the family was never contacted".

Since the positive identification in 2024 detectives have been trying to identify a suspect in the killing but as of this writing they are still searching for answers.

A couple of final notes. People love a good mystery. Tell your cold case stories. Build a website. List your agency's cold cases. Link as many photos and videos as you can.

Never forget.

Paul Wagner
Reporter
News4
May 2025

Selected Bibliography and Weblinks

https ://www.fox5dc.com/news/fauquier-county-investigators-say-there-is-new-evidence-in-1988-cold-case

https://www.youtube.com/watch?v=iSlEgUpWJNE

https://mpdc.dc.gov/sites/default/files/dc/sites/mpdc/publication/attachments/pratt_mary.pdf

The murder of John Pernell. https://www.fox5dc.com/news/dc-police-arrest-murder-suspect-in-john-pernell-cold-case
The murder of Semo Rich. https://www.fox5dc.com/news/rewind-to-the-crime-who-killed-norman-semo-rich
https://www.nbcwashington.com/news/local/prince-georges-county/newly-found-witness-account-describes-decades-old-unsolved-murder-at-prince-georges-hospital/2592747/
https://americannightmarepodcast.com/shows/season-2/
https://wtop.com/shows/american-nightmare-series/
https://www.nbcwashington.com/news/local/cold-case-solved-investigators-identify-woman-found-killed-on-maryland-farm-in-1998/3573739/

Digital Evidence Investigations in Cold Case Homicides

21

TREVOR BUCHANAN

Introduction

The digital revolution has fundamentally transformed the way people live, work, and communicate. In today's interconnected world, individuals maintain constant connectivity through their mobile devices, whether at home, traveling, or even sleeping. This dependency has become so pronounced that researchers identified "nomophobia," the fear of being without a working cell phone, in the UK in 2008, after discovering that nearly two-thirds of the population experienced this anxiety (Merriam-Webster, 2025).

The cellular telephone's evolution from a basic communication tool to a multifunctional device has revolutionized daily life, enabling users to access information and communicate from virtually anywhere at any time. This technological shift has profound implications for criminal investigations, as recognized by the United States Supreme Court in their landmark ruling on Cell Site Location Information (CSLI). The Court emphasized the ubiquity of mobile devices, noting that "There are 396 million cell phone service accounts in the United States for a nation of 326 million people" (Carpenter v. United States, 585 U.S. 1, 2018).

The volume of information stored by third-party electronic communications and remote computing service providers, including cellular carriers, social media platforms, and email or internet service providers, has grown exponentially over the past three decades. Society's reliance on these services continues to accelerate, creating both opportunities and challenges for criminal investigators.

Evolution of Criminal Investigation Methods

Traditional police work historically relied on fundamental investigative techniques: canvassing for witnesses, conducting interviews and interrogations, and performing comprehensive crime scene analyses. As technology advanced, new tools emerged to support investigations, including DNA

 DOI: 10.4324/9781003415633-24

analysis and the proliferation of surveillance cameras in residential and commercial properties. By the early 1990s, Call Detail Record (CDR) analysis began gaining prominence in criminal investigations as law enforcement agencies recognized the investigative value of cellular phone data.

The transformation from bulky "Zack Morris" mobile phones to analog models and eventually to modern smartphones dramatically increased both the types and volume of information retained by service providers. This evolution has created unprecedented opportunities for criminal investigators to gather evidence and reconstruct events.

Digital forensics analysis, like DNA analysis, does not replace traditional investigative techniques, tactics, and principles (TTPs). Instead, it adds a crucial layer to investigations that must be utilized to ensure comprehensive case examination. The insights gained from proper electronic data analysis can be transformative for a case. However, investigators must guard against over-reliance on technology within their agency's culture.

While analyzing CDRs can provide valuable inculpatory or exculpatory evidence, effective investigation still depends on solid police work. This includes gathering reliable case details and corroborative information through video surveillance, financial transactions, witness statements, physical evidence, and other electronic data sources.

Preservation Requests

After officers respond to and secure a crime scene, the immediate focus shifts to preserving all potential evidence. Law enforcement bears the responsibility of safeguarding all potential evidence during an investigation, including digital evidence. This aspect of scene preservation is frequently overlooked because the evidence may not be physically present at the crime scene—it could be stored thousands of miles away on servers belonging to various service providers.

When investigators believe relevant information exists that could contain evidence of a crime, they can request it through appropriate legal demands. Like physical evidence, such as surveillance videos from local businesses, digital evidence has limited retention periods and may not be available indefinitely. Different companies maintain varying policies regarding how long they retain specific information on their servers. While some companies provide their retention policies to law enforcement, information sometimes remains accessible well beyond their stated timeframes.

I consistently recommend attempting to collect this evidence. If you can clearly articulate your request in a legal demand, don't hesitate to ask for it. You won't know its availability until you try. Even if the information has been deleted, the effort demonstrates due diligence in your investigation.

Technical Evidence Review

Cases often reach investigators after initial investigation by other detectives. Reviewing previous work can be challenging, requiring investigators to sift through information to understand the case thoroughly, including all its nuances and details. The goal is to identify new avenues for exploration.

This already overwhelming and time-consuming task becomes further complicated by electronic evidence components such as forensic extractions from mobile devices, phone records, social media data, and more. Hidden within vast amounts of data may be crucial pieces of information essential for advancing the investigation. It's important to understand everything at your disposal and know how to extract case-relevant artifacts effectively.

Cold Case Homicide Investigations

Several years ago, I assisted with a homicide investigation that had occurred years earlier. At that time, I was a member of the police department's newly formed Technical Investigations Unit, where I supported other investigators primarily by analyzing CDRs and geolocation data.

The homicide investigator had collaborated with the prosecuting attorney's office to secure arrest warrants for the primary suspect, primarily based on circumstantial evidence and an unreliable eyewitness—neither of which provides an ideal foundation for securing a conviction. As the saying goes, you can't pick your case or your witness.

Before meeting with the prosecutor and lead detective a few months before trial, I reviewed the case file. I was pleased to find a comprehensive list of cellular records for numerous individuals involved in the investigation, including witnesses, the victim, and potential suspects or co-conspirators. Each record was neatly labeled, indicating who was believed to have possessed each cellular phone.

I cannot overemphasize the importance of maintaining a clean, organized case file, particularly regarding electronic data. It is easy to lose track of which data is associated with which item or individual. As I read through the case synopsis, I could easily match the records to the key players in the case.

Initial Analysis

I began analyzing the call data and geolocation information to see how they correlated with the established facts. Unfortunately, the records labeled for the suspect were inconclusive, as there was no data associated with that phone number during the requested timeframe outlined in the search warrant.

During my meeting with the prosecutor and detective, I presented the cell phone records we had collected. We examined approximately 15 records, displaying them on an overhead computer monitor using Google Earth. This allowed us to visualize the general locations of each phone during the evening hours surrounding the time of the homicide.

The Breakthrough

One record caught my attention: it belonged to the mother of the cooperative witness who lived near the crime scene. Since it was a pay-as-you-go phone, also known as a "burner phone," subscriber information wasn't available. The noteworthy aspect of these records was that the phone appeared in the vicinity of the crime scene shortly before the homicide occurred and left the area immediately afterward.

We reviewed the statements made by the witness's mother, which indicated that she had been home all day and was present at the crime scene afterward. This was in stark contrast to the cellular records. The crucial question became: whose records were we examining?

The detective began sifting through the overflowing three-ring binders filled with notes and case evidence. Eventually, a significant realization emerged: the phone number provided to investigators came from the witness's mother, but it was not her number. Instead, the mother had given it to the detective as the suspect's phone number. This was a breakthrough, as it meant we now had corroborative information linking the suspect's cell phone to the vicinity of the crime scene before the homicide and leaving immediately afterward, thus lending credibility to the witness's account.

Expanding the Investigation

This breakthrough opened new avenues for further investigation. Within the phone records, we located the International Mobile Equipment Identifier (IMEI), which serves as a unique identifier for electronic devices, like how a Vehicle Identification Number (VIN) identifies a car. The IMEI can be used to trace accounts associated with the device by various third-party service providers.

In this case, the IMEI number was linked to Google LLC, a major entity that handles personal data. With a search warrant, we aimed to gather information from Gmail accounts associated with the suspect's cell phone. The findings were incredibly valuable. One account was registered in the suspect's name and phone number, confirming their identity.

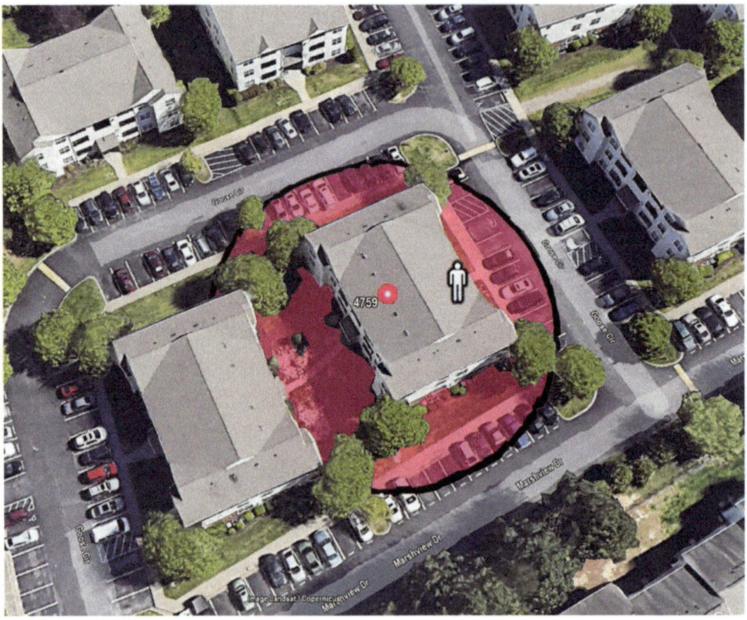

Figure 21.1 Location data from Google LLC for the time of the homicide. Wi-Fi sourced location with 21 m uncertainty radius around the center latitude and longitude point (pink dot).

Critical Evidence Discovery

The email content included receipts for a Lyft ride taken from the suspect's residence to the crime scene. Additionally, there was a subsequent pickup near the crime scene that returned them home after the homicide.

The Lyft emailed receipts included a map showing the routes taken for both trips. Additionally, during the month surrounding the homicide, there were over 12,000 location data points collected, primarily sourced from Wi-Fi and Global Positioning System (GPS) signals. These data points had a precision level that could pinpoint the device's location to within 3 m at a given time in some instances. At the time of the homicide, Google LLC's location data indicated a data point consistent with the crime scene, with an estimated uncertainty radius of 21 m (Figure 21.1).

Corroborative Evidence

Knowing that the suspect's Gmail was used for a Lyft ride share on the day of the homicide, a request was sent to Lyft for all information linked to that Google account. The information provided by Lyft resulted in another piece

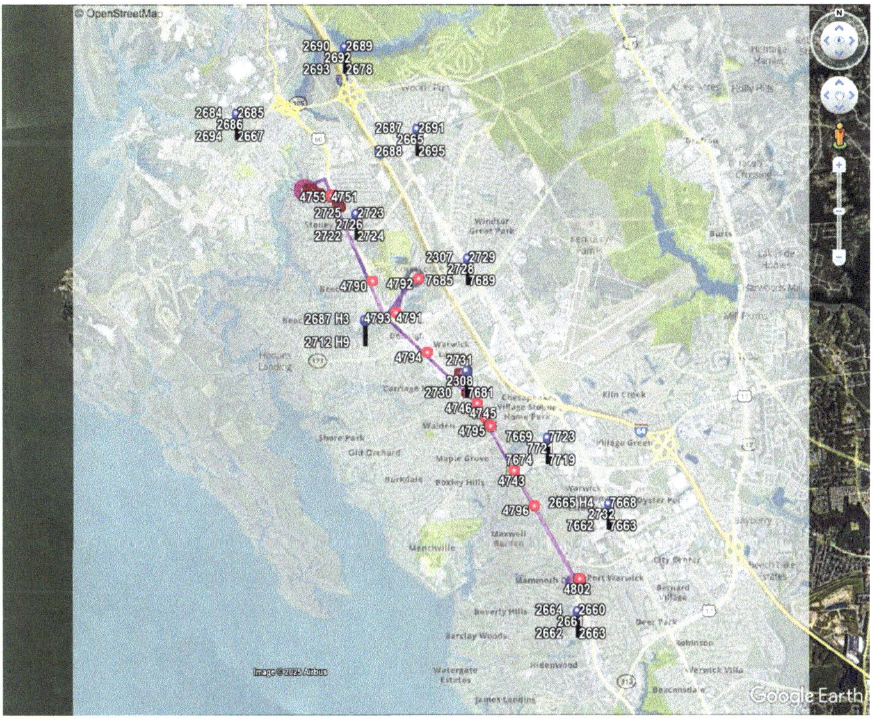

Figure 21.2 Location data from Google LLC (pink), cellular records from AT&T (blue), and Lyft receipt containing trip route overlayed in Google Earth (purple).

of corroborative evidence confirming the user of the cell phone linked to the Gmail account, and the phone number was recovered from the suspect's known residence and taken to the area of the crime scene before the homicide.

It also revealed the user was picked up several blocks from the homicide location shortly after the crime and dropped off at the known residence. When layering the corroborative location data sourced from three separate service providers, using three different types of data (GPS, Wi-Fi, and cellular), the results strongly supported the facts of the case and ultimately the outcome at trial (Figure 21.2).

Conclusion

The integration of digital evidence analysis into criminal investigations represents a paradigm shift in modern law enforcement. Third-party service providers hold vast amounts of potentially crucial evidence that can corroborate witness accounts, establish timelines, and provide location data with remarkable precision. However, this technological capability must be balanced with traditional investigative techniques and proper legal procedures.

The case study demonstrates how multiple data sources can be layered to create a comprehensive picture of events. The combination of cellular records, email communications, ride-sharing data, and GPS tracking provided overwhelming corroborative evidence that would have been impossible to obtain through traditional methods alone.

Success in digital evidence investigation requires meticulous organization, understanding of legal requirements for data preservation and collection, and the ability to synthesize complex technical information into coherent narratives that support case facts. As technology continues to evolve, so too must the investigative techniques used to harness its potential for justice.

References

Carpenter v. United States, 585 U.S. 1 (2018)

Merriam-Webster. Nomophobia (2025). Retrieved from https://www.merriam-webster.com/dictionary/nomophobia

Resources III

Victim Advocacy

22

RYAN BACKMANN

Introduction

This chapter discusses the importance of advocacy and including an advocate in any cold case unit, task force, review team, or victim/survivor communication. The value and benefit of using system-based and/or community-based advocates can sometimes be overlooked, but given the complex nature of sudden and violent loss, unsolved crimes, and traumatic grief, a dedicated, compassionate, experienced go-between can be a force multiplier for law enforcement.

Cold case advocacy is a critical element in the journey for answers and healing for the families involved. Advocates serve as a bridge between victims' families, law enforcement, and the broader community, ensuring that cases do not fade into obscurity with the passage of time. Unlike investigators or prosecutors, advocates are not tasked with solving crimes but with educating families, amplifying the voices of those impacted, rallying public and institutional support, providing resources for healing, and occasionally fostering accountability within the criminal justice system. Advocacy also provides an emotional anchor for families, offering comfort, reassurance, and an empathetic point of contact as they navigate a complex system. A system in place to enforce laws and punish offenders, but often leaving families on the outside looking in.

The challenges in cold case advocacy are vast. Advocates must address the stigma and misconceptions surrounding unsolved crimes, counter public apathy, and work within systems constrained by limited resources and competing priorities. However, advocacy also opens new opportunities—engaging communities in awareness campaigns, collaborating with media, and pushing for legislative changes that prioritize these cases. By shedding light on cold cases, advocacy not only honors the victims but also underscores the societal obligation to support victims and survivors and pursue justice, regardless of the passage of time.

This chapter explores the multifaceted role of advocacy, the strategies employed to support families and keep cases active, and the broader impact on the criminal justice system. Cold case advocacy is a testament to perseverance and compassion—a reminder that the pursuit of justice does not have an expiration date.

DOI: 10.4324/9781003415633-26

Definitions

Advocacy: The act of supporting, defending, or arguing on behalf of a cause, policy, or individual. In the context of long-term missing persons or cold, unsolved, or unresolved homicides, advocacy is about giving a voice to the voiceless and standing alongside the families of victims as they navigate the long, difficult journey for answers. Cold case advocacy is not just about pursuing judicial resolution; it's about addressing the victims' families' emotional, psychological, and social needs, in the moment they reach out, in a compassionate, respectful, and empowering way.

Victim/survivor/co-victim/secondary victim: These terms are often interchangeable in cold case advocacy and typically depend on regional or jurisdictional custom.

Victim: A legal term used in the criminal justice system to describe someone who has suffered harm from a destructive action.

Survivor: A term often used by surviving family members of homicide victims to identify themselves. It can also be used to empower someone who has experienced trauma.

Co-victim: A more technical term for a person who has been impacted by the death of a loved one in a homicide, such as a family member, friend, or partner.

Secondary victim: A person affected by a crime or violent act, but is not the direct victim.

Ambiguous loss: Often associated with families of long-term missing persons, describes a loss that remains unclear or unconfirmed and thus has no resolution.

Traumatic/unresolved/complicated grief: Often associated with families of homicide victims, it is the complex grief reaction that can occur after a violent death or loss. It can include symptoms of both grief and trauma, as well as preoccupation with the event and/or a prolonged and intense state of mourning that can interfere with a person's ability to function in their daily life.

System-based advocate: An individual employed by a public agency, such as a law enforcement agency or prosecutor's office, to help victims navigate the criminal justice system.

System-based advocates can screen calls from families, scan documents, return calls with specific information provided by detectives, make referrals to outside resources like support groups, prepare and send out communications, among other policy and procedure-driven tasks. An advocate's work can free up detectives to focus on the investigation.

Community-based advocate: An individual employed by a private organization, typically a nonprofit or non-governmental organization (NGO), to help victims navigate the criminal justice system and beyond.

Community-based advocates can provide similar services to system-based advocates and are particularly beneficial if public agencies lack advocates or are understaffed. A community-based organization may also provide more comprehensive and long-term resources and should not be viewed as competition, but as a community partner.

Advocacy educational requirements: While there are currently no specific degrees in advocacy, some positions may require a bachelor's degree. Studies in fields like Social Work, Psychology, Sociology, or Criminal Justice offer relevant academic preparation. Volunteering or interning with community organizations, attending training sessions, and pursuing certifications can provide valuable practical experience. The National Organization for Victim Advocacy offers a credentialing program for victim-serving professionals.

Lived experience is another factor. Some survivors/co-victims find healing in helping others who have experienced a similar trauma. Some of the best advocates are survivors who turn their pain into purpose. However, being a survivor does not automatically qualify one for work as an advocate. This work—deeply emotional and often triggering—can come at a cost. Engaging with the pain of others may re-traumatize advocates, especially those with their own histories of loss. Steps should be taken to ensure that any potential advocate is emotionally and mentally in a place to support others. See Self-Care for Advocates section.

What's Unique about Cold Case Survivors?

Cold case survivors are a unique victim population. They share many of the struggles of other victimizations, but also have added strains that other populations don't encounter. As time passes, the needs of those impacted evolve. The immediate and acute needs in the early days of victimization are different than the needs of someone struggling with an unresolved case. The consistent flow of grief is replaced by waves of grief at varying times and strengths. Needs often shift from self-preservation to an investigative focus. Perceived scenarios can become their "truth." From imagined motives to assumed conspiracies, families create scenarios in their heads that make sense to them or generate interest from third parties. A single-victim attempted robbery homicide is so common that it often generates little news or attention, but a complex conspiracy that includes dirty cops and relatives of elected officials not only generates interest but adds perceived value to the victim. As families plead with society to remember their loved one and care about the loss of life, they sometimes feel the need to exaggerate circumstances in order to match sensational headlines.

Added complexities like the loss being sudden, violent, and unsolved add layers of complication for families navigating a perpetual cycle of hope and despair. For most families, their only experience with the criminal justice world is television. They have been prepared for this journey with unrealistic expectations, forensic exaggerations, and over-simplified investigative processes. The result is often frustration for families and exasperation from law enforcement. The key to overcoming these issues is education and communication.

Additional challenges include a lack of specialized resources for families of cold case victims. While initial investigations may include victim services and some mental health options, this support often fades, or the needs change as the case goes cold. Families are left to navigate the emotional and psychological toll of unresolved grief on their own. The prolonged uncertainty of a cold case can lead to mental health struggles such as depression, anxiety, and post-traumatic stress, yet few resources are specifically tailored to address the unique needs of these individuals, years after the incident. Advocacy efforts are vital in filling this gap, providing consistent contact, emotional support, and connections to services like homicide or cold case support groups, which foster a sense of belonging in the company of others facing similar struggles.

The pie chart in Figure 22.1 shows the universally accepted "Critical Needs of Victims and Survivors." When analyzing these needs, we start to see why this population's struggles extend beyond other victimizations.

Safety: If the person who committed the crime has not been caught. How safe can they feel?

Support: Support from law enforcement, the media, the public, friends, and even some family members fades over time.

Information: Most details are withheld from survivors, even years later. Imagine being told that information about your loved one's death is so important that it cannot be shared with you.

Access: Open cases, even cold ones, are typically exempt from public records requests. Cold cases aren't closed, even when they are inactive. These exemptions are dependent on each state's public records law and each agency's interpretation of that law.

Figure 22.1 Critical needs of victims/survivors. (Courtesy of Project: Cold Case.)

Continuity: Agency turnover and poor inter-agency communication are among the least discussed issues in cold case investigations. Promotions, transfers, and retirements consistently cause cases to slip through the cracks. When turnover happens, this, along with antiquated or unfollowed agency policies, often results in lost communication with the family and may stall an active cold case investigation.

Voice: Families consistently say they don't feel like they are being heard throughout the criminal justice process.

Justice: Cold cases represent the antithesis of justice as it is commonly defined. We will discuss this in more detail later in the chapter.

What's Unique about Cold Case Advocacy?

Cold case advocacy is distinct from other forms of immediate or active case advocacy due to the advocates' necessity to navigate the profound and complex challenges families face due to the passage of time without answers. As days turn to weeks, weeks to months, months to years, and sometimes, those years become decades, families often feel that law enforcement has forgotten their loved one. An advocate's ability to prevent those feelings should not be undervalued. Cold case advocacy requires an understanding that despite the length of time since the loss, the grief remains and can manifest years later, sometimes in unhealthy ways. A lack of communication with law enforcement is often singled out as the biggest frustration for families. Advocates become a natural conduit between families and information. Cold case advocates should be prepared to answer questions about prior investigative efforts, new investigative technologies, facilitate meetings with detectives, understand agency policy on media participation, and connect with outside resources, including mental health professionals.

The uniqueness of cold case advocacy lies in its endurance and adaptability. It requires sustained effort in the face of systemic barriers, unwavering compassion for families navigating lifelong grief, the ability to maintain communication while nurturing relationships, and creative approaches to maintain visibility for cases that might otherwise be lost to time. It is advocacy in its purest form—a refusal to let victims be forgotten and an insistence that every victim deserves justice, no matter how long it takes.

Cold cases and their associated advocacy often contend with a lack of prioritization in the field. Only a fraction of law enforcement agencies have cold case units, and most of those units have added responsibilities, like in-custody deaths, officer-involved shootings, and child abductions, all of which take priority over active cold case investigations. Similarly, some agencies lack advocates or are understaffed, and with a lack of specific cold case advocacy training options, a void is sometimes left. Cold case advocacy is often relegated to the periphery of an agency's priorities. Community-based advocacy groups can assist with filling that void (Figure 22.2).

Figure 22.2 Navigating grief. (Courtesy of Project: Cold Case.)

Engaging with Cold Case Survivors

Agencies and organizations should create a policy on proactive engagement with survivors. Traditionally, communication with cold case families is reactive: responding to a phone call or email. However, proactive communication can build trust and repair prior damage. When speaking with those impacted, remember that empathy is the foundation of this advocacy, fostering trust and ensuring that survivors feel heard, validated, and supported as they navigate their journey.

Using a victim-centered, trauma-informed, and empathetic approach is crucial in supporting individuals affected by cold cases. It prioritizes their emotional and psychological well-being throughout the process and recognizes that each experience is unique and that trauma can manifest in different ways, often persisting long after the initial loss. By centering the needs and voices of victims, advocates can provide tailored support that acknowledges the complexities of grief, respects the autonomy of survivors, and avoids re-traumatization.

Communication

Communication is the cornerstone of effective advocacy. A respectful and consistent line of communication with survivors is vital to maintaining trust and cooperation.

Advocates should encourage survivors to keep an ongoing list as new questions, thoughts, or concerns arise. A best practice for survivors is using their phone to store the list, as it allows instant notetaking and is less likely to get misplaced or forgotten when a meeting with detectives takes place. Advocates should suggest that survivors keep detailed notes of communication with detectives or other officials to help ensure that nothing slips through the cracks. Advocates can assist by providing a brief email recap of meeting discussions to ensure important details are not forgotten, misunderstood, or misinterpreted. Setting a specific follow-up date for any unanswered questions or post-meeting information gathering can provide a sense of structure and accountability. It is recommended that the detective set the amount of time needed before the follow-up communication.

Advocates should also assist survivors in distinguishing between reality and perceived or assumed situations. Misinformation or misunderstandings can easily arise, particularly in the emotionally charged atmosphere of a cold case investigation. Addressing issues by respecting and utilizing the chain of command within law enforcement agencies is crucial for maintaining a constructive relationship. Rarely does a survivor going straight to the chief, sheriff, or media benefit the investigation or the relationship between family and law enforcement. If a detective is rude, disrespectful, apathetic, or refuses to communicate, using the chain of command to address the situation is the best way to establish accountability. Multiple steps up the chain of command are rarely needed to achieve cooperation.

The most important element of cold case advocacy is meeting the survivors where they are and supporting them in *that* moment. There is no roadmap for grief; each person processes and heals at their own unique pace. This means each call will be different. Each family member will be different. The ability to assist an individual without prior knowledge of what they need is an important part of cold case advocacy. Those needs evolve over time, and it is essential for advocates to remain flexible yet prepared. Being honest is paramount. There is a fine line between hope and false hope and telling survivors what they want to hear can jeopardize trust with the advocate and system. Saying you *don't know* or *can't say* is not a failure in advocacy.

Survivors often reach out requesting an update on their loved one's case. For system-based advocates, be clear and honest about the status of the investigation. Is it assigned to a detective? If so, provide that detective's desk number and email address. Is the case inactive? If so, provide insight into the agency's policy on case review and assignment. For community-based advocates, refer survivors to the investigating agency and prepare them with questions, such as case status and inquiring about review policies. Survivors also call about meeting with the detective assigned. Advocates can assist survivors with suggestions for questions. Survivors may call to vent. Let them explain without interruption. Listening to them and offering an empathetic response builds trust. Before ending the conversation, offer referrals to outside resources like counselors or support groups.

While being honest and transparent, you may find yourself answering questions about prior missteps, old policies, and/or investigative practices no longer acceptable. Common practices in the 1970s, 1980s, 1990s, etc. may be cringeworthy compared to new standards. Acknowledge any issues that may have happened in the past. Explain that evidence collection and investigative strategies have changed and advanced since their loved one's murder. If families continue to point out previous failures, real or perceived, try to redirect them to today and moving forward from this point.

A lack of communication can foster frustration, mistrust, and feelings of abandonment as law enforcement agencies juggle cold cases alongside newer, higher-prioritized investigations. For many families, the silence echoes the painful loss itself, amplifying their sense of helplessness.

Create a communication plan for your group that includes, at least, annual contact with survivors. Even if it is a form letter acknowledging that the case is not forgotten and reminding survivors that they can call at any time. For system-based advocates, including the assigned detective's name and desk number, along with the case number, is a great way to provide information and show concern. For community-based advocates, annual communication provides the opportunity to suggest that survivors reach out to their detective or offer support groups and mental health resources. Requesting updated contact information in the letter is another good idea. If your agency/organization is worried about families not wanting to be contacted, add an Opt-Out slip that they can return to avoid causing unwanted stress.

Defining Justice

Justice in regard to cold case investigations can take many forms. It is essential to educate survivors about the various possible outcomes of an investigation, including the reality that not every case will result in an arrest or conviction. Justice may mean different things to different people—whether it's having the truth acknowledged, the perpetrator held accountable, or simply knowing that every possible effort has been made to solve the case. Survivors may exhibit a very basic view of justice, guilt, or innocence. They often haven't considered that their loved ones' case could become inactive or go cold. If an arrest is made, they may not realize how long it takes to get to trial. Or that the death penalty, plea deals, dropped charges, or acquittals are out of their control. Advocates play a crucial role in helping survivors understand these different outcomes, ensuring the complexities of the criminal justice system do not blindside them.

Awareness

Survivors often feel forgotten by the media. While some victims may experience high-profile exposure within local media, it rarely stays in the public eye for long. Others remain frustrated that their loved one barely received any press. One way advocates can help is to encourage survivors to use social media to share their loved one's story. Also, referrals to local media can make survivors feel that the value of their loved one's life is being acknowledged. It is best to identify a journalist who has done cold case stories in the past. Specifically, one who interviews the family and law enforcement to ensure no protected details or inaccurate information is released. Local reporters are particularly easy to contact through social media and are often interested in producing cold case stories.

It is good to remind survivors of realistic media expectations. Television segments rarely exceed a few minutes. Print media struggles to retain readers these days, but may offer a more in-depth story. While media awareness has produced tips and new leads, that should be the hope, not the expectation.

As podcasting and video-producing equipment have become affordable for many, a new platform of media has grown in popularity. Many get their news and information through sites that are not run by professional journalists, but by influencers. With that can come extensive exposure and unethical sensationalism.

The rise of True Crime entertainment has brought increased attention to cold cases, but it has also perpetuated many unrealistic expectations. Reminding survivors that True Crime is a genre of entertainment may be necessary. Real crime is what they experienced.

True Crime takes very complex, painful, and traumatic incidents and transforms them into short, sensational, and often insensitive headlines, episodes, and docudramas. They often lack the victim's perspective and are sometimes created without the family's permission or the option to participate. Advocates can educate survivors on the potential adverse effects of engaging with this type of content and encourage them to be discerning consumers of True Crime content creation. The genre is rife with unethical creators looking for fame and money from stories that aren't theirs to tell.

Real Crime is far less entertaining and far more tragic. Victims and survivors endure traumatic stress-inducing encounters, followed by decades of efforts at healing. The rollercoaster of emotions accompanying investigations, the judiciary, and day-to-day life cannot be squeezed into a podcast, series, or movie.

While traditional media and social media can be powerful tools for raising awareness and keeping a case in the public eye, it's important to approach all opportunities with caution and a firm understanding of the expectations.

See **resources** for the link to a downloadable guidebook, *Collaborating for Justice*—a guide for families and creators spreading awareness for unsolved cases.

Family Fracture

Tragedy has a way of not only taking the life of a loved one but also shattering the very foundation of a family. For grieving parents, the loss of a child can strain even the strongest relationships, as each person navigates their pain differently. Guilt, resentment, and anger often rise to the surface—blaming oneself, blaming each other, or blaming the world for what was lost. In the absence of shared coping mechanisms, families may fracture, each member independently seeking their own path to healing. Some may turn to substances for relief, others to obsession or even thoughts of vigilantism, desperate for a sense of control. Tensions mount when one person feels alone in their fight, frustrated that others aren't grieving "hard enough" or taking action to find justice. These emotional divides can create lasting rifts, leaving isolated individuals mourning a loved one and the family that once was.

While advocating, one may find oneself in the middle of family feuds, accusations, and uncomfortable topics or conversations. You may also find that communicating with one point of contact exacerbates this fracture. Setting firm boundaries, declining to engage in family rumors or attacks, and setting up separate points of contact may be necessary.

Mental Health and Normalizing Counseling

One of the most crucial aspects of cold case advocacy is the recognition and promotion of mental health awareness. The trauma of losing a loved one to homicide, compounded by the lack of resolution, can have long-lasting psychological effects. It is important to normalize the need for counseling and therapy, even decades after the loss. Grief is not a linear process, and unresolved trauma can resurface unexpectedly. Encouraging survivors to seek professional mental health support can be a vital step in their healing process.

Support groups can also play a significant role in the well-being of survivors. While general grief groups can offer solace, there is immense value in participating in groups specifically focused on homicide grief, and even more so in those tailored to unresolved homicides. These groups provide a space where survivors can connect with others who truly understand their unique pain and challenges.

The Myth of Closure

The word "closure" is often used by media and high-ranking law enforcement officials to describe the benefit a family receives at the resolution of their loved one's case. However, this term creates unrealistic expectations for families. The idea that a case's resolution will bring an end to grief or provide a sense of finality is a myth. While law enforcement and prosecutors can "close" a case, grief and loss are complex, ongoing processes, and the suggestion that a family will "receive closure" implies an end to the suffering.

It is not an advocate's role to correct a survivor who uses the word, but educating the individual may help avoid an added emotional burden, long term. Advocacy should focus on supporting survivors in finding a new normal, where they can live with their grief in a way that honors their loved one and their own emotional needs. The journey of healing will last their lifetime, and at no point will an arrest or conviction fill the hole in their hearts.

Self-Care for Advocates

Working in the field of advocacy, especially when supporting those impacted by trauma and loss, requires a deep emotional investment that can take a significant toll on one's mental and physical well-being. Self-care is not a luxury in this work—it is a necessity. Advocates must prioritize their own health and set clear boundaries to avoid compassion fatigue and burnout. For survivor advocates, these issues can be magnified. Engaging in regular self-reflection, taking breaks, seeking peer support, and accessing mental health resources can help maintain a sustainable balance. When advocates care for themselves, they are better equipped to offer consistent, empathetic, and effective support to those they serve.

Acknowledgments

The knowledge I have shared in this chapter comes directly from lived experience. On October 10, 2009, my father, Clifford Backmann, was shot and killed during a robbery in Jacksonville, Florida. Before the one-year anniversary of his murder, I switched careers and became a victim advocate, working for a community-based nonprofit that served families that had lost a loved one due to violence. I spent 4½ years advocating for those families, with law enforcement, in court, at support meetings, and on the phone during moments of extreme grief and crisis. As my own father's case went cold, I recognized voids in service for families of unsolved homicides. In 2015, I started Project: Cold Case to help fill those voids and provide specific services and resources for families like mine.

Along the way, I have worked with hundreds of survivors, dozens of detectives and prosecutors, a number of elected officials, and countless media outlets. I have observed death penalty cases, plea deals, dedicated professionals, and apathetic ones. Project: Cold Case has seen 60+ cases featured on its platform achieve resolution, but far more remain unsolved. Each individual I came in contact with, each story I have heard, and every situation I have observed deserves acknowledgment. Without each, this chapter wouldn't exist. I humbly thank all those who have trusted me with their loved one's story, agreed to meet with me, let me present at their conference, and allowed this survivor a seat at the table so that I could take that information back to my office and use it to help others.

Resources

Annual Cold Case Symposium—coldcasesymposium.org

Collaborating for Justice Guidebook. A guide for families & creators spreading awareness of unsolved cases—tinyurl.com/cfjguidebook

The National Organization for Victim Advocacy—trynova.org & trynova.org/credentialing
The Office of Victims of Crime—ovc.ojp.gov
Parents of Murdered Children—pomc.org
Project: Cold Case—projectcoldcase.org
Resource Association for Missing People—ramissingpeople.org
Sexual Assault Kit Initiative, Other Violent Cold Case Crimes—sakitta.org/ovccc
Your State's Office of the Attorney General.

Establishing & Maintaining Cold Case Units

23

CHRISTOPHER FLANAGAN

A Duty, Not a Luxury

While most acute law enforcement crises receive immediate and sustained attention for as long as the situation exists, the crisis of unsolved homicides in the United States receives little attention. It is often addressed with ill-conceived approaches that fade with time and lack of success. The Murder Accountability Project estimated that from 1965 to 2023, there were nearly 346,000 unsolved homicides and non-negligent manslaughters based on their interpretation of the Federal Bureau of Investigation's (FBI) Uniform Crime Report data (Project: Cold Case Project, n.d.).

For decades, we have seen Cold Case Units come and go. The term itself is somewhat ambiguous. While many have allocated personnel and resources, some "Cold Case Units" would be more appropriately defined as a collateral assignment to an already full duty position. Not every law enforcement agency in the United States needs or can afford a dedicated Cold Case Unit; however, every agency with unsolved murders, sexual assaults, or long-term missing persons needs some mechanism in place to address those cases. Cold Case Units are not a one-size-fits-all solution. There are several investigative options suitable for small, medium, and large agencies, agencies with few or many unsolved cases, and agencies struggling with adequate funding. That said, as a profession, law enforcement must stop viewing Cold Case investigations as a luxury to be explored in "good times" but as a necessary duty intertwined in its promise to protect and serve.

The outcomes of Cold Case Units and the cases themselves are greatly impacted by the foundation on which the unit is established. Creating a Cold Case Unit for the wrong reasons and without protocols often leads to unattained goals and the dissolution of the unit. Thoughtful considerations of the protocols and expectations of the unit will provide the best opportunity for a successful unit that is both effective and sustainable.

One of, if not the first steps in creating a Cold Case Unit is for the agency to truly understand the proper motivation to form a Cold Case Unit. The primary reason to form a Cold Case Unit should be to review and resolve

 DOI: 10.4324/9781003415633-27

unsolved crimes. That may seem obvious, but too often Cold Case Units come to be as a result of an alternative agenda, such as agency public messaging, political gain, or data-driven policy, such as increasing closure rates. All of which can be significant positive byproducts of an effective Cold Case Unit, but when the unit is built on an alternative agenda, it often eventually collapses much like a structure built on a weak foundation. Across the United States there are numerous successful Cold Case Units doing exceptional work. Unfortunately, we have also seen far too many Cold Case Units created and dissolved within a year or so for a variety of reasons, including unrealistic expectations and little attention to best practices and protocols. For example, a Cold Case Unit is established in large part to close the most publicized and horrific murder under the agency's purview. While horrific and deserving of attention, the case is often the most comprehensive investigation in the agency's inventory. The murder is not unsolved because of a lack of investigation or the application of contemporary investigative techniques. The agency focuses the resources of the Cold Case Unit on the murder for six months to a year with little if any progress toward resolution. After a year, questions begin to arise about the effectiveness of Cold Case investigations and whether those resources should be transferred to the other pressing needs of the agency. The lack of short-term tangible "success" of the unit leads to the dissolution of the Cold Case Unit. Meanwhile, unsolved cases with a much higher probability of resolution sat on the same shelves but garnered no attention because they did not have the infamy. The unit was destined to fail due to ill-advised protocols to identify the most appropriate cases to investigate, as well as unrealistic expectations.

Likewise, if the primary reason to form a Cold Case Unit is for agency messaging like "We haven't forgotten" and "It's all about the victims" yet the agency fails to deploy the proper resources and protocols the unit will likely be unsuccessful, and those statements will be nothing more than unsupported slogans. If the commitment to unsolved cases is incongruent with that message, then at best, the actual message received is that unsolved murders and sexual assaults are not a priority; at worst, an acknowledgment of the crisis, yet not doing anything about it.

The commitment to creating a Cold Case Unit based on the primary objective of comprehensively reviewing and resolving unsolved cases leads to resolution for survivors, a measure of justice for victims and their families, and a safer community.

Historically, law enforcement has attempted to address Cold Cases with several approaches. A common and unfortunate approach is the "When You Have Time" concept. Essentially, current Homicide detectives are assigned to "take a look at this case when you have time." Anyone who has ever worked Homicide knows there is hardly enough time to comprehensively work their current cases, not to mention a 20-year-old case they are unfamiliar with. The default is that the current cases get all or nearly all of the time and attention, and the Cold Case gets little to no attention. Most Cold Cases are unsolved because of a lack of technology and/or the time and resources for a comprehensive investigation. The concept of resolving a complicated unsolved murder in the spare time of the detective has not been and will not be an effective approach to resolving Cold Cases, let alone building a strong prosecutable case.

Another approach to investigating Cold Cases is the Task Force approach. The Task Force approach can be an effective way to address and investigate unsolved cases. The Task Force approach can be beneficial to numerous smaller agencies in the same region that individually lack the personnel, resources, and funding to support their own Cold Case Unit. Typically, the agencies also have a smaller number of unsolved murders and sexual assaults. The Task Force approach does require the collaboration and cooperation of all the participating agencies, including a well-defined Memorandum of Understanding outlining the requirements of the participating agencies, such as personnel, supervision, equipment, case assignment protocols, investigative responsibilities, and funding.

Lastly, a dedicated Cold Case Unit within the agency is the most effective way to review, analyze, and execute successful Cold Case investigations. The size of the unit depends on the number of unsolved cases under the purview of the agency. While it's unrealistic to presume that a Cold Case Unit can be built out to work hundreds, let alone thousands of cases, it should be built out in consideration of effectively inventorying, reviewing, and resolving a significant number of cases. The unit should be developed to be sustainable, not just a short-term program expecting immediate success. The makeup and structure of the unit will be discussed later.

Before establishing the Cold Case Unit, it is critical to obtain "Buy In" from several entities that have a vested interest in unsolved cases. The "Buy In" begins with the top law enforcement leader of the agency down to the detectives working the cases. The unit also needs the "Buy In" and the support of the prosecuting authority, as well as the forensic laboratory utilized by the agency. Often overlooked is "Buy In" from Victim Advocacy groups and the citizens in the community. Quite often they are the most consistent and supportive of Cold Case investigations. Lastly, "Buy In" from local political leaders is important. The "Buy In" begins with in-person honest conversations about the goals, objectives, role responsibilities, funding, and expectations of the unit in general. Having conversations early not only gives the vested entities an inclusive role in the partnership but also an important level of responsibility and accountability. Getting the vested entities on the same page from the beginning reduces the risk of future weak links in support of the unit, which is essential to sustaining the unit in good times and bad times. Cold Case Units that lack support both internally and externally are vulnerable to breaks in commitment and continuity that can make the very existence of the unit fragile.

Cold Case Standard Operating Procedure

Most agencies have Standard Operating Procedures (SOPs) that govern how units within the agency will function. A Cold Case Unit is no different and should also have a written SOP. Not only to provide guidelines for the unit in real time but also to provide clarity of the operation of the unit in the future. While SOPs should not be so detailed or rigid that they impair the function and operation of the unit, they should provide a concrete structure for the unit that is not easily departed from without significant consideration. Cold Case Units without a SOP are susceptible to changes in operation and structure with changes in command and opinions. Not that agencies should not be open to changing or improving the operation of the unit, but it should not be done without careful consideration. Significant changes without careful consideration often result in repeating the same missteps of the past.

The SOP should at a minimum note a clear definition of a Cold Case and the types of cases that will be investigated by the unit, the protocol for the transfer of cases to the unit, the structure and personnel of the unit, case review protocols, investigative responsibilities, supervisory responsibilities, case management, and documentation protocols. The Charlotte Mecklenburg Police Department (NC) has a long-standing, successful Cold Case Unit governed by a SOP (Charlotte-Mecklenburg Police Department, 2023) (Ex. 1).

The agency should have a straightforward definition of Cold Cases and the timing of when they will come under the purview of the unit. Typical cases that fall under the purview of the Cold Case Unit are unsolved homicides, equivocal deaths, unsolved sexual assaults (usually so-called stranger cases or suspected serial cases), and long-term missing persons. Some Cold Case Units have the additional responsibility of investigating critical incidents such as Officer Involved Shootings and In-Custody Deaths. While it is understandable to place that investigative responsibility on the most experienced detectives, it is also a significant manpower and time-intensive duty that pulls detectives away from their core mission. When Cold Case investigations are interrupted by a critical incident investigation, the Cold Case not only gets set aside for months, but most investigations do not resume where they left off and need some secondary review to get back up to speed. It is important to define the types of cases under the purview of the unit; otherwise, additional collateral assignments are likely to be delegated to the unit. The written SOP will help deter the assignment of collateral duties to the unit.

It is essential to establish clear criteria for determining when a case transitions into the status of a Cold Case. Larger agencies with a significant number of murders and sexual assaults per year may require a term limit to stay with the initial investigating unit. The reality is that a detective who investigates more than six murders a year will have little time to refocus on previously unsolved murders assigned to him or her. As the detective becomes more tenured, they have even less, if any, time for work on older cases. The same is true for violent crime units that work murders, suicides, and other death investigations. A term of one to three years with no viable leads is an acceptable term for transferring an unsolved case to the Cold Case Unit. Agencies with fewer murders and sexual assaults per year may consider an alternative to the term limit. In this circumstance, the case will remain with the Homicide/Sex Crimes detective until which time he/she leaves the Homicide or Sex Crimes unit. The rationale behind this process is that the initial detective has fewer unsolved cases and has a greater understanding of the investigation in the event a new lead is developed. This option should not preclude the homicide unit from meeting with the Cold Case Unit and "Round tabling" the case to explore new investigative strategies.

Regardless of the timing of the transfer, a transfer protocol should be in place. The transfer should include a meeting of the original Homicide detective and his/her supervisor to brief the case, followed by a meeting of the Homicide supervisor and the Cold Case Supervisor to brief the case to complete the transfer. The Cold Case Unit should be provided with the entire case file at the time of the transfer. The physical case file should include a digital copy of the case file whenever possible. The Cold Case Supervisor is responsible for documenting the transfer of the case to the Cold Case Unit. The documentation can be as simple as adding the case information on a Cold Case Inventory spreadsheet (Ex. 2).

Structure of the Cold Case Unit

The Cold Case Unit should have a first-line supervisor responsible for the management of the personnel. It is most beneficial if the supervisor has homicide and/or sex crimes investigations experience. While not mandatory, it is helpful when the supervisor understands the work of their subordinates, not to mention the differences between Homicide investigations and Cold Case Homicide investigations. The nuances of Cold Case investigations are important for supervisors to understand. The Cold Case Unit supervisor will often be in meetings with command who may be familiar with violent crime investigations but not Cold Case investigations. The supervisor's knowledge and ability to brief command not only on the status of cases but also to articulate how cases are prioritized for investigation and how the life cycle of a Cold Case investigation differs from the initial homicide investigation. It is not uncommon for supervisors to have to explain why another case is not being investigated instead of or in addition to the current caseload. The supervisor should be respected by both his/her superiors and subordinates. If the superiors do not respect the Cold Case Supervisor, they are less likely to listen and allow him/her to lead their unit, particularly if they do not share the same opinion as the supervisor. The Cold Case Supervisor will also have to manage seasoned detectives. Quite often those detectives have strong personalities and require strong leadership to maximize the potential of the individuals and the entire unit.

The detectives selected for the Cold Case Unit should have experience in homicide and/or sex crimes, or a minimum experience in violent crimes investigations. It does not mean that other detectives cannot be successful; however, unsolved cases require the best the agency has to offer in that discipline. Seeing hundreds of death scenes in person cannot be matched by reading about them or looking at photographs. It's the in-person death scene experience that assists the Cold Case detective in analyzing the scene photographs of a Cold Case. Cold Case detectives should be self-motivated, methodical, detail-oriented, analytical, and require little supervision. Just as there are nuances to Cold Case investigations that differ from initial investigations there are differences in Cold Case detectives. Many very successful Homicide detectives thrive in the fast-paced world of Homicide where time is of the essence and new cases are constantly coming in. While they thrive in that environment the slower pace and methodical approach of Cold Case investigations is not necessarily appealing or compatible with them. The detectives should have strong interview skills and experience in crime scene analysis. A significant portion of the Cold Case investigation relies on the ability and necessity to be able to talk to people of all walks of life. In recent years, too many investigations have heavily relied on advances in forensic technologies to resolve cases and neglected interview strategies. Testimonial evidence is still to this day playing a dominant role in resolving Cold Cases, even though it does not receive much fanfare. That said, Cold Case detectives should also understand past forensic technologies and contemporary advanced technologies. As mentioned before, crime scene analysis experience is important for the Cold Case detective. The initial crime scene in its original form is no longer available, and detectives must rely on notes, photographs, and diagrams to interpret scenes. Having the experience of viewing hundreds of death scenes is critical as it relates to viewing older crime scene photographs to help determine who, what, when, and how the event transpired. The Cold Case detective should also have strong documentation skills. Unfortunately, not all cases will be resolved but the investigative steps taken should be well documented so the next generation of detectives who will revisit the case will not waste time trying to figure out what was done or repeat steps already taken.

The Cold Case Unit should also have a Crime Analyst. This position is often overlooked and underappreciated. The Crime Analyst should have extensive experience in open-source data mining and using state-of-the-art software for data tracking. This includes but is not limited to data mapping and timelines to condense volumes of information into short, useful evidence illustrations. The Crime Analyst should have a comprehensive understanding of current and past records management and evidence management systems of the agency. Many unsolved homicide case files are not complete and require extensive physical and electronic searching for documents. The ability of the Crime Analyst to effectively search for older documents and potentially related incidents is very important to the comprehensive review of a case and identifying viable leads. The addition of a Crime Analyst also allows detectives to allocate more time to following up on leads and less time in the office.

What was once thought of as an unheard-of prospect in homicide investigations is now known to be a valuable resource to any Cold Case Unit. That is the use of non-sworn personnel, including previous law enforcement and interns. Retired law enforcement or "hirebacks" can be volunteers or part-time employees. They have been effectively used to assist in the inventory, organization, and review of unsolved cases. As mentioned earlier, unsolved case files are rarely complete at first glance and require a measure of legwork to collect and organize all the documentation of previous investigations. Likewise, interns from local universities are an exceptional resource for Cold Case Units. It is recommended that college interns be selected from third- or fourth-year students, if not graduate students. The intern's education should be focused on a program appropriate for investigations, such as criminal justice, forensics, biology, chemistry, psychology, etc. This does not mean that the interns must be committed to a career as a police officer. They can merely show an interest and level of dedication to a field that could be beneficial to an unsolved homicide investigation. College interns have proved to be exceptional at reading comprehension, which is critical for reviewing thousands of pages of an investigation and condensing it to a brief Case Summary. Whether it's hirebacks or college intern all applicants should go through a stringent vetting process including a comprehensive background check and polygraph examination. Applicants who complete the process successfully should also be required to sign a comprehensive non-disclosure agreement to protect the sensitive information they will be exposed to. Not only are the hirebacks and interns productive, but they also free up sworn personnel to dedicate more time to other duties such as interviews, report writing, surveillance, and arrests. College interns like hirebacks require little training to understand reporting protocols and subsequent documentation of the case review. College interns' access to case files and case information should be restricted to in-office use only. College interns greatly benefit from the experience as well. Not only earning college course credits but hands-on experience and exposure to the real world of homicide investigations cannot be replicated in a text.

Many agencies across the country are now understanding the importance of Victim Services in unsolved homicides and sexual assaults. A Victim Advocate working with the Cold Case Unit can be just as effective in Cold Cases as in the Homicide or Sexual Assault Unit. The Victim Advocate working with the Cold Case Unit should have experience dealing with the victims and survivors of violent crimes and at least training for the nuances of Victim Advocacy for victims and survivors of unsolved crimes. The impact on a survivor of an unsolved crime can be significantly different than that of a crime that is solved just as the impact on a surviving family of a "no body homicide" is different. The lack of a resolution to a case often impacts the relationship between the survivors and law enforcement. The actions of the Cold Case Unit can greatly improve a strained relationship with proper communication protocols between detectives, victim advocates, and survivors.

When possible, a prosecutor should be embedded with the Cold Case Unit or at least designated to focus on Cold Case investigations and prosecutions. History and experience have shown that "turning a case over" to a prosecutor after the investigation is not best for a comprehensive investigation nor subsequent prosecution. A case file left on the desk of a prosecutor for review for prosecution will likely remain on the desk. It is not acceptable to deliver the case file and then say we have done our job as detectives. Prosecutors are just as overworked and understaffed and typically have current prosecutions underway that require their immediate attention. Vertical prosecutions are a very effective protocol to allow Cold Cases to get the appropriate attention in a timely fashion. Vertical prosecutions engage the prosecutor from the start of the Cold Case investigation through sentencing. That means detectives and prosecutors are communicating and assessing the unsolved case as soon as the investigation is initiated. Prosecutors can provide guidance on standard legal issues as well as legal issues that may be unique to long-term unresolved cases, including testimonial memory issues, chain of custody issues, and evidence admissibility issues. Early input from prosecutors can help detectives develop and execute an effective investigative strategy that can withstand the challenges of the legal process. Vertical prosecution also helps to build a strong rapport between prosecutors, detectives, victims, survivors, and witnesses. Vertical prosecutions allow prosecutors to be vested in the case early and are more likely to drive appropriate cases to prosecution.

While forensic lab personnel are typically not a basic component of the Cold Case Unit the relationship between "the lab" and the unit should be well established with both entities having at least a basic understanding of each other. Cold Case detectives and lab personnel should communicate regularly both on specific cases and new technologies. Cold Case detectives need to be able to rely on the expertise of the lab personnel to provide significant input to investigative strategies as it relates to physical evidence and forensic testing. Many Cold Cases require advanced testing beyond the current capabilities of the agency's lab. Having the ability to discuss private lab testing options with lab personnel is critical to making good evidence testing decisions. Doing what is best for the case is sometimes not moving forward with forensic testing and consuming valuable samples. Much like the relationship with the prosecutors' office, the relationship with the lab needs to be built early. Lab personnel should be engaged in case conversations early as opposed to showing up at the lab with a multitude of items to be tested with little to no discussion about the probative value of the evidence or testing options.

Passion, passion, passion! Passion should be the common attribute possessed by all those entrusted with investigating unsolved homicides and sexual assaults. A passion to fight for victims and survivors who are long overdue for answers, resolution, and some measure of justice. That passion drives detectives through, around, or over both internal and external obstacles that have stalled investigations in the past. Passion cannot be measured or scored on a matrix. Passion is found where the work is done when no one is watching, when you don't take no for an answer, when doing what is best for the case is truly the only thing that matters, when good enough is not good enough.

Workspace

Where the Cold Case Unit will be housed should also be a consideration before beginning the unit's work. The workspace should be located close to, but clearly separated from, the homicide unit. It should be located near the homicide unit to facilitate a good working relationship and information sharing but separated to prevent the Cold Case Unit from becoming a supplemental unit to Homicide more often than necessary. The size of the space will depend on the number of personnel needed to address the agencies' unsolved cases effectively, but there are also considerations unique to Cold Case Units. The workspace should include an area large enough to review and "roundtable" cases being investigated. The workspace should include room for poster-sized charts, timelines, photographs, tasks completed/incomplete, etc. At a minimum, the unit workspace should include a secure area to store case files currently being investigated. If the agency has a smaller number of cases and has the space, all unsolved case files should be secured in the Cold Case workspace.

Assessing Cases for Investigation

The SOP should also address how unsolved cases will be assessed and prioritized for investigation. It is highly recommended that there is a clear understanding that cases are prioritized based primarily on the solvability of the case. That is not to say that any one case is more important than any other murder, but the objective of the unit is to resolve as many cases as possible and that begins with prioritizing the cases most likely to be resolved with a contemporary comprehensive investigation. The SOP should not be so rigid that it does not allow for some flexibility within the unit. The unit will often receive leads on unsolved cases that are not currently being investigated. The supervisor and detectives need to be able to assess the value and time sensitivity of the lead and take appropriate action. The SOP should protect the unit from being assigned cases based strictly on the notoriety of the case or public/political pressure. Every unsolved murder has a victim who deserves justice and survivors who deserve answers. When the unit doesn't have a clear prioritization for assigning cases for investigation, many of the investigations will suffer the consequences. There is only so much time and so many resources and when those resources are spread thin it is counterproductive to applying maximum time and attention to specific unsolved cases. "If you're working ten cold cases, you're not effectively working any."

Cold Case detectives should not be working more than two unsolved murders per detective at a time. The strict focus on assigned cases allows the unit to properly review, analyze, strategize, and execute a comprehensive investigation. Understanding the possible outcomes of the investigations is important for Cold Case Unit and their cases. While the goal is to close the case with an arrest and prosecution, at a minimum, the case should undergo a comprehensive review to determine the solvability of the case. Additionally, the investigation may stall again after utilizing all contemporary investigative strategies. The agency needs to recognize this less-than-optimal result and consider moving on to the next prioritized case. This does not mean that a case gets shelved and forgotten but only means that resources are being reassigned to a case more likely to benefit from a comprehensive investigation. If new leads develop on the previous case the unit is already prepared to address them. Limiting the assigned caseload allows for time to follow up on leads that come into the unit on other cases as well as time for other investigations that may be assigned to the unit such as missing persons.

The solvability of the case should be determined by a comprehensive review of the case. The comprehensive review will be discussed in detail later but a protocol for the review process should be in place. A comprehensive review will identify the value of existing evidence, be it physical or testimonial, identify gaps in the investigation that require attention, and assess the evidence for the application of contemporary forensic testing. The comprehensive review should be documented in some format. The more common formats are either a Solvability Matrix or Case Summary format. The Solvability Matrix is typically a shorter form that assigns a numerical score to the case about solvability. Exhibit 3 is a Solvability Matrix similar to one used by the Chesterfield County (VA) Police Department Cold Case Squad (Chesterfield County Police Department, 2025). The Solvability Matrix is very good for a quick assessment of the Cold Units Inventory and as a snapshot of the cases' solvability based on a numerical score. The Solvability Matrix requires less time to produce than the Case Summary. The Solvability Matrix can lack details to definitively support the numerical score and be subjective in some respects—subjective in terms of the ambiguity of police terms, for instance, a named "suspect." The term "suspect" does not have a clear definition across law enforcement and often not even within the agency, currently or in the past. Furthermore, witnesses who once said they could recognize the suspect may later fail to do so, whereas those who originally could not may eventually identify the offender. Furthermore, the numerical score is based on the investigative techniques and forensic testing technology at the time of the review. For example, a murder with an unidentified victim and no known suspect was once considered to have a low probability of resolution. Today, the application of forensic genetic genealogy testing can identify victims, and many times lead to the development of a suspect, dramatically increasing the probability of resolution.

The Case Summary format is another option for documenting a comprehensive review. Exhibit #4 is like the Case Summary document used by the Fairfax County Police (VA) Cold Case Squad (Fairfax County Police Department, 2025). The Case Summary requires the same comprehensive review, but the results are documented in a text format with no numerical score. While a numerical score is not assigned, a significant amount of detail is documented as it relates to investigative steps already taken and their results, the available physical evidence and testing results, as well as the identification of all testimonial evidence with a brief of the content. The Case Summary does require more time to complete and does not give the agency a tangible "score" to classify the inventory of cases. The decision to prioritize a case for immediate work is based on the knowledge and experience of the multidisciplinary Cold Case team reviewing the Case Summary. The Case Summary provides more information to support the solvability of a case.

The Case Summary format also saves time in the future when leads come into the Cold Case Unit by allowing supervisors or detectives to quickly assess the value of the lead based on the previous investigations. It is not uncommon to have details in the Case Summary that come from handwritten notes, which are currently not effectively searchable in digital case files. It is much more efficient to review a Case Summary than search numerous boxes of documents only to learn later that the same lead has been vetted by previous investigations.

Regardless of the option selected by the agency, as mentioned previously, college interns and law enforcement hirebacks are a great resource to assist in the review and documentation of the comprehensive case review.

The determination of which cases will be assigned for investigation based on solvability should be made by both detectives in the unit and the supervisor. The comprehensive review and potential investigative strategies should be briefed within the unit, allowing the Cold Case Supervisor to determine the assignment of the case.

Investigative Responsibilities and Evaluation

Most agencies already have a SOP in place relating to investigative responsibilities for criminal investigations. The SOP should not be so rigid that it presumes all investigations are the same; however, it should establish guidelines for the minimum expectations of the duties of those investigating Cold Cases. For example, comprehensively reviewing unsolved cases to both assess and develop investigative strategies, executing a comprehensive investigation, utilizing a multidisciplinary team approach to address cases, maintaining appropriate contact with victims and survivors, and documentation. The SOP should consider the very nature of Cold Case investigations and how they differ from a "hot" homicide investigation. Daily updates and documentation requirements are not necessary for a Cold Case investigation. The Cold Case investigation typically moves much slower than a "hot" investigation and thus does not typically require short-term documentation requirements. Short-term documentation requirements will likely generate "check the box" reporting that often lacks new and important information. This does not mean that Cold Case detectives should not be contemporaneously documenting the investigation with both notes and reports. The reporting protocol should not be in place to "check the box" but should be a protocol that is productive for the investigation, supervisory oversight, and contemporaneous memorializing of the investigation. It should not be an unproductive mandated task taking time from other more productive investigative duties.

The SOP should address expectations of the unit for evaluation. It is important to have a protocol that allows for reasonable and effective assessment of the success of the unit. Cold Case Units and Cold Case detectives should not be judged solely on the closure of an unsolved case. While that is the goal not all investigations are equal. While all unsolved cases require a comprehensive investigation, some cases are jump-started with a Combined DNA Index System (CODIS) hit on the offender from a probative evidentiary sample. Other unsolved cases may require other investigative strategies that require a much longer investigation just to advance the case, let alone resolve it. As mentioned before, sometimes a comprehensive investigation will lead to the identification of the offender who is deceased. This investigation may require less time and post-arrest investigation since there will be no trial. Other unsolved cases have been resolved after a comprehensive investigation has shown that the death is in fact not a crime but a death by some other manner. While it is impractical to assign a specific number of cases that should be resolved each year, the supervisor can assess the work of unit and individual detectives based on the cases they are working. The productivity of the Cold Case Unit should also be assessed based on the number of unsolved cases that are reviewed, and the number of unsolved cases that are reviewed and brought up to contemporary investigative standards, even though the case is not resolved.

Evidence Handling and Storage

Protocols for evidence handling and storage are critical to all investigations. Most agencies already have written protocols for evidence handling. Over the decades, Cold Case Investigations have seen more than their fair share of investigations stall due to inappropriate evidence handling and storage. Too often evidence has been lost, destroyed, or misplaced in older cases. It is a bitter pill but one that law enforcement, in particular Cold Case Units, must acknowledge. That said, acknowledging the issue is just the first step. Cold Case Units must put into effect practices that secure evidence and prevent future mistaken destruction or release of property. Once all the unsolved homicides and sexual assaults are identified, all evidence in every Cold Case should be flagged in the Evidence Management System as a Cold Case. The Cold Case Supervisor should be identified in the system as the "gatekeeper." In other words, that evidence cannot be destroyed or returned to an owner without prior authorization of the Cold Case Supervisor. It is also a good practice to have all evidence in Cold Cases stored in the same area of the evidence facility and not comingled with other criminal cases.

The SOP should address Cold Case Unit meetings. Very few successful detectives and supervisors enjoy meetings. That said, meetings serve several purposes and when executed properly can have a positive impact on the unit. The meetings should be minimized in both frequency and duration. The SOP does not need to identify specific dates and times but can generally refer to a monthly meeting to discuss case updates and issues affecting the unit. From a practical application standpoint, assigned dates and a time limit on the meetings are most effective, for instance, a maximum of an hour on the second Tuesday of every month at 9 a.m. The detectives know when the meeting will be and can plan according. Most detectives will find an interview, surveillance, or trial prep meeting to avoid unplanned meetings or meetings that are too frequent and thought to be unproductive. Meetings that focus on targeted case updates and strategy discussions are most productive. The meetings should be concise and address new information, and not a rehash of updates already discussed. Detectives need to appreciate the importance of the meetings. Supervisors need to be updated on cases not only for oversight but to be able to update command staff at any given moment. Supervisors who aren't given the necessary information to effectively update command staff often lead to questions like "What exactly is the Cold Case Unit doing, and are they really necessary when we are so short?" If command staff is only aware of the statistics they can view on a dashboard, the unit runs the risk of being evaluated based on a fraction of the work being done. This uninformed assessment can lead to concerns over the value of the unit compared to other pressing needs of the agency.

Funding

Funding is always an issue for the law enforcement profession. It was not long ago that there was actual public debate regarding defunding law enforcement. When politics invade the realm of law enforcement and the administration of justice, victims and communities pay the price. Denying funding does not promote institutional reflection, nor does it facilitate positive change. A lack of funding does directly impact the quality and quantity of investigations. Most would agree that funding has a major impact on Cold Case investigations. A lack of funding is often the reason agencies don't give proper attention to unsolved homicides and sexual assaults. Not because agency leaders and policymakers don't care about victims and survivors but because Cold Case investigations have not risen to the top of the agency's priority list for funding. Many agencies are just trying to make ends meet and handle this month's demands. Herein lies the problem, our profession has become too comfortable living with the identified lack of funding but not doing much to address a solution as it relates to Cold Case Units. Law enforcement has kicked the funding can down the road for far too long. It is essential that law enforcement, leadership in particular, raise their collective voices and demand that funding for Cold Case investigations be part of the agency budget. Law enforcement needs to hold local, state, and federal political leaders accountable for underfunding the investigation of unsolved homicides and sexual assaults. We can no longer allow leaders and politicians to stand shoulder to shoulder with law enforcement at press conferences proclaiming, "It's all about the victims and their families," and "We haven't forgotten" if they will not support agency budgets that fully fund the investigation of Cold Cases. It's the responsibility of law enforcement leadership to collectively and publicly speak clearly, even at the risk of jeopardizing career advancement. Likewise, it is equally important and likely even more impactful when victim advocates and survivors speak publicly. Not only to hold local, state, and federal politicians accountable for any lack of support but also to hold the law enforcement profession accountable for their commitment or lack thereof to investigating unsolved homicides and sexual assaults.

Funding a Cold Case Unit is not inexpensive. The agency must understand spending expectations to run a successful Cold Case Unit. Those expectations should include operational, investigative, and training costs. The operational costs will depend on the needs of the agency, including personnel salaries and benefits, equipment, and additional workspace. Budgeting for operational costs for new units is not unique or new to law enforcement. What is often underestimated are investigative and training expenses. Most unsolved homicides require travel to conduct numerous interviews and other investigative strategies to execute a comprehensive investigation. Most unsolved cases also require forensic testing using the most advanced state-of-the-art technology. Often, agency labs and public labs are not equipped to conduct these examinations. This requires the use of accredited private labs, which can be very costly even on a case-by-case basis. The use of any private lab should be thoroughly vetted in consultation with the agency, state, or federal public lab utilized by the agency for traditional testing.

While the Cold Case Unit should be staffed with well-trained and experienced personnel, it does not mean that they no longer need training. Training with a curriculum focusing on Cold Case investigations is essential. Investigating an unsolved murder or sexual assault is not the same as investigating a case that occurred two hours prior. Cold Case detectives need training to understand the nuances of Cold Case investigations. Training helps them understand the hurdles of the lapse of time and how to turn that hurdle into an investigative advantage. Training in the latest advances in forensic technologies that can help resolve a case once thought unsolvable. And training that guides the unit through the nuances of supporting a family who not only had their loved one taken from them but have had to grieve with no resolution. Cold Case training also builds the detectives' Cold Case network. Over time, witnesses and suspects move across the country. Cold Case detectives need a cross-country network that is ready and willing to step up and assist in their investigation when the phone rings. Cold Case personnel should attend yearly trainings such as the Mid-Atlantic Cold Case Homicide Investigator's Association and the International Homicide Investigator's Association that focus on Cold Case investigations.

The most beneficial funding for building and sustaining a Cold Case Unit is from the agency budget. Other funding resources can significantly assist Cold Case Units in getting started, staffed, and investigating cases. There are federal grants from the Bureau of Justice Assistance as well as non-profits that raise money to fund the investigation of individual cases.

The Bureau of Justice Assistance provides funding grants including The Edward Byrne Memorial Justice Assistance Grant (JAG) program which can fund operational, investigative, and training needs of the unit. The National Sexual Assault Kit Initiative (SAKI) can also be used to fund the operational, investigative, and training needs of the Cold Case Unit including kit testing backlogs, unsolved homicides with a sexual assault component, and more recently any violent crime Cold Case without a suspected sexual assault component (Purpose Area 6). The Bureau of Justice Assistance also provides a grant funds for the investigation of missing persons and unidentified human remains under the Missing and Unidentified Human Remains (MUHR) Program (Bureau of Justice Assistance, 2025).

Law enforcement agencies should also explore Community Project Funding (Houlahan, 2023). These funds previously referred to as "earmarks" are awarded to states or districts through Congress in support of public safety initiatives among other programs. The establishment of Cold Case Units and the resolution of the Cold Cases has a direct impact not only on victims and survivors but on the community as well. The resolution of Cold Cases protects the community from dangerous offenders and prevents future crimes. The establishment of Cold Case Units also builds trust within the community and confidence that law enforcement truly hasn't forgotten and that every life taken in the community deserves a proper investigation. When communities have high numbers of unsolved violent crimes and the perception or reality that not enough is being done to address the issue the citizens lose confidence in law enforcement and the safety of their own community.

There are non-profit organizations that assist in funding Cold Case investigations such as Season of Justice (Season of Justice, 2025). Season of Justice can assist agencies on a case-by-case basis providing funding for forensic testing. The process only requires a short online application including basic case information, the testing requested, and the cost of the testing.

The applications are reviewed by Season of Justice with grants awarded quarterly. The National Center for Missing and Exploited Children assists agencies find funding as well as resources to investigate Cold Cases involving minors (The National Center for Missing and Exploited Children, 2025). There are other non-profits who support Cold Case investigations and offer funding, but with any strategy implemented in an investigation the opportunity and the non-profit organization should be thoroughly vetted.

Media Messaging

It is important for Cold Case Units to have a media protocol or at least a basic understanding of how the Cold Case Unit and the agency media relations team will work together. Initial considerations should include how the agency will develop and manage a dedicated agency webpage identifying unsolved cases. It is important to understand who in the agency will have decision-making authority on what case information is released and when it is released on cases that are actively being worked. Use of the media can be a very effective strategy in Cold Case investigations and is also an effective way to engage the community as well as garner support for Cold Case investigations. Agencies should explore many social platforms to both share and elicit information, engage with the community, and indirectly develop support for the Cold Case Unit. A dedicated anonymous tipline is highly recommended. The "tipline" should be capable of receiving texts, calls, and emails. All "tipline" correspondence should go directly to the Cold Case Unit, meaning a phone/voicemail in the Cold Case office and an email/text inbox should be accessible to the Cold Case Supervisor and detectives. All detectives should monitor the "tipline," but the Cold Case Supervisor should be responsible for checking the "tipline" daily.

Summary

The approach to resolving unsolved homicides and sexual assaults begins with an honest and thorough assessment of the agency's needs and capabilities. Properly investigating unsolved homicides and sexual assaults is a duty of law enforcement, not a luxury. A lack of current resources should not outweigh the need to properly investigate unsolved violent crimes. The proper initial assessment will guide the agency to establish a plan and protocols that provide the operation with the best chance at sustainable success. It is critical to begin with garnering support and "Buy In" from all the vested entities including agency leadership, the prosecuting authority, forensic laboratory personnel, local political leaders, community members, and victim advocates. Time must be spent planning the establishment of the unit prior to jumping forward into casework. The planning includes a SOP with protocols to guide the work of the unit, funding and resources of the unit, and the expectations of the unit. A solid foundation for the Cold Case Unit will give the unit the best chance at sustainable success and will minimize future roadblocks and hurdles not in the best interest of resolving Cold Cases.

Resources

Bureau of Justice Assistance, https://bja.ojp.gov. Inside Congress, https://www.youtube.com/watch?v=nH646XUM7uQ.

Project: The Cold Case Project https://projectcoldcase.org/cold-case-homicide-stats/ and The Murder Accountability Project.

(Ex. 1) Charlotte-Mecklenburg Police Department Cold Case Unit Standard Operating Procedure, Courtesy of Sergeant Darrell Price (Ret.) Charlotte-Mecklenburg Police Department, Cold Case Supervisor.

(Ex. 2) Cold Case Inventory Spreadsheet, Courtesy of Detective Chris Flanagan (Ret.), President, Mid-Atlantic Cold Case Homicide Investigators Association.

(Ex. 3) Solvability Matrix-Courtesy of Corporal Detective Johnny Capocelli, Chesterfield County Police Department.

(Ex. 4) Case Summary-Courtesy of Detective Chris Flanagan (Ret.), Fairfax County Police Department.

Season of Justice, https://seasonofjustice.org.

The National Center for Missing for Missing and Exploited Children, https://www.missingkids.org/home.

The Role of Academia 24

DAVID A. KEATLEY

Introduction

The purpose of this chapter is to provide investigators with an overview of the interaction and excellent opportunities for opening cold case investigations to academics. From the start, for transparency, my position should be clarified. I am both an academic and an international cold case analyst working with police and investigators. This chapter, however, is not a "sales pitch" to tempt more investigators into opening up their files to academics. Similarly, while this chapter is written with investigators as a primary audience, academics reading this chapter will also hopefully gain insight into what is expected, required, and necessary to successfully work with police and law enforcement organizations (LEOs). Expectation management from both sides is essential to fostering long-term, successful partnerships. While this chapter is not meant to be an autobiographical account, it may help to further explain a little of my background so that practitioners in policing and academia may understand the perspectives I have. From there, the chapter will provide several insights into the process of positive police-academic collaborations. The chapter will end with a case study based on a real-world cold case collaboration. The main aim is to understand the roles, remits, and possible roadblocks that may occur. Finally, I do not give advice; however, throughout the chapter I shall attempt to give "Lessons" that I have learned—sometimes the hard way.

The Doctor and the Detective

While many academics claim their research is applied, there remains a large gap between many academics and LEOs. Thankfully, growing numbers in both industries are attempting to narrow this gap. Several years ago, I was asked to present my academic research to a closed-door seminar involving law enforcement representatives from various departments around the United States. I presented the outcome of a very technical, quantitative, and complicated method for statistically mapping criminals' life histories that I had been developing for several years. This is not a boast, it is simply how many academics present their ideas—as being

 DOI: 10.4324/9781003415633-28

complex, complicated, and the type of work that takes elevated expertise to understand. Understandably, the reception was not as great as I had hoped for. I had wrongly thought that attempting to show-off my statistical skills and fancy erudite language was going to impress the room. I was wrong. I learned a valuable lesson: *No one is interested if you are not speaking their language.*

As the seminar wound down, I was approached by a detective. The detective suggested my research, while very limited,[1] had potential. When I tell this story to academics, with the actual words used, they often appear aghast at such a harsh review. Looking back, it was the best review I have ever received. While I was dealing with statistical significance, the detective was dealing with murderers, rapists, and other criminals. She had every right to call me and my research out. In academia, we get used to reviewers who while sometimes critical are often courteous. In applied work, prepare for sometimes brutal honesty. A paper with limitations may be improved through further iterations and development. A cold case review with limitations may have devastating consequences.

First Steps

There is typically and understandably various concerns from the police perspective about opening their files to non-uniformed entities, especially academics. This concern or apprehension is not without cause. There have been several examples of police being burned by academics. This is not meant as a warning to police officers—there are good academics out there who are capable and willing to help effectively. Academics can provide fresh insights, new ideas, new leads, current research perspectives, and the potential for larger "workforces" (e.g., student review groups [SRGs]). Like everything in life, a weighing-up judgment is essential and must be done on a case-by-case basis.

It would be naïve, however, to suggest that all cold case investigators should open their files to any academic who shows an interest in helping. Similarly, before approaching police, academics are encouraged to read the later sections of this chapter to consider whether the position of cold case reviewer is one that you really want to engage in. This is important because I fear that every time an academic approaches a police group or case and is given an opportunity that they do not see through to completion, it harms the reputation of other academics. Within my experience, I have heard many stories of police officers giving their files to academics, only to never hear from them again—or worse—to hear from them again when the media comes knocking.

Media

The true crime genre is one of the fastest growing areas in popular media. New podcasts and social media channels seem to appear daily. On each one is a steady stream of academics who speak at length about various cases and investigative areas. There are, of course, many police officers who also appear on these shows. But there is a difference. The detectives typically gain permission from the media/PR team in their department, alongside permission from their Chief/Commissioner. Academics seldom seek or need approval from a Dean or media team. The big difference, of course, is that the officer knows what can and cannot be said. The academic may not understand the nuance or nature of the investigation at that point in time. In my view, the case is more important than the carnival. Academics should be prepared to work on cases without any fame, note, or notoriety—something worth considering and discussing.

The allure of publicity and being on television is attractive to some academics and some universities. This is something that academics should be aware of from the outset (and engage in very open discussions with Deans and senior staff). Working with police on cold cases is often done behind the scenes. The details of the cases are often not made publicly available, nor is the academic's role in the case. I have heard of academics that did not clarify this to begin and had a hard time later in their career explaining why they were using work hours on cases. While the allure of saying, *our staff work with police* may seem appealing, the reality is that staff are split between university-related jobs and the cold case reviews. Negotiations regarding time allocations and workload should be conducted preferably *before* approaching police.

I am not suggesting that academics should avoid all media appearances. It can be helpful to your career, and it can help to get good, solid information out to the wider world. It may also raise awareness and lead to more leads. So, I am all in favor of it. I simply do not participate in it unless asked to do so by police. This is a discussion that should be had at the start of a collaboration. There are some academics who can traverse both the popular media and the cold case review work, but they number fewer than those who work behind the scenes and remain unknown there.

Non-Disclosure Agreements

Non-disclosure agreements (NDAs) are a staple of many cold case homicide investigations. These provide some security for police investigators, but they are far from foolproof. I have no qualms with signing them and have never come close to breaching one. As a rule, I do not engage with media nor talk about any case I work—even if the detective involved has already name-dropped me in media stories. The few times that I have appeared in the media discussing cases was done so at the request of the investigators involved—but this seldom happens. I do wonder, however, what happens when an NDA is broken? This is another issue that detectives must contend with, and academics should be aware of.

If a detective gives an entire case file to an academic, along with an NDA, what guarantee does the detective have? At the most extreme, the NDA may come with a legal ramification of prosecution. The reality is that few if any academics are prosecuted for breaking NDAs. For one thing, the damage will have already, perhaps irrevocably, been done. If the academic reads the files and leaks or otherwise talks about the case material, then prosecuting the academic will not change the fact that the case may have been ruined.

Data Storage

A further issue with academic involvement in cold case reviews is where the data or evidence is stored. Some police departments and review groups put the files behind a protective layer that does not allow direct downloading of materials. This is a fair attempt at maintaining security but is undermined by the fact that nothing stops an academic from taking a picture of the screen they are staring at. Reviewers may still discuss the material and thus release sensitive "holdback" information. Discussion of what materials are available for download or transfer is something that is required and should be adhered to. Use of a separate laptop may assist with separating work/everyday files from police work files.

Finances

I have heard of several academics offering their services to police at a cost. This is understandable if the academic wants to be bought out of teaching. This should be done at the start of collaborative interactions. I am not about to claim that being paid for reviews is an issue. I am simply going to make my position known. I have never been paid to review a cold case—and I have no intention of changing that. This is not always a popular position among academics. I leave it to police departments and academics to come to an agreement on this. Investigators should be aware that academics may need to be bought out of their teaching commitments. Academics should be aware that most police departments do not have money for outside reviews. Also, if you are being paid, it is wise to have an agreement on what is expected (i.e., what if you cannot find any new leads?) What is the financial outcome of you, as an academic, having spent a hundred hours reviewing a case, with no new leads or opinions?

On this last note, it is worth mentioning expectations of academic reviews. To begin with, I often felt the pressure of feeling like I had to solve the case. I felt a failure if I could add nothing. I felt useless if I could not point to someone and triumphantly shout, "*that's the suspect*!" It took me some time to realize that is not what the police wanted. For the most part, they wisely would not have listened if I had said that. Instead, they often simply want a new perspective, a new thread to pull on, a new line of investigation to follow up. That is their job—to investigate. Ours, perhaps, is to shine a spotlight on where to investigate. Put simply, police do not want us to "solve" their cases, they just want our help.

Breaching the Blue Wall

I am often asked, by academics, *how do you get into working with the police*? Here is where opportunity meets preparation. My advice is while you wait for the opportunity, focus on the preparation. There are hundreds of cases available for academics to work on. The world is over-saturated with real-world cold cases, many of which have a lot of information and evidence openly available—including police files, court documents, statements, etc. The pushback I almost immediately hear from colleagues is, *yes, but we don't have all the information*. To put it nicely: welcome to cold cases. Yes, police often have some "holdback" information about a case, but they too are often missing lots of vital information. If your main restraint to working on open access cold cases bereft of the police is not having all the information, then perhaps cold cases are not for you.

The reality is that I have yet to work a cold case wherein we have all the information we need. Countless are the times I have asked; *do you have x or y?* To be met with, *if we had that, we'd have solved it ourselves*. The point is this: in academia we are spoilt with complete, rich datasets. In the real world of cold cases, much is missing. The question is: how are we going to deal with that? There is nothing stopping you from attempting to develop methods that would help. Develop a method, and then when the detective comes calling—you have something to offer. There's a large difference between saying, "this is what I can do with an incomplete case" versus "please give me all your files and I'll see what I can do."

Coming full circle, that was the key part of my presentation that the detective saw all those years ago. While I was basing my analyses on serial killers—because we knew lots about their entire life story so had rich datasets—the world of cold cases is filled with unknowns. The question was how far I could push my methods into the unknown. I am not saying I have solved that enigma, but I am constantly attempting to narrow the gaps of the unknown.

Student Review Groups

There is a growing rise in student groups that assist in cold case reviews. While several police departments, typically in the United States, have forged close contacts with local university SRGs, there are also larger international groups, such as the International Cold Case Analysis Project (ICCAP), of which I am a core member. These student groups can be excellent resources for investigators, providing fresh insight and many more eyes and minds to pore over the work. Many times, I have been amazed by how hardworking the students are, and at times, what keen insights they have. Please do not be put-off working with students—they can provide great insights, and I have often been in awe of their hard work and dedication.

While I am honored to be a part of several SRGs, it is important that investigators understand what the role/remit of the group is and what the expectations are. Many SRGs, including ICCAP, are primarily focused on being educational for the students. The main goal is to train and teach students. Of course, there can be symbiosis in this process. There are occasions where the training and education of students can still lead to breakthroughs, but this is not the primary focus. Often, the students are getting their first experience of working on real-world cases. I am all for this exposure, hence being a part of these groups. There are, however, inherent limitations.

The role of the group is to teach and train the students. To that extent, the focus is more on developing the students than the case. Some recent research has shown that students typically enjoy these groups and do learn some valuable lessons. From a pedagogical perspective, this is great news. But if the goal is to teach and train students, then solving the case is sometimes secondary. This is sometimes misunderstood by the investigators. Transparency and openness about the goal and perspective of the groups is essential to fostering lasting partnerships or walking separate paths early on. Some police enjoy teaching and training students, so the symbiosis can be mutually rewarding.

The next potential issue relates back to NDAs outlined previously. If academic staff are seldom held to account for breaking NDAs, then the penalty to students is further diminished. Several years ago, a student group I heard about was tasked with investigating an unsolved series of crimes. Some members of the group later broke the limits of the NDA they had signed. Several of the students took it upon themselves to contact the suspect and attempt to gain a confession. The harm to the investigation was incalculable. The repercussions to the students were negligible. The point is this: while we ask students to sign an NDA, we can seldom enforce it. The most likely recourse is to remove the student from the review group. Furthermore, when does an NDA end? If the student graduates, are they still bound by the NDA? What happens if they decide to start a podcast and talk about it? These, of course, are not reasons to avoid SRGs, but they should be taken into consideration *before* collaboration.

Discovery

Another issue connected to the dissemination and source of information is that of discovery. If the case being reviewed does make it to court, wherein evidence is open to discovery, is there an issue that the key breakthrough came from a SRG? This is certainly worth considering. Some police departments I know of are very sensitive about "brand protection" and refuse outside help for fear it will shame the department if an outsider makes the breakthrough—especially a student! While I can partially understand this, I think having an unsolved case on the file potentially reflects worse on the department.

Overall, SRGs are an excellent way to train students and possibly help cold cases. When they work, as they often do, the results are excellent for all involved. Investigators gain a lot of input from a lot of eager and educated minds. Students gain great experience and possibly an interest to pursue a career in the area—and policing worldwide is in desperate need of recruitment! However, as ever, a balancing analysis needs to be considered. Typically, students are offered the "low-risk" cold cases in which in the worst of outcomes—a broken NDA—the effect is not overly detrimental to the case.

Police-Academia Cold Case Review: A Case Study

It would be easy to cherry pick a successful cold case collaboration. Collaborations between police and academics are occurring increasingly frequently and are a good sign that academic-practitioner connections are worth pursuing. In discussing this chapter with colleagues, however, such a case study often felt superficial. *What of the times wherein the collaborations do not work out so well?* I was often asked. I would not want to end this chapter on such a negative note, which would be unfair and not a true representation of the possibilities for success. Therefore, I shall end this chapter with a case study I was made aware of some years ago. The point is to help facilitate successful interactions between investigators and academics by confronting you with questions you should ask each other before embarking on a collaboration.

To begin, I will outline the premise of the cold case, and then provide you with the interaction between the police and the academic, as it transpired and expired. The case had been cold for some 30 years by the time the academic was invited into the task force room. In my experience, 30 years places the case in the position of being old enough that all leads had been exhausted multiple times across several reviews, but recent enough for family members to still be alive and actively pursuing updates. To this extent, the police reached out to a local academic for any insights or review that may offer some new thread on which to pull.

Case Synopsis

John Doe was a 10-year-old boy who went to play in a local park with his sister. They told their parents they'd be back by lunch time. This, of course, occurred before the time when every child had a phone and most had tracking apps built-in. John's mom, believing the suburb to be safe, lovingly kissed her children goodbye. She had no way of knowing: it was the last time she would ever see John alive.

Children, especially siblings, are competitive. John and his sister were no different, and they had barely left the house before she ran ahead, taunting him to keep up. She was older and faster. As she ran ahead, he fell behind. Joyous at her victory, she had no way of knowing: it was the last time she would ever see John alive.

John's sister arrived at the park approximately 15 minutes after leaving the house. She waited for another 10 minutes before beginning to back-track her path. At 12 years old, she had no real concept of *stranger danger* and so she was more annoyed than concerned—John was wasting precious park play time. It was only when she got back to her home that worry began to creep in. She was the older sister, her parents trusted her to look after John. What was she going to tell them?

The parents, having heard John was missing, presumed he had likely wandered off or been distracted. So, they got in their car and began searching the neighborhood. It was already too late. The emergency call came in to police at approximately midday. The police responded immediately, and a local officer was dispatched to take a statement and assist with the search. It would be another 24 hours before John was found. He had been bludgeoned multiple times and his body left in a desolate wooded area approximately 5 km from where he lived.

Despite numerous potential leads, sightings, accusations, and conspiracies spanning the decades, no solid suspect was ever developed, and the case grew colder. The police, to their credit, provided input to various documentaries and true crime productions in an attempt to raise awareness and leads. Eventually, having exhausted all "in-house" expertise and media appeals, the police looked further afield—to a local university wherein a criminologist with some experience in cold case reviews worked.

I appreciate that readers will want to know more about the case details. That is not the point of this case study. So, what is? This: it is more important to ask the right questions than believe the wrong answers. You see, the academic agreed to consult with the police and review the case. He came into the task force room and was shown the case files. Of particular interest to the academic was the body deposition site and the injuries to the victim. John had suffered numerous blunt force trauma wounds, including and especially to the face. Owing to the extent and type of injuries and postmortem behaviors, the academic posed a simple question: do you have any other cases like this in your books around the time?

This is nothing groundbreaking. Of course, the police will likely have considered this themselves. A couple of the detectives, though, were interested about *why* the academic wanted to know about other cases. The extent of the different injuries, postmortem behaviors, and movement and positioning of the body indicated to the academic that the offender may have committed other crimes. It was not lost on the academic that there was a notable awkwardness suddenly arising in the task force room. The academic was used to this reception. By asking if there are other cases, it may be misinterpreted as the academic suggesting that the police had "failed" in other cases, too.

Rather discretely, a couple of detectives took the academic to one side and discussed another case, involving another young boy that had happened some years prior. The other boy had also been playing in the local area and had also gone missing. Nothing major to connect the dots, yet. However, the other victim was also found a short time later having suffered numerous blunt force trauma wounds and other similar postmortem behaviors. Of course, crime linkage based on behavioral analysis is not an exact science. This, however, is what the academic specialized in—behavioral analysis. He asked for more information about the other case. The detectives suggested that it was not related, because they had made an arrest for the murder of the other child soon after he was found. The other child's murderer was, at the time of the currently unresolved cold case, in prison serving his sentence. This, the detectives suggested, answered the academic's questions and ended that potential lead.

Take a moment to consider: if you are a detective, would you consider this pathway a dead end? Would you accept that an arrest was made and thus the academic must be mistaken or simply wrong? If you are an academic, would this answer be satisfactory? Would you cease your four lines of questioning here and consider other leads? While sitting in the comfort of wherever you are reading this, it may be easy to contemplate. But consider what the situation was like in the task force room. Let's be blunt about this. The officers were being confronted with the potential of a wrongful conviction for the other victim—a terrible enough situation but made far worse by the potential that the real suspect had been left to offend again. The academic, for his part, was simply trying to help by asking questions that he would have been remiss not to ask.

The academic, for better or worse, kept asking for more information about this other case and their arrest. Did the detectives have access to the other case files? Did they have the statements and evidence from that trial? Was it worth spending at least a little time reviewing it—as much to learn about similar cases as to link them to a suspect. These questions did not go unnoticed by the wider task force members. Midway through a question regarding the convicted suspect's police interview, a senior officer requested the academic to leave the task force room. He was escorted from the room and the building. To date, he has not been asked back, nor has the case been solved.

So, in many ways, there ends the case study. Unsatisfactory, I know. But in my experience this case study is one of the most important cases I have come across when considering collaborations with police. Are investigators open to new leads being developed, even if they may harm "brand protection"? Similarly, we academics need to remember our role. We are not investigators; we are not there to pursue leads or push police into pursuing them. We, at best, offer suggestions or opinions, and I have found that this is often best done by asking questions.

These are issues worth considering before embarking on collaborations. If you are an officer, be open to the expertise and fresh insights that an academic and perhaps an SRG may bring. But consider that they may ask difficult questions. If you are an academic, consider how you might react in a situation like this. You may have views or leads that you think are worthy of investigation; but how will you respond to being told "no"? Can you walk away and never mention the case, or your suspicions, to anyone? If nothing else, I hope that this case study provides a foundation on which to have a discussion *before* the situation arises.

Note

1 The word the detective chose was actually less charitable. However, mapping criminal histories and using that to prioritize suspects is what the detective found potentially useful.

The Use of Human Remains Detection Canines

25

KACY ROBINSON AND
BRET SAYER

Clarifying Terms

HRD means human remains detection, commonly referred to as cadaver dogs. These dogs are also often referred to as recovery canines.

Canine Unit means the human remains detection canine and his or her handler working as a team on a search.

Police Canines are those canines specifically trained for explosive detection, substance detection, and/or tracking and apprehension. They are utilized by agencies and handlers who are sworn officers.

Search and Rescue/Recovery Canines are those canines specifically trained to assist with missing persons cases, including live find wilderness, tracking and trailing, avalanche recovery, water recovery, and human remains detection. These canines are trained in specialties ranging from live scent to skeletal remains.

Handler refers to the person responsible for maintaining and training a canine. Handlers are also responsible for deploying with the canine on search missions. Handlers focus on the "animation" of the canine in order to determine when the canine has located scent and when the canine begins to provide indication they are in scent. The handler has the ultimate responsibility for determining when the canine provides a final alert and articulating that to the agency requesting their assistance.

Scent/Canine in Scent is the term used when the canine is exhibiting behavioral indications that they have detected the odor for which they are searching.

Indication is the term used when a canine handler recognizes their canine is in scent.

Search Command is the term used to indicate to the canine that they are to go to work. Typically, these words are unique and not a word the canine will hear during the normal course of his or her day.

Alert/Final Alert is the term used when a canine handler recognizes that the canine has located the source of the odor for which they are searching. These alerts can range from barking to sitting or lying down at the source.

 DOI: 10.4324/9781003415633-29

Recall/Refind Alert is the term used when a canine will find the source of the odor for which it is searching, leave the odor, and provide a specific indication for the handler such as jumping, touching a hand, or barking, before then taking the handler back into the source of the scent and providing a final alert.

Why Utilize Canines for Search and Rescue/Recovery?

There is nothing more important to a search and rescue handler than his or her canine. Handlers have multiple tools at their disposal depending on the circumstances of the search, but without their canine partners, they are not searchers. Our canine partners are the single greatest tool we have, but they are not simply a tool, they are our greatest asset.

Canine handlers find themselves in a world where their focus must be on their canine partner and the bond they share—not maintaining skills at the highest level, but ensuring that the innate abilities of the canine are being properly honed and interpreted thus utilizing this unique team to the best of both of their abilities.

When in the field searching or training for a search, the canine handler must be able to completely trust his or her canine partner in every situation, and in turn the canine must trust the handler fully. Their safety and lives depend upon the trust they have for one another. Relying on the canine's abilities and skills allows the canine unit to be successful as a team and to bring resolution on the case in which they are working. It is imperative that the canine handler deploy the canine in situations where the canine will be safe and successful.

While it might take days or weeks to search a large area by humans, canines can quickly and efficiently cover large areas in a fraction of the amount of time it would take a human. Also, canines can deploy to a wide variety of situations including buried (snow, dirt, cement), water, shoreline, wilderness, urban, suburban, buildings, etc.

Why Are Canines the Perfect Search and Rescue/Recovery Tool?

Canines are not magic. The job of the handler would be much easier if they were, but they cannot be successful without a seasoned and highly skilled handler. Canines have innate abilities with scent that allow them to complete search work in ways no human can. The job of the human searcher is to utilize those skills in ways that will result in the greatest success.

This is accomplished in several different ways, one of which is taking all the variables of the search (i.e. terrain, weather, vegetation, missing person, victimology, circumstances of the search, wind speed and direction, etc.) and the other is training for all probable search scenarios.

Properly maintaining a canine unit means spending hundreds of hours consulting cases and researching real-world missing persons scenarios. This information is then incorporated into the training conducted from the very beginning when potential canines are puppies. While every handler has their own way of training their canine, the greatest success comes from training the canines by enhancing and interpreting their innate abilities.

Canines are born with this innate ability to scent in phenomenal ways. It has been proven that they can scent a single fingerprint on a pane of glass left in the elements for two weeks. Training a canine for search work means harnessing this ability and interpreting it, all the while not speaking the same language. This means the handler must learn to read the canine's body language and decipher all those clues they provide. It requires both the canine and the handler to form a bond beyond that is unbreakable. This bond is the most important part of training a search canine.

As most animal lovers understand, animals provide unconditional love and companionship that is unlike any other relationship. Working with a search canine requires an even greater bond. This requires the canine unit to depend upon one another in difficult situations and deepens the bond. The most successful handlers have an unbreakable bond with their working canine.

How Does One Choose a Search and Rescue/Recovery Canine?

Although it seems counterintuitive, the naughtiest dogs make the best search and rescue/recovery canines. Often canines who have failed at other service endeavors (i.e. guide dogs, explosive detection, etc.) due to extremely high prey drives and/or excessive energy become highly successful search canines.

From a litter, the canine handler will look for the puppy who is energetic and interested in their surroundings. Puppies who can focus on people but also enjoy exploring on their own are beginning to exhibit characteristics essential to a search canine. Canines who are observant yet willing to redirect their focus back to humans will allow the handler to continue teasing out those innate characteristics, making training more efficient.

Canines who also have an inborn prey drive will allow the handler to redirect the drive from prey to humans. Because of this, beginning with a canine breed known for a high prey drive is the first step. Breeds such as sporting or hunting canines tend to allow for easier and more efficient training because they already have the energy necessary and a high prey drive.

Canine handlers will also look for the puppy who is comfortable in multiple different scenarios. Search canines are exposed to every type of surface as well as every weather element. Puppies who show an adventurous spirit and are willing to play in all types of situations will be easily transitioned to training and searching in every scenario they may face when deployed on a search.

How Does One Train a Search and Rescue/Recovery Canine?

On average it takes approximately 1,200 solid hours to train a canine for basic search deployment. Further, it takes at least 600 hours per year to maintain deployment status. This essentially means the canine handler must constantly and consistently be training his or her canine in every situation they could potentially face during a search and then maintaining that training throughout the life of the canine.

There are many different types of canine search training. Some teams only search for missing people who are living. Some train for those who have died. Some do a combination of both. Some teams train to recover evidence. And finally, others train for aged missing persons. The focus of the training depends upon the types of searching in which the canine will be involved.

If the search team focuses mainly on live find searches, the canine will train on live human scent. Those who mainly deploy on searches for deceased individuals will train on cadaver scent. Those involved in both types of searches will incorporate both live and cadaver scent into the canine training. And for those who are specialized in cold case recovery, the training focuses on decomposed remains up to and including skeletal remains. On any given search mission a combination of these factors may be present. It is critical for the handler and canine to train for those specific scenarios they will face when deployed.

For canine handlers who are consistently focused on real-world training scenarios, the greater the likelihood their canine will be successful when deployed on an actual search. It is critically important for canine handlers to ensure they are training their canines for any and all potential possibilities.

Beginning training includes working on basic obedience commands and working on the bond between the canine and the handler, trust being the most important training element. Train the canine to be intelligently disobedient which means allowing the canine to disobey those basic commands when the canine is in scent. If the canine is too focused on the handler and easily distracted by commands or the actions of the handler, the canine could potentially leave or miss a source. This means the canine needs to learn to listen when necessary but ignore the handler when they are going in the wrong direction or leading the canine away from the scent. Having a good balance between basic obedience and control of the canine while allowing him or her the freedom to disobey when in scent is difficult to train but a key element in training an exceptional search canine.

One canine handler's story about intelligent disobedience:

> *I was working with my first search canine, Uintah. We were on our second deployment together searching for an individual who had been missing for ten days. We began the search at the victim's point last seen (the area where his car was found and he was last known to be). The other canines on the search began leading their handlers toward the city. Uintah began leading me to the highway. We continued our search towards the highway. Uintah was providing indication that she was on scent, so we continued.*
>
> *When we reached the highway, I glanced at my search map. The highway was the boundary for my search area. However, I noticed there were large drainage pipes under the highway. Thinking the victim may have used the pipes for shelter, I placed Uintah in a sit-stay and began to search the pipes. Uintah broke her sit-stay three times. Each time I would place her back into the sit-stay, she would break and come to my side.*
>
> *After realizing she was not going to stay, I placed her by my side and we searched the pipes together. We cleared the pipes and found no indication the victim had sheltered there. I then consulted my search map again. As it was the boundary of my area, I attempted to formulate our next steps. In my mind, I was trying to decide whether to double-back into the area where there were more points where the victim could shelter or to return to incident command and await further instructions from our commander.*
>
> *I placed Uintah back to work with her search command. It was at this point she decided to take action and leave me behind. She knew all along that the victim was on the other side of the highway and the only way we were going to reach him was if she didn't listen to me but trusted her own instincts and her training.*
>
> *Without warning, she bolted across the highway. By the time I reached her, she was twenty feet on the other side of the highway with the deceased individual. If she wasn't willing to leave me behind, we would not have found the missing person. I am forever grateful for the lessons she taught me that day.*
>
> *Not only did she teach me to allow my canine to have independence and agency to leave me when I walk away from a victim, but she taught me to trust her, to trust her instincts and that we are partners. As her handler, I must do everything I can to ensure she can be successful, but without her abilities, instincts, and independence, we cannot be successful.*

Training for independence can be difficult for canine handlers because they want to control for all variables, yet they are often most successful when training canines to utilize their innate abilities and to trust handlers to place them into situations where they can be the most successful. This means handlers must trust canines just as they trust their handlers.

Once a foundation of basic obedience and independence have been established, the scent source can be introduced. Introducing scent source, whatever the focus of the search canine may be, is a gradual process. The scent is first introduced to the canine and the canine is rewarded with whatever is their favorite reward. This can be a favorite toy or treat. The goal is to make the ending the best thing in the world to the canine, a "puppy party."

As the canine becomes more familiar with the source and is readily focusing on the source in order to obtain the reward, the source can then be moved and placed in different areas and scenarios from areas where the source can be seen to areas where it is hidden and out of the predominant wind direction. Gradually moving toward more and more difficult scenarios ensures the canine is searching for the source of the scent and providing the required indications and alerts when in scent. This also allows the handler to become familiar with the canine animation, indications, and alerts and can accurately articulate the actions of the canine. This training continues throughout the life of the canine. Introducing new and different scenarios keeps the canine from becoming complacent and helps the handler understand the canine's behavior in multiple different situations.

In What Situations Is It Appropriate to Deploy Cold Case Recovery Canines?

For first responders and investigators, some of the most compelling cases are not the ones that got away, but the ones that disappeared without a trace. They are the people missing for decades, the bodies that were never found, the searches that began with everyone knowing it would be a recovery mission, not a rescue. Cold case investigators are a tiny, dedicated band. The living matter to them, but so do the dead, because every case was once someone who was alive and loved, and closure matters to their families.

Search and recovery work is different than any other search and rescue discipline. With search and rescue, you have hope of life, but those focused on search and recovery understand one basic fact while going into every search mission: this victim will not be found alive. Yet, the motivations for continuing to do search and recovery work are like the motivations of those who do search and rescue: to bring a loved one "home," even if decades have passed.

Even when cases are cold and law enforcement resources have been depleted, families do not lose hope. They never lose hope. They live in limbo every single day, days suspended, not knowing what happened or where their loved one is.

Working with a cold case recovery team allows these families to know that someone cares, someone still thinks of their loved one, says their name, and wants to see that they are brought home. Utilizing cold case recovery canines in the location of missing persons allows the families to have some hope that someday their loved one will be returned to them.

There are, however, cases where the use of recovery canines is more advantageous than others. Many agencies have established cold case teams and states have begun legislating cold case databases. In cases where there has been no body recovered and there is adequate information, specialized cold case recovery handlers can analyze the case information in conjunction with the current investigators. In cold cases, time can be an advantage: relationships end, people begin talking; new technology allows for a deeper understanding of the case; and previously disregarding information can lead to new tips. When new information comes to light when a case is reopened or new tips are received, an opportunity to reexamine the case is presented.

No two cold cases are ever the same, whether for a missing child in the wilderness, an older adult suffering a medical issue in an urban setting, a suicidal individual, or a victim of homicide. Each search is as different as the missing person is and requires in-depth case research prior to deployment. Ensuring the use of specialized handlers who have this ability and the knowledge to conduct such an in-depth analysis is the first step.

Those who are properly trained and able to conduct these types of in-depth analysis will use their skills in lost person behavior, crime scene analysis, psychology, psycholinguistic profiling, criminology, forensics, navigation, digital forensics, victimology, and search and rescue. These skills are necessary to conduct a deep dive into each case prior to setting boots and paws on the ground.

Completing an in-depth analysis such as this allows the recovery canine handler not only to prepare for potential deployment but also determine the probability of finding the missing person. Information scrutinized includes but is not limited to entire case files, prior search information including GPS or search data, satellite maps of the area, and victimology. Sometimes the smallest piece of information, such as whether the person was right or left handed, can lead to the recovery of a missing person (when lost, right-handed people tend to make right turns, while left-handed people make left turns).

For homicide cases, understanding where searches have previously been conducted is the most pertinent piece of information. Together with information regarding the skills of those who previously searched and the certifications of the previous canine searches will help limit search areas and focus on areas where the probability of detection is the greatest.

Once this in-depth analysis and consultation is complete, recovery canine handlers can then make a determination as to the necessity of deployment. Together with the investigators, this deployment plan can be implemented. If a boots and paws deployment is deemed necessary, the next phase of the search begins.

The next phase includes the planning of the actual search. Taking into consideration multiple variables, the recovery canine handlers design a plan to deploy into the designated areas. Some of the variables which must be considered are:

Safety of canine and handler
Hazards in and around the area
Size of area to be searched
Terrain features
Wind speed/direction
Weather
Date person went missing
Animal activity in the area

Once deployed and in the area, canine handlers will then conduct a hasty search of the area. This can include a walk-through with the requesting law enforcement agency in order to identify any hazards. This step can also be conducted via drone. Once the hasty search of the area is complete, one handler and canine are then deployed into the area. The handler gives his or her canine their search command appropriate to the particular search. The canine unit will then devise a search strategy working into the winds if possible and conducting a fine-grid search so as not to miss any pertinent items of evidence. Should any items of evidence be found, the handler should mark the item on his or her GPS noting exactly what the item is. Photos should also be taken and law enforcement contacted as to the location of each item. Handlers should understand proper crime scene etiquette and should ensure that each item located is preserved and maintained for testing.

If there are areas of indication or alerts, these must be marked on GPS, noted specifically and relayed to law enforcement. Everything should be thoroughly documented, and law enforcement should be informed.

What Defines a Success?

Recovering the missing person is understandably the outcome any search team is seeking when they deploy. However, there are other types of success which may be less apparent. For example, some cases are too dangerous for human or canine search. These cases also include areas where the probability of detection is minuscule, including places like unstable mine shafts and caves. Determining the probability of detection in these cases can help law enforcement prioritize cases where recovery is possible.

Another unconventional type of success is providing canine assistance simply to clear an area. Clearing an area means utilizing canines to determine the missing person is not within the boundaries of a specific area. This allows law enforcement and the search and recovery team to shift focus to other areas of interest where the probability of detection of remains could be greater.

The greatest success search and recovery teams have is simply providing services to and engaging with law enforcement and families of the missing on cold cases, whether it be consulting on a case, deploying, or ultimately recovering a loved one. Families of long-term missing persons cases often feel no one cares. Letting them know that someone cares is the ultimate success.

Failures and Mistakes

Like humans, canines can have bad or "off" days. There will be instances when a canine is not willing or able to work in a given situation. The job of the canine handler is to recognize that their canine partner is not up to the task at that moment and allow another handler and their canine to search in their place. It is imperative that canine recovery teams build in redundancy so in the event a canine is unable or unwilling to search, other canine units can search the area.

Having multiple canine units available to search also allows for better coverage of an area as well as redundancy should there be scent in the area. It is far easier to explain to law enforcement and the court that multiple canines alerted in one particular area, than just one canine. It is always better to build in that redundancy, which can be documented and later presented should the case go to trial.

Another mistake canine handlers have made is making cuing their canine and causing a false indication or alert. In order to avoid doing so, it is always best to search an area blind. That is to say, the handler should never be present in the same area, while other canines are searching and the handler should not be provided with any prior knowledge which could cause him or her to make an assumption that there is evidence or a body in a particular location. If multiple canines have a final alert in one particular area, documented by GPS and handler observation, there is a greater likelihood of a recovery. This is particularly important when looking for small items or items of evidence.

The pitfall of assuming can also lead handlers to state that a body was in a location and moved which can lead to issues in court. Handlers must use proper language such as, "the canine indicated there was the odor of human remains in the area, however no body/evidence/etc. was recovered" rather than stating, "due to canine indications, a body was in the area and subsequently moved therefore no body/evidence/etc. was recovered."

Also worth noting is that a properly trained, certified recovery canine should never alert on scent sources that are not human. That is to say, if there are animal bones or remains in a search area, the recovery canine is expected to ignore those sources of scent. They should also ignore other live animals in the area both wild and domestic in order to focus on the task at hand.

Being humble and willing to admit when your canine is unable to perform on a specific search is of upmost importance. Hubris and arrogance are the enemy of any canine unit.

Considerations When Choosing to Work with Canines

In choosing to work with a canine team, there are several factors to consider. Keeping in mind that canines are not magic and must be trained properly and placed in situations in which they are highly skilled, consider the following before utilizing any canine team to help in searching for an aged missing person:

- Specific canine certifications
- Search and rescue canines should not be utilized on a cold case unless the canines are specifically trained in locating aged missing persons in the situation in which the case requires (i.e. wilderness, cement, water, etc.)
- Certifications should require the canine locate aged human remains up to and including skeletal remains and should match the specific case circumstances
- Canines should be certified in finding minute pieces of evidence
- Handler qualifications
- At a minimum, handlers who are working cold cases should be law enforcement or forensically certified
- Handlers should be trained in forensic anthropology
- Handlers should be crime scene analysts or equivalent
- Handlers should have blood borne pathogens certifications
- Handlers should understand the incident command system and structure
- Handlers should be able to fully integrate with law enforcement when deployed
- Handlers should have exceptional navigation skills
- Handlers should understand canine scent theory, detection, and location
- Handlers should have a strong working understanding of climatology
- Handlers are expected to qualify as expert witnesses should the case go to trial

It is important to remember that canine units are expected to integrate seamlessly with law enforcement. Canine units should not deploy to a search without the expressed consent and supervision of law enforcement.

Cadaver Dogs, Law Enforcement, and the Courts: A Case Study

The People of the State of Colorado v. Mark Allen Redwine Case # 17CR343

This case involves a missing child, Dylan Redwine, 13 years of age, who was last seen alive on November 18, 2012, during a court-ordered visit with his father, Mark Redwine. He and his father were flying and landed in Colorado supposedly on that date. They purportedly arrived in Colorado and then went to their residence in Bayfield, Colorado, on November 18th. Following arrival at home, Dylan sent an electronic communication at 2137 on the 18th. Following this communication, he was neither seen nor heard from again.

Later, blood was found in the home which was confirmed by DNA to be Dylan's in one area of the living room. The other areas of blood were not confirmed by DNA to be Dylan's. In June of 2013, portions of Dylan's remains were discovered less than 10 miles from the home. In November of 2015, Dylan's skull was found by hikers. Between November of 2012 and June of 2013, 13 portions of remains were discovered.

Throughout the investigation and subsequent searches, 16 "cadaver" canines were deployed. Only some of these deployed canines had any training in human remains detection. There are no national standards for human remains detection canines, and standards vary widely between teams purporting to be "cadaver" canines. Such was the case with the canines deployed in this case. Additionally, few of the handlers deployed in this case were certified in any form of human remains detection or forensics.

During the 16 searches, following recovery of portions of Dylan's remains, which included those areas where remains had been discovered along with searches near the home, canine handlers reported that their "cadaver" canines alerted in these areas, though no additional remains were recovered.

During the search of the home, one handler stated their canine could not work in a smoky environment and left the search area. Other handlers and their canines positively alerted in the home in areas including a hamper in the master bedroom and a washing machine. Additional searches provided canine alerts on the vehicle of Mr. Redvine. Additional canines alerted on an entirely different vehicle as well. Additional canines, during additional searches, did not alert on any areas at the home.

Nine months following the disappearance, another canine and handler were deployed to the home and alerted to the presence of human remains in several areas of the home. No remains were recovered during this search as well. Unfortunately, two days later, the same canine and handler were deployed into an area where Dylan's remains had been recovered and no alerts were identified by the handler. Yet, one year later, the same handler and canine alerted to human remains in a vehicle.

Mark Redwine was indicted by a grand jury in Colorado for second-degree murder and child abuse, largely due to the purported canine evidence. This occurred on July 20, 2017, which was five years after Redwine's son, Dylan Redwine, went missing. Due to the lack of evidence following the disappearance of Dylan, several "cadaver" canines were deployed in the hopes they would be able to locate Dylan's remains.

At issue in this case is not whether canines are able to scent odors and then alert to the presence of those odors, but the ability of a canine to locate and alert on a cadaver after a significant amount of time has passed and the cadaver has been removed from the area in which the canines are alerting.

Because the canine handlers believed their dogs had alerted them to the odor of the cadaver in those areas, the State of Colorado argued that the evidence of their alerts should be admissible as evidence during the trial. No remains or any evidence were ever recovered from any of the sites where the canines "alerted" and these alerts occurred 10 days to more than a year following the disappearance of Dylan. Unfortunately, in this case, no evidence was presented as to the reliability of these canines as to their ability to detect such scent in the conditions in which they were presented.

Also unfortunately in this case, not only was the reliability of the canines suspect, but the canine handlers were lacking in relevant qualifications. Due to these circumstances, the canine alerts were then called into question both for lack of reliability and ability to scent and alert in an area where no remains were found yet alerts were present, and in time frames that call into question whether this is even possible. It was argued, during the trial, that the state failed to prove that the canines could reliably detect such scent in these difficult circumstances. Yet, the State of Colorado's case hinged on the skills of these "cadaver" canines and their handlers. Canine and handlers such as these have led to states permanently excluding "cadaver" canine evidence due to reliability errors which can call into question the work of properly trained, vetted, and certified canines.

In 2019, the judge in this case allowed the "cadaver" canine alerts to be entered into evidence. In 2021, Mark Redwine was found guilty of second-degree murder and child abuse leading to death. He was sentenced to 48 years in prison. Cases such as this could have far-reaching effects and set precedence leading to the exclusion of reliable human remains detection canine evidence. Therefore, it is imperative to ensure the canines and handlers with whom you are working are highly trained and properly vetted.

Reliably identifying human remains' prior locations is a pitfall properly trained and certified canine handlers should avoid. As mentioned previously in this chapter, all human remains detection canines should be properly trained, and their handlers should be law enforcement or forensically trained. The reliability of the canine and the handler should be demonstrated in detailed, consistent, and constant training logs, along with demonstrated reliability on actual searches. The canine handlers should also strive for consistent and updated training in current forensic techniques. Properly vetted certification standards should be maintained and documented. And canine handlers should be certified as expert witnesses prior to testifying in any trial where their canine's alerts will be used as evidence. Caution should always be taken in working with human remains detection canines and proper vetting of all teams should be a top priority of any law enforcement agency prior to deployment on any case.

Unfortunately, there are many "cadaver" dog hobby teams who are not dedicated to the proper training and certifications necessary in dealing with human remains detection and recovery. It is incumbent upon law enforcement to ensure the teams in which they are utilizing will be an asset and not a liability should the case be tried in court.

Professional Networking in Cold Case Murders 26

JOHN R. ELLIOTT

Importance

One of the most important aspects of cold case investigations is working with other people. This can vary from other Law Enforcement agencies, prosecutors, forensic specialists, and civilians. In every cold case, there will be challenges. There could be difficulties with finding witnesses, the original investigators, case files, and evidence. To overcome these obstacles, modern investigators need to identify these issues and develop a strategy to proceed with their investigation.

Learning for other investigators and prosecutors can be invaluable and asking for assistance should not be an obstacle. Some of the biggest Police Departments with thousands of officers can learn from small departments who have almost no resources.

Other professions rely on networking to make progress. Large corporations regularly meet with investors, experts, and stakeholders for the success of their operation and attend industry-specific conferences to learn from each other.

Law Enforcement should be no exception in regard to communicating with experts and interested parties outside of their department. However, this has been obstacle with modern-day cases and cold cases. Investigators want to keep their investigative knowledge close and, in some instances, for good reason. It's not unusual with high-profile cases to hear a news report where a reporter is heard saying "law enforcement sources state…" with a reveal of information only investigators and their officials were aware of.

Investigators have ownership of their investigations and take pride in the information and investigative leads they develop. This work is not easy and for it to be prematurely released can be troubling. It can create problems for other parts of the investigation, identifying witnesses who are not corrupted by publicly released information and the possibility of evidence being destroyed. This is why investigators need to be selective, but open to who they share information with, and cautious of any potential fallout or secondary effects that information could cause. Something as a simple conversation could lead to a major breakthrough or a setback which takes time to overcome with rehabilitating trust with a victim's family or witness.

DOI: 10.4324/9781003415633-30

Unfortunately, many investigators keep information close and are very reluctant to share investigative files. Some for good reason, such as compromising details which are only known to the suspects and that information becoming publicly known.

In recent times, there has been a paradigm shift with cold cases. If a case is 10, 20, or maybe 30 years old, there is a rhetorical question with "what could possibly be compromised or lost" with releasing information or allowing family members to review a case file. These concerns have initiated legislation which has forced investigating agencies to be transparent. In 2021, the Homicide Victims' Families Rights Act was passed. In summary, the legislation states:

> This bill establishes a framework for immediate family members of a victim of murder under federal law to request a review of the victim's case file if the murder was committed more than three years prior, the murder was investigated by a federal law enforcement entity, all probative investigative leads have been exhausted, and no likely perpetrator has been identified.
>
> *(H.R.3359—Homicide Victims' Families' Rights Act of 2021, 2025)*

This legislation is related to Federal cases, but it has inspired legislation in other states throughout the nation. As of this writing, Florida **Senate Bill 694: Cold Case Murders** was in the legislative process. This legislation details specific requirements for cold case reviews, time requirements for the reviews, and specific tracking requirements.

With the legislation moving in the direction of "openness" with cold cases, old investigators and new investigators have to embrace the change. While some may not like it, there is a reason this legislation was introduced and like other industries and professions, there has been resistance to change.

One of many obstacles to this paradigm shift in openness is staffing levels. In 2025, almost every Law Enforcement agency in the United States is struggling with hiring and retention of qualified and competent police officers. Generally, cold case investigators are experienced investigators with years of homicide and death investigation cases. With the staffing and experience shortage, these qualified investigators are often re-assigned to active cases, forced into promotion or transferred to other so-called "critical, operational" positions. If there are no cold case investigators, then reviews and information sharing is non-existent.

The challenges of cold case investigations are well known. The case information, investigative techniques, and new forensic procedures cannot be shared among Law Enforcement professionals if agencies do not dedicate the resources to them. Networking among cold investigators is important, but the same concern needs to be communicated among law enforcement executives. Access to experts with specialized knowledge and experience has to go beyond the traditional walls of law enforcement.

Professional Organizations

There are dozens of organizations and groups which are dedicated to cold cases. Most groups are considered non-profit organizations and are formed through an overall interest in bringing resolution to the thousands of unsolved cases. Unfortunately, there are almost 350,000 unsolved homicides in the United States. This number is only as accurate as what is being reported to the FBI through the Uniform Crime Report. This number or estimate does not account for the death investigations which were classified as "undetermined" by medical examiners' and coroners' offices. There are probably thousands more which fall into this category or were wrongly classified due to the condition of the deceased, lack of experience of the investigators, and an incomplete forensic autopsy. Because of the high number of unresolved cases, several people have taken an interest in trying to resolve these murders.

Some of the organizations are volunteer groups who offer consultation and experts in various forensic specialties. Other organizations provide funding for advanced testing, which some Law Enforcement agencies cannot afford. Some organizations include the Vidocq Society, the Mid Atlantic Cold Case Homicide Investigators Association (MACCHIA), The Pennsylvania Homicide Investigators Association, the Southeastern Homicide Investigators Association (SEHIA), and Season of Justice—just to name a few. The regional organizations were formed in an effort to give investigators the ability to come together more easily since they are closer.

The Vidocq Society, formed in 1990 and named after Eugène François Vidocq, is one of the longest-running groups to maintain its existence. Historians consider Eugène François Vidocq one of the first people to specialize in criminal investigations. Located in Philadelphia, Pennsylvania, the group meets once a month to review cold case homicides during lunch at the Union League of Philadelphia. Investigators are invited to present their cases and solicit investigative ideas.

> Vidocq Society members come from all walks of life and include experienced investigators from federal, state and local law enforcement agencies and the private sector; internationally renowned forensic experts in the fields of pathology, criminology, dactylography, forensic dentistry, psychology, polygraphy and anthropological facial reconstruction; and many former federal, state and local career prosecutors.
>
> *(The founding of the Vidocq Society, 2025)*

Unique characteristics of the Vidocq Society are that membership is by invitation only and consists of special members and 82 "full members". The 82

Figure 26.1 The Union League of Philadelphia. (Photograph by the author.)

full members represent the number of years Eugène François Vidocq lived (Figure 26.1 and 26.2).

The MACCHIA is described as an "esprit d'corps among cold case homicide investigators within the Mid-Atlantic Region as well as national" (About Us/Join, 2025). The group is open to Law Enforcement members and hosts an annual conference in Annapolis, MD. The conference discusses investigative strategies, best practices, new technology, case presentations, and success stories. In addition to the conference, two "round tables" are held in the region in which investigators gather to review open, unsolved cases. Investigators review the cases and offer investigative strategies to bring resolution or forward their cases into new technology (Figures 26.3–26.5).

The MACCHIA is just one of many and follows the same principles and goals of other groups. Most states have their own homicide investigators association, but few are specifically dedicated to cold cases.

Figure 26.2 Cold case briefing during lunch at the Union League of Philadelphia. (Photograph by the author.)

Figure 26.3 Mid Atlantic Cold Case Homicide Investigators Association logo.

Figure 26.4 RoundTable presentation by Detective Dan Grassi of the Delaware State Police. (Photo by the author.)

Figure 26.5 Social gathering at the MACCHIA annual conference in Annapolis, MD. (Photo by the author.)

One of the most important elements of each of these organizations and their conferences is the encouragement of socialization among attendees. Anyone can sit through a training lecture or case review and walk away at the end of the day with increased knowledge and lessons learned. However, interaction with investigators and professionals from other agencies and other parts of the country allows attendees to discuss the uniqueness of their cases and challenges. Many conferences offer hospitality nights and excursions to bring people together.

Community Networking and Social Media

Involving the community with open, unsolved homicides and other serious crimes can be useful. However, agencies need to be guarded. So-called "keyboard sleuths" and regular citizens can create discussions and present meaningful ideas; however, they can also introduce distractions to the investigation. The distractions can be problematic, with people being named or accused of the crime when they had no involvement. With social media, these theories and accusations can take a life of their own to be played out over the internet. All it takes is an anonymous person to present a plausible theory along with the name of an uninvolved person, and the internet takes over. However, if the case is resolved, the postings, accusations, and theories become a blueprint for the defense. This also creates more work for the investigators to try and disprove during the pre-trial and prosecution phase.

In the last couple of years, the word "transparency" has been a popular term among elected officials and law enforcement executives. This can be damaging when attempting to be transparent with current investigations and specific case information, which must be maintained for case integrity. While most agencies are transparent, there does have to be some information that remains confidential. It's a balance between transparency and case confidentiality.

Another form of public information has been the use of social media. Some agencies self-produce stories regarding cold cases and publish the information through pictures and videos on various platforms. Some of the more popular platforms, as of 2025, were Facebook, Instagram, X, and TikTok. However, one of the challenges with a social media campaign is having qualified people who have the time to research, produce, and publish the case information. Some departments have officers who are good at social media productions and can do it "on the side" or have a reputation of being "tech savvy". But, the reality is for Law Enforcement agencies to have a qualified person whose main job is to produce social media information. This is just not for cold cases, but active investigations. We live in a society where people demand information almost instantly, and if the agency doesn't produce information, other people will produce a narrative before them. Unfortunately, this may not be an option for smaller departments where funding and staffing are problematic and usually these duties fall onto officers as a collateral duty.

Other social media or multimedia considerations are the use of podcasts. Mainstream media has taken a back seat to self-produced stories seen on YouTube or audio through podcasts. According to Gabriel Soto, Senior Director of Research, Edison Research, "Podcasting is transforming True Crime, helping to solve cases and to bring in donations for nonprofits at a higher rate. It's a movement that listeners associate with not just their favorite hosts but advertisers on these shows as well" (Edison Research, 2025). Some of these podcasts are simultaneously video recorded to reach both media paths.

However, Law Enforcement needs to be careful with selecting the right podcast or show to have a case profiled on. Not all podcasts or hosts are created equal, and each one must be vetted before agreeing to an interview or story. Considerations or information you should look for are online reviews regarding the show, the number of downloads to determine reach and popularity, and their purpose. Prior to any agreement, listen to what is currently published, look for previous interviews, and try to make contact with the other agencies and investigators who have been interviewed. Ask their opinion regarding the production and professionalism of the final product before agreeing to participate.

One such podcast is Anatomy of Murder which "is a weekly true crime podcast examining homicide cases and paths to justice for the victims" (Anatomy of Murder, 2025). The show is hosted by a former prosecutor and a former police officer. The show usually interviews a member of the victim's family, the investigating officer, or a prosecutor. The information is produced through the lens of people who have been involved in Law Enforcement and are familiar with the reality of cold case investigations and challenges. The podcast details both solved cases and unsolved ones, and the hosts promote the devoted work of investigators, forensic specialists, and prosecutors (Figure 26.6).

People love to hear about cold cases and are generally intrigued. As of 2025, mainstream media is not completely dead. However, the news cycle changes by the second, and trying to get a cold case produced by a local news station can be challenging. Producers and reporters constantly change, along with the news. Depending on the size of the agency and if there is a dedicated public information officer or media relations specialist, that person might develop relationships with reporters and producers. Often, these relationships can lead to news stories when asked by the agency. One example is

Figure 26.6 AOM logo.

Diane Richardson, media specialist with Charles County, MD Sheriff's Office. Over 25 years ago, she began working with a new reporter, Megan McGrath, who is currently a general assignment reporter with NBC4 Washington in Washington, DC. Since then, the two have worked together and shared information in each of their roles. In June of 2023, while working with Richardson, McGrath produced a new story regarding an unidentified female who was found murdered in Charles County, MD, in 1998. The victim's identity was unknown, but she was the victim of a homicide, and investigators worked countless leads over the years; however, they were never able to identify her. On June 23, 2023, the story aired on the evening news in the Washington, DC area, and days later, a tip was received with a possible name. Forensic testing was later completed, and she was identified as LaQuanda Denise Williams, a resident of Washington, DC.

Because of the working relationship between Richardson and McGrath, the two had open communication, a level of trust with a willingness to work with each other, which led to a homicide victim being identified after 25 years. The case remains open (Figure 26.7).

Communication

There should be no boundaries among Law Enforcement agencies regarding cold cases and information sharing; however, the reality is that there are countless obstacles. They include institutional policies, archaic practices, the routine of "this is how we've always done it", silos of secrecy, hoarding of investigative files, in-fighting between different agencies, and the egos of those involved.

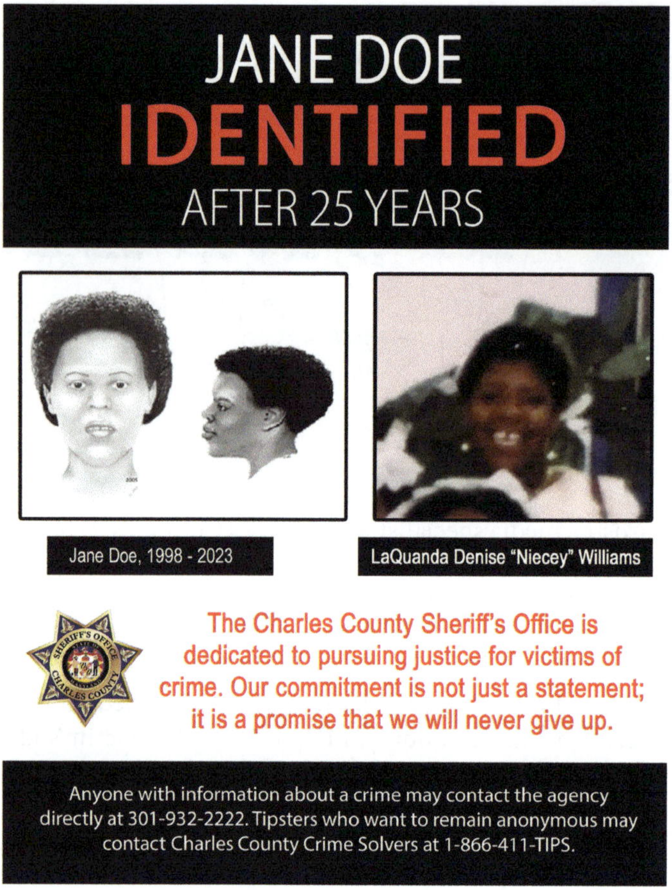

Figure 26.7 Jane Doe identified poster.

With modern communication, networking among professionals has become easier. Emails, video conferences, the conversion of old reports into electronic formats, and file sharing have made investigations easier, but in some respects more difficult. One element that cannot be removed is the human factor. There has to be a willingness to share information, collaborate, and learn from successes and failures, along with support from law enforcement executives. There has to be buy-in from everyone involved and sometimes an acknowledgment of mistakes and errors.

Establishing relationships with other like-minded professionals can make the difference in resources and finding the right information. Attempting to make a "cold call" to an agency may not have the best result, but knowing someone in a large or small department can be more efficient in obtaining information and investigative leads.

Groups who specialize or focus on cold cases exclusively can also be informal. A group of investigators who get together and meet regularly can be very productive. In some states there is a hybrid of investigators who are responsible for investigating homicides. There could be a municipality, a county Police of Sheriff's Department, and an investigating agency or group within the local prosecutor's office. Each one of these groups could have a so-called "piece of the puzzle" which could lead to a resolution, but there has to be communication between all of the involved parties. Especially in cold cases, where evidence could be scattered among everyone who was involved in the original case. It's not unheard of that evidence which was classified as lost or destroyed has been later found to be comingled with another case or found in an old storage closet. There have even been stories of agencies that threw evidence away because they ran out of storage and real detectives who knew the value and kept the evidence themselves in an effort to preserve it.

When cold cases are solved, the stories make headlines. Their success stories are celebrated by Law Enforcement executives and they bring positive attention to the hard work of police officers everywhere. However, they are usually the last to receive needed resources and staffing. Community police and other "boutique" programs have become expected at times when staffing levels are critically low. Cold case units are usually the ones that get investigators pulled out of or completely eliminated.

Case Study

In August of 1979, Vickie Lynn Belk was reported missing to the Prince George's County, MD Police Department. Investigators believed she was last seen in Washington, DC, after she left work at the Department of Agriculture. Belk would commute to the city with her boyfriend from Maryland, park her car at Robert F. Kennedy Memorial Stadium, and take the METRO train downtown to her office building.

Vickie left work the afternoon of August 27, 1979, but was never seen again. Her boyfriend, friends, and family looked for her, but she never returned home. Her vehicle was later located abandoned, not far from the stadium on August 28, 1979.

On August 29, 1979, Vickie was found dead on the side of the road in an isolated area of Charles County, MD, about 25 miles south of Washington, DC. Based on information from early reports, it appeared Vickie had been sexually assaulted and was shot in the head. The original investigators pursued leads and tips; however, the suspect was never identified and her case went unsolved for decades. Fortunately, most of the evidence was retained.

Forensic specialists and detectives re-visited the case in the early 2000s and began to evaluate the remaining evidence. Several pieces of evidence were submitted to the Maryland State Police, Forensics Sciences Division, for DNA analysis. Due to current cases and backlogs, the forensic specialist could only test a few items at a time.

Through collaboration and case review, detectives and forensic scientists would evaluate which items they thought would be the most probative. Testing continued for several years; however, no known DNA profile was identified or extracted from the evidence. In 2012, one of the forensic scientists recommended to stop any further testing. It was her recommendation to wait until technology got better regarding DNA analysis and testing.

In 2022, forensic specialists with the Charles County, MD Sheriff's Office re-evaluated the evidence and submitted several items to Sorenson Forensics, a private lab in Utah. It was requested that Sorenson Forensics process the clothing Vickie was wearing in 1979 using an M-VAC.

> The M-vac uses wet-vacuum principles to cause the DNA material to release from the substrate and to capture the cells. DNA free buffer is sprayed directly onto the surface while simultaneously vacuum is applied around the spray pattern to collect the buffer with the suspended particles and transfer it into a sterile collection bottle.
>
> *(How Does the M-Vac Work? 2025)*

A simple comparison to understand the M-VAC would be similar to a handheld carpet cleaner. The area of interest is covered with a sterile solution and vacuumed onto a sterile filter. The filter is then tested for DNA.

The clothes from 1979 were processed using the M-VAC and the filters tested for DNA. A full DNA profile was obtained from a filter and later entered into CODIS, the combined DNA index system. Once it was entered into CODIS, there was an offender match to a person named Andre Tayor of Washington, DC.

Taylor was a lifelong criminal, in and out of jail with several arrests, including two other unrelated murders. He was never named in the original investigation and was unknown to the Belk family. From historical records, it was learned Taylor lived for a short period of time a few miles from where Vickie's body was found in Charles County, MD. The same records also revealed he spent most of his life in the surrounding area where her car was found abandoned in Washington, DC.

Once investigators learned of his name, they needed to locate him for a confirmatory DNA standard. It took some time, but Taylor was located in a nursing home. In March of 2023, investigators obtained a search warrant to get Taylor's DNA. Contact was made with Taylor in his room and he was questioned. Taylor denied knowing Vickie and denied having any type of relationship with her. The interior of his mouth was swabbed and the test results later confirmed it was his DNA found on her clothes in 1979.

Taylor was subsequently indicted and arrested. In July of 2024, Taylor went to trial and was found guilty of the murder and sexual assault of Vickie in 1979.

None of this work could have been completed without established relationships with other investigators and agencies. Some relationships were established as this case unfolded, while others had been long-standing. These relationships allowed investigators to make one phone call when resources were needed during the homicide investigation of Vickie. This collaboration and efficiency with working with other agencies didn't happen overnight. These bonds are formed over time while working on cases together. Investigators got to know each other and through those established relationships, work was done much faster and more efficiently.

Just some of the agencies involved included the Maryland State Police Forensic Sciences Division, The Metropolitan Police Department, Washington, DC, the United States Secret Service, the Department of Homeland Security—Homeland Security Investigations, and the United States Marshals Service. Most of these agencies had a working relationship with the investigators of the Charles County Sheriff's Office and were familiar with each other and how they worked (Figures 26.8–26.10).

Figure 26.8 Photograph of the investigators, forensic specialists, prosecutors, and the Belk family the day the suspect was convicted. (Photograph by the author.)

Figure 26.9 Picture of Vickie Belk.

Figure 26.10 Arrest photographs of Andre Taylor.

Resources

The Vidocq Society—https://vidocq.org/
Mid Atlantic Cold Case Homicide Investigators Association—https://coldcasehomicidc.org/
South East Homicide Investigators Association—https://sehia.org/
Pennsylvania Homicide Investigators Association—https://www.pahia.us/
National Missing and Unidentified Persons System—https://namus.nij.ojp.gov/

References

About Us/Join. (2025, May 27). Retrieved from The Mid Atlantic Cold Case Homicide Investigators Association: https://coldcasehomicide.org/about-us-%2F-join-us

Anatomy of Murder. (2025, May 27). Retrieved from Anatomy of Murder: https://anatomyofmurder.com/

Edison Research. (2025, May 27). The True Crime Consumer Report by Edison Research and audiochuck. Retrieved from Edison Research: https://www.edisonresearch.com/the-true-crime-consumer-report-by-edison-research-and-audiochuck/

H.R.3359—Homicide Victims' Families' Rights Act of 2021. (2025, May 27). Retrieved from congress.gov: https://www.congress.gov/bill/117th-congress/house-bill/3359

How Does the M-Vac Work?. (2025, May 27). Retrieved from M-Vac Systems, Inc: https://www.m-vac.com/why-mvac/how-it-works

The Founding of the Vidocq Society. (2025, May 27). Retrieved from The Vidocq Society: https://vidocq.org/

Afterword

FRANK P. TONA

I began my career in law enforcement in 2002 in Charles County, Maryland. As someone born and raised in Buffalo, New York, I was a fish out of water in those early days, new to the region, the agency, and my organization's culture. But one thing was certain: I wanted to be an investigator. From the start, I was driven by a need to understand the deeper "why" behind every crime, every motive, and every unanswered question. I've always been obsessed with learning and have a lifelong passion for history, so when I found my way into the cold case work, it felt like a natural fit, a kind of marriage between curiosity and purpose.

I stepped into the world of cold case investigations in 2007 with more determination than direction. Like many in this field, my introduction was a mix of curiosity, a sense of justice, and a fair share of trial and error. I quickly discovered that working cold cases is not glamorous. It's tedious, at times maddening, and often deeply humbling. Files don't solve themselves. Leads vanish. Witnesses disappear. Evidence ages, and so do expectations. But what remains, what always remains, is the responsibility to speak for those who no longer can, and to stand alongside their families in their long wait for answers.

My first cold case was the sexual assault of a 68-year-old retired schoolteacher. She had lived a quiet life of service to her community, only to become the victim of a brutal crime that, to this day, remains unsolved. That case taught me just how heavy a file can feel when the victim's voice is missing, and the trail has gone cold. I've also witnessed the gut-wrenching complexities of resolution. In a 1985 cold case sexual assault that we successfully reopened, our investigation led to a long-awaited arrest, only to end in the heartbreaking acquittal of the defendant. It was a stark reminder that closure does not always follow answers.

And yet, hope continues to shine through the shadows. I think often of the 1980 murder of a 17-year-old girl whose battered remains told a silent story of violence and loss. Despite the decades that have passed, there is still active hope, hope that new forensic tools and renewed investigative focus will finally bring justice to her memory. These are not just cases. They are people. And they are the reason this work cannot be allowed to fade into the background.

Still, there are moments of light, moments when answers come, and peace can finally begin to take root. I had the privilege of assisting in the closure of a 1979 rape and murder of a 28-year-old woman. Helping bring resolution to that case was an honor, but the true privilege was meeting the victim's family. In all my years, I have never met a group more gracious, resilient, and dignified. Their strength left a lasting impression on me, and I carry their story with me always.

The National Institute of Justice has called cold case homicides "the nation's silent mass disaster," a description that resonates deeply with those of us who carry these investigations forward. These are not isolated tragedies, they are part of a national backlog of unresolved violence. It is imperative that law enforcement executives recognize the magnitude of this crisis. Cold cases must be prioritized with the same seriousness given to community relations and public-facing initiatives. Justice cannot be selective. If we believe in our duty to serve and protect, then that duty must extend to every victim, regardless of how long ago the crime occurred or how difficult the path forward may be.

Along the way, I've had the honor of advocating for victims and their loved ones, forming enduring partnerships with dedicated forensic scientists, and building bridges with professionals in allied agencies who share the same unwavering resolve. These relationships have not only shaped my career, but they have also grounded it. In a profession that often walks the line between heartbreak and hope, collaboration becomes both a shield and a guide.

I have been incredibly fortunate to learn from some of the very best. Law enforcement professionals like John Elliott, Noelle Gehrman, Jeff Bryant, Paul Gregory, Kevin Leahy, Tim Miner, George Higgs, Kevin Keelan, Christopher Shankster, Tom McAndrew, Shawn Williams, Christopher Flanagan, Darrell Price, Richard Lumb, Gary Metz, and the late Frank Colaprete each played a pivotal role in my development. They were mentors in the truest sense, generous with their knowledge, steadfast in their support, and unflinching in their dedication to justice. Their influence helped me move beyond the early missteps and begin to approach these cases with the patience, strategy, and compassion they deserve.

In 2012, I met Dr. Rachel Walton, and that moment changed the course of my career. She was not only brilliant but deeply committed to ethical, evidence-based investigations. Over the years, we stayed in touch, and I continued to learn from her, through our conversations, her writings, and the example she set. Her belief in me and her invitation to continue her legacy in being a coauthor of this textbook remains one of the greatest honors of my life. I was deeply saddened by her passing in 2025. Her absence is felt by many, but her impact lives on in the work she inspired and the lives she touched.

I am more convinced than ever that the answers we seek still exist. Technology continues to evolve, offering tools we once only dreamed of. But at the heart of it all, it's still gumshoe police work, boots on the ground, interviews, timelines, files revisited, or leads reexamined, that moves these cases forward. The combination of old-school detective work and modern innovation can, and does, resolve what once seemed unsolvable.

This third edition brings together the very best of what was presented in the first two, updated with new investigative approaches, expanded insights, and the latest forensic advancements. It stands as both a record of progress and a reminder that the mission is far from over. The past is still speaking. We just must keep listening.

I still believe in the quiet power of persistence. I still believe that every case, no matter how old, holds the possibility of resolution. And I remain committed, to the work, to the victims, and to the families who never stop hoping.

Finally, I leave this quote from author Michael Connelly's famed literary character, Detective Hieronymus "Harry" Bosch, "Everybody Counts or No One Counts."

Lt. Frank P. Tona
Charles County Sheriff's Office
La Plata, MD

Index

Note: **Bold** page numbers refer to tables and *italic* page numbers refer to figures.

For Product Safety Concerns and Information please contact our EU representative GPSR@taylorandfrancis.com Taylor & Francis Verlag GmbH, Kaufingerstraße 24, 80331 München, Germany

* 9 7 8 1 0 3 2 5 4 1 9 5 2 *

T - #0043 - 180226 - C638 - 234/156/30 [32] - CB - 9781032541952 - Gloss Lamination